Catharine

Parr

Traill's

The Female

Emigrant's

Guide

Y0-BDT-163

CARLETON LIBRARY SERIES

The Carleton Library Series publishes books about Canadian economics, geography, history, politics, public policy, society and culture, and related topics, in the form of leading new scholarship and reprints of classics in these fields. The series is funded by Carleton University, published by McGill-Queen's University Press, and is under the guidance of the Carleton Library Series Editorial Board, which consists of faculty members of Carleton University. Suggestions and proposals for manuscripts and new editions of classic works are welcome and may be directed to the Carleton Library Series Editorial Board c/o the Library, Carleton University, Ottawa K1S 5B6, at cls@carleton.ca, or on the web at www.carleton.ca/cls.

CLS board members:

John Clarke
Ross Eaman
Jennifer Henderson
Laura Macdonald
Paul Litt
Stanley Winer
Barry Wright

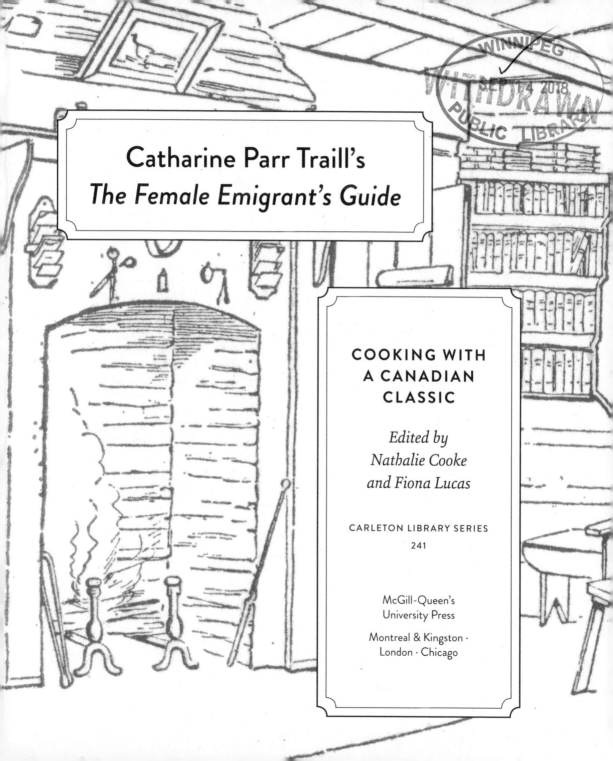

Catharine Parr Traill's
The Female Emigrant's Guide

COOKING WITH A CANADIAN CLASSIC

Edited by
Nathalie Cooke
and Fiona Lucas

CARLETON LIBRARY SERIES

241

McGill-Queen's
University Press

Montreal & Kingston ·
London · Chicago

WINNIPEG PFD 4 2018 WITHDRAWN PUBLIC LIBRARY

© McGill-Queen's University Press 2017

ISBN 978-0-7735-4929-6 (cloth)
ISBN 978-0-7735-4930-2 (paper)
ISBN 978-0-7735-4931-9 (ePDF)
ISBN 978-0-7735-4932-6 (ePUB)

Legal deposit second quarter 2017
Bibliothèque nationale du Québec

Printed in Canada on acid-free paper that is
100% ancient forest free (100% post-consumer
recycled), processed chlorine free

This book has been published with the help of
a grant from the Canadian Federation for the
Humanities and Social Sciences, through the
Awards to Scholarly Publications Program,
using funds provided by the Social Sciences and
Humanities Research Council of Canada.

McGill-Queen's University Press acknowledges
the support of the Canada Council for the Arts
for our publishing program. We also acknowledge
the financial support of the Government of
Canada through the Canada Book Fund for our
publishing activities.

Set in 10.5/13 Sina Nova and 10.5/13
Filosofia with Brandon Grotesque

Book design & typesetting by
Garet Markvoort, zijn digital

LIBRARY AND ARCHIVES CANADA
CATALOGUING IN PUBLICATION

Catharine Parr Traill's The female emigrant's
guide : cooking with a Canadian classic /
edited by Nathalie Cooke and Fiona Lucas.

(Carleton library series ; 241)
Includes bibliographical references and index.
Issued in print and electronic formats.
ISBN 978-0-7735-4929-6 (hardcover). –
ISBN 978-0-7735-4930-2 (softcover). –
ISBN 978-0-7735-4931-9 (ePDF). –
ISBN 978-0-7735-4932-6 (ePUB)

1. Traill, Catharine Parr, 1802–1899.
Canadian settler's guide.   2. Cooking –
Canada – History – 19th century.
3. Cooking, Canadian – History – 19th
century.   4. Food – Canada – History –
19th century.   5. Canada – Social life and
customs – 19th century.   6. Dinners and
dining – Canada – History – 19th century.
7. Kitchens – Canada – History – 19th
century.   8. Cookbooks.   I. Cooke,
Nathalie, editor   II. Lucas, Fiona, editor
III. Series: Carleton library series ; 241

TX715.6.C381 2017   641.597109'034
C2017-901483-8

C2017-901484-6

Contents

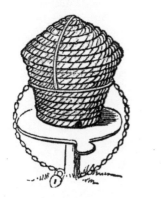

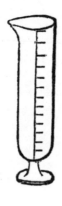

Figures

Acknowledgments

We are grateful to a wide range of friends and colleagues who helped us prepare the materials for this new edition of Catharine Parr Traill's *The Female Emigrant's Guide*.

Our thanks to Renaud Roussel for his close reading and attention to detail, and to Iain Childerhose, whose resourcefulness and interest in photography and culinary experimentation brought an additional dimension to the volume. Iain's summer internship working on this project at McGill University in 2015 was funded by the inaugural Len Blum Award. Our thanks to Len Blum for the funding support and to the McGill Institute for the Study of Canada, which administers the award. Our appreciation too for research assistance from Étienne Gratton and Saundra Tobman, as well as insights into the influence of First Nations traditions and foodways on backwoods settlers from colleagues Margery Fee and Toby Morantz, and feedback on terminology from Glyne Piggott and Jacques Leroux. This project was supported by McGill's wonderful library staff who helped us ferret out historical materials (Raynald Lepage, Richard Virr, Lonnie Weatherby), source digital images (Greg Houston, Sarah Severson), think through questions about mapping Traill's world (Deena Yanofsky), and resolve questions of copyright (Jillian Thom). Ryan Kirkby of the University of Guelph's Archival and Special Collections and Elizabeth Ridolfo at the University of Toronto's Thomas Fisher Rare Book Library helped us source illustrations, for which we are very grateful. Erin Yanota provided invaluable editing support as we prepared the manuscript for initial submission.

We are especially grateful to two anonymous reviewers who offered thoughtful and immensely helpful feedback. The final manuscript is far stronger thanks to their generous comments. It has also benefitted enormously from the careful attention and thoughtful editing of Joan McGilvray.

Jonathan Crago of McGill-Queen's University Press has offered wise counsel throughout this project's development. In the earliest stages, we believed our task was to make Traill's first edition of the *Guide* more readily available and to introduce readers to the culinary knowledge it provided. It was Jonathan who urged us to think more about how the contemporary reader and culinary enthusiast might understand the cookbook – about what its real treasures were. The result is this current volume, which is more toolkit for historical cookery than reprint of a textual source. We hope it will serve as a useful guide for the contemporary cook and prompt readers to try out its recipes.

Introduction

For the majority of us, food is an important consideration – where to find it, how to pay for it, how to cook it, how to provide basic nutrition for our family and ourselves. For those of us who are privileged to be food secure, it means challenging ourselves to eat mindfully, seasonally, locally, and sustainably. This challenge has been laid down by those advocating the "100-mile diet," as well as by psychologists like Susan Albers, food writers like Michael Pollan, popular chefs like Jamie Oliver, and even celebrities like Gwyneth Paltrow. And it is a challenge, for the alternative to thinking about, sourcing, preparing, and serving healthy, home-prepared meals is often a quick trip to the local supermarket, with its many remarkably affordable packaged food items lining the shelves of its centre aisles. Despite, and perhaps because of, such an easy alternative, our world is crowded with government food guides outlining the basics of a healthy diet, attractive cookbooks devoted to healthy eating, lavishly illustrated blogs extolling the virtues and rewards of such eating, and celebrities who voice their support for the uphill climb towards mindful foodways. The industry around healthy eating is robust because most of us lose momentum on the uphill climb and need to reach out to guides, cookbooks, blogs, and authorities for inspiration.

That we lose momentum is inevitable because, in the twenty-first century, for those who are food secure, mindful eating is a choice rather than a necessity. By contrast, for those newcomers who emigrated to the Americas,[1] both in the early decades of settlement and in subsequent waves of immigration, mindful eating was a necessity. It was already a central tenet of life for the First Nations peoples, although new settlers may not have fully recognized the extent to which they practised sustainable food sourcing and harvesting. Many of the foodstuffs native to North America, and therefore more economical and available, seemed new and unfamiliar to an immigrant palate. But even later, when food was more readily available, the immigrant reality continued to involve mindful eating, as settlers learned new foodways and transformed their previous practices to suit a new agricultural and social landscape.

---

1 We use "the Americas" rather than the "New World" in this volume to distance our discussion from the myth that North America was "new," that it was unpopulated and virgin territory.

In many ways, our current turn to mindful eating has much in common with the immigrant experience. As twenty-first-century citizens, we have begun to turn away from the world of technological advancement that, during the past century, developed the urban, processed foodways we find around us. Most North Americans now live in urban environments. We are familiar with frozen, dried, pre-mixed, pre-baked, canned, packaged, and bottled processed foods, and with the layout of a supermarket. We are blasé about the miracle of microwave technology and the variety of cuisines on offer in our globalized world. We are used to having foods planted and harvested for us, manufactured for us, wrapped and transported for us, but are often unfamiliar with food sourcing possibilities nearer home or with what is edible in the immediate landscape. But this is changing, as shown by the rise of the locavore movement, the increasing numbers of farmers' markets and customers who support them, and the popularity of foraging. It is a wonderful discovery to learn that young dandelion leaves, for example, make a nice salad in early summer or that dandelion roots can be the basis of a pleasant hot drink, similar in taste to coffee. Or that wood sorrel leaves are edible, and a tea made from them can taste like lemonade if one adds a touch of sweetener. Or that edible berries can be plucked from that bush we walk past every day. We venture into mindful eating as a journey of discovery of new foodways and of rediscovery of the world around us. Slowly, we begin to inhabit the world of scratch cooking and local, seasonal food sourcing.

What better guide for such a journey of rediscovery than an astutely observant early immigrant to the Americas who had an eye for botanical detail, a fine skill with her pen, and the diligence to keep detailed accounts of household practices? For the contemporary reader interested in edible possibilities in the northeast, Catharine Parr Traill provides detailed instructions on nurturing fruit and vegetables in a harsh climate like the backwoods of Upper Canada. She writes of the ease with which hops can be grown up the pillars of one's house and of the advantages of having them readily at hand to use in making bread rise. She describes how to identify wild berries for puddings and pies. And for the contemporary reader who is curious about whether the weather differs in our day from what it was in the nineteenth century, Traill provides detailed notes about weather patterns in order to advise her readers about safe dates for planting and transplanting seeds.

Traill learned much from her First Nations neighbours, the Hiawatha First Nation, formerly known as the Mississauga Anishinaabe. The *Guide* provides a detailed glimpse of the way Upper Canada functioned as what Alison Norman has called a culinary "contact zone," characterized by the exchange of foods and cooking styles between First Nations and settlers and the creation of "hybrid" cuisines.[2] The "back-woods" where Traill settled were the sacred homelands of the Mississauga Anishi-naabe First Nations, and Rice Lake (or Pimadashkodeyong), where Traill made her home, had gained its name because it was the site of *minomiin* (wild rice) harvesting by the Mississauga Anishinaabe people. In one letter, Traill wrote that First Nations women "have been several times to see me; sometimes from curiosity, sometimes with the view of bartering their baskets, mats, ducks, or venison, for pork, flour, po-tatoes, or articles of wearing apparel. Sometimes their object is to borrow 'kettle to cook,' which they are very punctual in returning."[3] Such exchanges were typical of the period, since First Nations peoples living in close proximity to British settlements had come to depend on trade to obtain provisions.[4] The particular items for which they traded – wheat flour and pork, for example – provide evidence that their food-ways were adapting just as much as those of the settlers. One example involves a common First Nations food, bannock, a quick flat bread that had been adapted from a Scottish dish.[5] The shift from consumption of local foods such as game meat, ber-ries, and wild rice to consumption of flour, sugar, and lard signals the beginnings of a transition from a healthy diet to a deficient industrialized one. Margery Fee makes this point when she writes that the "history of colonization in North America is the history of the ongoing 'nutrition transition,'"[6] a transition that was underway in Traill's time and can be seen in her observations about interactions with her Anishi-naabe neighbours.

Traill referred to her Mississauga Anishinaabe neighbours as "Indians" and the women as "squaws," terms that are now understood to be offensive, although they were part of the common speech of Traill's day. However, in her writing, including the *Guide,* Traill notes that her First Nations neighbours were generous and reliable exchange partners who took the obligations of reciprocity seriously. For example, she describes how it was quite common for a group of First Nations hunters to take refuge overnight in a settler cabin while travelling to or from their hunting grounds. Typ-ically they would be careful to leave their weapons outside, to come and go quietly,

2 Norman, "'Fit for the Table of the Most Fastidious Epicure,'" 38–69.
3 Traill, *Backwoods of Canada*, 135.
4 Peter Jones, *History of the Ojebway Indians*, 73.
5 Fee, "Stories of Traditional Aboriginal Food, Territory, and Health," 55–78.
6 Ibid., 56.

and would often leave "a leash of wild ducks" or "haunch of venison" as tokens of gratitude [54]. Leanne Simpson, in *Dancing on Our Turtle's Back*, provides insights into the Anishinaabeg[7] peoples' deeply held respect for exchange and reciprocity. Traill's sister Susanna Moodie had cause to be very grateful for this generosity during a particularly dire period when her family lacked food, recounting how an Anishinaabe neighbour from Curve Lake, John Nogan, was one of the friends who left food on her doorstep, slipping away quietly so as not to give offence to someone who was not able to reciprocate.[8]

Recipes in the *Guide* reveal how settlers made use of Indigenous food items, both borrowing and adapting First Nations' preparation techniques. Check in the index for recipes that use masquinonge (a kind of pike), cranberries, pumpkin, maple syrup, and cornmeal. Other influences of First Nations foodways are more indirect. For instance, Traill includes her sister's recipe for dandelion root coffee [142–3]. Could this drink have been an adaptation of the Haudenosaunee practice of making what Alison Norman describes as a "coffeelike brew out of burned corn"?[9] Certainly Traill remarks on the variety of drinks made from local produce, including sassafras, both for their taste and for their medicinal properties.

In some cases, Traill provides detailed observations of the Mississauga Anishinaabe methods for food harvesting and preparation – for example, for harvesting wild rice in September [112], or preparing maple syrup during the spring thaw [151], both of which would have been unfamiliar – and extremely useful – to the British female settlers she imagined would be using her *Guide*. Wild rice is nutritious and Traill knew well that when circumstances were grim it would be important to understand how to benefit from such an excellent food source. However, while Traill's observations are astute, she did not always understand the guiding principles behind First Nations planting and harvesting techniques. For example, when describing what she calls "Indian corn," she notes that it is always planted alongside pumpkin [118] but fails to mention beans, the third of the "three sisters" and traditionally planted with the other two crops. Nor does she discuss the benefits of such combined planting. The Haudenosaunee knew that planting the "three sisters" together made for efficient

---

7 We are grateful to Jacques Leroux, who points out that the plural form can be written as "Anishinaabek" or "Anishinaabeg." It is the same phoneme, though spelling varies according to the writing traditions of particular communities.

8 Moodie, *Roughing It in the Bush*, 280.

9 Norman, "'Fit for the Table of the Most Fastidious Epicure,'" 42.

use of space and minimal watering and weeding, as well as eliminating the need for staking: the beans could climb the corn stalks while providing nitrogen for the soil, while the squash provided cover that inhibited weed growth and encouraged water retention.

Much of the land of the Mississauga Anishinaabe First Nations' territory had been lost to them during the nineteenth century, when their people began to be forced to live on reserves such as the one at Rice Lake. The 1818 Rice Lake Treaty No. 20 is only one example of the treaties Aboriginal peoples signed with the Crown, which often contained clauses that had not been fully understood and whose acceptance rested on assumptions of reciprocity that were not consistent with the Treaty terms, leading to loss of land and of hunting and fishing territories. George Copway describes the misunderstanding involved in Treaty negotiations, explaining the situation in which his ancestors found themselves in 1818: "As they could neither read nor write, they were ignorant of the fact that these islands [in Rice Lake] were included in the sale. They were repeatedly told by those who purchased for the government, that the islands were not included in the articles of agreement. But since that time, some of us have learned to read, and to our utter astonishment, and to the everlasting disgrace of that pseudo Christian nation, we find that we have been most grossly abused, deceived and cheated. Appeals have been frequently made but all in vain."[10]

Not able to appeal to the Treaty to regain their traditional land, the Mississauga Anishinaabe peoples attempted to secure another area for cultivating wild rice. Bonita Lawrence tells the story of Mary Buckshot, who in 1880 took wild rice and mud from Rice Lake to nearby Mud Lake. Lawrence notes that the rice supply at Rice Lake was badly affected by the construction of the Trent-Severn waterway, but wild rice could still be gathered from Mud Lake. In 1983, however, the right to harvest wild rice was again threatened, this time because the Ontario government began issuing licenses for its harvesting to non-Indians and non-status Indians in areas of Kenora and Dryden districts where Indigenous communities had previously had exclusive harvesting rights.[11] The resulting "Rice War" testified to the continued central role of wild rice in Anishinaabeg foodways.

---

10 Copway, *The Life, History, and Travels of Kab-ge-ga-gah-bowh*, 66.
11 Lawrence, *Fractured Homeland*, 139–43. The 1983 decision followed a five-year moratorium decreed in May 1978 (DeLisle, "Coming out of the Shadows," 50). Commercial licenses had been issued for outside Treaty 3 territory as early as 1960.

In the 1830s through 1850s, during the time the Traills and Moodies were settlers in the backwoods, the Mississauga Anishinaabe no longer had stewardship of the land. In Traill's description of harvesting wild rice [112], it is unclear whether she fully understood how carefully the Mississauga Anishinaabe had nurtured this resource to ensure its sustainability[12] and how much settler society had disrupted their sustainable food practices. In fact, rather than attributing the dwindling supply of wild rice to the impact of new settlement on traditional harvesting practices, Traill concluded it was due to the "Indian" being "indolent, or possibly, employed in agricultural pursuits or household work" [112]. As Fee points out, European settlers found it hard to understand – or even to see – the "modifications" Indigenous peoples made to the land to enable sustainability.[13] English settlers, Traill included, were unaware of the impact settler colonialism and the lack of careful stewardship had on natural resources. Other examples of changes include the disappearance of wild game from the area and the extinction of the passenger pigeon.

One of the greatest treasures for contemporary readers is Traill's detailed explanation of food traditions shared by nineteenth-century Canadian bush settlers, which accompany recipes that, for the period, provide remarkably detailed instructions. Through personal experience she was acutely aware that the newest arrivals would not be familiar with cooking techniques suitable to the Americas and her attempts to help them adjust mean that, among all the early Canadian cookbooks, Traill's *The Female Emigrant's Guide, and Hints on Canadian Housekeeping* – to give its full original title – offers particular riches for contemporary readers hoping to find details of the northeast's edible landscape, seasonal patterns, and foodways.

We address this new edition of Traill's *Guide* to those curious to do more than just read about history. We speak to those who want to reach out and experience history; to taste, touch, feel, and smell a nineteenth-century backwoods kitchen; to roll up their sleeves and actively participate in recreating the world of women who settled in the Americas and cooked in the backwoods, as Catharine Parr Traill did from 1832 through 1854. Traill's *Guide* is as much about cooking over the open hearth (pre-1850) as it is about cooking with the new iron cookstoves, which began to enter kitchens in the 1830s but were not fixtures in most kitchens until about 1850, and sometimes

---

12 Simpson, "Land & Reconciliation."
13 Fee, "Stories of Traditional Aboriginal Food, Territory, and Health," 58.

later in some areas. This new edition of Traill's *Guide*, more than a history or a textbook, is an explorer's toolkit.

Household guides were practical books, written to provide clear and helpful instruction for the author's contemporaries, as well as to earn money and attention for the author. But there are huge benefits to reading such a book more than a century and a half after it was written, especially when it provides the precise and extensive information available here. It allows one to become a time traveller, journeying back after a century of urbanization to a time when "Canada" was being settled, largely by immigrants from Great Britain and America, its territory only beginning to be cultivated using western European farming techniques. Readers can glimpse the gamut of challenges settlers faced: hordes of mosquitoes, a harsh climate, looming poverty, the loneliness of a vast land with a small population, the dangers of disease, drink, and laziness. There are unexpected insights here as well, as when Traill gives prudent advice to the women settlers to whom her *Guide* was primarily addressed. For instance, when she discusses the critical difference between sharing and "borrowing," the latter a ruse used by experienced settlers to take advantage of the naiveté of newcomers [35–7]. Or when she identifies the differences between British and Canadian pumpkin pie [133]. In these moments, when Traill describes the finer points of life in the Americas, a twenty-first-century reader can begin to understand the daily challenges of settler life for women in the bush and on struggling farms.

The *Guide* was not only a treasure trove of information about how to survive for those embarking on a journey into the backwoods: it also provides a treasure trove of knowledge about scratch cooking and food sourcing for those interested in self-sufficiency and practical housekeeping. It is full of fundamental knowledge about seasonal eating, local sourcing, foraging, small-scale farming, kitchen gardening, and how to preserve the bounty for future seasons and generations – a wonderful tool for those interested in reviving long-forgotten and little-used culinary techniques. In this regional cookbook, Traill identifies foods available in what is now Ontario and provides clear and detailed instructions for how to grow, preserve, and prepare them. In her day, such knowledge was the key to the survival, health, and comfort of settler families. Dried huckleberries, cranberries, strawberries, and apples provided much needed sustenance during the long winters, particularly as they include what would be identified at the turn of the twentieth century as vitamin C. Dried fruit, less vital today because of the wealth of foods available to us, has become a handy snack or an addition to breakfast cereal. But preparing it at home, in the way Traill suggests, can still be valuable, providing an enjoyable activity as well as an economical way to control the level of contaminants in the food we eat.

Recipes that Traill copied from other publications, such as those for cakes, typically do not include the detail and personal information that she adds to her own recipes. She included the recipes in the *Guide* because she had identified them as particularly useful and knew that the publications in which they had first appeared might be too expensive for new settlers to purchase. She chose them because they were representative of the typical fare of her day but provides less information about them because she knew that most household cooks would have been familiar with how to assemble and bake such commonplace dishes and needed only a reminder of ingredients and minimal information about measurements.

Traill's detailed instructions and our updated recipes and menus allow readers to actively use the *Guide* – to embark on an exercise of imagination and experimentation with nineteenth-century recipes. The rewards are plentiful and involve a new awareness of our own food practices, as well as insight into things about our daily life that often go unnoticed. Today's readers will gain new appreciation for the convenience and joy of frozen corn and peas for winter stews, for ready-to-use flour that needs no drying or sifting, for wax candles that don't smell of tallow. When preparing bread dough, for example, today's readers will find that tap water, which now usually contains chlorine and other additions like fluoride, does not work as well as distilled water. And they will notice that some of the old food preservation techniques are no longer viable. For instance, it is now recognized that covering the surface of fruit conserves with a brandy-infused circle of paper does not fully inhibit contamination. With the huge revival of interest in the home-preserving of jams, marmalades, chutneys, and pickles, demonstrably safer techniques have been developed, but attention to the details of safe food preservation is still a critical concern for the home food provider.

Recognizing the appetite for culinary journeys of discovery and a curiosity for rediscovering lost foodways, publishers have offered new editions of historical cookbooks, with and without supporting materials. But contemporary cooks quickly discover that using these books is often not straightforward. To correct this, we provide supporting materials and three primary tools in this historical cookery toolkit. Think of Traill's *Guide* as a laboratory manual, providing both tips and instructions for experiments in your modern kitchen and garden as well as occasional narratives about the resulting chemical reactions. Recognizing that every laboratory manual, especially one over a hundred years old, has passages that seem confusing – moments when a teacher is needed to offer additional explanation – we provide a selection of updated recipes, suggesting which modern ingredients might be substituted for those now unavailable, or explaining what is now an unusual food preparation technique. Finally, we offer what might be construed as a dictionary of terms, which explains some of the technical terms and cookery concepts unfamiliar to most modern readers. While we have developed our tools for an interpretation of Traill's *Guide*, our "Glossary of Food and Cooking Terms" is useful for the exploration of other early cookbooks as well.

Why did we choose Traill's *Guide* as an example of an early Canadian cookbook that would be of interest to culinary explorers? There were actually six other contenders, all English-language cookbooks published before 1870, but the choice of Traill's *Guide* was easy. Most significantly, the content in all the others had been taken largely from other works.[14] Technically, the first cookbook published in English Canada was the anonymous *The Cook Not Mad or Rational Cookery*,[15] a reprint of an American text, presumably used by Upper Canadian town women, both those of Yankee origin as well as British newcomers. It offers a considerable view of the range of Canadian fare at the time but provides little information about the foodways of poor backwoods farm families. Another charming little book is *The Frugal Housewife's Manual*. However, its contents were unabashedly and almost entirely cribbed, so it does not provide a reliable portrait of specifically Canadian foodways of the period.[16] Its author, A. B. of Grimsby, who called herself "A Canadian Lady" in a small advertisement in *The Christian Guardian* of 19 August 1840,[17] compiled her tiny manual from other cookbooks, both English and American. Some of the recipes she chose are repeated verbatim, some paraphrased, and several include her editorial insertions,

14 Driver, *Culinary Landmarks*, 19–39.

15 *The Cook Not Mad or Rational Cookery*. Published in Kingston, Upper Canada, in 1831 by James Macfarlane from an 1830 book of the same title published in a small town across the border, Watertown, New York (Driver, *Culinary Landmarks*, 286–7).

16 Much of the culinary material in *The Frugal Housewife's Manual* was taken from two sources: Colin MacKenzie's *Five Thousand Receipts* (1823), which was reissued in an enlarged version many times from 1829 to 1860, especially in Philadelphia, and Lydia Maria Child's *The American Frugal Housewife* (1832). The vegetable garden section was drawn from Charles Crosman, *The Gardener's Manual* (1835). For details on *The Frugal Housewife's Manual* see Driver, *Culinary Landmarks*, 287–8, and Lucas and Williamson, "Frolics with Food."

17 In advertisements, beginning 8 April 1840, *The Frugal Housewife's Manual* is attributed to a "Canadian Lady" who, like many women authors of the time, preferred anonymity. Eleven advertisements for the cookbook appeared in *The Christian Guardian* between 8 April and 4 November 1840.

but few of her recipes seem to be clearly original. As well, her entire section on gardening is almost identical to an American Shaker pamphlet, Charles Crosman's *The Gardener's Manual*.[18]

Three other books were interesting possibilities and worth mentioning but were ruled out because they were Canadian editions of foreign titles: an 1845 Montreal edition of *Modern Practical Cookery* by the Edinburgh cookery teacher Mrs Nourse, an 1846 Niagara edition of *Every Lady's Cook Book*, uncredited but by American Mrs Crowen, and an 1848 Montreal edition of *The Skilful Housewife's Guide: A Book of Domestic Cookery, Compiled from the Best Authors*, also uncredited but assembled by American author Mrs Abell, which includes recipes from her American edition but, as Mary F. Williamson notes, excludes the preface to the American edition as well as the non-culinary material (sections on gardening, botany, and ornithology).[19] In 1861, seven years after Traill's *Guide* appeared, the *Hamilton Spectator* published *The Canadian Housewife's Manual of Cookery*, another compilation of previously published recipes by an anonymous author. With the exception of Traill's *Guide*, all these early cookbooks describe the basic cookery of the town households and farmsteads of the aspiring and middling classes in the countries from which their authors had emigrated. Traill's *Guide* is the best example of a detailed published account of settler life in Canada's backwoods during the 1850s, especially from the female point of view. None of the men's guides (of which there were dozens) addressed women's daily duties in any meaningful and practical way, although a few included some passing advice. Only Traill's *Guide* details the food tastes and practices of Canadian bush settlers of the period, especially in the Peterborough area, even if she addressed her guide to her primarily English, Irish, Scots, and Welsh readers.

We settled on Traill's *Guide* to illustrate the food sourcing, preservation, and preparation techniques of the period. It is also arguably the first authentically Canadian cookbook, as it gathers the collective knowledge of Traill's friends and United Empire Loyalist neighbours and focuses on the foods and food preparation techniques of her region, informed by her hard-won personal experiences. Thanks to McClelland and Stewart, a 1969 paperback version of the 1855 edition, which was retitled *The Canadian Settler's Guide* without Traill's knowledge or permission, is currently available through antiquarian book dealers. However, as a small paperback edition, it is not ideally suited for use in the kitchen. Its introduction, by literary critic Clara Thomas,

---

18 Lucas and Williamson, "Frolics with Food," 147–68.
19 Driver, *Culinary Landmarks*, 92.

provides insights into the literary context of the *Guide* but does not invite readers to think about the ways in which the back-to-the-land movement of the late 1960s/early 1970s related to Traill's experiences, nor (obviously) does it address how more recent concerns about mindful eating and local food sourcing are similar to the concerns of early settlers. We chose to work with the earliest version of Traill's *Guide,* primarily because this is the book that she constructed in the way she wanted it to appear, unlike future editions over which she had no control. As well, until recently this first version was available in printed form only in archives and rare book libraries:[20] only one copy (now housed at University of Toronto's Fisher Rare Book Library) survives of the first thousand printed, and two copies of the second thousand. The first edition is dated 1854 on the title page, but was actually published in a single volume only early in 1855, although the book's text had been made available previously in four separate parts, which had appeared monthly, as evidenced by advertisements in the *Old Countryman,* as well as Traill's correspondence.[21] The re-set text in the present book is taken from the "second thousand" printing.

In this earliest edition we glimpse a world in flux. Traill provides rich insights into the forces at play during the period, which may challenge some of our assumptions about the mid-nineteenth century. When reading an early cookbook, one is tempted to make a comparison between then and now as if they were two static moments in time. But just as "now" feels to us like a moment in a world changing at dizzying speed, so too the "then" of Traill's *Guide* appeared to be a moment in a situation of radical and profound change. Mention in the earliest edition of the *Guide* of challenges to the class structure and the arrival of brand names and products provides evidence of a world in the process of changing, as do its variations in punctuation, spelling, cooking measurements, cooking techniques, and equipment. Readers will

20 That said, Traill's *Guide* was widely distributed during her time. Her agent and publisher, Henry Hope, arranged for bulk sales of the book to the Canadian and British governments, both of whom purchased it in an effort to encourage emigration (Driver, *Culinary Landmarks,* 294; Gray, *Sisters in the Wilderness,* 239; Letters and Memoranda, Library, Library Archives Canada, 1855, RG1, E7, vol. 43). An abridged version was published by the Alcuin Society in 1971–75, but only 450 copies were printed, so it is difficult to find and would not be useful in the kitchen. Alternatively there is an online version of the original edition, taken from the "second thousand" print run, reproduced by the Canadian Institute of Historical Microreproductions (https://archive.org/details/cihm_41417), which can be ordered as a bound paper copy. Neither the CIHM or Alcuin texts provide any guidance in understanding or using the *Guide.*

21 Traill, *I Bless You in My Heart,* 24.

notice that Traill offers her readers British spelling for some words, American for others. For example, in the section describing Female Energy, Traill uses the Canadian spelling for "neighbour" [34–5], whereas in the section on Candle-Making, she uses the American spelling, "neighbor" [177–9].[22]

More generally, manuals like Traill's were guidebooks for a new way of life. Their readers were witnessing an emerging middle class and a society in which men and women lived and worked in separate spheres. These guidebooks were not preserving an old way of life but charting a new course. The domestic instruction manual for housewives was a hugely popular and useful form of writing from 1850 to 1950 precisely because it offered possible models of behaviour at a time when one generation was not necessarily following in the footsteps of the previous one. In America, for example, Lizzie Kander's *The Settlement Cookbook*, aimed at introducing new Jewish immigrants to American foodways, was first published in 1901 with a print run of one thousand copies. By 1984 it had sold almost two million copies.[23]

Despite the oversimplification involved in assuming a "then" completely distinct from "now," one can still make some general observations about the shifts in taste and thinking between the moment captured by the *Guide* and our own. Readers will notice the absence of garlic, for example, and of vanilla flavouring. They will find no mention of Thanksgiving celebrations either, although Traill does describe celebrating Christmas in the backwoods.[24] Settlers celebrated the harvest bounty, the Harvest Festival being part of the Church calendar, but Traill notes that the tone of celebrations was different from those in England; there were "no harvest frolics" [144] in the Americas. Further, the October date for Thanksgiving that Canadians know today is a very recent innovation, put in place only in 1957.[25]

In 1854, when Traill wrote her *Guide*, "Canada" for her meant Upper Canada. In the early 1850s, Canada West (previously Upper Canada, now Ontario) and Canada

---

22 For a much more detailed discussion of different measurement conventions referenced in the *Guide*, see "Measurements for Cooking" (303).

23 Abella, *A Coat of Many Colours*, 283–4; Abusch-Magder, "Cookbooks," 281–7. Our thanks to Lara Rabinovitch for alerting us to the popularity of Kander's book.

24 We cannot help but mention one memorable Christmas in early Canada. It took place in 1847 in Fort Edmonton and consisted of "boiled buffalo hump and calf, dried moose nose, white fish, buffalo tongue, beavers' tails, roast wild goose, potatoes, turnips and bread, but no pies or dessert" (see Murray, *A Taste of Canada*, 59).

25 For information on early Canadian Thanksgiving, see Lucas, "'The Condition of Turkey Will Be Seriously Considered by Canadians Today,'" 1, 6–8; and Smith and Boyd, "Talking Turkey," 116–44.

East (previously Lower Canada, now Quebec) were the two administrative halves of the colony of Canada. Nova Scotia, New Brunswick, Prince Edward Island, and British Columbia were separate colonies, as were Rupert's Land and the Northwest Territory, now sub-divided into Manitoba, Alberta, and Saskatchewan. The western provinces opened up only in Traill's sons' generation – her sons William and Walter both moved west in the 1860s– especially with the coming of the railroad. Not surprisingly, then, Traill mentions none of these places. All eight of her Canadian books and most of her periodical sketches are set in the woods and on the waters of the Townships of Douro, Otonobee, and Hamilton, which are between Lake Ontario and Lake Katchewanooka. Peterborough and Lakefield were the nearest towns. She lived her long Canadian life in these areas and it is to them she is referring when she uses the word "Canada."

In the mid-1880s, recognizing that changes were happening and that her 1854–55 text was largely outdated, Traill half-heartedly planned a revision. Was she perhaps thinking of her two Prairie daughters-in-law? Her alterations, additions, and deletions were handwritten throughout the pages of several incomplete editions of her *Guide* that are held in the Traill Family Collection at Library and Archives Canada. We tell you a bit about her proposed changes in relevant entries of the glossary and include three facsimile pages in this new edition. The revised edition, however, never appeared, perhaps because of the challenges such a large project involved for an author who was then in her eighties.

The *Guide* itself is provided in its original form and without intrusive editorial commentary in the text because one of the unique pleasures of cookbooks lies in the moments when one can hear the voice of the author or various contributors who offer favourite recipes or cooking tips. These are moments of rare intimacy, when we sense we are not just looking through a window to the past or reading a historian's account, but are looking inside a *particular* kitchen window and catching sight of a *particular* cook at work. For this reason, too, we have made the editorial decision to leave idiosyncrasies in place, while flagging their presence to invite readers to pay attention to the voice speaking through them. Imagine then, if you will, Catharine Parr Traill leading you on a journey of discovery, stepping out ahead while we, as editors, through the supporting materials of this edition, shine a flashlight (or oil lamp?) not only on the direction she pursues but also on paths not taken.

Idiosyncrasies of spelling and phrase, a table of contents organized thematically rather than alphabetically [7–9], and leisurely sections on favourite foods (such as bread) or tenets of personal belief (the evils of drink) offer glimpses of Traill herself.

Traill's *Guide* is full of such moments of intimacy, where we come to understand her food preferences, trust her tips, and learn the ins and outs of backwoods cookery under her tutelage. She had a knack of reaching out to her readers with a well-turned phrase to provide clear, reassuring instructions. Having made the difficult transition from genteel middle-class life in England to the harsh rural existence of Upper Canada's backwoods, she was well aware of the need to extend a hand to other women who would be feeling lost and unsure of themselves as they joined their husbands and children in emigrating to the Americas.

Traill was also well aware that some of the skills she had learned the hard way, through experience, might be difficult for a newcomer to master. Bread making using hops-rising is one such important skill, so the *Guide* pauses to discuss the topic at length. While we are now unfamiliar with making bread from our own homemade rising – which has to be carefully nurtured to remain viable – instead of with yeast purchased at a nearby store, we must remember that her contemporary readers would also have been unfamiliar with the whole range of knowledge needed in Canada's backwoods. Traill's reassuring tone anticipates a reader who had come to the backwoods from a long distance, in terms of both geography and expectations. Given this, Traill's *Guide* is ideal for the twenty-first century, when we find ourselves looking for guidance about the basic principles of food sourcing and scratch preparation after having for so long inhabited a world of easily sourced prepared foods.

In many ways, Traill can be seen as the Canadian Mrs Beeton.[26] We are not the first to suggest this comparison: the late Canadian literary critic Clara Thomas made the same observation in 1967, at a time when Canada's centenary was spurring Canadians to explore the details of their national past. She writes that "Catharine Traill is the Mrs. Beeton and the Fannie Farmer of nineteenth-century Canada, but she goes beyond either of these worthy pattern-makers. The pioneer wife's knowledge and capabilities had to extend far beyond the home, the kitchen and the promotion of gracious and thrifty living – ideally, she must also be competent in the garden, the

26 Isabella Mary Beeton became a household name in Britain following the 1861 publication of her cookbook, *The Book of Household Management*. She died in 1865 at age twenty-nine from complications following childbirth. Due to the careful stewardship of her publishing persona by her publisher husband, S.O. Beeton, and the company that later acquired the rights from him, Ward, Lock, Publishers, as well as other companies once copyright ran out, her encyclopedic book has been revised, enlarged, and reissued in whole and in parts in an astonishing range of publications. In 2000, Oxford University Press published an abridged edition edited by Nicola Humble, whose introduction is superb.

fields, with the animals, as nurse and mid-wife, as manufacturer of clothing and, in emergencies, she must have hands as strong and head as clear as a man's. To wear out was frightfully common for the female pioneer; only the incorrigibly slovenly could rust out."[27]

Thomas's point is that Traill distinguished herself by going further than the rest – beyond the house to the fields and the bush of Canada's backcountry. Like Beeton, who published her famous *Book of Household Management* five years after Traill's *Guide* appeared, she saw herself as one who gathered information rather than generating or authoring it herself. "Now this requires more arrangement than invention," she wrote to her sister Susanna, "I must get all my friends to help me with good recipes about Canadian management ... I want to supply a book that will give instruction in every branch that may be needed by the family of a new settler, a book such as I should have been glad to have myself when I came out."[28]

What are some of the best recipes here for modern kitchens? Simple, nutritious, and now forgotten recipes? Try the recipes for Excellent Hot Tea-cakes [100] or Common Bush Tea-cakes [109] or Lemon Cake [106, 108]. Also Indian Pudding [126] – the apple version has become one of our favourites. After all, one reason for deciding to use Traill's *Guide* as an exemplar was because of its detailed and tasty recipes.

Although we revive and comment on a few of Traill's recipes, we frequently turn to Traill's descriptions of dishes and meals and their particular appeal to sketch out what they tell us about nineteenth-century diners, particularly their preferences for seasoning. In some cases, of course, these taste preferences are markedly different from our own and such differences are revealing in and of themselves. For example, Traill did not use garlic and not because the flavouring was unavailable. Field garlic was actually readily available, often to settlers' dismay, because it tainted the taste of milk and butter if cows grazed near it. This is not to suggest that the foods Traill prepared were bland. She mentions using "savory, thyme, marjoram, and the like" [164], as well as a range of spices, and suggests that it is useful to keep on hand bottled vinegar into which has been put scraped horseradish [164].

Despite its extensive list of recipes, the *Guide* omitted many foods that would have been typical of the period. Most notably, Traill provides no recipe for pastry, presumably because she felt readers would already be familiar with its preparation:

27 Thomas, "Happily Ever After," 43–53.
28 Traill to Susanna Moodie, *I Bless You in My Heart*, 6 January 1854, 88. See also Driver, *Culinary Landmarks*, 291–2.

it would have been a staple in kitchens everywhere.[29] Traill's intention was not to create an enormous, expensive, and comprehensive tome. Rather, she was careful to collect practical recipes in an edition that would be affordable for poor families in Upper Canada. She emphasized her curatorial decisions explicitly in the cake section, saying "As this work is not intended for a regular cookery-book, I have limited myself to cakes as are in common use in the farm-houses" [110]. And throughout the *Guide* she was careful to point out practical substitutes for expensive or rare foodstuffs, as when she signals the nutritive value of wild rice, for example, or provides a recipe for Farmer's Rice as a substitute when the farmer did not have enough cash to buy real Carolina rice.

Some familiar British recipes were not included, presumably because they were so much a part of day-to-day cooking they required no written instructions. There is no Scrapple, for example, or Bubble and Squeak. Scrapple is an American dish of fried pork sausage, and Bubble and Squeak is the English version of the Irish and Highland Scots colcannon, a hash of boiled or fried cabbage and potatoes, sometimes with mashed turnips and carrots, and meat scraps. Both were economical recipes made from easily available ingredients, often leftovers. Neither was likely to appear in recipe books, but both were well known. Traill does, however, give a recipe for another popular recipe for leftovers, Irish Mash, which she described as a more economical version of Irish Stew [131].

Simple egg preparations are also absent, although eggs were an essential ingredient in many recipes and egg preservation was a key concern. By contrast, everyday food dishes that would have been unfamiliar to British immigrants are mentioned, including Supporne [121–2], Buckwheat Pancakes [114], and Farmer's Rice [103].

Focusing on the unfamiliar is also the guiding principle for Traill's discussion of meat dishes. For instance, there are remarkably few mentions of "butcher's meat," as it was called then, which would have been familiar to new settlers, even though Traill explains that in "Canadian farm-houses meat is generally cooked twice and sometimes thrice a day" [129]. Instead she provides methods for preparing a variety of wild meats such as bear, venison, and squirrel, all of which would have been unfamiliar to Anglo settlers. At the same time there is no mention of the much more familiar chicken, which was sometimes roasted by hanging it from a string over the fire or by being skewered and turned before the fire in a tin heat-reflector oven. Similarly,

---

29 For those interested in a good, historical recipe for pastry, see Maria Rundell's recipe, provided in this edition [360]. This recipe dates from 1806, but stands up well against the test of time.

there is no mention of meat roasts, although Traill does provide a variant of Yorkshire Pudding (an accompaniment to roast beef) made with cornmeal, which was available to settlers [126]. With the exception of Boiled Ham, there is little discussion of boiled meats, although, as our discussion of settler foodways explains, these would have been common fare in the period. Interestingly, there is also no mention of eating chipmunk, raccoon, eel, or beaver, although poor finances certainly made these attractive sources of nourishment. Catharine's sister, Susanna Moodie, fed them to her family, and Anne Langton mentions that her family once tried porcupine meat, deciding it was similar to lamb.[30]

There are, however, a number of recipes that provide variants of dishes that would have been familiar fare for emigrants, for example, hot drinks, salads, and meat pies. Warm drinks include Labrador tea and dandelion (root) coffee. Celery is described as a "much esteemed" ingredient in salads [60]. Suggested fillings for pie include fish [167–8] and game readily available to settlers: venison [159], pigeon [161], and blackbird [163].

At first glance, then, it might seem that there is a contradiction in Traill's method. Her *Guide* was addressed to new female settlers and assumed they needed instruction. On the other hand, the selection of recipes suggests that she assumed certain foods and food preparation techniques would have been familiar and were therefore not a necessary part of a cookbook aiming to be affordable. Similarly, she provides brief mention of preparation methods in some recipes and much greater precision in others, which is both endearing and exasperating for today's readers. But it is important to remember that this was a very reasonable approach to take in her own time, when some things were common knowledge but backwoods ingredients and methods needed to be carefully explained to the emigrant.

The value of this new edition, this toolkit for historical cookery, lies not only in Traill's original recipes, with their rare level of detail and her distinctive voice, but in the range of documents provided to help translate the nineteenth-century recipes and foodways of settlement in the Americas into achievable dishes in today's kitchens. We hope to revive interest in some simple, nutritious, and forgotten nineteenth-century recipes and menus. For some of Traill's most popular recipes, we provide updated versions, replacing ingredients that are not available today (such as saltpetre) with modern-day equivalents. These updated recipes follow the common format of

30 Anne Langton, *A Gentlewoman in Upper Canada*, 16 September 1842, 351.

modern recipes, providing standardized measurements and detailed description of method of preparation. For cooks attempting a nineteenth-century recipe for the first time, the comparative measurement chart will demystify nuances of different spoon and cup sizes, while explanations of modern ingredients that can be used to approximate historical ones will help while shopping. The annotated list of food terms also offers descriptions of unfamiliar food items. Happy exploration!

A Short Biography of Catharine Parr Traill

Catharine Parr Traill[1] (1802–1899), her sister Susanna Moodie (1803–1885), and their brother Samuel Strickland (1805–1867) were remarkable siblings who recorded their experiences as Canadian backwoods colonists; taken together, their many books and stories document a vivid, multi-faceted picture of mid-nineteenth-century Ontario.

Their parents were Thomas Strickland (1758–1818), a successful merchant, and Elizabeth Homer Strickland (1772–1864). The eight Strickland siblings – Elizabeth, Agnes, Sarah, Jane, Catharine, Susanna, Samuel, and Thomas – grew up happily in the "sylvan wilderness"[2] of agricultural Suffolk. Emphasizing the virtues of resourcefulness, "industry, observation and self-reliance," their father instructed them in history, literature, languages, geography, mathematics, and sciences, while their mother taught the girls to sew, mend, embroider, and bake. Included in this wide-ranging education were ghost stories, daily Bible readings, and evangelical Anglican catechisms.[3] Catharine even learned to fish under her fond father's tutelage. Also somewhat unusually, Catharine and Susanna learned to milk cows, make butter and cheese, and cultivate garden vegetables, unintentional preparation for their later lives as impoverished and often servantless settlers in the rough backwoods of Upper Canada. Another factor that, ironically enough, must have helped them in their later lives was learning to deal with the unforeseen genteel penury caused by their father's sudden death.

Elizabeth (called Eliza) and Agnes co-authored many biographies of royal women (although Agnes was and still is much better known), while Catharine and Susanna became prolific, well-known poets and children's writers in the flowery style of the

---

1 The Strickland family claimed descent from Catherine (Kateryn) Parr, Henry VIII's wife, but that has been disputed and is now generally not accepted.

2 Traill Family Collection, 7.

3 Traill Family Collection, 8854, 8860, 10857, 10896; "Strickland, Catharine Parr (Traill)," *Dictionary of Canadian Biography*, 12:996; Ballstadt, *Catharine Parr Traill and Her Works*, 2; Traill, *I Bless You in My Heart*, 3, 4.

Fig. 1 · Village of Peterborough, 1828. Sketch by Captain Basil Hall, who visited the area in the late 1820s.

Georgian period.[4] Susanna was also involved with the Congregational church and the anti-slavery movement. Sarah was nicknamed "the Baker" for her domestic skills.[5] Adventurous young men, Sam went to Upper Canada in 1825 to join family friends and Thomas went into the merchant navy. In April 1831 Susanna married Lieutenant John Dunbar Moodie and a year later thirty-year-old Catharine married his friend and fellow Orcadian, Lieutenant Thomas Traill. Both Moodie and Traill had been officers in the 21st Scottish Regiment of Fusiliers during the last years of the Napoleonic Wars but had retired on half-pay pensions to pursue non-military careers. Catharine's family was not enthusiastic about her choice of Thomas Traill as a husband. A recent widower, father to two teenage sons, the older, well-travelled, and well-read Traill possessed an Oxford degree and an unhappy disposition that left him prone to depression and ennui. Seeking a solution to the precariousness of their financial status in genteel middle-class England, the two young couples, like so many other hopefuls, immigrated to Upper Canada in summer 1832, taking their maids with them. By

4 "Strickland, Catharine Parr (Traill)," *Dictionary of Canadian Biography*, 12:996. For Catharine and Susanna's writings for young readers, see Ballstadt, *Catharine Parr Traill and Her Works*, 2–4, and Schieder's introduction to his edition of Traill's *Canadian Crusoes*.

5 Peterman, *Sisters in Two Worlds*, 12.

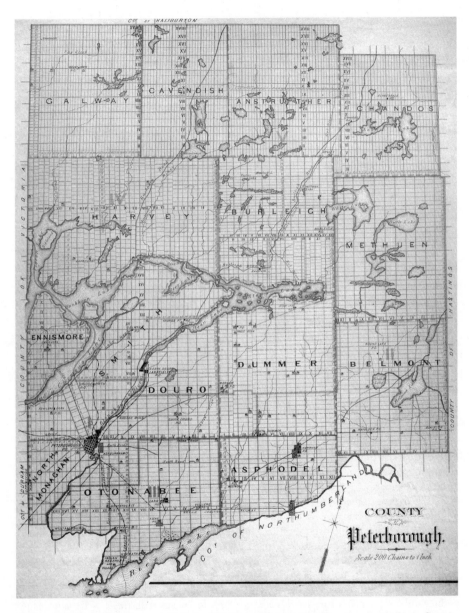

Fig. 2 · 1879 Map of Peterborough County, which is located about forty kilometres north of Lake Ontario on the Otonobee River in what was Douro Township, Newcastle District.

Christmas the Traills were settled in a neat log house on Lake Katchewanooka's east shore in Douro Township, ten miles north of present-day Peterborough,[6] neighbours of their brother Sam and his second wife, backwoods-raised Mary Reid. The Moodies lived first in a cramped hut outside Cobourg, but moved to land beside the Traills in February 1834.

At first Catharine "breathe[d] nothing but domestic happiness,"[7] but, unlike Sam and Mary who were thriving despite hardships, the Traills and Moodies were ill-equipped to be bush farmers, regardless of their youth and hope.[8] Their husbands' agricultural ineptitude and economic bumbling frequently left their expanding families without money, so both sisters returned to writing as a source of income for their families and as a literary outlet for the emotional tensions of their gruelling settlement efforts. Already well-known, though minor, authors, they were able to capitalize on their small literary reputations.

Catharine was the first Strickland to be published. Before coming to Canada, she had written many short stories as well as fourteen books for young audiences, including the juvenile novel *The Young Emigrants; or, Pictures of Canada* (1826), which can be claimed to be her first Canadian book, even though it appeared long before she arrived, since it tells the story of a refined English family called Clarence who retreat from unexpected poverty into the wilds of Canada. Its myriad details about pioneering had been gathered from emigration books,[9] letters written by the Blacks – "valuable" and "amiable"[10] family friends who had emigrated earlier in the decade – and letters to twenty-year-old Sam, who had joined the Blacks in 1825 and later married their daughter Emma. The fictional Clarences succeed through foresighted

6   The city of Peterborough is located about forty kilometres north of Lake Ontario on the Otonobee River in what was Douro Township, Newcastle District, an area in what was the traditional land of the Anishinaabe. The earliest colonists included the Reid and Stewart families, Irish gentry, who arrived in February 1823. In 1825, a large number of other Irish immigrants followed under the leadership of Peter Robinson. The community prospered throughout the nineteenth century. Today it is the largest city in the Trent-Severn Waterway system, which includes the Otonobee.

7   Describing Catharine's happiness, her sister Sarah used this phrase in a letter to their mother dated 23 March 1834. Quoted in Traill, *Backwoods of Canada*, xxvi, lxiv n19.

8   Moodie, *Roughing It in the Bush*, 64. Also Traill's letter of rueful remembrance to her brother-in-law Richard Gwillym, *I Bless You in My Heart*, 9 March 1845, 51–2.

9   In the footnotes Traill scattered through her novel, she credits the *Encyclopedia Britannica* as well as three authors: John Howison, *Sketches of Upper Canada*; Francis Hall, *Travels in Canada and the United States in 1816 and 1817*; and Charles William Janson, *Stranger in America*.

10   Catharine Strickland, *The Young Emigrants*, iii.

preparation, perseverance, good luck, and a belief in God's efficacy, helped by Catharine's youthful inability to comprehend the actual hardships entailed by emigration. Her early fascination with pioneer life may have made the decision to come to Canada more compelling. In 1836 she wrote *The Backwoods of Canada: Being Letters from the Wife of an Emigrant Officer, Illustrative of the Domestic Economy of British America,* the book on which her literary reputation is largely based. A carefully composed epistolary account covering the period from July 1832, when she and her new husband sailed, to May 1835, five months after they moved into their first log house, still anticipating a promising future, it was a practical book for fellow gentlewomen who could have no true idea of the actual primitive colonial conditions, even if they were well-versed in emigrant literature. It reflects both Catharine's naive enthusiasm and her acute powers of observation; part memoir, part natural history treatise, and part settlement guide, it was published by the Society for the Diffusion of Useful Knowledge, which specialized in inexpensive scientific and educational books.[11] When the Society requested more material to increase the book's size to match others in the series, she sent detailed information on manufacturing maple sugar, vinegar, soft soap, candles and pickles, as well as on how to succeed with hop-rising and salt-rising for bread, but because the information arrived too late to be included in the original book, this material was attached as a domestic Appendix.[12] It established what were to become the three themes of Traill's adult writing: the study of the "natural history and botany of the new country," its "imperative domestic duties," and descriptions of local life, all intended to help diminish the sense of alienation felt by "female sojourners in the backwoods of Canada."[13] Susanna's writing, in contrast, would focus on emotional and psychological character studies.

Traill enjoyed the novelties of homemaking and cooking, at first in a situation where her servant did most of the housework and money was available to purchase most necessities. As money dwindled in the late 1830s, she gradually took on the cooking and housekeeping duties. The first Traill child, James, was born in 1833, fol-

---

11 Traill, *Backwoods of Canada*, xxvii. The book was enormously popular: 11,000 copies were printed in 1836, and it was reprinted at least eight times over the next twenty years and translated into German and French (ibid., xxxiv, xl).

12 Ibid., lvii–lviii. The New Canadian Library (1989) edition of *Backwoods* retains the housewifery items as an appendix, but the Centre for Editing Early Canadian Texts edition places them individually at the ends of the relevant letters, as Traill had intended.

13 Ibid., 3.

Fig. 3 · Yellow anemone, photographed by Geraldine Moodie (granddaughter of Susanna).

lowed by eight more over the next fifteen years. During the 1840s and 1850s, her busiest decades as a mother, housewife, and author, and the period when the family had the least money, she published numerous short stories, anecdotes, poems, and essays about bush farm life, including her 1852–53 "Forest Gleaning" series for the Toronto-based *Anglo-American Magazine. Canadian Crusoes, A Tale of the Rice Lake Plains* (1852) was an adventure novel and survival handbook that told the story of three bush-raised adolescents lost in the woods on Rice Lake who successfully adapt to the environment. Unlike the entirely second-hand *Young Emigrants, Canadian Crusoes* conveyed her own local knowledge; both books were didactic fables aimed at Christian youth. *The Female Emigrant's Guide, and Hints on Canadian Housekeeping* was Traill's next book. (For a summary of its publication history see pages xxxix–

Fig. 4 · "Absolutely Pure White Vetch," photographed by Geraldine Moodie.

xliii.) *Lady Mary and Her Nurse*[14] (1856) details how a middle-class pioneer woman explains pioneer skills to Mary, the young daughter of her well-to-do employer. Next came Traill's two studies of Canadian (that is, Ontario) botany – *Canadian Wild Flowers* (1868) and *Studies in Plant Life in Canada* (1885) both written with her niece Agnes (Moodie) Fitzgibbon Chamberlin – which include many culinary notes.

Traill continued to write until her very last years. In the 1880s, she pursued several unrealized projects, from which some manuscripts survive, including an updated *Backwoods of Canada,* a second edition of *The Female Emigrant's Guide,* and a family

14 It was originally published in 1853 as "The Governor's Daughter," a twelve-part serial in *The Maple Leaf.* See Canadian Institute for Historic Microreproductions 18728.

memoir called "Under the Pines."[15] In her nineties she published two children's books, *Pearls and Pebbles* (1894) and *Cot and Cradle Stories* (1895), a combination of memoirs and sketches about flowers, birds, and squirrels, but without any reference to old-fashioned pioneer life skills.

Although the Traills never achieved the prosperity they had assumed would be theirs – and which Catharine initially assured her readers they would find if they were industrious and persevered – she never lost her naturally optimistic temperament or abandoned her devout Christianity. "It has ever been my way to extract the sweet rather than the bitter in the cup of life, and surely it is the best and wisest to do so." As an old woman, she wrote, "To me there was *always* a silver lining to the cloud – and surely it was a gift from God ... in days of trouble and sorrow ... I could look upwards and say – Lord, thy will be done."[16] Through many tribulations – including the loss of two children as babies, the murder of her eldest son, many other family deaths, chronic illness and physical disability, her husband's severe depressions, and stretches of terrible poverty – Catharine continued to write copious family and business letters, journal entries, and anecdotes and articles for Canadian, American, and British periodicals, as well as eight books that presented the natural history and domestic reality of her life in Canada. She and her sister Susanna Moodie became foundational authors in Canadian literature.

Outliving all her siblings, Catharine Parr Traill died at home in Lakefield on 29 August 1899, age ninety-seven, still poor, but having recently been fêted for being the "oldest author in the British Empire" at a public testimonial organized by her good friend Sir Sandford Fleming. Traill was much admired and respected for her contributions to Canadian literature and nature studies.[17]

For more details on Traill's life, see Michael Peterman's entry in the *Dictionary of Canadian Biography* and his beautifully illustrated *Sisters in Two Worlds*, Charlotte Gray's *Sisters in the Wilderness*, and Audrey Morris's *The Gentle Pioneers*, among other works on Traill listed in our bibliography.

---

15 Traill, *Backwoods of Canada*, xlix; Traill Family Collection, revised *Female Emigrant's Guide* ms, 5829–6252; Traill Family Collection, "Under the Pines," 8638–773.
16 Traill, *Backwoods of Canada*, 226; Traill Family Collection, 8875.
17 Traill to Sir Sandford Fleming, *I Bless You in My Heart*, 21 December 1898, 392.

A Publication History of *The Female Emigrant's Guide*

After Traill had decided that she "want[ed] to supply a book that will give instructions in every branch that may be needed by the family of a new settler, a book such as I should have been glad to have had myself when I came out,"[1] she approached her sister Agnes Strickland, a well-known and experienced author in her own right, for assistance in finding a London publisher. When she eventually gave the manuscript to the Toronto firm of Thomas Maclear and Company, the well-off Agnes, not appreciating her sister's desperate circumstances, was annoyed, despite her own failure to find a British publisher willing to take it on. She snipped, "nothing that is first published in Canada will sell in England. So never deceive yourself again with the idea that it will."[2]

At the project's earliest stages, Agnes presciently advised Traill not to sell the copyright for the *Guide*, understanding that if the book "succeeds it will be a good milch cow."[3] Her prediction proved to be accurate, but for the book's publisher rather than, sadly, its author. The *Guide* was produced at considerable cost to Catharine at a time when she was in no position for such an outlay of effort and money. In a letter written in 1855, prior to the release of the last section of the book, Catharine wrote about her fading energy, saying, "I never do any thing now myself. I grow old and indolent. However I sew a good deal and write when I am able or see any good end in view."[4]

---

1 Traill to Susanna Moodie, *I Bless You in My Heart*, 6 January 1854, 88.
2 Agnes Strickland to Traill, 2 June 1855, Traill Family Collection, 568. A series of letters in 1854 and 1855 delineate Strickland's attempts to find a willing publisher and her remonstrations against Traill for deciding on a Canadian firm. (Two of Traill's later books were published with the essential partnership of her widowed niece Agnes Moodie Fitzgibbon, who created the beautiful lithographs for *Canadian Wildflowers* [1868] and, under the name Agnes Chamberlin, her name following her second marriage, for *Studies of Plant Life in Canada* [1885].)
3 Agnes Strickland to Traill, summer 1854, Traill Family Collection, 553.
4 Traill to Ellen Dunlop, *I Bless You in My Heart*, 20 June 1854, 94.

In another letter of the period to her sister Susanna, she explained, "I am not well enough to write long stories and have no brains left."[5]

Only Traill would have described herself as indolent and brainless at a time when she was producing what would become a watershed culinary publication; evidence from other letters suggests the energy she brought to the project. From the start, she understood that the *Guide* would involve gathering information, that it would be a project of "arrangement" rather than "invention.[6] She began by writing to family and friends to ask for material for the book, starting with Susanna herself. "I must get all my friends to help me with good recipes about Canadian m[anage]ment and all such things, in cooking and making and baking, as are needful. Any good useful practical receipts that you can glean up for me among farmers wives will be faithfully received but I do not want you to travel about writing them because you have too much to do but if you can get any written for me I shall be equally obliged."[7]

Next came the task of marketing the project. Once the publisher had agreed to take on the *Guide,* he still asked Traill to help sell subscriptions to the various installments. The terms he offered her initially were remarkably onerous given the level of her involvement. She wrote in a letter to Ellen Dunlop that her publisher wanted her to "bring it out" at her own risk "and get subscription lists opened up the principal towns for the work."[8] Luckily, Traill managed to renegotiate the terms of publication, so by the time she wrote this letter, she was able to say that she had no liability for the publication costs but she was still expected to come up with a subscription list. The logistics that made it possible for her to visit towns in order to "get subscription lists" were complicated to say the least. In the same letter she admitted that she would very much like to go to Toronto, but had "not the means either for supplying myself with decent outer clothes – such as I could present myself in at the houses of the gentry who are desirous of seeing me – or to pay for a weeks board and lodging at some decent house."[9] However, by the end of that same letter, she had convinced herself to go, deciding to stay with a friend to keep costs down.

Although raising funds by subscription was a method commonly employed by publishers to ensure sales of at least a specific number of copies, it was difficult for

5 Traill to Susanna Moodie, *I Bless You in My Heart*, 6 January 1854, 89.
6 Ibid., 88.
7 Ibid.
8 Traill to Ellen Dunlop, *I Bless You in My Heart*, 20 June 1854, 92.
9 Ibid.

the reticent Catharine to accomplish, especially given her geographically isolated location. Nevertheless she succeeded in raising a good-sized subscription list of local "good men and true," such as the doctor, who bought it "for housekeepers young and old" and young men "to buy it for their wives and sweethearts."[10]

The book's actual production was bedevilled by difficulties, particularly a lack of money because not all subscribers pre-paid on time; the printer wanted prepayment for the paper, and then ran out of it. "We have been stopped in issuing the last part of my book for want of paper for the printing," she wrote in a letter of early 1855, "few of the subscribers having paid in advance on the second part. This has been a drawback for we relied on some of the proceeds to get out the last part."[11] This led to a decision to bring the book out in four parts. The first part was dated 1 December 1854, although it did not actually appear until the end of the month. The three other parts were scheduled for publication every three weeks, but were also delayed. Thus, although the title page of the first edition is dated 1854 – the year generally assigned to it – the completed book was actually available only in mid-March 1855.[12] This new re-set edition reproduces the text as it appears in the "second thousand" series of copies, also produced in 1855 but dated 1854.

The Reverend Henry Payne Hope (1803–1868), an Englishman recently arrived in Toronto who had started the *Old Countryman* newspaper in June 1853, acted as Traill's agent, but proved to be a self-serving scoundrel. At first he had been very friendly toward Traill and accepted items for inclusion in his newspaper, but over the years he failed to pay her her full share of the profits from the hundreds of copies of the *Guide* purchased by both the Department of Agriculture and the British government.[13] In later editions he, and other unscrupulous publishers, even excised her name from the title page. The usually charitable Traill expressed her unhappiness with Reverend Hope: "1854 The Emigrants Guide [*sic*] printed in Toronto by subscription, badly got up – a vexatious failure – [I] sold the copyright to Rev^d Mr Hope for

10 Ibid., and Traill Family Collection, 17 September 1854, 1953.
11 Traill to Ellen Dunlop, *I Bless You in My Heart*, 19 February 1854, 94.
12 Ibid.; Driver, *Culinary Landmarks*, 292–3.
13 For a comprehensive and detailed chronology of the complicated publication history of *The Female Emigrant's Guide*, see Driver, *Culinary Landmarks*, 291–300, as well as Traill, *I Bless You in My Heart*, 24–5; Traill Family Correspondence, Reverend G. Warren, "The Life of Catharine Parr Traill," published in the *Ottawa Citizen* on 27 June 1898, 12857; and a manuscript fragment, not dated but apparently from late in her life, given the shaky hand, Toronto Reference Library, Special Collections.

which he paid me with a bad note of hand & 50 unbound copies[.] Afterwards he treated with an Eng[h] [English] printer and got a situation for his son in Liverpool – I was told after his death that he had obtained a money grant from the Can[n] Gov[t] as in my behalf but I never received or was told of the gift."[14] The book sold well during her lifetime, but the dishonest Hope continued to cheat Traill. In a letter dated 21 July 1861, Agnes Strickland informed Traill "that Mr Hope your foxlike friend is selling your Emigrants Guide at a great rate for it has been [taken?] up by government ... How is it that you have no benefit from your own work? Your name is not even appended to it."[15] Nor had she been sufficiently aggressive in claiming what was rightfully hers for any of her books. Traill was, she claimed, a "poor country mouse" about publishing negotiations.[16] Strickland seems not to have recognized that Traill and her daughters were often busy performing the very household tasks the *Guide* was about. As well, in addition to being retiring and often ill, neither Catharine nor her husband had a head for business.[17]

There were several reprints and editions published throughout the 1850s and 1860s, although, as bibliographer Elizabeth Driver notes, it is difficult to be sure how many, since Hope's numbering system was inconsistent. The fifth edition, published sometime later in 1855, was retitled *The Canadian Settler's Guide*, although it was not Traill's choice. It was reprinted several times under this title. In 1861 and 1862 it was reprinted under the title *The Canadian Emigrant Housekeeper's Guide,* in 1861 by James Lovell and in 1862 by Lovell & Gibson.

McClelland and Stewart's decision to use *The Canadian Settler's Guide* as the title for their 1969 reprint, which they list on the copyright page as the 5th edition, has led to it being best known under this title. This printing includes an introduction by Clara Thomas. The Alcuin Society produced an abridged edition under this title in 1971, but only in a limited edition of 450 books.

The Female Emigrant's Guide was produced rapidly, indeed hastily, in under a year because the Traills were then particularly badly off financially, which may explain its organizational flaws. The tone is uneven, sometimes conversational and full of

---

14 Traill Family Collection, manuscript fragment, Traill, no date, 8967.
15 Traill Family Collection, Agnes Strickland to Traill, 21 July 1861, 653–6.
16 Traill to Frances Stewart, 5 May 1862 (?), Baldwin Room, quoted in Peterman, "Splendid Anachronism," 181; Traill to Agnes Fitzgibbon, 29 October 1861, Thomas Fisher Rare Book Library, University of Toronto.
17 Peterman, "Splendid Anachronism," 181.

asides like "Try it!" [89], sometimes neutral, sometimes expansive, sometimes brief (especially with regard to recipes taken from other publications). Editing could have tightened some sentences, eliminated many repetitions, and caught a few egregious errors, such as misplacement of the peaches section [86–7], but, once typeset, these could not easily be corrected. The book would also have benefited from an index, and Catharine's sister Jane had offered to teach her the art of indexing – "always done after the book is printed, a plague to do, but easy when learned" – but economic pressures or a lack of time may have prevented her from taking this on.[18] The *Guide* has an ad hoc, cobbled feeling that could have been improved if given time, but its informality, spontaneity, and chattiness must have inspired warmth, confidence, belief, and relief in her intended readers, as it does today.

18 Jane Strickland to Traill, 4 April 1854, excerpt quoted in Driver, *Culinary Landmarks*, 292.

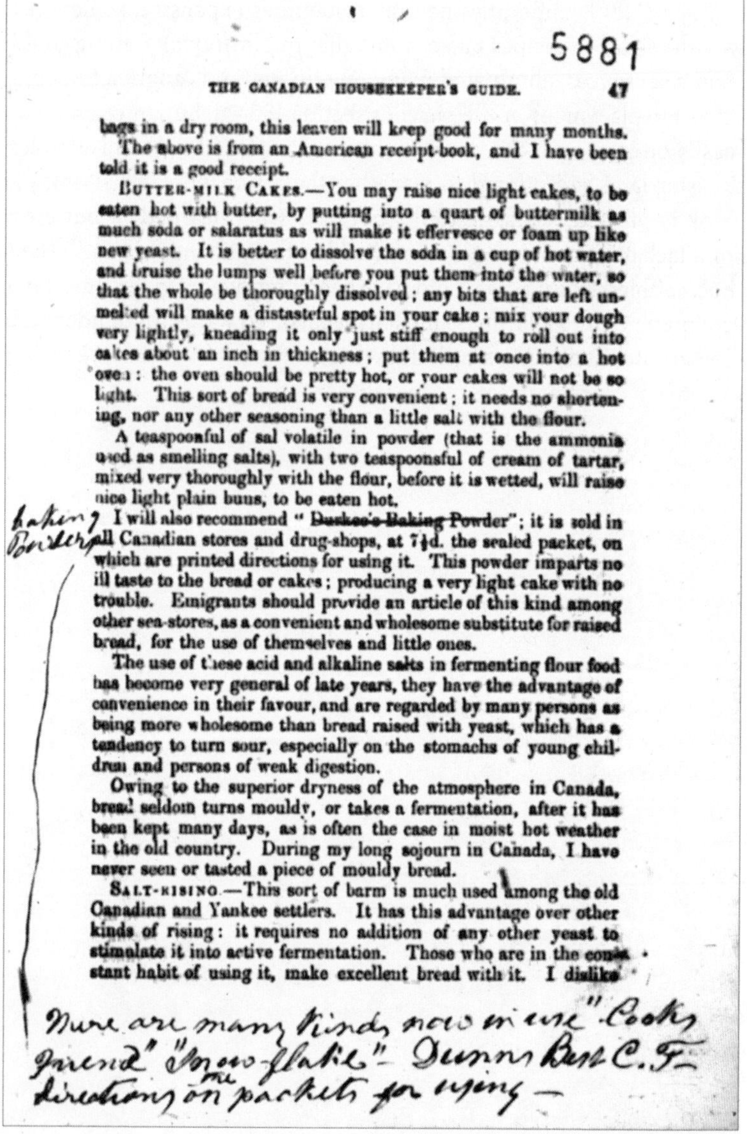

5881

bags in a dry room, this leaven will keep good for many months.

The above is from an American receipt-book, and I have been told it is a good receipt.

BUTTER-MILK CAKES.—You may raise nice light cakes, to be eaten hot with butter, by putting into a quart of buttermilk as much soda or salaratus as will make it effervesce or foam up like new yeast. It is better to dissolve the soda in a cup of hot water, and bruise the lumps well before you put them into the water, so that the whole be thoroughly dissolved; any bits that are left unmelted will make a distasteful spot in your cake; mix your dough very lightly, kneading it only just stiff enough to roll out into cakes about an inch in thickness; put them at once into a hot oven: the oven should be pretty hot, or your cakes will not be so light. This sort of bread is very convenient; it needs no shortening, nor any other seasoning than a little salt with the flour.

A teaspoonful of sal volatile in powder (that is the ammonia used as smelling salts), with two teaspoonsful of cream of tartar, mixed very thoroughly with the flour, before it is wetted, will raise nice light plain buns, to be eaten hot.

baking *Powder* I will also recommend "~~Buskee's Baking Powder~~"; it is sold in all Canadian stores and drug-shops, at 7½d. the sealed packet, on which are printed directions for using it. This powder imparts no ill taste to the bread or cakes; producing a very light cake with no trouble. Emigrants should provide an article of this kind among other sea-stores, as a convenient and wholesome substitute for raised bread, for the use of themselves and little ones.

The use of these acid and alkaline salts in fermenting flour food has become very general of late years, they have the advantage of convenience in their favour, and are regarded by many persons as being more wholesome than bread raised with yeast, which has a tendency to turn sour, especially on the stomachs of young children and persons of weak digestion.

Owing to the superior dryness of the atmosphere in Canada, bread seldom turns mouldy, or takes a fermentation, after it has been kept many days, as is often the case in moist hot weather in the old country. During my long sojourn in Canada, I have never seen or tasted a piece of mouldy bread.

SALT-RISING.—This sort of barm is much used among the old Canadian and Yankee settlers. It has this advantage over other kinds of rising: it requires no addition of any other yeast to stimulate it into active fermentation. Those who are in the constant habit of using it, make excellent bread with it. I dislike

There are many kinds now in use "Cook's Friend" "Snow-flake" – Dunns Best C. F. directions on the packets for using –

Fig. 5 · Traill's proposed revision to the discussion of baking powder brand names, made in the early 1880s. Her note reads: "There are many kinds now in use. 'Cook's Friend' 'Snow Flake' – 'Dunns Best C. F.' – Directions on the packets for using –"

Editors' Note

The present edition of Catharine Parr Traill's *The Female Emigrant's Guide*, with the subtitle *Cooking with a Canadian Classic,* is based on the first edition, which was released in 1855 but carries the publication date of 1854. It reproduces the text in the "second thousand" printing, but has been re-set for ease of reading as well as for efficient use of space on the page. Ease of reading also prompted our decision to use the typeface Filosofia. The original text was altered as little as possible: where clarification or explanation was necessary, rather than modify the text, we chose to either insert the information within parentheses or add a footnote. References to the *Guide* in our accompanying essays and glossaries are indicated by square brackets within the text. Thus, for example, [100] refers to page 100 of this new edition. Every effort has been made to produce a text that respects Traill's voice and prose.

In order to give readers a sense of the original book, we reproduce three facsimile pages (figs 8, 10, and 11). The pages appear in their original dimensions. We also reproduce some of the images in the original edition: clearing the land (fig. 9), Indian rice (fig. 12), a settler family undertaking their annual harvest of maple syrup and sugar (fig. 13), provincial division diagram (fig. 14), a diagram of the Canadian "side line" (fig. 15), and children in a sleigh (fig. 16).

In the 1880s, Traill revisited the *Guide* with an eye to producing another, updated volume, although this was never published. Three facsimile pages from this second manuscript are reproduced here, to suggest how Traill's thinking had changed in the thirty or so years since she first drafted the *Guide*. These three pages refer to recipes involving baking powder (fig. 5), cakes (fig. 6), and tomato catsup (fig. 7). The numbers stamped in the top right corner indicate that they are part of the Traill Family Collection at Library and Archives Canada.

Since we concentrate on the culinary content and context of the *Guide*, we have not attempted to identify sources for Traill's many quotations from poems, plays, and Bible verses.

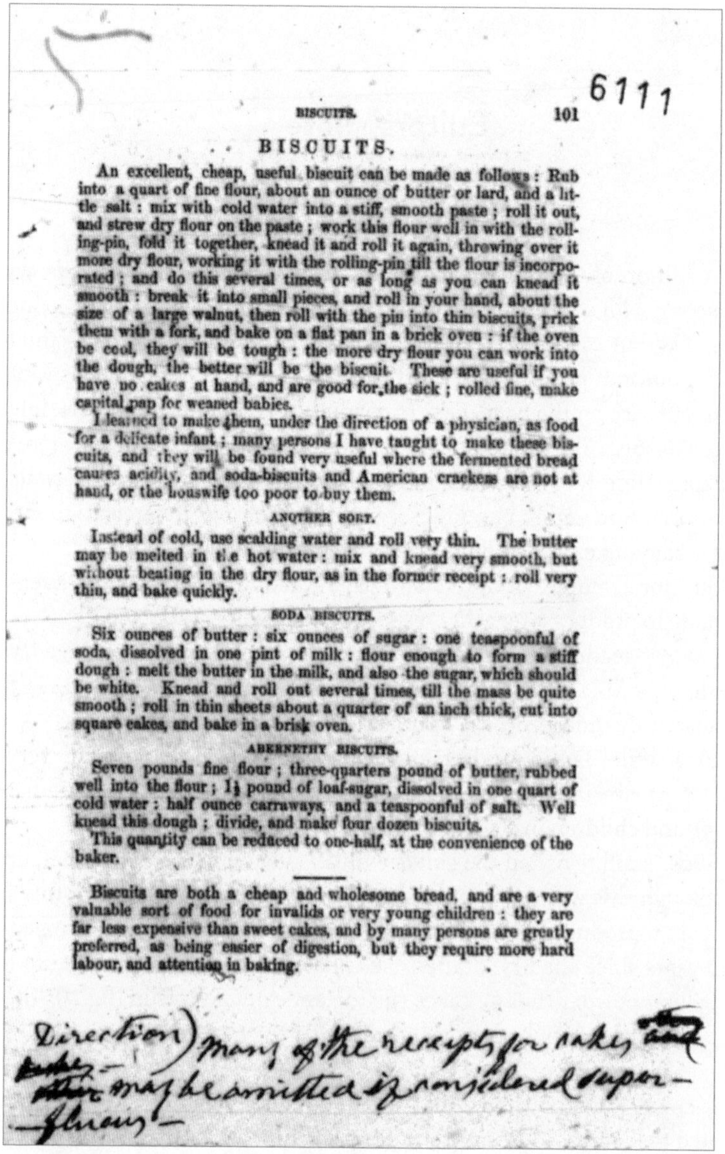

6111

BISCUITS.

An excellent, cheap, useful biscuit can be made as follows: Rub into a quart of fine flour, about an ounce of butter or lard, and a little salt: mix with cold water into a stiff, smooth paste; roll it out, and strew dry flour on the paste; work this flour well in with the rolling-pin, fold it together, knead it and roll it again, throwing over it more dry flour, working it with the rolling-pin till the flour is incorporated; and do this several times, or as long as you can knead it smooth: break it into small pieces, and roll in your hand, about the size of a large walnut, then roll with the pin into thin biscuits, prick them with a fork, and bake on a flat pan in a brick oven: if the oven be cool, they will be tough: the more dry flour you can work into the dough, the better will be the biscuit. These are useful if you have no cakes at hand, and are good for the sick; rolled fine, make capital pap for weaned babies.

I learned to make them, under the direction of a physician, as food for a delicate infant; many persons I have taught to make these biscuits, and they will be found very useful where the fermented bread causes acidity, and soda-biscuits and American crackers are not at hand, or the houswife too poor to buy them.

ANOTHER SORT.

Instead of cold, use scalding water and roll very thin. The butter may be melted in the hot water: mix and knead very smooth, but without beating in the dry flour, as in the former receipt: roll very thin, and bake quickly.

SODA BISCUITS.

Six ounces of butter: six ounces of sugar: one teaspoonful of soda, dissolved in one pint of milk: flour enough to form a stiff dough: melt the butter in the milk, and also the sugar, which should be white. Knead and roll out several times, till the mass be quite smooth; roll in thin sheets about a quarter of an inch thick, cut into square cakes, and bake in a brisk oven.

ABERNETHY BISCUITS.

Seven pounds fine flour; three-quarters pound of butter, rubbed well into the flour; 1½ pound of loaf-sugar, dissolved in one quart of cold water: half ounce carraways, and a teaspoonful of salt. Well knead this dough; divide, and make four dozen biscuits.

This quantity can be reduced to one-half, at the convenience of the baker.

Biscuits are both a cheap and wholesome bread, and are a very valuable sort of food for invalids or very young children: they are far less expensive than sweet cakes, and by many persons are greatly preferred, as being easier of digestion, but they require more hard labour, and attention in baking.

Direction) Many of the receipts for cakes ~~and others~~ may be omitted if considered super-fluous –

Fig. 6 · Traill's proposed revisions to cake recipes, made in the early 1880s. Her note reads: "Direction Many of the receipts for cakes ~~and others~~ (?) may be omitted if considered superfluous –"

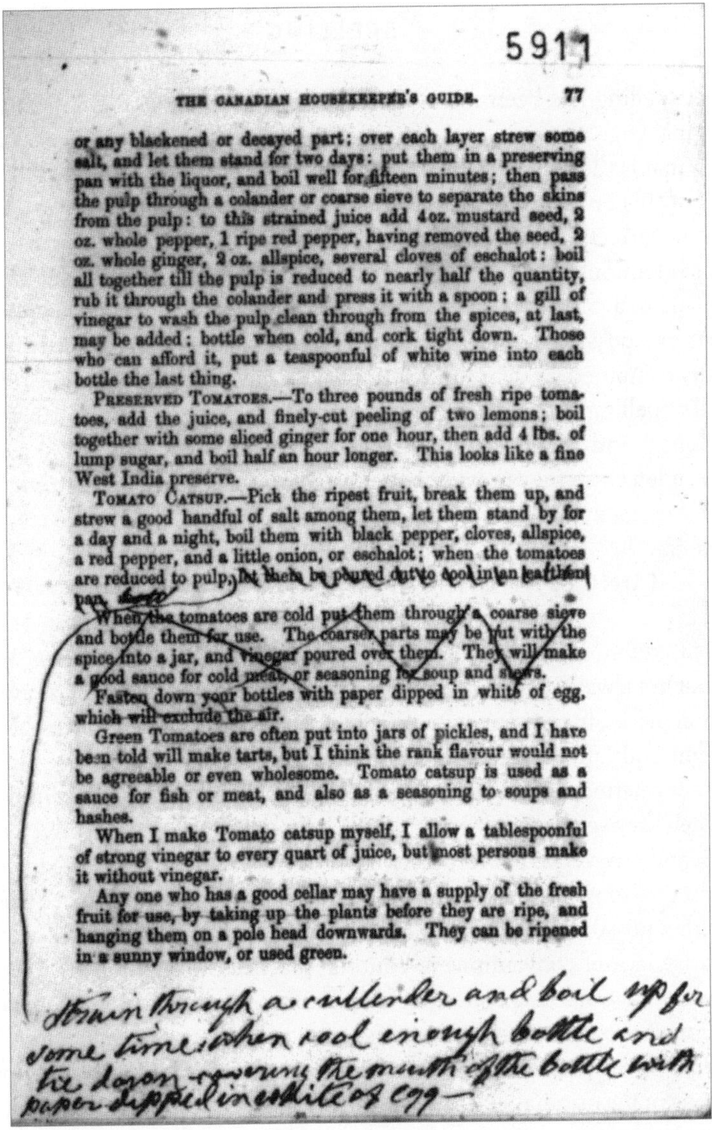

5911

or any blackened or decayed part; over each layer strew some salt, and let them stand for two days: put them in a preserving pan with the liquor, and boil well for fifteen minutes; then pass the pulp through a colander or coarse sieve to separate the skins from the pulp: to this strained juice add 4oz. mustard seed, 2 oz. whole pepper, 1 ripe red pepper, having removed the seed, 2 oz. whole ginger, 2 oz. allspice, several cloves of eschalot: boil all together till the pulp is reduced to nearly half the quantity, rub it through the colander and press it with a spoon; a gill of vinegar to wash the pulp clean through from the spices, at last, may be added: bottle when cold, and cork tight down. Those who can afford it, put a teaspoonful of white wine into each bottle the last thing.

PRESERVED TOMATOES.—To three pounds of fresh ripe tomatoes, add the juice, and finely-cut peeling of two lemons; boil together with some sliced ginger for one hour, then add 4 lbs. of lump sugar, and boil half an hour longer. This looks like a fine West India preserve.

TOMATO CATSUP.—Pick the ripest fruit, break them up, and strew a good handful of salt among them, let them stand by for a day and a night, boil them with black pepper, cloves, allspice, a red pepper, and a little onion, or eschalot; when the tomatoes are reduced to pulp, let them be poured out to cool in an earthen pan.

When the tomatoes are cold put them through a coarse sieve and bottle them for use. The coarser parts may be put with the spice into a jar, and vinegar poured over them. They will make a good sauce for cold meat, or seasoning for soup and stews.

Fasten down your bottles with paper dipped in white of egg, which will exclude the air.

Green Tomatoes are often put into jars of pickles, and I have been told will make tarts, but I think the rank flavour would not be agreeable or even wholesome. Tomato catsup is used as a sauce for fish or meat, and also as a seasoning to soups and hashes.

When I make Tomato catsup myself, I allow a tablespoonful of strong vinegar to every quart of juice, but most persons make it without vinegar.

Any one who has a good cellar may have a supply of the fresh fruit for use, by taking up the plants before they are ripe, and hanging them on a pole head downwards. They can be ripened in a sunny window, or used green.

strain through a cullinder and boil up for some time. When cool enough bottle and tie down covering the mouth of the bottle with paper dipped in white of egg —

Fig. 7 · Traill's proposed revision to the recipe for tomato catsup, made in the early 1880s. Her note reads: "strain through a cullinder and boil up for some time. When cool enough bottle and tie down covering the mouth of the bottle with paper dipped in white of egg –"

SPELLING

Original spelling has been retained throughout to preserve the tone and charm of the original (e.g. "musquitoes," "waggons," or "thorouly"). Where there is inconsistent spelling that is the result of obvious typographical error (e.g. "far" instead of "for," "i" instead of "it") or that impedes readers' understanding of the text (e.g. "ley" instead of "lye"), a correction is entered in square brackets following the original. Where the author's intentions are ambiguous (e.g. "within side my fence"), no modification has been made to avoid altering the original meaning. Instead, an explanatory footnote suggests one possible correct phrasing or spelling. Many paired words that are now generally combined, such as "under" and "side," have been left as in the original.

Traill's spelling fluctuated between standard American and British conventions (e.g. "honor" and "honour" or "neighbor" and "neighbour"). These inconsistencies have been left since they provide some insight into the sense of linguistic flux at this historical moment in the Americas.

PUNCTUATION, CAPITALIZATION, AND LAYOUT

The 1854 edition followed no strict rules of punctuation and layout. Spaces were often, but not always, added before commas and semi-colons, as well as after opening quotation marks, in part but not entirely due to the original text having been set with both right and left justification. These spaces have been removed, as have double spaces after periods. Commas, however, have been left as they were in the original, even when they separate subject and verb. A few commas were incorrectly typeset as periods, and vice versa. In most cases they have been silently corrected. The font size of headings also varies from one part to another. Since this edition has been re-set, it was neither possible nor appropriate to retain all such inconsistencies, which convey the relative lack of conventions in editorial practices at the time. However, since in many ways the *Guide* is a collection from multiple sources, conventions for the capitalization of proper nouns are inconsistent in ways that often signal a shift in voice. In order to give contemporary readers access to such moments of shift, capitalization appears as in the original.

Quotation marks often appeared at the end of long quotations but rarely at the beginning. For the sake of consistency and to help readers distinguish between Traill's own words and secondary sources, the missing quotation marks have been added, with the change indicated in a footnote. If no quotation marks accompanied quotations in the original, none have been added here. In the original text, a narrower spacing distinguishes quotations from Traill's own text, but in this re-set edition, we have indented quotations for the sake of clarity.

The thematic sections generally follow the original edition but in a few cases we have provided a new title in square brackets, such as [B E A N S.]. The initial typesetter was also inconsistent about the format used to indicate first- and second-level themes, and we have regularized these indicators in this edition.

TERMINOLOGY

The 1854 edition referred to the First Nations people of Canada by the outdated and vexing term "Indian" and even the derogatory "squaw." Traill signals unease with this last term and also uses the phrase "Indian-women," adding the qualification that "they don't like to be called squaws since they have become Christians."[1] We have decided to leave these terms in the *Guide* to accurately present the world in which Catharine Parr Traill lived, referencing the relationship between settler and First Nations peoples of the period. To recognize that "Indian" was a name imposed by settler communities, outside direct quotations, titles, recipes, and names for historical ingredients we refer either to the First Nations or, where appropriate, to a specific First Nation, recognizing and respecting the diverse ways in which First Nations, Métis, Inuit, and other Indigenous peoples choose to identify themselves. Traill wrote the *Guide* in her family's home near Rice Lake, traditional territory of the present Hiawatha First Nation, formerly known as the Mississauga Anishinaabe of Rice Lake. The Mississauga belong to the larger Ojibwa (Ojibwe) language group that refers to itself as anissina.pe, which we render as Anishinaabe.[2] Other Anishinaabe groups, as well as the Haudenosaunee (Six Nations), also have long histories in this area.[3]

NOTES

We have used numbered notes to distinguish our editorial comments from Traill's original footnotes, which have been retained and, as in the original, are denoted with

---

1 Traill, *Studies of Plant Life in Canada*, 104.
2 Rogers, "Southeastern Ojibwa," 760–71.
3 See Laviolette, "Notes on the Aborigines of the Province of Ontario." For additional detail on the history of the Hiawatha First Nation see http://www.hiawathafirstnation.com/about-us/history/.

asterisks. In addition to indicating changes made to the original text and suggesting the correct spelling of words misspelled by Traill, our footnotes provide additional historical context for Traill's *Guide*. We have also occasionally commented on Traill's footnotes – these comments appear in square brackets.

RESOURCE MATERIALS

The resource materials are aimed at providing readers with further information about nineteenth-century cooking and housekeeping. They draw from subject-specific dictionaries and guides, many nineteenth-century commentators and cookbooks, as well as Traill's published and unpublished papers and other works, and the extensive Traill Family archives. To keep these references as unobtrusive as possible, short titles have been used in the footnotes and a bibliography included.

The Female
Emigrant's
Guide

THE
FEMALE EMIGRANT'S
GUIDE,
AND
Hints on Canadian Housekeeping.

BY MRS. C. P. TRAILL,

AUTHORESS OF

THE "BACKWOODS OF CANADA," "FOREST GLEANINGS,"

"THE CANADIAN CRUSOES," &c., &c.

SECOND THOUSAND.

TORONTO, C.W.:

SOLD BY MACLEAR AND COMPANY

AND ALL THE PRINICIPAL BOOKSELLERS THROUGHOUT CANADA,

THE BRITISH AMERICAN PROVINCES, AND THE UNITED STATES.

1854.

Price Twenty-Five Cents, or One Shilling and Three-pence, each part, postpaid to any
part of Canada, the British American Provinces, and the United States.

TO THE RIGHT HONOURABLE
THE EARL OF ELGIN AND KINCARDINE, K. T.

&c., &c., &c.

GOVERNOR-GENERAL OF BRITISH NORTH AMERICA,

THE FIRST PART OF THIS LITTLE HOUSEHOLD VOLUME

IS DEDICATED

AS A RESPECTFUL TRIBUTE OF LOYAL ESTEEM,

BY HIS LORDSHIP'S

FAITHFUL FRIEND,

THE AUTHORESS.

TABLE OF CONTENTS[1]

——————

1 This alphabetical Table of Contents follows the original text, but page numbers refer to this new, re-set edition.

PREFACE.

Among the many books that have been written for the instruction of the Canadian emigrant, there are none exclusively devoted for the use of the wives and daughters of the future settler, who for the most part, possess but a very vague idea of the particular duties which they are destined to undertake, and are often totally unprepared to meet the emergencies of their new mode of life.

As a general thing they are told that they must prepare their minds for some hardships and privations, and that they will have to exert themselves in a variety of ways to which they have hitherto been strangers ; but the exact nature of that work, and how it is to be performed, is left untold. The consequence of this is, that the females have everything to learn, with few opportunities of acquiring the requisite knowledge, which is often obtained under circumstances, and in situations the most discouraging ; while their hearts are yet filled with natural yearnings after the land of their birth, (dear even to the poorest emigrant), with grief for the friends of their early days, and while every object in this new country is strange to them. Disheartened by repeated failures, unused to the expedients which the older inhabitants adopt in any case of difficulty, repining and disgust take the place of cheerful activity ; troubles increase, and the power to overcome them decreases ; domestic happiness disappears. The wo-

B

PREFACE.

Among the many books that have been written for the instruction of the Canadian emigrant, there are none exclusively devoted for the use of the wives and daughters of the future settler, who for the most part, possess but a very vague idea of the particular duties which they are destined to undertake, and are often totally unprepared to meet the emergencies of their new mode of life.

As a general thing they are told that they must prepare their minds for some hardships and privations, and that they will have to exert themselves in a variety of ways to

Fig. 8 (*facing page*) · First page of original preface; Fig. 9 (*above*) · A new colonist chops a log for the fence that surrounds his clearing. Behind him is a log cabin and a cow shelter. Notice the big exterior stone fireplace and the rain barrel.

which they have hitherto been strangers; but the exact nature of that work, and how it is to be performed, is left untold. The consequence of this is, that the females have everything to learn, with few opportunities of acquiring the requisite knowledge, which is often obtained under circumstances, and in situations the most discouraging; while their hearts are yet filled with natural yearnings after the land of their birth, (dear even to the poorest emigrant), with grief for the friends of their early days, and while every object in this new country is strange to them. Disheartened by repeated failures, unused to the expedients which the older inhabitants adopt in any case of difficulty, repining and disgust take the place of cheerful activity; troubles increase, and the power to overcome them decreases; domestic happiness disappears. The woman toils on heart-sick and pining for the home she left behind her. The husband reproaches his broken-hearted partner, and both blame the Colony for the failure of the individual.

Having myself suffered from the disadvantage of acquiring all my knowledge of Canadian housekeeping by personal experience, and having heard other females similarly situated lament the want of some simple useful book to give them an insight into the customs and occupations incidental to a Canadian settler's life, I have taken upon me to endeavor to supply this want, and have with much labour collected such useful matter as I thought best calculated to afford the instruction required.

As even the materials differ, and the method of preparing food varies greatly between the colony and the Mother-country, I have given in this little book the most approved recipes for cooking certain dishes, the usual mode of manufacturing maple-sugar, soap, candles, bread and other articles of household expenditure; in short, whatever subject is in any way connected with the management of a Canadian settler's house, either as regards economy or profit, I have introduced into the work for the benefit of the future settler's wife and family.

As this little work has been written for all classes, and more particularly for the wives and daughters of the small farmers, and a part of it is also addressed to the wives of the labourer and mechanics, I aimed at no beauty of style. It was not written with the intention of amusing, but simply of instructing and advising.

I might have offered my female friends a work of fiction or of amusing facts, into which it would have been an easy matter to have interwoven a mass of personal adventure, with useful information drawn from my own experience during twenty-two years sojourn in the Colony; but I well knew that knowledge conveyed through such a medium is seldom attended with practical results; it is indeed something like searching through a bushel of chaff to discover a few solitary grains of wheat. I therefore preferred collating my instruction into the more homely but satisfactory form of a Manual of Canadian housewifery, well contented to abandon the paths of literary fame, if I could render a solid benefit to those of my own sex who through duty or necessity are about to become sojourners in the Western Wilderness.

It is now twenty years ago since I wrote a work with the view of preparing females of my own class more particularly, for the changes that awaited them in the life of a Canadian emigrant's wife. This book was entitled "Letters from the Backwoods of Canada," and made one of the volumes in Knight's "Library of Useful and Entertaining Knowledge," and was, I believe, well received by the public; but as I had then been but a short time resident in the country, it was necessarily deficient in many points of knowledge which I have since become aware were essential for the instruction of the emigrant's wife. These deficiencies I have endeavoured to supply in the present work, and must here acknowledge with thanks the assistance that I have received from several ladies of my acquaintance, who have kindly supplied me with hints from their own experience on various matters.

To Mr. W. McKyes, Mrs. McKyes and Miss McKyes I am largely indebted for much useful information; also to Mrs. Stewart of Auburn, Douro, and her kind family; and to Misses A. and M. Ferguson; with many others, by whose instruction I have been largely benefitted; and take the present opportunity of publicly acknowledging my obligations.

Hoping that my little volume may prove a useful guide, I dedicate it with heartfelt good wishes to the Wives and Daughters of the
CANADIAN EMIGRANT.

INTRODUCTORY REMARKS,

Addressed to Husbands and Fathers.

Before the master of the household fully decides upon taking so important a step as leaving his native land to become a settler in Canada, let him first commune with himself and ask the important question, Have I sufficient energy of character to enable me to conform to the changes that may await me in my new mode of life?—Let him next consider the capabilities of his partner; her health and general temper; for a sickly, peevish, discontented person will make but a poor settler's wife in a country where cheerfulness of mind and activity of body are very essential to the prosperity of the household.

In Canada persevering energy and industry, with sobriety, will overcome all obstacles, and in time will place the very poorest family in a position of substantial comfort that no personal exertions alone could have procured for them elsewhere.

To the indolent or to the intemperate man Canada offers no such promise; but where is the country in which such a person will thrive or grow wealthy? He has not the elements of success within him.—It is in vain for such a one to cross the Atlantic; for he will bear with him that fatal enemy which kept him poor at home. The active, hard-working inhabitants who are earning their bread honestly by the sweat of their brow, or by the exertion of mental power, have no sympathy with such men. Canada is not the land for the idle sensualist. He must forsake the error of his ways at once, or he will sink into ruin here as he would have done had he staid in the old country. But it is not for such persons that our book is intended.

To Wives and Daughters.

As soon as the fitness of emigrating to Canada has been fully decided upon, let the females of the family ask God's blessing upon their undertaking; ever bearing in mind that "unless the Lord build the house, their labour is but lost that build it; unless the Lord keep the city, the watchman waketh but in vain." In all their trials let them look to Him who can bring all things to pass in His good time, and who can guard them from every peril, if they will only believe in His promises, and commit their ways to Him.

As soon, then, as the resolution to emigrate has been fixed, let the females of the house make up their minds to take a cheerful and active part in the work of preparation. Let them at once cast aside all vain opposition and selfish regrets, and hopefully look to their future country as to a land of promise, soberly and quietly turning their attention to making the necessary arrangements for the important change that is before them.

Let them remember that all practical knowledge is highly valuable in the land to which they are going. An acquaintance with the homely art of baking and making bread, which most servants and small housekeepers know how to practice, but which many young females that live in large towns and cities where the baker supplies the bread to the family, do not, is necessary to be acquired.

Cooking, curing meat, making butter and cheese, knitting, dressmaking and tailoring—for most of the country-people here make the everyday clothing of their husbands, brothers or sons—are good to be learned. By ripping to pieces any well-fitting old garment, a suitable pattern may be obtained of men's clothes; and many a fair hand I have seen occupied in making garments of this description. For a quarter of a dollar, 1s. 3d., a tailor will cut out a pair of fine cloth trowsers; for a coat they charge more; but a good cloth is always better to have made up by a regular tailor: loose summer coats may be made at home, but may be bought cheap, ready-made, in the stores.

My female friends must bear in mind that it is one of the settler's great objects to make as little outlay of money as possible. I allude to such as come out to Canada with very little available capital excepting what arises from the actual labour of their own hands, by which they must realize the means of paying for their land or the rental of a farm. Everything that is done in the house by the hands of the family, is so much saved or so much earned towards the paying for the land or building houses and barns, buying stock or carrying on the necessary improvements on the place: the sooner this great object is accomplished, the sooner will the settler and his family realize the comfort of feeling themselves independent.

The necessity of becoming acquainted with the common branches of household work may not at first be quite agreeable to such as have been unaccustomed to take an active part in the duties of the house. Though their position in society may have been such as to exempt them from what they consider menial occupations, still they will be wise to lay aside their pride and refinement, and apply themselves practically to the acquirement of such useful matters as those I have named—if they are destined to a life in a colony—even though their friends may be so well off as to have it in their power to keep servants, and live in ease and comfort. But if they live in a country place, they may be left without the assistance of a female-servant in the house, a contingency which has often happened from sudden illness, a servant's parents sending for them home, which they will often do without consulting either your convenience or their daughter's wishes, or some act on the part of the servant may induce her to be discharged before her place can be filled; in such an emergency the settler's wife may find herself greatly at a loss, without some knowledge of what her family requires at her hands. I have before now seen a ragged Irish boy called in from the clearing by his lady-mistress, to assist her in the mystery of making a loaf of bread, and teaching her how to bake it in the bake-kettle. She had all the requisite materials, but was ignorant of the simple practical art of making bread.

Another who knew quite well how to make a loaf and bake it too, yet knew nothing of the art of making yeast to raise it with, and so the family lived upon unleavened cakes, or dampers, as the Australians call them, till they were heartily tired of them: at last a settler's wife calling in to rest herself, and seeing the flat cakes baking, asked the servant why they did not make raised bread: "Because we have no yeast, and do not know how to make any here in these horrible backwoods," was the girl's reply. The neighbour, I dare say, was astonished at the ignorance of both mistress and maid; but she gave them some hops and a little barm, and told the girl how to make the yeast called hop-rising; and this valuable piece of knowledge stood them in good stead: from that time they were able to make light bread; the girl shrewdly remarking to her mistress, that a little help was worth a deal of pity. A few simple directions for making barm as it is here practiced, would have obviated the difficulty at, first. As this is one of the very first things that the housewife has to attend to in the cooking department, I have placed the raising and making of bread at the beginning of the work. The making and baking of REALLY GOOD HOUSEHOLD BREAD is a thing of the greatest consequence to the health and comfort of a family.

As the young learn more quickly than the old, I would advise the daughters of the intending emigrant to acquire whatever useful arts they think likely to prove serviceable to them in their new country. Instead of suffering a false pride to stand in their way of acquiring practical "household knowledge, let it be their pride—their noble, honest pride—to fit themselves for the state which they will be called upon to fill—a part in the active drama of life; to put in practice that which they learned to repeat with their lips in childhood as a portion of the catechism, "To do my duty in that state of life, unto which it may please God to call me." Let them earnestly believe that it is by the will of God that they are called to share the fortunes of their parents in the land they have chosen, and that as that is the state of life they are called to by his will, they are bound to strive to do their duty in it with cheerfulness.

There should therefore be no wavering on their part; no yielding to prejudices and pride. Old things are passed away. The greatest heroine in life is she who knowing her duty, resolves not only to do it, but to do it to the best of her abilities, with heart and mind bent upon the work.

I address this passage more especially to the daughters of the emigrant, for to them belongs the task of cheering and upholding their mother in the trials that may await her. It is often in consideration of the future welfare of their children, that the parents are, after many painful struggles, induced to quit the land of their birth and the home that was endeared to them alike by their cares and their joys; and though the children may not know this to be the main-spring that urges them to make the sacrifice, in most cases it is so; and this consideration should have its full weight, and induce the children to do all in their power to repay their parents for the love that urges them to such a decision.

The young learn to conform more readily to change of country than the old. Novelty has for them a great charm: and then hope is more lively in the young heart than in the old. To them a field of healthy enterprise is open, which they have only to enter upon with a cheerful heart and plenty of determination, and they will hardly fail of reaching a respectable state of independence.

———————

The wives and daughters of the small farmers and of the working class, should feel the difficulties of a settler's life far less keenly than any other, as their habits and general knowledge of rural affairs have fitted them for the active labours that may fall to their lot in Canada. Though much that they have to perform will be new to them, it will only be the manner of doing it, and the difference of some of the materials that they will have to make use of: enured from childhood to toil, they may soon learn to conform to their change of life. The position of servants is much improved in one respect: their services are more valuable in a country where there is less competition among the working class. They can soon save enough to be independent. They have the cheering prospect always before them: It depends upon ourselves to better our own condition. In this country honest industry always commands respect: by it we can in time raise ourselves, and no-one can keep us down.

Yet I have observed with much surprize that there is no class of emigrants more discontented than the wives and daughters of those men who were accustomed to earn their bread by the severest toil, in which they too were by necessity obliged to share, often with patience and cheerfulness under privations the most heartbreaking, with no hope of amendment, no refuge but the grave from poverty and all its miseries. Surely to persons thus situated, the change of country should be regarded with hopeful feelings; seeing that it opens a gate which leads from poverty to independence, from present misery to future comfort.

At first the strangeness of all things around them, the loss of familiar faces and familiar objects, and the want of all their little household conveniences, are sensibly felt; and these things make them uncomfortable and peevish: but a little reasoning with themselves would show that such inconveniences belong to the nature of their new position, and that a little time will do away with the evil they complain of.

After a while new feelings, new attachments to persons and things, come to fill up the void: they begin to take an interest in the new duties that are before them, and by degrees conform to the change; and an era in their lives commences, which is the beginning to them of a better and more prosperous state of things.

It frequently happens that before the poor emigrant can settle upon land of his own, he is obliged to send the older children out to service. Perhaps he gets employment for himself and his wife, on some farm, where they can manage to keep the younger members of the family with them, if there is a small house or shanty convenient, on or near the farm on which they are hired. Sometimes a farmer can get a small farm on shares; but it is seldom a satisfactory mode of rental, and often ends in disagreement. As no man can serve two masters, neither can one farm support two, unless both parties are which rarely happens, quite disinterested and free from selfishness, each exacting no more than his due. It is seldom these partnerships turn out well.

There is an error which female servants are very apt to fall into in this country, which as a true friend, I would guard them against committing. This is adopting a free and easy manner, often bordering upon impertinence, towards their employers. They are apt to think that because they are entitled to a higher rate of wages, they are not bound to render their mistresses the same respect of manners as was usual in the old country. Now, as they receive more, they ought not to be less thankful to those who pay them well, and should be equally zealous in doing their duty. They should bear in mind that they are commanded to render "honor to whom honor is due." A female servant in Canada whose manners are respectful and well-behaved, will always be treated with consideration and even with affection. After all, good-breeding is as charming a trait in a servant as it is in a lady. Were there more of that kindly feeling existing between the upper and lower classes, both parties would be benefitted, and a bond of union established, which would extend beyond the duration of a few months or a few years, and be continued through life: how much more satisfactory than that unloving strife where the mistress is haughty and the servant insolent.

But while I would recommend respect and obedience on the part of the servant, to her employer I would say, treat your servants with consideration: if you respect her she will also respect you; if she does her duty, she is inferior to no one living as a member of the great human family. The same Lord who says by the mouth of his apostle, "Servants obey your masters," has also added, "and ye masters do ye also the same, forbearing threatening; knowing that your master also is in heaven, and that with him there is no respect of persons."

Your servants as long as they are with you, are of your household, and should be so treated that they should learn to look up to you in love as well as reverence.

If they are new comers to Canada, they have everything to learn; and will of course feel strange and awkward to the ways of the colony, and require to be patiently dealt with. They may have their regrets and sorrows yet rankling in their hearts for those dear friends they have left behind them, and require kindness and sympathy. — Remember that you also are a stranger and sojourner in a strange land, and should feel for them and bear with them as becomes Christians.

Servants in Canada are seldom hired excepting by the month.—The female servant by the full calendar month; the men and boys' month is four weeks only. From three to four dollars a month is the usual wages given to female servants; and two, and two dollars and a half, to girls of fourteen and sixteen years of age, unless they are very small, and very ignorant of the work of the country; then less is given. Indeed, if a young girl were to give her services for a month or two, with a good clever mistress, for her board alone, she would be the gainer by the bargain, in the useful knowledge which she would acquire, and which would enable her to take a better place, and command higher wages. It is a common error in girls coming direct from the old country, and who have all Canada's ways to learn, to ask the highest rate of wages, expecting the same as those who are twice as efficient. This is not reasonable; and if the demand be yielded to from necessity, there is seldom much satisfaction or harmony, both parties being respectively discontented with the other. The one gives too much, the other does too little in return for high wages.

Very little if any alteration has taken place nominally in the rate of servants' wages during twenty-one years that I have lived in Canada, but a great increase in point of fact.* Twenty years ago the servant-girl gave from 1s. 6d. to 2s. 6d. a yard for cotton prints, 10s. and 12s. a pair for very coarse shoes and boots: common white calico was 1s. and 1s. 3d. per yard, and other articles of clothing in proportion. Now she can buy good fast prints at 9d. and 10d., and some as low as 7½d. and 8d. per yard, calicoes and factory cottons from 4½d. to 9d. or 10d.; shoes, light American-made and very pretty, from 4s. 6d. to 7s. 6d., and those made to order 6s. 3d. to 7s. 6d.; boots 10s.; straw bonnets from 1s. 6d., coarse beehive plat, to such as are very tasteful and elegant in shape and quality, of the most delicate fancy chips and straws, proportionably cheap.

Thus while her wages remain the same, her outlay is decreased nearly one-half.

Ribbons and light fancy goods are still much higher in price than they are in the old country; so are stuffs and merinos. A very poor, thin Coburg cloth, or Orleans, fetches 1s. or 1s. 3d. per yard; mousselin de laines vary from 9d. to 1s. 6d. Probably the time will come when woollen goods will be manufactured in the colony; but the time for that is not yet at hand. The country flannel, home-spun, home-dyed and sometimes home-woven, is the sort of material worn in the house by the farmer's family when at work. Nothing can be more suitable to the climate, and the labours of a Canadian settler's wife or daughter, than gowns made of this country flannel: it is very durable, lasting often two or three seasons. When worn out as a decent working dress, it makes good sleigh-quilts for travelling, or can be cut up into rag-carpets, for a description of which see the article—*Rag-Carpets:* and for instructions in dyeing the wool or yarn for the flannel see *Dyeing.* I have been thus minute in naming the prices of women's wearing apparel, that the careful wife may be enabled to calculate the expediency of purchasing a stock of clothes, before leaving home, or waiting till she arrives in Canada, to make her needful purchases. To such as can prudently spare a small sum for buying clothes, I may point out a few purchases that would be made more advantageously in England or Scotland than in Canada: 1st. A stock, say two pairs a piece for each person, of good shoes.—The leather here is not nearly so durable as what is prepared at home, and consequently the shoes wear out much sooner, where the roads are rough and the work hard. No one need encumber themselves with clogs or pattens: the rough roads render them worse than useless, even

---

* Since the above statement was written the wages both of men and women have borne a higher rate; and some articles of clothing have been raised in price. See the tables of rates of wages and goods for 1854. [The 1854 table Traill refers to in this footnote was part of the extensive Appendix added by the publisher, Maclear, and is not included in this re-set edition.]

dangerous, in the spring and fall, the only wet seasons: in winter the snow clogs them up, and you could not walk ten yards in them; and in summer there is no need of them: buy shoes instead; or for winter wear, a good pair of duffle boots, the sole overlaid with india-rubber or gutta percha.[2]

India-rubber boots and over-shoes can be bought from 4s. to 7s. 6d., if extra good, and lined with fur or fine flannel. Gentlemen's boots, long or short, can be had also, but I do not know at what cost. Old women's list shoes are good for the house in the snowy season, or good, strongly-made carpet shoes; but these last, with a little ingenuity, you can make for yourself.

Flannel I also recommend, as an advisable purchase: you must give from 1s. 9d. to 2s. 6d. for either white or red, and a still higher price for fine fabrics; which I know is much higher than they can be bought for at home. Good scarlet or blue flannel shirts are worn by all the emigrants that work on land or at trades in Canada; and even through the hottest summer weather the men still prefer them to cotton or linen.

A superior quality, twilled and of some delicate check, as pale blue, pink or green, are much the fashion among the gentlemen; this material however is more costly, and can hardly be bought under 3s. 6d. or 4s. a yard. A sort of overshirt made full and belted in at the waist, is frequently worn, made of homespun flannel, dyed brown or blue, and looks neat and comfortable; others of coarse brown linen, or canvas, called logging-shirts, are adopted by the choppers in their rough work of clearing up the fallows: these are not very unlike the short loose slop frocks of the peasants of the Eastern Counties of England, reaching no lower than the hips.

Merino or cottage stuffs are also good to bring out, also Scotch plaids and tweeds, strong checks for aprons, and fine white cotton stockings: those who wear silk, had better bring a supply for holiday wear: satin shoes are very high, but are only needed by the wealthy, or those ladies who expect to live in some of the larger towns or cities; but the farmer's wife in Canada has little need of such luxuries—they are out of place and keeping.

ON DRESS.

It is one of the blessings of this new country, that a young person's respectability does by no means depend upon these points of style in dress; and many a pleasant little evening dance I have seen, where the young ladies wore merino frocks, cut high

---

2 Gutta percha was made from the sap of trees of the genus *Palaquium*, which produce a natural form of latex widely used in the nineteenth century.

or low, and prunella shoes,[3] and no disparaging remarks were made by any of the party. How much more sensible I thought these young people, than if they had made themselves slaves to the tyrant fashion. Nevertheless, in some of the large towns the young people do dress extravagantly, and even exceed those of Britain in their devotion to fine and costly apparel. The folly of this is apparent to every sensible person. When I hear women talk of nothing but dress, I cannot help thinking that it is because they have nothing more interesting to talk about; that their minds are uninformed, and bare, while their bodies are clothed with purple and fine linen. To dress neatly and with taste and even elegance is an accomplishment which I should desire to see practised by all females; but to make dress the one engrossing business and thought of life, is vain and foolish. One thing is certain, that a lady will be a lady, even in the plainest dress; a vulgar minded woman will never be a lady, in the most costly garments. Good sense is as much marked by the style of a person's dress, as by their conversation. The servant-girl who expends half her wages on a costly shawl, or mantilla, and bonnet to wear over a fine shabby gown, or with coarse shoes and stockings, does not show as much sense as she who purchases at less cost a complete dress, each article suited to the other. They both attract attention, it is true; but in a different degree. The man of sense will notice the one for her wisdom; the other for her folly.—To plead fashion, is like following a multitude to do evil.

CANADA A FIELD FOR YOUNGER WORKING FEMALES.

Quitting the subject of dress, which perhaps I have dwelt too long upon, I will go to a subject of more importance: the field which Canada opens for the employment of the younger female emigrants of the working class. At this very minute I was assured by one of the best and most intelligent of our farmers, that the Township of Hamilton alone could give immediate employment to five hundred females; and most other townships in the same degree. What an inducement to young girls to emigrate is this![4] good wages, in a healthy and improving country; and what is better, in one where idleness and immorality are not the characteristics of the inhabitants: where steady industry is sure to be rewarded by marriage with young men who are able to place their wives in a very different station from that of servitude. How many young

3 Prunella was a strong cloth used for gowns worn by barristers and clergymen as well as the top halves of women's shoes.
4 The exclamation point was typeset in the original text – its location is clearly an error but a charming one.

women who were formerly servants in my house, are now farmers' wives, going to church or the market towns with their own sleighs or light waggons, and in point of dress, better clothed than myself.

Though Australia may offer the temptation of greater wages to female servants; yet the discomforts they are exposed to, must be a great drawback; and the immoral, disjointed state of domestic life, for decent, well-conducted young women, I should think, would more than counterbalance the nominal advantages from greater wages.—The industrious, sober-minded labourer, with a numerous family of daughters, one would imagine would rather bring them to Canada, where they can get immediate employment in respectable families; where they will get good wages and have every chance of bettering their condition and rising in the world, by becoming the wives of thriving farmers' sons or industrious artizans; than form connexions with such characters as swarm the streets of Melbourne and Geelong, though these may be able to fill their hands with gold, and clothe them with satin and velvet.

In the one country there is a steady progress to prosperity and lasting comfort, where they may see their children become landowners after them, while in the other, there is little real stability, and small prospect of a life of domestic happiness to look forward to. I might say, as the great lawgiver said to the Israelites, "Good and evil are before you, choose ye between them."

Those whose destination is intended to be in the Canadian towns will find little difference in regard to their personal comforts to what they were accustomed to enjoy at home. If they have capital they can employ it to advantage; if they are mechanics, or artizans they will have little difficulty in obtaining employment as journeymen.—The stores in Canada are well furnished with every species of goods; groceries, hardware and food of all kinds can also be obtained. With health and industry, they will have little real cause of complaint. It is those who go into the woods and into distant settlements in the uncleared wilderness that need have any fear of encountering hardships and privations; and such persons should carefully consider their own qualifications and those of their wives and children before they decide upon embarking in the laborious occupation of backwoodsmen in a new country like Canada. Strong, patient, enduring, hopeful men and women, able to bear hardships and any amount of bodily toil, (and there are many such,) these may be pioneers to open out the forestlands; while the old-country farmer will find it much better to purchase cleared farms or farms that are partially cleared, in improving townships, where there are villages and markets and good roads; by so doing they will escape much of the disappointment and loss, as well as the bodily hardships that are too often the lot of those who go back into the unreclaimed forest lands.

Whatever be the determination of the intended emigrant, let him not exclude from his entire confidence the wife of his bosom, the natural sharer of his fortunes, be the path which leads to them rough or smooth. She ought not to be dragged as an unwilling sacrifice at the shrine of duty from home, kindred and friends, without her full consent: the difficulties as well as the apparent advantages ought to be laid candidly before her, and her advice and opinion asked; or how can she be expected to enter heart and soul into her husband's hopes and plans; nor should such of the children as are capable of forming opinions on the subject be shut out from the family council; for let parents bear this fact in mind, that much of their own future prosperity will depend upon the exertion of their children in the land to which they are going; and also let them consider that those children's lot in life is involved in the important decision they are about to make. Let perfect confidence be established in the family: it will avoid much future domestic misery and unavailing repining.—Family union is like the key-stone of an arch: it keeps all the rest of the building from falling asunder. A man's friends should be those of his own household.

Woman, whose nature is to love home and to cling to all home ties and associations, cannot be torn from that spot that is the little centre of joy and peace and comfort to her, without many painful regrets. No matter however poor she may be, how low her lot in life may be cast, home to her is dear, the thought of it and the love of it clings closely to her wherever she goes. The remembrance of it never leaves her; it is graven on her heart. Her thoughts wander back to it across the broad waters of the ocean that are bearing her far from it. In the new land it is still present to her mental eye, and years after she has formed another home for herself she can still recal the bowery lane, the daisied meadow, the mossgrown well, the simple hawthorn hedge that bound the garden-plot, the woodbine porch, the thatched roof and narrow casement window of her early home. She hears the singing of the birds, the murmuring of the bees, the tinkling of the rill, and busy hum of cheerful labour from the village or the farm, when those beside her can hear only the deep cadence of the wind among the lofty forest-trees, the jangling of the cattle-bells, or strokes of the chopper's axe in the woods. As the seasons return she thinks of the flowers that she loved in childhood; the pale primrose, the cowslip and the bluebell, with the humble daisy and heath-flowers; and what would she not give for one, *just one* of those old familiar flowers! No wonder that the heart of the emigrant's wife is sometimes sad, and needs to be dealt gently with by her less sensitive partner; who if she were less devoted to home, would hardly love her more, for in this attachment to home lies much of her charm as a wife and mother in his eyes.—But kindness and sympathy, which she has need of, in time reconciles her to her change of life; new ties, new interests, new comforts arise; and she ceases to repine, if she does not cease to love, that which she has lost: in after life the recollection comes like some pleasant dream or a fair picture to her mind, but she has ceased to grieve or to regret; and perhaps like a wise woman she says—"All things are for the best. It is good for us to be here."

ADORNMENT OF HOME.

What effect should this love of her old home produce in the emigrant-wife? Surely an earnest endeavour to render her new dwelling equally charming; to adorn it within and without as much as circumstances will permit, not expending her husband's means in the purchase of costly furniture which would be out of keeping in a log-house, but adopting such things as are suitable, neat and simple; studying comfort and convenience before show and finery. Many inconveniences must be expected at the outset; but the industrious female will endeavor to supply these wants by the exercise of a little ingenuity and taste. It is a great mistake to neglect those little household adornments which will give a look of cheerfulness to the very humblest home.

Nothing contributes so much to comfort and to the outward appearance of a Canadian house as the erection of the verandah or stoup, as the Dutch settlers call it, round the building. It affords a grateful shade from the summer heat, a shelter from the cold, and is a source of cleanliness to the interior. It gives a pretty, rural look to the poorest log-house, and as it can be put up with little expense, it should never be omitted. A few unbarked cedar posts, with a slab or shingled roof, costs very little. The floor should be of plank; but even with a hard dry earthen floor, swept every day with an Indian broom, it will still prove a great comfort. Those who build frame or stone or brick houses seldom neglect the addition of a verandah; to the common log-house it is equally desirable; nor need any one want for climbers with which to adorn the pillars.

SHADE PLANTS.

Among the wild plants of Canada there are many graceful climbers, which are to be found in almost every locality. Nature, as if to invite you to ornament your cottage-homes, has kindly provided so many varieties of shade-plants, that you may choose at will. First, then, I will point out to your attention the wild grape, which is to be found luxuriating in every swamp, near the margin of lakes and rivers, wreathing the trees and tall bushes with its abundant foliage and purple clusters. The Fox-grape and the Frost-grape* are among the common wild varieties, and will produce a great quantity of fruit, which, though very acid, is far from being unpalatable when cooked with a sufficiency of sugar.

From the wild grape a fine jelly can be made by pressing the juice from the husks and seeds and boiling it with the proportion of sugar usual in making currant-jelly, i.e., one pound of sugar to one pint of juice. An excellent home-made wine can also be manufactured from these grapes. They are not ripe till the middle of October, and should not be gathered till the frost has softened them; from this circumstance, no doubt, the name of Frost-grape has been given to one species. The wild vine planted at the foot of some dead and unsightly tree, will cover it with its luxuriant growth, and convert that which would otherwise have been an unseemly object into one of great ornament. I knew a gentleman who caused a small dead tree to be cut down and planted near a big oak stump in his garden, round which a young grape was twining: the vine soon ascended the dead tree, covering every branch and twig, and forming a bower above the stump, and affording an abundant crop of fruit.

The commonest climber for a log-house is the hop, which is, as you will find, an indispensable plant in a Canadian garden, it being the principal ingredient in making the yeast with which the household bread is raised. Planted near the pillars of your verandah, it forms a graceful drapery of leaves and flowers, which are pleasing to look upon, and valuable either for use or sale.

The Canadian Ivy, or Virginian Creeper, is another charming climber, which if planted near the walls of your house, will quickly cover the rough logs with its dark glossy leaves in summer, and in the fall delight the eye with its gorgeous crimson tints.

The Wild Clematis or Traveller's Joy may be found growing in the beaver meadows and other open thickets. This also is most ornamental as a shade-plant for a verandah. Then there is the climbing Fumatory, better known by the name by which its seeds are sold by the gardener, "Cypress vine." This elegant creeper is a native of Canada, and may be seen in old neglected clearings near the water, running up the stems of trees and flinging its graceful tendrils and leaves of tender green over the

---

* There are many other varieties of wild grapes, some of which have, by careful garden cultivation, been greatly improved. Cuttings may be made early in April, or the young vines planted in September or October.

old grey mossy branches of cedar or pine, adorning the hoary boughs with garlands of the loveliest pink flowers. I have seen this climbing Fumatory in great quantities in the woods, but found it no easy matter to obtain the ripe seeds, unless purchased from a seedsman: it is much cultivated in towns as a shade plant near the verandahs.

Besides those already described I may here mention the scarlet-runner, a flower the humming-birds love to visit. The wild cucumber, a very graceful trailing plant. The Major Colvolvulus or Morning Glory. The wild honeysuckle, sweet pea and prairie-rose. These last-named are not natives, with the exception of the wild or bush honeysuckle, which is to be found in the forest. The flowers are pale red, but scentless; nevertheless it is very well worth cultivating.

I am the more particular in pointing out to you how you may improve the outside of your dwellings, because the log-house is rough and unsightly; and I know well that your comfort and cheerfulness of mind will be increased by the care you are led to bestow upon your new home in endeavouring to ornament it and render it more agreeable to the eye. The cultivation of a few flowers, of vegetables and fruit, will be a source of continual pleasure and interest to yourself and children, and you will soon learn to love your home, and cease to regret that dear one you have left.

I write from my own experience. I too have felt all the painful regrets incidental to a long separation from my native land and my beloved early home. I have experienced all that you who read this book can ever feel, and perhaps far more than you will ever have cause for feeling.

CONTRAST NOW TO PERIOD OF EARLY SETTLEMENT.

The emigrants of the present day can hardly now meet with the trials and hardships that were the lot of those who came to the Province twenty years ago, and these last infinitely less than those who preceded them at a still earlier period.

When I listen, as I often do, to the experiences of the old settlers of forty or fifty years standing, at a time when the backwoodsman shared the almost unbroken wilderness with the unchristianized Indian, the wolf and the bear; when his seed-corn had to be carried a distance of thirty miles upon his shoulders, and his family were dependent upon the game and fish that he brought home till the time of the harvest; when there were no mills to grind his flour save the little handmill, which kept the children busy to obtain enough coarse flour to make bread from day to day; when no sabbath-bell was ever heard to mark the holy day, and all was lonely, wild and savage around him. Then my own first trials seemed to sink into utter insignificance, and I was almost ashamed to think how severely they had been felt.

Many a tale of trial and of enterprize I have listened to with breathless interest, related by these patriarchs of the colony, while seated beside the blazing log-fire, surrounded by the comforts which they had won for their children by every species of toil and privation. Yet they too had overcome the hardships incidental to a first settlement, and were at rest, and could look back on their former struggles with that sort of pride which is felt by the war-worn soldier in fighting over again his battles by his own peaceful hearth.

These old settlers and their children have seen the whole face of the country changed. They have seen the forest disappear before the axe of the industrious emigrant; they have seen towns and villages spring up where the bear and the wolf had their lair. They have seen the white-sailed vessel and the steamer plough those lakes and rivers where the solitary Indian silently glided over their lonely waters in his frail canoe. They have seen highways opened out through impenetrable swamps where human foot however adventurous had never trod. The busy mill-wheels have dashed where only the foaming rocks broke the onward flow of the forest stream. They have seen God's holy temples rise, pointing upwards with their glittering spires above the lowlier habitations of men, and have heard the sabbath-bell calling the Christian worshippers to prayer. They have seen the savage Indian bending there in mute reverence, or lifting his voice in hymns of praise to that blessed Redeemer who had called him out of darkness into his marvellous light. And stranger things he may now behold in that mysterious wire, that now conveys a whispered message from one end of the Province to the other with lightning swiftness; and see the iron railway already traversing the Province, and bringing the far-off produce of the woods to the store of the merchant and to the city mart.

Such are the changes which the old settler has witnessed; and I have noted them for your encouragement and satisfaction, and that you may form some little notion of what is going on in this comparatively newly-settled country; and that you may form some idea of what it is likely to become in the course of a few more years, when its commerce and agriculture and its population shall have increased, and its internal resources shall have been more perfectly developed.

In the long-settled portions of the Province a traveller may almost imagine that he is in England; there are no stumps to disfigure the fields, and but very few of the old log-houses remaining: these have for the most part given place to neat painted frame, brick or stone cottages, surrounded with orchards, cornfields and pastures. Some peculiarities he will notice, which will strike him as unlike what he has been used to see in the old country; and there are old familiar objects which will be missed in the landscape, such as the venerable grey tower of the old church, the ancient ruins, the old castles and fine old manor-houses, with many other things which exist in the old country. Here all is new; time has not yet laid its mellowing touch upon the land. We are but in our infancy; but it is a vigorous and healthy one, full of promise for future greatness and strength.

FURNISHING [A] LOG HOUSE.

In furnishing a Canadian log-house the main study should be to unite simplicity with cheapness and comfort. It would be strangely out of character to introduce gay, showy, or rich and costly articles of furniture into so rough and homely a dwelling. A log-house is better to be simply furnished. Those who begin with moderation are more likely to be able to increase their comforts in the course of a few years.

Let us see now what can be done towards making your log parlour comfortable at a small cost. A dozen of painted Canadian chairs, such as are in common use here, will cost you £2 10s. You can get plainer ones for 2s. 9d. or 3s. a chair: of course you may get very excellent articles if you give a higher price; but we are not going to buy drawing-room furniture. You can buy rocking chairs, small, at 7s. 6d.; large, with elbows, 15s.: you can cushion them yourself. A good drugget,[5] which I would advise you to bring with you, or Scotch carpet, will cover your rough floor; when you lay it down, spread straw or hay over the boards; this will save your carpet from cutting. A stained pine table may be had for 12s. or 15s. Walnut or cherry wood costs more; but the pine with a nice cover will answer at first. For a flowered mohair you must give five or six dollars. A piece of chintz of suitable pattern will cost you 16s. the piece of twenty-eight yards. This will curtain your windows: and a common pine sofa stuffed with wool, though many use fine hay for the back and sides, can be bought cheap, if covered by your own hands. If your husband or elder sons are at all skilled in the use of tools, they can make out of common pine boards the frame-work or couches, or sofas, which look when covered and stuffed, as well as what the cabinet-maker will charge several pounds for. A common box or two stuffed so as to form a cushion on the top, and finished with a flounce of chintz, will fill the recess of the windows.

---

5 Drugget was a coarse woolen cloth for clothing, aprons, or tablecloths, although by Traill's time, the word was also used for a coarsely woven woolen rug. In Canada, it had a handwoven linen (and later a commercial cotton) warp and a wool weft in the simplest of weaves. Some drugget underclothes survive in historical clothing collections (Burnham, *Keep Me Warm One Night*, 62).

A set of book-shelves stained with Spanish brown, to hold your library.—A set of corner shelves, fitted into the angles of the room, one above the other, diminishing in size, form an useful receptacle for any little ornamental matters, or for flowers in the summer, and gives a pleasant finish and an air of taste to the room. A few prints, or pictures, in frames of oak or black walnut, should not be omitted, if you can bring such ornaments with you. These things are sources of pleasure to yourselves, and of interest to others. They are intellectual luxuries, that even the very poorest man regards with delight, and possesses if he can, to adorn his cottage walls, however lowly that cottage may be.

I am going to add another comfort to your little parlour—a clock: very neat dials in cherry or oak frames, may be bought from 7s. 6d. to $5. The cheapest will keep *good time*, but do not strike. Very handsome clocks may be bought for ten dollars, in elegant frames; but we must not be too extravagant in our notions.

I would recommend a good cooking-stove in your kitchen: it is more convenient, and is not so destructive to clothes as the great log fires. A stove large enough to cook food for a family of ten or twelve persons, will cost from twenty to thirty dollars. This will include every necessary cooking utensil. Cheap stoves are often like other cheap articles, the dearest in the end: a good, weighty casting should be preferred to a thinner and lighter one; though the latter will look just as good as the former: they are apt to crack, and the inner plates wear out soon.

There are now a great variety of patterns in cooking-stoves, many of which I know to be good. I will mention a few:—"The Lion," "Farmers' Friend," "Burr," "Canadian Hot-Air," "Clinton Hot-Air;" these two last require dry wood; and the common "Premium" stove, which is a good useful stove, but seldom a good casting, and sold at a low price. If you buy a small-sized stove, you will not be able to bake a good joint of meat or good-sized loaves of bread in it.

If you have a chimney, and prefer relying on cooking with the bake-kettle, I would also recommend a roaster, or bachelor's oven: this will cost only a few shillings, and prove a great convenience, as you can bake rolls, cakes, pies and meat in it. An outside oven, built of stones, bricks, or clay, is put up at small cost, and is a great comfort.* The heating [of] it once or twice a week, will save you much work, and you will enjoy bread much better and sweeter than any baked in a stove, oven or bake-kettle.

---

* Two men, or a man and a boy will build a common-sized clay oven in a day or less, if they understand the work and prepare the materials beforehand.

Many persons who have large houses of stone or brick, now adopt the plan of heating them with hot air, which is conveyed by means of pipes into the rooms. An ornamented, circular grating admits the heated air, by opening or shutting the grates. The furnace is in the cellar, and is made large enough to allow of a considerable quantity of wood being put in at once.

A house thus heated is kept at summer heat in the coldest weather; and can be made cooler by shutting the grates in any room.

The temperature of houses heated thus is very pleasant, and certainly does not seem so unhealthy as those warmed by metal stoves, besides there being far less risk from fire.

Those who wish to enjoy the cheerful appearance of a fire in their sitting room, can have one; as little wood is required in such case.

The poorer settlers, to whom the outlay of a dollar is often an object, make very good washing tubs out of old barrels, by sawing one in half, leaving two of the staves a few inches higher than the rest, for handles. Painted washing-tubs made of pine, iron hooped, cost a dollar; painted water-pails only 1s. 6d. a piece; but they are not very durable. Owing to the dryness of the air, great care is requisite to keep your tubs, barrels and pails in proper order. Many a good vessel of this kind is lost for want of a little attention.

The washing tubs should be kept in the cellar, or with water in them. Those who keep servants must not forget to warn them of this fact.

In fitting up your house, do not sacrifice all comfort in the kitchen, for the sake of a best room for receiving company.

If you wish to enjoy a cheerful room, by all means have a fireplace in it. A blazing log-fire is an object that inspires cheerfulness. A stove in the hall or passage is a great comfort in winter; and the pipe conducted rightly will warm the upper rooms; but do not let the stove supersede the cheering fire in the sitting-room. Or if your house has been built only to be heated by stoves, choose one that, with a grate in front, can be opened to show the fire. A handsome parlour-stove can now be got for twelve dollars. Tanned and dyed sheep-skins make excellent door mats, and warm hearth-rugs. With small outlay of money your room will thus be comfortably furnished.

A delightful easy-chair can be made out of a very rough material—nothing better than a common flour barrel. I will, as well as I can, direct you how these barrel-chairs are made. The first four or five staves of a good, sound, clean flour barrel are to be sawn off, level, within two feet of the ground, or higher, if you think that will be too low for the seat: this is for the front: leave the two staves on either side a few inches higher for the elbows; the staves that remain are left to form the hollow back: augur holes are next made all round, on a level with the seat, in all the staves; through these holes ropes are passed and interlaced, so as to form a secure seat: a bit of thin board may then be nailed, flat, on the rough edge of the elbow staves, and a coarse covering, of linen or sacking, tacked on over the back and arms: this is stuffed with cotton-wool, soft hay, or sheep's wool, and then a chintz cover over the whole, and well-filled cushion for the seat, completes the chair. Two or three of such seats in a sitting-room, give it an air of great comfort at a small cost.

Those settlers who come out with sufficient means, and go at once on cleared farms, which is by far the best plan, will be able to purchase very handsome furniture of black walnut or cherry wood at moderate cost. Furniture, new and handsome, and even costly, is to be met with in any of the large towns; and it would be impertinent in me to offer advice as to the style to be observed by such persons: it is to the small farmer, and poorer class, that my hints are addressed.

The shanty, or small log-house of the poorer emigrant, is often entirely furnished by his own hands. A rude bedstead, formed of cedar poles, a coarse linen bag filled with hay or dried moss, and bolster of the same, is the bed he lies on; his seats are benches, nailed together; a table of deal boards, a few stools, a few shelves for the crockery and tinware; these are often all that the poor emigrant can call his own in the way of furniture. Little enough and rude enough. Yet let not the heart of the wife despond. It is only the first trial; better things are in store for her.

Many an officer's wife, and the wives of Scotch and English gentlemen, in the early state of the colony have been no better off.—Many a wealthy landowner in Canada was born in circumstances as unfavourable. Men who now occupy the highest situations in the country, have been brought up in a rude log-shanty, little better than an Indian wigwam. Let these things serve to cheer the heart and smooth the rough ways of the settler's first outset in Canadian life.—And let me add that now there is more facility for the incoming emigrant's settling with comfort, than there was twenty or thirty years ago; unless he goes very far back into the uncivilized portions of the country, he cannot now meet with the trials and privations that were the lot of the first settlers in the Province. And there is no necessity for him to place himself and family beyond the outskirts of civilization. Those who have the command of a little capital can generally buy land with some clearing and buildings; and the working man can obtain good employment for his wife and elder girls or boys, so as to enable them by their united savings, to get a lot of land for themselves, to settle upon. This is more prudent than plunging at once into the bush, without possessing the experience which is necessary for their future welfare, almost for their very existence, in their new mode of life. When they have earned a little money and some knowledge of the ways of the country, they may then start fair, and by industry and sobriety, in a few years become independent.

To pay for his land by instalments, is the only way a poor man can manage to acquire property: to obtain his deed, is the height of his ambition: to compass this desirable end all the energies of the household are directed. For this the husband, the wife, the sons and the daughters all toil: each contributes his or her mite: for this they endure all sorts of privations, without murmuring. In a few years the battle is won. Poverty is no longer to be feared.

The land is their own: with what pride they now speak of it; with what honest delight they contemplate every blade of wheat, every ear of corn, and the cattle that feed upon their pastures. No rent is now to be paid for it. God has blessed the labours of their hands. Let them not forget that to him is the glory and praise due.

When they have acquired land and cattle, let them not in the pride of their hearts say—"My hand and the power of my arm has gotten me all these;" for it is God that giveth the increase in all these things.

ON TEMPERANCE.

With habits of industry long practiced, cheered by a reasonable hope, and with experience gained, no one need despair of obtaining all the essential comforts of life; but strict sobriety is indispensably necessary to the attainment of his hopes. Let not the drunkard flatter himself that success will attend his exertions. A curse is in the cup; it lingers in the dregs to embitter his own life and that of his hapless partner and children. As of the sluggard, so also may it be said of the intemperate—"The *drunkard* shall starve in harvest." It is in vain for the women of the household to work hard and to bear their part of the hardships incidental to a settler's life, if the husband gives himself up as a slave to this miserable vice.

I dwell more earnestly upon this painful subject, because unfortunately the poison sold to the public under the name of whiskey, is so cheap, that for a few pence a man may degrade himself below the beasts that perish, and barter away his soul for that which profiteth not; bring shame and disgrace upon his name, and bitterness of heart into the bosom of his family. I have known sad instances of this abhorrent vice, even among the women; and they have justified themselves with saying—"We do it in self-defence, and because our husbands set us the example: it is in vain for us to strive and strive; for everything is going to ruin." Alas that such a plea should ever be made by a wife. Let the man remember that God has set him for the support of the wife: he is the head, and should set an example of virtue, and strength, rather than of vice and weakness. Let both avoid this deadly sin, if they would prosper in life, and steadfastly resist the temptation that besets them on every side. And not to the poor man alone would I speak; for this evil habit pervades all classes; and many a young man of fair expectations is ruined by this indulgence, and many a flourishing home is made desolate by him who founded it. The last state of this man is worse than the first.

FEMALE ENERGY.

It is a matter of surprize to many persons to see the great amount of energy of mind and personal exertion that women will make under the most adverse circumstances in this country. I have marked with astonishment and admiration acts of female heroism, for such it may be termed in women whose former habits of life had exempted them from any kind of laborious work, urged by some unforeseen exigency, perform tasks from which many men would have shrunk. Sometimes aroused by the indolence and inactivity of their husbands or sons, they have resolutely set their own shoulders to the wheel, and borne the burden with unshrinking perseverence unaided; forming a bright example to all around them, and showing what can be done when the mind is capable of overcoming the weakness of the body.

A poor settler was killed by the fall of a tree, in his fallow. The wife was left with six children, the youngest a babe, the eldest a boy of fourteen. This family belonged to the labouring class. The widow did not sit down and fold her hands in utter despair, in this sad situation; but when the first natural grief had subsided, she roused herself to do what she could for the sake of her infants. Some help no doubt she got from kind neighbours; but she did not depend on them alone. She and her eldest son together, piled the brush on the new fallow; and with their united exertions and the help of the oxen, they managed to log and burn off the Spring fallow. I dare say they got some help, or called a logging Bee, to aid in this work.—They managed, this poor widow and her children, to get two or three acres of wheat in, and potatoes, and a patch of corn; and to raise a few vegetables. They made a brush fence and secured the fields from cattle breaking in, and then harvested the crops in due time, the lad working out sometimes for a week or so, to help earn a trifle to assist them.

That fall they underbrushed a few acres more land, the mother helping to chop the small trees herself, and young ones piling the brush. They had some ague, and lost one cow, during that year; but still they fainted not, and put trust in Him who is the helper of the widow and fatherless. Many little sums of money were earned by the boys shaping axe-handles, which they sold at the stores, and beech brooms: these are much used about barns and in rough work. They are like the Indian brooms, peeled from a stick of iron-wood, blue-beech, or oak. Whip-handles of hickory, too, they made. They sold that winter maple sugar and molasses; and the widow knitted socks for some of the neighbours, and made slippers of listing. The boys also made some money by carrying in loads of oak and hemlock bark, to the tanners, from whom they got orders on the stores for groceries, clothes and such things. By degrees their stock increased, and they managed by dint of care and incessant labour to pay up small instalments on their land. How this was all done by a weak woman and her children, seems almost a miracle, but they brought the strong will to help the weak arm.

I heard this story from good authority, from the physician who attended upon one of the children in sickness, and who had been called in at the inquest that was held on the body of her husband.

Dr. H.[6] often named this woman as an example of female energy under the most trying circumstances; and I give it to show what even a poor, desolate widow may do, even in a situation of such dire distress.

BORROWING.

And now I would say a few words about borrowing—a subject on which so much has been said by different writers who have touched upon the domestic peculiarities of the Canadians and Yankees.

In a new settlement where people live scattered, and far from stores and villages, the most careful of housewives will sometimes run out of necessaries, and may be glad of the accommodation of a cupful of tea, or a little sugar; of barm to raise fresh rising, or flour to bake with. Perhaps the mill is far off and the good man has been

---

6 A Scot who came to Upper Canada in 1818, Dr John Hutchison (1797–1847) moved to Peterborough in 1830. He often treated the Traill and Moodie families; their names appear in the extant ledgers held at his home, now an historic house museum in Peterborough called Hutchison House. He was a good friend to Thomas Traill. In her story "The Old Doctor: A Backwoods Sketch" (Traill, *Forest and Other Gleanings*, 187–94), Traill describes him as benevolent and sarcastic, eloquent and "a model of strength, both mental and physical" (188). Susanna refers to him in *Roughing It in the Bush*: he was the doctor who lanced her infected breast after childbirth. He sponsored his young cousin Sandford Fleming, who became a great friend to Catharine in her old age. Dr Hutchison died in the typhus epidemic that swept through Canada in the late 1840s.

too much occupied to take in a grist. Or medicine may be needed in a case of sudden illness.

Well, all these are legitimate reasons for borrowing, and all kindly, well-disposed neighbours will lend with hearty good-will: it is one of the exigencies of a remote settlement, and happens over and over again.

But as there are many who are not over scrupulous in these matters, it is best to keep a true account in black and white, and let the borrowed things be weighed or measured, and returned by the same weight and measure. This method will save much heart-burning and some unpleasant wrangling with neighbours; and if the same measure is meted to you withal, there will be no cause of complaint on either side. On your part be honest and punctual in returning, and then you can with a better face demand similar treatment.

Do not refuse your neighbors in their hour of need, for you also may be glad of a similar favour. In the Backwoods especially, people cannot be independent of the help and sympathy of their fellow creatures. Nevertheless do not accustom yourself to depend too much upon any one.

Because you find by experience that you can borrow a pot or a pan, a bake-kettle or a washing-tub, at a neighbour's house, that is no good reason for not buying one for yourself, and wearing out Mrs. So-and-so's in your own service. Once in a while, or till you have supplied the want, is all very well; but do not wear out the face of friendship, and be taxed with meanness.

Servants have a passion for borrowing, and will often carry on a system of the kind for months, unsanctioned by their mistresses; and sometimes coolness will arise between friends through this cause. In towns there is little excuse for borrowing: the same absolute necessity for it does not exist.

If a neighbour, or one who is hardly to be so called, comes to borrow articles of wearing apparel, or things that they have no justifiable cause for asking the loan of, refuse at once and unhesitatingly.

I once lived near a family who made a dead set at me in the borrowing way. One day a little damsel of thirteen years of age, came up quite out of breath to ask the loan of a best night-cap, as she was going out on a visit; also three nice worked-lace or muslin collars—one for herself, one for her sister, and the third was for a cousin, a new-arrival; a pair of walking-boots to go to the fair in at ————, and a straw hat for her brother Sam, who had worn out his; and to crown all, a small-tooth comb, "to redd up their hair with, to make them nice."

I refused all with very little remorse; but the little damsel looked so rueful and begged so hard about the collars, that I *gave* her two, leaving the cousin to shift as she best could; but I told her not to return them, as I never *lent clothes,* and warned her to come no more on such an errand. She got the shoes elsewhere, and, as I heard they were worn out in the service before they were returned. Now against such a shameless abuse of the borrowing system, every one is justified in making a stand: it is an imposition, and by no means to be tolerated.

Another woman came to borrow a best baby-robe, lace-cap and fine flannel petticoat, as she said she had nothing grand enough to take the baby to church to be christened in. Perhaps she thought it would make the sacrifice more complete if she gave ocular demonstration of the pomps and vanities being his to renounce and forsake.

I declined to lend the things, at which she grew angry, and departed in a great pet, but got a present of a handsome suit; from a lady who thought me very hard-hearted. Had the woman been poor, which she was not, and had begged for a decent dress for the little Christian, she should have had it; but I did not respect the motive for borrowing finer clothes than she had herself, for the occasion.

I give these instances that the new comer may distinguish between the use and the abuse of the system; that they may neither suffer their good nature and inexperience to be imposed upon, nor fall into the same evil way themselves, or become churlish and unfriendly as the manner of some is.

One of the worst points in the borrowing system is, the loss of time and inconvenience that arises from the want of punctuality in returning the thing lent: unless this is insisted upon and rigorously enforced, it will always remain, in Canada as elsewhere, a practical demonstration of the old adage—"Those who go borrowing, go sorrowing;" they generally lose a friend.

There is one occasion on which the loan of household utensils is always expected: this is at "Bees", where the assemblage always exceeds the ways and means of the party; and as in country places these acts of reciprocity cannot be dispensed with, it is best cheerfully to accord your help to a neighbour, taking care to count knives, forks, spoons, and crockery, or whatever it may be that is lent carefully, and make a note of the same, to avoid confusion. Such was always my practice, and I lived happily with neighbours, relations and friends, and never had any misunderstanding with any of them.

I might write an amusing chapter on the subject of borrowing; but I leave it to those who have abler pens than mine, and more lively talents, for amusing their readers.

CHOICE OF A VESSEL.

In the choice of a vessel in which to embark for Canada, those persons who can afford to do so, will find better accommodations and more satisfaction in the steamers that ply between Liverpool and Quebec, than in any of the emigrant ships. The latter may charge a smaller sum per head, but the difference in point of health, comfort and respectability will more than make up for the difference of the charge. The usual terms are five or six pounds for grown persons; but doubtless a reduction on this rate would be made, if a family were coming out. To reach the land of their adoption in health and comfort, is in itself a great step towards success. The commanders of this line of ships are all men of the highest respectability, and the poor emigrant need fear no unfair dealing, if they place themselves and family under their care. At any rate the greatest caution should be practiced in ascertaining the character borne by the captains and owners of the vessels in which the emigrant is about to embark; even the ship itself should have a character for safety, and good speed. Those persons who provide their own sea-stores, had better consult some careful and experienced friend on the subject. There are many who are better qualified than myself, to afford them this valuable information.

LUGGAGE.

As to furniture, and iron-ware, I would by no means advise the emigrant to burden himself with such matters; for he will find that by the time he reaches his port of destination, the freightage, warehouse room, custom-house duties, and injury that they have sustained in the transit, will have made them dear bargains, besides not being as suitable to the country as those things that are sold in the towns in Canada. Good clothing and plenty of good shoes and boots, are your best stores, and for personal luggage you will have no freight to pay. A list of the contents of each box or trunk, being put within the lid, and showed to the custom-house officer, will save a great deal of unpacking and trouble. Any of your friends sending out a box to you, by forwarding an invoice and a low estimate of the value of the goods, the address of the party, and the bill of lading, properly signed by the captain to whose care it is assigned, to the forwarder at Montreal, will save both delay and expence. Macpherson Crane & Co., Montreal, or Gillespie & Company, with many others of equal respectability, may be relied upon. For upwards of twenty years I have had boxes and packages forwarded through Macpherson, Crane & Co., Montreal, without a single instance of loss: the bill of lading and invoice being always sent by post as soon as obtained: by attention to this advice much vexatious delay is saved, and the boxes pass unopened through the custom-house.

———————

I now copy for the instruction of the emigrant, the following advice which was published in the "Old Countryman", an excellent Toronto bi-weekly paper:

EMIGRATION TO CANADA.—The arrangements made by the Government of Canada for the reception and protection of emigrants on their arrival at Quebec contrast in a remarkable manner with the want of such arrangements at New York, and the other ports of the United States, to which emigrants are conveyed from Europe. On the arrival of each emigrant ship in the river St. Lawrence, she is boarded by the medical officer of the Emigrant Hospital at Grosse Isle, situated a few miles below Quebec, and, whenever disease prevails in a ship, the emigrants are landed, and remain at the hospital, at the expense of the Colonial Government, until they are cured.—On the ship's arrival at Quebec, Mr. Buchanan,[7] the government agent of emigrants, proceeds at once on board, for it is his duty to advise and protect each emigrant on his arrival. He inquires into all complaints, and sees that the provisions of the Passenger Act are strictly enforced. This he is enabled to do in a most effectual manner, as under an arrangement sanctioned by the Commissioners of Emigration in Great Britain, whenever an emigrant vessel leaves any British port for Quebec, the emigration officer of that port forwards to Mr. Buchanan, by mail steamer, a duplicate list of her passengers, with their names, age, sex, trade, &c. This list is usually received by him two or three weeks before the vessel reaches Quebec, so that he is not only fully prepared for her arrival, but is furnished with every particular which may be useful to him in protecting the emigrants.—If just cause of complaint exist, he institutes, under a very summary law of the Province of Canada, legal proceedings against the master: but so thoroughly are the value and efficiency of this officer felt, that since a very short period subsequent to his appointment, it has very rarely been found necessary to take such proceedings. In cases where emigrants have arrived without sufficient funds to take them

———————

7 Alexander Carlisle Buchanan (1808–1868) was the Crown Agent for emigrants in Quebec, responsible for offering advice, solving complaints, and enforcing the Passenger Act of 1828 (Knowles, *Strangers at Our Gates*, 57).

to places where employment is abundant and remunerative, their fares have been paid by Mr. Buchanan, out of the funds in his possession for the purpose. Emigrants from other than British ports experience precisely the same protection at the hands of Mr. Buchanan.—In 1858 about one-sixth of the emigration to Canada was German and Norwegian.

IMPORTANT TO EMIGRANTS.—The many fatal cases of cholera which have taken place on board emigrant vessels, will impress upon all who contemplate emigrating the propriety of adopting the salutary precautions set down by orders of her Majesty's Land and Emigration Commissioners, and widely circulated by placard. These precautions state:—That the sea-sickness, consequent on the rough weather which ships must encounter at this season, joined to the cold and damp of a sea-voyage, will render persons who are not very strong more susceptible to the attacks of this disease. To those who may emigrate at this season, the Commissioners strongly recommend that they should provide themselves with as much warm clothing as they can, and especially with flannel, to be worn next the skin; that they should have both their clothes and their persons quite clean before embarking, and should be careful to do so during the voyage—and that they should provide themselves with as much solid and wholesome food as they can procure, in addition to the ship's allowance, to be used on the voyage, and that it would, of course, be desirable, if they can arrange it, that they should not go in a ship that is much crowded, or that is not provided with a medical man.

EXTRACT FROM MR. VERE FOSTER'S ADVICE TO EMIGRANTS AS TO
SHIP STORES AND OTHER ESSENTIALS FOR THE VOYAGE.

I have been allowed by the author of a most useful and comprehensive little pamphlet on emigration, written for the use of poor emigrants by Vere Foster, Esq., and circulated at the low price of one penny, to make the following extracts, which I think must be of much value to families preparing to embark for this country, and contains some points of information which I was not able myself to supply:—
Mr. Foster says:—

"The lowest prices of passage from Liverpool to the different Ports in America, are much as follows:—
Quebec....................£ 3   0   0   to   £4   10   0

| Philadelphia............... | 3 | 0 | 0 | to | 4 | 10 | 0 |
| New Orleans............... | 3 | 5 | 0 | to | 4 | 10 | 0 |

"To the United States 10s. less is charged for any passenger under fourteen years of age; to Canada one-half less is charged; under twelve months often free of all charge.

"From London £1 higher is charged than the above rates.

"The rates of passage are higher than they were last year, on account of the high prices of provisions and increased expenses in the fitting up of ships, caused by the regulations of the late acts of parliament.

"Some steamers take passengers from Liverpool to Philadelphia for £8 8s. 0d. Others go in summer from Liverpool to Montreal, in Canada, for £7 7s. 0d., including provisions. In the winter months they go to Portland in Maine, where the fare, including railway fare, also is £7 7s. 0d.: to New York it is £8 8s. 0d.

"PURCHASE OF PASSAGE TICKETS.

"I would recommend emigrants to employ *no one*, but purchase for themselves at the Head Agency Office of the ship at the port of embarkation; or from the master of the ship in which they are about to sail; where they will be more likely to be charged the market rate. This ticket should be given up to *no one*, but should be kept till after the end of the voyage by the passenger, in order that he may at all times know his rights.

"Ships with but one sleeping deck are preferable to those with two, on account of health; and the less crowded with passengers the better for comfort.*

"As to those who wish to buy land, let them see it first, and avoid the neighbourhood of marshes, and rivers, where sickness is sure to prevail.* In the States of America, the price of Government land is One dollar and a quarter per acre. In Canada the government land is 7s. 6d. per acre.

---

* The humane writer of the "Advice to Emigrants" from which the above remarks are taken, though a person of education and refinement, and in delicate health, voluntarily chose to come out to Canada as a steerage passenger, that he might test in his own person the privations and discomforts to which the poorer emigrant passengers are exposed, and be enabled to afford suitable advice respecting the voyage-out to others.

* This rather belongs to small lakes and slow-flowing waters with low flat shores. Rapid rivers with high steep banks are not so unhealthy.

"OUTFIT OF PROVISIONS, UTENSILS AND BEDDING.

"The quantities of provisions which each passenger, fourteen years of age and upwards, is entitled to receive on the voyage to America, including the time of detention, if any, at the port of embarkation, are according to

British Law,

3 quarts of water daily.	1½ lb sugar.................. weekly.
2½ lbs of bread or biscuit weekly.	2 oz. tea, or 4 oz. coffee or
1 lb wheaten flour.......... "	cocoa...................... "
5 lb oatmeal................. "	2 oz. Salt.................... "
2 lb rice...................... "	

American Law.

3 qts. of water daily.	½ lb sugar.................. weekly.
2½ lb navy bread........... weekly.	2 oz. tea...................... "
1 lb wheaten flour.......... "	8 oz. of molasses and vinegar. "
6 lbs oatmeal................. "	
1 lb of salt pork............. "	
(free from bone.)	

"According to an act of Parliament which came in force on 1st October, 1852, certain articles may be substituted for the oatmeal and rice at the option of the master of the ship.

"In every Passenger ship issues of provisions shall be made daily before two o'clock in the afternoon, as near as may be in the proportion of one-seventh of the weekly allowance on each day. The first of such issues shall be made before two o'clock in the afternoon of the day of embarkation to such passengers as shall be then on board, and all articles that require to be cooked shall be issued in a cooked state. This excellent Parliamentary regulation is often evaded.— Each passenger is entitled to lodgings and provisions on board from the day appointed for sailing in his ticket, or else to 1s. per day, for every day of detention, and the same for forty-eight hours after arriving in America.

"EXTRA PROVISIONS FOR THE VOYAGE.

"As respects extra provisions, as great a quantity as heretofore will probably not be required, if the ship's provisions are issued according to law, cooked.

"In my recent voyage in the Washington from Liverpool to New York, which voyage occupied thirty-seven days, I took out the following extras, which I found quite sufficient. 1½ stone wheaten flour; 6 lbs bacon; 2½ lbs butter; a 4-lb loaf, hard baked; ½ lb tea; 2 lbs brown sugar; salt, soap, and bread soda for raising cakes. These extras cost 10s. 6d. I also took the following articles—the prices as follows:—

	s.	d.
Tin water-can holding six quarts	8	
Large tin hooked-saucepan	6	
Frying pan	8	
Tin wash-basin	6	
Tin tea-pot	4	
Tin kettle	9	
Two deep tin-plates	3	
Two pint-mugs	3	
Two knives, forks and spoons	9	
Barrel and padlock for holding provisions	1	0
Straw mattress	1	0
Blanket, single	2	0
Rugs	1	3
Sheets, each	10½	

"The handles and spouts of the tin-ware should be rivetted as well as soldered. Families would do well to take out a covered slop-pail and a broom. The bottoms of the chests and trunks should have two strips of wood nailed to them to keep them from the damp floor. In addition to the extra stores, a cheese, a few herrings, with some potatoes and onions may be added. [The eyes or shoots can be destroyed by drying the roots in an oven after the baking heat is off, for a few minutes; or they may be rubbed off with a coarse cloth from time to time.] Preserved milk is also a good thing; it can be kept good for some time.*

---

* Fresh milk put into a close jar and set in a pot of water, kept boiling for six or eight hours, and when cool bottled and corked with waxed corks, will keep some time. An ounce of white sugar boiled with the milk or cream will help to preserve it; and just before bottling, a small quantity—half a tea-spoonful—of carbonate of soda, may be added.

"As little luggage as possible should be taken, as the carriage often comes to as much as the first cost: woollen, and shoes, however, are cheaper at home, and therefore it is advisable to bring a good supply. Fruits and green vegetables should be eaten very sparingly at first: the free indulgence in fresh meat is also apt to bring on diarrhœa.—Many deaths happen in consequence of want of prudent attention to temperance in meats and drinks on first coming ashore.

"EMIGRANTS ON LANDING, should not linger about the suburbs of the ports and large towns, but go at once into the interior, for it is one hundred chances to one against their getting employment at these seaports. There is a great propensity in the poorer sort of emigrants to linger idling about the cities, spending their time and their little means, often refusing work when it is offered them, till their last penny is spent, when the trunks and other property are seized to pay for lodging. It is best to get work as fast as possible, and it is unreasonable to look for the highest rate of wages till a little experience in the work of the country has made them expert in the handling of the tools, which are often very different to those with which they have been used to labour.

"Intoxicating drinks are unfortunately very cheap in America and Canada. They are a great curse to the emigrant, and the main obstacle to his bettering his condition. Emigrants would do well to take the temperance pledge before sailing; as no liquors are allowed on board ship, they will have a beautiful opportunity of breaking themselves in to total abstinence of a practice which is injurious to health, expensive and selfish, as it robs them of the power of maintaining their families and adding to their comforts."—*Abridged from "Emigration to America" by Vere Foster, Esq.*

I have given you the substance of this valuable advice to emigrants, with here and there a few words added or omitted as the case might be.

I have omitted saying that the most eligible part of Canada for emigrants desiring to buy wild land, is the western portion of the Upper Province, or that peninsula that lies between the great waters of Lakes Ontario, Erie, Huron and the smaller lake Simcoe. Railroads and public works are being carried on in this part of the country; the land is of the richest and most fertile description, and the climate is less severe. The new townships afford excellent chances for mechanics settling in small villages, where such trades as the shoemaker, blacksmith, carpenter, wheelwright and others, are much needed, and in these new settlements labour of this kind pays well, because there is less competition to regulate the prices. It is a good thing for those who grow up with a new place; they are sure to become rich men.

I will also add a piece of additional advice. Let the immigrant on landing at any of the frontier towns ask for the Government agent but if none be resident in the place, and he is at a loss for advice as to the best mode of proceeding, let him then enquire for the clergyman, the mayor or one of the head gentlemen or merchants of the town. These persons have no interest to deceive or mislead in any way, and will give you all the information that you may need as to the best way of lodging and disposing of your family, and also the most likely persons to afford you employment.

In Toronto Mr. Hawke, the Crown Agent, will give all attention to you: he is a man whose knowledge is only surpassed by his uprightness and benevolence. You have only to ask his address; any one will direct you to his office.

One more piece of advice I would give to mothers who have young girls whom they may think proper to put to service; or to servant girls who come out without parents to act for them. Be careful how you enter into low families such as the keepers of low boarding houses or taverns, without endeavouring to learn something of the character of the parties, and by no means let relations or friends separate in a strange place without making some written note of their place of abode or future destination: by such carelessness many young people have lost all trace of their fathers and mothers, sisters and brothers, or of the friend under whose care they were placed by their relatives, and have suffered the most painful anxiety. Negligence of this kind is very much to be condemned and should be avoided. This is an error that often arises from ignorance and want of proper consideration. Perhaps you who read this book may deem such advice uncalled for, and so it may be in the case of all careful and thoughtful persons; but these may come out in the same vessel with others who are of a reckless, improvident nature, on whom they may impress the value of the advice here given. Among the Irish and even more cautious Scotch emigrants I have met with many many instances of children being left in a strange land without a trace of their place of residence being preserved,—the children in their turn having no clue by which to discover their parents.

POSTAGE.

In Canada the rates of postage are not high, though still they are greater than in the old country. Three-pence will pay a single letter to any part of the Province, and 7½d. to Great Britain, if marked Via Halifax: if sent unmarked it goes through the United States and costs 10d. postage.

In every large town once or twice a month a printed list of unclaimed letters lying at the Post-Office is published in one of the newspapers, by which regulation very few letters are lost.

_____

VALUE OF LAND

Owing to the rapid progress made in the Province during the last few years in population, trade, agriculture and general improvement, lands have increased in value, and it now requires as many pounds to purchase a farm as formerly it cost dollars.

The growth of towns and villages, the making of roads, gravel, plank and now railroads; the building of bridges, the improvement of inland navigation, mills of all sorts, cloth factories, and the opportunities of attending public worship have, under a peaceful government, effected this change; and wise men will consider that the increased value of lands is a convincing proof of the flourishing condition of the people and the resources of the country, and feel encouraged by the prospect of a fair return for capital invested either in land or any other speculation connected with the merchandize of the country.

The crown lands to the Westward, in the newly surveyed counties, are selling at 12s. 6d. currency per acre. The soil is of great fertility; and to this portion of the Province vast numbers are directing their steps; certain that in a few years the value of these bush farms will be increased fourfold; but let none but the strong in arm and will go upon wild land. The giants of the forest are not brought down without much severe toil; and many hardships must be endured in a backwoodsman's life, especially by the wife and children. If all pull together, and the women will be content to bear their part with cheerfulness, no doubt success will follow their honest endeavours.—But a wild farm is not to be made in one, two or even five years.—The new soil will indeed yield her increase to a large amount, but it takes years to clear enough to make a really good farm, to get barns and sheds and fences and a comfortable dwelling-house: few persons accomplish all this under ten, fifteen and sometimes even twenty years. I am speaking now of the poor man, whose only capital is his labour and that of his family; and many a farmer who now rides to market or church in his own waggon and with his wife and children, well and even handsomely clad, by his side, has begun the world in Canada with no other capital. It is true his head has grown grey while these comforts were being earned, but he has no parish poor-house in the distance to look forward to as his last resource, or the bitter legacy of poverty to bequeath to his famishing children and broken-hearted widow. And with so fair a prospect for the future, wives and mothers will strive to bear with patience the trials and toils which lead to so desirable an end, but let not the men rashly and unadvisedly adopt the life of settlers in the Bush, without carefully considering the advantages and disadvantages that this mode of life offer over any other; next his own capabilities for successfully carrying it into effect, and also those of his wife and family: if he be by nature indolent, and in temper desponding, easily daunted by difficulties and of a weak frame of body, such a life would not suit him. If his wife be a weakly woman, destitute of mental energy, unable to bear up under the trials of life, she is not fit for a life of hardship—it will be useless cruelty to expose her to it. If the children are very young and helpless, they can only increase the settler's difficulties, and render no assistance in the work of clearing; but if on the contrary the man be of a hardy, healthy, vigorous frame of body, and of a cheerful, hopeful temper, with a kind partner, willing to aid both within doors and without, the mother of healthy children, then there is every chance that they will become prosperous settlers, an honor to the country of their adoption. The sons and daughters will be a help to them instead of a drawback, and the more there are from six years old and upwards to lend a hand in the work of clearing, the better for them: they will soon be beyond the reach of poverty. It is such settlers as these that Canada requires and will receive with joy. To all such she bids a hearty welcome and God speed; and I trust the intelligent wives and daughters of such settlers may derive some assistance in their household labours from the instruction conveyed to them as well as to others in the pages of this book, which is not intended to induce any one to emigrate to Canada, but to instruct them in certain points of household economy, that they may not have to learn as many have done, by repeated failures and losses, the simple elements of Canadian housekeeping.

Among the many works most particularly valuable for affording the best information for Emigrants, I would point out "Brown's View's of Canada and the Colonists, Second Edition, Edinburgh, 1851," and Major Strickland's "Twenty-seven years' residence in Canada." The former supplies all necessary statistics, written with much good sense judgment and ability, while the latter, besides being very amusing, contains the best practical advice for all classes of settlers; but unfortunately is published at a price that places it out of the reach of the "People." It is a pity that the plain, practical portion of the work is not issued in a pamphlet form, at a rate which would place it at once within the means of the poorer class of emigrants, to whom it would be invaluable, as it gives every possible instruction that they require as back-woods settlers.

DESCRIPTION OF A NEW SETTLEMENT.

Extracted from Major Strickland's "Twenty-seven years' Residence in Canada West"[8]

"On the 16th of May, 1826, I moved up with all my goods and chattels, which were then easily packed into a single-horse waggon, and consisted of a plough-iron, six pails, a sugar-kettle, two iron pots, a frying-pan with a long handle, a tea-kettle, a few cups and saucers,* a chest of carpenter's tools, a Canadian axe, and a cross-cut saw.

"My stock of provisions comprised a parcel of groceries, half a barrel of pork, and a barrel of flour. "The roads were so bad (in those days when there were no roads) that it took me three days to perform a journey of little more than fifty miles. [This was twenty-eight years ago, let it be remembered, when travelling was a matter of great difficulty.[9]] We, that is my two labourers and myself, had numerous upsets, but reached at last the promised land.

"My friends in Douro turned out the next day and assisted me to put up the walls of my shanty and roof it with basswood troughs, and it was completed before dark. [This shanty was for a temporary shelter only, while working on the chopping, and preparing for the building of a good log-house.]

"I was kept busy for more than a week chinking between the logs, and plastering up all the crevices, cutting out the doorway and place for the window-casing, then making a door and hanging it on wooden hinges. I also made a rough table and some stools, which answered better than they looked.

"Four thick slabs of limestone placed upright in one corner of the shanty, with clay packed between them to keep the fire off the logs, answered very well for a chimney, with a hole cut through the roof above to vent the smoke.

"I made a tolerable bedstead out of some ironwood poles, by stretching strips of elmwood bark across, which I plaited strongly together to support my bed, which was a good one, and the only article of luxury in my possession.

"I had foolishly hired two Irish emigrants who had not been in Canada longer than myself, and of course knew nothing of either chopping, logging or fencing, or indeed of any work belonging to the country. The consequence of this

---

* Instead of crockery, the old bush-settler's plates and dishes, cups, &c. were of tin, which stood the rough travel of the forest roads better than the more brittle ware.

8 Traill has not used Samuel Strickland's material verbatim. Some of his phrases are excised and a few of hers inserted in square brackets.

9 This interjection and others in square brackets are Traill's comments to readers.

imprudence was that the first ten acres I cleared cost me nearly £5 an acre—at least £2 more than it should have done.*

"I found chopping in the summer months very laborious. I should have underbrushed my fallow in the fall before the leaves fell, and chopped the large timber during the winter months, when I should have had the warm weather for logging and burning, which should be completed by the first day of September. For want of experience it was all uphill work with me.

"A person who understands chopping can save himself a good deal of trouble and hard work by making what is called a *Plan* heap. Three or four of these may be made on an acre, but not more. The largest and most difficult trees are felled, the limbs only being cut off and piled. Then all the trees that will fall in the same direction should be thrown along on the top of the others, the more the better chance of burning well.

"If you succeed in getting a good fallow, the chances are, if your plan-heaps are well made, that the timber will be for the most part consumed, which will save a great many blows with the axe, and some heavy logging.*

"As soon as the ground was cool enough after the burn was over, I made a Logging Bee, at which I had five yoke of oxen and twenty men. The teamster selects a large log to commence a heap—one which is too pondrous for the cattle to draw: against this the other logs are drawn and piled: the men with handspikes roll them up one above the other, until the heap is seven or eight feet high and ten or twelve broad—all the chips, sticks, roots, and other rubbish are thrown up on the top of the heap. A team and four men can pick and log an acre a day if the burn has been good.

"My hive worked well, for we had five acres logged and fired that night. On a dark night a hundred or two of such heaps all on fire at once have a very

---

* The usual price for chopping, logging and fencing an acre of hardwood land is from eleven to twelve dollars; but if the pine, hemlock and spruce predominate, fourteen dollars is given. [This is a shorter version of Strickland's original footnote.]

* I have been told that in the western townships where the land is very heavily timbered, the usual plan now adopted by the settlers is to chop one year and let the timber lie till the following year when it is fired. The fire burns all up, so that a few charred logs and brands which are easily logged up is all that remain. This lightens the labour I am told very much; it is practised in the "Queen's Bush." [Footnote added by Traill.]

fine effect, and shed a broad glare of light over the country for a consider-able distance.

———————

"My next steps towards my house-building was to build a lime heap for the plastering of my walls and building my chimneys. We set to work, and built an immense log heap: we made a frame of logs on the top of the heap to keep the stone from falling over the side. We drew twenty cart loads of limestone broken up small with a sledge hammer, which was piled into the frame, and fire applied below. This is the easiest way in the bush of getting a supply of this useful material.

"I built my house of elm logs, thirty-six feet long by twenty-four feet wide, which I divided into three rooms on the ground floor besides an entrance-hall and staircase, and three bed-rooms above. I was busy till October making shin-gles, roofing, cutting out the door and windows, and hewing the logs smooth inside with broad axe." [Then follows a description and direction for making shingles.]

In the XII chapter we have an excellent passage about the choice of land, but I must refer my reader to the work itself for that, and many other most valuable hints, and go on to select another passage or two on building &c.

"The best time of the year to commence operations is early in Sept. The weather is then moderately warm and pleasant, and there are no flies in the bush to annoy you.

"A log-shanty twenty-four feet long by sixteen feet wide is large enough to begin with, and should be roofed with shingles or troughs.* A cellar should be dug near the fire-place commodious enough to contain twenty or thirty bushels of potatoes, a barrel or two of pork or other matters.

"As soon as your shanty is completed, measure off as many acres as you intend to chop during the winter, and mark the boundaries by a blazed-line [notched trees] on each side. The next operation is to cut down all the small trees and brush—this is called under-brushing. The rule is, to cut down every thing close to the ground from the diameter of six inches and under.

"There are two modes of piling, either in heaps or windrows. If your fallow be full of pine, hemlock, balsam, cedar and the like, then I should advise

———————

* This is a chopper's shanty: a good shelter for those who are clearing in the bush or lumbering. It should be chinked, and made wind and water tight. [This is Traill's, not Strickland's, note.]

windrows; and when hardwood predominates, heaps are better. The brush should be carefully piled and laid all one way, by which means it packs and burns better.

"The chopping now begins, and may be followed without interruption until the season for sugar-making commences. The heads of the trees should be thrown on the heaps, or windrow; this a skilful chopper will seldom fail to do.

"The trunks of the trees must be cut into lengths from fourteen to sixteen feet, according to the size of the timber."

"The emigrant should endeavour to get as much chopping done the first three years as possible, as after that time, he will have many other things to attend to. [It is a mistake to clear more wild land than a man and his family can work, as it is apt to get overrun with a second growth of brush and the fire-weed, and give a great deal of trouble, besides making a dirty-looking, slovenly farm.]

"In the month of May, the settlers should log up three or four acres for spring crops, such as potatoes, (which are always a great crop in the new soil,) Indian corn and turnips, which last require to be pitted or stored from the effects of the severe winter frost.

"The remainder of the fallow should be burnt off and logged up in July; the rail-cuts split into quarters and drawn aside ready for splitting up into rails. After the log-heaps are burned out, rake the ashes while hot into heaps, if you intend to make potash.*

"As soon as the settler is ready to build, let him if he can command the means, put up a good frame, rough-cast, or a good stone-house. With the addition of £150 in cash, and the raw material, a substantial family-house can be built which will last a vast number of years."

So far my brother. I will now add a few remarks myself. There are many very substantial dwellings now seen on the old clearings, built of stone collected from the

---

* See chap. xiii. page 170, "Twenty-seven years residence in Canada West." I could, with great advantage to the emigrant, have made more copious extracts from my brother's useful work, but I must content myself with such as more especially bear upon the subject of the first settlement. It is much to be regretted that the high price of these volumes places the work out of the power of the poorer class of the settlers, who would have found much that was practically useful to them, as well as to the reader to whom it is more particularly addressed. A cheap abridgment would be very useful to all classes of emigrants, and I hope may be published soon.

surface of the field. These are faced with a proper instrument into form, and in skilful hands are used as a proper building material. They have rather a motley surface, unless the building is rough-cast, but are very warm in winter and cool in summer. I like the deep recesses which the windows form in this sort of building; they remind one of some of the old-fashioned houses at home, with low window seats. I enjoy to sit in these gossiping corners. A good verandah round takes off from the patchy look of these stone-houses. Then there is the strip-house, and the vertical clapboard, or plank-house, and the block-house, either upright or horizontally laid; all these are preferable in every respect to the common log-house or to the shanty; but persons must be guided by their circumstances in building. But those who can afford a hundred or two pounds to make themselves comfortable, do so at once, but it is not wise to expend all their ready money in building a frame house at first. Among other reasons I would urge one, which is:—in building on wild land, owing to the nature of the forest land, it is very difficult to select a good site for a house or the best; and it is mortifying to find out that you have selected the very least eligible on the land for the residence: it is better to bear with cheerfulness a small evil for a year or two than have a ceaseless cause of regret for many years. It is always necessary to have water both for household purposes and near the cattle-yard. Good chain pumps can now be bought at a cost of a few dollars; and for soft water, tanks lined with water-lime can be constructed to any size. This is a great comfort if properly finished with a pump—the coldest water can be obtained; the expense is proportioned to the size.

In building a house a cellar lined with stone or cedar slabs or vertical squared posts, and well lighted and ventilated, is a great object: it will be found the most valuable room in the house. The comfort of such an addition to the dwelling is incalculable; and I strongly commend the utility of it to every person who would enjoy sweet wholesome milk, butter or any sort of provisions. A good house is nothing, wanting this convenience, and the poorest log-house is the better for it; but the access to the under-ground apartment should not be in the floor of the kitchen or any public passage: many limbs are broken yearly by this careless management. An entrance below the stairs or in some distant corner, with a post and rail to guard it, is just as easy as in the centre of a floor where it forms a fatal trap for the careless and unwary.

An ice-house in so warm a climate as the summer months present, is also a great luxury. The construction is neither expensive nor difficult, and it would soon pay itself. Fresh meat can be hung up for any time uninjured in the ice-house, when it would be spoiled by the ordinary summer-heat in any other situation. A lump of ice put into the drinking water, cools it to a delightful temperature, and every one who has experienced the comfort of iced butter, and the luxury of iced cream, will agree with me it is a pity every housewife has not such a convenience at her command as an ice-house.

I have placed my notice of this article in the chapter that is more particularly addressed to the men, because it depends upon them and not upon their wives, having these comforts constructed. A little attention to the conveniences of the house, and to the wishes of the mistress in its fitting up and arrangements, would save much loss and greatly promote the general happiness. Where there is a willingness on the husband's part to do all that is reasonable to promote the internal comfort; the wife on hers must cheerfully make the best of her lot—remembering that no state in life, however luxurious, is without its trials. Nay, many a rich woman would exchange her aching heart and weary spirit, for one cheerful, active, healthy day spent so usefully and tranquilly as in the Canadian settler's humble log-house, surrounded by a happy, busy family, enjoying what she cannot amid all her dear bought luxuries, have the satisfaction of a hopeful and contented heart.

REMARKS OF SECURITY OF PERSON AND PROPERTY IN CANADA.

There is one thing which can hardly fail to strike an emigrant from the Old Country, on his arrival in Canada. It is this,—The feeling of complete security which he enjoys, whether in his own dwelling or in his journeys abroad through the land. He sees no fear—he need see none. He is not in a land spoiled and robbed, where every man's hand is against his fellow—where envy and distrust beset him on every side. At first indeed he is surprised at the apparently stupid neglect of the proper means of security that he notices in the dwellings of all classes of people, especially in the lonely country places, where the want of security would really invite rapine and murder. "How is this," he says, "you use neither bolt, nor lock, nor bar. I see no shutter to your windows; nay, you sleep often with your doors open upon the latch, and in summer with open doors and windows. Surely this is fool-hardy and imprudent." "We need no such precautions," will his friend reply smiling; "here they are uncalled for. Our safety lies neither in bars nor bolts, but in our consciousness that we are among people whose necessities are not such as to urge them to violate the laws; neither are our riches such as to tempt the poor man to rob us, for they consist not in glittering jewels, nor silver, nor gold."

"But even food and clothes thus carelessly guarded are temptations."

"But where others possess these requisites as well as ourselves, they are not likely to steal them from us."

And what is the inference that the new comer draws from this statement?

That he is in a country where the inhabitants are essentially honest, because they are enabled, by the exertion of their own hands, to obtain in abundance the necessaries of life. Does it not also prove to him that it is the miseries arising from poverty that induce crime.—Men do not often violate the law of honesty, unless driven to do so by necessity. Place the poor Irish peasant in the way of earning his bread in Canada, where he sees his reward before him, in broad lands that he can win by honest toil, and where he can hold up his head and look beyond that grave of a poor man's hope—the parish work house—and see in the far-off vista a home of comfort which his own hands have reared, and can go down to his grave with the thought, that he has left a name and a blessing for his children after him:—men like this do not steal.

Robbery is not a crime of common occurrence in Canada. In large towns such acts will occasionally be committed, for it is there that poverty is to be found, but it is not common in country places. There you may sleep with your door unbarred for years. Your confidence is rarely, if ever, abused; your hospitality never violated.

When I lived in the backwoods, out of sight of any other habitation, the door has often been opened at midnight, a stranger has entered and lain down before the kitchen fire, and departed in the morning unquestioned. In the early state of the settlement in Douro, now twenty years ago, it was no uncommon occurrence for a party of Indians to enter the house, (they never knock at any man's door,) leave their hunting weapons outside, spread their blankets on the floor, and pass the night with or without leave, arise by the first dawn of day, gather their garments about them, resume their weapons, and silently and noiselessly depart. Sometimes a leash of wild ducks hung to the door-latch, or a haunch of venison left in the kitchen, would be found as a token of gratitude for the warmth and shelter afforded them.

Many strangers, both male and female, have found shelter under our roof, and never were we led to regret that we had not turned the houseless wanderer from our door.

It is delightful this consciousness of perfect security: your hand is against no man, and no man's hand is against you. We dwell in peace among our own people. What a contrast to my home, in England, where by sunset every door was secured with locks and heavy bars and bolts; every window carefully barricaded, and every room and corner in and around the dwelling duly searched, before we ventured to lie down to rest, lest our sleep should be broken in upon by the midnight thief. As night drew on, an atmosphere of doubt and dread seemed to encompass one. The approach of a stranger was beheld with suspicion; and however great his need, we dared not afford him the shelter of our roof, lest our so doing should open the door to robber or murderer. At first I could hardly understand why it happened that I never felt the same sensation of fear in Canada is I had done in England. My mind seemed lightened of a heavy burden; and I, who had been so timid, grew brave and fearless amid the gloomy forests of Canada. Now, I know how to value this great blessing. Let the traveller seek shelter in the poorest shanty, among the lowest Irish settlers, and he need fear no evil, for never have I heard of the rites of hospitality being violated, or the country disgraced by such acts of cold-blooded atrocity as are recorded by the public papers in the Old Country.

Here we have no bush-rangers, no convicts to disturb the peace of the inhabitants of the land, as in Australia. No savage hordes of Caffres[10] to invade and carry off our cattle and stores of grain as of the Cape; but peace and industry are on every side. "The land is at rest and breaks forth into singing." Surely we ought to be a happy and a contented people, full of gratitude to that Almighty God who has given us this fair and fruitful land to dwell in.

NATURAL PRODUCTIONS OF THE WOODS.—HOW MADE AVAILABLE TO THE SETTLER.

When the Backwoodsman first beholds the dense mass of dark forest which his hands must clear from the face of the ground, he sees in it nothing more than a wilderness of vegetation which it is his lot to destroy: he does not know then how much that is essential to the comfort of his household is contained in the wild forest.

Let us now pause for a few minutes while we consider what raw material is there ready to be worked up for the use of the Emigrant and his family.

Here is timber for all purposes; for building houses, barns, sheds, fencing and firewood.

The ashes contain potash, and the ley added to the refuse of the kitchen is manufactured by the women into soap, both hard and soft: or if spread abroad in the new fallow, it assists in neutralizing the acid of the virgin soil, rendering it more fertile and suitable for raising grain crops. From the young tough saplings of the oak, beech

10 Caffre or Kaffir refers to Black Africans. In South Africa, since 2000 (following the passing of Act No. 4), it and other derogatory racial terms are now included in legislation relating to hate speech.

and ironwood, his boys by the help of a common clasp knife, can make brooms to sweep the house, or to be used about the doors.—The hickory, oak and rock-elm supply axe handles and other useful articles. From the pine and cedar he obtains the shingles with which his log-house is roofed. The inner bark of the bass-wood, oak and many other forest trees can be made into baskets and mats. Dyes of all hues are extracted from various barks, roots and flowers. The hemlock and oak furnish bark for tanning the shoes he wears. Many kinds of wild fruits are the spontaneous growth of the woods and wilds.

The forest shelters game for his use; the lakes and streams wild fowl and fish.

The skins of the wild animals reward the hunter and trapper. From the birch a thousand useful utensils can be made, and the light canoe that many a white settler has learned to make with as much skill as the native Indian.

Nor must we omit the product of the sugar-maple, which yields to the settler its luxuries in the shape of sugar, molasses and vinegar.

These are a few of the native resources of the forest. True they are not to be obtained without toil, neither is the costly product of the silkworm, the gems of the mine, or even the coarsest woollen garment made without labour and care.

A FEW HINTS ON GARDENING.

Owing to the frosts and chilling winds that prevail during the month of April, and often into the early part of May, very little work is done in the garden excepting it be in the matter of planting out trees and bushes; grafting and pruning, and preparing the ground by rough digging or bringing in manure. The second week in May is generally the time for putting in all kinds of garden seeds: any time from the first week in May to the last, sowing may be carried on. Kidney beans are seldom quite secure from frost before the 25th. I have seen both beans, melons, and cucumbers cut off in one night, when they were in six or eight leaves. If the season be warm and showery early sowing may succeed, but unless guarded by glass, or oiled-paper frames, the tender vegetables should hardly be put in the open ground before the 18th or 20th May: corn is never safe before that time. The coldness of the ground and the sharpness of the air, in some seasons, check vegetation, so that the late sowers often succeed better than they who put the seeds in early. Having given some directions in various places about planting corn, potatoes, melons, and some other vegetables, I shall now add a few memoranda that may be useful to the emigrant-gardener. If you wish to have strong and early cabbage-plants, sow in any old boxes or even old sugar-troughs, putting some manure at the bottom, and six or eight inches of good black leaf-mould on the top, and set in a sunny aspect. The plants thus sown will not be touched by the fly. If sown later in May, set your trough on some raised place, and water them from time to time. Or you may sow on the open ground, and sprinkle wood-ashes or soot over the ground: this will protect the plants.—The fly also eats off seedling tomatoes, and the same sprinkling will be necessary to preserve them.

In sowing peas, single rows are better in this country than double ones, as unless there be a good current of air among the plants they are apt to be mildewed. Lettuces sow themselves in the fall, and you may plant them out early in a bed, when they will have the start of those sown in the middle of May.

Those who have a root-house or cellar usually store their cabbages in the following way: they tie several together by the stem near the root, and then hang them across a line or pole head downwards: others pit [put] them head downwards in a pit in the earth, and cover them first with dry straw and then with earth above that. The stem with the root should be stored by till spring, when if planted out, they will afford good, early, tender greens at a season when vegetables are not to be had.

There are many substitutes for greens used in Canada. The most common one is the Wild Spinach, better known by its local name of Lamb's-quarter. It grows spontaneously in all garden grounds, and may be safely used as a vegetable. It is tender, and when thrown into boiling water with a little salt, and cooked for five minutes, and drained, and sent to table like spinach, is much esteemed by the country people.

The Mayweed, a large yellow ranunculus that grows in marshy wet places, is also freely used: but be careful to use no wild plant unless you have full assurance of its being wholesome and that no mistake has been made about it. There is another wild green called Cow-cabbage that is eaten, but this also requires an experienced settler to point it out.

It is always well to save your own seeds if you can. A few large carrots should be laid by to plant out early in Spring for seed. Onions the same, also beets, parsnips, and some of your best cabbages.—Seeds will always fetch money at the stores, if good and fresh, and you can change with neighbours.

If you have more than a sufficiency for yourself do not begrudge a friend a share of your superfluous garden seeds. In a new country like Canada a kind and liberal spirit should be encouraged; in out-of-the-way, country places people are dependent upon each other for many acts of friendship. Freely ye will receive, freely give, and do not forget the advice given in the scriptures, "Use hospitality one to another," and help one another when you see any one in distress; for these are opportunities cast in your way by God himself, and He will require the use or abuse of them at your hands.

———————

Rhubarbs should always find a place in your garden; a cool, shady place and rich soil is best: throw on the bed in the Fall a good supply of long dung, and dig it in in the Spring. A barrel without a bottom put over a good plant, or a frame of an old box, will make the stalks very tender and less acid. The Giant Rhubarb is the best kind to plant.

A bed of Carraways should also find a place in your garden; it is always useful, and the seeds sell well, besides being valuable as a cattle medicine.

A good bed of pot-herbs is essential. I would bring out seeds of Balm, Thyme, and Sweet Basil, for these are rarely met with here.—Sage, Savoury, Mint and Pepper-mint, are easily got.

Sweet Marjoram is not commonly met with. I would also bring out some nice flower-seeds, and also vegetable seeds of good kinds, especially fine sorts of cabbage. You should learn to save your own seeds. Good seeds will meet with a market at the stores.

———————

The following plain, practical hints on the cultivation of ordinary garden vege-tables, taken from Fleming's printed catalogue, will be found useful to many of our readers.—

"Most kinds of seeds grow more freely if soaked in soft water from twelve to forty-eight hours before sowing; seeds of hard nature such as blood-beet, mangel and sugar beets, nasturtium, &c, often fail from want of attention to this circumstance. Rolling the ground after sowing is very beneficial, and will assist in making the seeds vegetate more freely; when a roller is not at hand, it may be done with the back of the spade, by flattening the earth and beating it lightly.—Kidney or French beans, may be planted any time in May in drills two inches deep, the beans two inches from each other, the drills about eighteen inches apart. If a regular succession is required, sow a few every few weeks from the first of May, to the first July. For climbers the best sorts are the white Lima, dwarf white haricot, bush bean and speckled red. Broad or Windsor beans, do not succeed well in this climate, the summer heat coming on them before they are podded, which causes the blossoms to drop off.

The best soil to grow them in is a rich, stiff clay, and on a northern border shaded from the mid-day sun: sow in drills two feet apart, two inches deep, and the seed three inches asunder.

Blood Beet, Long and Short Turnips, may be sown in a good, rich, deep soil, about the first week in May. Draw drills about one foot apart, and one inch deep; sow moderately thick: when the plants are up strong, thin them out the distance of six inches from each other in the rows. Brocoli and Cauliflower require a deep rich soil of a clayey nature, and highly manured. To procure Cauliflower or Brocoli the seed ought to be sown in a hot-bed early in March; when the plants are quite strong and healthy, they may be planted out in the garden about the middle of May. Plant in rows two feet square. The kinds that will do well in this climate are the Early London, and French Cauliflower, Purple Cape and Walcheren Brocoli.

Cabbage, both early and late, may be sown any time in May. The best situation for raising the plant is a rich, damp piece of ground, shaded. Seed sown in a situation of this kind is not so likely to be destroyed by the fly. When the plants are strong they may be planted in rows, and managed the same as directed for cauliflower.

The best kinds for summer use are the Early York, Battersea and Vannack: for winter use the Drumhead, Large Bergen and Flat Dutch.

Cucumbers may be sown in the open ground any time in May.—They require a good rich soil. Sow in hills four feet apart, leaving only four plants on each hill. The cucumber and melon vines are liable to be attacked by a yellow fly or bug. Soot, charcoal-dust or soap-suds, applied to the plants, will assist in keeping them off. Musk cantaloupe, nutmeg and water melons may also be sown at the same time, taking care to sow the different kinds a good distance apart from each other, as they are apt to mix. Plant in hills three feet square, leaving only three plants on each hill. When the plants have grown about six inches, stop or pinch the leading shoot, which will make the plants throw out side shoots, on which you may expect to have fruit.

Carrots.—The most suitable ground for growing Carrots, is a deep rich soil, that has been well manured the previous year. Sow any time in May, in drills one foot apart and one inch deep.

When the Carrots are up, thin them out, four inches apart, and keep them free of weeds. The kinds that are generally sown in the garden are the Early Horn, Long Orange, and Red Surrey: for field culture the white Belgian and

Altringham. The produce of one acre of field carrots, when properly cultivated, may be rated at from five hundred to eight hundred bushels. In cultivating them on the field system the drills ought to be two feet apart, and the carrots thinned out at least twelve inches asunder.

CELERY.—This vegetable is much esteemed as a salad. To have early Celery the seed should be sown in a hot-bed, in the month of March; for winter celery, the seed may be sown any time before the middle of May. Sow on a small bed of fine rich earth; beat the bed a little with the back of the spade; sift a little fine earth over the seed; shade the bed with a mat or board till the seeds begin to appear. Celery plants ought to be picked out into a nursery-bed, as soon as they are two or three inches high. Cut their roots and tops a little, before planting: water them well, and shade them from the sun, until they begin to grow. Let them remain in the nursery-bed for one month, after which they will be fit to transplant into the "trenches."—*(Fleming's Printed Catalogue)*

As a corrective to the sourness of very damp rich new soil, a light sprinkling of wood ashes is very useful. Leeched ashes are very good on some soil. The most splendid cabbages I ever saw were raised on ground where the spent ashes from a leech barrel had been ploughed into the soil. The kinds grown were the Conical cabbage and Portugal ivory-stemmed. The plants were from new seed from the Chiswick gardens, and my cabbages caused quite a sensation among the country gardeners.

HOPS.—This most useful plant no settler's house can dispense with: they are generally grown about the fences of the garden, around the pillars of the verandah, or porch, of the dwelling-house; or in hills in the garden. When in open ground, the hop must be supported with poles at least ten or fifteen feet high, set firmly in the ground.—The hop must be planted in very rich mould, and early in the Spring, that is before the sprouts begin to shoot above the ground. Two good buds at least are required for every root that you set. The Hop seldom is of much benefit the first year that it is planted, though if the ground be very rich, and the roots strong, the vines will produce even the first year. A little stirring of the mould, and a spadeful or two of fresh manure thrown on the plant in the fall, when the old runners have been cut down, will ensure you a fine crop the second year. Hops will always sell well if carefully harvested. In another part of the book[11] I mention that they should be gathered fresh and green: dull, faded, frost-bitten hops are of little worth. When plucked they

11 [92] in this new edition.

should be carefully picked from leaves and stalks, and spread out on a clean floor in a
dry chamber; and when quite dry packed closely into bags and hung up in a dry place.
Many persons content themselves with cutting the vines long after they are ripe for
gathering, and throwing them into a lumber room, there to be plucked as they are
required; but this is a very slovenly way. Children can pick hops at the proper season,
and store them by when dry, without much labour, and just as well as the mother
could do it herself.

The following article I have selected from the *Old Countryman*, a popular and useful
Canadian paper:—

GARDENING.

"We feel bound constantly to urge upon the attention of our readers the profit
and importance of a good garden. Its influence is good every way. It spreads the
table with palatable and nutritious food, and fills the dessert dishes with luxuries, and thus saves the cash which must otherwise be paid for beef, ham, veal,
and lamb; besides promoting the health and spirits more than the meat would.
Then a good garden is a civilizer. The garden and orchard beautify the home
wonderfully and kindle emotions which never die out of the heart.

But we must say a word or two on individual plants, and first of—

ASPARAGUS. This is a delicious vegetable. What the old bed requires in the
Spring is to cut off the last year's stalks just above the ground, and burn them;
loosen the earth about the roots, and clean up the whole bed. As the sweetness and tenderness of this plant depends upon its rapidity of growth, the soil
should be made very rich.

BEANS should be planted as soon as you feel secure from frost. They are
ornamental when planted in hills two or more feet apart, with birch sticks stuck
about the edge, and tied together at the top.

Then there are peas and beets of two or three kinds, parsnips, carrots, lettuce, radishes, cucumbers, rhubarb, pepper-grass, spinach, salsify, parsley,
tomato, turnips, celery, early corn, early potatoes, melons, onions, summer
squash, and cabbage, all affording the proper summer nutriment, and requiring a similar soil for their production. Sow and cultivate well a few of each, and
you will find your account in it.

SMALL FRUITS.—Set red and white raspberries, thimbleberries, black and
white, also currants and gooseberries. They are cheap and wholesome food,
and as easily raised as potatoes. Any home will have charms for children where
these are plentifully grown.

ORNAMENTAL. Do not allow the lusty teams and the broad acres,—the grass, the grain, and the tree to occupy all your time, but give a thought and an eye occasionally to the beautiful. Spread out a sunny space for the daughters, where the boys will cheerfully assist them with the spade. What a charming spot! Here are the mixed balsams and carnations; the mignionette, mourning bride, and columbine; there, love-lies-bleeding, and, in the corner, love-in-a-mist, the candy-tuft, and Canterbury bell. Why, you resume your youth here. Time almost ceases to make its mark. Old scenes come thronging to the soul, such as when you sat on the rustic seat in the garden, and dissected flowers with her who is now the mother of these beautiful and happy daughters. Such are the influences of the flower garden. We need not go to the books for poetry, it is nature every-where, but especially in such a group as this,—

> "There's beauty all around our paths,
> If but our watchful eyes
> Can trace it midst familiar things,
> And through their lowly guise."

We insist upon it, that there is time with all to be given to the ornamental. It will make you richer, better, happier, more cheerful, and enable you to die easier, and will have the same influences upon your family, by creating some-thing of the beautiful around you.—*New-England Farmer."*

The new settler will be surprised at the facility with which in the open ground he can raise the finest sorts of melons, with as little labour bestowed upon the plants as he has been accustomed to give to cabbages, lettuce or any of the commonest pot-herbs. The rich black mould of the virgin soil, and the superior heat of the sun in a climate where the thermometer often ranges from 80 ° to 95 ° for many days together during the summer months, brings both vegetables and fruit to perfection very rapidly. In the Western part of the country, or that portion lying between the great lakes Ontario, Erie and Huron, fruit is grown and ripened that is with difficulty perfected east of Toronto, where the heat is not so ardent, and late and early frosts nip the fair promise of the wall fruit. The peach, apricot and grape, with many other kinds are rarely met with in the eastern portion of the Province, unless trained on south walls, and protected during the cold season. Pears, however, will grow well: Apples of the finest quality, and many other fruits in the townships between Toronto and Montreal. I have heard that the apples of the Lower Province are considered by horticulturists to be of the finest quality. There are several sorts of apples in great repute in our orchards, and should be cultivated by those who are planting trees— "Pomme-gris," "Canada-red", "St. Lawrence" and "Hawley's Pippin", with some others of excellent reputation; but as I have devoted a separate section to Apples and the Orchard, I need say no more on this head in this place.

With a little attention and labour, the vegetable garden may be carried to great perfection by the women and children, with a little assistance from the men at the outset, in digging the ground, and securing the fences, or any work that may require strength to effect. In the new ground the surface is often encumbered with large stones, and these must either remain a blot on the fair features of the garden plot, or be rolled away by the strong arm of the men, aided by the lever. These surface stones may be made very serviceable in filling up the lower part of the fence, or, piled in large heaps, be rendered ornamental by giving them the effect of rockwork. I know many gardeners whose rustic seats, overarched by climbing plants, have been made both useful and ornamental with these blocks of granite and limestone forming the seat. Stone-crop, orpine, and many other plants, set in a little soil among the crevices, have transformed the unsightly masses into an interesting and sightly object. The Wild Cucumber, Orange Gourd, Wild Clematis, and a number of other shrubby climbing-plants, will thrive and cover the rocky pile with luxuriant foliage. Thus by the exertion of a little ingenuity, the garden of the settler may be rendered not only highly useful, but very ornamental. A little taste displayed about the rudest dwelling, will raise the inmates in the eyes of their neighbours. There are very few persons totally insensible to the enjoyment of the beautiful, either in nature or art, and still fewer who are insensible to the approbation of their fellow men; this feeling is no doubt implanted in them by the Great Creator, to encourage them in the pursuit of purer, more intellectual pleasures than belong to their grosser natures. As men cultivate the mind they rise in the scale of creation, and become more capable of adoring the Almighty through the works of his hands—I think there can be no doubt but that whatever elevates the higher faculties of the soul, brings man a step nearer to his Maker.

How much pleasanter is the aspect of a house surrounded by a garden, nicely weeded and kept, than the desolate chip-yard, unrelieved by any green tree or flower, that is so often seen in the new settlements in Canada. What cheerful feelings can such a barren spot excite; what home affections can it nourish in the heart of the emigrant wife? Even though she may have to labour to rear it with her own hands, let her plant a garden.

APPLES.

The planting of an orchard, which is a matter of great importance to the future comfort of the settler's family, is often delayed year after year, and that is done last, which should have been attended to at the outset.

Not only are apples valuable as a most palatable and convenient article of diet, but also as one of the most wholesome. In a climate where great heat prevails during the summer months, and even later in the fall, the cooling acid of fruit becomes essentially necessary for the preservation of health.

During the first years of the emigrant's life, this want is painfully felt by those who settle down in the backwoods; and a supply should be provided for as early as possible, by planting trees in the first or second year of the settlement.

I cannot too forcibly impress upon the emigrant the advantage he will derive from thus securing to his household, the comforts, I might almost say the blessing, of an orchard.

I would therefore advise him to fence in securely the first acre, or even half acre, of cleared ground about his house, and plant it with young apple-trees. In all the towns now he will find nurseries, where the choicest and best sorts of apples, pears, cherries, and plums, can be bought.

For good root-grafted apples of good character, which will begin to fruit in three years from the planting, the usual price is 1s. 3d. (a quarter dollar.) Pears, plums, and budded cherries, of good sorts, are dearer, say 2s. 6d. the tree. Ungrafted apple-trees, or seedlings of three years growth cost 7½d. (or a York shilling). These last will bear good kitchen fruit, and by chance, if well cared for, a very fine table-apple may be found among them; but those who can afford to lay out a few dollars in securing apples of the first quality will be wise to do so. But there may be some who are unable to make even this small outlay, and can hardly venture to purchase the ungrafted trees. Let such sow every apple-pip they can obtain, on a bed, set apart in the garden enclosure for that purpose. The Fall is the best time to put the pips into the ground; they will come up in the following Spring: but if you sow them in Spring they rarely come up till the following season, while those sown in the Fall come up in the ensuing Spring.

When these nurslings are well up in six or eight leaves, weed them carefully by hand, or with an old knife. The pips should be sown in drills, a foot apart; the seeds six or eight inches apart; but as ground is no object, and the young trees will be twice as strong and straight with room allowed to grow in, I would rather weed them out so that each sapling stood eighteen inches apart each way; you may plant out those you remove, and they will be none the worse for the resetting.

By the third year these young trees may be grafted, or else they may be removed to the situation in the garden or orchard they are meant to occupy; and after this removal good well-formed branches may be encouraged, but spurs and sprouts are better kept from filling up the middle of the tree. Seedlings thus managed, and the roots kept well worked about at the surface with the hoe, will stand a fair chance of becoming a valuable orchard. You will be surprised at the rapid advance of these trees in a few years time. A scattering of wood-ashes on the ground, or a little manure, well worked in with the hoe in the Fall, will do great things for your plantation. Many persons grow young nurseries for the sake of grafting on the young vigorous stocks. In Canada root grafting is very much practiced.

My female readers will say, these directions are all very well, but this is men's work; we women have nothing to do with nurseries, except in the house; but let me now say a few words on this head.

In Canada where the heavy labour of felling trees and cultivating the ground falls to the lot of the men, who have for some years enough to do to clear ground to support the family and raise means towards paying instalments on the land, little leisure is left for the garden and orchard: the consequence is that these most necessary appendages to a farm-house are either totally neglected or left to the management of women and children. That there is a miserable want of foresight in this, there can be no doubt, for the garden when well cultivated produces as large an amount of valuable crop as any part of the farm.—In any of the towns in the Fall or in Winter, a head of good cabbage will fetch 3d or 4d., onions a dollar a bushel, carrots from 3s. to 4s. a bushel, and other vegetables in like manner; and as food for the household consumption, they cannot be too highly valued, even for the sake of preserving the health. Nevertheless if the men will not devote a portion of time to the cultivation of the garden, and orchard, the women must, or else forego all the comfort that they would otherwise enjoy.

After all, when the enclosure is made, and the ground levelled and laid out in walks, and plots, the sowing of the seeds, and keeping the crops weeded and hoed, is not so very heavy a task: with the aid of the children and occasional help of one of the elder boys, a good piece of garden may be cultivated. The tending of a nursery of young trees from the first sowing of the seeds in the ground, is rather a pleasure than a labour; and one which I have taken a delight in from my earliest years.

When I was a child of eight years old, I assisted one of my sisters two years older than myself, under my father's direction, in planting a nursery of walnuts. Those trees now form a fine avenue, and have borne fruit for many years.

Little children can be made to sow the stones of plums, cherries, and apple-pips, in the nursery; these in time will increase and bear fruit in due season: they will all bear fruit without grafting or budding, and they are growing while you are sleeping. In a few years they will be a source of comfort and luxury to your family, and you will not then lament the care that you bestowed upon them.

In the early years of our infant settlement on the banks of the Otonabee river, above the town of Peterboro, all the ladies worked in their gardens, raised their own vegetables, and flowers, and reared the fruit trees which in after years almost over-shadowed their dwellings. They felt this work as no disgrace to them, but took pride and pleasure in the success of their labours.

My own garden was full of stumps, and stones, roots and wild bushes, and it cost some trouble to reduce it to smooth working order. I got some help to overcome the first difficulties. The stones, some of them of large dimensions, were removed with a handspike, and built up into a heap. Around the stumps, turf and rubbish of all kinds were heaped, and finally covered with a depth of fine black mould, on which gourds, cucumbers, or melons, were planted, the grass roots and weeds nourishing them as well as a regular hot-bed would have done: by this simple contrivance we got rid of much rubbish, which by degrees was converted into the best of manure, and hid many an unsightly object; the vines of the cucumbers &c. running down the steep sloping sides of the mound, and also covering the stumps with their leaves and fruit.

As I disliked the rough unsightly look of the rail fences, I got an old English set-tler to enclose my garden (which swept in a bold curved line from each corner of the house) with a wattled fence: this looked very picturesque, but did not last more than three years good. I then collected wild gooseberry bushes, currants, bush honey suckles, hawthorns, wild cherry and plum trees, with all sorts of young bushes, and planted them within side my fence,[12] to make a living fence, when the other should have decayed; and had I remained long enough to complete my plans, I should have

12 This charming phrase describes Traill's practice of interweaving live bushes together with wattle fencing to produce an attractive and longer lasting living fence.

had a nice hedge. If we could have procured the proper sort of wands, fit for the purpose, I have no doubt my fence would have proved as lasting as it was pretty to look at. It was the admiration of all my neighbours, and many came to look at "Mrs. Traill's fence."

Next to a picket fence made of split cedars, with cedar posts, a log fence is the best in situations where sawn lumber is not easily procured, but the logs should be secured from rolling by stakes and riders. These fences are only suitable to bush settlements, but as my book is intended for emigrants of all sorts, and conditions, and especially for the working hands, I have dwelt more minutely on such things as may suit their particular circumstances, though I trust it may also contain matter of valuable instruction to all classes.

I must now return to the subject from which I first started, Apple-Orchards and Apples.

I again repeat my advice to buy grafted trees if you can afford to do so. There are agents who travel the country, and penetrate even to the verge of the forest, to collect orders for trees, from different nursery-gardens in the United States, and also from the large towns in Canada. I recommend you to deal with the latter, for this reason: your trees are likely to reach your hands sooner after being taken out of the ground: give your strict orders to have the trees well rooted, and the roots matted; and deal with men of good character, who are well known, and have an established reputation. I will give you a list of the most approved and valuable Apples, at the end of this article.

In planting your trees do not be afraid to make the hole wide enough; it is better to dig the soil well, and let every part be thoroughly worked till it be fine and mellow: this is better than putting manure to the roots, which gardeners do not recommend. With a sharp knife cut the bruised roots, and if the top be large, and the roots small, reduce the branches: if the roots be large and spreading, little pruning is requisite: the young trees that have thriven best have been uncut when planted.

The careful planter will make holes deep, that a good bed of friable, sandy loam may be spread at the bottom to set the trees on. It makes a great difference on what soil the roots are bedded.

Let the tree be held up by one person, while another carefully arranges the roots, so that they lie in a natural way in contact with the soil; then lightly strew in the earth, with the hands, and fill up the hole with good soil, pressing the earth down: when planted, a quantity of half-decayed litter should be placed round the tree, as far as the roots extend: this is called by the gardeners mulching, and serves to keep the ground moist and mellow. If you think it needful to support the tree from the action of the wind, tie it to a stake, but place a bit of old cloth between the stake and the young tree, to keep the bark from being rubbed. "In most cases," says a skilful American horticulturist, "it is better to thin out, than to shorten the branches of the newly taken-up trees; leaves are necessary to the formation of roots, and if you deprive the young tree of all its boughs, you stop its resources for root-growth."

There are two seasons for orchard planting; in the Fall, and the Spring. Now I am myself rather in favour of the Fall planting, if it be not put off too late.* Many persons plant late, and lose their trees. October is the usual time, and I think it should be done as early in the month as possible. My own idea is that just at the season when the leaf begins to turn yellow, is the safest time for transplanting. If it be put off till the frosts harden the ground, injury to the tender nurslings must follow. In Spring the ground is often too wet, and cold, and the trees get too forward to be removed safely.— April is the Spring month for transplanting, and October in the Fall.

I will now, as well as I can, give you some simple directions about grafting, which is an art often practised by the female hand, as well as that of the professed gardener.

Cut the stock or branch which you design to graft upon, smooth and even, with a sharp knife, or if too large for the knife, with a small fine-toothed pruning saw; with your knife make a cleft of about an inch deep through the crown of the stock, dividing it clean through the bark on either side, into which cleft insert the handle of a budding-knife, which is smooth, and wedge-shaped; or if you are without this useful instrument, have ready a narrow wedge of wood, which will answer all the purposes; this is to keep the cleft open, while you insert the scions or grafts. Select your grafts from any good sorts, from healthy trees, the new, or youngest, growth of wood being chosen. Most grafters cut the scions some days or even weeks before. With a sharp knife pare away the wood on each side, taking care to leave a ridge of bark on your scion, as on this simple circumstance depends the life of the graft. The graft should be about a finger's length, with three distinct buds, one from the base of which you begin to shape the lower part or wedge, which is to be introduced into the cleft. Two grafts, one on each side of the stock, are generally inserted, unless it be in seedling apples, when one will be sufficient. I have seen as many as four scions on the large limbs, but one or two good grafts are better than more.

---

* Fall planting is now getting more into favour than it was, and earlier planting, say the last week in September.

With your grafting wax at hand, (for clay does not answer in this country as in England,) insert your scions at the edge of the cleft, so that the strip of bark left on it, fills up the opening like a slender gore let into the stock, taking care to bring the edges of the bark of the cleft and the bark of the graft close together, and even, so that neither one shall project beyond the other. Proceed in like manner to your other graft, and then remove the wedge from the centre of the stock; the crack will close, and hold your scions tight: then apply the wax to the sides, covering every part of the seam and a little below, where you see the cracking of the bark; also round the part where the lowest bud rests on the stock: do this effectually, and spread the wax over the crack on the crown of the stock, bringing a little of it all round the edge of the bark, to keep it from drying up. Some wind a strip of cloth, or thread, round, to secure the graft from being moved by any accident: others leave it to chance. You can do so if you like, only there is an old proverb in favor of the binding:

"Safe bind, safe find."

I have only described one method of grafting, but there are many equally simple and safe, which any one conversant with the practice of grafting, will describe, or what is still better, cut a branch, and a scion, and show you the process. I learned to graft from a Canadian lady in her own parlour. I will now give you the receipt for preparing the grafting wax.

GRAFTING WAX

is made in the following proportions: one part of common beef-tallow; two parts bees' wax; and four parts resin. Melt the whole together, pour into a pail of cold water; rub a little of the grease on your hands, to prevent the wax from sticking, and then as it cools work it well with your hands, first in the water and then on a bit of board, till it is thoroughly kneaded, and will be soft and plastic, without adhering to the fingers or running thin. This wax is spread over the sawn limb and round the graft, and down the wounded bark, so as to exclude the air and moisture; if too soft add a little more wax, or if too hard a little more tallow.

Some use cobbler's wax, some apply pitch, and the common turpentine from the pines; but the wax is neatest, cleanest, and best.—Clay is of little use, as it either dries with the sun, or cracks with the frost. Some use bass bark to bind round the grafts.

The tools used by those persons who make grafting a business, or have large orchards, are a grafting saw, a pruning knife, a wedge-handled knife, a small hammer with an axe at one end, for making clefts in the large boughs, and a bag for the tools, with a strap to pass about the shoulder, and a box for the wax, with string, or a coil of wet bass or cedar bark for binding; but many trees are grafted with only a knife, a saw, and the wax.

———————

Those who know how to graft should early sow the seeds of apples, pears, plums and cherries in a nursery bed, that they may have good vigorous stocks to graft upon. Not long since I met with an old-fashioned book on orchard-planting, where the following direction was given:

"Sow apple-seeds in a ring, at distances of twenty-five feet from ring to ring, on a space intended for an orchard. When your young trees are up, thin out, to two feet apart, keeping them stirred with the hoe, and free from weeds. At the end of three years graft your young stocks. The following year remove all but one healthy tree from each ring, choosing the very best to become your standard.—The rest of your young grafted trees may be set out in suitable places or sold, but you will find the advantage of never having transplanted your seedling, by the superior growth, and vigour, of your graft over the young stocks that have been checked by transplantation from the native soil."

As a manure for orchard-trees, wood soot, wood ashes, and a small quantity of lime is strongly recommended, especially in wet soil. A dead level, unless drained, is not so favourable for apple trees, as the side of a hill facing south or west. Soap-suds are recommended to wash or scrub the bark of apple and pear trees, to prevent scaly bark, and remove moss. In the Fall, a careful person should examine all the trees, and remove the nests of the caterpillars, which will be found adhering to the young twigs, like a gummy swelling of the bark. These are easily taken off like a brittle, varnished crust. Early in Spring search the trees again; if any escape they will show themselves in the leafing time, and unless the webs which they spin for a shelter, are removed in time, these caterpillars will injure the crop and tree, by devouring the foliage and blossoms.

Having given you some directions for the management of your orchard-trees, I will now furnish you with a list of the most highly approved sorts to select for planting, as the names differ much from those you have been accustomed to see in the English orchards.—America is famous for the excellence of her apples, and those that are the natives of the climate, are always most hardy, prolific, and best adapted for orchard planting in Canadian soil.

SUMMER APPLES.

Early Harvest, Yellow Harvest, Early Joe, Summer Queen, Sweet Bough, Summer Bellflower, (good cooking apple,) Summer Pearmain, Canada Red, Snow Apple; this last is not ripe till September, but can be used for pies or puddings much earlier; it is a great bearer, and the thinning out is no real sacrifice, as it improves the size of those left to ripen. It is known in the Lower Province as La Fameuse; it is a great bearer, and a fine, sweet, juicy apple.

AUTUMN APPLES.

Autumn Strawberry*,[13] Fall Pippin*, Holland* (kitchen apple), Red Astracan*, Hawley's Pippin*, Twenty-ounce Apple*, Burassa* (late Fall), Baldwin, St. Lawrence, Nonpareil Russet, Golden Russet*, York Quincy, Hawthornden*, Gravestien*.

WINTER APPLES.

Winter Strawberry*, Northern Spy*, Rambo, Baldwin*, Roxbury Russet*, Swaar*, Winter Pippin*, Rhode Island Greening*, Ribstone Pippin*, Newtown Pippin*, Pomme Grise, Spitzenburg*, White Winter Pearmain, Yellow Bellflower, Ladies' Sweeting. These are all choice sorts.

There are many other capital apples, but these are the most celebrated, and therefore I have selected them. Those marked with a star are of the best quality, but all are good. The mulching the trees as before noticed, is of great utility, but not too deeply. Or if much litter be laid round in the Fall, remove it in the Spring, and stir the ground with the hoe: covering the roots too thickly keeps the sun from warming the earth about them.

Having done with the planting, I will now give some good recipes for the cooking, and end with some remarks on the storing of Apples.

APPLE-PIE.

Every one knows how to make a common apple pie or pudding.—But in case there may be a few among my emigrant friends, who have been unused even to this simple process in cooking, I will say: peel and core your apples; good acid cooking-apples are better than sweet ones; drop them into a pan of clean water as you pare them; in the pie-dish place a tea-cup, turned bottom upwards; put in a large table-spoonful

---

13　In the next entry, Traill explains that her asterisks identify apples she thinks are "of the best quality." The McIntosh apple is not on this list because it came onto the commercial market later.

of sugar, and two or three cloves, or a bit of lemon peel, if you have these things at hand; fill your dish with the cored apples; a very small quantity of water—a large table-spoonful will suffice; add two or three more cloves, and more sugar; cover with your paste, rolled thin; finely crimp the edge, and scallop with your finger and the edge of the knife. A few delicate leaves, cut and marked to resemble apple leaves, placed in the centre, give a pretty look to the dish; but this is a mere matter of taste. If you have any cause to think that the fruit is not quite soft, when the crust is baked, set the dish on the top of one of your stove griddles, and let it simmer a while. Some persons stew the apples first, season and put them into the dish, and when cool, cover and bake; but I think the apples never taste so well as when baked in the old way.

The reason for inserting a cup in the pie is this: the juice and sugar draws under the cup, and is thus kept from boiling out: paring the apples into the dish of water preserves them from turning brown or black, and the moisture they imbibe renders no other water necessary, or very little. The Canadians season their pies with nutmeg and allspice, making them sickly tasted; they stew the apples till they are an insipid pulp, and sweeten them till the fine acid is destroyed. A good, juicy, fine-flavoured apple-pie is a rare dish to meet with in hotels and among the old Canadian and Yankee settlers.

DRIED APPLES.

The drying of apples is a great business in the houses of the Canadian farmers, where they have orchards, or live near those who have large orchards, who will sell the inferior fruit very cheap, as low as 7¹/₂d. a bushel, if you gather them yourself. Those who revel in an abundance of this useful fruit, often call their young friends together to an Apple-paring "Bee". Bushels and bushels of apples are pared, cored and strung on Dutch thread, by the young men and maidens, and the walls of the kitchen festooned round with the apples, where they hang till dry and shrivelled. They should be dipped into boiling water as they are hung up; this preserves the colour. Some expose them to the action of the sun and wind, on the walls of the house, or spread them on clean boards or trays; when thoroughly dry, they are stored in bags, and hung in a dry place, out of the dust. These dried apples find ready sale at 1s. 6d. per lb., and even higher, if the season be far advanced, and apples scarce. When required for use, they are steeped for some time in hot water. Stewed till tender, with a seasoning of cloves, these apples form a delightful preserve, and rarely need any sugar; but if too sour, a small quantity is easily added.—Some add molasses. Tarts, pies and many pleasant dishes are made with these dried apples: a delicious fever drink is made by pouring off the liquor after the apples have boiled a few minutes. By this simple process of drying, you may have apples to make use of all the year round, long after the fruit has decayed, and lost its flavour, in the apple chamber. In England this process of drying apples might be adopted to advantage.

PRESERVED APPLES.

Take equal quantities of good brown sugar and of good boiling apples; i.e. a pound to a pound; cut the apples up fine, put on your skillet, and to every three pounds of sugar allow a pint of water; scum the syrup as it boils up, add the apples, with a little essence of lemon, or lemon peel; a few cloves, or a bit of ginger: boil till the apples are tender and look clear.

The small American crabs will be excellent done the same way.—For common everyday use, half the quantity of sugar will do.

APPLE JELLIES.

Allow a pound of crushed sugar (this is an inferior sort of loaf sugar, which sells at 7½d. a pound) to a pound of chopped apples, boil the sugar to a syrup, with a few cloves and a stick of cinnamon; throw in the apples, and boil till the fruit is dissolved. If you wish to have it coloured, add in, while boiling, a slice or two of blood beet; this will give a beautiful rich tint to the jelly; or a little saffron steeped in a cup of boiling water, which will tinge it a deep yellow; strain the jelly through a coarse sieve of net or fine canvas. When potted, cut paper dipped in spirits, and lay on the top, the size of the inner rim of the jar: have a larger round cut, so as to cover the outer rim: beat up the white of an egg, and with a feather brush this paper over; press the edges close to the jar: to do this well, snip the edge with the scissors, which will make it form to the shape of the jar.

Preserves thus secured from the air, do not mould as in the ordinary mode of tying them up, and the trouble is not more than tying with string.

APPLES IN SYRUP.

Make a thin syrup with sugar and water, season with spice or lemon peel; pare some small-sized apples, whole, and let them boil till tender, but do not let them break if you can help it. Set the apples and syrup by in a deep dish till cold. This makes a cheap dish to eat with bread at tea. It is easily prepared, and is very agreeable, besides being very wholesome.

APPLE BUTTER, OR APPLE SAUCE.

This is often made in the houses of settlers where there is an abundance of apples, on a large scale; several bushels of pared apples being boiled down, either in cider or with water, for several hours, till the whole mass is thoroughly incorporated. Great care is needful to keep it stirred, so as to prevent burning. There are several ways of making this apple-butter: some make it with cider, others without, some use sugar, others do not; and some boil sliced pumpkin with the apples, if the latter are very acid. It is a standing dish in most American houses, and is very convenient.

ANOTHER METHOD.

Take three pails of cider, and boil down into one; have ready a quantity of sweet apples pared, and quartered, with the peel of one or two lemons; throw the apples into the cider, and as they boil down, add more, till your cider will boil down no more; keep the apples stirred well from the bottom of your skillet, to prevent burning: it will take some time to boil down quite smooth, say three or four hours: when done put it into a clean wooden or stone vessel, and keep covered in a dry place.

You may take out some of this pulp and spread on dishes or tins, and dry in the sun or before the fire, and pack away: it makes a nice dry sweetmeat, or, steeped and boiled up, a delicious wet preserve.—The Canadians who have large orchards, make as much as a barrel of this apple sauce for daily use.

CIDER.

Some persons have cider presses, which forms a part of their business in the Fall. The usual charge for making cider is 1s. per barrel for the use of the press, you finding the labour, &c., and, of course, the barrels and fruit.

Cider sells at from $2½ to $3, if good. Where a farmer has an extensive orchard, the house should be well supplied with this cooling beverage. In harvest time it supplies a valuable drink: in a country where beer is not brewed in private families, and where the exhaustion, and waste on the system, by excessive heat and labour, must require a supply of moisture, cider is very useful. The grateful acid must be preferable to the spirits, which are often mixed with the water, or drunk in fiery drams in the harvest field.

RED APPLE JELLY.

Take the small scarlet American crab apples, and boil down with a small quantity of water. The best plan is to put the apples with a little water, into a jar with a lid to it, and set it into a pot of boiling water; let it remain in this water-bath till the apples are quite soft; pulp them through a sieve; and add one pound of fine sugar to each pint of the apple-pulp, with a stick of cinnamon and a few cloves; boil for half an hour, or till the jelly will stiffen when cooled on a plate; put in jars or glasses, and when cold, pour a teaspoonful of spirits on the top. Wet a paper with white of egg, and fasten down so as to cover the edges of the jar quite tight. When well done, this jelly has the most beautiful transparency and lovely scarlet color.

The nice dishes that can be made with apples would fill in description a small volume; such as puddings, pies, tarts, puffs, turnovers, dumplings, &c., &c. I will only add one more, which is very simple, agreeable and cheap.

APPLE RICE.

Wet a pudding-cloth; place it in a basin or colander, having [in it a] previously well washed and picked a pound of rice, if your family be large: half the quantity will be sufficient if small: place some of the wetted rice so as to line the cloth in the mould all round, saving a handful to strew on the top; fill the hollow up with cored apples, and a bit of lemon peel shred fine, or six cloves; throw on the remainder of the rice; tie the bag, not too tight, as the rice swells much; and boil a full hour, or longer if the pudding be large. Eaten with sugar this is an excellent, and very wholesome, dish: acid apples are best, and are so softened by the rice as to need very little sugar to sweeten them.

APPLE-PARING MACHINE.

This useful invention saves much time and labour: it is an American invention, and can be bought in the hardware stores for 7s. 6d.

NOTE.—I strongly recommend to the attention of any one who takes an interest in orchard culture, a small volume called The American Fruit Book: it contains the best practical advice for the management of all the common fruits of Canada and the States. It is to be found in most of the district libraries. A small book and a cheap one, but a treasure to the inexperienced fruit grower.

Apple trees are subject to a disease of the bark, which is produced by the small scaly insect called bark-louse (or cocus): it resembles a brown shell, or a seed of flax, though hardly so large; young seed-apple trees are rendered sickly and stinted by this affection: to remedy the disease and destroy its cause, use—one part soft soap, four of water, and a little fresh slacked [slaked] lime: apply in the month of June, or indeed at any season; it may be used without injury to the tree. For removing the webs of caterpillars situated on high branches, tie some woollen rags to a tall staff; wet this mop in water or suds, and apply it to the branch, and by giving a twirl to the stick, you will remove the nest and its contents.

Apples for making cider should be well ripened and picked, free from decay, wood and leaves; if left in a heap to sweat for a week, they are the better, as they mellow and ripen; but they must not lie long enough to decay.

I copy a few directions for preserving and gathering apples, from the "American Fruit Book," which may be useful:

"The fruit" (says the author) "is of a finer quality for remaining on the tree till well ripened, though it will often keep better by gathering before quite or over ripe. Some in the warm parts of the country gather in the last week in September, others in October.—

"Gather your apples in dry weather, and pick winter or keeping fruit and dessert fruit by hand carefully. Some persons are so careful as to line the fruit baskets with cloth, or cotton, to prevent bruising. Do not let your fruit lie out in heaps, exposed to the weather, nor yet stand in barrels in the sun.

"In packing in barrels, settle the fruit gently, and head up full, pressing the head in carefully, so as not to injure the fruit.

"After barrelling, apples are generally left in an open shed on their sides, till the frost is beginning to set in, when they may be removed to a cool dry cellar. Apples will bear any degree of cold above freezing point; and headed up in barrels, even ten or twelve degrees below freezing point."

Some pack apples in bran, sawdust, dry sand, moss, fern, and many other substances. I have generally preferred laying very light layers of dry straw, and layers of apples, alternately.

I have not tried it, but I think fresh wood-ashes would preserve apples from frost. Heat and moisture, united, are destructive to apples, inducing bitter rot. I lost several barrels of lovely apples, by allowing them to remain in a warm kitchen for a month after gathering.

PEARS.

Pears are beginning to be largely cultivated all through the country, and though some sorts are more tender than the apple, others will thrive well, and in good situations produce abundance of delicious fruit. A good, deep, yellow loam, on an inclined plane, sheltered from the north, may be considered the best situation for planting pear-trees.

Like the apple, the ungrafted seedlings well cared-for will bear fruit. The seedling pear and the quince are the best adapted to grafting upon, though the native thorn is sometimes used for grafting the pear upon. It would be advisable to buy good grafted trees to begin with, of the most approved kinds. After they have been proved, you can increase your stock by grafting, yourself.

I will now select a few of the most approved pears for you to choose from. 2s. 6d. is the price usually charged for grafted pears, cherries and plums, of the best varieties: this is double the price of the best apples.

FOR SUMMER PEARS:—Madeline, Bartlett, Summer Frankreal, Belle of Brussels.

FALL:—Belle Lucrative, Flemish Beauty, Seckel, Louise, Yin de Jersey, Virgalien, Maria Louisa, White Dozenne, Vicar of Winkfield, Beurre Diel.

WINTER PEARS:—Easter Beurre, Winter Nelis Charmonte.

Many of these are very beautiful both to eye, and taste, and if you are at any loss which to select, consult the salesman, or some honest nursery-gardener, to choose for you. The names should be cut on a lead, or a tin ticket, fastened to a limb of the tree by a copper wire, as it is provoking not to know the name of a favourite fruit.

If insects, as the slug, attack the leaves of the pear, dust with ashes or sulphur, which will kill them.

CHERRIES.

The cherry thrives well in Canada, in spite of the frosty winters.—There are many excellent sorts, sold at the nursery gardens, as Tartarian Black, Black-heart, Bigaroux, Mayduke and many others.—There is a red cherry that grows and bears very freely from seed: it ripens in July, is middle sized, of a full dark red, not black, but rather crimson; sends up a vast number of shoots, which will bear in a few years abundance of fruit, if set out, trimmed up, and kept in order.—Suckers should be removed from the roots, as soon as they appear, as they weaken the larger trees, and absorb the nourishment that is required to perfect the fruit.

PLUMS.

The native or wild plum, if introduced into the garden, and kept in order, produces a very useful fruit for preserving, but is not so good for general purposes as the Gages, and Damascenes, Orleans, or several other of the cultivated sorts; it will, however, grow where the better sorts will not—in wet marshy ground, in hollows, and near water courses.

Owing to some causes which I am not able to explain, the plum is short-lived, and often perishes from diseases that attack the sap-vessels, or from insects that cause blight to the blossom, rendering the fruit useless, or utterly preventing its forming. Still, with care, much of this may be prevented, and in some situations plums are healthy, and yield abundantly. The Green-gage, Blue-gage, Yellow-gage, Golden-drop, Egg Plum, Imperial Gage, Washington, and the common Blue Damson Plum are among the best sorts. The soil may be light rich loam, not too dry.

WILD FRUITS.

In the long cultivated districts of Canada, especially in townships lying west of Toronto, where the seasons are warmer, and the winters compartively [comparatively] mild, great pains are now taken in planting orchards of the choicest fruits. Apples, pears, plums, cherries, peaches, and even grapes ripen and come to perfection, as well as the small summer fruits. Extensive orchards of all these fruits, are attached to most of the old farms, west of Toronto; but in the more northerly portions of Canada this is not yet the case. Orchards are, it is true, now generally planted, and gardens are more cared for than they were some years ago, but those who settle down in newly-surveyed townships, and far from the vicinity of large towns, which the hardy and adventurous emigrants, eager to secure a larger quantity of land, still do, must secure this advantage by early planting. The absence of fruit from their diet would be most severely felt, were it not that Nature has bounteously scattered abroad some of these blessings in the shape of wild fruits, which are met with in many situations, and often brought as it were almost miraculously, to the settler's very door, springing up without his care or culture.

The year or two after a fallow has been chopped, and logged, and cropped, in all the corners of his rail fence, and by the rude road that he has hewed out to his dwelling, spring up the red raspberry, black raspberry, the blackberry, and often the strawberry. The wild gooseberry, both smooth and prickly, is seen on upturned roots, at the edge of the clearing. Wild currants, both black and red, are found in moist swampy spots: here also are often to be found wild plums and choke-cherries, (the last not very fit to eat;) and a tangled growth of wild grapes, near creeks and lakes; fox and frost grapes entwine the trees, near the shores of lakes and rivers; while the high-bush cranberry shows its transparent clusters of scarlet berries, from among the fading foliage, or on the utterly leafless bough. On open lands, as on those parts called Plains, the abundance of wild fruits is yet greater than on the forest clearings. Here the ground is purple with the sweet and wholesome fruit of the huckleberry, the luscious bilberry; and strawberries of the most-delicious flavour carpet the ground.—The May-apple in moist rich soil springs up, both in the bush and on any shady lands. On summer fallows on these plains, and in the first and second years' ploughed lands, the strawberries attain a size that is remarkable for wild fruits of this kind, and quantities are gathered for home consumption, and also carried into the towns for sale.—There are besides the eatable fruits that I have named, many other small berries, that are wholesome, and eaten freely by the Indians, but which require a knowledge of their nature and growth, to be ventured upon by any but the natives, and botanists whose knowledge of the structure of plants enables them fearlessly to venture upon using the wild fruits, and roots and leaves of plants, that would be dangerous to be used as food by the unlearned. This is indeed the main use of botany as a study, though many persons foolishly despise it, because they are really not aware of the value of the science, and the benefit that mankind has derived from it. It is easy to see how useful these wild fruits are to the settler, in the absence of the cultivated sorts; and though the earliest efforts should be made for planting a garden and orchard, yet supposing circumstances should have prevented the obtaining of good trees, and bushes, something may be done towards improving the wild fruits by cultivation. The wild gooseberry, planted in good soil, and in a *shady, cool* part of the enclosure, will thrive well, and in time the thorns that beset the outer coat of the berry, will disappear. There are smooth red gooseberries, as well as those so appropriately called *Thornberries,* that can be found. On old neglected clearings; by forest roads and wastes; in open spots, and the edges of beaver-meadows, you may procure many varieties. If you have a straight fence, plant the wild bushes near it, as it serves to shelter them, not from the cold, for that they prefer, but from too much heat. The cultivated gooseberry is liable to mildew, which often destroys the promise of a fine crop.

The wild raspberry I do not advise you to cultivate: it grows too weedy, and there is no rooting it out; besides you will find it in all your fields, fences, and even in the very forest. But the grape is much improved by cultivation, and if you have an unsightly upturned root, or tall jagged stump, near the house, plant the vine beside it, or plant a small dead tree firmly in the ground, with all its branches on, (a sapling, of course, it must be,) for the vine to climb up. Thus you will have a beautiful object, and fruit, which after the frost has softened it, will make a fine rich jelly, or wine, if you like it.

The wild red plum is greatly improved by garden culture: it is, when ripe, a valuable fruit: skinned, it makes good pies, and puddings, and, boiled down in sugar, a capital preserve. The bush settlers' wives boil down these plums in maple molasses, or with a proportion of maple sugar. This is one of the comforts of having a good store of maple sugar: you can have plenty of preserves from wild raspberries, strawberries, plums, and wild gooseberries. The wild plum loses much of its astringency by cultivation; it is so hardy that it can be moved even when in flower; though early in Spring, or Fall, is better. This plum is not subject to the disease called black canker, or black knot, which destroys the cultivated sorts soon after they arrive at maturity; indeed it destroys even young trees, where the disease is unchecked. The wild plum forms the best and most healthy stock for grafting or budding the finer sorts upon, and is less liable to disease. Of late, nursery-men have greatly recommended this stock as producing healthier trees. While upon the subject of plums, let me strongly recommend to emigrants coming out, to bring with them small canvas-bags containing the stones of all sorts of plums—damsons, bullace cherries, and nuts of various sorts: even the peach will produce fruit from seed in the western parts of Canada: seeds of apples, pears, quinces, medlars, and indeed of all fruits that you can collect. If these grow you may obtain something for your surplus trees; and, if well treated, they will amply repay your trouble, and you will enjoy the great satisfaction of watching them come to perfection, and regarding them with that affectionate interest which those only experience who have raised seedlings from fruit grown in their beloved native land, and, perhaps, from the tree that they played under, and ate the produce of, when they were little children. In enumerating the blessings that awaited the returning Jews from their captivity, the prophet says—"And every man shall eat of the fruit of his own vine, and sit under the shadow of his own fig-tree." He could hardly promise them a greater blessing.

I also recommend you to bring out the seeds of raspberries, gooseberries, currants, and strawberries. Pulp the ripe fruit into cold water; wash away the fruity part, and drain dry; expose the seed in a sieve turned bottom upwards, or on a dry clean board, in the sun and wind, till well assured that all moisture is removed; mix with a little dry white sand; put the seeds into vials or dry paper bags, writing the name on each sort; and let a good bed be prepared in your new garden, by stirring well with the hoe if in quite new soil; or trench-in good rich earth in old; keep your nurslings, when up, well weeded, and thinned, so as to leave each plant room to grow.

The high bush cranberry, or single American Guelder-rose, is a very ornamental shrub in your garden; it likes a rich moist soil and a shady situation. The flowers are handsome in Spring, and every period of ripening in the fruit, is beautiful to see, from the pale orange tint, to the glowing scarlet when fully ripe, and, after the frost has touched them, to a light crimson. The berry when fully ripe is almost transparent. The flat, hard seeds in this juicy fruit make it unsuitable for jam, but as a jelly nothing can be finer, particularly as a sauce for venison or mutton. The native soil of the high bush-cranberry is at the edge of swamps, or near rivers and lakes, where the soil is black and spongy; but they also thrive in shady flats in dry ground in our gardens.

The large spurred hawthorn, also, may be found near creeks, and on the banks of rivers, on gravelly soil. This is if anything, more beautiful than the common English white thorn, the "May" of the poets. The Canadian hawthorn will grow to a considerable height, bears abundance of fragrant flowers, and is followed by fruit as large as a cherry, and when ripe very agreeable to the taste. The thorns are so large and so strong that it would make a formidable hedge, if any one would plant it; but few will take the time and trouble.—Some of our English labourers from the wooded counties in the East of England, where the culture of the thorn hedges is much attended to, might try the plan for a garden hedge. The long winter in Canada, the great value of labour, and the continued pressure of work in the open seasons of the year, are bars to many experiments of this kind being carried into effect. But hedge or no hedge, I recommend the hawthorn as an ornament for your garden.

On old grassy clearings, which have once been burned and cropped, strawberries spring up in abundance, of several kinds; among which may be found a very pretty, delicate, trailing plant, with light crimson berries, in grains of a fine acid: these are known by the name of creeping raspberry:—they are thornless, and trail in delicate wreaths upon the ground.

The black raspberry makes fine pies: it is richer and sweeter than the red; the branches are long and weak; the bark red, with a whitish bloom on them. They are something between the raspberry and blackberry of the English hedges. The Canada blackberry or thimble-berry, is not so deadly sweet as the fruit of the common bramble, but is a very pleasant berry, and lately has been cultivated in gardens, and made to produce a fruit superior in quality to the mulberry. The huckleberry is, among all the wild fruits, one of the most wholesome; eaten as they come from the bush, or stewed with, or without sugar, they are a nice dish; but with a few red currants added, they are much better, the tartness of the currant improving the sweetness of the huckleberry. A pudding, or pie, or preserve, made with equal parts of red currants, huckleberries, and the fruit of the bush bilberry, is delightful, the bilberry giving an almond-like flavor, and increasing the richness of the other fruits.

The bilberry grows on high bushes, the large fruited from six feet to ten feet high, the fruit being the size and colour of small smooth red gooseberries: the dwarf kind seldom exceeds three or four feet in height, and the tall bilberry, or Juneberry, is a beautiful-growing shrub, with reddish bark, elegant white blossoms, and rose-coloured fruit, smaller in size than the other two, though the bush attains the height of fifteen and twenty feet. These bushes grow chiefly on dry gravelly, or sandy soil; seldom in the rich black soil of the dense forest.

I am particular in noticing these peculiarities of soil, and habits, in describing the wild fruits, that you may not look for them in situations foreign to their natures, and feel disappointed if you do not find on your own immediate locality every one of the native fruits that I have described and recommended to your notice. Every spot has its peculiar vegetables, flowers, and fruits, and we must recollect in counting our blessings, what an old poet says:—

"Who least has some, who most, has never all."

It is our wisest part to receive with gratitude that which our Heavenly Father has prepared for us, and not weary him by discontented repinings, remembering in humbleness of heart, that we are unworthy even of the least of his mercies.

Of wild cherries there are many different species, but they are more medicinal than palatable: steeped in whiskey, with syrup added, the black cherry is used as a flavour for cordials; and the inner bark made into an extract, is given for agues, and intermittents,[14] and also in chest diseases. All these wild cherry trees are beautiful objects, either in flower or fruit, especially the red choke-cherry, with its bright transparent fruit; but the excessive astringency of the juice causes a spasmodic contraction of the throat, which is painful, and to delicate persons almost dangerous, from whence its name of choke-cherry.—The bark is tonic and bitter: when steeped in whiskey it is given for ague. No doubt it is from this that the common term of "taking his bitters," as applied to dram-drinking, has been derived. Bitter indeed are the effects of such habits upon the emigrant.

The reason why the native plants often fail to grow and thrive when removed to the garden, arises from the change in the soil and situation: to remove a plant from deep shade and light rich soil, to sunshine and common earth, without any attention to their previous habits, is hardly reasonable. A fine leaf mould, water, and shelter should be afforded till the tender stranger has become inured to its change of soil and position: those that neglect to observe the habits and natures of wild plants, rarely succeed in their attempts to naturalize them to the garden, and improve them by domestic culture.

I will now give some recipes for drying and preserving the native fruits:—

DRIED APPLES.

(See that article.)

DRIED GREEN GAGES, OR ANY KIND OF PLUMS.

Gather your plums when not too ripe; split with a knife, and remove the stone: put a little fine sugar into the cavity, and set your plums on a dish, or tray, to dry in the sun, or below the kitchen-stove. At night put them into a *cool* stove, or into a brick oven, after the bread has been withdrawn. If you have neither stove nor oven let them dry in a sunny window of a warm room.

---

14 Another word for malarial ague, in which the patient alternated between cold shivering fits and a high fever. The eyes became red and dry, the neck was often stiff, and there was a severe headache. Folk remedies included the inner bark of the wild black cherry. Quinine was another remedy.

When quite dry, pack in paper-bags or boxes. In some stores, there are sold nice round white wooden boxes, with a lid and handle, which are excellent for keeping cakes, sugar or dried fruits: they are cheap, and very convenient.

These dried plums are very little, if at all, inferior to the dried Portugal plums, and are excellent either as a dry sweetmeat, or, steeped and boiled up, as a preserve. Plums or any other fruit, crushed and spread out on a flat pan to dry, with a little fine white sugar sifted over them, are also good, and economical, as they take little sugar.

HUCKLEBERRIES, RASPBERRIES, CHERRIES, OR ANY SMALL FRUIT,

may be dried either in a cool stove, or before the fire, or in a warm, sunny window; but fire-heat is the best, as the sun is more apt to draw the flavour from the fruit, and increase the acidity.

Boil huckleberries, currants, and bilberries for half an hour, or longer; spread them out on tin pans, and let them dry in the oven, or below the stove, or out of doors; cut into squares, when dry enough to move; turn the pieces and let them dry on the underside; sift a little white sugar upon each piece, and pack by pressing the fruit-cakes closely: keep in dry bags or boxes: stew down one or more of these cakes as you want them for use. These dried fruits are very useful in sickness: a portion of one of the cakes put into a jug, and boiling water poured on, makes a delightful acid drink: black currants cured this way, are very good. The drink taken warm is a fine remedy for a cold or sore throat.

Many persons use the dried fruit of currants or huckleberries, as a substitute, in cakes and puddings, for the Zante currants.

WILD GOOSEBERRIES.

These are not often dried, as they become hard and flavourless; but either green or ripe, they can be used as pies or puddings, or boiled down to jam.

The wild green gooseberry, or thornberry, is often beset with real sharp thorns; not on the branches, for they are generally smooth; but on the berry itself: to avail yourself of the fruit, you must pour boiling water on them: let them lie in it a minute; then rub them in a coarse clean dry cloth on the table: this will remove, or soften the spines so that their roughness will be taken away: make into pies, and sweeten with maple-sugar or molasses.

To make either the unripe or ripe gooseberries into jam, boil them down till soft, in a water-bath first, closely covered: when quite soft, add half a pound of sugar to each pint of fruit, and boil one hour longer. Some allow to eight pints of fruit, six pounds of sugar.

RASPBERRIES.

This fruit is most abundant in Canada where a clearing has once been made. The birds sow the seeds. The raspberry seems to follow the steps of the settler, and springs up in his path as if to supply the fruit which is so needful to his health and comfort. Ripening in July, the raspberry affords a constant and daily supply for his table, till the beginning of September. Large quantities of this fruit are sold in the towns by the bush-settlers' wives and children, who get from 4d. to 5d. a quart for the berries.

A dish of raspberries and milk, with sugar, or a pie, gives many an emigrant family a supper. The black raspberry makes the best pie, and this fruit dries better than the red, as it is sweeter and richer in quality: it can be greatly improved by culture.

Raspberry vinegar, too, is a cheap luxury to those who have homemade vinegar and home-made sugar.

RASPBERRY VINEGAR.

To every quart of good vinegar put two quarts of raspberries: let them stand for twenty-four hours; drain them off through a sieve, but do not squeeze them; add the same quantity of raspberries to the strained vinegar a second time; let them stand as before; drain and add a third quantity: when you have drained the fruit off a third time, measure the liquor into a stone covered-jar, and to each pint of juice add a pound of lump sugar: set the jar in a pot of boiling water, and let the vinegar boil for ten minutes, stirring it to mix the sugar well through: when cold, bottle it for use: it is all the better for standing for some months before being used.

A cheaper sort might be made with fine moist sugar, or with crushed sugar, but must be well scummed. Raspberry vinegar makes an excellent fever drink, a small quantity being mixed in a tumbler of cold water: it is very refreshing in hot weather, and is made in considerable quantities by those who have wild raspberries growing near the clearings, and plenty of sugar at command.

PLUM JAM.

Take any quantity of the red plums, and put them into a stone jar: set this into a pot of water, having first tied a piece of clean cloth over the top of the jar; bladder is best if you have it at hand. Let your fruit-jar remain till the fruit is soft; remove all the stones that you can find; measure your pulp into a preserving pan, and to every six pints of fruit add four pounds of good soft sugar: break some of the stones, and add the kernels to the fruit: boil all up for nearly an hour, and put by in jars; cover when cold with papers dipped in white of egg.

ANOTHER WAY.

To each pound of fruit, either blue, green or red plums, add a pound of sugar: boil till the fruit begins to sink, and the juice looks thick and ropy. Some open the fruit with a sharp knife, and remove the stone, before boiling; but many do not take that trouble, but allow somewhat less sugar.

There is not a finer preserve, or one that keeps better, than plum jam: it may be made with maple-sugar, or the plums boiled in molasses.

For Dried Plums see that article. The red plum will not answer so well for drying, being too acid and juicy.

I recommend the emigrant to bring out stones of all varieties; even the hedge-bullace and damson, which are not found here, and would thrive well.

PEACHES.*

This delightful fruit cannot be grown in every part of the Province. The Peach orchards begin to be cultivated westward of Toronto, where all kinds of fruit grow and flourish, the climate being warmer, and the winters not so long or so severe. With the culture of the peach I have had no experience; but there are many excellent directions given in a charming work, published in Rochester, entitled "The Horticulturist," a magazine on rural art and rural taste,* in which the cultivation of the Peach is much attended to. To any one who can afford to buy it, this beautifully embellished work would afford much excellent information on the cultivation of fruit and flowers: it comes out monthly. It is to be regretted that so few plain practical gardening-books have as yet been published in Canada, devoted to vegetable and fruit culture, suited expressly for the climate and soil of Canada.

---

* The Peach has been improperly introduced here, among the Wild Fruits of Canada.—EDITOR.

* The price of this work is two dollars per annum, the uncoloured, and four dollars the coloured numbers.

Ripe peaches are brought over during the season, from the States, in large quantities: they sell high, and are often in bad order. By and by, I trust that Western Canada will supply the home market.—

Peaches are dried in the same way as green gages. They also make a delicious wet preserve.

_____

CRANBERRIES.

The low-bush cranberry is not to be found about your clearings, or in the woods: it is peculiar to low sandy marshes, near lakes and river-flats. The Indians are the cranberry gatherers: they will trade them away for old clothes, pork or flour. This fruit is sometimes met with in stores; but it is of rare occurrence now: formerly we used to procure them without difficulty. The fruit is, when ripe, of a dark purplish red; smooth and shining; the size of a champaigne gooseberry; oblong in form. I have never seen the plants growing, but have a dried specimen of the blossom and leaves: they are very delicate and elegant, and must be beautiful either in flower or fruit, seen covering large extents of ground known as cranberry marshes.— At Buckhorn-lake, one of the chain of small lakes to the northwest of Peterboro', they abound; and at the back of Kingston, there is a large cranberry marsh of great extent. It is in such localities that the cranberry in its native state is to be looked for. The cranberry will keep a long time just spread out upon the dry floor of a room, and can be used as required, or put into jars or barrels in cold water. This fruit is now cultivated to some extent in the United States: directions for the culture are given in "The Genesee Farmer," published in Rochester at one dollar per annum.

CRANBERRY SAUCE.

A quart of the ripe picked berries, stewed with as much water as will keep them from drying to the pan, closely covered: a pound of soft sugar must be added when the fruit is burst; boil half an hour after you add the sugar, and stir them well. When quite stewed enough, pour them into a basin or mould: when cold they will be jellied so as to turn out whole in the form of the mould.

This jam is usually served with roasted venison, mutton and beef. It makes rich open-tarts, or can be served at tea-table in glass plates, to eat with bread.

The Indians attribute great medicinal virtues to the cranberry, either cooked or raw: in the uncooked state the berry is harsh and very astringent: they use it in dysentery, and also in applications as a poultice to wounds and inflammatory tumours, with great effect.

HIGH-BUSH CRANBERRY.

This ornamental shrub, which is the single guelder-rose, is found in all damp soil near lakes, and creeks, and rivers: it is very showy in blossom, and most lovely to behold in fruit; it bears transplantation into gardens and shrubberies, but a low and shady situation suits its habits best, and in this only it will thrive and bear fruit to perfection. The flat seeds render the fruit less proper for jam; but it is so fine as jelly, and so little trouble to make, that I shall give directions for it as follows:—

CRANBERRY JELLY.

Gather the fruit as soon as the frost has touched it, any time in October or November: pick the berries into a jar, and set the jar on the stove, or in a vessel of boiling water, covered down, till they burst; pass the fruit through a sieve or colander; the seeds being large, will not go through: boil the juice up, with a pound of sugar to a pint of juice: if you want it for immediate use, a smaller quantity of sugar will be sufficient, as it jellies very readily; but any fruit jelly that has to be kept for weeks and months, requires equal quantities of sugar and fruit to preserve it from fermentation.

STRAWBERRY JAM.

Boil as many pounds of sugar as you have pints of ripe fresh fruit, with a pint of water; boil and scum the sugar; then add your fruit, and boil well for an hour: if you use white sugar, three-quarters of an hour will do. The fine colour of the fruit, and its delicate flavour, are injured by coarse sugar, and too long boiling.

I have lately heard that adding a pound of sifted sugar to every pint of whole fruit, merely strewing the sugar with the fruit as you pack it in the jars, will make a fine preserve, without boiling at all.

RASPBERRY JAM.

Pursue the same plan as directed for strawberries; but for family use, raspberries may be boiled into jam, with brown or even maple sugar: boil an hour after adding them to the syrup. Some persons mix currants and raspberries together: this improves both.

CURRANT JAM.

String the currants and boil with equal parts of sugar, as directed for raspberry jam.

ANOTHER WAY.

Stew the currants till they burst; then add three-quarters of a pound of sugar; boil till the seeds begin to sink, and the jam is thickened, so that it stiffens when cold.

A MIXED-FRUIT JAM.

Take equal parts of bilberries, huckleberries, and red currants; stew well with half a pound of sugar to each pint of fruit, when burst. This is a fine preserve, most excellent in flavour. These fruits boiled in a crust, or baked as a pie, are very delicious.

CURRANT JELLY.

To every pint of clear juice add a pound of lump sugar: boil together for an hour, or till the mixture will jelly when cold. Raspberry-jelly is made in the same way. Cold currant-jelly is made by mixing one pound of juice, and merely stirring well together. The process of jellying commences at the bottom of the vessel, and of course is slower, but equally effectual as boiling would be. Try it!

CURRANT VINEGAR.

Gather ripe red or white currants, string them, and put them into a vessel: to four quarts of the fruit allow a gallon of water; let them stand in a warm kitchen to ferment for some days, stirring the fruit with a stick to prevent mould gathering on the surface: when the fermentation has continued for some time, strain off the liquor from the fruit: bruise the latter, or squeeze it well with your hands, while straining it. Add two pounds of coarse sugar to each gallon of liquor, and put it into a cask or any suitable vessel, and let it remain in a warm room. I had in six weeks strong fine-coloured vinegar, fit for pickling, with only one pound of sugar to the gallon.

BLACK CURRANTS.

This useful fruit may be dried whole, or boiled down and spread on tin plates and dried, with or without sugar; made into jam or jelly, or merely stewed with a little sugar, sufficient to sweeten, not preserve them. The convenience of this method is very apparent. In Canada, preserves are always placed on table at the evening meal, and often in the form of tarts. This method enables any one who has ripe fruit to prepare an agreeable dish at a small expense, and very little trouble, if a party of friends arrive unexpectedly to tea.

CURRANTS AND SUGAR.

This is a favourite dish to set on at tea-time—ripe currants strung into cold water, from which they are drained immediately, and sugar, brown or white, strewn over them. A rich natural syrup is thus formed, which improves the acidity of the currants, besides giving a bright fresh look to the dish of fruit which is very agreeable to the eye.

CURRANTS AND RICE.

Prepare rice as in the directions for apple-rice pudding, using ripe currants instead: boil in a cloth or mould, and serve with sugar and butter.

BAKED CURRANT PUDDING.

Make a fine batter with eggs and milk and flour sufficient to thicken to the consistency of cream: throw in a pint of ripe red currants, and a little finely shred suet, or some small bits of butter, on the top of the pudding: bake, and serve with soft sugar.

An Indian-meal pudding, with ripe currants, either baked or boiled, is very nice: if boiled and tied in a cloth, it requires long boiling—two or three hours, if large.

MANDRAKE, OR MAY-APPLE. *(Ripe in August.)*

This was the first native fruit that I tasted, after my arrival in Canada. It attracted my attention as I was journeying through the woods to my forest-home. The driver of the team plucked it for me, and told me it was good to eat, bidding me throw aside the outer rind, which he said was not fit to be eaten. The May-apple when ripe is about the size of an egg-plum, which it resembles in shape and colour. The pulp of the fruit is of a fine sub-acid flavour, but it is better not gathered too ripe: it should be allowed to ripen in a sunny window. The time of its ripening is in August: the rich moist lands at the edge of the forest, and just within its shade, is the place where the May-apple abounds. In the month of May, it may be seen breaking the black soil, the leaves folded round the stem like a closed parasol. The fruit-bearing plant has two large palmated leaves, i. e., leaves spread out like a hand; the stalk supports the leaf from the centre; in the fork formed by the leaves a large rose-shaped flower, of a strong scent, rises. Very fragrant at a little distance it is, but rank and overpowering when held too near. The colour of the blossom is a greenish white.

The May-apple makes a delicious preserve. Gather the fruit as soon as it begins to shew [show] any yellow tint on the green rind: lay them by in a sunny window for a day or two; cut them in quarters and throw them into a syrup of white sugar, in which ginger sliced, and cloves, have been boiled: boil the fruit till the outer rind is tender: take the fruit out, lay them in a basin, sift a handful of pounded sugar over them, and let them lie till cold. Next day boil your syrup a second time, pour it over the fruit, and when cold put it into jars or glasses, and tie down. It should not be used till a month or six weeks after making: if well spiced this preserve is more like some foreign fruit. It is very fine. Some only make use of the soft acid pulp, but though the outer part is not fit to be eaten in a raw state, it is very good when preserved, and may safely be made use of, boiled with sugar and spices.

This fruit might I think be introduced into garden-culture, and prove a valuable addition to our tables; but in event of planting it in the garden, a very rich light mould must be given to feed the plant, which grows by nature in the rich vegetable leaf-mould.

FERMENTATIONS FOR BREAD.

The making and baking of good, nourishing, palatable bread, is perhaps one of the most important duties of the practical housewife: so much of the comfort and health of a family depends on the constant supply of this most essential article of diet, that I shall give it a first place in the instructions that I am about to furnish to my female readers.

Many of the settlers' families for whom this little volume is intended, may have emigrated from large towns or cities, where the baker's shop supplies all the bread that is daily consumed by the inhabitants: or it may be placed in the hands of one, who from her position in life has been totally unacquainted with labour of any kind, and who may be glad to profit by the directions I am about to give. Even to the active, industrious wife, or daughter of the labourer, well skilled in the mystery of making bread, both brown and white, something new may be gleaned from these pages, for there is a great difference in the materials she will have to make use of, and in the managing of them.—First then I shall say something about the different modes of fermenting, or raising the bread, and give directions for making the various kinds of barm that are used in Canadian houses; that in circumstances where one fails, another may be adopted. To those who reside in towns, and have no garden of their own in which hops can be cultivated, it is better, if they wish to make their own rising, to buy hops at the store, which can be got good at from 1s. 6d. to 2s 6d. per lb., varying in price as the previous season has been good or bad for the supply. Country people will often sell hops as low as 1s. or 1s. 3d., but they are not so good as those you buy at the stores, few persons knowing the right time to gather them. This should be done when the hop is full blown, and when the yellow dust, at the base of each of the fine thin leaves that make the blossom, is well formed, of a bright yellow colour, and a little glutinous to the touch. If the hop begins to lose its colour and fade, much of the fine bitter flavour is gone: it is over ripe.

Some persons prefer having recourse to brewer's yeast or distiller's yeast; the latter is not so good or sure, and obtaining the former is uncertain, as the demand is often greater than the supply; while if you make your own hop-rising, you are not subject to disappointment, unless you are careless and let your stock run out. For a penny or three half-pence you may obtain about half a pint of fresh beer-yeast at the brewer's.

CURING BREWER'S YEAST.

This yeast is very bitter, and those who do not relish the bitterness that it is apt to impart to the bread, should remedy the defect by pouring about half a pint or more of lukewarm water on the yeast, and letting it stand a few hours previous to using it: this draws a portion of the bitterness away. Pour off the water clear from the yeast, then stir the yeast up, adding a little warm water, and a tablespoonful of flour, mixing it well; let it stand a short time, till it begins to rise in bubbles. A large cupful of this will raise you about ten pounds of flour. The residue may be bottled and set by in a cool place for a second baking. This sort of yeast does not keep so well as the hop-rising; for the making of which I will now give you directions.

HOP-RISING.

Boil down two large handfuls of hops, in three quarts of water, till the hops begin to sink to the bottom of the vessel, which they do after an hour's fast boiling. Put about a quart of flour in an earthen pan, or any convenient vessel, not too shallow, and strain the liquor, boiling off the fire, into the flour, stirring the batter quickly as you do so. The flour will thicken up like paste: stir it as smoothly as you can, then let it stand till blood warm; mix in a tea-cupful of the old stock of barm, and let the vessel stand covered up near the fire till it begins to show that fermentation has taken place. In summer you need only cover the jar or pan; it will rise in a few hours; but new barm

Fig. 10 (*opposite*) · Hop-Rising, page 93 of the first edition (1854 [1855]), reproduced from the printing of the second thousand.

ten pounds of flour. The residue may be bottled and set by in a cool place for a second baking. This sort of yeast does not keep so well as the hop-rising ; for the making of which I will now give you directions.

HOP-RISING.

Boil down two large handfuls of hops, in three quarts of water, till the hops begin to sink to the bottom of the vessel, which they do after an hour's fast boiling. Put about a quart of flour in an earthen pan, or any convenient vessel, not too shallow, and strain the liquor, boiling off the fire, into the flour, stirring the batter quickly as you do so. The flour will thicken up like paste : stir it as smoothly as you can, then let it stand till blood warm ; mix in a tea-cupful of the old stock of barm, and let the vessel stand covered up near the fire till it begins to show that fermentation has taken place. In summer you need only cover the jar or pan ; it will rise in a few hours ; but new barm is not so good as after it has worked for some days. A large earthen pitcher tied down from the air, or a stone jar with a cover, is best for keeping the rising in. The vessel should be well cleaned before refilling.

ANOTHER SORT.

Boil your hops for two hours. With a pint of the liquid cooled down to moderate heat, mix a pint-basinful of flour to a batter, very smoothly ; next strain in the remaining scalding hop-liquor, stirring the whole till it is about the thickness of cream : set this mixture on the stove, or some hot coals on the hearth, in a clean pot ; the one you have just used for boiling the hops, well rinced and wiped clean, will do ; keep the mixture stirring till the whole begins to thicken and assume the appearance of a thick gruel. Some do not think it necessary to boil it after it thickens, but it keeps better if it remains on the fire a few minutes after it comes to the boil : if it be too thick to stir easily, thin with a little boiling water : add a large tea-spoonful of salt. Pour this hop-gruel into your jar, and when cooled down so that you can bear a finger in it comfortably, add a cupful of rising, and set it by. Some add a table-spoonful of brown sugar.

This sort of barm keeps longer without souring than the common sort. Remember that for keeping yeast in summer, a cool dairy or cellar is best ; and in winter some warm closet or cellar, which is too close to admit of frost, is most advisable. A teaspoonful of soda or salaratus, dissolved in a little water, and stirred into yeast that is a little sour, will reclaim it, but it must be done just at the time you are going to make use of the yeast, or it will lose its good effect.

HOP-YEAST WITH POTATOES.

Pare and wash a dozen good-sized potatoes ; set them on with about a quart or three pints of water, with a heaped tea-spoonful of salt ; boil till they are soft enough to mix through the water like is not so good as after it has worked for some days. A large earthen pitcher tied down from the air, or a stone jar with a cover, is best for keeping the rising in. The vessel should be well cleaned before refilling.

ANOTHER SORT.

Boil your hops for two hours. With a pint of the liquid cooled down to moderate heat, mix a pint-basinful of flour to a batter, very smoothly; next strain in the remaining scalding hop-liquor, stirring the whole till it is about the thickness of cream: set this mixture on the stove, or some hot coals on the hearth, in a clean pot; the one you have just used for boiling the hops, well rinced and wiped clean, will do; keep the mixture stirring till the whole begins to thicken and assume the appearance of a thick gruel. Some do not think it necessary to boil it after it thickens, but it keeps better if it remains on the fire a few minutes after it comes to the boil: if it be too thick to stir easily, thin with a little boiling water: add a large tea-spoonful of salt. Pour this hop-gruel into your jar, and when cooled down so that you can bear a finger in it comfortably, add a cupful of rising, and set it by. Some add a table-spoonful of brown sugar.

This sort of barm keeps longer without souring than the common sort. Remember that for keeping yeast in summer, a cool dairy or cellar is best; and in winter some warm closet or cellar, which is too close to admit of frost, is most advisable. A tea-spoonful of soda or salaratus, dissolved in a little water, and stirred into yeast that is a little sour, will reclaim it, but it must be done just at the time you are going to make use of the yeast, or it will lose its good effect.

HOP-YEAST WITH POTATOES.

Pare and wash a dozen good-sized potatoes; set them on with about a quart or three pints of water, with a heaped tea-spoonful of salt; boil till they are soft enough to mix through the water like gruel. Pour into your rising-jar or pan, and mix in, as smoothly as you can, flour enough to make a thick batter; have your hops boiling, as in the former receipts, stir the strained liquor into your potato and flour batter, add a large spoonful of sugar, and mix all smoothly; when cooled down, add a couple of large spoonfuls of rising, to work i' [in]. After it has worked, it is strained into a bottle, and set by for use.

A large cupful will raise about ten pounds of flour. Some persons give the preference to this potato-barm, but either of the recipes is good for fermenting bread.

SUGAR-YEAST.

Boil two handfuls of hops in a gallon of water for an hour; strain off and add two table-spoons of salt; mix in one pound of flour and two pounds of soft sugar; stir all together when milk warm; add two spoonfuls of good yeast; let it rise for two days, then bottle and cork lightly, and put in a cool cellar: a large cupful will raise about ten pounds of flour, or more.

This recipe I have not tested myself, but I am told it is good, and has the advantage of fermenting itself, without the addition of other barm to set it to work.

LEAVEN CAKES.

Boil three ounces of hops in three gallons of water, till reduced to a quart: while boiling, hot strain the liquor into one quart of rye-meal, stirring it well. Let it cool: add a cupful of good yeast: when it has begun to work well, stir in as much Indian-meal as will thicken the mass to a stiff dough; knead it upon a board well, roll it into cakes about an inch in thickness, and let them dry on a clean board in the sun, for two or three days: do not leave them out after sunset. Two inches square of this yeast-cake dissolved in warm water, and thickened with a table-spoonful of flour, will raise one or two good-sized loaves. If hung up in bags in a dry room, this leaven will keep good for many months.

The above is from an American receipt-book, and I have been told it is a good receipt.

ANOTHER AMERICAN-YEAST.

Boil very soft and mash four large potatoes; mash them very fine; pour over them one pint of boiling water; when only warm, stir in two large spoons of flour, two of molasses, a tea-spoonful of salt, and a cup of good yeast. This must be used fresh: the above will raise a baking of bread for a family. Set in a sponge over night.

BUTTER-MILK CAKES.

You may raise nice light cakes, to be eaten hot with butter, by putting into a quart of buttermilk as much soda or salaratus as will make it effervesce or foam up like new yeast. It is better to dissolve the soda in a cup of hot water; and bruise the lumps well, before you put them into the water, so that the whole be thoroughly dissolved; any bits that are left unmelted will make a distasteful spot in your cake; mix your dough very lightly, kneading it only just stiff enough to roll out into cakes about an inch in thickness: put them at once into a hot oven: the oven should be pretty hot, or your cakes will not be so light. This sort of bread is very convenient; it needs no shortening, nor any other seasoning than a little salt with the flour.

A teaspoonful of sal volatile in powder (that is the ammonia used as smelling salts), with two teaspoonfuls of cream of tartar, mixed very thoroughly with the flour, before it is wetted, will raise nice light plain buns, to be eaten hot.

I will also recommend "Durkee's Baking Powder": it is sold in all Canadian stores and drug-shops, at 7½ d. the sealed packet, on which are printed directions for using it. This powder imparts no ill taste to the bread or cakes; producing a very light cake with no trouble.—Emigrants should provide an article of this kind among other sea-stores, as a convenient and wholesome substitute for raised bread, for the use of themselves and little ones.

The use of these acid and alkaline salts in fermenting flour food has become very general of late years; they have the advantage of convenience in their favour, and are regarded by many persons as being more wholesome than bread raised with yeast, which has a tendency to turn sour, especially on the stomachs of young children and persons of weak digestion.

Owing to the superior dryness of the atmosphere in Canada, bread seldom turns mouldy, or takes a fermentation, after it has been kept many days, as is often the case in moist hot weather in the old country. During my long sojourn in Canada, I have never seen or tasted a piece of mouldy bread.

SALT-RISING.

This sort of barm is much used among the old Canadian and Yankee settlers. It has this advantage over other kinds of rising; it requires no addition of any other yeast to stimulate it into active fermentation. Those who are in the constant habit of using it, make excellent bread with it. I dislike the peculiar flavour it imparts, and if it is not really well managed, it is neither pleasant nor wholesome; but many persons prefer it to all other modes of fermenting bread, so I shall furnish the instructions for making it.

Take one teaspoonful of salt, one pint of warm water or new milk, rather more than blood-heat; thicken with as much flour as will make a batter the thickness of good cream; mix in a jug that will hold about a quart; set the jug in a pan or pot half filled with water, warm, but not too hot; cover your mixture close, and set it in a warm place near to the stove or fire: in about four hours bubbles will begin to rise on the surface, and in about two more the yeast will begin to rise in a fine soft creamy head. The nice point in making salt-rising bread is to know when the yeast is risen enough:

after a certain time it goes down, and will not raise the bread, or turns it sour.—Experience will guide you after one or two trials. But we will suppose the yeast is risen nearly to the brim of the jug; then take as much flour, say four quarts, as will make you two loaves, or one good bake-kettle loaf; make a hole in the flour, add a little salt, and pour your barm in; mingle it thoroughly, and knead your dough smoothly and well with your hands, as you would make up any other loaf: let your bake-can be well greased before putting your loaf in; cover it with the lid. In baking in the bake-kettle, do not fill it much more than half full, that your dough may have room to swell; many a good loaf is spoiled by being crowded into too small a space. Set the pan with your loaf at a moderate distance from the fire, covered up; when it rises, which you see by its occupying a larger space, and cracking on the top, you may advance it nearer the fire, turning the bake-kettle round gradually from time to time, till every side has felt the influence of the heat. When within two inches of the top, put a scattering of coals (live wood-embers) below the kettle and on the lid; or heat the lid on the fire, but not too hot at first, and then add live coals. You must keep your kettle turned gradually, that the sides may brown, and do not put too many hot coals below at once. You will soon learn the art of baking a shanty-loaf: a little attention and care is the main thing. When the crust is hard and bears pressure without sinking in, the bread is done.

Many a beautiful loaf I have eaten, baked before a wood fire in a bake-kettle. The bush-settlers seldom can afford to buy cooking-stoves during the first few years, unless they are better off than the labouring class usually are when they come to Canada.

BREAD.

Having given you a chapter on the different modes of making yeast, for the rising of your bread, collected from the best sources, I shall now proceed to the making and baking of the bread. I can hardly furnish a more excellent receipt for good bread, than that which is used in my own house; which indeed I can recommend to all housekeepers, as fine in quality and appearance, while at the same time it is decidedly economical. It can be made purely white; or brown, by the addition of two or three handfuls of coarse bran.

Should the quantity here mentioned prove too large in proportion to the number of the family, a little experience will enable the person who attends to the making of the bread, to reduce it one-half or one-third.

MRS. TRAILL'S BREAD.

Wash and pare half a pail of potatoes, taking care to remove all dark specks; throw them into a vessel of clean water as you pare them, as they are apt to acquire a brownish colour, which spoils the white and delicate appearance of the bread. Boil the potatoes till reduced to a pulp, bruising any lumps smooth with a wooden beetle or pounder: it will then have the consistency of thick gruel: when cool enough to bear your hand in it, stir in as much flour as will make the mixture the thickness of thick batter; add a good handful of salt, and two cupfuls of your hop barm or any good rising that you may have. A deep, red earthen pot, or a wooden pail, will be a good vessel to contain your sponge. It is a wise precaution to stand your vessel in a pan, as it is apt to flow over. If set to rise over-night, it will be risen time enough to work up in the morning early: in summer we seldom make this potato-bread, on account of the potatoes then not being so fit for the purpose, for, while young, they will not boil down so smoothly; but from the month of August till May, it may be made with great advantage. The quantity of sponge, above, will raise two large milk-dishes of flour, or about twenty pounds of flour. If you have a large kneading-trough, you can mix the whole at once, and knead it well and thoroughly; but if your trough be too small for convenience, divide your sponge, and make two masses of dough, working it very stiff on your board, scoring the top with a knife, and cover it up by the fire with a clean cloth; or you may make only half the quantity, using of course, less potatoes and water. In about two hours, or may-be longer, you will have a light dough, like a honeycomb, to make into loaves. When baked, take your bread out of the pan, wet the crust of your loaves over with clean water or milk, and wrap them in a clean cloth, setting them up on one side against a shelf till cold. This plan keeps the bread from becoming hard and dry. For lightness, sweetness and economy this is the best bread I know, resembling really-good baker's bread in texture and look. I cordially recommend it to the attention of the Canadian housewife.

INDIAN-MEAL BREAD.

Add six pounds of sifted Indian-meal to six pounds of wheaten flour; one gallon of water, pour, boiling-hot, on the Indian-meal; when cool enough to work with the hand, mix in the wheaten flour, and a cup of yeast, with a little salt; knead the mass, and set it to rise near the fire. This bread has a fine yellow colour, and is best used pretty fresh, as the Indian-meal is of a drying quality.

ANOTHER BREAD WITH INDIAN-MEAL.

Take as much good flour as will fill a good-sized milk-dish; add to the flour a quart of Indian-meal, and a tablespoonful of salt; mix the meal and flour well together: make a hole in the midst, and pour in a large cup of good rising, adding warm water; mingle stiff enough to knead on your flour-board; then when your mass of dough is worked smooth, lay it back in the pan or trough that you mixed it in, and let it lie covered near the fire to rise; when well-risen, divide, and bake in your oven or bake-kettle.

Some persons wet the Indian-meal with hot water first, but either way can be tried. I have used any supporne, or Indian-meal porridge, that has been left after breakfast, in making bread, and found it a very good addition. A good bread can also be made of equal proportions of rye, Indian-meal, and wheaten flour; rye alone does not make such good bread, the rye being very glutinous, which a mixture of Indian-meal corrects.

BRAN BREAD.

A sweet and economical, and most wholesome bread may be made by pouring water, either warm or cold, on to bran, stirring it up, and leaving it to steep for an hour; then strain the bran off through a sieve or strainer, pressing all the moisture out. There should be liquor enough to mix your bread, without any water, unless it be too cold, and a little hot water is required to raise the temperature; add the usual quantities of salt and yeast, and mix and knead as in other bread. The most wholesome and nutritive parts of the bran will thus be preserved and added to your bread.

Cobbett recommends this bread, and I have proved its good and wholesome qualities myself. All the fine flour and bran that passes through the sieve, should be put into your bread, along with the liquor, for this constitutes part of its excellence. If you wish for *browner* bread, throw in a handful of dry sweet bran, and mix with your flour, in addition, but not that from which the gluten and fine sugary particles have been extracted by the water.

Many persons who do not use potatoes in their bread, as directed in the first receipt, set a sponge over night, merely mingling the flour, warm water, salt and yeast, and when well risen, (which it is known to be by the air-bubbles that rise on the top,) thicken with flour, and knead well; when the dough is of sufficient lightness, make up into loaves; let them rise a second time in the bread pan or bake-kettle, and bake.

I have now given the best simple receipts for making bread, that I am acquainted with. There are methods of making light bread without using the yeast to ferment the flour.

I will now give an American receipt for unfermented bread, which I have not myself tested:—

EXCELLENT BREAD WITHOUT YEAST.

Scald about two handfuls of Indian-meal, into which put a teaspoonful of salt, and as much cold water as will reduce the mixture of meal to blood-heat; then stir in wheaten flour till it is as thick as hasty-pudding, and set it before the fire to rise. In about half an hour it generally begins to thin and look watery on the top. Sprinkle in a little more flour, and mind and keep the pot turned from time to time, taking care not to let it be too near the fire, or it will bake at the sides before it is risen. In about four hours it will rise and ferment, as if you had set it with hop-yeast; when it is light enough, mix in as much flour as will make it into a soft dough: grease a pan, put in your loaf, and let it rise, covering it up warm, and turning it so that the heat affects it equally; in less than an hour it will be ready for the oven: bake as soon as it is risen. Some bake in a Dutch-oven before the fire.—*From Mrs. Child's Frugal Housewife.*

EXCELLENT HOT TEA-CAKES.

One quart of fine flour: two ounces of butter: two teaspoonfuls of cream of tartar, mixed dry through the flour: one teaspoonful of salaratus or soda: moisten the latter in milk or water till dissolved: mix with sweet milk or cold water.

These cakes to be rolled, and cut out with a tumbler, about an inch in thickness, served hot and buttered.

SHORTS OR CANAILLE.

This is the common name given to the inferior flour which is separated in bolting,[15] at the mill, from the bran and fine flour, and is seldom used as a mixture in bread. This is not economical management: for mixed with fine flour, it makes sweet good bread; and many a loaf made from it I have seen, when other flour was scarce. The bread is closer in texture, and does not rise as light as brown bread with a mix-

15 Sifting.

ture of bran in it; but still it is by no means to be despised. As unleavened cakes, it is perhaps more agreeable than raised bread. The Irish call these coarse cakes by the odd name of "fudge."

BROWN CAKES.

Mingle a handful of fine flour, with as much of the coarse shorts as will make a baking of cakes for tea, say about three pints of the coarse, to half a pint of the fine: a little fine flour must also be used in kneading on the board, and rubbing the dough from your hands.—Rub a good bit of shortening into your dry flour, as if you were going to make short cakes: dissolve a teaspoonful of salaratus or soda, in a cup of hot water; add this to as much buttermilk, or sour milk, as will mix the flour into a light dough: do not omit salt, and do not knead the mass too stiff; only stiff enough to enable you to roll it out about an inch thick; cut into round or square cakes, and bake in a quick oven.

Eaten hot, with a little butter, these are good, plain, houshold [household] tea-cakes; with molasses and ginger they are very good.

BROWN SUPPORNE.

This is porridge, made entirely with shorts, and eaten with cold butter or new milk. It is made in the same way as Indian-meal supporne (see that article). In the absence of corn-meal or oatmeal, children will eat this dish very readily, and it is often a convenient substitute for bread, when flour runs out, and you are unable to obtain an immediate supply. It is most commonly made with water, but may be mixed with milk, or milk and water, the flour being stirred in as the water or milk boils.

MILK PORRIDGE.

Have your milk boiling, and a basinful of flour, into which a little salt may be mixed: with one hand sprinkle in your flour, and stir with a wooden stick or a spoon, till you have made your porridge as thick as you desire it to be: remove it from the fire to the top of the stove, or place the pot on a few hot embers, not near enough to the fire to scorch, and let it simmer for some time, stirring it carefully. This makes a very satisfying meal for children.

Eaten hot, with a little butter, these are good, plain, houshold tea-cakes ; with molasses and ginger they are very good.

BROWN SUPPORNE.

This is porridge, made entirely with shorts, and eaten with cold butter or new milk. It is made in the same way as Indian-meal supporne (see that article). In the absence of corn-meal or oatmeal, children will eat this dish very readily, and it is often a convenient substitute for bread, when flour runs out, and you are unable to obtain an immediate supply. It is most commonly made with water, but may be mixed with milk, or milk and water, the flour being stirred in as the water or milk boils.

MILK PORRIDGE.

Have your milk boiling, and a basinful of flour, into which a little salt may be mixed : with one hand sprinkle in your flour, and stir with a wooden stick or a spoon, till you have made your porridge as thick as you desire it to be : remove it from the fire to the top of the stove, or place the pot on a few hot embers, not near enough to the fire to scorch, and let it simmer for some time, stirring it carefully. This makes a very satisfying meal for children.

FARMERS' RICE.

Set milk on the fire, in a clean skillet, to boil, with half a tea-spoonful of salt in it. Take dry fine flour in a basin ; into this sprinkle cold milk, a few drops at a time, till it is damp, but not wet like dough : rub the damp flour in your hands, which must, of course, be delicately clean. The wetted flour must be rubbed till it adheres in small pieces like grains of rice ; if not damp enough scatter in a little more moisture, or, if too wet, add a little flour : when ready, throw this mock-rice into your milk, stirring it in by degrees : let it boil quick while mixing ; then set it at a little distance, say outside the griddle of the stove, and let it boil for fifteen minutes or half an hour; a little nutmeg, sugar and butter makes this a nice dish ; but some prefer it unseasoned, or with salt and butter.

These are homely dishes ; but they are intended for homely people, who have not the materials for luxuries at their command, but who may be glad to learn how to vary the method of dressing such simple food as they can obtain, so as to render it palatable and pleasant.

FARMERS' RICE.

Set milk on the fire, in a clean skillet, to boil, with half a tea-spoonful of salt in it. Take dry fine flour in a basin; into this sprinkle cold milk, a few drops at a time, till it is damp, but not wet like dough: rub the damp flour in your hands, which must, of course, be delicately clean. The wetted flour must be rubbed till it adheres in small pieces like grains of rice; if not damp enough scatter in a little more moisture, or, if too wet, add a little flour: when ready, throw this mock-rice into your milk, stirring it in by degrees: let it boil quick while mixing; then set it at a little distance, say outside the griddle of the stove, and let it boil for fifteen minutes or half an hour; a little nutmeg, sugar and butter makes this a nice dish; but some prefer it unseasoned, or with salt and butter.

––––––––––

These are homely dishes; but they are intended for homely people, who have not the materials for luxuries at their command, but who may be glad to learn how to vary the method of dressing such simple food as they can obtain, so as to render it palatable and pleasant.

BISCUITS.

An excellent, cheap, useful biscuit can be made as follows: Rub into a quart of fine flour, about an ounce of butter or lard, and a little salt: mix with cold water into a stiff, smooth paste; roll it out, and strew dry flour on the paste; work this flour well in with the rolling-pin, fold it together, knead it and roll it again, throwing over it more dry flour, working it with the rolling-pin till the flour is incorporated; and do this several times, or as long as you can knead it smooth: break it into small pieces, and roll in your hand, about the size of a large walnut, then roll with the pin into thin biscuits, prick them with a fork, and bake on a flat pan in a brick oven: if the oven be cool, they will be tough: the more dry flour you can work into the dough, the better will be the biscuit. These are useful if you have no cakes at hand, and are good for the sick; rolled fine, make capital pap for weaned babies.

I learned to make them, under the direction of a physician, as food for a delicate infant; many persons I have taught to make these biscuits, and they will be found very

Fig. 11 (*opposite*) · Brown Supporne, Milk Porridge and Farmer's Rice, page 100 of the first edition (1854 [1855]), reproduced from the printing of the second thousand.

useful where the fermented bread causes acidity, and soda-biscuits and American crackers are not at hand, or the housewife [housewife] too poor to buy them.

ANOTHER SORT.

Instead of cold, use scalding water and roll very thin. The butter may be melted in the hot water: mix and knead very smooth, but without beating in the dry flour, as in the former receipt: roll very thin, and bake quickly.

SODA BISCUITS.

Six ounces of butter: six ounces of sugar: one teaspoonful of soda, dissolved in one pint of milk: flour enough to form a stiff dough: melt the butter in the milk, and also the sugar, which should be white. Knead and roll out several times, till the mass be quite smooth; roll in thin sheets about a quarter of an inch thick, cut into square cakes, and bake in a brisk oven.

ABERNETHY BISCUITS.

Seven pounds fine flour; three-quarters pound of butter, rubbed well into the flour; 1½ pound of loaf-sugar, dissolved in one quart of cold water: half ounce carraways, and a teaspoonful of salt. Well knead this dough; divide, and make four dozen biscuits.

This quantity can be reduced to one-half, at the convenience of the baker.

––––––––––

Biscuits are both a cheap and wholesome bread, and are a very valuable sort of food for invalids or very young children: they are far less expensive than sweet cakes, and by many persons are greatly preferred, as being easier of digestion, but they require more hard labour, and attention in baking.

The American crackers are sold in many of the stores at 7½ d. a pound, but they can be home-made almost as well.

Those who have a stone or brick oven, can make their biscuits much finer and crisper, besides giving them the real biscuit flavour, by putting them into the oven after the bread, pie, &c. have been baked, and leaving them for some hours on the oven floor, while any warmth remains. Thus they are twice baked, and will keep for weeks and months. Bread of any kind does not mould, as in the damper climate of Britain; even in very hot weather, bread, cakes and other flour food will keep un-injured for many days. I have rarely seen mouldy bread or cake, during twenty years' sojourn in Canada. Next to biscuits there is nothing better than rusks: some call them "tops and bottoms," others "twice-baked cakes."

RUSKS.

Half-a-pound of butter or lard (butter is best), or half the quantity of each, dissolved in a pint of hot milk, six eggs well beaten, a little salt, as much yeast as will raise these ingredients; add as much flour as will stiffen into a very thick batter; cover warm, and when risen, stiffen just enough to admit of rolling lightly, about an inch in thickness: cut out with a tumbler or small round cutter: set to rise a few minutes; bake, but not *over*bake, cut them in two pieces, or, if very thick, make three slices with a sharp knife: return to the oven, and bake till each piece is crisp. Some lay on the top of a stove, turning them twice or thrice.

HARD RUSKS.

Dissolve half a pound of butter or lard (the latter will do), in *boiling* water, with a little salt: mix with a spoon as much flour as you can stir into the water and lard smoothly: as the mixture will be scalding-hot, you must wait till it cools down low enough to admit of your hand, working in a tea-cup not quite full of yeast; then knead the mass thoroughly, and cover it down near the fire till it rises.—When light, roll out, and cut into thin cakes, not quite an inch thick; bake and split them; return to the oven, and when dry, lay them out to cool; when cold, put by in a bag or canister for use. These rusks are as sweet as if sugar had been mixed with the flour. They will keep for weeks, and are excellent grated down for pap or panada for the sick, or a gruel made by boiling them, adding a teaspoonful or two of new milk, and seasoning with spice, for a sick person, where bread, however good, would be rejected.

TO MAKE AMERICAN CRACKERS.

One quart of flour, into which rub two ounces of butter; dissolve one teaspoonful of saleratus in a wine-glass or cup of warm water; half a teaspoonful of salt, and milk sufficient to mix it into a stiff, smooth dough: beat it for half an hour, working it well with the rolling-pin; make into thin biscuits, or small round balls flatted in the middle with the thumb, and bake till dry and crisp.

CAKES.

EXCELLENT GINGERBREAD.

Take three pounds of flour, one and a half pound of brown sugar; one pound of butter, six eggs, two tablespoonfuls of ginger, and a teaspoonful of salt: bake on tin sheets rolled very thin.

COMMON GINGERBREAD.

Treacle 1½ lb: seconds flour 2 lb: butter 2 oz: ginger 1 oz: spices 2 oz: of pearl-ash one dessert-spoonful; mix with milk warmed, into a dough; let it stand till it rises, bake on tins, and cut in squares.

GINGER CUP-CAKE.

Five eggs; two large cups of molasses: the same of rolled soft-sugar: two ditto butter: one cup of new milk: five cups of flour: half a cup of ground-ginger: a small teaspoonful of pearl-ash, dissolved in vinegar or cider. Cut up the butter in the milk, warm so as to melt; also warm the molasses, stir it into the milk and butter; stir in the sugar: let it cool. Beat the eggs light; stir in alternately with the flour, add the ginger and other spices, with the pearl-ash: stir the mass well; butter tins to bake it in.

GINGER BREAD.

To a pint of molasses add half cup butter, three eggs, half cup sour-milk, one tea-spoonful salaratus, one ditto cream of tartar, two cups flour, two table-spoonfuls of ginger.

PLAIN PLUM-CAKE.

One pound of flour: quarter pound of sugar; quarter pound butter; half a pound currants or raisins; three eggs; half a pint of milk or sour-cream, and a small tea-spoonful of carbonate of soda and spice to taste.

LEMON CAKE.

One tea-cup of butter, three of powdered sugar, beat together to a cream; stir in the yolks of five eggs, well beaten; dissolve a teaspoonful of soda in a tea-cup of milk, and add to the above: also the juice and grated-peel of one lemon, the whites of three of the eggs, beaten to a froth, and four cups of flour. Bake in two pans about half an hour.

COOKIES.

One pound of flour; half pound butter, rubbed well in: ¾ lb sugar: two eggs: half a cup of sour cream: one teaspoonful salaratus: a few carraways: nutmeg or ginger if you like. Roll out thin, and cut in round cakes.

DROP SWEET-CAKES.

Four eggs well beaten: a large cupful of sugar: the same of butter melted: flour enough to thicken to a thick batter; a few currants or seeds, or essence of lemon: beat for a few minutes, drop on tin sheets, and bake in a good hot oven.

If the batter spread[s] too much, add a little more flour.

CHEAP FAMILY CAKE.

To one egg and four ounces of butter, well beaten together, add a teaspoonful of allspice, half a teaspoonful of pepper, a pint of molasses, a teaspoonful of salaratus dissolved in a cup of cream or milk, and flour enough to make it the consistence of fritters; set in a warm place to rise, and when perfectly light, bake moderately.

SILVER CAKE. (*From the "Maple-Leaf"*)

One pound crushed sugar, three quarters of a pound of dried and sifted flour; six ounces of butter: mace and citron; the whites of fourteen eggs. Beat the sugar and butter to a cream; add the whites, cut to a stiff froth, and then the flour. It is a beautiful looking cake.

GOLDEN CAKE.

This and silver cake should be made together, to use both portions of the eggs. Take one pound of flour dried, one pound white sugar, three-quarters of a pound of butter: the yolks of fourteen eggs, the yellow part of two lemons, grated, and the juice also. Beat the sugar and butter to a cream, and add the yolks, well beaten and strained. Then add the lemon-peel and flour, and a tea-spoonful of sal-volatile dissolved in hot water. Beat it well, and, just before putting in the oven, add the lemon-juice, beating it in thoroughly. Bake in square, flat pans, ice it thickly, and cut it in square, thick pieces. It looks nicely on a plate with silver cake.

CALIFORNIA CAKE.

One cup of butter, three of sugar, one cup sour milk, one teaspoonful saleratus, and two of cream of tartar, six eggs and five cups of flour.

LADY CAKE.

Five oz. butter, half pound sugar, the whites of eight eggs, half pound of flour. Flavour with almonds—one ounce bitter, two sweet.

SODA CAKE.

One pound of flour, four ounces of butter, six ounces sugar, three eggs, one spoonful of sour cream, with one of saleratus, spices and fruit to taste. Bake in a very slow oven at first.

LEMON CAKE.

Six eggs, five cups of flour, three cups of sugar, one cup of butter, one cup of milk, one teaspoonful of saleratus, and the peel and juice of a lemon.

FARMERS' SPONGE CAKE.

One teaspoonful of carbonate of soda dissolved in a tea-cupful of sweet milk, two tea-spoonfuls of cream of tartar, mixed dry into the flour, one egg, one cup of soft sugar, one cup of butter melted: it can be made richer by the addition of a cup of currants, or spice to flavour it. Mix to a thickish batter, and pour into a flat pan; or bake in tins.

CUP CAKE.

Cup-cake is about as good as pound-cake, and a great deal cheaper. Three cups of flour, one cup of butter, two cups of sugar, and four eggs, well beat in together, and baked in pans or cups.

NOTE.—This is a regular American cake.

DOUGH NUTS.

Three pounds flour: one pound sugar: ¾ lb butter: four eggs: 1½ pint of milk: nutmeg and cinnamon, one teaspoonful: two large tablespoonfuls of barm: knead lightly: cut in strips, and twist and throw into boiling lard; when they are of a fine light brown, take the dough-nuts out: sift sugar over them while hot.

ANOTHER.

Take one pint of flour, half a pint of sugar, three eggs, a piece of butter as big as an egg, and a teaspoonful of dissolved pearl-ash; when you have no eggs, a gill of lively yeast will do; but in that case they must be made over-night. Cinnamon, rose-water, or lemon-brandy, to season, if you have it.

If you use half lard instead of butter, add a little salt.

Do not put them in till the lard is boiling-hot. The more fat they are fried in, the crisper they will be.

COMMON BUSH TEA-CAKES.

Scrape down a large cupful of maple-sugar, and dissolve in warm water, into which also put a teaspoonful of salaratus, well powdered; rub into two basins of flour, a good bit of butter, or some lard or dripping, and throw in a few carraways, or any spice you may have, and a teaspoonful of salt: knead lightly, cut out with a tumbler, the lid of an old tin tea-pot, or any other convenient cutter, and bake before the fire in the frying-pan, or in the bake-pan. The frying-pan is often used in the backwoods, for baking cakes or bread. In Canada they are generally made with a very long handle, in which there is a loop, through which a strong cord is passed, which is again passed over a nail in the chimney-board; or a machine called a pan-jack, is placed behind it, with notches which allows the cook to raise or lower the pan to the fire. A few hot embers are placed below the pan, to heat the bottom. This is a shanty-oven, often made use of in the backwoodsman's house.

CANADIAN CROQUETS.

Sift a teaspoonful of white sugar through a bit of muslin; add to the sugar three or four drops of essence of lemon, or almonds: beat up two eggs with the sugar, and to these add as much very-fine flour as will make the eggs into a stiff paste. It is better to work it with a spoon till it is smooth and stiff enough to handle: knead it, and roll it out as thin as paper. With a sharp penknife cut out leaves and shells, and roses; or, twist narrow slips into braids, cutting the veinings of the leaves and the edgings.

Have ready a clean tin-pan, half full of boiling lard: you can try the heat by throwing in a little bit of your paste; if hot enough, it will rise directly to the surface, and become stiff in about a minute or two. Throw in your croquets, one or two at a time; two minutes will cook them: take them out with a slice, drain and lay them on a dish, sift a little fine white sugar on them as you take them out.—From these materials you will have a heaped dish of most elegant-looking cakes, at a very small cost.

SWEET FRUIT-CAKE.

This is made by rolling out a fine short crust very thin, and spreading about an inch thickness of apple-marmalade, made by boiling down dried-apples to a pulp;

over this lay another thin crust of pastry: it should be baked in shallow tin-pans, and, when quite cold, cut into squares, or vandyke-shaped pieces, by cutting squares from corner to corner. This is sold in the confectioners under the name of mince-pie, and pie-cake.

As this work is not intended for a regular cookery-book, I have limited myself to such cakes as are in common use in the farm-houses. Canada is the land of cakes. A tea-table is generally furnished with several varieties of cakes and preserves. I have given you as many receipts as will enable you to make a selection: if you require more costly luxuries, there are plenty of good receipts to be had, by referring to any of the popular cookery-books.

[G R A I N S.]

INDIAN RICE.

Indian Rice is a wholesome and nourishing article of diet, which deserves to be better known than it is at present. It grows in vast beds, in still waters, in a depth from three to eight feet, where there is a great deposit of mud and sand. In many places where there is little current, these beds increase so as to materially fill up the shallow lakes, and impede the progress of boats on their surface.

When the rice begins to shew [show] its tender green blade above the water, you would think the lake was studded with low verdant islands. In the months of July and August, the rice comes in flower, and a very beautiful sight it is for those who have an eye to enjoy the beauties of Nature. The leaves, which are grassy, attain a great length, and float upon the surface of the water; I have seen the leaves of the rice measured to

Fig. 12 (*above*) · Indian rice, page 107 of the first edition (1854 [1855]), reproduced from the printing of the second thousand.

the amazing extent of eleven, twelve and thirteen feet. The deer come down at night to feed on the rice-beds, and there the hunter often shoots them. The Indians track them to their feeding-places, and shoot them by torchlight.

In the month of September is the Indian's rice harvest: by that time it is fully ripe and withered. The squaws collect it by paddling through the rice-beds, and with a stick in one hand, and a sort of sharp-edged, curved paddle in the other, striking the ripe heads down into the canoe, the ripe grain falling to the bottom. Many bushels are thus collected. They then make an enclosure on a square area of dry ground, by sticking branches of pine or cedar close together, to form a sort of hedge; in the centre of this place they drive in forked sticks, in a square of several feet, across which they lay others, and on this rude frame they extend mats of bass or cedar, for the manufacture of which the Indian women are renowned: they light a fire beneath this frame, and when reduced to hot, glowing coals, the rice is spread on the mats above the fire: the green enclosure is to keep the heat from escaping: the rice is kept stirred and turned with a wooden shovel or paddle, and, after it is dried, the husk is winnowed from it in large open baskets, shaken in the wind. This is the mere drying process of the green rice.

The parched Indian-rice is heated in pots over a slow fire, till it bursts and shows the white floury part within the dark skin. This sort is eaten by the Indians in soups and stews, and often dry, by handfuls, when on journeys, as the parched corn of the Israelites.

Indian-rice is sold in the stores at 10s. a bushel: it affords a great quantity of food. The Indians sow it up in mats or coarse birch bark baskets: it is dearer now than it used to be, as the Indians are indolent, or possibly, employed in agricultural pursuits or household work.

In appearance this rice is not the least like the white rice of commerce, being long, narrow, and of an olive-green colour outside, but when cooked, is white within. The gathering of wild rice is a tedious process, and one rarely practised by the settlers, whose time can be more profitably employed on their farms; but I have nevertheless given this description of harvesting it, as it is not devoid of interest, and, should this book fall into the hands of any person, who by accident was reduced to having recourse to such expedients as the wild country afforded, for food to keep themselves from starving, they might be able to avail themselves of the knowledge.

Men who have gone up lumbering, on the shores of lonely lakes and rivers, far from the haunts of civilized men, have sometimes been reduced to worse shifts than gathering wild rice to supply their wants.

I will now give the most approved recipes for cooking the Indian-rice.

WILD-RICE PUDDING.

A basinful of Indian-rice carefully washed and picked, should be soaked for some hours; the water being poured off twice during that time. Put it on in a covered vessel, with plenty of water, which should be drained off after it has boiled for half an hour, as there is a weedy, fishy taste with the rice, unless this is done. Milk may now be added in place of the water, with a little salt, and the rice simmered for an hour or more, till every grain has burst, and the milk is absorbed. Now add, when cool, four eggs, a bit of butter, sugar, and a little nutmeg or cinnamon. This makes an excellent baked or boiled pudding: and, leaving out the sugar, and spice, and eggs, and adding more salt, is a good vegetable dish.

STEWED-RICE THICKENED.

Boil or stew in a bake-kettle your rice, and milk as above, keeping a few hot embers above and below it. When nearly ready, mix a large table-spoonful of fine flour with some cold milk, in a basin, and stir into the rice, and let it boil up for five or ten minutes.

This may be sweetened, or eaten with salt, and is an excellent dish. To make it a savoury dish, put butter, salt and pepper, leaving out the sugar.

INDIAN-RICE IN SOUP.

The Indians use the parched rice in their soups and stews, which are chiefly made of game, venison and wild fowl. As an ingredient in fresh soup it is very good, but must be well soaked and carefully picked. Many persons prefer the wild rice to the white Carolina rice, in venison-soup.

NOTE.—The wild rice, commonly called Indian Rice, is by botanists called Water Oats (*Zizania aquatica*). The flower-stem comes up sheathed in a delicate green, hollow, membraneous leaf, and displays the elegant awned flowers:[16] from these the anthers depend, of a delicate straw colour and purple, which have a most graceful effect, waving in the wind. The upper or spiked part is the one that bears the seed: as the flowers approach maturity, the green, grassy leaves fall back from the stem, and float upon the surface: they are no longer needed to protect the fruit.

---

16 An awn is "a bristle-like projection growing from the grain-sheath of barley, oats, and other grasses" (*Canadian Oxford Dictionary*, 88).

BUCKWHEAT.

This grain is grown in Canada for the fine flour which is used as an article of food in the form of pancakes. It is the same grain that at home is known by the name of French-wheat; and in some counties of England, by the name of Branck. In England it is chiefly grown for feeding of fowls and game. In France I have heard it is used by the peasants as bread, probably in the way that the Canadians use it, as pancakes. Buckwheat is of easy culture: it is sown late, and cut early. Hogs are fed with it, in the straw: sometimes it is sown by the farmer to enrich the soil, by being ploughed down whilst in flower.

When intended as a crop for harvesting, it is cut and bound in sheaves, thrashed and ground into flour, which must be sifted with a fine sieve, as the husky part is quite black, and any portion mixing with the flour would render it unsightly. I will now give the best receipt for cooking

BUCKWHEAT PANCAKES.

The usual mode of preparing this favourite article of food, which the Americans and Canadians consider a national dainty, is as follows:

Take about a quart or three pints of the finely-sifted flour, mix to a batter with warm milk or water, a teaspoonful of salt, and half a teacupful of good barm: beat it well for a few minutes, till it is smooth, and leave it in a warm place all night, covered in an earthen pot or tin-pail, with a cover. In the morning have ready your griddle or frying-pan, wiped clean, and some lard or butter, made quite hot; into this drop a large spoonful or small teacupful at a time, of your light batter, till your pan be full, but do not let them touch: if the lard be very hot, the pancakes will set as you pour them in, and be well shaped, and as light as a honey-comb: fry of a light brown, and turn them; lay them on a hot plate, and serve quite hot, with maple molasses, treacle or butter.

If the batter have worked sour, melt half a teaspoonful of saleratus or soda, and stir in.

The buckwheat pancakes should be served hot and hot to table. Buckwheat pancakes are a favourite breakfast-dish with the old Canadian settlers.

These pancakes may be raised by mixing in three teaspoonfuls of the baking powder, just before frying, instead of using yeast to ferment the batter.

OATMEAL PANCAKES.

Mix one part of flour with three parts of oatmeal, and set with warm water and a little salt, into a thin batter; add a little barm, and let it rise; pour your batter on a hot, well-greased griddle or frying-pan, or drop into hot lard, as in buckwheat pancakes.

It is a mistake to suppose that oatmeal or buckwheat-flour will not rise. I believe that the flour of any grain will rise and make leavened bread, and, in scarcity of wheaten flour, a mixture may be made to great advantage, of rye, maize, oatmeal, or barley-flour. At all events, it is well to know how to make good food out of the inferior grains. The English peasantry who live on the best wheaten flour, are not more healthy, and hardly so strong in muscle, as the natives of Scotland and Ireland, whose diet is chiefly oatmeal and potatoes. Most medical men agree in the opinion, that brown bread, or bread with a part of the bran left in, is much more conducive to health, unless to very weakly persons of lax habit, than the pure white bread; and that were brown bread more common as a staple article of diet, there would be fewer calls upon them for medicines.—Habitually costive persons should adopt the constant use of brown bread, and abstain as much as possible from white bread, especially bakers' bread, in the composition of which alum and other astringents are often introduced.

OAT-MEAL PORRIDGE.

This wholesome dish is prepared as follows:—

Have ready boiling water, as much as will be required for your family; into this throw some salt; experience will guide you in the quantity, for it must depend upon taste, and the necessity for a large or small cooking. Have ready your oatmeal in a dish or basin, and a thick wooden round stick, which any boy can make for you with a good knife, and smoothing it off with a spoke-shave or a bit of glass. While you throw the meal slowly into the boiling water with one hand, keep stirring it with the stick with the other, till your porridge is thick and smooth; then let it boil for about ten minutes, and serve it in plates, with a cup of milk to each person. Some, however, prefer butter to eat with it, others molasses: it is a matter of taste and convenience.

MILK-PORRIDGE WITH OATMEAL

is made as above, only substituting milk for water, and less oatmeal. In making milk-gruel, it is better to mix the meal in a basin, smoothly, with water, and when the milk in the pot boils, pour and stir in the mixture.

Children are fond of this dish for supper and breakfast, and it is nourishing, light and wholesome, unless there be acidity of stomach; then it is not so good, as oatmeal has a tendency to create heartburn, when the digestion is deranged.

OAT CAKE.

It would seem presumptuous in an Englishwoman to give a recipe for making Oat-cakes. The North of England people know how to make them. The Scots and Irish are famous for them, and the inhabitants of the South, East and West of England would not eat them.

In Canada they are made by all classes of Irish and Scotch—some the plain, old-fashioned way, and others with shortening, as butter or lard. I like them best with a good deal of butter in them; they are less hard, and, I think, more palatable: and some put soda in the water, which I have been recommended to try. I have seen persons in ague, throw a handful of toasted or fresh oatmeal into a jug of cold water, and take it, not as a cure, but as a drink in the fever. I have seen very good results; in violent pains in the body alleviated, by oatmeal made hot in the oven or pan, slightly sprinkled with water to create a steam, put in a flannel-bag or a coarse cloth, and applied to the sufferer: or an oat-cake toasted and wrapped up in a damp cloth, laid over the stomach. Simple as such remedies are, in case of sudden illness it is well to remember them, especially in a country where doctors are few and far off, besides being very expensive visitors in a poor emigrant's log-house or shanty.

I might enumerate many other uses to which oatmeal can be put, and furnish a long list of dishes in which it figures as a principal ingredient, but these hardly belong to my plan: therefore I leave Oatmeal to more experienced housewives, and proceed to give instructions on the cultivation and uses of

INDIAN-CORN.

With the exception of wheat, there is not a more valuable grain, or one more various and valuable in its uses to man, than Indian-corn. It enters into the composition of many most nourishing and excellent compounds, and is equally palatable and wholesome in its green or ripened state, as food for man or the domestic animals about his homestead: while the wild creatures gather their portion, from the big black bear, down to the active and predaceous chipmunk. It comes amiss to none of God's creatures, and if it costs some labour to plant and harvest, it amply repays the care bestowed upon it. There are seasons when it does not arrive at perfection, as in the cold, wet harvests of 1835, 1836, and 1837, but those were years when the wheat grew in the sheaves, and grain of all kinds was with difficulty brought to perfection.

Even when the Indian-corn does not succeed so well, it still produces a great amount of sweet and nourishing food for animals, and though the grain may not come to its fullest state of perfection, it will be equally good for cattle, and the fattening of swine; so that after all, the loss is really not so great, as the failure in any other of the green crops would be.

CULTURE OF INDIAN-CORN.

The best soil is light, good loam, and lands that have been cultivated for some years, open and sunny, rather than the virgin soil of new lands: in the latter case the plant is apt to be too rank, running more to straw than grain. Indian-corn will bear soil well manured.—The best sort of corn (of which, however, there are many varieties) is the yellow eight-rowed corn, i. e. eight rows of grain on each cob. You will see varieties in the colour of the grain on the same cob; such as pale straw color, white and yellow, sometimes red, and even bluish green; but a good unmixed seed is better.

The time of planting is generally from the 20th to the 25th of May, though I have often known it planted as early as the 18th, in very warm dry seasons. The greatest danger the young plant has to encounter, is frost, which often nips the tender, green blade, when it is some inches above the ground.

Some persons steep the grain twelve or sixteen hours before planting, but this should only be done when the sowing has been retarded, to hasten vegetation, and if the ground be very dry. If the soil be wet from recent rains, it is not prudent to steep the seed, as it is liable to rot in the ground, and never come up.

The corn dropper should be supplied with a lap bag, of coarse canvas, tied round the waist, or slung across the shoulders, the mouth being wide enough to admit the hand freely; or a basket with two handles on one side, and one on the outer side; through these handles straps are passed, which are slung over the left shoulder, the basket; hanging a little under the left arm, which arrangement admits of the readiest access to the corn with the right hand: the outside handle serves for the dropper to steady the basket. One person should open the earth slightly with the hoe, into which four grains of corn are dropped, in a square of about two inches, as near as possible, from each other: the person who hoes, then draws the earth over the corn. Some merely let the grains fall on the surface, while the other covers them with earth, forming a slight hill over them: others again draw a furrow, and plant the corn in rows, at certain distances. These things are better learned by experience, and the advice of old settlers—sound, practical men, who have no interest in misleading the inexperienced emigrant.

The distance in planting corn, when it is the usual hill culture, is three feet from hill to hill, and three feet from row to row. Some allow a few inches more, considering that the plant having more space and air, repays them by an increase of luxuriance. The first hoeing generally takes place when the plant is about a foot high, when the earth is drawn towards the stems of the plants, and stirred well about them. The next hoeing should be before the plant begins to run up to flower. Where the fields are free of stumps, a one-horse plough is generally preferred to the hoe, as being a great saving of labour, and equally efficacious in earthing up the corn. Some cross-plough, but I do not think this is very often practised. Women and children take great part in the culture of the corn-crop, especially in the bush-farms, where the roots and stumps obstruct the plough, and the hoe alone can be made use of. Pumpkins are usually planted along with Indian-corn: the broad leaves of the pumpkin spreading over the ground, serves to shade it, and retain its moisture for the benefit of the Indian-corn, acting as a sort of wet-nurse to the tender plant.

The pumpkin-seed is planted in every other hill, and in every other row; which allows free space for the plants to run over the ground, without choking each other.

Some farmers remove the unfruitful shoots and suckers from the stem of the plants, that are thrown up; while others, who regard the fodder for their cattle as a matter of importance, think that they lose more than they gain.

As soon as the grain begins to fill with milk, and has acquired some substance, it is fit for the table; but the white, sweet, garden-corn is best for cooking, and should be cultivated for that purpose, instead of robbing your field-crop.

The first week in October is the usual time for harvesting Indian-corn, which is done by cutting it near the root, or pulling it: it is then set round in bundles, so as to form a large circular stook, which is tied with a band at the top, and these stooks are left to dry in the field till the farmer has leisure to house them. The common way is then to pull the cobs off the stalk, and throw them in heaps, when they are carted home to the barn or corn-crib.

The corn-crib should be raised from the ground, and made of logs or boards, close enough to keep out squirrels, but so as to admit the air, which is essential to its keeping well. The crib is made small at bottom, and wide at top, and roofed over.

Before threshing, it is necessary to husk the corn, which is simply stripping off the fine sheathing that surrounds the cob or ear; to effect this, "Husking Bees" are often called. Neighbours and friends, especially young folks, meet and sit round, and pull off the husk.—

The meeting usually ends in an evening frolic, a dance and supper.—This is seldom had recourse to excepting by the small farmers.

The choicest cobs should be selected for seed: these are only partially husked; the husk that remains is turned back, and the cobs are braided together in ropes, and hung across a pole or beam, to be kept against the spring. When rasping your seed-corn, break off about an inch or more from the cob, as the grains at the end of the cob are not so fine, or fit for planting, as the rest.

There are various ways of thrashing Indian-corn, but the usual method is simply with the flail; some tread it out with horses, on the barn floor. This is an ancient mode of thrashing, practised in the East, and also in Portugal and Spain. The first crop of Indian-corn I ever saw, was rasped by means of a bit of iron-hoop, set in the edge of a barrel; but this was a slow process. In the States there are machines on purpose for rasping corn, that work very expeditiously, and are a great saving of labour.

Four quarts of good seed will plant an acre of bush land, with the stumps on it: six quarts are allowed for old land, where the ground is not encumbered by stumps or trees.

I have been particular in describing, as minutely as I could, all these things relating to the cultivation of this crop, so universally grown in Canada; for though it is not often left to the management of females, yet such things have sometimes occurred through sickness or accident befalling the head of the family, that the work or the direction of it, has fallen upon the wives and daughters of the farmer.

I have known women in Canada, who have not only planted and hoed the corn, but have also harvested it. I knew the wife of an officer, who had settled on a government grant in the backwoods: she was a young woman who had never been accustomed to any other work than such light labour as the most delicate female may take pleasure in, such as the culture of flowers, and making pastry and preserves, and such matters; but of laborious work she knew nothing. Well, it so happened, that her female servant, her husband, and also the man-servant, all fell sick with intermittent fever: in a few days both the man and the maid went home to their own friends, and this young wife, who was also a mother, and had a baby of ten months old, was left to nurse her sick husband and the child, and do all the work of the house. At first she was inclined to fret, and give up in despair, but when she looked upon her sick husband and her helpless babe, she remembered that duty required better things from her than to lie down and weep, and lament: she knew that other women had their trials, and she braced up her mind to do what was before her, praying to God to give her strength to do her duty, and she went on cheerfully and with a brave spirit.

The spot where these people lived was very lonely; it was a new clearing in the forest, and there were not many settlers near them: it is now full eighteen years ago, and emigrants were not as well off then as they are now in their new settlements, and often had to put up with great privation, and encounter great hardships.

Besides a few acres of fall wheat, they had half an acre of Indian-corn, on which they depended in part for food for the household, and also for fatting some pigs for winter meat.

The corn was just ripe, for it was the last week in September; the great golden pumpkins showed like gigantic oranges on the ground, between the rows of ripened corn; but, alas! the fence was not very secure, and the hogs of a settler about half a mile off, came through the woods and destroyed the corn.

The blue jays, and the racoons from the forest, came to share in the spoil; the grain was fast diminishing, which was to have done so much for the support of the little household. The poor wife looked at her fever-stricken husband, and at her baby boy; neither could help her, and at first she hesitated before she could decide upon which plan to pursue. However she left plenty of cooling drink by the bed-side of her sick partner, and with baby in her arms she set out to the field; fortunately it was close at hand, just beside the garden. She spread a shawl on the ground at the foot of a pine tree that stood on the clearing, and setting up an umbrella to shade the little one from the heat of the sun, she set to work on her task of gathering the corn. She soon became interested in the work, and though her soft hands, unused to rough labour, were blistered and chafed, in a few hours she had stripped the cobs from a large portion of the corn, and thrown them into heaps, running back from time to time to speak to her baby, and amuse him by rolling towards him the big yellow golden pumpkins, with which in a short time she had effectually fenced him round, while the little fellow, shouting with joy, patted and slapped the cool rind of the orange-coloured fruit with his fat white hands, and laughed with infant glee.

Between gathering the corn, playing with the baby, and going to visit her sick husband, she had enough to do.

She next brought out some large Indian baskets, into which she gathered up her corn. At sunset she dragged her little one home, mounted in great state on the top of one of the loads; weary enough she was in body, but well satisfied in mind, at her day's work.

In this way she harvested and housed her first crop of Indian-corn. Her husband was well enough to aid in storing the pumpkins by the time her task was finished.

In after years she has often with honest pride related to her children how she gathered in the first Indian corn crop that was raised on their bush farm. Possibly this very circumstance gave a tone of energy and manly independence of spirit to her children, which will mark them in their progress in after life. I will now proceed to giving some improved [approved] recipes for the cooking of Indian corn.

HOMINY.

This is the Indian name for a preparation of corn either slightly broken in a crushing mill, or whole. The whole corn is steeped for some hours, twelve at least; it is then boiled in what is commonly called white lye, which is made with a small portion of ashes tied up in a cloth, or a clean bag, but a large tea-spoonful of salaratus, or a bit of pearl-ash would, I think, answer as well or better than the ashes, and be less trouble. Drain off the water when the corn has boiled an hour or so, and lay the corn on a pan before the fire to dry. When the fine skin begins to strip a little, put it into a clean bag, and beat it till the scales fall off. Sift or fan the bran away, rubbing it through your hands. When clean, return it to the pot, and boil it with plenty of water for six or eight hours, keeping it closely covered till it is quite soft. This dish is eaten with milk, or with meat seasoned with pepper and salt. If to be eaten as a vegetable, a piece of meat may be boiled with the corn; but if too salt, the meat should be steeped and parboiled.

When hominy is made of crushed corn, it may be steeped and then pressed through a coarse sieve: the scales will float, and can be skimmed off. The water must be kept to boil the hominy in, as it contains the flour. This must be boiled many hours, and is eaten with milk.

SUPPORNE.

This is a thick sort of porridge, made from Indian meal, very similar to oatmeal porridge, only it is boiled rather longer. The sifted Indian meal is sprinkled into the boiling water, and stirred quickly,—rather more salt is used than for oatmeal porridge,—and when boiled, about twenty minutes, is taken up in a dish, and is eaten with milk, sugar, butter, or any other seasoning that is prepared. If there be any left from the breakfast or supper, it may be cut (for it becomes quite solid when cold) in slices an inch thick, and fried for breakfast, and buttered hot, or eaten with meat gravy.

Supporne to the Americans and Canadians is what oatmeal porridge is to the Scotch and Irish. It is the national dish, and very good and wholesome food it makes. One bushel of Indian meal will go as far as two of flour in puddings and cakes, bread and porridge, as it absorbs a great deal more water or milk, swells in bulk, and satisfies the appetite sooner. Supporne is better for long boiling.

MILK SUPPORNE.

A very nice sort of hasty pudding is made in the following manner:—to three handfuls of Indian meal add one of wheaten flour, and mix them well: set on the fire a quart of sweet milk and a pint of water, with a tea-spoonful of salt. As soon as the milk and water boils, throw in and stir your flour and meal, and let them boil a few minutes, fast. After the meal has been all stirred in, if not quite thick enough, you can throw in a little more meal,—remove from the stove or fire, and let it simmer on a few embers on the hearth, or on the outside of the stove, for a quarter of an hour longer, or even half an hour. This needs no seasoning otherwise than the salt that you put in, and is very delicious, being richer and more satisfying than the common supporne. It makes a good pudding for children, and, if seasoned with nutmeg or cinnamon, four or five beaten eggs, and sweetened, it is an excellent baked or boiled pudding.

GREEN CORN.

Green Corn can be preserved by simply turning back the husk, all but the last thin layer, and then hanging it in the sun or in a very warm room. When it is to be used boil it soft, and then cut off the cob and mix it with butter. The summer sweet corn is the proper kind.

Another is to par-boil sweet corn: cut it from the cobs and dry it in the sun, then store it in a cool dry place, in a bag for use.

GREEN CORN PATTIES.

Twelve ears of sweet corn grated, one tea-spoonful of salt, and one of pepper, one egg beaten into two table-spoonfuls of flour; mix, make into small cakes, and fry brown in butter or sweet lard.

GREEN CORN FRITTERS.

One tea-cupful of milk, three eggs, one pint of green corn grated, a little salt, and as much flour as will form a batter. Beat the eggs, the yolks, and whites separate. To the yolks of the eggs add the corn, salt, milk, and flour enough to form a batter. Beat the whole very hard, then stir in the whites, and drop the batter a spoonful at a time into hot lard, and fry them on both sides, of a bright brown colour.

BOILED CORN.

This is a favourite dish in Canada and the States. When the grains are sufficiently swollen and beginning to harden, but not to become hard, break off the cob, and boil for two hours or till they become tender. Some like corn best boiled with salt at meat, but that is a matter of taste or convenience. As a vegetable it is much admired, especially the sweet garden corn: the grain of this is of milky whiteness, and is very nice even in its corn state, being full of rich, *sugary* milk. It is of green *sweet* corn that the preceding dishes are made.

Some people cut the grains from the cob and boil them like peas, with butter and pepper for seasoning; this obviates the ungraceful mode of eating corn so much objected to by particular persons.

STEWED CORN.

This is a nice dish: cut the corn from the cob, boil for an hour and a half, reducing the liquid that you boil it in to a quart; cut some slices or steaks of any fresh meat, adding young onions, carrots, and sweet herbs, with pepper, salt, and a couple of tomatoes cut up; stew till the vegetables are tender. Should the gravy be too much reduced in quantity, add a little boiling water or cream.

FRIED CORN.

Green sweet corn fried in butter and seasoned is excellent: the corn should be boiled first till tender.

INDIAN MEAL PANCAKES.

Make a batter with one part flour, and three parts Indian meal, a little salt, and some warm (not hot) water or milk, half a tea-spoonful of salaratus dissolved in butter-milk if you have any, if not, milk will do, if sour so much the better; stir into your bowl or pan with the batter, and beat it a few minutes; heat your griddle or frying pan quite hot, with butter or lard, and drop in your pancakes. As soon as browned on one side turn them: keep them from burning by adding a little more fat or melted butter. Strew sugar on the surface as you lay them on the dish. Some butter them hot, and sift sugar also. These pancakes are far lighter for the stomach than flour pancakes.

It is a simple dish—easily made—very economical—and makes a wholesome variety at dinner or supper. A handful of currants strewn in, or a few ripe garden currants makes them nicer, or eaten with preserved apples where you have an orchard, and fruit of this kind is plentiful.

INDIAN MEAL PUDDING WITH MEAT.

This is a good substantial dinner when you have fat meat in the spring, and no vegetables. Mix Indian meal, seasoned with salt, to a thick batter with hot water or cold milk, add a little tea-spoonful of soda, but it is not indispensable; grease your bake-kettle or stove-pan, pour in your batter, stirring it well, slice some ham or fat bacon, pepper them, (a grate of nutmeg is an improvement if you have it at hand,) and lay them on the batter. Your slices of meat must not be very thin: half an inch thick at least. When the meat is brown on one side, turn the slice, and if done too quickly, remove to a hot dish and keep them covered up till the pudding is done. Some do not put the meat in till the batter is well set, but the pudding is best when both are done together. The Indian meal absorbs the fat from the meat without tasting greasy, and a very savoury and relishing dish is made out of very homely ingredients. Fresh meat, a small joint of mutton or beef, can be thus cooked, the pudding making an excellent addition to the dinner; and by this mode of cooking a small portion of meat will give an ample provision for a large family.

INDIAN POUND CAKE.

8 eggs, beaten, 1 pint of powdered sugar, 1 pint of sifted Indian meal, ½ a pint of fine flour, ½lb. of butter; stir the butter and sugar to a cream, beat the eggs apart, stir the meal and flour to the eggs and sugar and butter, add nutmeg and lemon peel, or essence of lemon, with a glass of wine and brandy; butter a flat pan or little tart tins, and bake. This may be eaten the same day or as soon as cold.

INDIAN TEA-CAKE.

A pint basinful of Indian meal sifted, four well-beaten eggs, a teacupful of butter melted, a cupful of sugar, and a table-spoonful of treacle or molasses, (but if you have none, this last can be omitted; the cake will be good without, though it looks richer,) a table-spoonful of carraway seeds, or a cupful of currants; a teaspoonful each of ginger and nutmeg grated, and half a teaspoonful of salt. Dissolve a teaspoonful of soda or salaratus, in some milk, and mix these ingredients to a pretty thick batter;

bake in a stove pan, in a brisk oven. When done, cut the cake into squares: it should be about two inches thick when baked.

This is a very nice cake, quickly made, and is rich and light, without injuring the digestion.

A fine cake can be made of Indian meal, eggs, butter, molasses and ginger, with soda and sour milk or cream.

Allspice makes a good seasoning for a plain cake; and dried garden-currants or huckleberries are good put in.

INDIAN-MEAL BREAKFAST-CAKES.

One quart of sifted Indian meal, one handful of fine flour, three eggs well beaten, a cup of yeast, one tea-spoonful of salt, one quart of milk made pretty hot; put in the yeast, eggs and salt, and then stir in your meal. Mix into a batter overnight, adding in the morning a little pearl-ash, or soda or saleratus, just before baking, but be careful to roll and dissolve before putting it to your batter, and stir it well through.

Pour the batter on a hot, buttered griddle, and turn when browned on the under side: serve hot.

JOHNNY-CAKE.

One quart of Indian meal: two tablespoonfuls of molasses, or a cup of coarse sugar; one cup of butter melted, a teaspoonful of salt, and one of ginger; two eggs: make these ingredients into a batter with scalding water or milk: pour the batter into a flat pan, and bake brown: cut in squares, and serve hot with butter or preserves.

PLAIN JOHNNY-CAKE.

Take a quart of sour milk or buttermilk, to which add as much soda or pearl-ash as will make it froth up well; thicken this milk with Indian meal; add a little salt; pour the batter into a flat pan, and bake it brown; cut in pieces, and eat it hot with butter or molasses. A few seeds are an improvement to Johnny-cake.

BAKED INDIAN-MEAL PUDDING.

Scald a quart of milk, and stir in seven or eight table-spoonfuls of Indian meal, a little salt, sugar or molasses to sweeten it, a cup of beef or veal suet, nicely shred, a teaspoonful of ginger or any spice you prefer, a tea-cupful of currants or chopped apples, and four eggs beaten to froth; sprinkle a little fine suet on the top and grate a little nutmeg.

PLAIN INDIAN PUDDING.

The same as above, only omitting the eggs and fruit. The same pudding may be boiled instead of baked, but the cloth must be tied so as to allow of the meal swelling, and requires to be boiled two or three hours.

INDIAN PUDDING TO EAT WITH MEAT.

This is simply a batter made with Indian meal, a little salt, and scalding milk or water, tied up, not too tightly, and boiled three hours.

INDIAN-MEAL YORKSHIRE PUDDING.

Make a batter of Indian meal, with milk and two or three eggs, and pour into the pan, when you are roasting beef, pork, mutton, or any fresh meat: it absorbs the gravy, and is very nice. It is as well to pour off some of the gravy before you put your batter in with the meat, as it is apt to rob the meat of all that runs from it. When you serve the meat, pour over it the reserved gravy, made hot.

INDIAN FRUIT PUDDING.

Make your batter with hot milk, a little suet, shred fine, or butter rubbed with the meal, six eggs, and a pint of any green or ripe fruit, (as currants, gooseberries, cherries, huckleberries, or apples chopped fine,) a little sugar, and a tea-spoonful of salt; boil for two hours, or longer if your pudding be large.

CORN STARCH.

This is a most truly valuable article of diet, as well as being used in the dressing of fine linen. It is prepared in the United States, and sold in all Canadian stores, in packets, on which are printed directions for using it.

It is quite as palatable as arrow-root—much cheaper—and as easily prepared. As diet for the sick, it is very valuable; and also for young children. It would form a most admirable sea-store for emigrants.—A half pound packet of this fine light powder costs 7½ d., or a York-shilling. It makes delightful custards and puddings.

CORN-STRAW BEDS AND MATS.

The sheathing which envelopes the grain of the Indian corn is often used for filling beds, or loose mattrasses [mattresses], to put below feather beds; and is preferred by many people to straw or any other material. The best method of preparing it is this:— after the corn has been husked, or the cob stripped of the dry sheath that protects it, take a few nails and drive them quite through a piece of board,—the bottom of an old box will do for the purpose: the nails must project so as to present the points an inch or two beyond the surface, and several, say six or eight, must be driven in so as to form a sort of comb, having a double row of teeth. Gather up a handful of the dry husks, and draw them quickly across the nails so as to tear them into strips: with a little practice this work can be carried on very quickly. A bag of coarse brown linen, with an opening in the middle seam, large enough to admit of a person's hand, and furnished with strings or large buttons, is the best receptacle for the straw. The persons who makes the beds stirs the contents of these mattrasses by putting in her hand. Mats for laying under beds are also made by braiding the sheathing into thick ropes, and sewing them together with a wooden needle or a large iron needle, with an eye large enough to admit of a single blade of the husk being threaded through it. This is then tied; but those who do not care for the trouble of constantly threading and tying, use twine, or the tough inner part of the cedar tree. Round and oval mats are made for the doors, of the corn sheathing. The rough ends of the husk are left projecting about an inch. The braid is made in this fashion:—you take nine blades of the sheathing and tie them at the top, to keep your work from coming undone: the braid is the simple three ply; but you use three blades together, instead of one. To make it thick enough, every time you come to the left side, insert there a fresh blade, leaving a little bit of the end to project at the edge. About twenty yards is sufficient for a door mat: it is sown together with the big needle, and twine or bark. Children can be taught to make these things; and they cost nothing but the time, and can be made of an evening or on wet days, when other work cannot be attended to.

This is one among the many uses to which this valuable plant can be applied: even the cobs themselves are of service after the grain has been taken from them. They make excellent corks for bottles; and a bag of them of all sizes should be kept for such purpose. Burnt slowly in the smoke-house, the corn-cob is in high repute, as affording the finest flavouring for hams and bacon; and burnt to fine white ashes, they afford a very excellent alkali for raising gingerbread, and other cakes. I have seen Canadian housewives make a pure white ley [lye] of the ashes, for that purpose.

POTATOES.

The most common method of planting potatoes in the new soil, is in hills: on the older farms, in ridges, earthed up by the means of a single-horse plough. The potato is set all through the month of May and the early part of June, and even later than this; but the earlier they are planted, the better chance you will have of a fair crop.

In the bush-farms potatoes are generally planted in hills: the method is simple. One person drops the seed on the ground, at a distance of sixteen or eighteen inches apart, and two feet between the rows: another follows, and with a hoe, draws the earth each way over the set: some flatten the top of the hill with the hoe, and shape them like little mole-hills. When the shoot breaks the ground, and the leaves expand, the earth is again drawn up to the plant. In the fresh virgin soil, once [one] hoeing is all the crop receives; but in gardens, we give the potatoes a second, and sometimes a third hoeing. The hills are preferred in new clearings, where the roots and stumps would prevent the ridges from being straight, and interrupt the ploughing. The Irish plan of lazy-beds is seldom practised in Canada, unless it be to improve a piece of turfy or weedy soil. The field-crop of potatoes is seldom fit for use before August, but earlier sorts may be planted in the garden for table, which will be fit in July. The sorts usually set are early kidneys, for garden culture. Pink-eyes, the common white and red apple potato; rough-skinned purple, and cups, for the main crop. There are many others that I could name. I would advise any settler coming out early in the Spring, to bring a small quantity of good potatoes for seed, in a box of dry sand. New seed will fetch high prices, and pay well if the crop succeeds. There is always an eagerness to obtain new sorts of an approved potato, especially early kinds.

The month of October is the general one for storing the field potatoes, which should be taken up in dry weather. I feel assured that a vast deal of loss, both in quantity and quality, is caused by storing potatoes wet.

The cellar, the root-house, and pits in the ground, are the storing-places. There are objections to the cellarage, as the cellars, which are, for the most part, pits dug under the flooring of the kitchen-part of the log-house, are often too warm, and the potato heats, or exhausts itself, by throwing out sprouts, besides, in the Spring, causing a bad smell and impure air, very injurious to the health of the inmates of the dwelling.

The root-house is better, but requires to be constructed with due attention for excluding the frost. In pitting potatoes, the mode observed by some of the most careful farmers, is this:—the potatoes are suffered to lie spread on the ground, to dry in the sun and wind, as long as possible, during the day: they are then gathered in large heaps, on a dry spot, sandy, if possible, and the ground slightly inclining towards the south, or east: no pit is dug—the potatoes lie on the ground only: over the heap is spread a good quantity of dry litter or straw; on this earth is thrown, about a foot in depth; on this more straw or the dry stalks of the potatoes, and another bank-ing of earth. A few boards placed slanting, so as to throw off the rain, is sometimes added; but the frost seldom penetrates the second layer of straw. Those who have a good safe root-house, or large cellars, seldom pit: but if it is unavoidable, the way I have recommended is the best, for securing this valuable root from the severe frosts of a Canadian winter.

NOTE.—A highly intelligent Scotchman, in our vicinity, tells me that he has found from long experience, the following plan is the best for preserving the quality of the potato:—when taking up the crop, he lays the roots in heaps of eight or ten bushels on the surface, covers them with dry haum [haulm[17]] and earth, but leaves a vent or space at the top, with no earth on it, to allow the steam that rises from the potatoes to escape, till the cold weather comes on, when the pits are either removed to the root-house or cellar, or secured by an additional quantity of litter, and an outer banking up of earth.

POTATO BREAD.
(See Bread.)

Every body knows how to cook a potato; but every one does not know that it is better to put them on in cold than in warm water, and also, that cutting a slice off the rose-end—in the end which is beset with eyes, will greatly improve the mealiness of the potato. A cup of cold water thrown in a few minutes before they are done, also is good. After the water has been drained off, and the pot returned open to the fire, to dry them for a few minutes, a sprinkle of salt is a decided improvement; then let them be served up as hot as possible.

After dinner, let any potatoes that remain be peeled while yet warm, and set aside for breakfast; sliced and fried, with pepper and salt to season them, or placed whole in the oven or bake kettle, with a little dripping or butter, and made nicely brown, forms a good dish to eat with meat in the morning, and saves the trouble of boiling. In Canadian farm-houses meat is generally cooked twice and sometimes thrice a day. Or the potatoes may be put on the fire in a frying-pan or spider; (this is a conven-ient little pan with three legs, that is used to fry or stew in, which accompanys all cooking-stoves: it has a comical name; but the little pan is a very convenient utensil;)

---

17 A collective term for the leftover stalks of threshed grains, peas, grasses and beans, used as roof thatch, cattle bed-straw, or mud floor cover (*Canadian Oxford Dictionary*, 645).

a little butter, pepper, salt, and a little chopped onion being added, the cook, as she stirs the potatoes, minces them or mashes them fine with the blade of the knife, keeping them from burning by constant stirring, till they are nicely browned. This is a favourite way of cooking potatoes a second time: I learned it from an American lady.

MASHED POTATOES.

Pare the potatoes very free from spots; throw them into cold salt-and-water as you pare them; when all are done, put them into clean, cold water, and boil till soft, carefully skimming the pot: pour off dry; then mash fine, adding a cup of milk or thin cream, and a little more salt, or you may put in a bit of butter: dish, and smooth the potatoes on the top and sides, and put into the oven or before the fire to brown. Cold mashed potatoes, cut in slices an inch thick, and browned in the oven like toast, and buttered, is a nice dish for breakfast.

POTATO SOUP.

Set on the fire, bones of beef, or any fresh meat, with a gallon of water, into which slice onions, carrots, and turnips; a little salt and pepper: boil till the vegetables are soft. Have ready, potatoes finely mashed—a quart basin full; add them to the soup, from which the bones may now be removed; boil an hour, slowly; pass the soup through a colander; if too thick, add a little boiling water or liquor in which meat has been boiled; return the soup after straining it to the pot; shred in a little green parsley and savory; give it a boil up, and serve it with toasted bread. If you have no meat, a piece of butter rolled in flour, will do to enrich the soup instead.

POTATO FISH-CAKES.

This is an excellent dish. If salt cod, or fish of any kind, salted or fresh, be left cold, remove the bones and skin carefully; pound the fish in a clean pot with the beetle, till every piece is separated; if too dry, add a little hot water or melted butter; when thoroughly reduced, and well picked from the bones, add mashed potatoes, nicely seasoned with pepper—some add cayenne, but as children dislike such hot seasoning, it is better omitted in the mass; pound the fish and potatoes till they are well mixed; throw a little flour on a clean board, and taking out a small portion, *mould* it with your hands into a round cake; flatten on the top, and roll it in the flour. When you have a dishful made, fry the fish-cakes in hot dripping, butter, or lard, on a brisk fire: when neatly made and nicely browned, this is a nice way of cooking fish. If fresh fish is used, you must season with a little salt: some persons add an *egg* and a little finely chopped parsley, when pounding the potatoes and fish. The same preparation put in a deep dish, and browned before the fire or in the oven, is, I believe, called Chowder by the American cooks: it is less trouble, but the fish-cakes both look and eat better.

POTATO-CAKES.

A very favourite cake with the Irish. They are simply made with potatoes boiled very soft, and kneaded with flour and a little salt, rolled thin; cut in squares, and baked quickly. The goodness of this cake depends on the making and baking: some persons use twice as much flour in making them as others. A nicer potato-cake is made by adding a little cream to moisten the potatoes and flour, making the dough stiff and rolling it thin, and working a piece of butter in, as in making pastry; bake lightly in the oven, or fry, and sift over them a little fine sugar.—All potato-cakes are best eaten hot.

POTATO-DUMPLINGS.

Make a dough with mashed potatoes and flour, wetting the mass with a very little milk, to enable you to knead it smooth; make dumplings, and boil in milk. Some boil the dumplings in milk, till the dough is boiled down, and the milk thickened like hasty pudding. This should be done in a bake-kettle placed over a few hot embers, and the lid heated on a clear fire; but it requires great care to keep the milk from scorching: when nicely done, it is a good sort of pudding for children: with the addition of sugar, eggs, and spice, it is as good as custard.

IRISH MASH.

This is not the dish commonly known as Irish stew, but a more economical one; though certainly very inferior in goodness. It is made with a large quantity of potatoes, seasoned with onion and pepper; cold meat chopped up and mixed through the potatoes: there is no gravy, or very little, and the dish is rather recommended for its satisfying than its delicate qualities; nevertheless it is a useful sort of dish where the meat is scarce in a large family. Many a savoury dish can be made with potatoes and a small portion of meat, either as pie or stew; but I think it better to confine my recipes to dishes that are more peculiar to the cookery of Canada.

POTATO-STARCH.

As I have before observed, it is a great object with the Canadian settlers to manufacture everything they consume, if it be practicable. The careful emigrant's wife buys no starch; but makes all she uses, either from potatoes or bran.

Potato starch is the fine flour that is obtained from the potato by grating it down in water.

Pare some large potatoes; white skinned are preferable to red or purple; grate them down to pulp on a coarse rasp, or the large-holed side of a bread grater; let the pulp fall into a pan of clean cold water. When you have reduced all your potatoes by grating, stir the mass well up with your hand; lay a clean coarse cloth in your colander over a vessel, and strain the whole mass; squeezing it till the pulp is quite dry. The liquor that remains after the straining must then be left to settle for an hour or more, or till it looks clear, and shows a sediment at the bottom. It may then be poured off, and a second water put on; stir this, and leave it again for some hours. A third water should be added; pouring off the former one as before: three waters is generally sufficient. The last time you pour the water off, you will perceive a slightly discoloured crust on the top of your starch, or some of the fine fibrous matter that has passed through: remove it with a clean spoon, and the pure, spotless, white substance below is the starch. This must be taken out, and spread to dry in a warm, sunny place, stirring it very frequently, till the whole is perfectly dry. It may then be put in paper bags, and hung up in a dry room.—Be sure that it is quite dry before bagging it.

Not only does this make the clearest and best of starch for muslins and linens; but is a good substitute for arrow-root, boiled in milk, either for invalids or babes; and is valuable in places where delicacies for sick persons cannot easily be procured.

CORN STARCH.

This is an American preparation of Indian corn, which is sold in small packets, in most of the Canadian stores. It is used not only for starching clothes, but as an article of diet; for puddings, custards, and mixed with milk for pap for very young children. I should think a similar preparation could be made by steeping corn, till it be swelled and fermented; bruising it, and pouring off the white floury sediment, as in potato starch; bleaching it, and drying.

BRAN STARCH.

A large supply of good starch can be made by the following process: steep half a bushel of bran in a clean tub or barrel, pouring over it several pailfuls of water. Let it stand in the sun or in the warm kitchen, till it begins to ferment: this is known by the bran swelling, and throwing up bubbles. At the end of a week, if the weather be very warm, it will ferment; but sometimes it will take a fortnight to sour. Stir the mass well up several times; then strain off, squeezing the bran through a canvass cloth, coarse, but quite clean. When the liquor that has been strained has settled, pour off the top, and throw on more fair water; stir up, and again leave it to settle. After repeating the washing process three times, strain once more through a fine sieve or canvass cloth; and when you pour off again, remove the brown, discoloured starch from the surface of the cake that remains in the bottom of the vessel: dry thoroughly, as for potato starch, and tie it in bags for use. Cows or hogs will eat the refuse bran. If you like to blue your starch, it must be done by bluing the last water that you put on, and stirring well; but it is better to blue the water you boil your starch with.

Those who understand the art of dying, use the sour, fermented water that is poured off, in colouring red and scarlet, which are brightened by acid.

PUMPKINS.

This vegetable, or rather fruit, is extensively grown in Canada; being always planted with Indian corn. It is given in the fall of the year to the cattle and swine, which feed upon it eagerly: it is fattening and nourishing, and imparts no bad flavour to the milk, as turnips are apt to do.

Among the old-fashioned settlers, the pumpkin is much esteemed for pies, and a sort of molasses, which they prepare from the fruit by long boiling. When properly made, there is not a better dish eaten than a good pumpkin-pie. Now I must tell you, that an English pumpkin-pie, and a Canadian one, are very differently made, and I must give the preference, most decidedly, to the American dish; which is something between a custard and a cheese-cake, in taste and appearance. I will now give you a recipe or two for

PUMPKIN-PIE.*

Select a good, sweet pumpkin, fully ripe: to ascertain if it be a sweet one, for there is a great difference in this respect, cut a piece of the rind and taste it, or cut several, and then you can judge which is best. The sweetest pumpkins require less sugar, and are much richer.

Pare and cut the fruit into slices, removing the seeds and also the fibrous, spongy part, next to the seeds. Cut it into small pieces, and put it on the fire with about a pint of water, covering the pot close: you are not to bruise or stir it. Should the water boil

---

* I had this recipe from a Canadian lady who is celebrated for the excellence of her pumpkin-pies. I can vouch for their goodness from my own experience.

away so as to endanger the pumpkin burning to the bottom of the pot, a small quantity more of water may be added. It will take three or four hours to boil quite soft, and of a fine brownish yellow. Some improve the colour and richness by setting the pot on a few embers, near the fire, and keeping the pot turned as the pulp browns at the sides: but this requires to be carefully attended to.

When the pumpkin is as soft as mashed turnips, pass it through a hair-sieve or a colander; then add new milk and two or three eggs well beaten, with grated ginger; as much sugar as will make it sweet enough to be pleasant. Pounded and sifted cinnamon is frequently used as spice or nutmeg; but ginger and cinnamon are preferable to any other spice for pumpkin-pies. The milk must not be sufficient to thin the pumpkin too much: it should be about the consistence, when ready for the oven, of finely mashed turnips: if too thin you will need more eggs to set it; but it absorbs a great deal of milk, and is better to stand some little time after the milk is added, before being baked.

Make a nice light paste; line your dishes or plates, and then put in your mixture. These pies are always open; not with a cover of paste over them.

A very rich pumpkin-pie may be made by adding cream, lemon-peel, the juice of a lemon, and more eggs.

A finer dish, than a good pumpkin-pie, can hardly be eaten: and it is within the power of any poor man's family to enjoy this luxury. If you do not grow this fruit, any neighbour will give you one for the asking.

ANOTHER WAY.

Boil your pumpkin, as before directed, for three or four hours; bruise it fine with a beetle, such as you pound potatoes with; mix with new milk, and two or more eggs, as you like: add a little sugar, and ginger or all-spice, and bake in lined tins for half an hour. Some people grate the raw pumpkin on a coarse grater, boil it with a very little water for an hour or so, then add milk by degrees, as long as it will absorb it, keeping it simmering slowly. When well boiled and swelled, let it cool,—when cold, sweeten and season, and bake as in the other receipt.

DRIED PUMPKIN.

Boil down the pumpkin; and when soft, take it out of the pot, spread it on dishes or tins, and set them in the sun or under the stove to dry. When quite dried, pack in paper bags, and hang up in a dry room. This mode will enable you to make pumpkin-pies at any season, when required. Steep it in milk, till it swells and softens, and make your pies as usual.

Some cut the pumpkin in rings, and hang up to dry in the kitchen; but it is apt to mould and turn black: possibly, if dried at once in the sun outside the house, or at night in the oven, it would keep better.

PUMPKIN-MOLASSES.

This article is made by boiling down a quantity of ripe pumpkin for many hours, expressing the juice, and then boiling it down to molasses syrup.

SQUASH.

This is a vegetable of the gourd tribe of plants, and is in much repute with many of the Canadians. It grows very luxuriantly in the new bush-soil without any need of manure. The seeds are either set in a hollow basin, one or two in a place, or on hills; but hollows are considered preferable, as the loose soil dries too much. The same may be observed with respect to cucumbers and melons in new gardens.

Squashes are of various kinds and qualities, and are boiled green, like the vegetable-marrow, or mashed like turnips, with milk and pepper and salt. Squashes, when ripe, are made into pies, in the same manner as pumpkins.

In old gardens manure is necessary for the growth of all this tribe of plants. A good hot-bed for squashes or cucumbers may be made by piling the weeds and rubbish, dried leaves and stalks of vegetables, and covering the mound with several inches of fine mould. On this set your seeds, and you will have a fine crop; besides covering an unseemly object, and making an excellent bed, of the finest soil, for flowers or vegetables of any sort requiring good, rich, mould.

CUCUMBERS AND MELONS.
(Plant, if in open ground, from 18th to 25th May.)

Both these fruits can be raised in Canada without the trouble of making hot beds, and sheltering them with frames, provided your soil be rich enough, and the young plants are protected from the late frosts, which will sometimes, even in the latter part of May, cut both corn and the tender leaves of the melon. It is not commonly the case, but it has happened even in the early part of June. In general the seeds are put in about the 20th of May, and if you wish to bring them on safely, place a square of bricks about each plant: on this lay a pane of glass. Glass costs very little in Canada. This will serve as a frame-light, and you may open and close it at will. Water your plants, and keep the glass over them at night, or till your plants no longer require such care. Spread a little fine hay over the ground between the plants: this will keep in moisture to the roots, and help ripen the fruit. A bit of slate or glass is sometimes laid beneath the fruit to attract the sun's ray. I have seen splendid melons—musk, cantaloupe, rock, and nutmeg-melons—brought to great perfection in the open ground, on new soil. If the summer and fall are fine and sunny, which is generally the case in Canada, you may reckon on having ripe melons in plenty with a little care.

The ends of the shoots, of both melons and cucumbers, should be nipped as soon as the plant shows for bloom, this increases the size of the fruit very considerably.

There is a plan that I have seen recommended in horticultural books for growing cucumbers: this is on a frame of sticks, placed close together, slanting like the pickets of a ha-ha fence. On this the vines are trained, and suffered to grow, stopping the length of the end shoots, to keep them from trailing beyond the frame: or the top of a bush set in the ground for them to climb, has also been recommended: the former plan, if more trouble, is certainly the neatest.

MELONS PRESERVED.

Cut a ripe musk or cantaloupe melon in slices,—remove the seeds,—sprinkle a little white sugar on the fruit, and let it stand for an hour. To every pound of fruit allow three-quarters of a pound of sugar, white, it should be; a dozen cloves, and some ginger, sliced. Now pour off the ju ce [juice] that has run from your fruit,—put it along with the rest of your sugar and spice into a clean skillet or preserving-pan, and boil it up. When boiling put in your melon and boil for half an hour. The peel of a lemon, thinly pared and cut in strips, may be added. The juice of two, squeezed in, greatly improves the preserve, but it may be omitted. This makes a very beautiful looking preserve, of a fine apricot colour. It is very rich; but rather too luscious for some tastes.

The citron-melon is grown especially for preserving; and is a very elegant-looking dish on a supper-table.

TOMATOES.

Canada produces this fruit in great perfection. The culture is simple—a bed of light rich mould should be prepared, on which the seed should be sown in the early part of May; a light dressing of wood ashes sprinkled over the bed saves the young plants from the attack of the fly which is very apt to injure the first seed leaves unless guarded against. The tomato is very hardy and bears transplanting well, as the plant grows very large and bushy in a good soil. You must not set out your tomatoes nearer than three or four feet of each other; a border is best, as the sun and light have better access to them than when planted on a bed. I copy a passage from the "Rochester Horticulturist" which may be useful to the Canadian gardener.

The correspondent of the 'Horticulturist' says, "A trellis on which to train the tomato is easily made by setting stakes behind the row of plants, slanting very considerably backwards; on these laths may be nailed a foot apart, or wires may be stretched. Each branch of the tomatoes will need to be tied at first, but afterwards it will be sufficient to run twine from stake to stake in front of them. Mine have been trimmed and trained in that way for many years. The top buds should be shortened to check their growth. The fruit thus treated is remarkably fine in quality and abundant in quantity."

The tomato is used in many different ways as a dinner vegetable, as a sauce, and even as a tart and wine. I will now add the best receipts for dressing it as a vegetable, and for catsup.

TOMATOES PREPARED AS A VEGETABLE DISH.

Gather ripe tomatoes, remove the stalk, lay them in a deep pan, pour boiling water over them, and remove the skins; put them in a sauce-pan with a little salt, a bit of butter, cayenne pepper, or other pepper if preferred, and one table spoonful of vinegar, stew for half an hour. This is a good sauce for roasted meat.

DRIED TOMATOES.

This is for the convenience of having the benefit of the fruit at any season. The tomatoes are skinned and salted, and set into a vessel in a water bath, and stewed for half an hour; the excess of juice may be drained off, which will do for catsup, then spread the pulp on earthen dishes or plates, and dry them gradually in a cool stove or brick oven; when quite dry hang them in bags in a dry room, and soak when wanted to cook for sauce—but they will require seasoning with pepper and butter.

AN EXCELLENT TOMATO SAUCE.

Wash eight dozen ripe tomatoes, place them in an earthen pan, having divided them in one or two pieces, carefully removing any stalk that may adhere, or any blackened or decayed part; over each layer strew some salt, and let them stand for two days: put them in a preserving pan with the liquor, and boil well for fifteen minutes; then pass the pulp through a colander or coarse sieve to separate the skins from the pulp: to this strained juice add 4 oz. mustard seed, 2 oz. whole pepper, 1 ripe red pepper, having removed the seed; 2 oz. whole ginger, 2 oz. allspice, several cloves of eschalot; boil all together till the pulp is reduced to nearly half the quantity, rub it through the colander and press it with a spoon; a gill of vinegar to wash the pulp clean through from the spices, at last, may be added; bottle when cold, and cork tight down. Those who can afford it, put a teaspoonful of white wine into each bottle the last thing.

PRESERVED TOMATOES.

To three pounds of fresh ripe tomatoes, add the juice, and finely cut peeling of two lemons; boil together with some sliced ginger for one hour, then add 4 lbs. of lump sugar, and boil half an hour longer. This looks like a fine West India preserve.

TOMATO CATSUP.

Pick the ripest fruit, break them up, and strew a good handful of salt among them, let them stand by for a day and a night, boil them with black pepper, cloves, allspice, a red pepper, and a little onion, or eschalot; when the tomatoes are reduced to pulp, let them be poured out to cool in an earthen pan.

When the tomatoes are cold put them through a coarse sieve and bottle them for use. The coarser parts may be put with the spice into a jar, and vinegar poured over them. They will make a good sauce for cold meat, or seasoning for soup and stews.

Fasten down your bottles with paper dipped in white of egg, which will exclude the air.

Green Tomatoes are often put into jars of pickles, and I have been told will make tarts, but I think the rank flavour would not be agreeable, or even wholesome. Tomato catsup is used as a sauce for fish or meat, and also as a seasoning to soups and hashes.

When I make Tomato catsup myself, I allow a table spoonful of strong vinegar to every quart of juice, but most persons make it without vinegar.

Any one who has a good cellar may have a supply of the fresh fruit for use, by taking up the plants before they are ripe, and hanging them on a pole head downwards. They can be ripened in a sunny window, or used green.

[BEANS.]

PRESERVED GREEN FRENCH BEANS.

This is done by gathering the green beans while tender, and throwing them into strong brine, in which a bit of alum is dissolved: fill the vessel, a small cask is best, with the beans till it will hold no more, and is closely packed; lay some straw on the top to keep the beans from floating, and cover them down from the air. Some make no brine, but strew dry salt between the layers of beans:—they should be steeped for some hours to draw out the salt.

LIMA BEANS. *(Time to sow, 18th to 25th May.)*

There are no beans that are more truly valuable to cultivate than the white lima bean; it is a climber, and requires poles to cling to. It is better to be set in hills three feet apart, about four seeds in each hill; three slender poles, seven or eight feet in height, set so as to meet at the top, should be put in at the same time as the seed. With a small hoe earth up the plants when in six or eight leaves, and your labor is done. This bean bears profusely; the crop continues in succession till the oldest beans are ripe. The green beans are very large, and very tender; in moist rich ground they are excellent. The ripe beans are of a pure ivory white colour, flat and kidney-shaped. These beans form a favorite article of vegetable diet in America. The manner of preparing them is as follows:

STEWED BEANS.

Steep the beans, say a quart, in hot water for twenty-four hours, or even longer; boil them, and remove the skins; the water should be changed, and the beans when soft enough, drained and seasoned with pepper, salt and butter. They take three hours to boil soft. Another way is to par-boil a bit of pork, and put it to boil with the beans; then remove the beans to a deep pan or dish, put the pork in the middle, and brown all together in the oven. Beans are a good ingredient in soup, and also as a pudding, made in a similar manner to pease-pudding.

SUBSTITUTES FOR TEA AND COFFEE.

It sometimes happens to persons living at a distance from towns, that their stores of tea and coffee have been exhausted, before a fresh supply can be procured; or the want of ready-money for purchasing these necessary luxuries, has left the poor emigrant to such resources as the herbs of the field offer. Among the old Canadians there are persons intimately acquainted with the virtues of various plants which they frequently make use of instead of tea, and consider them more wholesome than the more palatable Chinese leaf, which we are so accustomed to regard as indispensable to our comfort.

Necessity, no doubt, has taught the old settlers, both in the States and Canada, to adopt certain leaves, roots and berries, as a substitute for the genuine article; and habit has reconciled them to the flavour. Some attribute valuable medicinal properties to their simple infusions, and, possibly, not without reason. The Indians boil the chips and bark of the sassafras, or spice-wood tree, as a luxury, as well as a medicine, and bring it from distant parts of the country. I once tasted the decoction, and found it very pleasant, besides tasting the bark, which had a fine aromatic flavour, like the nutmeg.

Tinctures, essences, and fermented drinks are in high repute, I have been told, in the States: the sassafras is regarded as a fine purifier of the blood.

There is a species of fern, known by the country people by the name of sweet-gale, and sweet fern: it is woody, growing in a slight, waving bush, about three or four feet from the ground: when the leaves are rubbed they give out a delightful, aromatic, spicy odour, which soon goes off. When boiled, it has a slightly resinous taste, with a bitter flavour, that is not very unpleasant. This sweet-fem is in high repute among the Yankee and old Canadian housewifes, as a diet-drink: they attribute to it many excellent virtues, and drink it as we do tea.

It grows only on very light, sandy soil, by wastes on the road side, or at the edge of pine woods. At dewfall, at night, or early in the morning, this shrub gives out a delightful perfume: it is very elegant in form, and in quality tonic and astringent: it has been recommended as a specific for ague. The botanical name is Comptonia asplenifolia.

CEANOTHERS.—NEW-JERSEY TEA.—MOUNTAIN SWEET.

These are the names of another very pretty and fragrant shrub, with white feathery flowers, that have the scent of the flower we used to call Meadow-sweet, and, Queen of the Meadows. It does not grow in the thick forest, but on open plain-lands, such as the Rice-Lake, Brantford, Monaghan and other open, shrubby lands.

The natives use the leaves of this plant as a substitute for tea.—There is nothing injurious in this plant; and like the former one, it is tonic and astringent. I have never tasted the tea made from the leaves of this shrub, but I intend to cure some as a trial of its flavour, adopting the method, as near as I can, practised by the Chinese in drying their teas, heating the leaves in a pan for a few minutes, rolling them with the hand, and letting them cool, and heating them again.

The lumbermen use the New-Jersey tea, when out at their work, and also the Labrador-tea.

LEDUM LATIFOLIUM.—LABRADOR TEA.

This very pretty and singular shrub grows chiefly on the low level banks of swampy, half dried-up lakes. There are two kinds; one that is called marsh rosemary, the leaves bearing a strong resemblance to the shrub rosemary: it has pale, lilac flowers, and bluish-coloured, hard berries, resinous in taste, not unlike juniper-berries in taste and appearance; but it is the broader-leaved that is used as tea by the lumber-ers. The under side of the leaves of this plant, are of a deep rust colour, and soft and cottony: the outer surface is hard and dry, of a deep, dull green: the flowers are white, and very prickly: the whole plant has an aromatic scent, which is rather too powerful in the decoction, for it must be boiled for a few minutes.—Some people highly approve of this beverage. I have tasted it, but disliked the resinous flavour.

PINUS CANADENSIS.—HEMLOCK TEA.

The tops of the hemlock are used by some persons as tea, but I think very few would drink hemlock-tea if they could get a more palatable beverage.

As a remedy for a severe cold, I believe a cup or two of hemlock tea, drunk quite warm in bed, is excellent, as it promotes perspiration; it is also a powerful diuretic, as well as sudorific. Do not be alarmed at the name of *hemlock*; it is not the poisonous plant known by that name, that is here spoken of; but a very beautiful species of pine tree, called the hemlock-spruce, which grows in Canada, in the forests, on poor, rocky soil: it is very hard to cut down, and difficult to burn up: the wood of the hemlock is not much used, it being full of resinous knots, tough and stringy.

There are many other herbs used as tea, but it is better to obtain information from those who are in the practice of testing their qualities.

For substitutes for coffee, the list is endless. Beans, peas, corn, potatoes raw, cut small, and dried-to a brown colour, all through; rye, wheat, and even bread. The very best that I can recommend, is made from the root of the common dandelion.

DANDELION COFFEE.

Dr. Harrison, of Edinburgh, recommended the use of this root, many years ago. It possesses, he says, all the fine flavour and exhilarating properties of coffee, without any of its deleterious effects.—The plant being of a soporific nature, the coffee made from it, when taken in the evening, produces a tendency to sleep, instead of exciting wakefulness, and may be safely used as a substitute for the Arabian berry, (he adds,) "being equal in substance and flavour to the best Mocha coffee." This is going too far: it is the best substitute that has been found, but certainly not equal in flavour to really fine coffee: I will now give my sister, Mrs. Moodie's, recipe for preparing the dandelion-root, and her method of cooking it. "The roots should be carefully washed, but not so as to remove the fine, brown skin which covers them, and which contains the aromatic flavour. The roots, when dry, should be cut up into small pieces, about the size of a kidney-bean, and roasted either in a Dutch-oven, before the fire, or in the stove, stirring them from time to time, to prevent burning: when they are brown through, and crisp, like freshly-roasted coffee, remove them, and let them cool; grind like coffee. Put a small cupful into the coffee-pot, and pour over it a quart of boiling water, letting it boil again for a few minutes: drunk with sugar and cream, this preparation is very little inferior to good coffee."

"Experience," she says, "taught me that the root of this valuable plant was not so good in the Spring as in the Fall. In new clearings this herb abounds, and grows most luxuriantly in the fine new soil.—The best season to collect it is in the month of October, when the potato-crop is being taken up. To persons residing in the bush, to whom tea and coffee may happen to be an expensive article of consumption, the knowledge of this valuable property in a plant spread so abundantly over their fields, may be very useful."

I can speak to the excellence of the dandelion-coffee, having often drunk it, though I do not think I ever succeeded in making it myself, so well as my sister did. I believe that I scraped as well as washed the root, and thus injured instead of improving the flavour. The addition of a small quantity of good coffee would be an improvement, and would be very economical, as the difference would then hardly be detected, between the substitute and the genuine article. The small haricot-bean, browned, and a small quantity of coffee added to it, gives a respectable imitation. The acorns of the white-oak, browned and ground, are also used.

Before I leave the subject of the dandelion, let me observe that it is sometimes blanched, and used as a salad, instead of endive; or boiled as a vegetable.

COFFEE.

The best coffee, or what is here *called so,* sells at 1s. 3d. per lb, in the country stores; but a better article may be got at 1s. per lb, in any of the larger towns, and at 10d., unroasted.

"The reason," says an agricultural journal now before me, "that coffee is seldom well made, is, first, the berries are too hastily roasted, or roasted too much: a light cinnamon is their proper colour. Secondly, the coffee is ground too fine; and thirdly, it is often boiled too much; by which the bitter principle is extracted, and the finer flavour flies off; and fourthly not enough coffee is allowed in the pot."

A FEW REMARKS ABOUT BEER.

There is nothing that the new settler complains more feelingly of, than the want of good beer and ale. Nobody brews beer in their own homes in Canada. Beer can be got in all towns, it is true; but it is not, the emigrants say, like the sweet, well-flavoured, home-brewed beer of the English farm-houses. The reason why so few of the Canadians brew their own beer, arises from several causes: first, that there are so few maltsters; that barley is not very generally grown as a rotation crop: and then, the want of vessels and conveniences for brewing, is an obstacle which it often takes years to overcome; and by that time, the taste for beer has often unhappily been superseded by that of whiskey. I feel assured that if there were more private families who brewed beer, there would be a thousandfold less whisky drunk in this colony. As there is no prohibition in Canada, against people malting their own barley, I think it would be wise for every farmer to grow a small quantity of this useful grain, and learn the practice of malting it: they might not perhaps, produce at first, as fine a flavoured malt as what they had been accustomed to purchase at home, from the malster; but one that would supply them with a very palatable beer, and at a very little cost: the hops they can grow in their own garden; every one cultivates this plant on account of it being an indispensable ingredient in making barm for raising the household bread, besides shading and adorning their verandahs, by its luxuriant foliage and graceful flowers. The bush-settler has, however, little time to attend to malting and brewing; but those who reside upon old cleared farms, would find no great difficulty in supplying themselves with beer of their own manufacturing, at a small expenditure of time and trouble. Many of the cotters' wives in Suffolk, used to make a cheap sort of beer for the use of their families, from treacle, hops, bran and water, with yeast to ferment it.—This they might also make in Canada. During the very hot weather, some cooling and strengthening beverage is much required by men who have to work out in the heat of the sun; and the want of it is often supplied by whisky diluted with water, or by cold water, which, when drunk in large quantities, is dangerous to the health, and should, if possible, be avoided.

Instead of the usual allowance of strong beer and harvest-cakes, at four o'clock in the afternoon; tea or coffee, with bread and butter, pancakes or cakes, are carried out into the field as a refreshment.—They have supper on their return, at seven or eight at night.

There are no harvest frolics held here, as in England. The practice seems altogether laid aside. No gleaners are ever seen in Canadian harvest-fields. Perhaps this very circumstance will show that the poor man does not require such a means of increasing his store: he reaps his own field, and his own hogs and fowls are the gleaners that gather up that which his own hand has scattered.

TREACLE-BEER.

To a five-gallon cask allow four pounds treacle: boil a large handful of hops in a gallon of water, for an hour: strain the liquor off the hops into your cask: add the treacle: fill up with water, to which put one pint of yeast: in two days bottle it, but do not cork till the third: it will be fit to drink in two days after corking.

MAPLE-BEER.
(See that article.)

BEET BEER.

Clean and well scrape and wash six sugar or white beets: cut them in slices, and boil for two or three hours in six gallons of spring water: when the liquor is as sweet as beer-wort, strain it into a small cask: add to this the liquor in which you have boiled down a good handful of hops: when cooled to blood-heat, add a teacupful of good rising: set your cask in a warm place, till the fermentation takes place: when the beer has worked for two or three days, fill up the cask, and set it in a cool cellar: it will be ready in a week or ten days for drinking.

BEET-VINEGAR.

This is made in the same way; only, instead of stopping, let the fermentation go on, and keep the vessel open in a warm place near the fire, for some weeks, and you will have a beautiful vinegar of a fine colour.

BEET–MOLASSES.

Boil down for some hours, white sugar-beets, with one or two blood-beets to colour the liquor of a fine red. When the liquor is very sweet, remove the beets, and strain through a flannel-bag: beat up two eggs, and pour into the beet-syrup, taking care that it be quite cool: return it to the fire; and when the scum rises, remove it carefully: it must now boil fast, and be reduced to a thick syrup, as in maple molasses. Those who dislike the sweetness of the beet-molasses, may sharpen it by adding a little lemon-juice, or the juice of any acid fruit: it is a lovely colour, and, in the absence of other preserve, is useful and wholesome, and costs nothing but the trouble of boiling down.

MAPLE–SUGAR.

This little volume would be incomplete unless it contained some instruction on the making of maple sugar, though the manufacturing of this Canadian luxury, is no longer considered so important a matter as it used formerly to be: the farmer, considering that his time can be more profitably employed in clearing his land, will not give his attention to it, for maple sugar is less an article of trade than it used to be. The West India sugars are now to be bought at 4d per lb., or if you pay a dollar you can get 14 lbs. of good soft sugar. The price of maple sugar is never less than 3d., but 5d. for many years, was the standard price if it were good, now there is little call for maple sugar, muscovado being quite as cheap. Still there are situations and circumstances under which the making of maple-sugar may be carried on with advantage.

Fig. 13 · A settler family undertaking their annual harvest of maple syrup and sugar, page 140 of the first edition (1854 [1855]), reproduced from the printing of the second thousand.

There will always be a class of emigrants who, for the sake of becoming the proprietors of land will locate themselves in the backwoods, far from the vicinity of towns and villages, who have little money to expend, and who are glad to avail themselves of so wholesome and so necessary a luxury at no greater cost than their own labour.

With the assistance of the children and the females of the house, a settler may, if he have a good sugar bush, make several hundred weight of sugar in a season, besides molasses and vinegar. Many a stout boy of fourteen or fifteen, with the aid of the mother and young ones, has made sugar enough to supply the family, besides selling a large quantity. In the backwoods the women do the chief of the sugar making; it is rough work, and fitter for men; but Canadians think little of that. I have seen women employed in stronger work than making sugar. I have seen women underbrushing, and even helping to lay up and burn a fallow, and it grieved me, for it was unfit for them.

We will suppose that the settler has resolved upon making sugar. The first thing is to look out for a good sugar bush, where he can be sure of a hundred or two hundred of good trees standing not very far from each other. In the centre of his bush he should fix upon a boiling place: a fallen pine, or any large tree should be chosen: if there be not one ready felled, he must cut one down, as he needs a good lasting back log against which to build his fire at the boiling time; but there are other requisites to be attended to: a certain number of troughs, hollowed out of small pine, black ash, basswood, and sundry other kinds of wood; one or more troughs to each tree; if the trees be large, two, and even three troughs are placed, and so many incisions made in the bark with the axe, into which spills of cedar are inserted; these are made with a hollow sort of chisel; but some do not take much pains, and only stick a flat slip of shingle, slanting from the gash in the bark, to direct the flow of the sap to the trough. The modes of tapping are various: some use the augur and bore a hole, which hurts the tree the least; some cut a chip out across the bark, and cut two sweeping lines down so as to give the sap two channels to flow in; others merely gash the bark with a slanting cut, and insert the spill.

My brother, Mr. Strickland, in his work on Canada, gives very good instructions on this subject.

There should be a large trough hewed out almost as big as an Indian canoe, or barrels, placed near the boiling place for a store trough; into this the sap is collected: as fast as the smaller ones fill, the boys and women empty their contents into pails, and the pails into the large receptacle. The boiling place is made by fixing two large stout forked posts into the ground, over which a pole is laid, stout enough to support the kettles; ironwood is good for this purpose; on this the kettles are hung at a certain height above the fire. A hoop, with a piece of clean coarse serge or flannel sewed over it, serves for a strainer; the edge of the pots should be rubbed with clean lard to prevent the sap boiling over. It is a common plan, but I think by no means a nice one, to keep a bit of pork or fat bacon suspended by a string above the sap kettles: when the boiling sap reaches this it goes down: but I think my plan is better, and certainly more delicate. If possible have more than one kettle for boiling down; a constant change from the pots facilitates the work: as the first boiling decreases, and becomes sweeter, keep adding from the others, and filling them up with cold sap. A ladleful of cold sap thrown in at boiling point, will keep it down. Attention and care is now all that is required. The one who attends to the boiling should never leave his business; others can gather the sap and collect wood for the fires. When there is a good run, the boiling down is often carried on far into the night. If heavy rain occurs, it is better to empty the sap-troughs, as the sap would be too much weakened for boiling. The usual month for sugar-making is March, though I have known some years in which sugar was made in February. By the middle of April the sap is apt to get sour if kept many hours, and will not grain. If you have sap kept rather long, put salaratus in till it foams a little; but it is seldom that good sugar is made from acid sap. A handful of quick-lime, some prefer to cure sour sap. The best run of sap occurs when a frosty night is followed by a warm sunny day. If cold weather set in after the trees have been tapped, it is sometimes necessary to tap them a second time.

After the sap has been boiled down to thin molasses, it is then brought in to be sugared off. The syrup must be carefully strained through a woollen strainer; eggs are then beaten up, with the shells, and poured into the cold syrup, which is now ready for boiling into thick syrup, or for sugaring off.

Where the sugar bush is far from the house, some persons prefer having a small shanty put up, of logs, and thatched with bark; it may be built so as to enclose a large stump, to which may be affixed a wooden crane, by means of a socket in which, the upright part of the crane can be made to move; to the cross beam of the crane the pots can be hung, and a fire, with a few large stones or a great log at the back, fixed, lighted beneath. The advantage of the crane is this: that if the syrup boil too fast to be kept down; by aid of a wooden hooked stick, or a bit of chain affixed to the upper limb, it can be moved forward in an instant from the fire.

Care must be taken to watch the syrup, ladle in hand, till the scum is seen to rise in a thick mass, which it does just a minute or two before boiling commences; this scum is then to be taken off with a skimmer or ladle, and if this part of the business be well done, the sugar will be good and bright, and clear-looking. It is the want of care in clarifying the sugar, that gives it the dark look and bitter taste that many persons object to in maple sugar. Keep removing the scum, as it rises from time to time; if it has been well scummed the syrup will look as clear as the finest Madeira wine. Rub the edge of the kettle with clean lard or butter when you first set it over the fire, but do not depend on this preventative for boiling over, as when near sugaring, the liquid is very thick, and rises rapidly. It is prudent always to keep a little cool stuff by you to throw in, should it rise too fast. Towards the close of the boiling, the greatest care and watchfulness is required. When the syrup boils in thick yellow foam, and the whole pot seems nothing but bubbles, the sugar is nearly come; it then drops ropy from the ladle, and experienced sugar makers can tell by blowing it off the edge of the ladle, if it be done; it then draws into long, bright threads that easily stiffen when cool. Others drop a little into a pail of cold water, when, if it hardens, they say it is ready to pour out into pails or pans, or any convenient vessel. Most persons grease the pans or moulds before they pour the syrup into them, that it may turn out easily.

Much maple sugar is spoiled in its quality by being over-boiled. It is true it hardens more readily, but loses in excellence of grain and colour.

In the course of two or three days the sugar will be formed into a solid cake, and may be turned out; but if you wish to have a good fine grained sugar, after turning it out of the moulds, pierce the bottoms of the cakes, and set them across sticks, over a clean vessel; a sugar trough will do, and the wet molasses will drain out, which will improve the look of your sugar, render it easier to break up for use, and removes any coarse taste, so that you may put it as a sweetener into cakes, puddings, tea, or coffee, and it will be as nice as the best muscovado.

The larger coarse-grained maple-sugar, which looks like sugar candy, is made by not over-boiling the syrup, pouring it into shallow pans, and letting it dry slowly in the sun, or a warm room. This I like better than the cake sugar, but it is not so convenient to store. To those who have few utensils or places to put things in, as a sweetmeat for eating, the dark heavy-looking sugar is liked the best, but I prefer the sparkling good grained sugar, myself, for all purposes.

The Indian sugar, which looks dry and yellow, and is not sold in cakes, but in birch boxes, or mowkowks, as they call them, I have been told, owes its peculiar taste to the birch bark vessels that the sap is gathered in, and its grain to being kept constantly stirred while cooling. I have been told that a small bit of lime put into the syrup whitens the sugar. Milk is used to clarify, when eggs are not to be had, but I only made use of eggs. Four eggs I found enough for one boiling of sugar.

As I know of no better authority for the process of making sugar than that of my brother, Major Strickland, I shall avail myself of his directions, and abridge from his last volume, 18th chapter, such passages as may add to the settler's knowledge, what I have already collected from my own experience, and other sources.

He says, "The settler having selected his sugar-bush, should underbrush, and clean the surface of the ground, by removing all rotten logs, and fallen trees. It should be surrounded by a fence, to hinder the cattle from drinking the sap, and upsetting the sap-troughs, which they are very apt to do to the great loss and annoyance of the sugar-boiler. The boiling site should be as near to the centre of the bush as possible, from which roads wide enough to admit of the movements of a sleigh and oxen, should be cut in every direction."

"Settlers commonly suspend the boilers over the fire, from a thick pole, by means of iron chains; but this is liable to accidents. The best plan is to build the sugar kettles into an arch,* either in the open air, or in a small shanty built for the purpose of sugaring off."

"A store trough should be made from the trunk of a large white pine, capable of holding from fifty to one hundred pails of sap. This should be placed near the boilers, and any empty casks or barrels may also be mustered in case of a good run."

"In a good season from eight to twelve hundred pounds of sugar and molasses can be made with five hundred sap troughs. Let the troughs be made of pine, black ash, cherry, or butternut, capable of holding three or four gallons each."

"No sap wood should be left in making the troughs as it is sure to rot them. As soon as the season is over, let the boys collect all the troughs, and set them upon end, against the North side of the tree, which preserves them from cracking with the sun."

"If the farmer desires, as of course he will, to preserve his sugar bush, the best way is to tap the tree on the South, or sunny side, with an inch and quarter augur, and use hollow spills. Care must be taken to set the trough directly under the drop, and as level as possible. Many use the axe only, in tapping, but this soon kills the tree."

---

* This no doubt is a good plan when sugaring is carried on with good help, and on a large scale; but where women and boys do the work, it would hardly, I fear, be carried into effect.—ED. [ED is the short form for editor. Here it refers to Traill's agent, Henry Hope.]

"The sap runs best after a frosty night, followed by a warm sunny day, and brisk westerly wind. The tap should be made in the early part of the season, on the South, and when it requires removing later, on the North."

"The most expeditious way of gathering the sap is to drive through the roads with the ox sled, on which a puncheon or barrel is securely fixed; in the bung-hole of this receptacle, a wooden tun dish should be inserted, large enough to hold a pail of sap; in the hollow of this a bit of tin or iron punched full of holes is inserted to act as a strainer."

"As soon as a sufficiency of sap has been stored, and the kettles filled, the fires are lighted, and boiling begins, and should now be kept up night and day, till a sufficiency for a batch of sugar has been boiled down into thin molasses. It is then allowed to cool, and settle, and should be poured into the sugaring vessel, free of the sediment. Eggs are then beaten up—six will clarify fifty pounds of sugar. The beaten eggs are stirred into the cool liquor, the pot slung on the crane, and *as it rises to the boil,* the thick black scum, must be instantly removed. If properly scummed, the liquor will be bright and clear as white wine."

"Great attention must now be paid by the sugar-boiler; he must not leave his station, unless his post be taken by a careful hand. The liquid, as it thickens, is continually rising to the surface, and unless watched with care, would boil over; it is well to keep a little always cooling at hand to dash in in case of a sudden rise."

"To the uninitiated, the greatest difficulty is to know when the liquid has attained a sugaring point. When it boils in one continued yellow froth, throwing up jets and puffs of steam, it is not far from being ready; but to try this, take a thin bit of wood, in this make a narrow hole an inch long, and an eighth of an inch wide, if this is dipped into the molasses, a fine thin film will fill the hole, which, if blown, will throws out a long-shaped bubble, if the sugar is sufficiently boiled. Some can tell by blowing a thread of it from the edge of a ladle, or by dropping it on the snow, when, if hard, it is done, and the sugar may be poured out into pans to granulate."

"Sugar-making," adds the writer of the above, "is one of the most laborious occupations, while it lasts, yet a vast quantity of maple sugar is yearly made in the back woods by the joint operations of the settlers' wives, and their children and though it takes place at the most changeable and unpleasant season of the year, when the frosts and thaws are alternate, and the work is done in the wet snow, it is very rarely that you hear of ague attacking the sugar-makers. March and April are not the seasons for ague; it is in the hotter months this disease prevails."

NOTE.—I have given this useful extract from Mr. Strickland's work, "Twenty-seven year's experience in Canada West," because it embraces some valuable points of advice on the subject, very clearly expressed, and as the price of his book places it beyond the reach of a large proportion of the emigrants and poorer settlers, I considered it was conferring a benefit upon my readers.

MAPLE SYRUP.

This beautiful addition to the table is simply a portion of the syrup, taken out when it begins to thicken to the consistency of virgin honey. It sells at nine pence or ten pence a-quart readily; if for use in your own family, boil it rather longer, and cork it tight, setting it by in a cool cellar to keep it from fermentation. It is used as sauce for pancakes, puddings, and to eat with bread. Those persons who do not think it worth their while to make sugar, will often make a gallon or two of molasses. Some call it maple honey, and indeed it comes nearer to honey in taste, and consistency, than to treacle.

MAPLE SUGAR SWEETIES.

When sugaring off, take a little of the thickest syrup into a saucer, stir in a very little fine flour, and a small bit of butter, and flavor with essence of lemon, peppermint, or ginger, as you like best; when cold, cut into little bricks about an inch in length. This makes a cheap treat for the little ones. By melting down a piece of maple sugar, and adding a bit of butter, and flavouring, you can always give them sweeties, if you think proper to allow them indulgencies of this sort.

MAPLE VINEGAR.

Those persons who make maple sugar generally make a keg of vinegar, which, indeed, is highly advisable; no house should be without it; it is valuable, both as an article of diet, and medicine; and as it is easily made, and costs nothing but the labour, I shall give directions how to make it.

At the close of the sugar-making season, in the month of April, the sap loses much of its sweetness, and when boiled down, will not make sugar, but it will make good vinegar:—for this purpose it will only be necessary to reduce five pails of sap to one by boiling; twenty-five gallons of sap, boiled down to five, will fill your little five gallon keg; but it is better to boil rather more, as you will need some after the fermentation is over to fill up the vessel. This is the common proportion, five pails reduced to one; but I do not think that six to one would be too much to allow in boiling down. While blood-warm, strain the liquor into the vessel, and pour in half a tea-cupful of rising; set the cask in the chimney corner, or at the back of the stove, and let it work as long as it will, then lay a bit of glass over the bunghole to keep out dust, and let it stand where it will keep moderately warm for some weeks. It will be fit for use by the summer; if it is too weak put a little more sugar to it.

In the hot weather a nice cooling drink can he made with a quart of hot water, a large spoonful of maple syrup, and as much vinegar as will sharpen it; when quite cold, grate a little nutmeg on it, or drop a little essence of lemon, to flavour it. This is very refreshing in harvest weather.

MAPLE BEER.

This is made with sap, boiled down as for vinegar, to which a large handful of hops boiled, and the liquor strained in, is added, with barm to ferment it; some add sprigs of spruce, others bruised ginger.

MAPLE WINE.

Boil down six pails of sap to one, in proportion to the quantity you wish to make. Set it to ferment with a little yeast, and stop it soon; let it stand in a cool cellar after it is bunged. It may be drunk in a few weeks, as it has not much body, and would soon sour. A finer wine may be made with sap, boiled down, adding a quarter of a pound of raisins split.

This wine should be made when the sap is at its best; it is not prudent to defer it till the end of the season. Birch wine can be made in the same way, only it requires sugar, as there is much less sweetness in the sap of the birch, than in that of the sugar maple. From the soft, or swamp-maple, no sugar can be made, but a strong black ink is made from boiling the bark, and setting the color with copperas; a little sugar is necessary, or a small quantity of gum-arabic to give it gloss, and consistency; many settlers use no ink, but that which they manufacture themselves.

CURING OF MEAT.

The cutting up and salting of meat is attended to in most farmhouses by the men, but sometimes it falls to the lot of the settlers' wives, and it is necessary that they should possess some knowledge of the process, as circumstances may oblige them to take an active part in the business, or give directions to their servants, as the case may be.

The meat should be hung in a cool place till it is stiff: it may then be cut up for salting. The usual way of dividing the hog is to take off the head; cut out the hams, and fore legs, ham shape; and divide the rest of the carcass in pieces, which are cut clean through, chine fashion. These are rubbed and packed in clean salt, as tight as the barrel can be packed, and the barrel is then filled up with strong brine. A barrel of pork, containing nothing but the side pieces, should contain two cwt. of *pork*. This sells at the highest market price, and goes by the name of "MESS PORK." "Prime mess" contains the hams and shoulders, as well as sides, and sells for less. And "PRIME," which is the whole hog cut up indiscriminately, is the lowest in market value; but a barrel of either must weigh two cwt. of meat.[18] Hams are sometimes sold separately at 6d. or 7d. per lb., dried or smoked. Pigs are often sent to market, or to the stores in a frozen state, and sold by the cwt. In purchasing a barrel of pork, it is necessary to ascertain the sort of meat you are buying, and not to pay for "Prime" or "Prime Mess" the same as for "Mess." As the emigrant, on first commencing house-keeping, is obliged to provide stores of this sort, it is well that he should be on his guard against imposition. And when the storekeeper sees that his customer is not ignorant of these matters, he will be less disposed to take unfair advantage of him. Always endeavour to make your dealings with persons of respectability of character. And now to return to the curing of the meat for household use.

18 "Cwt" is the short form for hundredweight. See page 315.

PICKLE FOR HAMS, CHEEKS, AND SHOULDERS.

*Fourteen pounds of good salt, half a pound of saltpetre, two quarts of molasses or four pounds of coarse brown sugar, with water enough to dissolve the salt, and a pint of good beer or of vinegar, if you can command either. Bring this liquor to a boil, and scum off all the impurities that may rise to the surface. When cold, pour this over your hams, which should be cold, but not frozen. The addition of pepper, allspice, and cloves is made by some who like a high flavour to the hams. The hams should remain in this pickle six or eight weeks; being turned and basted every two or three days, and then hung in the smoke-house. The best woods for smoking are: sugar-maple chips, hickory, birch, corn-cobs, white ash, and beech. When removed from the smoke-house, sew each ham in any old linen or cotton cloth, and if you give this covering a coating of whitewash, with a whitewash brush, it will preserve it from the flies. There is a small dusky beetle, with two dull red or orange bars across its body, which injures meat more than the flies: it deposits its eggs in the skin and joints. These eggs turn to a hairy worm, which destroy the meat; and unless some precautions are taken, will render it unfit for use. If you find by examining the hams, that the enemy has been at work, I would recommend a large boiler or kettle of water to be put on the fire, and when it boils, immerse each ham in it for five or even ten minutes. Take them out, and when dry, rub them over with bran or saw dust, and pack them in a box of wood ashes, or of oats, as the Yorkshire farmers do: you will have no trouble with the weevil again. To preserve pork free from taint, or to restore it if it be injured, pack charcoal in the barrels. The use of charcoal as a preserver of meat is very great: I have restored meat that was much injured, by first putting off the bad brine—scraping the meat—and washing it in cold water—burning some cedar-bark in the barrel, and repacking the meat, laying lumps of charcoal between the layers of meat, a strong brine being again poured on to cover it.

A pint of the drippings from the stove-pipe joints added to the brine will also re-store meat, and give it the flavour of smoke,— or a small quantity of pyroligneous acid. Where the brine has been allowed to stand in barrels too long, the burning of cedar-bark in them will purify them for use. A bad cellar may be purified by the same means, care being taken to secure the building from danger of fire. Where roots have

---

* This quantity will be sufficient for two cwt. of meat. In salting down meat, it is better to have one to rub the meat, and another strong hand to pack into the barrel. Some prefer meat dry-salted to pickling it.

been kept in a cellar for any time, such purification is very essential in the spring of the year.

PRIZE HAM.

Rub your ham, which should be of fine-grained, well-fed pork, when quite cold, with fine salt, to which add a little red pepper, and half a pint of molasses. Let it remain in the pickle, basting and turning it for six weeks. Then hang it up, and smoke for six weeks. About the first week in April take it down; wash it in cold water, and rub it over with unleached ashes.[19] If you have any number of hams, let them lie for a week, heaped together; then hang them in a cool room, having sewed them in canvass or old cotton covers. (Hamilton[20] prize ham.)

TO BOIL HAM.

Soak it over night in soft water; wrap a lock of sweet hay about it, and boil in plenty of water, three, or if very large, four hours: let the ham remain in the water to cool gradually. Next day remove the skin, and trim all unsightly parts away: the ham will retain its flavour and juice much better than if skinned hot: this of course can only be adopted when you do not require to serve the joint up hot to table: in that case skin it; grate crumbs of bread over the surface and let it stand a few minutes in the oven to crisp the bread crumbs.

BACON TO PREPARE FOR SMOKING OR DRYING.

Having taken off the hams from a side of pork, chop the rib-bones close to the back, so as to remove the back-bone the entire length of the side. With a sharp knife, raise all the small long bones from the meat, and trim all rugged portions carefully away. Then mix a pound of coarse sugar to 2 oz. of saltpetre, and 4 lb. of salt. Rub this well over the meat on all sides: two sides of bacon will not be too much for the above quantity. Cut them in two pieces, and lay each piece above the other, the rind downward, and strew the remainder of the salt mixture over the last piece. A shallow wooden-trough or tray, with a hole and peg at the bottom, is the best to salt your bacon in: it should be placed a little sloping forward. Every second day, draw off the liquor that runs from the meat, into a vessel, and carefully pour it over the meat

19 Unleached ashes refers to ashes straight from the hearth, which, not having been boiled, still contain lye.

20 This Hamilton is the township bordering Lake Ontario and the western part of Rice Lake, not the town on the escarpment at the western end of Lake Ontario.

again, having first shifted the bottom pieces to the top. In six weeks time, take them out; rub with bran, and lay on the rack to dry, or smoke them: this process makes excellent meat.

————————

Much of the goodness of pork, ham, and bacon depends upon the meat itself—the breed of hogs—and their treatment in fattening.

A great deal of the barrels of pork sold in the stores, is coarse, loose, flabby pork—distillery-fed, or else nut-fed; the swine having nearly fattened themselves in the woods on beech-mast, acorns, and such food. This pork is known by its soft, oily fat; the meat running away to oil, in the act of frying. Of course, meat like this is not profitable to the buyer. Such meat is better dried or smoked, than eaten fresh from the pickle. It is better to purchase your meat fresh of some respectable farmer, or salt it yourself, or buy well-dried meat, though you must, of course, give a higher price for it. By referring to the market-table,[21] you may ascertain the prices of meat, both salt and fresh.

————————

Here is an excellent recipe, furnished by a gentleman, who considers it the best in use: I have eaten excellent meat at his table thus treated.

PICKLE FOR BEEF OR PORK.

To three gallons of pickle, strong enough to float an egg, add ½lb. of alum, 1qt. of treacle, 1oz. of potash; mix them well together; pack the beef or pork, and pour the pickle on it; cover it close: in about three weeks it will be fit for use. *The meat must not be salted,* but packed as it comes from the butcher, and the pickle poured over it.

————————

LARD.

This is made from the inner or kidney-fat of the hog. It should be cut up in small portions, and boiled down on a slow fire. Let the fat boil till all the oil is extracted; but be careful not to let it burn. When it has ceased to make a noise, be on the watch:

21 This comment was probably added by Traill's publisher Thomas Maclear or her agent Henry Hope. The Appendix added to the first and second printings of Traill's text but not reproduced here contains a series of market tables showing such information as food prices, rail-road fees, agricultural advice, and equivalences between currencies.

it is ready to strain off into clean, dry jars. The best, are the stone-jars, with covers to them: these can be bought in any of the stores: they are made in this country, or in the States. The coarse red pottery is very cheap. It is manufactured in large quantites [quantities], in many parts of the Province; and is used in dairies, and for all kinds of household purposes.

Lard sells at 6d. and 7d. per lb. in the market at Toronto: it used formerly to be much cheaper. It is now used as a substitute for oil, in parlour lamps.

VENISON.

They who live in the backwoods, often have venison brought in, either by their own people or by the Indian hunters, who gladly exchange it for salt-pork, flour, or vegetables. A few hints as to the best method of dressing this meat may not be quite unacceptable to the Canadian settler's wife.

TO ROAST VENISON.

The best joints to roast are the haunch and the loins, which last should be cut saddle fashion, viz., both loins together.

If the deer be fat and in good season, the meat will need no other basting than the fat which runs from it; but as it is often lean, it will be necessary to use lard, butter, or slices of fat bacon to assist the roasting. Venison should be cooked with a brisk fire—basted often—and a little salt thrown over it: it is better not overdone. Being a meat very open in the grain and tender, it readily parts with its juices, and takes less time to roast than any other meat.

BROWN FRICASSEE OF VENISON.

Fry your steaks quite brown, in hot dripping; put them in a stew-pan with a very little water, a bunch of sweet herbs, a small onion, a clove or two, and pepper and salt. When it has boiled for a few minutes, roll a bit of butter in flour, with a table-spoon-ful of catsup or tomato-sauce, and a tea-spoonful of vinegar; stir this into the fricassee, and dish it quite hot.

FRIED VENISON.

Cut your meat in suitable pieces: dust them with flour, and season with pepper and salt; fry in boiling lard, or with some nice thin slices of ham or fat bacon. A little seasoning of onion in the gravy may be added, if not disagreeable. A little dust of flour in the pan, with a table-spoonful of boiling water, and a little tomato-catsup will make the gravy.

VENISON-PIE.

Season your pieces of venison with pepper and salt, a little allspice, and three or four cloves; flour each steak as you lay it in the dish; pour in a tea-cupful of water, and cover the dish with a nice short crust. If the meat be very lean, a few slices of ham or bacon will improve the pie.—Small balls made with crumbs of bread, chopped ham, parsley shred fine, seasoned with pepper, and made up with an egg improves the pie.

VENISON-SOUP.

The leanest and worst pieces of the deer will make an excellent soup, if boiled down long enough. A handful of Indian rice may be put in when first set on the fire, but should be soaked in water for an hour or two, and drained and picked clean before adding it to the soup. Season the soup with onions and sweet herbs, pepper and salt. The meat after long cooking will be of little worth, as all the good and nourishing qualities have been parted with in the soup.

CORNED VENISON.

When you have more fresh meat of this kind than you think will keep good, rub it with salt, and hang it in the root-house or dairy.

VENISON-HAM.

Make a mixture of sugar, salt, and a very little saltpetre; rub the haunch well with this every day, for three weeks; hang it to smoke for three more. It is very good grated, or if dried, cut in thin shavings, as a relish with bread and butter for tea or breakfast, with salad.

Jerked venison is the flesh cut in strips, and dried in the open air.

BEEF.

Beef needs to be well packed in the barrel, and a good deal of salt strewn at the bottom. Strew a handful of salt between each layer of meat, and then make a brine that will float a middle-sized potato. To this add a quarter of a pound of saltpetre, which always improves the colour of pickled meat, and four pounds of coarse sugar. Boil your brine; scum it, and when cold, pour over your beef: it should be quite covered, and a lid put on the barrel. Unless you need beef for immediate use, say a week or ten days, no salt need be rubbed on. If you want dried beef, remove a joint—the half leg is best—from the pickle, after a month's time, and hang it up to dry,—or season a leg with the same pickle as you use for hams, adding 2oz. of allspice, ¼ oz. of cloves, and 2oz. of black pepper to your pickle. Let it be turned and basted daily for six weeks, then hang it to dry and smoke. This is usually shaved, and eaten with no other cooking than what the drying process gives.

———

As this is not a regular cookery-book; but is confined to the preparing of food, as practised in this country, it will be unnecessary to give all the various methods of cooking beef or other meats, as commonly practised, and which can be taught by any cookery-book.—It is my aim, in this work, to supply the female settler with information to meet her daily wants; and to put her in the best way of acquiring the knowledge she needs in making use of what material she has at her command, and turning them to the best advantage, with the least expenditure of money and trouble.

———

CANADIAN PARTRIDGES.

These birds, which are of two different varieties,—the spruce partridge, and the ruffed grouse, are more like the pheasant than the English partridge—the meat being white instead of brown; but they have not the high gamy flavour of either the partridge or pheasant. They are, when in season, very good eating; but about the end of the winter, the flesh becomes dry and bitter. This arises from the nature of their food, which, in the thick woods, consists chiefly of the resinous buds of the spruce, the bark and buds of the birch, and some berries, which they find beneath the snow; with various mosses and lichens, which give an astringent taste to the flesh. At all other seasons they are very good and fleshy, and are excellent roasted and stuffed with fine bread crumbs, pepper, salt, a little butter, and sweet herbs. They require much basting, as they have no fat in themselves. Half an hour, with a good fire, will cook a partridge. To stew them, cut them up, dust with a little flour, pepper, salt, and stew gently with a small quantity of water; thicken with a little cream, flour, and a little nutmeg, grated; serve with toasted bread cut as sippets, at the edge of the dish.

———

PIGEONS.

During the spring and summer months, numbers of pigeons linger to breed in the Canadian woods, or pass over in straggling flocks, when they are shot in numbers by the settlers. These birds are good any way you cook them: roasted or in pies.

ROAST PIGEONS.

Pluck and draw your birds; mix bread crumbs with a little parsley chopped fine, some butter, pepper and salt; put a little into the body of each bird; lard and roast them: twenty minutes, with a good fire, is long enough. The basting will serve for gravy,—or add a little butter, and a very little boiling water after you have taken up the birds, and heat it in the pan your pigeons were roasted in.

PIGEONS IN CRUST.

Stuff your birds as above, and cover each one with a thin crust, of short pastry; bake half an hour.

PIGEON-PIE.

Season your pigeons well with pepper and salt; as many as will lie in your pie-dish; dust a little flour on, thin; add a cup of hot water; cover your pie, and bake an hour.

POT-PIE.

Pigeons stuffed, larded, and cooked in a bake-kettle, are very nice; and are tenderer, and more savoury than when baked in the stove. To make a pot-pie of them, line the bake-kettle with a good pie-crust; lay in your birds, with a little butter put on the breast of each, and a little pepper shaken over them, and pour in a tea-cupful of water—do not fill your pan too full; lay in a crust, about half an inch thick; cover your lid with hot embers, and put a few below. Keep your bake-kettle turned carefully, adding more hot coals on the top, till the crust is cooked. This makes a very savoury dish for a family.

Pigeons are best for table just after wheat harvest: the young birds are then very fat.

BLACK SQUIRRELS.

These little animals are often found in great numbers, in the beech and oak-woods in Canada, and are considered very delicate food; being free from any strong flavour. They are roasted like rabbits, or cut in pieces and fried, fricasseed, or made into stews or pies. Some people object to them, simply because they have not been accustomed to see them brought to table, or even to hear of their being used as an article of food, and others consider them as insipid. This last objection is, perhaps, the most weighty; but by seasoning them well, it may be overcome. Nothing can be more cleanly than the habits of these little creatures; their food consisting entirely of grain, or fruits, or vegetables. When fresh meat is scarce, as it often is in the woods, the black and even the red squirrel may be eaten, as a wholesome change of diet. The lumberers and hunters will use the musk-rat, porcupine, and beaver for food, and even the wood-chuck or groundhog, which is a species of marmot. But though its food is vegetable, it is very fat and oily; and does not make pleasant meat. The bear is also made meat of by the backwoodsman. The meat when cooked, either roasted or boiled, is like coarse beef, and would pass for such, if a person was not told to the contrary. The bear is certainly a more cleanly feeder than the hog. The hams, when well cured, are considered very excellent.

CANADIAN HARE.

This is another of the native wild animals. It is not so well-flavoured as the English hare, or so large; being in size and colour more like a white rabbit. The colour in spring and summer is brown, but it grows white at the approach of the cold weather. They are taken by snares set among the bushes, in their run-ways, which are easily detected in the snow. They frequent cedar-swamps, and also abound on the Plains-lands. The meat is dark coloured, like the common hare. They are inferior to that animal; but make a pleasant variety to the salt meat; and may be cooked either roasted like rabbits, stewed, fried, or made into pies. The fur of the Canadian hare is very worthless: it is loose, and comes off at a touch.

The snipe and woodcock are cooked the same as in other countries; and the quail, which abounds in some districts, may be dressed like the partridge.

WILD DUCKS.

Wild fowl of this kind abounds on the shores of lakes and rivers, or any open, marshy spots. Some of these birds are excellent; others fishy. The best are: the canvass-back, the red-headed duck, the swamp or blue-billed duck; the ring-necked, the mallard, the winter duck, wood-duck, and blue-winged teal, are among the best; but there are many others that can be eaten. The usual mode of cooking, and the best is, to roast them.

The feathers and down of all these water birds are valuable, and should not be thrown away; as they sell well, and are of great value in a household, for beds and pillows. It is best to put them in paper bags, and hang them in a dry place, till you have collected enough for putting into cases.

WILD GEESE.

Sometimes the flesh of the wild goose is fishy and oily, and it is best to parboil them for a few minutes, to extract the superfluous oil. They may then be stuffed with bread-crumbs, sage, onion, and a good deal of pepper and salt, and roasted. The fat is sufficient for roasting them, without any addition of lard or butter. The liver, head, pinions, and gizzard should be well parboiled; the water put off, and fresh added; and gravy made by boiling them a long time, with a few rings of onion, a crust of browned bread, and pepper and salt; pour into the dish when the goose is served up.

Most excellent pies may be made of the blackbirds of Canada, which come in great flocks upon the fields of ripe grain, in the summer, and commit great ravages on those farms in the vicinity of fresh lakes and rivers, where they assemble to breed, and bring up their young. They are of good size, fat, and tender, and are delicious eating at the harvest season; and make a dainty dish, either roasted or baked in a pie. They fly in large flocks, and are often mixed with the rice-bunting, redwing, and others of the same family. I have often seen these birds dressed for sick persons—who could bear no rich meats—who found them lighter, and more nourishing even than chickens. The Canada robin is also eaten. These birds are the size of a blackbird or starling.

ESSENCE OF BEEF.

This excellent form of nourishment, for sick persons, is procured by cutting up some lean beef in small pieces, and putting it into a covered jar, which is then set into a pot of boiling water, and suffered to remain for some time, till the juices of the meat are quite extracted. A single tea-spoonful of this extract, given from time to time, contains more actual strengthening matter than a pint of beef-tea or broth, made with water in the usual way. For sick infants, who have been reduced to great debility by ague or dysentery, a few drops from time to time, have restored them more rapidly than any other sort of food would have done. The juices of any meat may be obtained in the same way, and a little seasoning added if required. In cases of great debility, when the stomach is too weak to bear the weight of ordinary food, this essence of beef is of great value, and is so easily manufactured, that it is within the reach of the most common cook to obtain it, however unskilful in the culinary art she may be.

———————

All seasoning herbs, as savory, thyme, marjoram, and the like, should be gathered green, dried for a few minutes in the oven, and preserved in bottles for winter use. Horse-radish scraped down into vinegar and bottled, is very useful.

FISH.

To those who live near the shores of lakes or rivers, fish forms an important article of diet, in Canada. So plentifully supplied are the waters of this fine country with fish of the finest quality, and largest size, that they can be procured with little trouble by the most inexpert angler. In the months of April and May, the lakes and rivers swarm with myriads of perch, of all sizes, from an ounce to two or three pounds weight; sun-fish, a small flat fish, of splendid colours—gold, and blue, and red; pink-roach, a very delicate, silver-scaled fish—not very large, but very delicate; with rock-bass and black bass. These last are very fine fish—are taken near the shores with a hook and line, while the larger sorts, such as masquinonge, which varies from a few to thirty pounds in weight, are either speared by torchlight, or caught with a trolling line. As soon as the ice breaks up on the lakes, the dark nights are illumined by the lights used by the fishers, to aid them in spearing these noble fish, which furnish a delicious meal when fresh, either fried or boiled, and may be salted, dried, and smoked for future use; while those to whom money is an object of importance, sell the surplus, for which, if they live near a town or village, there is always a ready market. There is one thing more to mention. This is, that there are no laws restricting the poor man from casting his line into the waters, or launching his night-canoe or skiff upon the lake, to supply his family with the blessings which God has bestowed upon all, alike, in this free and happy land of plenty. But now having told you how easily your husbands and sons can obtain this most excellent article of diet, it is necessary for me to give you a little instruction in the best modes of dressing it for the table.

MASQUINONGE.

Scale and clean your fish, if possible before the skin becomes dry and hard; but should it not come to your hands for some time after being taken out of the water, lay it on some clean stones, in a cool place, and throw over it a bowl or two of cold salt and water: this will render the scales less difficult to remove. With a sharp knife remove the gills and the inside. Few people cook the head of the masquinonge unless the fish is to be boiled, or baked whole, when the head and tail are tied and skewered so as to form a circle. Be careful, in cleaning this fish, not to wound your flesh with his sharp teeth or fins, as the cut is difficult to heal. Take out the roe, and throw it into salt and water. It should be floured, peppered, and salted, and fried as a garnish to the dish, but requires to be thoroughly done through: if it be soft and jelly-like it is not sufficiently cooked. If you design to fry the fish, it must be cut in pieces, quite through the thickness of the fish, about three inches in width; dry on a board; flour the pieces, and sprinkle with salt and pepper; or, beat up an egg, dip the-pieces in the egg, and strew crumbs of bread, and lay them in the boiling lard: this is the best way. But sometimes the Canadian housewive [housewife] may be obliged to resort to a more homely method, that of frying some slices of fat pork, to obtain the dripping in which to cook her fish; and if well attended to, even thus, her fish will be no despicable dish for a hungry family.

TO BOIL MASQUINONGE.

Having cleaned your fish, strew a handful of salt within side, and let it lie all night. Tie the tail and head together, and place your fish in a shallow pan—a fish-kettle if you have one, of course, is best; cover it with cold water—the water should just cover it and no more; let it come to a boil, and be careful to remove all scum. If your fish be any size, let it boil slowly for five or ten minutes; but when the fish has boiled five minutes, pass a clean knife in the thick part, near the back-bone, and if it parts from the bone, and looks white and flaky, it is cooked enough; but if soft, and has a pinky look, and adheres to the bone, let it simmer longer, but not long enough to break the fish: a little salt thrown in, when boiling, helps to preserve the firmness, and improves the flavour. A very thick, heavy fish will require a longer time to cook; but by trying it as I have directed, you can ascertain the time it will take. There is nothing more unwholesome than under-done fish. Melted butter, and any fish-sauce may be served with masquinonge; but where persons are unprovided with such luxuries, vinegar and mustard may be eaten with it. To the poor man, no sauce seasons his dish so well as a good appetite, which makes every dish savoury.

FISH-SOUP.

In the month of May, the lakes and rivers abound with perch, sunfish, and many other kinds, which are caught by children with the simplest of all tackle—a stout thread and a small perch hook, tied to a wand cut from some green sapling on the lake-shore. Any bait will be seized: a bit of meat, a worm, a fish cut up in small pieces, will give your little angler as many fish as you can cook at two or three meals.

When you have abundance of the smaller sorts of fish, there is no better way of cooking, than making them into soup. To do this, lay aside the larger ones, and boil down the small fish till they are broken to pieces; strain them through a colander, and put on the liquor, with a crust of bread, into your stew-pan; season with pepper, salt, parsley, savory or thyme, and a few green chives cut up, or a young onion. Have ready about a dozen, or two dozen of the largest sized fish, ready cleaned and scaled; put these into your soup; mix a teaspoonful of fine flour, a slice of butter, and a table-spoonful of tomato-catsup, if you have it by you, and mix with a cup of thin cream or milk. When the soup boils up, stir this mixture in, and remove the pot from the fire. Your dish is now ready, and requires nothing more than a little toasted bread and a good appetite, to be found an excellent meal, at a very small expense, and far more wholesome than salted pork or beef.

The roes of the fish should be boiled in the soup to thicken it, or fried by themselves.

A few slices of fat bacon will serve to fry any of the small fresh fish, when lard or butter are not plentiful.

In frying fish, the fat should be quite hot, and the fish or pieces of fish, dry, when put into the pan. As sauces are not so easily procured in country places, and by those who are too poor, or too prudent to expend money upon luxuries, it is common to season fried fish with pepper and salt whilst frying them, and many serve them with gravy made with a little butter rolled in flour, half a tea-cupful of water, a table-spoonful of vinegar, and pepper and salt, heated in the pan, and poured into the dish with the fish.

For boiled fish, melted butter with mustard, vinegar, and an egg boiled hard and chopped fine, may be used. Tomato-sauce is served with fish, as mushrooms are not as common in the newly-cleared lands as on old farms, or as they are in the old country. The morel, which is often found in old beech-woods that have been partly cleared, is a very good substitute and quite wholesome, but not so high flavoured as a good mushroom. They are conical in shape, of a pale brown colour, and covered with hollow cavities like a honey-comb, on the outside. They are good, fried in butter with pepper and salt, and may be manufactured into catsup.

FISH-PIE.

Boil fresh bass, masquinonge, or white fish, till it will readily part from the back-bones, which must be carefully removed; pound the fish fine, adding as you do so a pint of cream, a small bit of butter rolled in flour, a table-spoonful of walnut, mushroom, or tomato-catsup, a table-spoonful of vinegar, a little parsley scalded and chopped fine, and the yolks of two eggs bruised fine; smooth in a pie-dish, and bake half an hour. A large masquinonge, trussed, with the head and tail tied or skewered together, and stuffed with bread-crumbs, butter, pepper, salt, and sweet herbs, and moistened with a couple of beaten eggs, with butter sufficient to baste the fish, if put into the oven or before the fire and baked, is a most excellent dish. To try if it be cooked, pass a knife in near the back-bone; if it parts directly, and the flesh looks white, it is ready; but if it adheres, and is soft and clear, it requires longer cooking.

POTTED FISH.

Boil any sort of fish—not too much; remove the bones from the back and fins;—this can be done by running a knife along the edge of the back and laying back the meat, first on one side and then the other, breaking it as little as you can help. You can easily separate the fins; any other bones are not of much consequence, unless your fish be of the larger sorts. As you cut your fish, lay the pieces in a deep dish or pot, and sprinkle between each layer, pepper, salt, a little cayenne, a few cloves, and whole allspice. When your dish is full, pour on good vinegar, as much as will just cover the fish, and set it in a slow oven all night, or for some hours, covering the dish close with a plate or a coarse crust of dough, just to keep in the steam. This potted fish should stand for several days: it may then be used as a breakfast or supper dish, with bread.

SALT HERRINGS POTTED.

Steep them for twenty-four hours; cut off the heads, tails, and back-bones; skin them and lay them, packed close, in a pan; pour boiling vinegar over them, in which you have boiled whole pepper, allspice, and ginger; let the pan be covered close, and stand in the oven for an hour; when not very hot, set aside, and use as required: it will keep for some weeks or months.

EELS.

The eels caught in the Canadian waters are of a very large size, and very rich, but coarse. The best way of cooking them is, first, to parboil them, then open, and carefully remove the oily fat which lines the back-bone; cut out the bone the whole length, and also the tail and head; wash the fish clean, and spread it open; strew over the whole inner surface plenty of chopped parsley and thyme, or summer savory, pepper and salt, with a little allspice; then, beginning at the tail end, roll the fish tight into a bolster, and bind it well with tape or strips of calico; over this fold a piece of clean cloth, and tie it at each end; put it into boiling salt and water; (a handful of salt will be enough;) boil slowly for four or five hours, if your fish be large and the roll thick: do not remove the binders till the fish is quite cold; pour over it half a pint of vinegar, and when served, cut it in slices; garnish with parsley.

TO DRY MASQUINONGE OR SALMON.

Split the fish down and remove the back-bone; having gutted and scaled it, wipe it dry, but do not wash it; lay it on a board, and strew salt on the inner side; let it lie for two days, turning each day; then wash the inside from the salt, string on a willow-wand, and hang up in the sun and wind to dry for several days; smoke it, but not to [too] much.

The Indians use but little salt in drying their fish, and smoke them with the wood or bark of red cedar; but this fragrant wood is not common, and other wood will answer. Some merely dry them in the sun, without smoking. Corn-cobs burnt give a fine flavour either to meat or fish, and should be laid aside for such purposes.

When required for the table, soak for a few hours in warm water, and boil or fry.

WHITE FISH.

This is, by most people, considered as the richest and finest of all our fresh water fish, and abounds in the lake Ontario. Vast quantities are caught every year, and salted for sale; when they may be bought by the barrel. A few years ago, a barrel of white fish could be bought for three dollars; but now the price is much increased.

The fresh white fish are so rich, that they require no other fat than that which they contain to fry them.

Before dressing the salted white fish they must be steeped many hours, and the water twice changed. Most persons parboil them before frying them, and season them with pepper:—slightly salted, dried and smoked, they are very fine, and are esteemed a great dainty.

BLACK BASS.

There are two kinds of bass—the rock-bass and the black bass—the latter are the largest; but both are good. The black bass may be taken with a hook and line, in deep water; the rock-bass, nearer to the shore. They vary from half a pound to three, four, and even five or six pounds weight. The flesh is firm and sweet:—by many people the bass is preferred to the masquinonge. The usual way of cooking these fish is frying; but they are excellent broiled or boiled.

———————

The best fish that are bred in our Canadian waters are the salmon-trout, the masquinonge, white fish, and black bass.

One of the most nutritious of all dishes is fish-soup; but this mode of cooking is very rarely adopted. Any fish may be dressed according to the recipe given for the small fish, and will be found excellent.

———————

SOAP MAKING.

Soap is made from a union of the lie[22] [lye] of wood ashes, and any sort of grease, the refuse of the kitchen; even bones are boiled down in strong lie, and reduced. The lime of the bones are, by many soapmakers, thought to improve the quality of the soap. The careful Canadian housewives procure a large portion of their soap-grease from the inside, and entrails of the hogs, and other beasts that are killed on the farm. Nothing in this country is allowed to go to waste, that can be turned to any good account. Before I give you directions respecting the manufacturing soap, it will be as well to say a few words about the ashes, and setting of the leech barrel.

THE LEECH.

The ashes made use of for soap-making, should be from hardwood: such as oak, maple, beech, hickory, and the like; the ashes of *none* of the pine tribe, nor any other soft woods, are to be made use of, such as pine, hemlock, spruce, larch, or soft maple; swamp maple, bass-wood, and some others are also not good. Too much care can hardly be taken with respect to storing ashes. An old iron or tin vessel, pot or pan is the safest thing to remove the hot ashes in from the hearth, as live coals are often taken up with them, which might burn any wooden utensil, and if left on a verandah or floor, endanger the safety of the house. Most persons put up a small covered hut, made shanty form, in which the ashes are stored. This building should be apart from any of the house offices.

The careful soap-maker never allows sweepings of the house to be mixed with the ashes for soap making.

The ash barrel is usually any old flour barrel, or a hollow log that has been burnt out, leaving only a shell; this is sawn into the proper length, and set upon a sloping board, raised from the ground high enough to admit of a trough or pail standing

---

22 The original spelling of "lie" is the variant spelling used throughout this section in the original text.

beneath it, to receive the lie; at the bottom of the leech, sticks of split lathing or twigs, are placed across each other; a handful of dry straw is next laid over the twigs, and about a pint of unslacked [unslaked] lime scattered upon that. Two quarts or more of good lime are allowed to each barrel of ashes. The lime has the effect of neutralizing some of the salts, which are prejudicial to the good qualities of the soap.

If a barrel is used for the leech, it will be necessary to bore three or four holes with a half inch augur at the edge of the bottom of the barrel, in the direction of that part which will be sloped towards the front of the stand. You may support this stand with logs or stones; or put legs of wood into holes bored, the two front legs being shorter than the hinder ones, to give a proper inclination for the lie to run off into the trough below. If you can manage to have two barrels set up, so as to collect a larger quantity of lie, it is better, especially if you have much grease to boil down. Do not be afraid of your lie being too strong: the stronger the better for consuming the grease. More soap is spoiled by weak lie, than any thing else; neither let the dark colour of the lie deceive you: the colour is not strength.

The ashes should be put into the leech barrel, and pounded down with a long beetle. You may distribute the lime as you fill it up, or dissolve the lime in a pail of boiling water, and pour on after the barrel is filled up, and you commence running the lie.

Make a hollow in the top of the ashes, and pour in your water; as it soaks in, keep adding more; it will not begin to drop into the trough or tub for many hours; some-times, if the ashes are packed down tight, for two or three days; but you must keep the hollow on the top of the barrel always supplied with water—soft water is best, if you are near a creek, or have a rain water tank (which is a great convenience to a house), and the water you run your leech with should be hot at first.

Remember that you should be careful to keep any wet from getting to your ashes, while collecting them, previous to making the lie, as that weakens and destroys its effect.

I have been told that twelve pounds of grease will make a barrel of soft soap, but I do not vouch for it. Some say three pounds of grease to a pail of strong lie is the proportion; but experience is the best teacher. Of one thing you may be sure: that the strongest lie will take up the most grease: and after boiling several hours, if there be a thick scum still upon the soap, you may know that the lie has taken up all it is capable of boiling in; or if it should happen that your lie is not strong enough to consume the grease, add more strong lie. This is the advantage of having two barrels of ashes; as it affords you the chance of increasing the strength of the lie, if required; but if the soap, after long boiling, does not thicken, and no scum is on the top, of any account, add more grease.

To try if the soap is too strong, for it will not thicken sufficiently if it be so, take, with an iron spoon, a small quantity, say two spoonfuls into a saucer, add one of water, and beat it—if it wants water, it will thicken the soap; add more water as long as it makes it thicker; if it thickens well with one spoonful of soap to one of water then your soap, when poured out into the soap barrel, may have as many pails of water added, as you have pails full of soap; if very good lie has been used, a double quantity of water may be added; but it is better not to thin it too much.

To try the lie, float an egg or a potato; it should be buoyed half up. You can always lessen the strength after the soap is made, by adding water. A pint of pure turpentine, such as runs from saw-logs, or from a gash cut in a large pine, may be boiled in with your soap; or some resin; but the turpentine is best.

So much depends on the size of your pot, and quantity of grease, that it would be difficult to tell you how much to put in with your lie, when about to boil off; but as the lie will only boil in so much grease, according to its strength, you need not mind having a good deal of grease, as it can be scummed off, after the soap is done boiling, and is all the better for boiling down when you have a fresh supply of lie.

No tin vessel should be used in soap-making, as the lie eats off the tinning: iron to boil the soap in, and wood to keep it in, answers best.

There is another method which requires no boiling at all; this is known as

COLD SOAP.

This is less trouble—the sun doing the work of the fire. The same process of running the lie must be gone through, and the grease to make good clean soap, should be boiled down in weak lie, and strained into the barrel, into which fresh run lie may be poured, and the barrel set in a warm sunny place, keeping it stirred from time to time, to mix the grease and the lie. This is all that is done in making cold soap. If it does not thicken after a week or ten days, add more grease, or more lie if there be too much grease; the lie should be poured hot on the grease. Some persons treat the grease in the following way: they have a barrel or tub in the cellar, or any convenient place, into which they put hot strong lie, and throw in all the grease, as it is collected, from time to time. When they have as much as they need, this half-made soap is boiled up for some hours, and strained off into a vessel, and if more grease floats than can be taken up, it is either boiled with more lie, or hot lie is thrown in to consume it, and set out in the sun for some time, and stirred, as above.

HARD SOAP.

This is made from good soft soap. I have not made it myself, but I give the directions of an experienced house-keeper on the subject.

If the soft soap be good, there is little difficulty in making it into hard soap. When you find the soap of a good thickness, take two or three good handfuls of salt, and stir into your pot or kettle: if it be a large kettle, you may put in six or seven handfuls: let it boil till you see the soap separating; boil it about ten minutes longer, and set it by till the next day, when the soap will have formed a thick cake on the top of the vessel, and the lie have separated and remain below, a dark reddish-brown fluid. Remove this cake of soap, and put it into a pot on the fire, adding to it a pint of turpentine or resin. When the soap begins to boil up, add more salt; if the soap cuts like soft putty when you put it into the pot, several handfuls of salt will be required; but if it cuts firm, one or two will be enough—but experience must be your guide, or, seeing the process, which is better than learning from books.

When the soap is boiled a few minutes after the salt has been stirred in, pour it into a flat wooden box, or mould, about three or four inches deep; it may be cut into bars, or square pieces, when perfectly cold, and set up on a shelf, in some dry place, to harden.

———————

To remove paint, pitch, cart-grease, or the resin from cedar or pine, which will stick to the hands and clothes, if touched, nothing more is required, than to rub the cloth, cotton, or flesh, with clear lard, butter, or grease, then wash it well with hot soap-suds; but it is useless if you wet the part with water first. A weak solution of pot-ash, or pearl-ash, will also remove stains of this sort, or grease spots from cloth, or silk. Spirits of sal volatile, or hartshorn, will remove acid stains from silks, and restore the lost colour.

SCOURING MIXTURE FOR BOARDS, OR TO BE USED AS THE WASHING MIXTURE.

Take about two pounds of quick lime: pour over it one-and-a-half gallon of boiling water; when cold, clear off one gallon: cut two pounds yellow soap into a gallon of water, and boil until melted. Into the gallon of lime water, put one pound of sal-soda,* and boil together for half an hour, covered close: then half an hour uncovered; pour it into an earthen pan, and when cold, cut it up in squares for use; it does not harden much.

---

* This is sold in most stores, by the name of washing soda. It costs 5d. per pound.

This quantity will make fifteen or twenty pounds. You may use it as for the Washing Mixtures *(which see.)* It is excellent for scouring boards.

POTASH SOAP.

I have no experience of the following compound, but I give it in case any one should feel disposed to make the experiment.

Six pounds of potash, which would be equal to as many pails of good lie, four pounds of lard, or fat, boiled down, and cleansed, one quarter-of-a-pound of rosin, pounded; mix these ingredients, and set aside, in a vessel, for five days; put the mixture into ten gallons of hot water, stir it twice a day, and you will have one hundred pounds of good soft soap. The cost, if you buy the fat, and other materials, is staffed to be about seven shillings and six pence. I should think that much larger proportion of grease would be required to make the quantity of soft-soap here mentioned; however, it can be tried first with four pounds, and more grease added, if it does not thicken into soap.

I will now give an excellent receipt, called

LABOUR-SAVING SOAP.

Take fourteen pounds of bar-soap, or five gallons of good common soft soap, three pounds of sal-soda, sold by the name of washing soda, one quarter-of-a-pound of rosin, pounded, two ounces spirits of turpentine, eight ounces salt; boil together in five gallons of soft water, till the ingredients are all melted, and well mixed. Let it cool, and cut out for use.

When required for use, melt a piece in a pint of soft water, and stir it into as much warm soft water as will be sufficient to soak the clothes, which may be done over night—the white clothes by themselves: pound them a little, and wring out; lay on a clean board, and put them into your boiler with a piece of soap dissolved; let them boil for half an hour: take them out into a clean Indian basket, set across two bars, over your tub; while the liquor drains off, wring the clothes into another tub of clean water; then wring again in blue water.

ANOTHER WASHING MIXTURE.

Soak the clothes in soft water, the night before washing; take half a-pound of sal-soda, four ounces of quick lime, and dissolve each separately, in a quart of soft water; boil twenty minutes, and set by to settle. On the washing morning, pour off your lime-water clear, and add to the soda; boil in a saucepan together for a few minutes;

cut a pound of soap into ten gallons of water, in your boiler, and add the soda mixture and lime to it; when the soap is melted put in your clothes, having wrung them out, and rubbed a little soap on the collars, and wrists of the shirts; let them boil half an hour; drain, and wring, and rinse as above.

It is sometimes necessary to rub the sleeves and collars of shirts, but this method is a very great saving of soap and of labour, a matter of great moment to such as have been unused to the hard work attending washing for a large family.

A washing board is always used in Canada. There are several kinds. Wooden rollers, set in a frame, are the most common, but those made of zinc are best. These last do not cost more than the wooden ones, wear longer, and being very smooth, injure the fabric of the clothes less. In Canada no servant will wash without a washing-board.

CANDLE MAKING.

There is no mystery and not much skill required in making candles; any girl of ten or twelve years of age, that is careful, can make candles.

Good candles require clean well strained tallow, and strong smooth wick. When suet, or fat of any kind, mutton, beef, or lamb, is to be tried down for tallow, let the vessel it is put into be clean, and a table-spoonful or two of water be put in with the fat; this keeps the fat from burning to the bottom, and goes off in steam, during the trying down. Cut the fat into small pieces, and throw into the pot; a stick should be put in, which enables you to stir it from time to time; the handle of a metal spoon or ladle is apt to get too hot. Let the suet boil on a slow fire till the whole fat is well rendered. Be careful not to let it burn; remember when it ceases to make a noise, and becomes quite still, it is then *really* boiling hot, and is more apt to burn. You had better now remove it, and with a ladle pour it all clean off into a pot or tin dish, through a sieve or colander, over which you have tied a flannel strainer. The last drop of fat, as long as it is not discolored, may be drained out of the scraps, and the refuse may be placed in the receptacle for soap grease—no refuse fat of any kind being allowed, in a Canadian farm-house, to go to waste.

When quite cold, the cake of tallow may be turned out of the dish and set by, ready for candle-making.

You have now the tallow—at any of the tinsmiths in the towns, you can buy a stand of moulds, or get them made to order, from a stand of four to two dozen; but six or eight are best, and easier cleaned and handled. Every house-keeper requires candle moulds, and it is a bad way to depend upon borrowing of a neighbor. In careless hands these things are easily injured. The wick is sold in the dry-goods stores in balls, from 3½ d to 7½ d a ball; the whitest and most thready looking is better than the soft yellow looking wick: this last is fitter for lamps.

When about to make your candles, measure a double length of the wick, allowing a bit for tying; you must have some slender sticks, a bit of pine wood cut like a skewer, will do; slip the double wick through the holes in the bottom of the mould, leaving the loop end uppermost, the stick having to go through the loops to support the wick and keep it straight, and also to draw out the candles from the mould, when cold, by.[23] Having run all your wicks, slip your sticks through the loops at the top and put them even, then turn up the mould, and tie the ends tight at the bottom; and be careful that all your wicks are set evenly: if the sticks are slanting in any way, your wick will not be in the middle of your candle; and this not only causes the candle to look ill, but affects its burning. You are now ready for the tallow: let this be melted, but not made *too* hot, and poured into the moulds. It is best to keep an iron or tin saucepan, holding from a pint to a quart, for melting your grease in; use it for no other purpose; also a small pitcher with a spout, a common delf [delft][24] cream pot will do, for pouring the fat into the moulds. A tin mug with a spout is still better. Set your moulds aside, to cool; when nearly cold, fill up each mould again, for, as the fat cools, it shrinks, and a vacancy is made at the top of each candle, to the depth of half an inch; this would make a difference in the time of the candles burning. When thoroughly cold, there is little difficulty in drawing your candles, if your tallow be good; but if it is of inferior quality, it will not harden so well, and requires other means than simply cutting off the knot at the bottom, and drawing them out by means of the stick which you passed through the wick. Hold your moulds over a pan, or your sink, and pour boiling water from a jug over the outsides of your moulds, and draw the candles as quickly as you can. Good housewives never make candles just as they want them. Things done in haste are seldom well done. When a large quantity of tallow has been rendered down, after the killing of beef or mutton, it is better to make it up into candles as soon as possible, packing them, as they cool, into a box, till all are made. This is the most economical method as well as the most satisfactory. Candles burn much longer and better that have been made some time; and you are spared the mortification of finding yourself out of this necessary article, perhaps, when it would be highly inconvenient for you to make more.

If you have lard, as well as tallow, a mixture of one part of lard, to three of beef or mutton suet, is an improvement; lard alone will not make candles: it is too soft. It is cheaper to buy tallow and make your own candles than to buy them ready made.

The farmer's wife gets six-pence or seven-pence a pound for clean hard mutton or beef tallow at the stores, but if she buys a pound of candles, she gives ten-pence, and in country stores one shilling per pound. Some time ago candles were eight-pence or

---

23 The sentence is incomplete.
24 Delftware was blue and white earthenware pottery originally from the Delft, Holland, but also manufactured in England.

nine-pence, varying in quality from very bad to good; but you pay for the ready-made article just as much for the bad as the good. It is much better to make your material up in your own house, and make it well.

In the backwoods where the poor emigrant has not yet cattle enough to afford to kill his own beef, the careful housewife burns no candle; a tin cup, or a simple tin lamp, holds any clean fat she can get from the pot where meat has been boiled, and a bit of twisted rag serves her for wick; but even this light is often dispensed with, and the girls knit or sew by the red light of the blazing log-fire, or the pine knots which yield a great deal of resin, and burn with a vivid light. These pine knots are gathered up about the fallow, by the children, where large dead trees have fallen and moul- dered away upon the earth. The substance called "Fat pine," which is picked up in the forest, is also sought for and burned. The old upturned roots of pine trees will burn with a strong light, for they also are saturated with the resinous substance. These things are the poor emigrant's candles. Candles should be kept in a dry cool place, and carefully covered from the mice.

The cleanings of the chamber candlesticks, should be put into any old crock, and melted down and strained, or else put to your soap grease.

I have been told that steeping the wicks of the candles, previous to making them up, in a strong solution of saltpetre, improved the brightness of the flame, and tended to destroy the strong smell which newly made candles, especially if not made of pure tallow, are apt to emit. I have not tried this plan; I merely suggest it. Very handsome globe lamps are now much used, in which melted lard is burned instead of oil, at half the expense of oil.

Much care however, is required in cleaning and lighting these sort of lamps. The destruction of the glass makes the saving between lard and candles somewhat doubt- ful. A portable tin lamp, for burning of fine lard in the kitchen, is considered a great saving, by careful housekeepers; and one of these can be bought for one shilling and six-pence at the tinsmiths.

If the fat that rises from boiling beef, be carefully clarified by boiling it down in clean water, letting it stand to be cold, and then boiling the cake of fat again, on the top of the stove, till all the watery part has gone off in steam, very good candles can be made. It must be strained before it is used, as all fat should be, to make good candles.

MANAGEMENT OF WOOL.

The usual time of shearing the sheep in Canada is about the latter end of May, if the weather is warm and dry. The sheep having been washed, are left in open dry pastures for a day or two, that the fleece may be well dried before shearing: the wool being removed, is generally left for some little time, and then carefully picked and sorted by the women and children: all dirty wool is thrown aside, and those who are very careful will sort the coarse from the fine in separate parcels. The wool when picked is then greased with lard, oil or refuse butter, which is first melted and then poured over the wool, and rubbed and stirred about with the hands till it is all greased: about three pounds of grease is allowed to seven or eight pounds of wool, it is then fit for the carding mill: very few persons card at home now, but when first I came to the colony there were very many farmers wives who carded their own wool, but now the greasing as well as the carding is done at the mills. The usual charge is two-pence per lb if the wool be greased and picked at home, and three-pence if it be done at the mill: this includes the carding.

Those that sell the wool do not pick it, but sell it in the fleece, just as it comes from the hands of the shearer. Some years ago wool was as low as nine-pence and one shilling per lb, but now it is more than double that price: one shilling and six-pence cash, per lb, was given last year, and one shilling and nine-pence, if you took the payment in cloth or yarn. Sheep are decidedly the most profitable stock that can be fed on a Canadian farm: the flock in favourable seasons usually doubles itself. The expense of feeding is not great: peastraw, a little hay and roots, with salt occasionally, and a warm winter yard being the chief requisites. The lambs should not come before the middle or latter end of April, as the cold March winds are very trying to the tender flock. Wool sells at a good price, and mutton and lamb always meet with a market. Sometimes neighbours kill sheep or lambs in the summer, and exchange meat, weight for weight; this is a great accommodation, as in hot weather the meat will not keep more than two or three days good. If however you must kill a sheep to yourself, rub salt on the legs, and hang them in a cool root-house or cellar, and they will be good at a week's end: turn back or remove the flap or skinny part between the loin and the leg. The skin of a sheep or lamb with the wool on it will sell from two to four shillings, according to its size and goodness. The pedlars that travel the country with tins are always willing to trade for skins of sheep or calves: they give you no ready money, but sell tinware, and also buy rags, old iron, bottles and many other things. These pedlars penetrate into the country in every direction: many of them are respectable men and fair dealers; the housewife often supplies herself with tin milk pans, pails, strainers, mugs and many other conveniences, by selling such things as would otherwise be lost.

———————

Many people think that there is little saving in manufacturing your own wool into cloth, and that it is as well to sell the raw material and buy the ready made cloth. But where there is a large family of girls who can spin on the large wheel (and any one can learn this useful art in a few lessons,) I should say that making home spun cloth and flannel was a decided advantage. The price of weaving flannel is five-pence per yard: it may be six-pence; as all labour has risen in price since the rise in breadstuffs; and full cloth seven-pence or eight-pence per yard. The cloth thus manufactured is generally much more durable than any that is bought at the factory or in the stores, for which you must pay from four shillings to six and three-pence per yard, narrow width. Flannels from two shillings and three-pence to two shillings and nine-pence per yard, yard wide. The home-spun flannel is a long-enduring article, either with cotton-warp or all wool. The usual dresses for home wear both for women and children, among the small farmers, is the country flannel. This is dyed in different colours in the yarn, or made plain grey with a mixture of black wool, in the proportion of one black fleece to three white ones: this is mixed for you at the carding mill, and carded together so as to make the proper colour called sheep's grey. In a subsequent article you will find some notice of dying. The thrifty industrious farmers' wives usually spin yarn for making into flannel sheets, which are very fine and soft and warm for winter wear, and last a very long time: home spun blankets too are made, sometimes on shares with the weaver. These are often checked with a blue or red cross bar, but sometimes are made plain, with only a broad red or blue border. Those families who know nothing of spinning can hire a spinning girl by the week, and this is frequently done and is a very good plan: these spinning girls are usually the daughters of farmers, and generally are respectable and honest.

———————

DYING.

Those who spin their own wool should also know something about dying it. The industrious economical Canadian farmers' wives generally possess some little knowledge of this kind, which enables them to have many varieties in the colours of their home spun garments. The common grey flannel and fulled cloth worn by the men is made by mixing the wool of the black sheep with the wool of the white: one part of black wool to three parts of white, makes a light grey; but the shade can be increased by adding a little more of the black; a dark brown may be produced by adding one fleece of white to three of black. The chief objection made to the black wool by itself, is that it is not so strong as white wool dyed, and is apt to fade in wearing. It is very useful as a grey cloth, for common home-wear, and also as a mixture for socks. This colour is commonly known as "sheep's-grey."

If you have black wool of your own, you can get it mixed at the carding-mill, light or dark, as you wish it; and even if you have no black wool of your own, they will generally change with you, if you desire it. By paying so much per pound, you can also get different colours dyed for you, if you name them, by your weaver; but most women prefer preparing their own yarn for weaving.

There are many vegetable dyes that are made use of here, such as the butternut, which dyes a rich, strong, coffee-brown, by steeping the inner bark in cold water for several days, and soaking the yarn in the strained liquor. The flowers of the golden-rod, a plant which grows abundantly in Canada, and blooms in the latter end of summer and fall, boiled down, gives a fine yellow; and yarn steeped first in this, and then in indigo, turns to a bright full green. The lie of wood-ashes, in which a bit of copperas has been dissolved, gives a nankeen-color or orange, if the strength of the lie be sufficient to deepen it; but it is hurtful from its corrosive qualities, if too strong. Logwood steeped for some days in house-lee, strained from the chips, and boiled with copperas, gives a permanent black. The yarn should be boiled in it half an hour, and then thrown into cold spring-water, and rinsed up and down many times: two or three waters may be used, and then the hanks hung upon a stick, in a shady place, to dry out of the sun.

The yarn before dying must be well and thoroughly washed, to remove the oil which is made use of in the carding-mill; and well rinsed, to take out the soap used in washing it; as the soap would interfere with the colours used in the dying process.

Horse-radish leaves boiled, give a good yellow; and the outer skins of onions, a beautiful fawn or pale brown.

To cloud your yarn of a light and dark blue, for mitts, socks or stockings, braid three skeins of yarn together, before you put them into the indigo-vat, and when dry and wound off, the yarn will be prettily clouded with different shades, from dark to very pale blue.

The same effect can be produced in dying with any other colours, if you braid or twist the yarn before you put it into your dye-stuff.

Yarns must be well scoured with hot soap-suds, and rinsed in soft water, before putting them into the dying liquor; and also wetted in soft water, before you proceed to dye them, or the colours will not be equal: most dark colours are prepared in iron vessels, but light and delicate tints in brass or tin. The dyers use a composition for bright blues, called "Chemists' Blue," a few drops of which will give a beautiful colour to silks, deepening the shade by adding more of the compound. Greens are easily dyed, by first steeping the articles in yellow dye, and then in the blue. The common yellow dye used by the settlers, is either a decoction of the Golden-rod; of a weed known as Smart-weed, (a wild persicaria it is;) or horse-radish leaves; and some others, which any of your neighbours that are used to dying, will describe to you. Fustic, which is sold in the drug-stores, dyes yellow. White-maple bark, boiled, and set with alum, gives a brown grey; but it must not be boiled in an iron vessel.

Logwood,[25] boiled in cider or vinegar, with a small bit of copperas, gives a black dye: it should be boiled in iron. These are only a very few of the dies [dyes] made use of: there are many others to be learned.

LOGWOOD DECOCTION

is made by boiling half a pound of logwood chips in two quarts of soft water, and dissolving in it a small bit of pearl-ash. The weed Purslain, boiled down, and the liquor mixed with the logwood, gives a bright blue: set with alum.

To brighten faded purples or lilacs, in cotton prints, rinse in water in which you have dissolved some pearl-ash. If you wish to restore reds or pinks, use vinegar, or a few drops of diluted acid of vitriol,[26] in the rinsing water.

---

25 A natural fabric dye derived from the heartwood of a Central American tree, *Haematoxylon campechianum*. Purchased as chips, it yields a range of dark blues and purples when dissolved in boiling water. Pearlash was the mordant (setting agent) commonly used with it.

26 Acid of vitriol is commonly known today as sulfuric acid.

A SLATE-DYE FOR COTTONS.

Having washed the goods to be dyed, clean, in soap-suds, rinse them well in warm water. Put a pound of sumach-bark in a sieve; pour boiling water over it, and let it drain into a pan; put in your goods, and let them steep for two hours, lifting them up and down, from time to time, that it may take the colour evenly. Then take it out, and steep it in a pan of warm water, in which half an ounce of green-copperas has been dissolved for five or six minutes. It will then be a full leaden-grey. But to turn it to a blue-slate colour, run the article through a weak decoction of log-wood, made by boiling an ounce of logwood in a quart of water, with a small lump of pearl-ash; then throw it into warm-water, and handle it, for some minutes. Dry in the shade. For lavender, add a little Brazil-wood.

[C A R P E T S]

Rag-carpets are among the many expedients adopted by the Canadian-settlers' wives, for procuring comforts at a small cost, and working up materials that would, by the thrifty housewives of England, only be deemed fit for the rag-merchant. Let us see now how a careful settler's wife will contrive, out of worn-out garments, mere shreds and patches, to make a warm, durable and very respectable covering for the floor of her log-parlour, staircase and bed-room.

I asked the wife of the resident-minister of P.,[27] what she was going to do with a basket of faded, ragged clothes, old red-flannel shirts, and pieces of all sorts and sizes; some old, some new, some linen and cotton, others woollen. "I am going to tear and cut them up, for making a rag-carpet," she replied; "they are not good enough to give away to any one."

I fancied she was going to sew the pieces like patch-work, and thought it would make a poor carpet, and last no time.

"I will shew [show] you," she said, "what I am going to do with these things." She then took a piece, and with the scissors began cutting it into long narrow strips, about a quarter of an inch wide, not wider; and indeed the narrower the strip, the better. She did not cut quite through, when she came to the end, but left just as much as would serve to hold it together with the next strip, turning the piece in her hand, and making another cut; and so she went on cutting or tearing, till that piece was disposed of: she then proceeded to a second, having first wound up the long strip: if a break occurred, she joined it with a needle and thread, by tacking it with a stitch or two. Sometimes she got a bit that would tear easily, and then she went on very quickly with her work. Instead of selecting her rags all of one shade, for the ball, she would join all kinds of colours and materials. "The more lively the contrast, the better the carpet would look," she said. Some persons, however, wind all the different colours

---

separately, in large balls, and then the carpet will be striped. A white and red ball, wound together, makes a pretty chain pattern, through dark stripes.

My friend continued to cut and tear, join the strips and wind up, till she had a ball as big as a baby's head; and I continued to watch her, still puzzling my brains to think how these big balls could be turned into a carpet; till she lightened my darkness, by telling me that these balls, when there was a sufficient weight of them, were sent to the weavers, with so much cotton-warp, which should be doubled and twisted on the spinning-wheel. If you double and twist the warp, yourself, the weaver will charge 6d. a yard for the weaving; but if he doubles and twists, he charges 8d. A pound and a half of rags will make one yard of carpet, with the warp. Many persons dye the warp themselves: lie of wood-ashes, with a little copperas, makes a deep yellow: logwood and copperas makes a black, and indigo and lee from the house, gives a full blue. Made up with the coloured warp, the carpet looks better, and does not dirty so soon.

The white cotton rags are better washed clean, and then dyed with any of these dyes. Those who do not care to take this trouble, use them as they are, but they soil soon.

The best sort of rag-carpet is made by intermitting the colours as much as possible, cutting the strips through, instead of turning the corners: you have more work in joining, but the effect is better; and there are no unsightly ends on the surface of the carpet. Bits of bright red flannel, of blue, green or pink mousselin-de-laine, or stuffs of any bright colour, old shawls and handkerchiefs, and green baize, will give you a good, long-enduring fabric, that will last for eight or ten years, with care. Children can be taught to cut the rags, and join and wind into balls, ready for the weaving.

To the more wealthy class this humble manufacture may seem a very contemptible affair; but it is not for the gay and luxurious that such things are suitable; though I have seen them in the houses of some of our best settlers, who were wise enough, like the wife of the rector, to value whatever was comfortable, and save buying. When well assorted, I assure you these rag-carpets make by no means a despicable appearance, on the rough floors of a Canadian farmer's house.

I would recommend the settler's wife to keep a basket or box, into which all scraps of woollen and cotton, and any worn-out clothes, can be put. A rainy day may be chosen for the cutting and winding.—Another box may be appropriated for the reception of the balls when wound up. The thinnest cottons, and even muslins, can be used for the purpose; only that the latter articles may be cut half an inch wide.

To wash a rag-carpet let it be ripped into breadths, and taken to a creek or river, and flounced up and down, and then laid out to dry: no rinsing is required: the edges should be well bound with a broad strip of cloth. Thirty pounds of rags will make about twenty yards of carpetting; and when you consider that you can buy no sort of carpet worth making up, under 4s. a yard, in any of the country stores, this simple substitute, made out of refuse materials, is not to be despised.

WOOLLEN HOME-SPUN CARPETS.

Those farmers who keep a good many sheep, and whose wives and daughters are well skilled in the homely but valuable art of spinning on the big-wheel, often turn the coarser wool to good account by spinning a stout yarn, dying it of various gay colours, and sending it to the weavers to be woven into carpetting. The warp and woof are of wool, and if well done, make a handsome appearance: a dark green ground, with checkers of red, yellow or blue, look well; or sheep's-grey and checked with red, like a drugget, looks neat and unpretending on the floor of a log-house.

Among the emigrants into whose hands this little book may go, there may be some who have followed weaving as a trade: to them no instruction is requisite on the simple art of weaving druggets; and let me tell such an one, that many a poor settler has become rich by setting up his loom in the backwoods of Canada, in their own house, or in the small villages. Blankets, shawls, plaids, cloaking, the country flannel, both white and grey, and carpets such as I have described, will give plenty of employment to the industrious man, while his sons carry on the labours of the farm.

Women often weave, and make a good living; and I have heard a very respectable farmer's daughter say, that she could weave from ten to twelve yards of plain flannel a day. Sometimes she wove the wool on shares.

Carding is not so often done in the settlers' houses as it used to be, so many carding-machines now being in operation, and mills in all the towns for fulling and carding;[28] but many years back this work was chiefly done by hand.

Neither flax nor hemp are much grown in Canada at present; consequently there is little home manufacture of that kind. The big wheel is generally substituted for the small spinning-wheel, as being more suitable to wool; though for fine yarn, perhaps, the latter is as good.

---

28 Making fabrics (ranging from utilitarian homespuns to fancy bed coverlets) was a vital element in the domestic economy of most rural and backwoods households before the carding, spinning, dying, and fulling mills took over by the end of the nineteenth century. Carding is combing the raw wool into straight lengths preparatory to spinning it into threads, and fulling is shrinking woven woolen cloth to make it thicker and water resistant.

KNITTING.

If you do not understand this useful art, I strongly advise you to turn your attention to it as soon as possible: children cannot learn to knit too soon. Those who are not already able to knit a sock or a mitt, will find some kind neighbour ready and willing to teach them; it will be nice work on the voyage out: a few pounds of coloured or white yarn is no ill store, for your boys and husband will need plenty of woollen socks and mitts in Canada.

There is no country where there is so much knitting-work done as in Canada, for when the household of the settler is supplied with socks, stockings, mitts, and gauntlets (these are long, thick mitts, that come halfway up the arm, and are used in driving), the surplus yarn meets with ready sale at the stores when manufactured into socks, &c. Men's socks sell at one shilling and six pence to two shillings and three pence, according to their goodness: the best article in Canada, as elsewhere, fetches the best price. The second or even third-rate wool, knitted up, can be made more profitable than the best wool sold in the fleece; and children and women will earn many a dollar if they are industrious, in the evening, between twilight and candle-light.

I knew a settler's daughter who knitted seventy-five pairs of socks one year, to provide clothes for her marriage,—and a complete wardrobe she made up, without any cost to her parents; for she had been given a ewe-lamb, and this in due time produced an increase, so that she had a little flock of her own, and clothed herself from the wool, which she could card, dye, spin, and knit herself.

It would be useless for me to describe all the different patterns that the skilful knitter can devise, for mitts and children's socks, or the colours chosen for that purpose; but I have seen striped mitts, flowered, spotted and plain, ribbed and unribbed. A young lady in my neighbourhood, has gained many a prize at the County and Provincial Agricultural Shows, by her socks and gauntlets: the same chance is open to every one who has skill and taste in this useful art.

A very young woman is prized in this country according to her usefulness; and a thriving young settler will rather marry a clever, industrious girl, who has the reputation for being a good spinner and knitter, than one who has nothing but a pretty face to recommend her. This is as it should be; and I would bid the young daughters of the emigrant to bear the fact in mind, if they wish to become the wives of steady young men, and wish to prosper in the world. Nor do I confine my advice, on this head, to the daughters of the poorer class of emigrants. In the new country to which they are going, knowledge of the simple art of knitting must form one of the occupations of the females of the higher or more educated class, who reside in the agricultural portion of the colony.

A family who are too proud or indolent to work in Canada, will sink into absolute poverty:—they had better never have crossed the Atlantic. To the mind of the well-regulated female, there is no disgrace in so feminine an occupation: she is kept in countenance by ladies of her own rank; and indeed would be considered as a very useless and foolish person, if she despised that which every one here practises. Here, as in Germany and Holland, young ladies take their knitting-bag out with them, and carry it to the house of a friend when they go out: it is certainly a very sociable employment. The earlier children learn to knit, the better; those who learn late in life, seldom acquire the same quickness, as those who learn in childhood. I have myself experienced the disadvantage of not learning this sort of work till I was old, and my finger joints had lost their flexibility, consequently I am a slow and unskilful knitter: I can hardly shape a sock or a stocking.

Many persons knit cradle-quilts, and large coverlets for beds, of coloured yarns, and among the town-bred young ladies, curtains, tidies for sofas, and toilet covers, of all sorts and patterns are manufactured with the knitting-needles, and cottons of suitable qualities.

Because store goods are now lower than they used to be formerly, and socks can be bought cheap, let not the farmer's daughter despise the useful art of knitting and spinning: they belong to her station in life, in this country, and few grow rich who abandon this homely occupation.

THE DAIRY.

The following remarks, on the management of the dairy, were published last year, under the title of an "Essay on Butter-Making;" and for which a prize was awarded to the authoress by the members of the "Hamilton Agricultural Association, and Farmers' Club." It was copied by several Agricultural periodicals, and weekly papers, which induced me to give it in an abridged form for the benefit of the female emigrant; its usefulness having received the sanction of many practical Canadian settlers.

The want of succulent food, during the long winter, is one of the causes of a deficiency in the butter-producing qualities of the milk. Where roots, such as good sound turnips, cannot be had, the deficiency might be supplied by boiling oats in a good quantity of water; a quart of oats thus given, morning and night, will keep a cow in good order, with her ordinary food, and greatly increase the quantity of her milk; or bran mashes made thin, with boiling water, left to cool down twice a-day, with a handful of salt once a week, will tell well. Some of the careful small farmers, will take the trouble of boiling a lock or two of hay with water, sufficient for a good drink; but I should think the boiled oats, or the bran, or a handful or two of indian meal, boiled in water would be preferable, affording nourishment, as well as milk. Having thus far spoken in behalf of the treatment of the animals, as respects their food, and general comfort, I would next observe, that regularity in the time of milking, is of great importance. In the morning, as early as possible, the milking hour should be established, that the cow may go forth to feed *while the dew yet lies fresh upon the herbage.* This is of great consequence in the hot dry summer weather: it is soon after sunrise, in the early spring time of the day, while the grass is wet with the clear refreshing dew of night, that the beasts of the field shake off their slumbers, and rise to feed; they then can afford time to lie down during the noon-day heat, to ruminate and digest their food. The wise man will consider this, and will derive advantage from studying the natural habits of the animals under his care. Those persons whose occupation is too small, to admit of keeping their cows in constant pasture, would find it an advantage to make an enclosure, even if the ground be but scantily provided with grass, as a night yard. The early milking will enable them to be let out to feed. I allude to such cows as roam at large in the woods and wastes, and on the plain land. A little occasional fodder, given to encourage them to return to the usual milking place, will generally ensure their coming home, and they should not be kept waiting, but be attended to at once. I recommend this plan because I have known much loss of time, caused by the looking up the cow, loss of milk and butter, and what may sound strangely to some persons, *loss of life*. How many of the children that have, at different times, been lost in this Province, have been sent out in the forest to seek for the cows, and straying from the beaten path, or bewildered by converging ones, have returned no more to their home, but have perished miserably.

Cows can be taught to come home at the sound of a horn: if food be given them at such times—the habit will be easily established. I have known this practised in Canada, and I have heard that it is common in the pastoral countries on the continent of Europe, for the herd boy to collect his cattle in that way. No doubt the shepherd's pipe was used for this purpose, as well as for the shepherd's own amusement. I have heard of cows coming home in towns regularly, at the sound of a factory bell, which they learned to regard as a signal for the milking hour. The advantage of establishing regular hours needs hardly to be further insisted on. We shall now proceed to make a few remarks on the next most important matter, which is the dairy.

The coolness in summer, and warmth in winter of the dairy, are two most essential points to be considered in the making of good butter. The dairy-maid may be skilful and orderly, and yet if the place in which the milk is stored, be not perfectly cool and airy, her labour will do her little credit; with her superior knowledge, she may make a *better* article than some of her neighbors, but not the best. In this country, the dairy women often work under the greatest disadvantages. Frequently she has nothing better to keep her milk in, than a close damp cellar or root-house, where to preserve thorough ventilation is impossible: without proper utensils, and conveniencies [conveniences] for carrying on the process, complete success can hardly be expected. Instead of being surprised that there is so little really fine butter sent to market, the wonder should be, that under such disadvantages, there is so much. Let the men look to the providing of a suitable place where the work of the dairy can be carried on, and the result would speedily repay the cost and labour bestowed upon it. The space allotted to the dairy is generally too limited: it should be large enough to admit of thorough ventilation, and room for carrying on the necessary work of churning, cheese-making, &c. A sunk floor, well paved with brick, or stone, and a covered drain, and grating, are advisable, to carry off any moisture. The floor can then be kept cool in hot weather, by throwing a few pails of water down, which is a constant practice in the dairies in the home country. I have seen dairies built with good stone foundations, and the walls of squared cedars, placed upright, forming a solid compact building, the windows latticed, and each window supplied with a wooden shutter, which could be lowered at pleasure, to exclude the sun, wind, or rain; by this simple arrangement, the sun's rays need never have access to the dairy. A porch, with shelves, and a bench, on which the empty pans, trays, pails, &c., can be set up to dry after scouring, are great conveniences.

Pans of thick glass are much used in home dairies; also pans lined with zinc, and a species of enamel, such as the iron-stone pan, and preserving pans, are coated with; trays of wood about four inches in depth, with peg holes for letting off the milk, used to be much the fashion, but I think wooden ware is liable to crack and warp, during hot weather, and is less easily cleansed from the sour particles of the milk.

With respect to the churn, a small volume might be written on the kinds: in my opinion the simpler the machinery the better. The old fashioned upright churn, worked with the staff and cross-dash, may be as effective in the end, but it imposes a greater amount of labour, than such as are wrought with a winch. The simplest churn, and one that I have heard much praised by every good dairy-women, is a box churn, the sides of which are sloped, so as to leave no acute angles and corners, always difficult to keep clean; the sides are provided with dashers, and a dasher also is affixed to the beam of the handle, which passes through the churn: this can be unscrewed, and the buttermilk is drawn off by means of a plug-hole, near the bottom of the churn. This churn may be bought at a cooper's for 12s 6d. I have also seen a churn with an iron wheel, turned with a winch, which is very easy to work. There is the old barrel-churn, which is also simple and effective, the advantage of this last being, that the butter can be washed before being removed from the churn, ready for salting. Earthenware pots, or good stoneware jars, are best for storing the cream in. With each jar there should be a clean, smooth, wooden staff, for stirring the cream; this is a matter that dairy-maids pay little attention to here, and yet it is of some importance, in thoroughly mixing the cream together, so as to prevent any sour milk, or whey from settling below, thus giving a disagreeable taste to the whole mass of butter. In cool weather, scalding the cream, just before churning, greatly facilitates the churning, and obviates the necessity of putting hot water into the cream, a practice in very common use, but which I believe is very injurious to the richness and good colour of the butter, giving it a white, greasy, poor appearance. In the winter season, the cream jars should be brought into a warm room over night, which will thicken the cream, and bring it to the required temperature for churning. Frozen cream will make frothy butter, or no butter will be obtained, after much labour. In hot weather the churn should be allowed to stand some time with clear cold water in it, and if the weather be very hot, immerse the churn in water; if a plunge churn be used, it can be place[d] in a tub of cold water, during the churning. Many excellent dairy women are in favour of churning cream and the strippings,[29] while others prefer the cream only; I think myself that the richest butter is produced from the cream alone, but possibly a larger return may be obtained from the former practice.

Where cows are fed on turnips, a small quantity of saltpetre, dissolved in a little warm water, and mixed with the cream before churning, is said to remove the flavour of the turnips from the butter. I knew a farmer's wife who always practised it in the winter season. This same person, who was celebrated in the part of the country where she lived, for good butter, used, during the hot weather, to put half a pint of cold spring water into each of the milk pans or trays, to raise the cream, and in winter she put the same quantity of boiling water to raise the temperature, for the same purpose.

Many approve of the Devonshire and Cornish plan of scalding the milk, but careless servants are apt to let the milk get over-heated, which decidedly injures the flavour of the butter; but very good butter is no doubt made by heating the milk, and the largest amount of cream is thus raised. The milk should stand some hours before it is heated. It has another advantage, that of keeping the skimmed milk sweet for the use of the family.

In a North-Lancashire paper, I saw the following advice to dairywomen, which, as it is easily tried, I will insert. "Heat two pans of the same size with boiling water, let them stand a few minutes, then pour off the water, and pour in the new milk; cover the pan that has the milk in it, with the empty heated pan; this will raise the cream in less time, and in larger quantity than if put into cold pans. Try it?"[30] Some persons never wash their butter, but absorb the buttermilk in the following way: They place a lump of butter in a coarse linen cloth, and beat against the sides of the churn, wringing the cloth from time to time in cold salt and water, repeating the beating process

---

29 "The last milk of a milking. It is much higher in fat percent than the foremilk or middle milk" (Frandsen, *Dairy Handbook and Dictionary*, 759).

30 The question mark appears in Traill's original 1854 text, but we suspect that in the original North-Lancashire paper, this was an exclamation mark.

until the milky particles are completely removed. The famous Epping butter is thus treated; this butter has the character in London, of being the finest in England; very little salt is used for seasoning it; but as the sale of it is so rapid, probably the keeping properties have hardly been tested.

The thorough extracting of the milky particles, and the working of the salt well through the mass cannot be too much insisted on. Attention to cleanliness, coolness in summer, and a moderate temperature in winter, are the three most important matters for securing good marketable butter.

The following recipe was given me by an old country farmer's wife, who was cele-brated for the excellent quality of her butter, both for flavour and keeping:—

To thirty-two pounds of well-washed butter, she allowed the following mixture: two and a-half pounds of finely-rolled salt, six ounces of saltpetre, and half a pound of fine, rolled, lump sugar; these materials were well ground together, and worked into the mass of butter, which was then packed into a stone jar; over the top of the butter, she poured a strong clear brine, sufficient to cover the whole surface two inches in depth; a white cloth was then laid over the jar, and above this the stone lid pressed tightly down. This butter, she said, would be as good at the end of the second year as the first.

Those cows that get their living all spring and summer, roaming at large through the forest, often feed upon the wild leeks, which spring up in the rich leafy soil of the woods; the flavour imparted to the milk by this sort of food is very odious. The milk is almost useless, excepting for the feeding and fattening of calves; but while this cir-cumstance annoys the settler not a little, there is one advantage that makes amends, in some measure, for the leek diet; which is, that the cattle that are poor and weak, and often in a diseased condition from poor feed, during the long winters, are re-stored to health and good condition very speedily, by feeding upon the green leeks.

A small piece of saltpetre dissolved in the cream, I have been told, will remedy the ill flavour, but of this I cannot speak from experience. There are other plants also, on which cows feed in the woods, that give a rank, weedy taste to the milk. These evils are confined to those who, having settled on the new land, cannot command pastures for the cattle to feed in.

During the chopping season, the cattle browse a great deal upon the shoots of the felled trees, particularly upon the sugar maple, the bass, elm, beech and other hard-wood trees. It used formerly to be the practice to let the calves run with the cows, but this is a very unwise one; and now it is more usual to take the calf from the mother before it has sucked at all, and feed it by finger; in a few days it may be taught to drink out of the pail, and is then put into some small enclosure where it can pick a little grass. A month's new milk is all that is allowed; then a sufficiency of skimmed milk all the summer. Many calves are killed by being given sour milk in hot weather. A little very thin flour gruel, with a little milk in it, is sometimes given, when there is a scarcity of its proper nourishment.

Salt is necessary for cattle and sheep in Canada, to keep them in health; it also induces them to return home.

In winter, wood ashes, and clay are left near the feeding places for the use of the sheep and cows.

Warm yards are of as much use as good feeding, and this is a point often miserably neglected by the small holders. The Irishman, however miserable his own dwelling may be, will generally take care that the cow and the pig are warmly housed. I actually once saw a patchwork quilt, pegged up in front of the shed where the cows were stabled, though from the appearance of the dwelling house, I should have supposed it could ill have been spared from the children's beds, but the cow must be sheltered whoever else suffered from the cold wind and snow.

A want of attention to the comfort of the cows also imposes much discomfort upon the females who have to milk them, exposed to the biting blast of cold and frost, and drifting snow. Men should bear this in mind, and provide as well as they can, against such evils; it is bad policy, as well as cruelty. A dairy-woman cannot execute her task perfectly with hands benumbed by cold. The excuse for the want of attention to these things is: "we have so much to do clearing land, and fencing, and building, cropping and harvesting, that we have no time to make sheds, and fence in cattle yards." The same thing is said about making gardens. "We really have no time for these things." But a wise man would rather clear an acre or two less land, and take the time for adding to the comfort and health of the family. I notice this error as a friendly hint to husbands, and masters of families, which I hope they will act upon.

CHEESE.

It is only of late years, that much of the attention of the Canadian settler has been turned to the subject of cheese-making. The reason of the neglect of this valuable portion of dairy produce, is evident. During the process of clearing wild land, the want of a sufficiency of pasture for the cows, obliges the prudent farmer to limit this branch of his stock, according to his supply of fresh grass or dry provender for their support; consequently, for some years, he is unable to keep cows enough for the profitable manufacturing of cheese as well as butter; but now that the country is opening out on every side, and there are many fine cleared farms of long standing, and under good cultivation, dairies are increasing everywhere, and the farmer's wife is beginning to see the great advantage of making good cheese, for which an excellent market can always be obtained.

Good rich cheese will sell at 7½ d per lb; inferior fetches 5d. Now this is of course encouraging, and it is well worth taking pains to make a superior article, when it meets with a remunerative price.

I will condense, as much plain instruction on the subject of cheese-making, as will afford a general knowledge of the subject, for the benefit of such of my female readers, who may be strangers to the process of making cheese; with a few hints on various subjects, which may prove useful to the bush settler's wife, whose operations are confined to making cheese upon a very limited scale; and, first, let me give directions as to the common method of preparing the rennet.

THE RENNET

is prepared from the first stomach or maw of the sucking calf.[31] Any milk-consuming animal will, I believe, answer the same purpose for curdling milk; such as the lamb, kid, and even the sucking pig; but the calf's maw alone is used in the dairy work of cheese-making.

The calf's maw being emptied of the curd and slime, is carefully turned, and well and thoroughly washed with clean water, then thrown into a brine of cold salt and water for about twelve hours; it is then rub-well with salt, and stretched upon a flexible stick, by bending it, and holding both ends in one hand: over this, the bag is drawn, and tied at the open end, near the ends of the stick; it may then be hung up to dry, in the house, or in the sun, on the house-wall in the open air, till quite hard; then take out the stick, and put the rennet bag into a paper bag, and hang up in a cool place: it is better for keeping a year, I have been told; but it may be used in a few weeks

---

31 Rennet is "curdled milk found in the stomach of an unweaned calf, used in curdling milk for cheese" as well as a "preparation made from the stomach membrane of a calf" (*Canadian Oxford Dictionary*, 1222). "Maw" refers here to "the stomach of an animal," although the term is more widely used today to refer to "the jaws or throat of a voracious animal" (Ibid., 894).

or months. Some persons, after washing, picking, and salting the bag, put it into a strong brine, in an earthen vessel, and tie it close down; others fill the bag quite full of salt, tie, and hang it up. In the second plan, a spoonful or two of the brine only is used, but if the rennet is dried, as in the first and last instance, a small piece is cut off, and steeped in warm water for some hours before putting it to the milk. Whether cheese is made, or not, in a family, the rennet should be preserved, as it is convenient to have a little sweet curd and whey, as an addition to the dinner or supper table, especially with a little ripe fruit; it makes a nice dish for the children. If the rennet brine be good, a dessert spoonful will set a good dish of milk; the milk should be as warm as when first drawn from the cow; if too hot, the curd will be tough; if cold, not firm enough to separate from the whey.

TO MAKE GOOD ONE-MEAL CHEESE.

This cheese is made entirely of the morning's new milk, strained into a well-cleaned cheese-tub. If the milk be too much cooled in its transit from the milking yard to the dairy, a portion of it must be heated, but not boiled, in a clean vessel, on the fire or stove, and returned to the tub, pouring in as much as will make the whole quantity the same heat as new milk just drawn from the cow; some add a small portion of hot water for bringing the milk to a right temperature, and say that the water comes off in the whey, without impoverishing the curd; it is certainly less trouble. The Wiltshire cheese, I have been told, is done so, and even has scalding water thrown upon the curd.

The rennet is then stirred in: if good, half a teacupful should curdle a good-sized cheese. In about twenty minutes, or half an hour, the curd will be formed, and with a saucer, a small wooden dish, or a wooden cheese-knife, the curd may be cut across in several directions, till the whey rise clear between the gashes you have made on the curd. It may then be broken lightly, and left for a few minutes longer. Have ready a cheese basket; this is a loose square, or round basket without a handle. Set it across your tub on a wooden frame, called a cheese-ladder, which is a simple contrivance: two long sticks, and two or three short bits, nailed across to support the basket or vat: a thin cloth being laid in, the basket being large enough to admit of the edges hanging over the sides; the curd is laded out of the tub, and to aid in the draining off the whey, from time to time bring the ends and sides of the cloth together gently, so as to give an increase of pressure; when the curd is well drained, bring your vat beside the basket; have a fresh cloth laid in it; remove the curd into the vat, breaking it up, as you put it in; mingle in it a little salt, not very much, and continue to fill till the vat is full; fold over the sides of the cloth, and turn it in the vat with care; tuck the sides and ends neatly in a little way, and set your cheese in the press, not putting on the full power of weight, at first: slow pressure is best, till you again cloth your cheese. Some break the curd up fine the second removal, and increase the pressure.

At the end of sixteen or eighteen hours, the cheese may be removed to a shallow tray: a little fine salt is sprinkled over the upper surface. Some make a brine, in which they lay the cheese, and turn it, after eight or ten hours time, washing the sides with the brine, before removing it to the shelf. If very rich, a linen binder, the full depth of the cheese, may be fastened round to prevent the cheese from cracking and bulging. Care is required in turning these rich cheeses at first, but in a few days the rind begins to harden, and it can be moved with less difficulty.

A RICH CHEESE.

This is made by adding the nights' milk with the cream, warmed to the heat of new milk, to the morning's milk, instead of making it of new milk alone. This cheese is generally considered richer than the new milk cheese, and is, I believe, the mode used in Cheshire.

The larger the quantity of milk, the better will be the quality of the cheese made. To make the fine, blue moulded cheeses, so much admired by some cheese-fanciers, sprinkle a little fine flour in between the layers of curd, when putting it into the vat. This was a secret told me by a dairy-woman, famous for the manufacture of the blue cheeses.

A BUSH CHEESE.

If the settler's wife desires to make a few cheeses during the hot weather, and yet has not a sufficient quantity of milk for the purpose, the following plan is often adopted. We will suppose that the dairy consists of only three cows, the milk of which would be insufficient to make a cheese of any size. Set out the night's milk, reserving only a bowl for the use of the family; add this to the morning's milk, warming it a little, to bring the whole to the proper heat; mix in a good spoonful of rennet, and set as usual; drain the curd, leave it in the cheese-basket, covering it over with several folds of clean cloth to prevent its getting dry and hard, and set it aside in a cool corner of the dairy, cellar, or root-house, or wherever you keep your milk. The following morning, do the same; add the night and morning's milk, and curdle as before; add this day's curd to that in the basket, and if you have enough curd with the two gatherings, braid and mix all with your hands; throw in a very little salt, and put into your vat, and press as before. Sometimes three of these double meals are required for making one good-sized cheese. A simple press is made by the bush farmers, with a long lever, and a big stone or two; but this can be seen at any of your neighbor's, and would be understood far better by sight than description. I used to press my bush cheese with heavy stones on a board put on the top of the vat; but it is not so regularly pressed this way. A far easier and readier way of preparing cheese was told me by a Sussex farmer's wife; the same as that practised in Stilton; which I recommend to be adopted by Canadian farmer's wives.

SELF-PRESSING CHEESE MOULD.

This consists of a tin cylinder, about a foot in depth, and eight inches in diameter; this is perforated with holes, at intervals of about two inches from each other, all over its surface. At each end is a moveable lid, that fits on like the lid of a common tin canister. The curd is put into this mould, when it has, been fully set, and drained from the whey; the whey that still remains with the curd, flowing freely out from the holes without any other pressure; all that is necessary being to turn the mould about every hour or so, bottom upwards, for a couple of days, or till it is firm enough to turn out, and put in the salting tray. Some persons have a broad wooden hoop, that they slip over the cheese, and suffer to remain round it till it is time to remove it to the shelf for drying. I have seen cheese brushed over with whitewash to preserve it from flies, and linen binders, passed round to keep it in shape.

A GOOD HOUSEHOLD CHEESE

Is made by skimming the night's milk, and adding the milk without the cream, to the new morning's milk. This is called by some, two-meal cheese, and is very good for household use; and eaten before it becomes very dry, is a pleasant cheese, equal to the single Gloucester. It has this advantage, that it enables you to make a little butter for the table, while you are making cheese. A small pinch of saffron, steeped in warm water, may be mixed in with the milk to give a richer colour to the cheese; but a really good rich cheese needs no colouring.

CREAM CHEESE.

Take one quart of rich cream, when well soured; put it in a linen cloth, and tie it as close as you can, as you would a batter-pudding; hang it upon a hook, with a pan below it, to drain for two days; then turn it into another clean cloth, and let it drain for another two days, till it becomes solid; then lay it on a clean fine cloth, spread on a plate; fold the cloth neatly over on each side, and turn it over in the cloth on the plate; lay another smaller plate over it, turning every six hours; sprinkle a little fine pounded salt, and lay vine leaves over and under to ripen; it is fit to eat in a few days, when slightly coated.

POTATO CHEESE.

This cheese is made with mashed potatoes, salted slightly, and mixed with cheese curd, taking care to braid it well together, and press as other cheese.

POULTRY.

In these days, when all the world is running after Cochin China and Shanghai, Bantams and Dorkings, Dutch, Spanish, and Poland fowls, the omission of a chapter on the poultry-yard would, I fear, be regarded as a grave neglect in a work that is chiefly devoted to instruction on points of rural economy.

Of the management of the rarer breeds of poultry, I have had no experience myself at present, but I have been assured by those who have been most successful in their rearing of Shanghai and Cochin China fowls, that they have had no more trouble with them than with the common barn-door fowls. The want of having good fowls and plenty of eggs, seems simply to consist in attention to their being well-supplied with good food, clean water, ashes, lime, rubbish and charcoal; a clean, airy pen in summer, and a warm, sheltered roost in winter. A supply of animal food seems greatly to promote vigor in fowls. Where fewer dogs are kept, the fowls come in for much valuable food, which tells well upon the richness and increase of their flesh and eggs. Those persons who succeed best with poultry, are careful to cater well for them, and will boil up all sorts of refuse vegetables, especially potatoes, carrots, parsnips, and other roots to mix with their grain. Boiled Indian corn, or crushed corn steeped, makes very satisfying food for fowls.

In this country, fowls in general, are left very much to take care for themselves. They have the run of the barn-yard, and are even allowed by some of the improvident, small growers, who are seldom the most economical managers, to have the run of the barn itself. That such a plan is a very wasteful one it hardly needs any one to declare. Not only is there a vast and unnecessary expenditure of valuable grain, but a considerable deal that is injured and made unsaleable. By a little care of the dross and refuse corn, the fowls would be equally well fed without that woful [woeful] waste which the want of a proper system of management produces. I have known this plan pursued even among farmers who were careful in other matters, but whose wives were so short sighted, as to persuade them into the belief that, because they were able to sell a few dozen of eggs at ten-pence or a shilling a dozen, in the early part of the season, that this was all clear gain—quite forgetful of the loss and injury to the valuable grain.

Fowls fed with scalded bran, or the coarse part of the flour, generally known here as sharps or canaille, mixed with potatoes or other vegetables, any scraps of meat and refuse grain, and curdled milk scalded so as to harden the curd, with access to ashes and gravelly substances, will ensure plenty of eggs without giving them access to the barn or granary.

Besides the eggs consumed in the family, since the commencement of the laying season, my children have sent to market upwards of one hundred dozen eggs, which have been sold at prices varying from one shilling to seven pence halfpenny per dozen. The fowls have received little grain, and not much attention—in number they were about thirty-five. They were shut out from the barn, and had no access to the seed in the fields. With more attention we might have had a still larger return, but this is sufficient to prove that fowls are well worthy of the attention of the Canadian housewife.

During the grain-sowing season, and if there be any wheat fields near the farm yard, it will be advisable to confine the fowls within an enclosure—a green yard, with a high picket fence round is the best sort of fowl-yard. A coarse thread, of common Dutch twine, tied from post to post, will effectually prevent any fowl from attempting to fly over the fence. A shelter at one end of this inclosure for roost and laying place; plenty of dust and ashes in a heap for them to roll in, with a trough for water, will be all-sufficient; a tree makes a good summer roost, and a few bushes for shelter from the great heat of the sun is also advisable for the comfort of this fowl-yard. The confinement need not last long at either season, and it is well worth the trouble of having such a convenience made to prevent loss and vexation of spirit. When once made it lasts for years, and would soon repay the farmer for the outlay of a few days labour, and a few nails for fastening up the pickets.

The young chickens are seldom cooped for more than a few days, if the weather be fine and warm: they will thrive as well abroad, or in the enclosed yard.

For the rearing of geese and ducks with profit, they should have access to a creek or pond of water, mill-dam or lake. On the rice-beds geese fatten finely, and do well; but as the goslings are hatched in the spring, a season which is usually very changeable, more care is required for keeping the tender goslings from the cold and wet, than is usually bestowed upon the chickens, which come later and are more hardy. The goose is usually cooped in a large coop, and this is surrounded with a fence, enclosing several square yards of green turf. A flat pan with some stones in it is given for the goslings to wash in: the stones enable them to stand and keep themselves dry while drinking, as too much wet is bad for them during the first week or ten days. Scalded bran, curds, and crumbs, or soaked and crushed Indian corn may be given them, which, with the grass in their yard, will be all-sufficient. At a fortnight's end, if the weather be dry, they may be let out.

Geese are often found great depredators[32] in the young wheat fields. The old gander and brood geese are treated with a yoke or neck-ring: this is simply an oblong piece of shingle, shaped into an oval form, with a hole in the centre. This is drawn over the head of the goose, and effectually keeps it from breaking into the fields through the rail-fences:—a goose is never at the trouble of climbing, so the remedy is always effectual.

I have known geese sold as low as one shilling and three pence a-piece; but now they are double that price.

To make geese profitable, the farmer's wife plucks them twice and sometimes thrice in the season; but the quills are not touched, so that the animal suffers but little from the operation. The head of the goose or gander is put into a bag; (an old sock is sometimes used;) this is tied about the neck—the darkness keeps the creature quiet—and the feathers are plucked into a basket: a still day and a warm one is chosen; and in the moulting season the feathers fall easily, and perhaps the loss of them may be a relief from the heat of such a thick covering.

Turnips chopped small; raw and boiled potatoes, with the run of the barn-yard, is the goose's fare in the winter. A low log-shed, with a door to shut them in at night, is necessary. They also, as all fowls do, require lime and ashes in their house in winter. The goose begins to lay in March or April; but if the season be at all mild, in the latter part of March. The egg should be brought in as soon as laid, as the frost chills it very quickly; placed in a box of bran or sawdust, till the goose is ready to sit, and the goose must be given water, or let out to wash and feed once a day—she sits thirty days. It is better to remove the early-hatched goslings, when strong enough, to a basket, but I would not feed them; return them at night to the mother, and you will most likely have the rest of the family by the following noon. Late-hatched goslings are often allowed to go abroad under the care of the old ones without any shelter, and in some dry seasons they will succeed as well as those that have had a great fuss made

32 Presumably she meant "predators."

with them; but in cold wet springs care and shelter are requisite to ensure the lives of the little family. If the cock be remarkable for his tender care of his wives, the gander is no less admirable as a father in protecting and cherishing his young ones. There is much that is interesting and admirable to be learned in the poultry-yard by the careful observer; and many a pleasant, cheerful hour may be passed in the care of the domestic birds about the farmer's yard: children learn lessons of care and kindness, and many a moral lesson the wise mother may inculcate, even from so homely a creature as the common hen.

In suitable localities the duck is easily managed; but they need a constant supply of water, and will not thrive unless they have free access to a stream or pond. The little ducklings require to be cooped with the mother, and fed with curds, bran, or some soft food for a few weeks. They are very useful in freeing a garden from insects; and thrive well in dry weather, while very young. Near lakes and millponds they get their own living on the weeds and shell-fish; but where no water is, they require a great deal of feeding.

The turkey breeds well in Canada; but the young ones are great ramblers, and do much hurt to the young grain; and for this reason the farmer is shy of breeding them. Some manage to confine them by tethering the hen to a stake, when the young will not ramble far from her.

The Guinea fowl are hardy enough to be kept; and even the tender pea-fowl prosper and breed well in Canada; roosting within the barn in the winter; and it is not often they die from cold if well fed. I know many farmer's wives who rear the young to sell, which they do at various prices, from seven shillings and six pence to three dollars a head.

Of late years poultry have been more attended to as a matter of profit, as well as of amusement, and no doubt will well repay the care bestowed upon them.

———

FIRE.

Among the casualties that bring danger and alarm into a Canadian settler's home-stead, there is none more frequent than fire—none more terrible; but, one, where a little presence of mind, and knowing what best to do on the spur of the moment, may save both life and property. As a timely care will often do more by preventing the danger, than much exertion after it has occurred, I will warn those whose houses are heated by stoves, to have the pipes taken down, especially where there are elbows or turns in them, twice during the long winter months; have a sheet of tin or iron nailed down on the floor below the stove:—this is less troublesome than a box, as in old times was the custom, filled with sand. The kitchen stoves are, from their con-struction, less liable to take fire than any other: the dampers being pushed in will stop the draught from ascending into the pipe. If it is a chimney that is on fire, after throwing water on the logs, hang up a cloth, rug, blanket, or anything you can get hold of, made wet, in front of the chimney, and keep the doors shut; a wisp of wet straw, or old woollen rags tied on a long staff, and put up the chimney, may extinguish the fire. All houses should have a ladder at hand; there are usually ledges left on the roof, near the chimney, to facilitate cleaning them; a bunch of pine-boughs, or a bundle of straw fastened to a rope, and drawn up and down by two persons, is the common chimney-sweep of a Canadian house. A quantity of salt thrown on the fire will damp flame. A mass of fire may be put out or kept down by covering it and pressing it down; and many a child has been saved by being wrapped tightly up, so as to exclude the access of air. Even a cotton garment, if pressed closely and the air excluded, has been safely used to smother fire; but linen or woollen is best of anything for this purpose. A table-cover, carpet, rug, any large thing should be caught up, unhesitatingly, to ex-tinguish fire.

One of the great causes of destruction of houses by fire, in Canada, may be traced to the want of care in removing ashes, among which some live embers will often be hidden. No wooden vessel, pail, or box should be used to take ashes away in, and no ash-barrel should stand on the verandah, or near a wall. A proper ash-shed, away from the house, should be made, and an earthen or stone floor should be below the ash-barrels.

Sometimes people are exposed to considerable peril in new clearings, from the running of fire in the woods, or new fallows. In such case, where there is any danger of the fire getting to the homestead or standing crops, and there is no near supply of water, much can be effected by beating out the advancing flames, and still more by opening the earth with hoes, spades, or better still, by men yolking [yoking] up the cattle and ploughing a few furrows, so as to interpose the new earth between the advancing fire and the combustible matter. Women, yes, weak women and children have battled against a wall of advancing fire, and with hoes and other instruments have kept it back till help could be obtained. This subject may seem out of place to dwell upon, but I have seen many instances where, if women had not roused themselves to exertion, *all* would have been lost.

––––––––––

The summer of 1845 was one of almost tropical heat. From the first week in July to the end of August the heat exceeded that of any season within the memory of the oldest settler.

For days together the temperature varied from ninety to ninety-six, and sometimes ninety-eight degrees in the shade. We began to think any degree of heat below ninety moderate. The earth became dust; the grass, stubble; the small creeks, and most of the springs were dried up. No rain fell for many weeks. The clouds when they rose were watched with longing eyes, and every one speculated, and hoped they were charged with rain. A thunder-storm was really looked forward to as a blessing; but none came to cool the glowing atmosphere, and cool the parched earth. The cattle wandered far for water—it was a bad summer for the dairy.

A new source of anxiety arose from the fires which, as usual, had been kindled on the newly-chopped fallows.

Encouraged by the dryness of the wood, and absence of moisture from the ground and herbage, it spread with fearful rapidity—driven onwards by a strong wind.

We were surrounded by fires on all sides of the clearing. At one time the log-barn was in imminent danger of being destroyed: the fire was burning among the roots, and had got to a log-fence near the barn. This had to be removed with all speed, or the building would have been destroyed. The fire ran among the standing grass, and old rotten stumps. At night the scene was very striking:—an old log-house, used as a hay-barn, was burnt down—it was full of new hay. The hay was saved; the horses stood patiently with the fires within a few yards of them while it was removed. A quarter of an hour afterwards the building was on fire, and a fine spectacle it made. Day after day the stumps and roots continued to burn. Sometimes the fences were on fire, and all hands were obliged to assist in subduing the destructive element. The springs were dry:—we had every day to open new holes to get water to put out the fires, and the supply was so small that, if it had been our only resource, we must have been burned out; but upon the hoe, the spade, and the plough was our main reliance placed.

Help from our neighbours we could not obtain. When we sent a messenger for one, he and all his family were battling with the fire on their own clearing; to a second, his fences were on fire—all hands were employed in saving the crops; a third, the barn was in danger; and so we were forced to rouse every energy that we could to overcome the danger. Ourselves, women, and little children—all had to help; and this continued day after day. At night we got rest; for as soon as the breeze went down, and the dews fell, the fires ceased to run. The air then became oppressive to a degree of suffocation, being loaded with the smell of the rank weeds, and burning roots and stumps of decayed trees. Each night the sun went down in a red haze; no rain fell, and still the fires burned on. The wind carried the sparks into a thick cedar-swamp, not far from the house, a few acres intervening, and there it blazed and leaped from tree to tree. The children were never tired of looking at it. I trembled lest the wind should change and bring it back upon us. Often we would wonder in such case how we should save our furniture, for the fires were around us on all sides. At last, in the month of September, rain fell, and the earth smoked and reeked as it came down. The Autumn rains finally extinguished the fires all over the country, and the dread of their ravages was at an end for that year; but it was neither the first time nor the last that I have seen the fire within a hundred feet of the dwelling-house, and been obliged to give my own feeble help to assist in subduing it.

In cases of emergency, it is folly to fold one's hands and sit down to bewail in abject terror: it is better to be up and doing.

———

A FEW WORDS ABOUT AGUE

Every one considers Canada a healthy country: it is so, generally speaking; but there are diseases, such as ague and rheumatism, which are more common here than in Britain. Dysentery in children prevails during the hot months, especially among very young infants; and erysipelas, among persons exposed to the great heat of the sun in summer, having the perspiration suddenly checked by cold bathing, drinking very cold water, or being suddenly chilled by change of atmosphere. These, however, are chances which only happen to the few. The same causes would produce similar effects in any country.

Many years ago it was a rare thing to hear of colds, coughs, or influenzas,—now it is very common, and I believe, with many medical men, that the stoves have to answer for these disorders. People heat their rooms like ovens, and go out into the sharp, frosty air; they return again from the keen frosty air into heated rooms; their tender organs of respiration are not fitted to stand such reverses, and pulmonary disease and colds in the head are the result, which not unfrequently end in consumption. Formerly open fireplaces were seen in every house, and the inmates of them were healthy;—now they have stoves in every part of the dwelling, even in the bed-rooms, and the result is sickness and loss of complexion. The largest log-fires, in an open fireplace, will not produce the same general heat; but it will be far more conducive to health. A Canadian house may be kept very comfortable, without being over heated, by means of a good hall-stove and fireplaces in the sitting rooms—a porch, enclosing the outer doors, also helps to keep the house warm in winter. The inhabitants of the Lower Province, where the cold is more intense, and the winters of longer duration, understand the art of warming their houses better, and constructing them so as to keep out the cold better than we do in Upper Canada. The commonest log-house should have a verandah—no matter how homely the construction;—if only made with unbarked poles of cedar, and shingled, it will add not a little to the comfort of the family. It makes the house cooler in summer and warmer in winter; it saves much work, as the house is kept cleaner; it serves for a summer eating-room; its pillars, wreathed with hops, give a pleasant, rustic look to the otherwise unsightly log-house,

and keeps off the glare of the sun through the long summer's day. At the kitchen-end
of the house, the stoop serves for a summer kitchen, and it is there that the housewife keeps her pails, and pots, and pans—her washing tubs and barrels. The want of
this convenience is often sorely felt by the females; and I would advise every settler
who builds, by no means to omit this addition, if he has any regard for the comfort
and tidiness of his house. And here I must observe, that it is the total inattention to
the comfort and convenience of women, that often makes them unhappy and discontented in their new homes. Like the captives of Israel, they are often expected to
make bricks without straw.—Let the men do all they can to make the house as convenient as circumstances will admit of their doing, and the females must, on their
part, put up with those wants that are the result of this new order of things. Let each
comfort and cheer the other, and bear the privations and trials that befal them as
cheerfully and as hopefully as they can, and thus the burden will fall lighter upon all.

The constitutional grumbler will, of course, find many causes of complaint in
Canada; but so she would do in Australia or any other colony, and so she would in her
own country. To such unhappy tempers, all climes, all countries, and all situations
are alike—for her there is no happy land; for she bears within her breast the seeds
of misery, which will cast its baneful shadow across the threshold of her home, to
embitter all its domestic joys. In her path, thorns and thistles spring up, and choke
life's fairest flowers.

Ague is the disease most dreaded by new settlers, and to many persons it has
proved a great drawback, especially to such as go into the uncleared lands. They who
live in the long-settled parts of Canada, seldom have ague: it arises from the exhala-
tions of the vegetable soil, when opened out to the action of the sun and air. As long
as the soil is unbroken, and the woods uncleared, no such effect is felt. I have heard
some of the hardy, old trappers say, that they never had ague in the woods; but on the
newly-cleared land, or by lakes and swamps, where the sun had access, there they
would have ague. Some people never have ague; others, only the first or second year
after coming to the country; but some seldom pass a year without an attack of it. A
singular error prevails among some of the old settlers, that those who put a stop to
the disease, when it first attacks them, will be subject to it for life:—believe it not;
but use vigorous means to check it as soon as, or before, it is confirmed. Remedies
for the ague are as plentiful as blackberries; but the following mode of treatment, I
believe, to be the best of any: I have experienced its efficiency in my own family, and
as it was the prescription of a skilful physician, well acquainted with the diseases of
this country, I do not hesitate to give it:—

AGUE.

For an adult female, divide six grains of calomel[33] into three doses; take one of these doses every two hours; at the end of the sixth hour take a large tea-spoonful of Epsom salts. On the following day take a wine-glassful of the following tonic mixture: dissolve twenty grains of quinine in a pint of water, to which add four drachms of diluted sulphuric acid: if too acid, add more water to reduce it. Take the dose at seven in the morning—at eleven—and again at four, as long as the bottle lasts. When you have finished it, take a dose of senna[34] and salts; and in most cases the ague will cease; but it generally returns at the end of twenty-one days. As it is sure to give you notice of its approach, have recourse to the same doses of calomel and salts, as before, followed by the quinine and sulphuric acid; or you may take three grains of calomel the second time, divided into two doses: it seldom fails of curing. Should the disorder shew [show] any symptoms of returning the third time, do not wait for a confirmed fit, but take a few doses of the tonic mixture, diminishing the quantity from two doses to one, till you leave it off altogether.

Rest is essential for ague patients: total rest from labour, if possible, and good nourishing diet, that is not hard to digest, and change of air if the patient can leave home. Poor diet is one of the causes of ague: those who can afford to live well, seldom suffer from ague, unless in low, marshy situations.

There is an Indian remedy sold in all drug stores, in Canada; it is called Indian Cologue; it is very nauseous; but I have been told it is very effectual as a cure.

The inner bark of the wild, black cherry, steeped in whiskey, is also taken as a tonic for ague; but I have more reliance on the treatment of the disorder, as I have given above.

For a man, the dose of calomel is seven grains, in three doses; and for a child, three grains, at intervals of two hours between each grain, and a dessert spoonful of castor oil at the end of the third dose; a tea-spoonful of the tonic mixture, diluted with water, thrice a day. I have found the fit much relieved in a young child, by putting it into a warm bath and wrapping it in warm blankets, and giving it a few drops of antimonial wine, in warm drink, to promote perspiration. An emetic is often administered previous to taking any other medicine.

33 "A compound of mercury and chlorine, formerly used medicinally as a purgative" (*Canadian Oxford Dictionary*, 202).

34 A laxative prepared from the dried pods of the cassia tree (*Canadian Oxford Dictionary*, 1318).

DYSENTERY IN CHILDREN.

This disease is often fatal to young children—frequently baffling the skill of the most experienced physician.

I lost two infants who were under the care of the most careful medical men; but saved another by the use of a wild herb, that was given me by a Yankee settler's wife. A plant called spikenard, (or spignet, as she called it,) that grows in the forest, with a long spindle root, scraped, and a small quantity boiled in milk, thickens it, as if flour had been put in: it has a sweet, astringent taste, slightly bitter. A tea-spoonful, thrice given in one day, cured the child, who was wasting fast under the disease. This spike-nard belongs to the same family of plants, as the sarsaparilla: it bears black berries, not unlike the elderberry in size and taste. There are many of the old settlers who know the plant. No one should use the wild herbs without the experience of a careful person, to whom their sanatory [sanitary] or hurtful qualities are well known. The old Canadian settlers are often well skilled in the use of the native plants—they may, possibly, have learned the value of them from the Indians, or from long experience, taught by necessity, in a country where, formerly, educated doctors were far from being as commonly met with, even in the towns, as they now are. Possibly, in those days, there were fewer diseases to cure, and the simple medicines that the forest af-forded were sufficient for all curative diseases. In lonely places, where the aid of a medical man is difficult to be obtained, even severe wounds are healed, and simple fractures are reduced by the inhabitants themselves. Some one among them who has more nerve, or more judgment than the rest, is consulted upon such occasions, and faith goes a great way with many patients in effecting a cure.

When emigrants first arrive in this country, they are apt to fall ill: the change of diet, of air, and many other causes, possibly the want of comfort on board the vessel, may operate upon them to induce disease. A little care, and some doses of simple medicine, will often save themselves and children from fevers or other serious com-plaints. Timely attention to health on landing is very advisable, and it would save many from much suffering if they went at once to a skilful medical man, and pro-cured medicine and advice, which is often supplied to the poorer class of emigrants free of all cost.

BEES.

Of late years the long established settlers have begun to turn their attention to the cultivation of bees. In the Eastern, or Lower part of Canada, honey has long been a source of commercial profit to the farmer.

As an article of luxury, it stands unrivalled at our tables. As a medicine it is invaluable in its soothing, purifying, healing qualities—nay, even moral lessons have long been associated in the mind of the young child with the labours of the "Busy Bee."

It is a pity that the cultivation and profitable management of the bee is so little attended to in a country where nature has strewn the wilderness with flowers for their sustenance.

If the Lower Canadians are able, with a little care, to cultivate the hive to advantage, there can be no doubt but that the inhabitants of the Western Province might derive a considerable profit from the proceeds of this stock.

Why should we import either honey or wax if by our own labours we could raise these valuable articles on our own farms.

The British peasantry generally contrive to keep bees, and understand the management of the hives—I mean the practical part, that of housing the young swarms and abstracting the honey from them at the close of the season. They would require to pay some attention to the difference of seasons. The extreme cold of the long Canadian winter, must, of course, be taken into consideration when removing the comb. The shortness of the flowering season must also be taken into account, and proper shelter provided for the hives during the cold weather. Those cultivators from whom the stock is bought will not refuse to impart their experience, which has the great value of having been acquired after many losses and vexatious failures; they will be your best guides and advisers in the management to be adopted. I know at present of no simple practical work that has been written by the bee-keeper in Canada, for the instruction of the public: unfortunately I have no experience of my own to offer on the subject.

[A TYPICAL YEAR]

The Canadian emigrants will naturally desire to know something of the natural productions and general features of the country to which they are about to direct their steps. To enter minutely into details of the natural history of so large a portion of country, which from its geographical extent includes many varieties of climate and productions, would far exceed the limits to which this small book must necessarily be confined. A few general remarks as to climate and the vegetables and animals indigenous to the Upper or Western portion of Canada may not be uninteresting to my readers. I shall convey these in the form of a notice of the months; at the same time observing that in the parts of Canada between the shores of Lakes Ontario, Erie and Huron, a difference exists in the coming on of the winter and the approaches of early spring, which are considerably in favour of that part of the Province; many kinds of fruit coming to perfection west of Toronto, which are cultivated only with great care and difficulty on the banks of the St. Lawrence and in the counties eastward and northward of it. Vegetation is thus a fortnight or three weeks earlier in the western part of the Province than in the eastern. Some forest trees grow there which are not found with us, such as the button-wood, the black-walnut, the sweet-chestnut, the sassafras and many others.

JANUARY.

This month, though we date our new year from its commencement, as in the old country, is not really the first month of our Canadian winter, which often commences as early as the first week in November: some years however it is later, and I have seen fine mild open weather far into December; yet you must not be surprised at snow showers and severe frosts in those two months, and winter clothing should all be prepared before the chances of a November cold setting in. The month of January forms, as it were, a break in the winter's cold. I have known many new year's days when there was not snow enough on the ground to make sleighing practicable: this present January, for instance, when the earth was brown and bare, and wheeled vehicles alone were seen on the road.

The first new year's day, viz., 1833, that I passed in Canada there was no snow to be seen, and the air was so warm that we sat with the outer door open, the heat of the stoves being too oppressive for comfort. We had had snow showers as early as November the 3rd, but no intense degree of cold till after the 27th of January; after that time we had heavy snow storms and intense cold all through the month of February and up to the 17th of March, when a warm rapid thaw set in and cleared the snow off by the middle of April, even in the woods.

In the year 1846 the new year's day was warm and we walked on the dead leaves in the woods. This year 1855,[35] there was snow about the middle of November which lay till the 22nd, then the weather was mild again. We had intense cold the week before Christmas, but a thaw commenced on the 23rd and the snow disappeared, the ground being bare till the 13th of January, when a scattering of about an inch fell, but it was not till the last week in that month that any quantity of snow fell, greatly to the discomfiture of the farmer, who reckons on the sleighing season for the easier transport of his grain to market, and as a season of recreation for his family.

There is always a January thaw in the early part of the month, when the December snows melt off. The frost then relaxes its iron bands, and a moist atmosphere takes the place of the keen frosts of early winter: rain frequently falls and high winds blow. A change is sure to take place again on or about the twelfth of January: snow again covers the ground. After heavy snow storms a cold north-west wind begins to blow; the new fallen snow is sent in clouds like smoke over the open fields, drifting in high banks on the road sides, filling up the corners of the rail fences, and blocking the narrow lanes: the cutting wind plays fantastic tricks on the edges of these snow drifts, sweeping them out in hollows and caves, sculpturing their spotless surfaces in curved lines of the most graceful forms, so that you would imagine some cunning hand had chiselled them with infinite care and pains. But while these changes are going on with the snow-falls in the open country, in the great forest it is very different. There undisturbed by the war of winds, the snow flakes fall in ceaseless silent showers till the whole dark unsightly mass of fallen trees and broken boughs are covered with the spotless deposit. The thick branches of the evergreens receive the load that falls from the lofty pines and naked hardwood trees, as moved by the

35 This should be 1854. In her extensive entry for *The Female Emigrant's Guide,* Driver notes that Traill sometimes mixed up the years (Driver, *Culinary Landmarks,* 293).

wind they shake of the feathery burden. Go into the forest the morning after a heavy snow storm and you will behold one of the purest, one of the loveliest scenes that nature can offer you. The young saplings bent down with the weight of snow, unable to lift their heads, are bent into the most graceful arches and hang like bowers of crystal above your path; the keen frost has frozen the light branches and holds them down to the hardening surface, so that these bent trees remain in this way till the breath of spring sets them once more free, but often they retain the bent form and never recover the upright shape entirely. The cedar swamp which is so crowded with trees, of all ages and sizes, from the tiny seedling, rooted on the decayed trunks of the old fallen trees, to the vigorous sapling striving to make its way upwards, and the hoary trunks, over the bleached and mossy heads of which centuries have passed, now presents a curious aspect, filled with masses of new fallen snow, which forms huge caverns and curtains lying in deep banks on the prostrate trunks, or adorning the extended fanlike branches with mimic flowers of purest white.

January parties, balls, pic-nics and sleigh rides are frequent in the towns and long settled parts of the country; so that though the cold is often intense, this season is not without its pleasures. The backwoodsman is protected in his drives by the ancient forest, which excludes the wind and is equal to a second great coat in travelling.

No vegetation is to be seen going on in this month: silence and stillness prevail. The bear, the raccoon, the porcupine, the groundhog, the flying squirrel and little striped chitmunk or ground squirrel, with many other smaller animals lie soundly sleeping in their nests or burrows. The woods are deserted by most of the feathered tribes, a solitary tree creeper, the little spotted woodpecker, with some of the hardy little birds called Chickadee-dee by the natives, are alone seen on sunny days in the thick shelter of the pines and hemlocks; while around the houses of the settlers the snow birds in lively flocks whirl hither and thither in the very wildest of the snow drifts, or a solitary whiskey jack (Canada Jay) ventures to gather up the crumbs which have been swept outside the door. Sometimes the graceful form of a black squirrel may be seen running along the outstretched branch of a tree, his deep sable fur contrasting very remarkably with the glittering silver snow, over which he gambols as gaily as if in the warmth of a July sun.

FEBRUARY.

This is indeed the coldest of the Canadian winter months and though the lengthening of the days gives you more sunshine it seems to add little to your warmth. Cold and clear the sun shines out in a blue and often cloudless sky, but the thermometer often indicates a very low temperature, 10, 12, 18, nay, sometimes as low as 28 and even 30 degrees below zero [Fahrenheit]. Warm wrappings are now indispensably necessary to the traveller. In event of any person finding their ears, hands or faces frozen, which accident can be seen as well as felt, the part becoming of a livid whiteness, and feeling hard and stiff, the remedy is at hand, and must be applied immediately to the frozen part, viz., snow rubbed on hard till the flesh resumes its former healthy appearance: some apply spirits of turpentine or brandy, or spirits of any kind, after the snow has been rubbed on well.

The care of the cattle and sheep, drawing in firewood, splitting of rails for fencing, and preparing sap troughs, are the usual operations in the settlements during this month.

MARCH.

The early part of March often resembles February, with this difference, the longer days cause a relaxation of the severe cold during the sunshining hours; the very surface of the snow thaws, patches of bare earth begin to appear towards the middle of the month; the weak but pleasant note of the little song sparrow and the neat snow sparrow in its quaker-like plumage may be heard and seen as they flit to and fro, picking the seeds of the rough green amaranth and tall woolly-stalked mullien which stand faded and dry in the garden patch or on the road side. The equinox is often attended with rough gales and snow storms: these past, the sun begins to melt off the snow, and a feeling of coming spring is experienced in the soft airs, and a look of life in the bark and birds. The rising of the sap is felt in the forest trees; frosty nights and sunny days call forth the activity of the settlers in the woods; sugar making is now at hand, and all is bustle and life in the shanty.

I have largely entered into the details of this busy season in the earlier part of my book. We will now proceed to April.

APRIL.

April in Canada is not the same month in its general features, as the lovely, showery, capricious April, that month of smiles and tears, of storms and sunshine, in dear old England. It is often cold, stern and harsh, yet with many hopeful changes that come to cheat us into the belief that winter is gone, and the season of buds and flowers is at hand, and some years it is so; but only once in five or ten years does the Canadian April prove a pleasant genial month.

Some warm, lovely, even sultry days, misty like Indian summer, are experienced, and the snow melts rapidly and a few flies creep out and sport awhile in the warm beams of the young sun, but "by-and-by a cloud takes all away." The wind blows chilly, snow showers fall, and all is cold, cheerless winter again.

In fine Aprils a few blossoms peep out from under the thick carpet of dead leaves, and then you see the pretty snow-flower or Hepatica lifting its starry head and waving in the spring breezes on the way sides, on upturned roots and in the shelter of the underwood where the forest is a little thinned out so as to admit of the warm beams of the sun; pale pink, blue of two shades, and snowy white are the varieties of this cheerful little flower. Violets, the small white, and a few pale blue ones, are next seen. The rich rank soil at the edges of your clearing produces the sanguinaria or blood-root—the modest white flower shrouded at its first breaking the soil in a vine-shaped leaf, veined with orange. The root of this plant affords a bright red dye to the Indians, with which they stain the bark of their mats and baskets. You may know the blood-root, on breaking the leaf or the root, by its red juice.

In low, open, moist ground the mottled leaf of the dog's-tooth violet (erythronium) comes up, and late in April the yellow bells, striped on the outside of the petal with purplish brown, come up in abundance. Spring-beauty, too, is an April flower, a delicate little flower with pale pink striped bells—Claytonia is its botanical name—but we love to call these wild flowers by some simple name, which simple folks may easily remember.

As the snow melts off in the woods, the leaves of various evergreen plants appear still fresh and green. Among these are the pyrolas or sweet-wintergreens, a numerous and lovely family of Canadian plants; several varieties of the club-moss, one of which is known as the festoon pine, and is used to make wreaths for ornamenting the settlers' houses with. The wild garlic, too, shows its bright green spear-shaped leaves early in this month. This plant so eagerly sought for by the cattle to which it is a very healing medicine, is dreaded by the dairy-maid, as it destroys the flavour of the milk and spoils the butter.

If the month of April should prove cold, many of the above named flowers put off their blossoming time, appearing in the ensuing month of May.

April unlocks the ice-bound lakes, and streams; and it is during this month, that the winter snows are dissolved: the warmth which in sunnier climes brings to perfection the bulbs, and gives odour to the violet and blue bell, the pale primrose, and the narcissus, here must be expended in loosing the frost-bound earth from its icy fetters, and the waters from their frozen chains. Let us therefore not despise our Canadian April, though she be not as winning and fair as her namesake at home.

MAY.

Clear skies, cold and bright, often mark this month: such weather is useful in drying up the moist earth, saturated by the snow which April has melted away, and hardening the soft earth which is to be made ready for the spring crops.

This is a busy month, the busiest in all the year, for the work of two must be crowded into it.

Ploughing, sowing, planting, goes on incessantly: no time now for the gardener or the husbandman to be idle. Every thing is full of life and activity, from the little squirrel and tiny titmouse running up and down the trees, gathering its moss and grey lichens to build its curious oven-shaped nest.

What crowds of birds now visit us. The green frogs are piping in the creeks and marshes. The ground is now yielding us flowers of all hue. Yellow, blue, and white violets; butter cups, anemones, or wind-flowers, the wood daffodil, or bell flower. The snow-white trillium, moose flower some call it, wild vetches, blue and white.

Vegetables of all kinds are sown during the month of May; and the grain, such as spring wheat, barley, oats, and peas, with early potatoes, and, later in the month, Indian corn, must be put in all through May.

The bright skies and sunshine, the singing of the birds, the bursting out of the leaves and buds of all kinds make May a charming month. There is far less rain in the Canadian Spring than in the same season in Britain. There is less need for it, as the earth has received so large a share of moisture in the form of snow, during the winter months. May is usually a dry month here—sometimes cold drying winds prevail, and frosty nights are not uncommon, which often check vegetation. The new growth of the pine takes place in May.

JUNE.

This month perfects the leafage of the late deciduous trees, such as the oak, butter-nut, ash, and some others. It is in this month that the forest trees are seen in their greatest beauty, so intensely green, so varied that the eye is never tired with wandering over their living verdure. Later in the summer these charming tints seem to lose their youthful freshness, and assume one uniform color of sober green. There are frequent thunder storms and often heavy rains early in June, and sultry heat: the musquitoes and black flies, in situations favourable to them now appear; but it is in July the mosquitoes are the most troublesome, especially in the close pine woods, and near lakes and streams. On open old cleared parts of the country these pests are less known and less heeded. Flies always attack the new comers with more virulence than old settlers, who scarcely feel the annoyance.

Some of our most beautiful flowers—I mean the wild flowers—blossom during this month, such as the yellow mocassin, (and later the white and purple,) the large orange lily, lilies of many kinds, the blue lupin, the splendid enchroma or painted cup, which may be known by the brilliant scarlet colour that tips the leaves and in-volucrum of the flowers; this beautiful plant is found chiefly on dry sandy soil, or on the open plain lands: it continues from June till September. The sweet scented round leafed winter green, called lily of the valley, (it should be lily of the woods), with several of the same lovely family, bloom all through June and July.

The evening air at dewfall is now filled with the perfume of the single red-rose, a dwarf rose with crimson stems and greyish thorns, which grows in vast profusion on the plains. The sweet scented shrub Ceanothers or New Jersey tea, with white feathery flowers, also adds its perfume along with the sweet scented Monarda or mountain sweet: but these are only a few and a very few of the blossoms that you will find springing in the open fields, the deep forest or the roadside wastes.

The wild strawberry which is sure to spring up in old clearings, and new meadows, now begins to ripen from the tenth to the end of the month; you will find them red and ripe and far finer in size and flavour, than any that are to be found in the woods in the old country.

Potatoes are often planted in the early part of this month, and hoeing both of corn and potatoes, is continued, with other work on the farm.

JULY.

July is the hottest month of the Canadian year: there is often a succession of heavy thunderstorms and showers, which give a sultry heat, which is less bearable than the clear dry atmosphere that marks the harvest month of August. The raspberry and huckleberry ripen during the month of July, the rice comes in flower with many other aquatic plants. On the still flowing lakes, now may be seen vast beds of that most beautiful flower, the large white nymphæa or double white water lily, looking down through the clear water: these flowers may be discovered in every stage of progression, from the soft young bud closely folded up in its oily olive coloured calyx, to the half opened blossom, showing its ivory petal, and the nearly full-blown flower still shielding the lemon-tinted anthers, which are seen only fully developed in the perfect blossom which sits as a crown upon the waters, giving out its exquisite odour to the soft breeze that gently stirs the limpid bosom of the lake. The deep golden cup of the yellow nymphæa may also be seen, seldom far removed from the white blossomed; and the arrow-shaped leaves of the blue spiked pondwort and rosy flowers of the persicaria, form a beautiful sight on hot sunny days.

The meadows are now mowed, and the hay harvest is in full operation; and if the weather have proved sufficiently warm, the earliest sown fall wheat will be now cradled, i. e. mown with the cradle scythe; an instrument which has quite set aside the old reaping hook and sickle. A good cradler will cut three acres of heavy wheat in a summer's day: one or more following in his steps to bind and stock up the sheaves.

The cherry, currant and garden raspberry, are now ripe—peas and some other vegetables—but early potatoes are still rare unless care has been taken to plant early kidneys, which should be put in early in May to ensure their being fit for table in the middle of July.

Many splendidly coloured butterflies are seen during the hot months of July and August, some of a superior size to any seen in England. The large brimstone swallow tail, the great scarlet and black; admirals of several sorts, with a variety of small gay winged species, and some very fine moths, one of a delicate green with coloured eyes in its wings, red feet, and a thick body covered with white feathery down; besides sphinges and tiger moths, with an endless list of dragon flies, and beetles of various hues appear.

The humming birds may now be seen, making frequent visits to the flower garden, hovering over the open blossoms of the larkspurs, morning-glories, scarlet bean, and any other honey yielding flowers. In the forest you may chance to see the gay glancing wings of that shy but splendid bird, the scarlet tanager or summer red-bird; while in the orchard and gardens, the blue-bird and the wild canary, or American gold-finch, dart to and fro in the sunshine; and at night, the rapid voice of the whip-poor-will is heard from eve till dawn, especially where there are groves of trees, near the house: you will know the oriole by its orange and black plumage; the cat-bird by its long tail, dark dove coloured coat, and squalling note, much like that of a cat calling her kittens. The saucy blue or crested jay, calls "Thate, Thate," and the "Phœbe," repeats its own name in a variety of tones.

It is pleasant to know even a bird or a flower by name, and though some of my readers may care for none of these things, there may be others, and perhaps not a few, who may be glad of the information I have given them about the wild flowers and wild creatures of the strange land they may be destined to sojourn in for many years. It may enable them to teach their children the names of the natural productions, and create an interest in their young minds in the new country, which will not be without its beneficial effects upon their minds. Little children love simple knowledge, and ask for it eagerly. To acquire the name of any object that strikes its fancy, is the first step on the young child's ladder to learning.

AUGUST.

Harvest, if not begun in the last-named month, commences the first week in this. The grain now ripens as fast as it can be cut and carried. The weather is generally hot, dry, and clear all through this month, with splendid sunsets; but the nights are often cool— almost chilly. It is during the wet season that agues and other intermittents usually prevail, more than in the moister months of the spring. The heavy dews should be avoided as much as possible. Towards the latter part of August, it is not very unusual to experience slight frosts at night. I have seen a change on some of the forest-leaves before this month was out. Some of the earlier sorts of apples may be used now—the early Harvest-Yellow, Harvest and Early Joe, with some others.

Sunflowers of many kinds are now in bloom, with many sorts of fruit. The mandrake or May-apple may now be gathered: the berries of many wild plants are ripe. The flower-garden is in all its glory. Melons ripe, and all kinds of vegetables. Nature is perfecting her great work. Not only is man busy with the harvest, but the wild animals are also garnering up their winter stores. The squirrels are busy from morning till night, gleaning the ripe grain, and laying it up on the rail fences and stumps to dry in the sun before they venture to carry it off to their granaries and burrows: they are a lively, busy race; ever at work or at play. They seem to me the happiest of all God's creatures, and the prettiest.

The flowers that are most commonly seen now are of the starry or syngenesian class—sunflowers, asters of many kinds, golden-rod, lion's-foot, liatris or gay-feather, with many others.

SEPTEMBER.

This is one of the most delightful months in the year. The heat is sometimes very great in the first week; but after that is past, a genial warmth, with a clear air, is felt. The warm rich tints steal by degrees over the trees, especially those that grow at the outer edges of the clearings, and the soft maples and dogwood bushes that skirt the water; but it is not till the rains of the equinox, and its subsequent frosts, that the glory of the autumnal foliage is seen in all its splendor.

The harvest is now over; and the fall ploughing has begun with great zeal: by the second week in this month, most of the wheat will have been sown, unless where sickness or other causes have delayed the work. September, like May, is a busy month in Canada. The Indian-rice is now ripe, and the squaw goes forth in her light bark canoe, to gather in her harvest—one which, like the birds of the air, she gathers, without having scattered the seed, or toiled for its increase.

OCTOBER.

There is generally a season of rain during the last week of September, lasting until the tenth or twelfth of October. This may be looked for almost as a certainty. The weather generally clears about that time, and frosty nights and mild days ensue. Indian-summer, for the most part, succeeds close upon the rainy season. Warm, sultry, hazy days. The autumn foliage is fast covering the earth with a thick carpet of variegated leaves, returning to her bosom that which was derived from her, to be again resumed in due season, to form fresh leaves and buds, and woody fibre. How much wisdom may be imparted to us even by the fall and decay of the leaves of the trees; and to man alone has been given the privilege of looking upon these things with the eye of faith and reason, that by the small and weak things of earth, his soul may be lifted up to Heaven, to adore God the Creator in all his works.

The last flowers that linger yet are the Gentians. These belong to the months of September and October, exclusively, and are among the most beautiful of the Canadian wild-flowers. The large, bright-blue, fringed gentian, may be seen lifting its azure blue and white-fringed bell, by shady banks and open woods, in size varying from the plant of two or four inches in height, to the tall branching one of two and three feet high, with flowers proportionably large. The pitcher-shaped gentian, of deep cerulean blue, closed at the lips, is found in damp spots; not in the close swamps of the forest, however, but in open places, a little marshy, and among small thickets. The pale lilac whorled Gentian grows more frequently in half-cultivated fields, and waste lands; while the full, deep-coloured purple of the large bell-flowered gentian, the Calathian violet, is found on dry sandy and gravelly soil. This is one of the most beautiful of all our wild-flowers, and is worthy of a place in any garden. I have seen it in conservatories at home, tenderly nursed and guarded with care, while here it braves the first chilling frosts, and may be said to lay its head almost on the lap of winter snows.

The lovely asters, the late everlasting, the golden-rod, and a few more hardy plants, linger on in bloom through the Indian-summer, and then wither with the first hard frosts.

It is during the Fall months that the Northern-lights are so frequently seen illumining the horizon—a novelty which will attract the attention of the emigrant, and fill him with pleasing admiration. It is seen at times all through the year, but in September, October and November more frequently, especially before the setting in of the Indian-summer.

Early in this month, the root-crops are stored, and such trees planted out, as you desire, in the orchard.

NOVEMBER.

Our year is fast drawing to a close: all Nature seems preparing for the change. The squirrel and wood-chuck have laid by their stores of nuts and grain and seeds. The musk-rats and beavers have built their houses, and the latter have repaired their dams. The summer birds have left us: the discordant cry of the blue jay is heard only at intervals. Only a few of our old feathered friends abide with us, and they seek the warm shelter of the woods, and doze away the long cold winter in silence and gloom.

November is very unlike the foggy, cheerless, dark, soul-depressing month, bearing that name in Britain: it often, it is true, wears the garb of winter, but this is by no means a certain characteristic of the season. There are often delightful days of sunshine and clear frost; and, in some years, Indian-summer falls into this month, and gives an aspect of warmth and loveliness to the very borders of Winter's frozen garments.

The plough is now busy preparing the fallows for the ensuing Spring crops, that the soil may be mellowed by the Winter frost and snow. This work continues as long as the ground is open. The only plants now of any interest are the wintergreens. The red berries of the cranberries, and the purple clusters of the frost grapes, give liveliness and beauty to the scenery.

DECEMBER.

Sometimes this month is open and fair during the first week or so; but it varies from moderate to intense cold. We must not be surprised at finding the streams ice-bound, the earth hardened into stone, or deep snow covering the earth; but this is according to our climate; and to those who look for its approach, and are in any way prepared for its severity, the Canadian winter is a cheerful season.

CLOSING REMARKS ON THE MONTHS

I have brought my year to its close. Some will think my sketch too fair a one, because they will experience many changes and discomforts; and seasons are brightened or darkened by our individual feelings and domestic circumstances. To the sad and sorrowful all seasons are alike gloomy.

"To feverish pulse each gale blows chill."

I have chosen a medium year from among those of which I have kept a faithful diary, and I consider it a fair average of the Canadian climate, or of that portion of Canada lying between Toronto and Kingston. Above, it is milder; below colder, but less variable.

Some decided changes I have marked in my time. The year 1834 the Spring came on very early: the snow was all gone in March, and earlier in the sun-exposed clearings: leaves were out in the first week in May; but a severe frost and snow took place on the 14th and 15th of May, and cut off vegetation for a time; nevertheless, we had a long, dry, hot Summer, and fine Fall.

We then had three successive wet harvests; which, with a visitation of cholera, checked emigration for several years: this, joined to the rebellion, proved a great drawback to the prosperity of the colony. Good, however, sprung out of evil, and many ills and abuses were remedied, which might have remained to this day, but for the attention of the rulers of the people being turned towards them.

We have had winters of comparative mildness, with plenty of snow, but no very intense cold. The Spring of 1839 was very early, but the Summer was hot and moist; and that year we had a long Indian summer; while some years we have had scarcely any weather corresponding to that uncertain season.

Spring is the most uncertain of our seasons. The Fall is the wettest, but often the most delightful of them; but to such as are of a contented spirit, there is good at all seasons, and in everything: for as the old poet says—

"Not always fall of leaf, nor ever Spring;
Not endless night, nor yet eternal day;
The saddest birds a season find to sing,
The roughest storms a calm may soon allay:
Thus with succeeding turns God tempers all,
That man may hope to rise, yet fear to fall."*

I now subjoin a few valuable extracts, selected from some well-written letters, which were published in 1853 as a supplementary sheet to a newspaper issued in Toronto, entitled the "Old Countryman."

These "Letters from Canada" are deserving of a wide circulation, as I think the selections I have made for my readers will prove. The limits of this work forbid my introducing a larger portion of the valuable matter contained in the original publication.

EXTRACTS FROM "LETTERS FROM CANADA."[36]

"All the favourable impressions of Canada, which I named to you before, have been fully confirmed upon a more accurate enquiry into her *wonderful* resources and capabilities; if there be any country which deserves to be known at home, that country is Canada. We seem never to have realized what Canada really is, and have always thought of her as a desolate and chilly place, the abode, of anthropophagi and musquitoes, from whence we got ice and pine timber; instead of which, it is a country about four times the size of the British Possessions in Europe, producing almost everything which can minister to the comforts and luxuries of life, and where, within the space of less than fifty years, millions of acres of land have been converted from forest and swamps into fruitful and well-cultivated farms, supplying not only the wants of its own rapidly-increasing population, but enabling us to export produce to the States and England to the value of some millions sterling every year. This, however,

---

* These lines form a portion of an admirable little poem called "Times Go by Turns," written by Father Robert Southwell, who was the victim of religious persecution during the reign of Queen Elizabeth.

36 These letters are unlikely to have been written by Traill herself.

it is desirable to prove by something more than mere assertion. Canada has a fruitful soil and a fine climate—she has before her a glorious prospect, and her sons and daughters a lofty mission—she is a land of kindling energies, and of untold and undeveloped resources, which will give her soon a place and a name among the nations of the earth: she entertains a warm and affectionate regard for the "old house at home," and a deep feeling of loyalty towards her Sovereign, and it would have delighted that distinguished Personage could she have seen the way in which her last Birth-day was celebrated on this side of the Atlantic.

"It is truly cheering to see how fondly "home" is spoken of here, for it is by that endearing word that England is known here, and when I say England, I mean of course the United Kingdom. It makes my old heart stir within me to hear our far-off home thus spoken of in the Provincial Parliament and in the shanty of the settler. There is indeed a mighty and enduring force in old and early associations, which time and distance cannot obliterate or diminish.— There is a magic in the word when uttered here which I cannot describe. It is a word that conjures up memories of the past on which the heart loves to linger—the memory of prayers uttered on bended knees at the feet of departed parents—who blessed our early and guided our advancing years—when the pas- sions of youth were unsubdued and the principles of manhood unconfirmed. It recals [recalls] the abode of distant, most loved, and loving friends, and brings back scenes on which the eye has not rested for many a year of anxious struggle and final success. I must tell you a little anecdote on this point which moved me exceedingly. I called, one day, while in the Bush, at the house of a venerable old man of eighty—a soldier and a gentleman—who had been here forty years, and seldom got any tidings from home. I happened to have in my pocket-book a primrose, which dearest —— sent me in a letter, and I placed it on the old man's knee and said, "Did you ever see a flower like that?" The old man took it up and when he recognised it he kissed the pale flower over and over again, and bending his aged head he wept like a child, so long and so violently that I was alarmed. Who can tell what thoughts this little flower awakened in the old man's mind? The thoughts of some shady lane, perchance, near the unforgotten home of his childhood—

"The first love-beat of his youthful heart,"

a mother's gentle look, a father's word of approbation or sign of reproof; a sister's gentle love, a brother's fond regard, handsful of flowers plucked in green and quiet meadows—birds' nests admired, but not touched—the Sabbath call to prayer and praise. It was too sacred a sight for a stranger's eye. I don't *think* he could have spoken, I am *sure* I could not. So I wrote in pencil a few words promising to see him again, and, if we should be both spared, that he should next spring, have a pale memorial of spring and home from the same green lane as the one which had, much to his honour, elicited, "A Soldier's Tear."

In order that you, and other friends at home, may known how this Province is divided, I send you a small diagram.

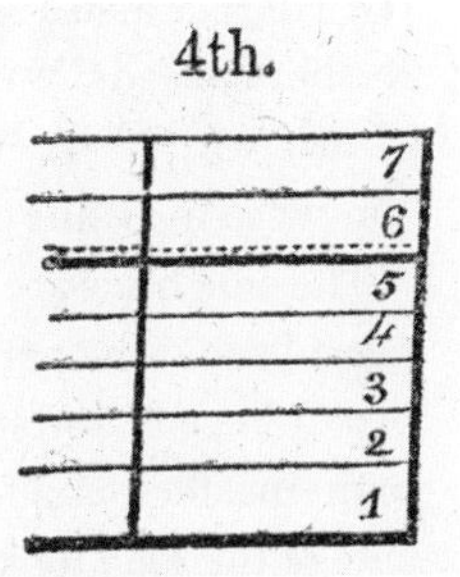

The dark lines, running North and South are road allowances, and called Concession lines, the others are side lines, the smaller lines are the division of each block into 200 acre lots, which are all numbered; and, on asking, you would be told that "the Old Countryman lived on Lot 3, on the 4th," meaning the 4th Concession.

Another thing has surprised me, and I want much to have it explained, viz, why a Medical School, conducted here by very eminent members of the profession, was done away with.[37] Canada is a very healthy country, no doubt, but accidents and diseases must happen; and nothing can be more important to a community than that we should have well informed, well instructed and cultivated medical men, to whom to entrust our lives and limbs. If any one will send me a temperate history of this matter you shall it; but there must be no personalities beyond those which are necessary to elucidate the matter. There are some cases of personal hardship connected with the matter I *know* of, where medical men having given up their private practice to become professors in

Fig. 14 · Provincial division diagram. This little diagram was in Traill's original text at this location.

---

37 The author was likely referring to the abrupt and controversial closure of the decade-old University of King's College Medical School in 1853. (King's College became the University of Toronto in 1849.) This prosperous medical school, and the law school too, were abolished by legislative order on the politically motivated grounds that the professions of medicine and law should not be supported by state funds but by private enterprise. The professors lost their university positions and went to teach at several private medical schools with lower standards, which led to many Canadian doctors with questionable credentials. The Faculty of Medicine at the University of Toronto was reinstated in 1887. See Shorter, *Partnership of Excellence*, 18–21, and Wallace, *A History of the University of Toronto*, 208–11.

the medical school, have little left them but hearty sympathy, blighted hopes, ruined prospects, and severe, though silent, suffering.

The consumption of timber here is most wonderful, and I shall write to you more at length on this subject.

There are scarcely any hedgerows here, and the long dreary miles of roads and fences, made of what are called snake fences, give a cold look to the country. There is also a sad want of clumps of trees for shade, and shelter also, about the homesteads. With the early settlers every tree was a weed of gigantic growth. "Down with it" was the universal motto. Many persons have wasted and burnt timber to the value of the fee simple of their estates.

The side lines are singularly long and dreary roads, and have not the advantage of the "long perspective view, with a church at the end of it"—the definition of a College Fellowship. I submit the following sketch very respectfully to the path-masters, and fence-viewers of Canada, and I leave them to consider which side of the road looks best.

A CANADIAN SIDE LINE.

AS IT IS.   AS IT MIGHT BE.

Fig. 15 · Canadian side line. This little diagram was in Traill's original text at this location.

There is glorious fishing and shooting in this country. Fish abound every-where. —— has caught them by the hundred weight on those lovely lakes, Simcoe and Couchiching. This is a beautiful and an interesting spot, and if there were hotels affording good accommodation at Atherley and Orillia, lots of people would go there. We shall soon be within three hours of it by the North-ern Railroad, and a Steamer in connection with it. The interests of the public and the railroads are identical, and we are looking forward to increased and cheap facilities for locomotion by the issue of season, day, and return tickets; and a reduction, by means of the railroad, in the price of cord-wood, which is now five dollars a cord here, and only one dollar on the lake shores of Simcoe and Couchiching. We shall soon see houses on the line of railroad, as we have at home; and writing of this, there are two classes of houses wanted here, some of about £25 per annum, for the gentry, and some of much less rental, for mech-anics. If the former could be had, many families would resort here to educate their children. They should be brick or stone houses, wooden houses should be discouraged, and, in some places, strictly *forbidden!*

At Mara and Rama we saw many Indians, of whom I will tell you more here-after. Poor Indians! the White Man has brought them disease, and taught them drunkenness, and they are dying out fast. Small Pox is very fatal to them. I do hope that the Indian Presents may not be discontinued, at least suddenly.[38] Even now the subject is forming matter of discussion at their Council, and they talk, poor simple-minded harmless, creatures, of sending a deputation to their Great Mother! Canada! thou art prosperous and prospering, set not your heart too much on riches! The Lords of the Soil have lost their hunting grounds and even the birch bark for their frail canoes is getting scarce. There will soon be no place for the Red Man's foot or the free bird's wing. You have asked for their broad lands and they have given them. What have you given *them?* Disease, and Whiskey and Death! I saw the bereaved parents of a young Indian, who was drowned when drunk, bending meekly in a Christian Church at Orillia, with a devotion that might be imitated by many a white Christian. The mourners were an Indian Chief and his wife. On my pointing the next day to the crape on his hat, he said with a tone of grief and resignation I shall never forget:—"Mine

---

38 "Indian Presents" probably refers to items such as tea and tobacco, often offered as placatory gestures of friendship to First Nations peoples. Some First Nations people came to rely on them.

first-born! Whiskey too much! Drowned!" Let them be weaned by kindness and persuasion from this horrid vice. Give the poor things their presents yet for a few years. Earth is *their* school as well as *ours*. Heaven their Home as much as ours! Fit them for both!

England and Canada should never forget the time when the Red Man was their Ally, and fought and bled in the fore front of many a stricken field; and now when they are comparatively a "feeble folk," their good services should not be forgotton [forgotten] for the sake of a few thousands a year. When National Faith has once been pledged or implied to any contract, it should *never be broken,* and the value of the pledge will be measured and estimated by the magnitude and character of the nation giving it. I will conclude this letter with an interesting anecdote on this subject.

St. George's day was this year celebrated in a very gratifying way, at New York, by Americans and English. In replying to a Toast, Major Sprague, of the U. S. army, said:—"Some years ago I was engaged in removing some Indians beyond the Mississippi, and one day when encamped I saw a party approaching me. I took my glass and found they were Indians. I sent out an Indian with the *Stars and Stripes* on a flag, and the leader of the Indians immediately displayed the RED CROSS OF ST. GEORGE! I wanted him to exchange flags, but the Savage would not, for said he—"I dwell near the Hudson's Bay Company, and they gave me this flag, and they told me that it came from my Great Mother across the great waters, and would protect me and my wife and children, wherever we might go; I have found it as the White Man said, and *I will never part with it!*" "I could not," added the gallant officer emphatically, "but admire the feeling of confidence and the sentiment."

I hope these letters won't tire you, but Canada is an exhaustless theme, and well deserves to be examined throughout and known. She presents a vast opening to the agriculturist, a most interesting field of study for the botanist, the naturalist, the geologist, and an interesting and much needed mission for the Divine.

You must bear in mind that when I name the price of any Canadian produce, the sum named is in *currency,* unless I distinctly call it sterling value; the simple way to bring which into sterling money is to deduct one fifth."

———

I have now brought my labours to an end, and will close my book with some lines, which, though copied from a translation of a Chinese poem, appear to be well suited to the flourishing state of the Canadian colony:—

> Where spades grow bright, and idle swords grow dull,
> Where jails are empty, and where barns are full;
> Where churchyards are with frequent feet outworn,
> Law courts are weedy, silent and forlorn.
> Where doctors foot it, and where farmers ride,
> Where age abounds, and youth is multiplied,
> Where these signs be, they clearly indicate,
> A happy people and well governed state!

THE GRAVES OF THE EMIGRANTS.[39]

———

They sleep not where their fathers sleep,
　　In the village churchyard's bound;
They rest not 'neath the ivied wall,
　　That shades that holy ground.

Not where the solemn organ's peal,
　　Pours music on the breeze,
Through the dim aisle at even hour,
　　And swells amid the trees.

Not where the turf is ever green,
　　And spring-flowers blossom fair,
Upon the graves of the ancient men,
　　Whose children sleep not there.

Where do they rest, those hardy men,
　　Who left their native shore?
To earn their bread in distant lands,
　　Beyond the Atlantic's roar?

They sleep on many a lonely spot,
　　Where the mighty forest grew,
Where the giant pine, and stately oak
　　A darkling shadow threw.

The wild bird pours her early song,
　　Above their grassy graves;

39　This poem and all the others are not in the first edition, but appear in the second.

And far away through the stilly night,
 Is heard the voice of waves.

And the breeze is softly sighing,
 The forest boughs among,
With mournful cadence dying,
 Like harps by angels strung.

And lilies nursed by weeping dew,
 Shed here their blossoms pale;
And spotless snow-flowers lightly bend,
 Low to the passing gale.

The fire-fly lights her sparkling lamp,
 In that deep forest-gloom;
Like Hope's blest light that breaks the night
 And darkness of the tomb.

The mossy stone, or simple cross,
 Its silent record keeps,
Where mouldering in the forest-shade,
 The lonely exile sleeps.

————————

(From the Old Countryman.)

A SONG FOR CHRISTMAS.[40]

THE OLD HOLLY-TREE.

Oh! the old holly-tree is a beautiful sight,
With its dark, glossy leaves, and its berries so bright;

---

40 Traill's poem was not included in the first edition, but in the second. The material between here and the conclusion was written by Traill but published earlier in *The Old Countryman*. We don't know whether she suggested its inclusion or whether the decision was made by the publisher Thomas Maclear or her agent Henry Hope.

It is gay in the winter, and green in the spring,
And the old holly-tree is a beautiful thing.

It gladdens the cottage, it brightens the hall,
For the gay holly-tree is beloved by us all:
It shadows the altar, it hallows the hearth—
An emblem of sacred and innocent mirth!

Spring blossoms are lovely, and summer flowers gay;
But the chill winds will wither and chase them away;
But the rude blasts of Autumn and Winter may rave
In vain round the holly, the holly so brave!

Though the "fine old English gentleman" no longer now is seen;
And customs old have passed away, as things that ne'er have been;
Though wassail shout is heard no more, nor missletoe [mistletoe] we see;
Yet they've left us yet the holly-green, the bonny holly-tree!

C. P. T.

Oaklands, Rice Lake.

MEMORIES OF CHRISTMAS DAY
IN THE BACKWOODS.

———

When first I came to Canada, I was much surprised at the cold indifference which most people showed in their observance of Christmas day—with the exception of the then few residing English families, the church was scantily attended. For in those days there was no dressing of the houses or churches with evergreens as is now so generally the custom, (long may it continue); and I missed the heartfelt cordiality that seems on that sacred day of Christian gladness to overflow all hearts, and break out into smiles of loving kindness to the poorest and least cared for of our fellow creatures. There be many—who with a scoffing eye look upon the decoration of our

Fig. 16 (*above*) · Children in a sleigh. Traill's Christmas essay was not included in the first thousand printing of the first edition of 1854 (1855), but appeared in the second thousand (early 1855), with this image above the essay title.

hearths and altars on that day, and loudly condemn it as a rag of Romanism. But are we really better Christians for casting aside all those old customs, that tended to hold us in the bond of unity and Christian love? I cannot but think that this old custom had its origin in the palm branches, that were strewed in the way of our Lord when the multitudes cut down branches from the trees, and strewed them in the way, crying "Hosannah to the son of David." Did Christ reprove the people for this simple sacrifice in honour of him?—Why then should our observance of this old custom draw down upon us the rebuke of our neighbours?

I remember the first Christmas day I passed in Canada—being laughed at because I wandered out on to the plains near Peterboro', and brought in a wreath of the box-leaved trailing wintergreen (which with its scarlet berries reminded me of the varnished holly with which we were wont to garnish the old house at home), and hanging it over the mantel piece, and above the pictures of my host's parlor, in honor of the day. It seemed to me these green branches might be held as emblems to remind us that we should keep faith bright and green within our hearts.

But while the *nativity* of our Lord was little regarded, all its honor and glory was conferred on the New Year's day. This is with the Canadians the day of days. The world claims that, which used to be given to Christ.

The increase of British settlers however has done something towards restoring a Christian feeling among us, and now our churches are duly dressed with evergreens, our hymns and anthems sung, and our friends and families meet together as of old.

I remember one Christmas day in the Bush. It was the year after the memorable rebellion in Canada: my brother-in-law had been appointed to a company in the Provincial Battalion then stationed in Toronto; my sister who had remained behind with her infant family was alone, and we were anxious that she should spend this day with us, and that it might look more like an English Christmas day, I despatched Martin, the boy, and old Malachi, the hired man, to bring a sleigh load of evergreens, from the swamp to dress the house with, but when all our green garlands were put up, we missed the bright varnished holly and its gay joy-inspiring red berries, and my English maid Hannah, who was greatly interested in all our decorations, remembered that there were high-bush cranberries, at the lake shore, and winter greens in the swamp, but these last were deep beneath a covering of two or three feet of snow. With the red transparent berries of the cranberry we were obliged therefore to content ourselves, and little Katie brought her string of coral beads and bade me twist it among the green hemlock boughs, clapping her hands for joy when she saw it twined into the Christmas wreath.

Then we sent off the ox sleigh for my sister, and her little ones, for be it known to you, my reader, that our settlement in those days was almost the Ultima Thule of civilization,[41] and our roads were no roads, only wide openings chopped through the heart of the forest, along which no better vehicle than an ox sleigh could make any progress without the continual chance of an overturn. We bush-settlers were brave folks then, and thankfully enjoyed every pleasure we could meet with, even though we had to seek it through means so humble as a ride in a rude vehicle like an ox sleigh, through the wild woods, with the snow above, and the snow below, and in good truth many a pleasant ride have we enjoyed travelling through that dim forest, through bowers of snow-laden hemlocks and dark spruce, which shut us out from the cold wind, like a good fur-lined cloak.

Reposing on a bed of hay covered with buffalo or bear skins, or good wool coverlets, and wrapped in plaids, with well wadded hoods, we were not a whit less happy than if we had been rolling along in a gay carriage, drawn by splendid horses, instead of the rudest of all vehicles, and the most awkward and clumsy of all steeds. At night our lamps, the pale stars and the moon, walking in brightness in the frosty sky, casting quaint shadows of gigantic form across the snowy path, or wading through misty wrack or silver-edged cloud.

A glorious goose fattened on the rice bed in our lake, was killed for the occasion: turkeys were only to be met with on old cleared farms in those days, and beef was rarely seen in the back woods,—excepting when some old ox that was considered as superannuated was slaughtered to save it from dying a natural death. Remember this was sixteen years ago,[42] and great changes have taken place since that time in the condition of all ranks of people in the Province; now there are luxuries, where before necessaries were scarce. However there was no lack of Christmas cheer in the shape of a large plum pudding, to which our little ones did ample justice. A merry day it was to them, for our boy Martin had made them a little sledge, and there was a famous snow drift against the garden fence, which was hard packed and frozen smooth and glare—up and down this frozen heap did James and Kate[43] with their playmates glide and roll. It was a Christmas treat to watch those joyous faces, buoyant with mirth, and brightened by the keen air, through the frosty panes; and often was the graver

41 "Ultima Thule" was a faraway land or the highest point attainable. To the Ancient Greeks, Thule was a far-distant land north of Britain, possibly Norway (*Canadian Oxford Dictionary*, 1573).

42 In other words, the Christmas of 1837.

43 Two of Traill's children.

converse of the parents interrupted by the merry shout and gleesome voices of their little ones; and if a sadder train of thought brought back the memory of former days, and home, country, and friends, from whom we were for ever parted; such sadness was not without its benefit, linking us in spirit to that home, and all that made it precious to our hearts; for we knew on that day our vacant places would be eyed with tender regret, and some kind voice would murmur,

'Ah would they were here.'

That night, unwilling to part too soon, I accompanied my sister and her little ones home. Just as we were issuing forth for our moonlight drive through the woods, our ears were saluted by a merry peal of sleigh bells, and a loud hurrah greeted our homely turn-out, as a party of lively boys and girls, crammed into a smart painted cutter, rushed past at full speed. They were returning from a Christmas merry-making at a neighbour's house, where they too had been enjoying a happy Christmas; and long the still woods echoed with the gay tones of their voices, and the clear jingle of their merry bells, as a bend in the river-road, brought them back on the night breeze to our ears. There then we were breaking the Sabbath stillness of the dark forest with the hum of joyous voices, and the wild bursts of mirth that gushed forth from those glad children, who had as yet known little of the cares and regrets that later years bring with them as the inevitable consequence of a mature age. But soon overpowered by excess of happiness, and lulled by the low monotonous creaking of the runners of the sleigh, and heavy footfall of the oxen, one by one, our happy companions dropped off to sleep, and we were left in silence to enjoy the peculiar beauties of that snow clad scene, by the dreamy light that stole down upon our narrow road through the snow laden branches above our heads. And often in after years, when far removed from those forest scenes, has that Christmas night returned to my memory, and still I love to recall it for it, brings with it the freshness of former days, and the array of infant faces now grown up and fulfilling the state of life into which they have been called by their Heavenly Father.

C. P. T.

Christmas, 1853 Oaklands, Rice Lake.

———

INDIAN SUMMER.[44]

This mysterious second summer comes for a brief season to quicken the vegetation of the new sown grain, and to perfect the buds that contain the embryo leaves and blossoms of the future year, before the frost of winter shall have bound up the earth with its fetters of ice. The misty warmth of the Indian Summer steals drowsily upon our senses. We linger lovingly over each soft day that comes to us, folded in a hazy veil, and fear each one will be the last. They seem to us

"Like joys that linger as they fail,
Whose last are dearest."—

We watch with anxious eye the sun go down in the smoky horizon, and wonder if we shall see another Indian Summer day arise on the morrow.

The earth is rendering up her increase on nature's great altar, giving back to us some of the teeming warmth that she had collected during the long hot days of July, August and September.

It is natural to suppose that the mist that softens the atmosphere at this peculiar season arises from vegetable decomposition.

Or may be it has its origin in a remoter cause: the commencement of the polar winter. This subject has puzzled wiser heads than mine; therefore I will dismiss that part of my subject to the natural philosophers of this enlightened, reasoning age.

Among the peculiarities of this season, may be noticed, frosty nights, followed by warm soft days; sometimes a hot stirring breeze comes on about noon, at other times a stillness almost sultry continues through the day. From notes made in my journal during a succession of years, I have remarked that the Indian Summer comes on directly after the rains which prevail during the equinox, and the first two weeks in October. From the tenth or 15th of October to the first week in November, I should fix as the usual period of Indian Summer. Old settlers say that it comes earlier now than in former years. The date used to be as late as the 20th of November, but it is rarely so late now, whatever be the cause.

The Northern lights are frequently seen about the commencement of the Indian Summer, often being visible for many successive nights. The termination of this lovely serene season is very generally accompanied with a tempest, a hurricane, a violent rain, ending in snow and sharp frost.

44 Not in first edition, but appears in the second.

Though so lovely to the senses, it is not always a season of health: autumnal fevers and agues, with affections of the chest, are common, Nevertheless, this Indian-Summer is hailed by the Indian people with joy. It is emphatically speaking, indeed the INDIAN'S SUMMER—his own peculiar season—his harvest in which he gathers in the winter-stores.

At this time the men forsake the villages and summer-lodges, and go off to their far-off hunting-grounds, for venison and furs. Now is their fishing-season; and it is in the month of October, that the lakes swarm with myriads of wild-fowl.

The term *Indian-Summer,* always sounds to me as so expressive of the wants, habits and circumstances of the race. Their summer is not our summer. Like the people it is peculiar to this continent.— *They* reap while *we* sow. While *they* collect, *we* scatter abroad the seed for the future harvest.

It is by minute observation upon the objects with which he is most familiar, that the Indian obtains his knowledge:—a knowledge which has hitherto been sufficient for the supply of his very limited wants. He knows by the thickness of the down on the breasts of the wild fowl, and the fur of his peltries, whether the coming winter will be a severe one or otherwise. By the number of small animals that congregate in their several haunts, and the stores which they lay up, whether the season will be of longer or shorter duration. By the beavers repairing their dams, and the muskrats building their houses earlier than usual, that the cold will also set in early.

In all these things the Indian trusts to the instinct of the lower animals, which is a knowledge given from God above—a great gift to help the weakest of his creatures.*

The unlettered Indian, in the simple faith of his heart, believes that the Almighty Creator—whom he adores as the GOOD SPIRIT, speaks to his creatures, tells them of his will, and guides them how to act, and provide for the winter's cold, be it little or be it much.

A great deal of the fruitfulness of the next year's harvest, may depend upon the length or shortness of the Indian-Summer.

It is during this season that the farmer stores his root-crops, and prepares his fallow lands. If as it sometimes happens, the Indian summer is short, and early frosts stop the ploughing operations, the Spring crops must suffer.

---

* "God's gift to the weak:" as says Mrs. Southey. [In the Explanatory Notes to Rupert Schieder's critical edition of Traill's *Canadian Crusoes* (note 129.23, page 265), Schieder cites the source of this phrase as the 1829 "The Reed-Sparrow's Nest" by Caroline Anne Bowles Southey, Robert Southey's second wife.]

Therefore the thoughtful settler naturally regards the length of the Indian-summer as a great blessing.

Nature has now exhausted her rich store of buds and blossoms.—The rains and winds of October have scattered the last bright leaves upon the earth. The scarlet maple, the crimson oak and cherry, the dark purple of the black-ash, the lighter yellow of the birch and beech, lie withering at our feet—"the fading glories of the dying year."

Is there nothing but sadness and decay, in those fallen leaves? In those grey, leafless branches, through which the wind is sighing a requiem over the faded flowers and foliage? In yon grey elder, those round knobs contain the embryo blossoms, closely packed like green seeds; yet each tiny flower-cup is as perfect as it will be in the month of May:—it is only abiding its time! Yes, truly, there is much of hope and promise, revealed to us at this season. There is a savour of death;—but it is a death unto LIFE !

Look on those broad fields of emerald verdure, brightening into Spring-like beauty, with the rays of the noonday sun. Do they not speak to us of the future harvest—of the fruits of the coming year, which the harvestman is to reap.

He, too, must bide the time: first the blade; then the ear; then the ripened grain; then, again, the seed cast upon the earth—the renewal of his toil and his trust. Thus, then, we perceive that the Fall of the year is the renewal of Hope. In its darkest gloom, there is ever a gleam of sunlight, pointing onward to future joys.—*Revised from the original copy published in the Old Countryman, Nov, 2d, 1853.*

THE SCOTTISH EMIGRANT'S SONG.[45]

———

She turns her wheel wi busy hand
    But her thoughts are far away
'Mid the bonnie braes o' her native land,
    While she sings this simple lay:—

"I think upon the heathery hills
    I ay hae lov'd sae dearly,
I think upon the wimpling burn
    That wandered by sae clearly.

The little gowans tipped wi dew
    That 'mang the grass shone brightly;
The harebell waving in the breeze
    That bowed its head sae lightly.

The lavrock singing in the cloud
    Wi' note sae blythe and cheery,
That made my heart forget its load
    O' grief and care sae eerie.

I think upon the moss grown grave
    O' those sae dear to me
Wha' slumber in the auld kirk yard—
    My bonnie bairnies three.

An' I would gie a mint o' gowd—
    If gowd were mine to gie—

45 Not in first edition, but appears in second.

To wander through that auld kirk yard
    Thae bairns' wee graves to see."

She ceased her sang—the briny tears
    Fell frae her glistening ee—
For her heart throbbed fast as she thought upon
    These graves ayont the sea.

CONCLUSION.[46]

And now, having touched upon almost every subject likely to prove useful to the emigrant's wife or daughter, in her Canadian home, I will take my leave, with the sincere hope that some among my readers may derive profit and assistance from the pages, which, with much toil and pains, I have written for their instruction. Very happy I shall be, if I find that my labours have not been entirely fruitless, and that my little book has been indeed, what it professes to be, a Guide and a Friend to the Female Emigrant.

If I have sometimes stepped aside to address the men, on matters that were connected with their department, it has still been with a view to serve their wives, daughters or sisters; and such hints I hope may be well taken, and acted upon, for the ultimate benefit and comfort of all. In writing this little book, I have been influenced by no other desire than that of benefitting my country women, and endeavouring to smooth for them the rough path which I have trodden before them, and in which, therefore, I may not be an incompetent guide.

I have urged upon no one the expediency of leaving their native land; but I have laboured to show them that Canada, especially the Western or Upper portion of the Province, is preferable in many respects, to any other country to which they might feel inclined to turn their steps. Here the capitalist will find safe investment for his surplus wealth: the agriculturist will find a large field open to him, for the exercise of his knowledge, with a ready market for his produce, and the protection of a mild government, under the name of Her whom Britons delight to call their Queen. Here the labour of the poor man is amply rewarded, and he has it in his power in a few years, to become independent, and owe no man anything but that debt of brotherly love, which all Christians are bound to pay to each other.

It is a pleasant thing to contemplate the growing prosperity of a new country. To see thriving farmers, with well-stored barns, and sunny pastures covered with flocks

46 Traill's Conclusion appears in the first edition.

and herds; with fruitful gardens and orchards, extending over spaces where once lay the trackless and impenetrable forest; and to reflect that these things have been the result of industry and well-directed energy;—that by far the greater number of the men who own these blessings, have raised themselves from a state of abject poverty to a respectable position among their fellow-men.

The Irish emigrant can now listen to tales of famine and misery endured by his countrymen, while he looks round with complacency and contentment upon his own healthy, well-fed, well-clothed family, and thinks how different is his lot from that of his less fortunate brethren at home.

He sees his wife and children warmly clad with the wool spun from the fleeces of the flock before his door; fed by the produce of his farm; and remembers the day when he landed in the strange country, hungry, naked, forlorn, and friendless; with drooping head, and crushed heart—scarcely even daring to hope that better things were in store for him and that pale, wasted creature at his side, his partner in misery and despair.

How many such have I seen and known! How many of those who came to this Province eighteen years ago, under such sad circumstances as I have described, were among the settlers who came forward, with willing mind and liberal hand, to offer their subscriptions towards the relief of the famine-stricken Irish peasantry, in those sad years when a funeral pall seemed to have fallen over their native land. Do not these facts speak well for Canada?

When I cast my eyes over this improving country, and behold such undoubted proofs of the prosperity of its inhabitants, I cannot but rejoice and feel glad in my very heart, that such things are; and naturally wish that the poor among my countrymen and women, were as happily situated as those I have described.

Let me add yet a few words ere we part, on a subject that doubtless is very dear to you—I mean your Church. If your lot be cast as a resident in any of the towns or villages, of which now there are so many; or in the long-cleared and populous portions of the Province; you will find churches and ministers of every denomination; with ready access to Sunday-schools, for the better instruction of your children: in the cleared townships services are held at stated times, in the school-houses, of which there are one or more in each section of every township: but you may be far from a church, and your opportunities may be few and far between, of attending divine worship. Nevertheless, suffer not your God to be forgotten in the lonely wilderness; for you have need of his fatherly care over you and yours.—His ear is ever open to hear, and his holy arm stretched over you to save. He is at hand in the desert, as well as in the busy city: forsake him not, and bring up your children in his love and in his ways; so shall his blessing be upon yourselves and your substance.

The first church in which I bent my knee in heartfelt thankfulness to the Almighty, for is saving care over me and my husband, in preserving us from the perils of the great deep, and the perils of the pestilence which had brought me down very low, almost to the very gates of Death—was in a log church of the rudest description; and subsequently, it was in a barn, where two of my elder children were baptized by the good rector of Peterboro', long since called away from his pastoral labours by his Heavenly Master. But there was no lack of reverence among the little flock in the wilderness, who were gathered together that day; for they felt that the rudest building can be made holy by the invisible presence of that Great God who has said, "Where two or three are gathered together in my name, there am I in the midst of them."

On that very spot, or within a few yards of it, the walls of a stone church are raised, and it will not be without a missionary of the Church, to administer the holy ordinances: so you see that while we were yet but a little flock, scattered and without frequent means of obtaining religious instruction, there were those who cared for the spiritual destitution of the poor colonists in the Backwoods; and many liberal donations were sent from the mother-country for the erection of this church: many others in like manner, have been built by funds supplied from England, and this fact will, I hope, encourage and cheer those whose first settlement may be made in remote and less-favoured situations. It is also encouraging to the poor Canadian emigrants to know that kind and pious hearts care for them.

Much has been effected by the government with respect to the establishing of schools in every township and in all the principal towns; and much improvement will yet be made; for we are what the Yankees would call a progressing people, *and must go forward*, till a satisfactory system of education has been established in the country, to meet this great want.

And now, farewell; and I trust you will find kind hearts and friends, and much prosperity, in the land of your adoption; never forgetting that you still belong to that land, which is the glory of all lands, and are subjects to a mild and merciful Sovereign, who is no less beloved in her Province of Canada, than she is by her loyal people of Britain.

———

Guide
to Traill's
World

Introduction

This section invites contemporary readers to learn more about the world in which Catharine Parr Traill lived, both to better understand the contents of the *Guide* in relation to the foodways of the period and for additional context and resources for their own experimenting with historical recipes.

In "Feeding Her Family," we describe the foodways of Traill and her family. We discuss the culinary skills and expectations Traill would have brought to Canada from late Georgian England and the attitude of eager apprenticeship toward new food practices that she adopted upon arrival. Drawing on clues in the *Guide* itself, as well as her other publications and correspondence, we identify some of Traill's own personal food preferences and practices. We describe what kinds of foods would have been available to the Traills through hunting, fishing, and foraging, as well as what they would have cultivated in the garden. We also identify what would have to be purchased at the village store. We invite readers to become better able to imagine the repertoires of taste in the period through learning about the ingredients Traill kept on hand and the annual routines of planting, harvesting, and preserving the foods settler families grew. "Farmhouse Foodways" extends the exploration by looking at typical menus of the period and locale to give readers a better sense of what would have made its way to the table during the different seasons, for both family meals and special occasions.

We anticipate that, armed with knowledge about typical foods and menus, readers will be interested in trying to prepare historical fare in the contemporary kitchen. Consequently, we offer a variety of resources. In "Measurements for Cooking" and the accompanying "Measurements Chart" we demystify the multiple measurement systems found in historical cookbooks and offer handy conversion information. In a section entitled "Interpreting Nineteenth-Century Recipes," we offer strategies for cooking from historical recipes and articulate realistic goals, since it is impossible to entirely replicate a nineteenth-century recipe in a twenty-first-century kitchen with twenty-first-century ingredients. However, we also include a list of historical ingredients, with tips about twenty-first-century ingredients that best approximate them.

Finally, we offer two selections of historical recipes – some based on recipes that appear in Traill's *Guide* itself and others from additional historical sources – written in the style of modern recipes, with clear instructions and specified measurements, cooking time, and temperatures. For readers intrigued by experimenting with hearth cooking, "Simple Fireplace Cooking at Home" offers advice about grilling on a gridiron, baking on a griddle and in a bake-kettle, roasting meat on a dangle string, and boiling puddings in a pot on a trivet.

If you are wondering exactly what a bake-kettle is, you will find the answer in the first of two glossaries that conclude this guide to Traill's world. The "Glossary of Food and Cooking Terms," as its title suggests, provides additional information about the culinary terms and phrases found in the *Guide*. The list is alphabetized, from Abernethy Biscuit to Yeast, and offers descriptions of such varied things as fruit varietals and rising agents of the period, as well as definitions of adjectives used in ways unfamiliar to contemporary audiences. Readers will learn, for example, what is meant by "fine" or "loaf" sugar.

A second glossary concludes this section on Traill's World, offering a list of the people and publications that provided information used in composing the *Guide*. In addition to providing specific information about sources described only vaguely, such as "an old-fashioned book on orchard-planting" [70], this section provides recipes sourced from other cookery books, such as the four from Lydia Maria Child, as well as acknowledging those individuals who contributed material directly to the project.

The aim of this current edition is to suggest ways of bringing Traill's recipes, indeed her culinary world, alive for contemporary readers. We hope that it may also inspire readers to take up the challenge of tracing the origins of other recipes that appear in the *Guide* – to date, there has been no definitive study of all the sources for the recipes Traill gathered for the volume.

Feeding Her Family

Catharine Parr Traill was interested in food, its flavours and textures, its preparation and presentation. Conscious of its social and cultural meanings, she found the food-stuffs, meals, and wild edibles in her new life such an interesting topic that it became a major theme in all her writing. Sharing her knowledge of Canadian domestic life to women about to emigrate was important to her.

Our imagining of what she fed her own family involved looking at the available evidence as well as informed speculation based on her own and her family's words, and that in other commentaries of the period. Traill intended her book to be for members of all social classes, ladies from her own genteel status to the families of mechanics, farmers, and the poorest crofters, all of whom would have had to deal with a lack of resources and minimal paid assistance in their new country, as well as with unfamiliar food words, ingredients, and cooking methods. Her family's experiences were similar to those of many immigrant families in rural Canada. However, although she explained to her readers that she wrote from first-hand knowledge, she did not acknowledge her own family's difficult circumstances, which we know about from the many letters exchanged with family and friends, as well as her journal entries and other surviving papers. At times in these writings she lamented her lack of money to buy salt pork, to pay the miller to grind their wheat, to go to town to replenish basic supplies. There are also many indirect but obvious allusions to poverty and its inherent trials in Traill's stories, books, articles, advice columns, and recipes. Annie Traill once remarked, "[T]here is not much money for a family of 7 as well as my mother and father to feed and clothe."[1]

Children of a respectable though not wealthy family in the first decade of the nineteenth century in Suffolk, England, Catharine and Susanna Strickland had an unusual upbringing that inadvertently prepared them for their experience as backwoods settlers.[2] Emphasizing the virtues of resourcefulness, "industry, observation and

---

1 Martin, McGillis, and Milne, *Gore's Landing*, 220.
2 Traill Family Collection, Afterword, n.d.

self-reliance," their father instructed all his children in history, literature, languages, geography, mathematics, and sciences, particularly botany, while their mother taught the girls the feminine skills of sewing, embroidery, and baking fine cakes.[3] Somewhat unusually for their time and class, they also learned to cultivate vegetables in the kitchen garden and make butter and cheese,[4] although Catharine and Susanna probably did not learn to milk until forced by necessity once they were in Canada. They probably understood how to make simple confectionary, still considered an appropriate culinary skill for a lady in a holdover from the seventeenth and eighteenth centuries.[5]

When the Stricklands emigrated in the early 1830s, the cooking of the affluent in Great Britain combined long-standing traditions (roast beef, Yorkshire pudding, spiced plum cake, suet pastry), fashionable eighteenth-century French cuisine (simplified versions of elaborate sauces, puff paste), and influences from other countries: Italy (macaroni, parmesan), Spain (olios – elaborate meat stews), the Americas (pumpkin, tomato, pineapple), Asia (rice, soy, ketchup, sago starch), and India (curry, mulaga-tawny/mulligatawny soup, chutney, punch). This wide range of international ingredients and dishes would have been quite familiar to the Strickland family, as well as to other well-off emigrant families such as the Langtons, the O'Briens, the Stewarts, and the Kings.

Breakfasts for prosperous British farmers, tradespeople, and professionals in the late Georgian period were simpler than the robust ones of the previous century or those of the upcoming Victorian era and usually involved hot cocoa, hot tea with milk and white sugar, buttered toast with marmalade, currant cakes, and the occasional broiled pork chop or boiled egg.[6] In Canada, in the same period, breakfast was more

---

3 Atwood, Florence – Transcript: Memoirs of Annie Atwood, Traill Family Collection, 10896; Atwood, Florence – C.P.T. Transcript, Traill Family Collection, 10857; Ballstadt, *Catharine Parr Traill and Her Works*, 2; Peterman, "Strickland, Catharine Parr (Traill)," 996.

4 Traill, *I Bless You in My Heart*, 3–4.

5 Simple confectionary consisted of biscuits, small cakes, candies, cheesecakes, fruit preserves, fruit cordials, etc. Anne Langton, part of a family that, like the Stricklands, suffered a serious decline in their financial well-being in the 1820s, recalls in her 1881 memoirs that she had been prepared to support herself if necessary: "I have already set down confectionary as one of the arts by which I might gain my bread if need be" (Anne Langton, *The Story of Our Family*, 87; Anne Langton, *A Gentlewoman in Upper Canada*, 346n14).

6 Quotations from Black, *Food and Cooking in 19th Century Britain*, 18; Lane, *Jane Austen and Food*, 26–8; Paston-Williams, *The Art of Dining*, 242–3; Stead, *Food and Cooking in 18th Century Britain*, 21, 24.

Fig. 17 · Interior of John Langton's cottage, looking north, 1837. Drawn by his sister Anne Langton

likely to be buckwheat or cornmeal pancakes with maple syrup, in addition to pork chops and eggs. And potatoes. Always potatoes.

The complex dinner etiquette of the period required two, sometimes three, courses, with multiple dishes. A roast meat at one end was balanced by boiled meat at the other, the four corners featured four different dishes and/or the two sides each held two dishes, or many more if the dinner was a particularly formal affair. Diners helped themselves or neighbours to nearby dishes, with limited assistance from servants. Gentlemen were expected to be politely attentive to the ladies' wants. A soup often preceded carving the main roast or serving a dressed fish. The second course – usually with an identical number and placement of dishes as the first – included a selection of meats prepared in a lighter way, such as patties, but also custards, tartlets, puddings, jellies, and other sweets. Dessert, if offered as a separate course, was dried fruit, fresh fruit, nuts and cheese, and sweetmeats, with tea and coffee. For the dessert course, the white tablecloth was removed to show the fine dining table. In the

Fig. 18 · Interior of John Langton's cottage, looking south, 1837. Drawn by his sister Anne Langton

1894 introduction to her Aunt Traill's *Pearls and Pebbles*, Mary Agnes Fitzgibbon said that at Stowe House the very young Catharine and her sisters "waited [in the small children's parlour] in their white dresses for the footman to summon them to the diningroom for dessert,"[7] an image that contrasts Georgian elegance with the Canadian log farmhouse, in which dining room and kitchen were one.

Even the simple family-only meals of middle-class families followed this general pattern. A typical early nineteenth-century British family dinner was "a couple of rabbits smothered with onions, a neck of mutton boiled and a goose roasted, with a currant pudding and a plain one," or "soup, fish, bouillée, partridges, and an apple tart," or "Mackerell, Soup, Neck of Venison, Chicken, Beans and Bacon, Pease and Cherry Tart," or "pease soup, a spare-rib, and a [savoury] pudding,"[8] all washed down by

---

7 Traill, *Pearls and Pebbles*, 155.
8 These early to mid-nineteenth-century family bills of fare are all taken from quotes from the period: Lane, *Jane Austen and Food*, 43–6; Stead, *Food and Cooking in 18th Century Britain*, 24, 29.

home-made fruit cordials, beers and ales, and imported wines. Vegetables and salads are not necessarily mentioned in such descriptions, but they would have appeared as other corner or side dishes and as garnishes to the meats and fish. Melted butter was the common sauce, either flavoured with herbs or anchovy for vegetables, or sugar and wine for puddings. A wide array of pickles was presented as accompaniment. Butter, cream, white flour and sugar, dried fruits, almonds, and sweet spices were used liberally in a remarkable variety of puddings, pies, tarts, and cakes, everything from delicate puff pastry that encased light egg custards to boiled, suet-enriched currant mixtures, yeasted spice and seed breads, airy sponge cakes baked in pretty moulds, or creams scented with rosewater.

As a Canadian housekeeper of good means, even if inexperienced, Traill expected to maintain these manners and standards and indeed did so for the first few years. But her natural curiosity led her to explore and appreciate the new ingredients, recipes, and wild foods around her. In mid-1834, Traill wrote this admiring description of a visit to a local farm family who took pride in their generous table: "We enjoyed during our sojourn many of the comforts of a cleared farm; poultry of every kind, beef of their own killing; excellent mutton and pork; we had a variety of preserves at our tea-table, with honey in the comb, delicious butter, and good cheese, with divers sorts of cakes; a kind of little pancake, made from the flour of buckwheat, which are made in a batter, and raised with barm, afterwards dropped in boiling lard, and fried; also a preparation made of Indian corn-flour, called supporne-cake, which is fried in slices, and eaten with maple syrup."[9]

Two decades later, as an experienced Canadian housekeeper with diminished means, Traill had become familiar with all sorts of ways to eke out meals through foraging, hunting, fishing, and adopting the simplest of preparations with minimal ingredients, more in line with what the legions of poor cottagers in Ireland, the Scottish Highlands, and the English Midlands existed on – hedge fruit, wildfowl, pottages, unleavened bannocks, pease puddings, root vegetables with herbs, pasties, cider, and beer. The landless British labourers in the city slums ate gristly bacon, hard cheese, lard, and inferior bread – its price high because wheat was expensive until the government was forced by the potato famine to reduce its cost – and drank sugared hot tea. Beer was expensive to purchase and awkward to brew in small homes. Oats and barley were the staple grains for a wide variety of British pottages, griddle breads, and cakes, while a bit of pork or a rabbit could roast from a dangle string in front

9 Traill, *Backwoods of Canada*, 197.

of the peat or coal fire. Milk and dried peas (pease) were fundamental foods. The incoming Irish settlers of the 1820s preferred potatoes to plum pudding,[10] but the Scots scorned the ubiquitous Irish potato and cabbage.[11] The choice of foodstuffs was restricted by a lack of money, fuel, and cooking space, as well as poor-quality or non-existent plots of land. Those of the yeoman class were accustomed to a higher level of daily fare, which included greater diversity and seasonal variations. They could afford white wheat flour, butchered beef and fresh mutton and their offal and blood, increased quantities of white sugar and treacle, and such imported groceries as sago, rosewater, spices, and almonds. A wide array of regional cakes, pastries, and breadstuffs emerged, and roast beef prevailed.

Traill's readers arrived in Canada in the 1850s and 1860s having had this range of culinary experience and were then introduced to Canadian foodways, a fusion of British and north-eastern American cooking that they needed to understand if they were to fit in and succeed. The earliest English-speaking Upper Canadian population, who had fled the American Revolution in the 1780s or sought new farming opportunities in the 1790s and 1800s, were mostly knowledgeable farm families from Pennsylvania, New York, and New England, usually of English, Scottish, and German ethnic background but American-raised for several generations. "Yankee," meaning "person from the northern United States," is a term frequently applied to them, often derogatorily, but not by Traill. For her, Yankees long-resident in Canada were Canadian and she willingly learned from them, as well as from her fellow nationals who had preceded her into the backwoods.

Although the roots of north-eastern American cooking are British, German, and Dutch, two centuries of physical separation from Europe as well as agricultural developments and trade stimuli had contributed to the development of an emerging national cuisine that included Indigenous foodstuffs, techniques, and terminology. Anglo-American foodways relied on the standard Anglo ingredients, recipes, and meal plans, but distinct differences defined the evolving culinary culture of the United States of America, the main one being the emphasis on Indian corn, the grain

---

10 "When Peter Robinson brought over one of his shiploads of impoverished Irish emigrants to take up new lives under his settlement scheme north of Rice Lake, feeding them on board proved to be a major challenge as offers of plum pudding and other treats were roundly spurned, with potatoes, and more potatoes being the only food they would eat." (Williamson, *"To Fare Sumptuously Every Day,"* 6.)

11 Black, *Food and Cooking in 19th Century Britain*, 6–7; Connery, *In an Irish Country Kitchen*, 17, 19; Stead, *Food and Cooking in 18th Century Britain*, 26–7.

of the Americas. To the dismay of the earliest English colonists, their grains and legumes – wheat, barley, peas, oats – did not thrive in what they called New England so they learned to depend on native corn instead, substituting it in their bread, griddle cake, pottage, porridge, pudding, and cake recipes. Similarly, beans often replaced peas, as in bean porridge (succotash). One signal that an American cuisine was maturing is the publication of Amelia Simmons's unpretentious *American Cookery*, whose subtitle is: "adapted to this country, and all grades of life." Beside recipes for the customary roasted and boiled meats, fruit pies and fruit preserves, boiled vegetables, wheat-based puddings and cakes, are the first printed recipes for dishes such as slapjacks and hoecakes made of cornmeal, custard-style pumpkin pie, cranberry sauce for roast turkey, soft gingerbread, and spruce beer, among others that had already had a long existence before appearing in print. Dutch influences are found in cookies, slaws, doughnuts, crullers, waffles, the use of buckwheat, and the blending of beans and molasses. Indigenous fruits and vegetables include pumpkins, Jerusalem artichokes, watermelon rind, and many more, but, interestingly, Simmons includes no maple products. By mid-century, other differences between the UK and the north-eastern states were the ubiquity and variety of quick breads and cakes that used chemical leavening powders (doughnuts, pancakes, teacakes), hasty puddings of cornmeal, porridges of beans, and brown bread blended from rye flour and cornmeal. A major German influence was found in drying apples. Canadian cooking, especially in the outback, included maple sugar and maple molasses, a flavour entirely alien to European palates. Adding herbs to maple syrup was an attempt to modify the flavour. In urban centres, the strongest influence was the standard Anglo-American diet of refined wheat, white sugar, and beef.

"On Sunday we have the inevitable New England fish balls for dinner with baked beans."[12] "The sirloin steak that has been kept for this occasion is cooked; a plate of the nicest cream toast dipped; the best mince pie, plum cake, doughnuts, cheese and preserves are placed on the table."[13] Another commentator wrote about the "relishing" breakfast supplied by "a farmer of the true old-fashioned stamp ... We have both coffee & a bowl of bread & milk, the true home made brown bread, 'punkin' pie, honey, pancakes & cider, excelent butter & cheese [and] ... excelent apples."[14] One Boston lawyer kept a diary that included meal references, such as these from summer

12 Caroline King, *When I Lived in Salem, 1822–1866*, quoted in Oliver, *Saltwater Foodways*, 13.
13 Emery, *Reminiscences of a Nonagenarian*, quoted in Oliver, *Saltwater Foodways*, 13.
14 Perkins, *John T. Perkins' Journal at Sea, 1845*, quoted in Oliver, *Saltwater Foodways*, 13.

fishing trips into the countryside: "Got us an excellent breakfast of corn cakes, poor tea, good butter and eggs, & unlimited supply of the best of milk." "We went to a farm house close to the river bank ... and took a plain lunch of eggs, bread & butter, and berries." "The people in the [inn] kitchen took our fish & we ordered supper ... of trout (of wh. I caught 16), excellent bread & butter, pie, doughnuts, blackberries and blueberries."[15] This is the kind of cookery that Catharine Traill learned from her established backwoods Yankee neighbours.

Settler women had so much house- and farm-work and childcare to accomplish daily that food preparation needed to be straightforward – something any working parent can still relate to. The activities that fill our present workdays may be different but the daily necessity of feeding the family continues. Before canned salmon and can openers, before microwave ovens and chest freezers, before the ubiquitous plastic-bottled tomato ketchup and plastic-wrapped sliced bread, the tasks associated with the daily necessity of food procurement, manufacture, and disposal were relentless. Today, it is hard to credit how much salted, smoked, dried, brined, pickled, spiced, sugared, candied, conserved, canned, potted, brewed, and fermented food was home-prepared for consumption in those refrigerator-less times. Stores provided some provisions – groceries and cooking equipment, both imported and locally made – but a huge proportion of food was made at home, even in well-to-do homes. Provided the household could afford salt, saltpetre, and sugar and had enough storage jars and jugs, bags, and barrels, the possibilities of food preservation were restricted only by the housewife's culinary ingenuity and those of her fellow housewives, often illiterate but skilled, who shared their discoveries and techniques. Today it is possible to eat well without using smoked, salted, pickled, or fermented food, although it is impossible to avoid opening the refrigerator regularly. Freezing has undisputedly supplanted all other preservation techniques.

WHAT KIND OF COOK WAS CATHARINE PARR TRAILL?

Traill seldom describes her daily or seasonal domestic routines or those of her daughters, but she implies much by her choice of recipes for the *Guide* and all the advice she supplies in her entire oeuvre on such female undertakings as making cheese, knitting socks, maintaining a flock of ducks, nursing a sick baby, or boiling puddings.

---

15 Dana, *The Journals of Richard Henry Jr.*, quoted in Oliver, *Saltwater Foodways*, 6.

When combined with the information in her published works, what she disclosed in her extant letters, and the housewifery comments from fellow settlers, such as Anne Langton, Anna Leveridge, Harriet Durnford King, Susanna Moodie, and many others, including men, a picture emerges of what the Traill family and their compatriots were eating in their new home of Upper Canada in the first half of the nineteenth century.

Traill was a good cook. She learned to feed her large young family fairly well, if not always with abundance or refinement. Her sister, Susanna Moodie, reminiscing about decades past, writes: "My dear Katie, I ... think you make delicious family roasts and pies and puddings."[16]

Although she preferred her recipes to be "simple, agreeable and cheap" [75], Traill often bids her readers to be economically careful, as she was. As a sensible and resourceful person in difficult circumstances, she favoured plain but tasty dishes easily prepared for a hungry family of young children, or, as they grew, girls and boys who did a lot of heavy housework and farm work. By the time she wrote the *Guide* in 1854, her three teenage daughters, Katie, Annie, and Mary, had undertaken responsibility for most of the housekeeping.[17]

Attentive to simple seasoning and nice appearance, even while in reduced circumstances, Traill always sought to make her food wholesome, palatable, and nourishing. These three adjectives are clues to her opinions about appropriate family food. She applied "wholesome" judiciously to fresh berries and cooked apples, bran bread, wild rice, oatmeal porridge, and dishes of cornmeal, even to black squirrel stew. Undercooked fish was unwholesome, but a light fish soup was more wholesome than the perpetual salt pork. Looking back from 1872, Susanna mentions "my old receipt for fish soup," which she had just made once more with perch and sunfish she had caught herself, pronouncing it "excellent, far richer and nicer than beef soup."[18] Apples were "valuable as a most palatable and convenient article of diet, but also as one of the most wholesome" [64]. Traill identified a variety of dishes as "convenient" – another

16 Moodie to Traill, *Letters of a Lifetime*, c. fall 1881, 348. And Moodie clearly felt she was qualified to judge: as an old widow boarding in Belleville, she wrote Traill: "Our diet is chiefly composed of stews and hashes, which never did agree with me, when I made them well. But these are fat and greasy, everything but nice ... It is quite a misfortune to have been a good cook. It makes one very dainty, but I can't help it. I don't care for luxuries. Plain food cooked well is a luxury, if only porridge" (Moodie, *Letters of a Lifetime*, 6 January 1871, 288).

17 Traill, *I Bless You in My Heart*, March 1846, 53 (Editors Ballstadt, Hopkins, and Peterman give March 1846, but the date is not specified in the original letter) and 19 February 1855, 94.

18 Moodie, *Letters of Love and Duty*, 13 June 1872, 338.

clue word – such as apple sauce, buttermilk cakes risen with saleratus, and curds and whey, all quick to prepare. Also convenient were hashes, stews, fricassees, roasts, and soups. Even Isabella, the Traills' Irish maid in 1834, was able to give a visiting lad "a good bowl of soup."[19] Other important descriptors are "pleasant" and "fine." For her, many ingredients and dishes – stewed blackberries, potato fish cakes – were "nice," while cornmeal pudding with ripe currants and stuffed pigeons were "very nice."[20]

As her family expanded to seven living children, she needed to get meals on the table in between mending trousers, making soap, scrubbing the worktable, milking the cows, harvesting the cabbages, gathering the berries, birthing babies – and writing, of course. Traill wrote continually, both as economic imperative and self-expression. At heart she was a teacher and storyteller, and women's domesticity was a recurring focus. One piece she wrote in the 1880s, "A Slight Sketch of the Early Life of Mrs. Moodie," says: "But while I notice her literary and artistic talents, I must not omit to record that they are not her only ones. She is as remarkable in her skill in domestic life, in her regulation of her household & her bread, pastry, preserves, etc. of the best. She excelled too in needlework, and all the many and various details that the life of a wife and mother involve are scrupulously attended to."[21]

WHAT DOES TRAILL REVEAL ABOUT HER TASTES?

Sometimes Traill expressed her likes and dislikes candidly; sometimes they can be inferred. Inevitably her personal tastes influenced what she chose to feed her family. Apples preserved with cloves were "delightful" [72], wild plums boiled with maple molasses were "capital" [80], and melon preserves were "rich" and "luscious" [136]. Labrador tea's taste was too resinous for her, and green tomatoes "rank" [138], although she liked cooked ripe tomatoes very much. She was quite particular too about the breads she enjoyed – salt-risen bread was "peculiar" [96], oatcakes "best [made] with a good deal of butter in them" [116], and potato bread "the best bread I know" [98], especially if baked in a brick oven [30]. She came to like cornmeal, several times pronouncing it "nice," and serving it as a pudding with meat was "savoury and

19 Traill, *Forest and Other Gleanings*, 105.
20 Ibid., 90, 154.
21 Traill, n.d.; as quoted in Traill, *Forest and Other Gleanings*, 55. The sketch was written in the late 1880s, but is found only in the Traill Family Collection since it was unpublished in Traill's own time.

relishing" [124]. Of custardy Canadian-style pumpkin pie flavoured with ginger and cinnamon, she said "a finer dish … can hardly be eaten" [134]; on the other hand, a Canadian-style apple pie with nutmeg and allspice was "sickly tasted" [72]. She preferred cloves and lemon peel. She claimed that during one illness "I lost my appetite entirely[,] living only on apples."[22]

When visiting the Young family at Young's Point on the Upper Katchewanook, Traill wrote glowingly of their success as settlers, farmers, grist millers, and hospitable hosts. Her description of the meal served to her and her husband suggests it suited her palate well: "Many are the apologies which are uttered by Betty and Nora for having no better fare to set before me than what are to us dainties, in the form of a fine, fat, tender boiled saddle of venison, delicately corned, and cooked most excellently, and served up with greens of the most verdant hue, and white floury potatoes, besides a dish of the finest and most delightful fried fish that I had ever tasted, the preparation of which did infinite credit to Nora's culinary skill. For my part, the voyage up the lakes, and the walk I have taken afterwards, have given me an excellent appetite, and I greatly relished my dinner."[23]

As for beverages, she liked coffee and quite liked dandelion coffee and approved of homemade beer, but scorned hard liquor. Her sister had noted that tea – "the inseparable beverage of every meal in New Brunswick"[24] as well as in Ontario – "is an article we cannot do without."[25] Water, apple cider, spruce beer, small beer, and maple water were all consumed.[26] The Moodies also drank sage and peppermint teas.[27]

Other preferences are easily surmised. Traill does not appear to have a sweet tooth, and was not overly fond of maple's taste, but she was aware that others liked sweetness so she suggests, for instance, that maple sugar pairs well with the tart native grapes to make grape jelly.[28] For her own meals, she favoured sharp foods: acidic apples [71], vinegar in her catsup [138], and lemon juice in beet molasses [145].

Both she and her sister disliked greasy dishes, a regular criticism levelled at Canadian home cooks, inns, and hotels. Frying with oil has to be managed carefully, she

22 Traill to her daughter Mary Traill, *I Bless You in My Heart*, 23 January 1858, 112.
23 Traill, *Forest and Other Gleanings*, 64.
24 Beavan, *Sketches and Tales*, 33–4.
25 Moodie, *Letters of a Lifetime*, 18 November 1866, 235.
26 Traill, *Canadian Crusoes*, 36
27 Moodie, *Roughing It in the Bush*, 353.
28 Traill, *Canadian Crusoes*, 145.

says, so that croquets can be fried crisp [159] and fish do not absorb the oil [165–7].[29] Many other commentators refer to the ubiquity of unpleasantly greasy food. Tiger Dunlop, for instance, famously quips, "The gridiron ... is usurped by the frying-pan, and everything is deluged with grease and butter."[30]

Interestingly, there is nothing to suggest Thomas Traill's personal tastes, which might have been fairly refined and expansive since he had lived for many years in France and Italy with his first family. Or perhaps he preferred plain foods, recalling his Scottish Orkney heritage. As a Scot, presumably he liked oatmeal and oatcakes, although in the *Guide* his wife suggests she was inexperienced at making them [116]. When she wrote that oatmeal can be served sweet with molasses but that "some, however, prefer butter to eat with it ... it's a matter of taste," was she specifying Thomas's preference? [115]. The Scots often preferred their oatmeal buttery and salty rather than sweet and there is some indication that the family had adopted some Scottish ways of preparing foods. For example, in *Canadian Crusoes*, Traill wrote that waterfowl was smoked "after the manner that the Shetlanders and Orkney people smoke the solan geese."[31] These are large sea-birds (gannets; *Sula bassana*) which were preserved for year-round consumption by being slightly salted, then wind dried; some considered them "too rank and fishy-flavoured for unpracticed palates,"[32] while others considered them a delicacy. They were served at breakfast, like smoked haddock and herrings.[33]

WHAT DID THE TRAILLS HARVEST FROM THEIR GARDENS, FIELDS, AND YARDS?

As a gardener, botanist, nature-lover, and very observant person, Traill dealt comfortably with the seasons, appreciating freshness when it was available and readying a large variety of fruits and vegetables for winter storage. Their fields, gardens, and orchards offered numerous options, which made it possible to provide a variety of colours, textures, and flavours. Products from their cattle, pigs, and poultry were also essential.

29 Among the handwritten recipes in the Traill papers at Library and Archives Canada are "Rules for frying fish crisp and brown," possibly by Traill's sister Jane, 4(22): unpaginated.
30 Dunlop, *Statistical Sketches of Upper Canada*, 55.
31 Traill, *Canadian Crusoes*, 131.
32 Dods, *The Cook and Housewife's Manual*, 108.
33 FitzGibbon, *A Taste of Scotland*, 68; Hawker, *Instructions to Young Sportsmen*, 133.

Traill lived in the Peterborough region for seven decades. Her first Canadian home of their own was Lake Cottage on Lake Katchewanook, deep in the bush. By November 1833, one month before they moved in, Thomas had twenty-five acres cleared and oats, corn, pumpkins, potatoes, and turnips planted. Catharine had a servant and was happily creating a home and enjoying the antics of their first baby, James. For a while they also employed a nursemaid. However, it was not long before the Traills' circumstances deteriorated – they were already desperate by 1838, which led to the first of many moves. Through the 1840s and early 1850s, and again in the early 1860s, they faced destitution several times, surviving by gifts of food, money, firewood, and clothing from friends and family. Such tremendous generosity with advice, gifts, and loans was characteristic of relationships in the backwoods and on farms.

But, according to the Traills' daughter Annie, even though they moved from house to house in the 1840s, they always had a garden plot and orchard. At Wolf Tower on the Rice Lake Plains, where they lived rent-free from mid-1846 to mid-1847 courtesy of a friend, there was "a beautiful garden laid out with currant bushes and black [raspberries] and gooseberries, white raspberries, and some fruit trees not yet in bearing."[34] Wanting to have their own farm again, they moved further up Rice Lake to rent Mount Ararat. Two years later, in May 1849, their next farm, Oaklands, was purchased already cleared and with what Annie describes as a "beautiful orchard [of] apples, pears, plums and cherries. I never have tasted such really delicious apples as there is in that orchard or *some* of the most *uneatable* ones either. There is a great many currant bushes, red, white and black and some white raspberries. So we have plenty of fruit of the best kind."[35] Traill wrote *Canadian Crusoes* and *The Female Emigrant's Guide* at Oaklands. In late 1859, after her husband's death, she was able to purchase a small property where she built her last house, Westove, and where she continued to cultivate her own fruitful garden, from which she still made jams and jellies, sharing some with her friends and neighbours.

Undoubtedly, like their neighbours, the Traills also planted and consumed plenty of carrots, parsnips, potatoes, cabbages, beets, onions, pumpkins, squash, and turnips and possibly even broccoli and cauliflower [59]. Although she quotes passages from published authorities on vegetable gardening, her personal knowledge is apparent in her comments and tips. Each family member had a part in planting and harvesting from their kitchen garden and from their fields: the girls stayed nearer

34 Martin, McGillis, and Milne, *Gore's Landing*, 216.
35 Ibid., 220.

the house, while the boys did the plowing, as was typical in most immigrant families. Even the littlest child helped by weeding.[36] In 1889 she told her sister Sarah, "I used to do the greater part of the garden work, the vegetables, my own self, the front garden and flowers – but now I find my strength is unequal to the work and I must hire help" from an Irish man.[37]

Fresh vegetables of all sorts were commonly boiled in salted water and served with a butter sauce seasoned with any number of flavours, such as mustard, anchovy, mushroom ketchup, onions, capers, or herbs, so few cookbooks provide instructions or recipes, and the *Guide* is similarly almost silent. Nor is it overly forthcoming on salads or pickles. Certainly, everyone consumed lots of fresh corn, scraped from the cob and served with butter or converted to patties and fritters. Corn on the cob slathered with butter and salt, as we happily eat it today, was considered uncouth. And the corn then was not as sweet or tender as modern varieties, so cutting it made it more accessible. Although vegetable pickles were considered essential and were ubiquitous at all meals, Traill supplied few recipes since what she called regular cookbooks included them. Likewise, her recipes say little about using herbs, although clearly she both grew and foraged for them. Despite saying "a good bed of pot-herbs is essential," along with recommendations of which to grow [58], few of her recipes include them – "a little green parsley and savory" in potato soup [130] and "parsley, savory or thyme, and a few green chives cut up, or a young onion" in fish soup [167]. A wide range are mentioned (see the full list under herbs in the index), particularly parsley, but their actual importance seemed so obvious that she did not need to explicate.

In some years, the Traills had rabbits, as well as geese, ducks, and chickens, for the eggs, of course, but also for meat, feathers, quills, fat, and fur. Farmwomen frequently took responsibility for the poultry yard, and indeed Traill seems to have gained this knowledge first hand, judging by the way she wrote about these birds. She learned the basics of butchery, as did others of her status in Upper Canada, such as Anne Langton and Mary O'Brien. Once pigs were butchered, she did her own pickling and brining of hams. Some families had shares in a cow and its milk, as the Traills did,

36 Traill to Ellen Dunlop, *I Bless You in My Heart*, 19 June 1853, 82.
37 Traill to sister Sarah Gwillym, 11 April 1889, Traill Family Collection, 2266–7.

at least in April 1853.[38] The Traill women often made their own butter and cheeses from the milk of their cows, which in 1846 were named Lady and Primrose.[39] Some years they could not afford fodder for a cow and had to go without dairy products.[40] As a new widow, she had "a few fowls but no cow having been too poor to buy one at present but I hope some chance will enable to supply that want."[41] Being without butter "is a great privation" and they "cannot buy" it.[42] "Milk, fresh butter, and eggs" and produce from the "very productive" garden, said Susanna when her husband was away on militia duty in summer 1838, "supplied the simple wants of our family."[43]

As farmers, the Traills tried sowing wheat (both winter and spring varieties), oats, and barley for sale. In some years, however, their yields were low because they had moved yet again and could not prepare the ground properly or harvest successfully. Not only did they need to provide for themselves, but they also needed to sell to others, such as the village store, to provide an income.

WHAT DID TRAILL PURCHASE FROM THE VILLAGE STORE?

As with all rural families, Traill and her family participated in the local economy as both sellers and purchasers, and were thereby part of the world-wide economy, since Upper Canada was linked by trade to both the British Empire and the continent. Her family's meals and well-being were dependent on several imported ingredients and items such as salt that they could not produce themselves. She also had food and non-food products to sell, exchange, or barter. Household self-sufficiency, although neither possible nor expected, was an ongoing ideal. A housewife's frugality was an important bulwark against economic disaster.

38 Traill to Frances Stewart, *I Bless You in My Heart*, 28 April 1853, 78. The Leveridge family in Hastings County north of Peterborough hired a cow before they could afford to buy their own. Tivy, *Your Loving Anna*, 31.

39 Martin, McGillis, and Milne, *Gore's Landing*, 217.

40 Traill to Susanna Moodie, *I Bless You in My Heart*, 26 July 1849, 59.

41 Traill to Agnes Fitzgibbon, 29 October 1861, Thomas Fisher Rare Book Library, University of Toronto.

42 Traill to Susanna Moodie, *I Bless You in My Heart*, 26 July 1849, 59.

43 Moodie, *Roughing It in the Bush*, 470.

While living near Gore's Landing from 1846 to 1857, the Traills shopped at William Brown's general store in the village.[44] She likely bought "groceries, salt, spices, and tea, and the finer sorts of wearing apparel" there.[45] She was also a customer at Sherin's general store in Lakefield after 1857 when she returned to live in the area.[46] The term "groceries" was used for foodstuffs imported from elsewhere because they were not grown locally, such as spices, currants and raisins, wines, sugars, bottled sauces, sago and tapioca, rice, tea leaves and coffee beans, and some cheeses. "Provisions" were perishable local foodstuffs, such as maple sugar, flour and other grains, wild rice, beer and cider, fresh fruits and vegetables, eggs, butter, and milk.[47] As was common, she sometimes had to delay payment.[48]

In exchange for bartering wild berries, she may have received pork or beef at times when they did not have their own hogs or cattle. Also, besides berries, the *Guide* is full of hints about other ways to gain a small income – selling caraway seeds [58], hops [60], goslings [202–4], tallow [178–9], and many other minor products in addition to such field crops as wheat and corn. Good quality cheeses could bring in a "remunerative price" [196], she notes. Also, home-crafted items such as dried flowers and ferns could be sold to collectors. The ever-resourceful Traill even took advantage of other people's botanical interest.

Traill's culinary and medical recipes required a minimum of imported goods (spices, lemons, essences, raisins, currants) and excluded other common items (wines, other spices such as for curries, sago, arrowroot, olive oil, macaroni, vermicelli, gelatine, oranges), which she and many of her readers might not have been able to buy with their limited funds. Lemons and lemon essence are suggested in several recipes, and almond and peppermint essences once each [109, 152], and all four appear in the account books of Peterborough area grocers.[49] Whole spices arrived in Canada in vast quantities from the earliest years, as can be seen in official import records, grocers' advertisements, and general store accounts. With the exception of caraway seeds, all spices came from tropical locations. Nutmeg and cinnamon were the most popular,

44 Martin, McGillis, and Milne, *Gore's Landing*, 51–2.
45 These are the words of a member of the Young family, as reported by Traill. The Youngs were a very successful farm family on the Upper Katchewanook. Traill, *Forest and Other Gleanings*, 63.
46 McCalla, *Consumers in the Bush*, 32.
47 Ibid., 68–9, 123.
48 Traill, Journal, 29 November 1862, Traill Family Collection, 2970.
49 McCalla, *Consumers in the Bush*, 205.

along with allspice and ginger, but they were not yet sold in the powdered form we are so accustomed to. Wild ginger, a plant common to the area, was widely used as a medicine by the local First Nations. Allspice, cinnamon, mustard, gingerroot, pepper, cayenne, and cloves appear in archival records. Traill probably bought cornstarch, since she remarks on it favourably twice as a substitute for arrowroot. Very likely she also bought the new chemical leaveners, such as saleratus. Until the early 1840s she bought China green tea, and then, once it became available in the 1840s, India black tea. Coffee beans would have been on her shopping list when she could afford them. She is silent on wine, although other settlers were not. The Langtons, for instance, purchased wines frequently.

Nineteenth-century rural families had a reputation for producing everything they needed, but the reality was more nuanced. Not only did they patronize the local general stores, they shopped in the bigger towns when possible. And many families looked forward to the arrival of wooden containers of goods and gifts from family and friends still in the UK. While Traill suggests that "To be up and doing, is the maxim of the Canadian; and it is this that nerves his arm to do and bear. The Canadian settler, following in the steps of the old Americans, learns to supply all his wants by the exercise of all his energy. He brings up his family to rely upon their own resources, instead of relying on his neighbours,"[50] the Traills certainly relied on their neighbours and provided assistance when they could; no farm family could be self-sufficient, despite the goal of independence.

WHAT DID THE TRAILLS HUNT, FISH, AND FORAGE FOR?

Stuck in the backwoods with little money and little opportunity to get to town for purchases, settlers needed to rely on wild food – roots and leaves, birds and their eggs, animals, berries, nuts, and wild rice. Local foraging, hunting, and fishing were skills learned by the earliest settlers and even in the mid-nineteenth-century were still a part of life for the many families down on their luck and attuned to nature. In the 1840s, we suspect that the Traills, due to their poverty, may have been more reliant on these skills than their friends. Catharine's knowledge in this area would have been extremely beneficial for feeding her family – her personal knowledge of cooking with wild berries, herbs, and meats was extensive. Frequent references to

50 Traill, *Canadian Crusoes*, 162.

the edibility of wild foods are also scattered through both her botanical books and her many short stories. Although a reader today might expect more recipes for wild game, greens, and fruits, we think Traill was careful to limit her discussion of this area, fascinating though she found the topic, because it might have demonstrated their penury and cast an unfavourable light on the breadwinning capabilities of her husband, as well as discouraging potential immigrants. While this knowledge is not obvious in the *Guide*, it is clear in her earlier book, *Canadian Crusoes*, which takes place in the deeply forested hills around her home Mount Ararat on Rice Lake.

The children in *Canadian Crusoes* manage to feed and clothe themselves for several seasons in the backwoods because they already have basic survival skills. They reassure themselves that they will not go hungry because "God cares for the creatures He has made, and supplies them with knowledge where they shall find food when they hunger and thirst."[51] "Truly, God hath, indeed, spread a table for us in the wilderness."[52] Not unexpectedly, their views echo Traill's own profound belief in God's gracious providence, since the young heroine, Catharine Maxwell, who makes these declarations, is to some extent a representation of Catharine Parr Traill. The benefits of the natural world have a significant place in the plot of *Canadian Crusoes*.

> "Let us, however, consider what we shall do for food; for, you know, God helps those that helps themselves," said Louis. "Let us consider a little. There must be plenty of fish in the lake, both small and great."
>
> "But how are we to get them out of it?" rejoined Catharine. "I doubt the fish will swim at their ease there, while we go hungry."
>
> "Do not interrupt me, ma chère. Then, we see the track of deer, and the holes of the woodchuck; we hear the cry of squirrels and chitmunks [sic], and there are plenty of partridges, and ducks, and quails, and snipes; of course, we have to contrive some way to kill them. Fruits there are in abundance, and plenty of nuts of different kinds. At present we have plenty of fine strawberries, and huckleberries will be ripe soon in profusion, and bilberries too, and you know how pleasant they are; as for raspberries, I see none; but by-and-by there will be May-apples – I see great quantities in the low grounds; grapes, high-bush cranberries, haws as large as cherries, and sweet too; squaw berries,

---

51 Ibid., 31.
52 Ibid., 49. On page 261 of the 1986 edition, the editor, Rupert Schneider, points out the similarity to Psalm 78:19 – "Can God furnish a table in the wilderness?"

wild plums, choke-cherries, and bird-cherries. As to sweet acorns, there will be bushels and bushels of them for the roasting, as good as chestnuts, to my taste; and butter-nuts, and hickory-nuts, with many other good things." And here Louis stopped for want of breath to continue his catalogue of forest dainties.[53]

The sunny plains, and the edges of forests and field clearings are a good source of wild fruit and Traill notes that purple grapes mixed with high bush cranberries and strewn with maple sugar "often formed an addition to our evening meal."[54] Judging by the number of times she comments on how delicious fresh and stewed berries are when eaten with maple sugar and cream, she must have liked them. Cranberries were a particular favourite for an extensive range of purposes: pie filling, jam on bread or jelly on toast, a piquant sauce for roast venison or mutton, a beverage. She recommends unusual combinations of mixed berries for pies, such as red currants, huckleberries, and bilberries – "delightful," she opines [82] and "requiring little sugar"[55] – and such a combination is still possible today for people living in areas where these berries grow naturally. The scarlet spice-berry was both "good to eat" and imbibed "as a tonic."[56] Hawthorns were "pulpy and of a pleasant flavour, not unlike tamarind."[57] Ripe red currants strewn with sugar develop a natural rich syrup, which both improves its flavour and appearance, so a bowl of them had a "bright fresh look … very agreeable to the eye" [90]. Even the astringent choke cherry was palatable to some. Its "leaves also have a pleasant aromatic, bitter flavor like those of the peach and almond, and form a good flavoring, resembling ratafia; when boiled in milk for puddings and custards one or two are sufficient, and may be removed when the milk has boiled. This flavoring is harmless and pleasant and easily obtained."[58] However, wild berries do not thrive in cool rainy years, so they are sometimes sparse or unavailable as a food source. Another wild fruit Traill liked is the mayapple, unfamiliar to city dwellers and gardeners today [90].

Lamb's quarter (wild spinach) was "much esteemed" and served with boiled pork [57].[59] Elsewhere, she writes that she uses the now little-known strawberry blite "I

---

53 Ibid., 31–2.
54 Traill, *Forest and Other Gleanings*, 163–4.
55 Traill, *Canadian Crusoes*, 73.
56 Ibid., 117.
57 Traill, *Pearls and Pebbles*, 170.
58 Traill, *Studies of Plant Life in Canada*, 119.
59 Traill, *Backwoods of Canada*, 174.

... boiled it as a vegetable."[60] Once boiled, it was salted and probably buttered. Dandelion leaves "if blanched to a beautiful cream-colour with straw, make an excellent salad, quite equal to endive."[61] Boiled with pork, dandelion leaves were a substitute for cabbage.[62] Great quantities of watercress "[grow] in bright round cushion-like tufts at the bottom" of brooks, and "are tender and wholesome" additions to salads.[63] Wood sorrel added a lemony taste to salads.[64] Spearmint, peppermint, and thyme, and hemlock twigs, were steeped into teas.[65] Wild garlic and wild leeks were known, since they tainted the milk when cows foraged for them, but Canadians had not developed a taste for them.

In the waters of Rice Lake, close to three of their homes, the Traill boys fished for eel, bass, muskellunge, and perch with "a rough staff cut with [their] knife from the woods, and a coarse linen thread or twine, neither float, nor plummet, nor reel, or any other assistance ... for the silly fish are *caught* not *snared* as with you, but this is well, where they form an article of subsistence, not luxury."[66] Willie Traill "caught a fine eel and a bass."[67] John Moodie said he "procure[s] many a good meal for my little family [from the Otonobee River], when all other means of obtaining food [has] failed us."[68] Moodie's children called Lake Katchewanook "Mama's pantry" because she enjoyed fishing in the early dawn.[69] Some backwoods residents waited for the local First Nations to supply fish – "I should say we used to get an accidental dish of fish when the Indians have been about."[70] The fish could be eaten fresh – such as black bass broiled upon coals – lightly smoked, or featured in a savoury pie. Moodie at least once "bake[s] an eel pie for dinner, which if prepared well is by no means an unsavoury dish."[71] Traill's sole eel recipe recommends parboiling and splitting them,

60 Traill, *Forest and Other Gleanings*, 163.
61 Moodie, *Roughing It in the Bush*, 355; Traill, *Studies of Plant Life in Canada*, 89.
62 Moodie, *Roughing It in the Bush*, 355.
63 Traill, *Backwoods of Canada*, 174; Traill, *Canadian Crusoes*, 91.
64 Traill, *Canadian Crusoes*, 235
65 Moodie, *Roughing It in the Bush*, 353; Traill, *Pearls and Pebbles*, 170; Stewart, *Our Forest Home*, 51, 68.
66 Traill to her brother-in-law Canon Richard Gwillym, *I Bless You in My Heart*, 9 March 1845, 51.
67 Traill, Journal, date unknown, 1859, Traill Family Collection, 2957.
68 Moodie, *Roughing It in the Bush*, 253.
69 Ibid., 356.
70 Anne Langton, *A Gentlewoman in Upper Canada*, 210.
71 Moodie, *Roughing It in the Bush*, 381. Susannah was familiar with cooking eels. As a young bride, she considered a gift of eels from an old fisherman "quite a treat." Moodie, *Flora Lyndsay*, 55–6.

then rolling them up ("collaring") for a long boil before serving with herbs and vinegar. Local mussels and crayfish roasted in their shells with a seasoning of salt and pepper "are good eating when nothing better is to be got," although one of the children in *Canadian Crusoes* declares them, despite a lack of salt, to be "very good, when well roasted, covered up with hot embers."[72]

The Traills also made their own maple sugar and molasses, and probably also sourced some wild honey. In *Canadian Crusoes*, Catharine says that wild honey is "a delicious addition" to wild rice and notes that it is possible to make "some very good vinegar with the refuse of the honey combs, by pouring water on it, and leaving it to ferment in a warm nook of the chimney, in one of the birch-bark vessels; this is an excellent substitute for salt as a seasoning to the fresh meat and fish."[73]

Wild birds and their eggs were easily available in the backwoods. The Traills probably ate quantities of partridges, ducks, and geese, and especially pigeons and squirrels. Anna Leveridge's family "had to-day a rabbit and a partridge stewed with sage and onions, and a pumpkin custard."[74] In *Canadian Crusoes*, the hungry children decide to boil partridge eggs instead of roasting them in the ashes, then declare them "better than those that are daily produced from the little hen-house."[75] Although she says that "some people" eat them, before she applies her giveaway clue of "wholesome" [162], Traill speaks approvingly of the edibility of blackbirds [163] and squirrels [163–4]; the inevitable conclusion is that her family ate them willingly. Certainly "the different variety of squirrels supplied" the Moodies "with pies, stews, and roasts" and "even the little chissmunk [chipmunk], is palatable when cooked."[76]

WHAT DID TRAILL FEED HER FAMILY IN DIFFICULT TIMES?

Having outlined the various influences and historical context of Traill's life in the mid-nineteenth century, what can we conclude about the Traill family's daily fare and how much it represents that of their compatriot immigrants? Answers come from various sources, not just what is revealed in the *Guide*. Their family meals were very Canadian, often quite meagre, but tasty nonetheless.

---

72 Trail, *Canadian Crusoes*, 27, 33, 71.
73 Ibid., 157, 161.
74 Tivy, Anna Leveridge to her mother, *Your Loving Anna*, 4 October 1885, 63.
75 Traill, *Canadian Crusoes*, 27.
76 Moodie, *Roughing It in the Bush*, 356.

One edifying indication of her family's meals are her comments about what children will willingly eat, suggestive of her own children's partialities. As weaned babies she fed them pap, cornstarch custard, and hard biscuits, as doctors recommended. As they grew older, curds and whey with a little ripe fruit made "a nice dish for the children" [197]; they showed a fondness for milk-porridge [115–16] and supporne [cornmeal porridge] [121–2]; and enjoyed potato dumplings "when nicely done" [131]. She was cautious about giving too much yeasted bread to children because it was sometimes indigestible if not well-baked [96], a complaint others made as well. Children were encouraged to drink fresh milk.

Two decades later Harriet Durnford King's grandchildren "can not touch the salt pork, and are heartily tired of boiled rice and dumplings, which are all the variety we can give them, with the exception of an occasional egg."[77] Some babies drank the sap from maple trees and Mary O'Brien was surprised "to see the avidity with which baby asked for the sap and the dexterity with which she lapped it up. It is quite clear, just pleasantly sweet."[78] It is not hard to imagine Traill's children also being tired of salt pork and enjoying maple sap.

In letters to her sister, Traill grieved that her sons' diets were so scanty.[79] During the 1840s, when the Traill children were young, did they know "every degree of hunger and nakedness" that the Maxwell and Perron children experienced during their exile on the Rice Lake plains? "During the first few years of their lives," were they also "compelled to subsist for days and weeks upon roots and herbs, wild fruits, and game which their [father] has learned to entrap, to decoy, and to shoot"?[80] Thomas Traill, like every man on backwoods farms, had a rifle, although as a gentle and repressed man it is hard to imagine him hunting with any success or relish, as so many of his contemporaries did. Perhaps the first two Traill sons, James (born 1833) and Thomas (born 1837), learned to "make deadfalls, and pits, and traps, and snares ... use the bow, ... pitch a stone, or fling a wooden dart at partridge, hare, and squirrel, with almost unerring aim."[81] They may have contributed to the family's larder, as so many boys and young men did. Catharine's older sister, Agnes Strickland, may have been

77 King, *Letters from Muskoka*, 96. See also Stewart, *Our Forest Home*, 95.
78 O'Brien, *Journals of Mary O'Brien*, 10 March 1829, 45.
79 Traill to Susanna Moodie, *I Bless You in My Heart*, March 1846, 54; to Susanna Moodie, 16 April 1846, 57; to Susanna Moodie, 26 July 1849, 59.
80 Traill, *Canadian Crusoes*, 28.
81 Ibid., 28, 56.

closer to truth than she would ever realize when she casually commented that "[a]n intimate acquaintance with [Canada's] rich vegetable and animal productions is most effectually made under the high pressure of difficulty and necessity."[82]

Besides Traill's personal tastes and those of her family members, other factors involved in her choice of food include practicality, palatability, and quantity. Inevitably, this included cornmeal at all meals, prepared in a wide variety of ways – cakes, porridges, breads, puddings. Meals that could fill up the yawning stomachs of children and growing farm boys were essential, such as puddings, porridges, and pancakes of corn, oats, buckwheat, and wheat flour, all easily assembled and cooked in boiling water or fried on a griddle in drippings. Pies too, simple breads, tea-cakes and crackers, all easily mixed and placed in the bake-kettle or plunked on the griddle. She called them "homely dishes" [103] [124] [166]. Dishes of one grain and a fruit, or hashes and fricassees with a little bit of meat, could be bulked up with root vegetables and onions. Others were a "simple fare of stewed rice sweetened with honey" and "a savory soup of hare or other game";[83] another was "some fine ripe strawberries … plenty of stewed [wild] rice, Indian meal cake [unleavened], and maple sugar."[84] Wild rice is called "very delicious,"[85] so clearly it was eaten in the Traill household. Since potatoes and pork were ubiquitous throughout Canada, we know the Traills also consumed quantities of both. Certainly potatoes were the basis of her favourite bread. Fried potatoes with minced onions and pepper and salt to season them became a new breakfast "favourite" to accompany the meat after she "learned it from an American lady" [130]. We suspect she deliberately boiled up enough potatoes to have some the next morning for frying [129]. As Anne Langton lamented, the "frying for breakfasts and suppers" is "everlasting."[86] Fried fish, potatoes, onions, pork chops, beefsteaks, hashes, bread, bacon, sausages, and eggs were mainstays at all meals. Meats were boiled or fried more often than roasted, since those methods required less wood and were generally quicker. And boiled meats could be left untended while other kitchen activities were taking place. There was lots of pork – bacon, sausage, ham, steaks (as in pork chops). "Our larder now allows us plenty of variety in that meal [dinner]. It is provoking that we should just have our best cheer at the season

82 Ibid., 322. Agnes Strickland's comment was part of a preface she wrote for the first edition.
83 Ibid., 161.
84 Ibid., 171.
85 Traill, *Pearls and Pebbles*, 214.
86 Anne Langton, *A Gentlewoman in Upper Canada*, 10 October 1838, 179.

when we have no one to partake of it, and in summer, when we saw more company, and wished for something more than boiled or fried pork, we have to run the changes upon roast chicken, boiled chicken, hashed chicken, chicken rice, and chicken pie."[87] An occasional option was venison with wild rice, flavoured with wild herbs.[88] The bones could be turned into a nice broth, said Anna Leveridge.[89]

Baking was done in the bake-kettle at the hearth, in a brick oven if the settler was lucky enough to have one, or in the cookstove oven. Bread was toasted on sticks or iron rods in front of the fire or fried in drippings or butter. Sandwiches were commonly taken out into the farm fields by the men. Traill needed to bake lots of bread for her growing family, and eventually her daughter Kate made good bread too.[90] Frances Stewart fed bread "every morn and evening [to] a panel of impatient little animals called children,"[91] a sentiment Traill undoubtedly and lovingly endorsed, and Anne Langton lamented the "eternal almost daily bread-baking."[92] Traill was "thankful if we can get bread sufficient for the wants of the day."[93] Countless emigrant and traveler accounts express either delight or dismay at the quality of bread available. Traill clearly preferred potato bread over salt-risen bread [96–8]; coarse bran bread was esteemed for its nutritious and digestive qualities [99].

Early chemical leaveners such as saleratus or pearlash were a real boon, often used in place of the time-consuming effort of whisking egg yolks and whites. They made it possible for busy housewives to bake cakes more frequently, and were especially effective when combined with molasses. Stacks of buckwheat or cornmeal pancakes accompanied by butter and maple syrup or molasses provided fortifying food for those involved in physically taxing farm work and housework. Making pastry for a pie, either savoury or sweet, was so fundamental a kitchen skill that Traill assumed her readers had that knowledge. If they did not, then she assumed they had another book to supply the necessary instructions. American white rice from Carolina kept well as a staple pantry item in the backwoods. Its main use was in popular rice puddings, with and without currants or raisins, or fresh berries, as attested by the frequency with

87 Ibid., 17 January 1839, 210.
88 Traill, *Canadian Crusoes*, 212.
89 Tivy, *Your Loving Anna*, undated letter from mid-1880s, 77.
90 Traill to Ellen Dunlop, *I Bless You in My Heart*, 7 August 1857, 106.
91 Stewart to Honora Edgeworth, *Revisiting "Our Forest Home,"* 19 August 1827, 124.
92 Anne Langton, *A Gentlewoman in Upper Canada*, 10 October 1838, 179.
93 Traill to Susanna Moodie, *I Bless You in My Heart*, March 1846, 54.

which it is mentioned in various settlers' accounts; all three Stricklands mention rice pudding. Beside the ubiquitous rice pudding, the Traills also ate considerable quantities of plain cornmeal and oatmeal puddings, and other everyday dishes, which seldom appear in cookbooks due to their ordinariness. Traill, probably more often than she cared to admit, fed her family the porridges more associated with breakfast for supper when nothing else was available. In January 1860, six years after publication of the *Guide* and a year after her husband died, Traill lamented that "[w]e had had only dry bread and tea without milk or sugar. It was not sufficient for the poor children. Mary must have felt the want of some more nourishing food and Willie too is dreadfully hungry[,] poor boy. Kate was ill but no one murmured. Today we had molasses and butter for dinner[.] It was greatly relished."[94] Mary was age nineteen, Willie sixteen, and Kate twenty-four.

In her published letters of the early 1870s, Harriet Durnford King outlined some evocative examples of what poor families ate. Her family had run out of money soon after emigrating to Muskoka. Having only one "attenuated" chicken: "with the help of lots of butter, onions and spices, I concocted a savoury stew which was much applauded. We had also a pudding! Well, the less said about that pudding the better. Nevertheless, I must record that it contained a *maximum* of flour and a *minimum* of currants and grease. The plums, sugar, spice, eggs, citron, and brandy were conspicuous by their absence. Still, the pudding was eaten – peace to its memory!"[95] The Kings bought "a bull calf for seven dollars" which "had a marvellous development of bone and gristle, but very little flesh; still we made much of it in the shape of nourishing broth and savoury stews."[96] Sometimes, potatoes were "roasted in the ashes and eaten with plenty of butter and salt."[97] In times of dire stress, dinner could be merely "bread-and-treacle and tea" or "porridge and potatoes"[98] or "'praties and pork' ... and a cup of tea, though there is only maple sugar to sweeten it and no milk to soften its harshness."[99] As a poor widow, Traill said, "I dig my little garden and eat my potatoes with a thankful heart."[100]

94 Traill, Journal, 31 January 1860, Traill Family Collection, 2965.
95 King, *Letters from Muskoka*, 52–3.
96 Ibid., 69–70.
97 Ibid., 126.
98 Ibid., 164.
99 Traill, *Pearls and Pebbles*, 98.
100 Traill to Agnes Fitzgibbon, 29 October 1861, Thomas Fisher Rare Book Library, University of Toronto.

In general, the Traills ate lots of fresh fruits and berries in season, often with cream, milk, or buttermilk. "A dish of raspberries and milk, with sugar, or a pie, gives many an emigrant family a supper" [85]. Apples were universally adaptable to any number of "nice dishes" [75] – either fresh or dried for winter storage – turned into turnovers, dumplings, puddings, pies, tarts, puffs, sauces, preserves, fever drinks, or jelly and used in syrup or cider. Clearly, Traill loved apples, particularly acidic ones, as she provided ten recipes for them and included apples in other recipes as well as expending a lot of effort on instructing readers about their cultivation in Canada. She lost her appetite during an illness in January 1858, but still ate lots of apples.[101] She also liked the acidic may-apple, particularly when preserved with cloves or lemon peel and/or ginger [90–1],[102] but also when unripe and roasted in embers.[103]

At times, the inexpensive and available foodstuffs were meagre and monotonous indeed. Traill and other cooks attempted to overcome this by considering how to make meals something tasty to look forward to. "To the poor man, no sauce seasons his dish so well as a good appetite, which makes every dish savoury" [166]. While certainly true, Traill wants even "homely dishes ... intended for homely people" to be "render[ed] ... palatable and pleasant" [103]. Suggestions about texture, colour, flavour, and presentation all featured in her recipes. With simple additions, such as herbs she grew herself, fresh cream, a sprinkling of maple sugar, a spoonful of her own tomato catsup enlivened with her own vinegar, or melted butter, she could supplement the dishes' basic flavours. Apple pie was improved if the apples were raw, not prebaked, and it was decorated with pastry leaves [72]. All good cooks know that these simple enhancements make a huge difference to a successful meal. A little nutmeg, sugar, and butter made the simplest of flour porridges pleasanter. Even in the bush, simple spicing was available for flavour and preservation – "a grate of nutmeg is an improvement if you have it at hand" [124]. Traill's spice shelf may seldom have had a nutmeg, but homegrown caraway seeds – "always useful" [58] – were readily available for seed cakes, one of the time-honored English cake recipes Traill omits since it was easily found in a regular cookbook. Cost meant that she could not be lavish with teaspoonfuls of black pepper or lemon essence, but she did encourage their use. Anna Leveridge was delighted with a custard pie "flavoured with ess[ence] of lemon on a short crust, on soup plates, and the whites beaten up and put on the top. You had

---

101 Traill to her daughter Mary Traill, *I Bless You in My Heart*, 23 January 1858, 112.
102 Traill, *Canadian Crusoes*, 75; Traill, *Studies of Plant Life in Canada*, 40–1.
103 Traill, *Canadian Crusoes*, 75.

better try it, it was very good."[104] Vinegar sauces, mustard, and catsups of mushroom, anchovy, or tomato were all handy flavour stimulants.

Sprinkling a little maple or white or brown sugar over puddings, tarts, griddle cakes, and fresh fruit added an extra sweetness, and was also a cost-saver if not much sugar was incorporated while baking. The buckwheat, cornmeal, and oatmeal pancake recipes, for instance, include no sugar, nor do any of the hasty puddings or porridges – the sugar, molasses, or syrup was added to the food once on the plate. The cake recipes published elsewhere – silver and gold cakes, Indian Pound Cake – however, typically include considerable amounts. An exception is the cup of maple sugar in bush tea-cakes [109]. Maple sugar is now an expensive commodity, but it was once associated with poverty because it was homemade in the bush. White sugar was prestigious, whereas nowadays it is cheap and available. If made at home today, raspberry vinegar is expensive, given the large quantity of fresh raspberries required (about six litres), but for the Traill family a store of raspberry vinegar concocted of fresh raspberries from their own garden and the forest clearings, like homemade maple sugar and homemade maple or red currant vinegar, was a "cheap luxury" [85].

Recalling the living standards of her youth at Reydon Hall farm and being innately class-conscious with gentle manners, Traill, even when experiencing financial distress in the bush, was disposed to make her table service as nice as possible. As the family's fortunes dwindled and they moved to ever smaller and cheaper farms, she was still conscious of how her table and her food appeared, both to her family and to guests. Her dear friend, Frances Stewart, summarized it well: "We always try to dress neatly & to be clean & and [sic] to have our tables decently and comfortably laid out & generally have a very plentiful supply of plain substantial wholesome food."[105] When Anne Langton writes that a dinner invitation has been accepted by friends, she and her mother set to "pondering upon the best method of manufacturing a top, bottom and four corners out of pork and poultry," their interminable staple meats. When they received a "present of veal from" an acquaintance, they could offer their guests the distinction of some variety.[106] Removing the tablecloth before dessert to reveal the dining room table continued to be proper etiquette.[107]

104 Tivy, Anna Leveridge to her mother and father, *Your Loving Anna*, 16 May 188[4?], 52.
105 Stewart, *Our Forest Home*, 5 May 1847, 212.
106 Anne Langton, *A Gentlewoman in Upper Canada*, 2 June 1840, 283.
107 Moodie, *Life in the Clearings*, 120, 332; Samuel Strickland, *Twenty-Seven Years in Canada West*, 310.

Typically, a log cabin meal was shared from bowls and platters placed on the table. The pot may even have been placed on the table. Growing up, the Stricklands would have eaten in the best Georgian manner, so did placing a cooking pot instead of a beautiful covered serving dish on the table cause Traill and Moodie pangs of regret for graciousness lost?

Enforced frugality was not new to Traill since she had already experienced it as a young woman when her father died unexpectedly, leaving his widow and eight children to suddenly need to penny-pinch when his investments faltered. Frugality is an ongoing theme in the history of feeding families, as a survey of cookbooks reveals clearly. Book titles, comments in prefaces and throughout recipes, pairs of rich and plain versions of recipes presented side by side, suggestions for less expensive ingredients, and other pointers all appear in many cookbooks and magazine recipe collections, even those without frugality as a theme. Traill's *Guide* is part of this honourable tradition.

Farmhouse Foodways:
Sample Seasonal Menus at Home

Fig. 19 · Canadian kitchen, 1864. A lively scene of a housewife at work, accompanied by a child and two cats. Notice the many containers on the shelves and mantel, and the big iron pot simmering on the hearth. An axe leans against the wall, a broom has fallen over, what might be pudding cloths hang from the shelf, and there are two three-legged stools, all suggestive of various kinds of work.

Immediately following her marriage, Catharine travelled with her new husband to his Scottish homeland, so she did not establish her own home until they arrived in Canada. The Moodies, however, had had their own home and their first child before leaving England and Susanna Moodie had had to think about planning meals for her husband and new family, even if she was not doing much of the actual cooking. She teased an old friend who supported her literary efforts by saying, "I have begun the pudding and dumpling discussions, and now find, that the noble art of housewifery is more to be desired than all the accomplishments, which are to be retailed by the literary and fashionable damsels who frequent these envied circles."[1] Once in their

1 Moodie, *Letters of a Lifetime*, 9 April 1831, 61.

backwoods cabins of Upper Canada, both women were necessarily "constantly engaged in the everyday cares of domestic life."[2]

Nowadays in Canada, we are clear on what foods constitute breakfast, lunch, and dinner. The overlap is minimal. Orange juice, instant oatmeal, or cold cereal with milk, yogurt and fruit, and the ubiquitous coffee are typical weekday morning foods, while a ham and lettuce or tuna fish sandwich with an apple, cookie, and soft drink or small carton of milk is an average lunch for both schoolchildren and office workers, unless they buy a take-out meal. Common dinners are pasta with a tomato sauce, or pizza, or a burger and fries, or microwaved curry, with or without a salad, all washed down with wine, coffee, or a soft drink. Of course many Canadians prefer a greater variety with healthier options, or the foods of their cultural heritages, but they still usually recognize a division of dishes among the meals. In Traill's day and place, the overlap between meals was constant. Buckwheat pancakes or supporne (cornmeal porridge) with maple syrup might appear at any meal, pie left over from dinner became part of breakfast the next day, grilled beefsteak or pork chops were as likely to be breakfast as part of the main meal at noon. Salt pork, shanty bread, cornmeal pudding, potatoes and cabbages, pickles, homemade fruit preserves of all kinds used as condiments or pie fillings, griddle cakes, maple molasses as sauce – all these foods appeared at any farmhouse or backwoods meal throughout the year. Bachelor settler Edward Talbot summarized it this way: "Their breakfasts not infrequently consist of twelve or fourteen different ingredients, which are of the most heterogeneous nature. Green tea and fried pork, honey-comb or salted salmon, pound-cake and pickled cucumbers, stewed chicken and apple tarts, maple-molasses and pease-pudding, ginger-bread and sour crout, are to be found at almost every table. The dinner differs not at all from the breakfast; and the afternoon repast, which they term 'supper,' is equally substantial."[3]

When outlining their menus in letters and journals, early Ontarians did not always include vegetables, although many were consumed, especially after the first few years of settlement and its deprivations. Farm families raised vegetables for themselves, for agricultural markets, and for general stores. A quotation from another bachelor, Thomas Need, provides an example of the inclusion of vegetables: "About noon, four [male] travellers arrived from Peterboro'; they were new to the Bush, and stared when

2 Ibid., 23 January 1835, 92.
3 Edward Talbot, *Five Year's Residence in the Canadas including a Tour through Part of the United States of America in the year 1823*, quoted in Williamson, "To Fare Sumptuously Every Day," 3.

I requested them to help me to prepare for their entertainment, but they soon entered into the spirit of the thing, and as in the good old patriarchal days, one baked, one attended to the roast, while a third prepared the vegetables. In due time, I set before them a repast of the usual forest fare – fish, fowl, and venison – which my guests pronounced sumptuous, and enjoyed not the less on account of its novelty."[4]

Abundant fresh fruit was much more likely to be itemized when described as part of a meal: "fresh melon, plums, strawberries, apples, grapes."[5]

MEAL TIMES

By the mid-nineteenth century in Canada, a day's housework and farm work were generally divided by three meals, with timing similar to our own day – breakfast, midday, and early evening. The pattern in England in the previous century had been quite different: breakfast in mid-morning and dinner in late afternoon, with a very light repast mid-evening before retiring.

In summer, men in a farm family often went out to the fields before eating, giving the women time to prepare breakfast. The "best time for hard work in a hot country is before six in the morning, and after the heat of the day in the evening."[6] Frances Steward added: "We have very substantial breakfasts as soon after six o'clock as all can be assembled." Before eating commenced, "Tom reads a portion of Scripture & prayers."[7]

A farm family's midday meal – dinner – was generally the day's heartiest. In town, the midday meal was luncheon, taken about one o'clock, with dinner at four, five, or six o'clock, much more in line with the English pattern. Although the Traills surely had a clock, some families did not, so they relied on the sun: "By the accustomed sun-mark on the floor, which Sybel prefers to the clock, she sees 'tis now the hungry hour of noon, and blows the [conch shell] horn for Lank to come to dinner."[8] Sam Strickland called the supper-horn a "sound of civilized life."[9]

During the winter, when darkness arrived in the late afternoon, supper started anytime between five and six o'clock, but it moved to mid-evening in the summer

4 Need, *Six Years in the Bush*, 71.
5 Ibid., 99.
6 Moodie, *Life in the Clearings*, 25.
7 Stewart, *Revisiting "Our Forest Home,"* 144. In the 1902 publication, "Tom" was changed to "Mr Stewart" (Stewart, *Our Forest Home*, 212).
8 Beavan, *Sketches and Tales*, 32.
9 Samuel Strickland, *Twenty-Seven Years in Canada West*, 1:153.

months so that the men could stay in the fields until just before dark. Their women-folk brought them a substantial snack about four o'clock [144]. Supper was a lighter meal than the substantial midday one, and often people ate the same dishes for breakfast and supper. Supper was often called tea or tea-time by genteel folk. Frances Stewart writes, "6 o'clock ... Our early tea is over. Bessie has gone to her garden for a little while & I will take the quiet time before all the *labourers* come in for their supper [to write a letter]."[10] Supper could also refer to a light meal late in the evening, such as the meal that accompanied an evening dance or ball. "The evening generally closes with a splendid supper," writes Susanna Moodie, "in which there is no lack of the good things which the season affords."[11]

BACKWOODS MENUS

We have devised some backwoods "menus" based on information about meals provided in the *Guide,* in Traill's other writings (especially *Canadian Crusoes*) and those of her sister Susanna Moodie, and in accounts by their bush farm contemporaries, primarily Anne Langton, Frances Stewart, Harriet Durnford King, Mary O'Brien, and Frances Beaven (of New Brunswick). Three family scenarios are presented to describe some rural Canadians' seasonal menus for breakfast, the midday dinner, and the late afternoon or early evening supper or tea.

Family One represents the families who struggled to put food on the table. Their daily experience included a level of repetition and simplicity typical of the earliest settlers' meals or those who were poor, even destitute, as the Moodies and Traills sometimes were in the 1830s and 1840s. Traill said their spirits were: "sinking under the load of mental anxiety ... and want of strengthening diet – bread, a few potatoes, given us by dear good Mr Stewart, and a few small fishes from day to day and week to week have been our fare ... the dear children eat it with single and contented hearts but baby and I grow thin ... I have a few small hams." A barrel of flour had also been given to them.[12]

Family Two depicts the more generous and varied meals of a large and expanding farm family who sat down together at a big, homely, but plentifully spread table. "We

10 Stewart, *Revisiting "Our Forest Home,"* 5 May 1847, 142. This opening sentence is not included in the 1902 book.
11 Moodie, *Life in the Clearings,* 90.
12 Traill to Susanna Moodie, *I Bless You in My Heart,* 16 April 1846, 57.

sit down 15 to every meal."[13] The Traills sat fewer, but would have been at least nine if all seven children were present.

Family Three exemplifies the meals of a small farm or town family with more financial resources who have guests. At dinner they want to demonstrate that they remember the old formal table service of their ancestral home, which would have been a first course with a soup, top dish, bottom dish, and several sides and/or corners, followed by a dessert course. In this case they had someone help serve: "Our dinner was served very comfortably by a neat maidservant, but [we] were waited upon principally by the children, and the attention of the host supplied whatever might otherwise have been wanting to the arrangements."[14] This recalls what the Stricklands did at home at Reydon Hall in Suffolk, and what the Langtons sometimes achieved in Upper Canada.

Several historical statements have helped inform us while creating these menus. The first four are from the *Guide*:

"In Canada, preserves are always placed on the table at the evening meal, and often in the form of tarts" [89].

"Canada is the land of cakes. A tea-table is generally furnished with several varieties of cakes and preserves" [110].

"In Canadian farm-houses meat is generally cooked twice and sometimes thrice a day" [129].

"Beef was rarely seen in the backwoods" [237].

"Meat was provided twice and often thrice a day; it being more a matter of taste than economy as to the number of times it was served."[15]

"We consume more in the way of ketchups, sauces, curry-powder, etc., than we used to at home, on account of the many months we are without fresh meat."[16]

---

13 Stewart, *Revisiting "Our Forest Home,"* 25 August 1866, 213.
14 O'Brien, *Journals of Mary O'Brien,* 1 January 1829, 30.
15 Haight, *Country Life in Canada,* 86.
16 Anne Langton, *A Gentlewoman in Upper Canada,* 3 August 1839, 252.

"Bread, salt pork, potatoes, tea and maple sugar were the staples of life in the backwoods. [F]or anything else the settlers went without or substituted anything they could invent or adapt."[17]

"A dinner in the country of Canada, taken at the house of some substantial yeoman, is a very different affair from a dinner in town. The table literally groans with good cheer; and you cannot offer a greater affront to your hostess, than to eat sparingly of the dainties set before you ... Fowls of several sorts, ham, and joints of roast and boiled meats, beside quantities of pies, puddings, custards, and cakes. Cheese is invariably offered to you with your apple pie; and several little glass dishes are ranged around your plate, for preserves, honey, and apple sauce, which latter dainty is never wanting at a country feast."[18]

"My readers should see a table laid out in a wealthy Canadian farmer's house before they have any idea of the profusion displayed ... Beside venison, pork, chickens, ducks, and fish of several kinds, cooked in a variety of ways, there was a number of pumpkin, raspberry, cherry, and currant pies, with fresh butter and green cheese (as the new cream cheese is called), molasses, preserves, and pickled cucumbers, besides tea and coffee ... We were all very hungry, having tasted nothing since five o'clock in the morning, and contrived, out of the variety of good things before us, to make an excellent dinner."[19]

Spring (Mid- to Late May)

By April, the cows would have been producing enough milk to permit butter-churning and cheese-making again, so milk, butter, cream, and fresh cheese, along with eggs, began to be plentiful again. The kitchen garden would be somewhat planted, albeit still yielding very little, so the ever-diminishing stock of preserves, pickles, salt meat, and salt fish would still be essential. The forest and lakes, however, would have

---

17 Traill, "Tom Nixon's Forest Home," Traill Family Collection, 4912.
18 Moodie, *Life in the Clearings*, 93.
19 Moodie, *Roughing It in the Bush*, 333.

yielded early wild greens and plenty of fish. Grain harvests are months away, but there would still be enough flour and cornmeal in the barrels.

Family One

BREAKFAST
Food: slices of salt pork with eggs fried in dripping; boiled lima bean pudding with salt pork [139]; wild morels fried in dripping [167]; applesauce (from reconstituted dried apples)

Accompaniments: a sprinkling of currant vinegar for the bean pudding [89]

Beverages: Labrador tea [141], maple beer [153]

DINNER
Food: fried pork chops; boiled potatoes; pickled cabbage; pickled cucumbers

Beverages: hops beer or apple cider

SUPPER / TEA
Food: fried bacon; the last of the previous year's potatoes and cabbage fried in the bacon fat; salt-risen shanty bread spread with the remaining bacon fat; applesauce [72–4]

Beverages: dandelion coffee [142], green tea sweetened with maple sugar but no milk

Family Two

BREAKFAST
Food: brown supporne (cornmeal porridge) made with milk [101]; "nice smiling pota-toes," fried;[20] cold salt pork; new-laid eggs, boiled; stewed rhubarb with maple sugar; toasted salt-risen shanty bread spread with early spring butter and/or potted white-fish, or lashings of raspberry and strawberry jams (perhaps with the mould scraped off the surface first); apple and pumpkin pies left over from dinner the day before [71–2, 133]

---

20 Stewart, *Our Forest Home*, 5 May 1847, 144. This was the wording in Stewart's original letter, but the 1902 publication eliminated "nice."

Accompaniments: cold butter and milk for the supporne [101]; mustard for the pork; bush cheese for the apple pie [198–9]

Beverages: milk for the children, green tea sweetened with white sugar and milk for others

(This breakfast is partially based on one mentioned in Stewart.[21])

DINNER

Food: salad of blanched young dandelion greens dressed with red currant vinegar and perhaps a bit of melted lard or drippings and mustard; squirrel hash made with onions; black or rock bass fried in fat pork drippings; early spring radishes; salt-risen shanty bread made of shorts[22] with butter and wild plum preserve (made with maple molasses); Indian pound cake [124]; bush tea-cakes [109]

Accompaniments: mushroom ketchup; pickled green beans [139] and pickled beets; fresh cream and lots of maple molasses for the cake

Beverages: raspberry vinegar for the children; hops beer; green tea sweetened with white sugar and milk for others

SUPPER / TEA

Food: perch lightly fried or grilled [167]; morels fried in early butter [167]; cold smoked ham slices; plain Indian pudding without eggs [126]; a pie of cranberry preserves (with lard pastry) [87]; bush tea-cakes [109]

Accompaniments: a sauce of blended beet vinegar [145] and mustard for the perch; beet pickles and sweet pickled citron melon.[23]

---

21 Ibid., 212; Stewart, *Revisiting "Our Forest Home,"* 144.
22 Shorts refers to coarse wheat flour. See page 464–5 in the glossary of food terms.
23 Surprisingly versatile and delicious, this sweet pickle is almost forgotten now in Canada, but candied watermelon rind was once familiar as a substitute for candied citron. Amelia Simmons provides one recipe for "American Citron." "Take the rine [*sic*] of a large watermelon not too ripe, cut it into small pieces, take two pound of loaf sugar, one pint of water, put it all into a kettle, let it boil gently for four hours, then put it into pots for use" (*The First American Cookbook*, 40). A similar method of preparation is "Take the rind of a large watermelon, cut it in small pieces, allow loaf sugar pound for pound, make a sirop of the sugar, boil two hours slowly, put into pots for use" (*The Cook Not Mad*, 181). The most detailed description appears in *The Canadian Receipt Book*: "The harder part of watermelon; next the skin, made into preserves, with sugar, equal weights; cooking down the syrup rather more for common use causes it to granulate, like citron which is kept for sale."

Beverage: green tea sweetened with white sugar and milk

Family Three

BREAKFAST

Food: hash of corned beef or salt pork with wild morels; hominy [121], or Indian meal pancakes with butter and strewn sugar (maybe with a few dried currants) [123–4]; fried potatoes or slices of leftover mashed potatoes browned in the bake-kettle; radishes; warm gingerbread cupcakes [106]

Accompaniments: mushroom ketchup for the hash [167]; maple syrup for the gingerbread

Beverages: green tea served with white sugar and milk, real coffee served with white sugar and rich cream

DINNER

First course: top dish of fish soup [166–7], followed by a boiled fillet of veal; bottom dish of roast pork, with parsnips and carrots roasted in the dripping pan under the pork; corners of spring chicken, ham steaks, veal steaks, and macaroni; wild rice pudding [113]

Accompaniments: toast sippets for the fish soup; gravy and applesauce for the pork; tomato catsup for the macaroni; pickled green beans [139] and pickled cabbage

Second course: baked Indian fruit pudding with dried huckleberries and cranberries [126], tart of dried apples [72–3], trifle, almond cheesecakes

Dessert: raisins and almonds, also butternuts

Beverages: red wine for the first and second courses; green tea and coffee for dessert; madeira for dessert

(This dinner is partially based on a meal outlined in Anne Langton's journal.)[24]

This chopped fine as citron make excellent substitute for that article; and for much less cost. Call in the neighbours to help eat about a dozen good sized melons, and you have outside enough for the experiment; and if the doctor is near he will help without a fee. They are nice, also, in mince pies in place of raisins" (*The Canadian Receipt Book*, 159).

24 Anne Langton, *A Gentlewoman in Upper Canada*, 5 June 1840, 284.

SUPPER / TEA
Food: cold sliced roast beef or roast venison [87]; roasted wild duck or stuffed pigeons [161, 163]; browned mashed potatoes [130]; radishes; apple-rice pudding [75, 329–30] with cranberry jelly [89]; gingerbread [106]

Accompaniments: horseradish for the beef or cranberry sauce for the venison [87]; onion-flavoured butter gravy for the roasted birds [161]; honey for the gingerbread

Beverage: cider, green tea sweetened with white sugar and milk.

Summer (Early to Mid-August)

Despite the heat, fires would still have been lit in the cookstoves, although they were often moved to the back kitchen or onto the back stoup, which served as a summer kitchen. Some fresh beef, especially veal, and lamb would have been available through the summer but most meat would have been butchered and quickly set to be smoked or brined. A chicken would have been easily turned into dinner. Numerous vegetables and fruit would have been at their peak, even fresh potatoes, which Traill declared "rare in July" [220]. Usually, the men would have headed out to the fields in the pre-dawn coolness, giving the women time to milk the cows and prepare breakfast.

Family One

BREAKFAST
Food: buckwheat pancakes with maple molasses [152]; huckleberries and fresh-picked raspberries; thick slices of cucumber quickly stewed in fat gravy; slices of watermelon

Beverage: wild peppermint tea[25]

DINNER
Food: stewed chicken with wild rice; boiled carrots and corn; salad of lettuce, cucumber, endive, celery, wild watercress, and just a little bit of wild peppermint, dressed

---

25 Moodie, *Roughing It in the Bush*, 353.

with a salad sauce;[26] wild mussels and crayfish roasted in ashes; hot Indian corn cakes [125] or gingerbread cakes [106] with stewed wild plums

Accompaniments: butter for the carrots and corn; butter for the cakes; maple syrup for the cakes

Beverage: sage leaf tea[27]

SUPPER / TEA
Food: fried corn [123]; milk porridge flavoured with chokecherry leaves and served with wild chokecherry jam;[28] fresh raspberries with milk or cream

Beverages: hop beer or beet beer [144–5], maple vinegar water flavoured with nutmeg and lemon essence [153]

Family Two

BREAKFAST
Food: buttermilk cakes with maple molasses [152]; pork sausages and bacon; boiled Indian meal pudding with a blend of fresh red currants, raspberries and blackberries; slices of watermelon

Beverages: buttermilk for the children, Labrador tea and coffee for others

DINNER
Food: salad of lettuce, cucumber, endive and wild watercress dressed with maple sap vinegar; fried or grilled trout; fried ham; little potatoes boiled; young French beans; broccoli; Indian tea cakes with milk and dried blueberries [124–5]; raspberry pie; "a splendid dish of strawberries and cream"[29]

Accompaniments: iced butter for the potatoes; strawberry jam for the tea cakes

Beverage: green tea

---

26 See page 358–9.
27 Moodie, *Roughing It in the Bush*, 353.
28 Traill, *Studies of Plant Life in Canada*, 118–19.
29 Beavan, *Sketches and Tales*, 34.

(This meal is based on one described in Frances Beavan's story of her New Brunswick life.)[30]

SUPPER / TEA

Food: pigeon pot pie baked in the bake-kettle [161]; stewed corn with meat [123]; boiled green peas flavoured with mint; drop sweet cakes flavoured with essence of lemon [107]; fresh melon; early apples and pears; stewed huckleberries and red currants with a little maple or muscovado sugar [82]

Accompaniments: butter for the green peas; pickled cabbage; pickled beets; pickled peaches

Beverage: maple vinegar water flavoured with nutmeg and lemon essence [153]

Family Three

BREAKFAST

Food: milk curds made with that morning's milk [197] and huckleberries; duck or goose eggs fried in butter; toasted potato bread, huckleberry jam; slices of watermelon

Beverages: milk for the children, green tea and coffee for others

DINNER

First course: top dish of potato soup followed by a chicken, rabbit, or veal curry;[31] bottom dish of boiled pork; two sides of fried pork and ham with corn patties [122]; green garden peas; green string beans

Accompaniments: applesauce for the boiled pork; mustard for the fried pork; iced butter for the peas

Second course: baked currant pudding [90]; tart of wild red plum preserves [80, 89]; caraway cookies [107]

Dessert: almonds, raisins, oranges, red raspberries, black raspberries

Beverages: red wine, green tea

30 Ibid., 33–4.
31 See page 356–8.

(The first and second courses are partially derived from Anne Langton's journal;[32] the dessert course is from Sam Strickland, remembering "a capital dinner" and "a nice dessert" that was "laid out" "after the cloth was removed."[33])

SUPPER / TEA

Food: cold ham; buttered eggs; boiled carrots; raspberry tarts; "nice light" buttermilk cakes [114–15] and lady cakes [108] served with black currant preserves made with maple molasses [152]

Accompaniments: mustard for the ham, good fresh butter for the cakes

Beverages: raspberry vinegar [85]

(This menu blends summer suppers mentioned in Langton and in Traill's story "The Mill of the Rapids."[34])

Autumn (Mid- to Late October)

The glut of autumn vegetables would have been converted into pickles, but plenty of fresh vegetables were still available in the underground cool room or cellar for a few months. Autumn was "the time of the pig-killing," when you could "hardly walk a quarter of a mile without meeting a waggon loaded more or less with carcasses of pigs."[35]

Family One

BREAKFAST

Food: pork sausage; pease pudding or Indian meal porridge (supporne) served with milk and maple sugar [121–2] or muscovado

Beverages: dandelion coffee [142–3], raspberry vinegar [85]

---

32 Anne Langton, *A Gentlewoman in Upper Canada*, 9 July 1839, 241. She includes an actual recipe for her "carroway" biscuits in her journal entry.

33 Samuel Strickland, *Twenty-Seven Years in Canada West*, 1:310.

34 Anne Langton, *A Gentlewoman in Upper Canada*, 9 July 1839, 241; Traill, *Forest and Other Gleanings*, 64.

35 O'Brien, *Journals of Mary O'Brien*, 13 November 1829, 78.

DINNER

Food: oatmeal porridge with butter; American crackers [105] with butter and a "one-meal" cheese [197–8] and potato cheese [200]; a little salad with the last of the fresh cucumbers, with wild watercress; pumpkin pie [133–4]

Accompaniments: green tomato pickle made with maple vinegar; cucumber pickles; beet pickles

Beverages: dandelion coffee, acorn coffee

SUPPER / TEA

Food: buckwheat pancakes fried in lard, baked apples with muscovado sugar

Beverage: cider

Family Two

BREAKFAST

Food: potatoes fried in dripping or butter with onion (left over from boiled dinner night before) [129–30]; oatmeal porridge with milk and maple molasses or moscavado sugar [115]; toasted hop-risen shanty bread with lots of butter and a potato cheese [200]; fresh grapes from the cold cellar

Beverages: milk for the children, dandelion coffee [142–3] for others

DINNER

Food: roast pork with Indian meal Yorkshire pudding in the dripping pan below [126]; stewed tomatoes (flavoured with cayenne and vinegar) [137]; boiled cauliflower with cheese sauce; apple pie with a pressed bush cheese [198–9]; green beans

Accompaniments: may-apple preserves and crab apple jelly for the roast pork

Beverage: green tea

SUPPER / TEA

Food: potato soup with toasted salt-risen bread [96–7] or Indian bread [98–9]; grilled pork chops with gravy; apple and plum pudding [125, 126]; more toast; butternuts

Accompaniments: tomato catsup sauce for the pork chops; wild grape jelly for the toast

Beverages: green tea and cider

Family Three

BREAKFAST
Food: beef and onion hash; fried pork liver; oatmeal porridge; apples and pears

Beverages: coffee, hops beer

DINNER
First course: top dish of mullagatawny soup,[36] followed by boiled pork; bottom dish of stewed goose; two sides of chicken pie and roasted stuffed partridge [160]; boiled cauliflower; boiled carrots

Accompaniments: toast sippets for the partridge, applesauce for the pork and goose

Second course: plum pudding;[37] apple tart; trifle

Accompaniments: sweet sauce for the pudding [see 359–60]

Beverages: red wine for the first course and green tea for the second

(This menu is also partially based on Anne Langton's journal.[38])

SUPPER / TEA
Food: pigeon stuffed with butter and parsley in a pastry crust [161], potato dumplings [131], cornstarch egg-custard pudding [126]; autumn grapes

Accompaniments: tomato ketchup for the stuffed pigeon; pickled cabbage; pickled beets

Beverages: green tea and cider

36 See page 356–7.
37 See page 356.
38 Anne Langton, *A Gentlewoman in Upper Canada*, 21 October 1838, 189.

Winter (Mid- to Late January)

Winter meals could not be based on fresh meat unless it was taken from the forest or defrosted from the icehouse, but "plenty of variety" and indeed "our best cheer" was possible using pickled, smoked, and frozen meat.[39] Almost no fresh fruit or vegetables would have been available, although one exception would be citron melon, which keeps well for months in cold cellars or root-houses. Meals tended to be stodgier, with quantities of breads, potatoes, and flour puddings, and saltier from the pickles and hams. Eggs would have been used only sporadically in the cold months but were occasionally available since warmly housed chickens sometimes continue to lay,[40] but they tended to be fried instead of used in puddings or cakes. Lots of pickles and preserves would have appeared on the table.

Family One

BREAKFAST
Food: rashers of fried bacon; buckwheat pancakes with maple molasses [114]; dried apples cooked in cider to make a rich applesauce [74]

Beverages: beer or cider and dandelion coffee [142–3]

DINNER
Food: boiled wild goose; pea soup; shanty bread made with old potatoes and spread with drippings; the last of the shriveled fresh apples cooked in cider to make a rich applesauce [74]

Accompaniments: gravy for the goose made of its liver, head, pinions, and gizzard [163]; pickled green beans

Beverage: hot whisky toddy

39 Ibid., 17 January 1839, 210.
40 Ibid., 12 April 1839, 226.

SUPPER / TEA

Food: bread and butter with shaved venison ham [159] and smoked salmon trout [169]; oatmeal porridge [115]; baked apples

Accompaniments: mustard and homemade-mushroom ketchup for the ham

Beverage: green tea, dandelion coffee

Family Two

BREAKFAST

Food: fried eggs and ham; buckwheat pancakes fried in lard and served with maple molasses [114]; stewed dried apples seasoned with cloves [72]; toasted shanty bread with drippings; dried-apple pie [71–2]

Accompaniments: mushroom ketchup and tomato ketchup for the fried eggs and ham; wild raspberry or huckleberry jam [88], and wild grape jelly for the toast [26]

Beverages: beer, dandelion coffee [142–3]

DINNER

Food: venison and wild rice stew with kidney beans and dried tomatoes, topped with potato dumplings [131]; stewed cabbage sprinkled with cider vinegar for flavour; roasted squash; mashed turnip; reconstituted dried apples and black currants for pie [72, 89], Canadian croquettes [109]

Accompaniments: pickled beets; pickled green beans; pickled mushrooms

Beverage: beer

SUPPER / TEA

Food: leftover supporne (cornmeal porridge) [121–2] with fried eggs and leftover meat gravy thickened with mushroom ketchup; potato bread [98]; preserved lima beans with pork [139]; pumpkin pie with lard pastry [133–4]; hot buttered johnny-cake [125]

Accompaniments: more mushroom ketchup, also black walnut catsup; salted butter for the bread; apple preserves [73] and wild honey for the johnny-cake

Beverages: raspberry vinegar [85], green tea

Family Three

BREAKFAST
Food: hominy [121] with mutton hash; potato cakes [131]; slices of citron melon

Accompaniments: tomato catsup

Beverages: coffee, tea, raspberry vinegar

DINNER
First course: top dish of roast venison [158] or mutton; bottom dish of rolled pig's head with bread and butter;[41] four corner dishes of stewed cabbage, mashed squash [135], mashed turnip, and boiled carrots

Accompaniments: cranberry jelly sauce for the venison or mutton; mustard for the pig's head; butter for the carrots; pickled beets

Second course: boiled suet pudding with raisins; apple pie [71–2]

Accompaniments: sweet sauce for the pudding

Dessert course: almonds in the shell, raisins, cheese and biscuits [103], bush tea-cakes [109]

Beverages: wine for the first and second course, coffee and green tea for dessert

SUPPER / TEA
Food: mutton or boiled salt ham; pickled eggs; rusks [105] with potted whitefish [168]; baked apples; sago pudding; melon preserves [136], and cranberry preserves [87] in individual tarts

Accompaniments: pickled mushrooms; mustard for the mutton or ham; cream and muscovado sugar for the apples

Beverage: whisky-punch

41 Ibid., 22 January 1839, 212.

Farmhouse Foodways:
Sample Menus for Special Occasions

Festive occasions call for their own celebratory menus. Then as now, abundance and generosity were the hallmark of these communal events.

SUMMER PICNICS

Picnics were very popular, even in winter, as we know from the many mentions in the historic sources.

"A plentiful supply of all our backwoods delicacies" for a September 1840 picnic shared by the Langton family and friends, consisted of "two roast fowls, two roast wild ducks, a chicken, a piece of ham, a cranberry tart, two moulds of boiled rice with cranberry jelly, a bun loaf, bread, melons, etc. all most beautifully packed in a tin box."[1] To an earlier picnic, Anne had taken asparagus and gingerbread.

Traill and her young children enjoyed "our little treat of milk and bread, and ripe-red strawberries gathered on the heights above by the children's busy hands."[2]

Frances Stewart comments on the "abundance of cool meats, pastry[,] cakes and fruits as well as wine &c." at an 1833 regatta on Sturgeon Lake.[3] Susanna Moodie writes, "there are always regular pic-nics, each party contributing their share of eatables and drinkables to the general stock. They commonly select some pretty island in the bay, or shady retired spot on the main land, for the

---

1 Anne Langton, *A Gentlewoman in Upper Canada*, 9 September 1840, 298–9.
2 Traill, "Rice Lake Plains," in *Forest and Other Gleanings*, 206.
3 Stewart, *Revisiting "Our Forest Home,"* 5 October 1838, 133.

general rendezvous, where they light a fire, boil their kettles, and cook the vegetables to eat with their cold prog [food], which usually consists of hams, fowls, meat pies, cold joints of meat, and [an] abundance of tarts and cakes, while the luxury of ice is conveyed in a blanket at the bottom of one of the boats. These water parties are delightful. The ladies stroll about and gather wild fruit and flowers, while the gentlemen fish."[4]

CHRISTMAS DINNERS

Many of the foods we associate with a Canadian Christmas were well established by the mid-nineteenth century, as can be seen in these historical quotes.

The Traills' Christmas meal of 1839 consisted of "a glorious goose fattened on the [wild] rice bed in our lake" and "a large plum pudding, to which our little ones did ample justice" [237].

Susanna Moodie says their 1853 Christmas dinner included "mince pies and Christmas cake and [plum] pudding."[5]

Wondering about the wisdom of her tenant's return to Ireland, Frances Stewart asked if her Irish Christmas meal would be as good as her Canadian one of "a good fat Goose & plum pudding & plum cake too."[6]

Of their first Christmas dinner in Canada (1871), Harriet King says "all our provisions for Christmas festivities consisted of plenty of potatoes and a modicum of flour ... [and] some hot tea."[7]

Of their last Canadian Christmas dinner (1874), Harriet King writes that she had "two very small salt herrings ... , and a huge vegetable marrow ... We borrowed, without hesitation, some butter from our friend ... Our guests

---

4 Moodie, *Life in the Clearing*, 91.
5 Moodie, *Letters of a Lifetime*, 25 December 1853, 137.
6 Stewart, *Revisiting "Our Forest Home,"* 7 December 1846, 142–3.
7 King, *Letters from Muskoka*, 174.

assembled and dinner-time arrived, I placed on the table a large and savory dish of vegetable-marrow mashed, with potatoes well buttered, peppered, salted and baked in the oven; the two herrings carefully cooked and with a steaming dish of potatoes, with plenty of tea, made up a repast which we much enjoyed … When tea-time came, my daughter … supplied us with relays of 'dampers,' which met with universal approbation."[8]

King adds that it was, "Very different was our fare on New Year's Day 1875 – a sumptuous wild turkey, which we roasted."[9]

COMMUNAL BEES

Most pioneers had the help of others to erect their first log house, and often for barns too. As hosts, the family had to provide substantial food and drink to the assembled workers. For days ahead, the women gathered in their kitchens to make the necessary repast.

Of their housing bee in April 1833, Traill quips that: "the work went merrily on with the help of plenty of nectar (whiskey), the honey that our *bees* are solaced with. Some huge joints of salt pork, a peck of potatoes, with a rice-pudding, and a loaf as big as an enormous Cheshire cheese, formed the feast that was to regale them during the raising. This was spread out in the shanty, in a *very rural style*. In short, we laughed and called it a *pic-nic in the backwoods*; and rude as was the fare, I can assure you, great was the satisfaction expressed by all the guests at every degree, our "bee" being as considered as very well conducted."[10]

Sam Strickland describes a similar event: "At eleven o'clock, cakes and pail-fuls of teas were served round. At one, we were summoned by the sound of a tin bugle to dinner, which we found laid out in the barn. Some long pine-boards resting on tressels served for a table, which almost groaned with the good things of this earth, in the shape of roast lamb and green peas, roast

---

8 Ibid., 175. Dampers were unleavened breads baked in ashes. See page 16.
9 Ibid., 179.
10 Traill, *Backwoods of Canada*, 18 April 1833, 98.

sucking-pig, shoulder of mutton, apple-sauce, and pies, puddings, and preserves in abundance, with plenty of beer and Canadian whiskey." [11]

Susanna Moodie also includes a description: "Our [thirty-two] men worked well until dinner-time, when, after washing in the lake, they all sat down to the rude board which I had prepared for them, loaded with the best fare that could be procured in the bush. Pease soup, legs of pork, venison, eel, and raspberry pies, garnished with plenty of potatoes, and whiskey to wash them down, besides a large iron kettle of tea. To pour out the latter, and dispense it round, devolved upon me. My brother and his friends, who are all temperance men, kept me and the maid actively employed in replenishing their cups." [12]

WEDDING FEASTS

Samuel Strickland said of one mid-1820s wedding, "The dinner was very good, though not served exactly in the English fashion" [13] but in the American instead. As has been true throughout European history, a wedding feast featured a cake, which until recent decades was usually a dense spiced fruitcake redolent of brandy with a hard egg-white icing.

As Traill describes it: "But the best of the fun was making the bride-cake. There was a regular 'Bee' for the occasion ... A home-made bride-cake, and the bride one of the compounders thereof! – who ever heard or even dreamed of such a thing? ... – but remember, ye fair and fastidious critics! – [this] was a 'Bush-Wedding.' The grand difficulty was in the icing [of] the cake. It was quite amusing for a looker-on to watch the curious anxious faces peeping over one another's shoulders into the various cookery-books, English and American, that had been privily borrowed from the most accomplished housewives in the neighbourhood. The gentlemen were of course excluded from these mysterious conferences, ... [except] little Harry ... [who] soon returned with a triumphant air, bearing in his hand a sort of flat trowel which he had carved out of a clean

11 Samuel Strickland, *Twenty-Seven Years in Canada West*, 1:36–7.
12 Moodie, *Roughing It in the Bush*, 319.
13 Samuel Strickland, *Twenty-Seven Years in Canada West*, 1:82.

shingle [to spread the icing] ... Harry's expedient was highly applauded by all present ... Then there was much anxiety about the baking of the precious compound, and the turning of it out of the bake-kettle ... The cake exceeded all expectations; ...and the ice looked almost like snow itself ... In short, it was a splendid achievement in the way of a home-made bride-cake; and, as all the boys declared, looked gloriously when decorated with the wreath of white roses ... and orange blossoms."[14]

There are other descriptions as well.

"A famous feast there was; roast, boiled and fried; pies, cakes and tarts of all imaginable sorts and sizes, and at the head of the table a most uncommon fine roast goose swimming in gravy ... well cooked."[15]

Served at the wedding tea of Bessie Stewart in May 1848 were tea, coffee, "bread & butter, buttered buns, plum cake, little Shrewsbury cakes & some other kind ... The Brides cake ... too was *home made* & excellent & nicely iced & ornamented with coloured comfits ... & just as good & rich looking as any bought plum cake." The tea was followed by a musical entertainment provided by the neighbours and concluded at 11:00 pm with "a little supper [of] cold fowl & lamb & ham & salad & some tarts & Raisins, Almonds and Apples, &c & &c & the Bride and Bridegroom[']s health were drank, & we left the gentlemen after which we heard great cheering and hurrahing."[16]

Kate Stewart's wedding supper in 1856 "looked very nice as there were two long tables & a handsome 3 storied cake on each table. These cakes were placed in the middle & then there were all sorts of jellies & custard, Russian Trifle, tarts & pies &c, besides turkeys and fowls, tongues, &c, &c. Every one said it was

14 Traill, "The Interrupted Bridal" (1849) in *Forest and Other Gleanings*, 132, 140. For more detailed discussion of "bride cake" (originally "bride pye"), "royal icing" (so named to honour the cake made for Queen Victoria's wedding in 1840), and "wedding cake," see Wilson, "Wedding Cake," 69–72.
15 Traill, "Bush Wedding and Wooing," *Forest and Other Gleanings*, 185–6.
16 Stewart, *Revisiting "Our Forest Home,"* 31 May 1848, 162, 163. Most of these culinary details were edited out of the published version of 1902.

excellent & plentiful & everyone seemed pleased & satisfied with the whole proceedings of the evening which was extremely gratifying to me."[17]

Mary O'Brien relates this story: "Drove to York in less than two hours ... We called on Dr. Diehl who begged to introduce us to his bride. We were accordingly ushered into a little parlour where she sat with her bridesmaids in bridal state. There was wine and brides cake on the table and another plate of little white rolls. We talked of the weather, the state of the roads, and our journey. The party exclaimed at our robustness when we said that we had come and intended returning the same day. The bride said she could have not enjoyment living so far from neighbours. Then came Mrs. Sheriff Ridout and her daughter. I thought that the silence which ensued would never be broken. I am not sure that Mrs. Sherriff had spoken yet, but the bride inquired of the young lady in a half whisper if she had heard that Edith had got the nutmeg. This I learned was concealed in the cake and the happy person who cut the piece containing it was the next to be married. They all seemed think that being married excellent fun, except the bridegroom who looked rather more serious about it."[18]

17 Ibid., 10 November 1856, 197–8. This letter was not included in the 1902 publication.
18 O'Brien, *Journals of Mary O'Brien*, 28 October 1829, 77.

Measurements for Cooking

Since the history of measurements is complicated, understanding historical culinary measurements can remove an obstacle to interpreting them in today's kitchens. We hope this explanation of times, weights, volumes, and temperatures historically used in cooking will help you interpret and recreate the recipes in *The Female Emigrant's Guide*.

A practiced cook relies on accumulated experience when reading a recipe, judging texture and flavour, testing doneness, and so on. Nowadays, Canadian recipes are usually written in the more-or-less universal format of a list of ingredients preceded by a definite quantity, in the order they will be used and followed by clear step-by-step instructions that include cooking time and temperature. A certain stylistic uniformity is expected. This was not always the case, as the *Guide* and all other pre-twentieth-century cookbooks make clear. Directions and quantities were often inexact, which can exasperate an inexperienced cook. A direction such as "flour enough to form a stiff dough" [154] assumes the cook already knows what a stiff dough feels like and what can happen if too little or too much flour is incorporated. Other instructions depend on the cook's preference, as in "spice to flavour it" [108]. Helpful comparatives are sometimes provided, such as "a piece of butter as big as an egg," but this famous adage is more likely to amuse than aid contemporary cooks [108]. Traill's inexactitude was typical of her time, although a few cookbook writers, such as American Eliza Leslie, did encourage careful measuring and in the 1880s Boston's Fannie Farmer began to insist on exact measurement as a cornerstone of culinary success. During Traill's time most home cooks learned via the mentorship of experienced female family members. Toward the end of the nineteenth century, however, a cultural shift led to the idea that rational judgment should be applied to the daily tasks of cleaning, child-rearing, and cooking. The domestic science movement (later called home economics) argued that cooking was a suitable subject for girls in public schools and for housewives in cooking schools, and promoted a scientific approach to the subject, including the introduction of standard measurements. In the United States in particular this resulted in adoption of an 8-ounce cup, replacing the previous varyingly sized teacups, and insistence on the dip and sweep method of measuring: "A cupful of dry material should be filled and heaped slightly (not shaken down), then levelled off even with the top," advised Mary Lincoln, director of the Boston Cooking School.[1] A legacy of the domestic science movement is that home cooks now generally prefer recipes that provide specific amounts and indicate a predetermined cooking time at a set temperature; without this the recipe feels inadequate and the cook may feel insecure. We imagine that Traill, as an experienced cook, would have been surprised at this development but, given her general interest and curiosity about scientific topics, suspect that she would have approved.

MEASUREMENT SYSTEMS

Until the Imperial Statute System of Weights and Measures was enacted on 1 January 1826, Great Britain used four main intertwined systems: Apothecary, Avoirdupois, Imperial, and Winchester. For centuries, commodities such as grains, ale, wine, salt, oil, fish, apples, and honey had been packed in bushels or barrels that varied in capacity; British North American industries, businesses, and households continued to use the familiar, if confusing, sizes and terminology. The Traills and Moodies learned Avoirdupois and Winchester in their formative years, but Imperial had been introduced by the time they left England in 1832.

The definitions that follow are in a roughly chronological sequence.

The Winchester System

The Traills and Moodies would have been familiar with the term "Winchester" for amounts of wine and wheat. The system began with Henry VII, continued with revisions under Elizabeth I, Queen Anne, and William III, and went out of use officially in 1826. In the United States, the conventional American system incorporates the Queen Anne Winchester Wine Gallon System and the William III Winchester Corn Capacity System. The Winchester Wine gallon was used throughout the Canadian colonies until 1880.

---

1 Lincoln, *Boston Cooking School Cook Book*, 29. Lincoln's successor as director of the Boston Cooking School was Fannie Farmer, who is generally credited with the most influential insistence on measuring accurately in the kitchen.

The Apothecary System

Those in medical professions characteristically combined small and precise quantities (drachms, drops, grains, minims, ounces) of ingredients for medicines. To be accurate, medicines required a druggist's glass to measure the exact quantities. Women often became familiar with this system in their role as family doctor and nurse. It was almost identical to the Troy Weight System used for precious stones and metals, gold and silver in particular. An Apothecary and Troy pound equals 5,760 grains or 12 ounces. Traill's ague remedy [210] from her doctor is the only recipe in her book that uses this system.

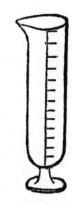

Fig. 20 · Druggist's glass

The Avoirdupois Weight System

In French, *avoir du poids* means "to have weight." In 1582, Elizabeth I decreed that one Avoirdupois pound equaled 7,000 grains or 16 ounces, distinguishing it from the Apothecary pound of 5,760 grains or 12 ounces. By the late sixteenth century Avoirdupois was the primary standard in England for weights (volume was incorporated into it later) and continued to be so until superseded by the Imperial System, which very closely resembled it. It was brought to British North America and remained legal in Canada until replaced by Imperial in 1877. It continues to be the base of the American Customary Unit System. Although Traill understood the system, she does not use the term Avoirdupois in her *Guide*; however, it appears in the appendix that her publisher inserted, starting with the second edition.

The Imperial System

Officially adopted into British law and trade on 1 January 1826 (although in legal use for two years before that) the Imperial System replaced all the archaic regional, local, and commodity systems used throughout the British Isles. Canada, despite being a British colony, did not legislate its use until 1873. Its culinary applications were for dry capacity, fluid capacity, and later, baking pan sizes. It was closely based on the Avoirdupois Weight System of one pound weight equalling sixteen dry ounces. An Imperial pint, however, is twenty fluid ounces.

The Imperial Statute imposed a single, logical measurement system on longstanding commercial and domestic customs throughout the British Empire, including the colonies of Nova Scotia, New Brunswick, and Upper and Lower Canada.[2] However, only in 1873, six years after these four colonies confederated into the Dominion of Canada, was the Canadian Uniform Weights and Measures Act (mass, capacity, line, area), commonly called the Canadian Imperial System, officially adopted in the face of increasing pressure from American commercial interests.

Decades passed before the official Imperial Statute became fully integrated into English and Scottish cookbooks and into home kitchens. Cookbooks originally published in the eighteenth and early nineteenth centuries that continued to be issued through the mid-nineteenth century were seldom converted, and new books did not necessarily reflect the new decree. The first, second, and third editions of *The Cook and Housewife's Manual* (1826, 1827, 1828) by Mistress Dods use Avoirdupois, but newly inserted recipes in the expanded fourth edition of 1829 use Imperial. Eliza Acton specifies Imperial in some of her recipes in *Modern Cookery for Private Families* (1845, 1855). However, by the time Isabella Beeton's *Book of Household Management* was published in London in 1860–61, the transition was more or less complete in Great Britain. Canadian cookbooks did not address the issue of different systems, but reflected the recipes' sources. By the 1890s, some Canadian, American, English, and Scottish cookbooks were providing tables of weights and measures, often with conflicting comparative quantities due to differing local usage.

The Metric System

A further transition occurred late in the twentieth century when the metric system was instituted in Britain and Canada and started appearing in those countries' cookbooks. The metric system is founded on the unit of ten. All calculations to increase or decrease quantities in recipes thus became simplified and streamlined, unlike previous systems, which were based on multiples of two, four, twelve, and sixteen, leading to awkward fractions such as $5/8$ and $3/16$ in recipes. Culinary metric volumes are measured in millilitres (mL) and litres (L), instead of saltspoons, teaspoons,

---

2 In 1836 and 1866, the American government consolidated and ratified a few simplifications to the previous standards that had been brought from Britain, which the new United States of America had retained after the Revolution and which became known as the American Customary Unit System.

dessertspoons, tablespoons, basting spoons, gills, wineglasses, teacups, cups, pints, quarts, or gallons. Weights are shown as grams (g) and kilograms (kg), instead of ounces (oz) and pounds (lb), and their fractions. Temperatures are given in degrees Celsius (°C) instead of degrees Fahrenheit (°F): water freezes at 0°C and boils at 100°C (32°F and 212°F).

Metrication had been introduced by the French National Assembly in the 1790s and formally legalized in 1840 to replace the many archaic systems that co-existed throughout France. Eventually the system was implemented almost worldwide, excluding only places like the United States, where conversion has been either partial or nonexistent. Interestingly, the French Metric System (Le Système International d'Unitiés – SI) was recognized as legally acceptable in Canada in 1871, even though a full century would pass before its modern form was adopted officially for international trade and domestic commerce, including cookbooks. By the time Catharine Parr Traill was contemplating a revised edition of her *Guide* in the 1880s, the metric system was legally acceptable in Canada, although cooks did not use it yet. In 1977 the Canadian Federal Government introduced the international metric system and by December 1983 Canadian grocery stores had switched to metric sizing.

In practice, the Imperial System was never fully adopted in English Canadian kitchens, given the influence of so many American cookbooks, because what Canadians casually consider "culinary Imperial" is actually the American Customary Unit System, basically unchanged since the late eighteenth century. Many of us can confidently cook in either non-interchangeable system, and in true Imperial also if we have a British recipe, but since numerous people still avoid metric, Canadian recipes usually provide a choice of either metric or what is known as the Imperial measuring system. Throughout the 1980s, during the transition to metric, Canadian home cooks were constantly reassured by home economists, food writers, and government officials that volume would continue to be the main measuring technique for the kitchen and could be easily managed by purchasing up-to-date sets of metric measures, since the sets were "replacements rather than direct equivalents"[3] of the familiar cups and spoons. Bakeware and oven thermometers were still viable because direct mathematical conversion from Imperial and American made them usable. Many conversion charts were included in cookbooks and recipe columns, just as they had been decades earlier during the incomplete switch to Imperial. However, cooks were

3 Spicer, *The Metric Kitchen*, 1.

often cautioned to neither substitute nor convert, but rather to use one system or the other. Today's readers may feel more comfortable with one or the other, depending on whether they learned to cook and bake in a North American or non–North American home.

WEIGHT

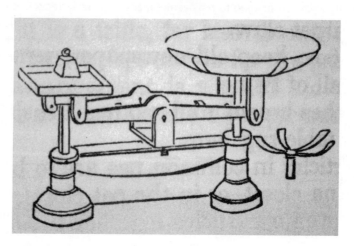

Fig. 21 · Balance scale

Around the world, dry ingredients are mostly given in terms of weight, the assumption being that every kitchen has a weight scale of some kind. Small balance scales, which featured a rounded dish for an ingredient on one side and a flat pan for a weight on the other, came with a full boxed set of weights that ranged from one drachm up to as much as five pounds. A spring scale was a hook attached to a wall that used gravity to weigh large things, such as beef haunches. Even in the backwoods, some sort of scale would have been common. Presumably the Traills had a scale, and Catharine expected her female emigrant readers to have one also, because many recipes in the *Guide* give measure by weight.

Measuring by weight has been done for centuries, since weighing is more accurate, especially for recipes that require chemical precision to be successful, notably baked goods. A look at eighteenth- and nineteenth-century recipes shows that quantities of flour, sugar, dry peas, rice, breadcrumbs, meat and fish, sago, butter, and almost every other non-fluid ingredient are primarily given in ounces and pounds – that is, if any quantity at all is specified, as many recipes don't suggest quantities. Very occasionally, a volume is suggested instead. For instance, some pastry recipes in the first edition of *The Art of Cookery* (1747) by Hannah Glasse vary between exact weight (three pounds), exact volume (a quarter of a peck), and inexact volume (a handful).[4] Five of Amelia Simmons's puff pastry recipes in her *American Cookery* (1796) list flour in pounds, while one inexplicably uses quarts instead.[5] Similar inconsistencies are found in many eighteenth-century and Victorian cookbooks. In North America, by the early twentieth century measuring flour, sugar, oats, beans, raisins, and almost every dry ingredient by weight had practically disappeared.

After being out of fashion in household kitchens for decades, weighing is increasingly popular today, especially with the arrival of digital scales. Commercial and restaurant kitchens, as well as food manufacturers, have long preferred the precision of weight when measuring ingredients.

VOLUME

For culinary purposes, the pint became slightly but significantly different in the British and American measuring systems when the Imperial system was formalized in the early 1820s. In both, one cup equals eight fluid ounces. But a US fluid pint – a pre-Imperial (Avoirdupois/Winchester/Wine) pint – holds two cups, while an Imperial fluid pint holds two and a half cups. And therein lies the source of the Canadian cook's confusion ever since, as demonstrated in this 1926 comment in a Canadian cookbook: "In accordance with that usage which appears to be most common ... we have used the Imperial gallon, quart and pint, but the Wine measure cup and spoons."[6] Similar comments appeared in other books, but plenty of unwary cooks with fallen cakes might well have been puzzled about one of the possible causes.

---

4 Glasse, *The Art of Cookery*: puff paste, 75, a cold crust, 75, and curd fritters, 81. Similarly, for Glasse, almonds could be measured by pounds, pints, or handfuls.
5 Simmons, *The First American Cookbook*, 29.
6 Women's Association of Trinity Memorial Church, *Systematic Cookery*, 7, quoted in entry Q156.1, Driver, *Culinary Landmarks*, 188.

Two pints is always one quart, but if the pint capacity varies, so then does everything else. As a general rule: American amounts are always smaller. A US quart has four cups, but an Imperial has five. A US gallon contains four quarts or sixteen cups, while a UK gallon has four quarts but twenty cups. It is important when reading and cooking from Traill's *Guide*, or from other older British, American, and Canadian books, to know the pint capacity and understand that "cups" were tin cups or china teacups that varied in size, not the eight-ounce American measuring cup that emerged at the end of the nineteenth century and became widely used after 1900, although it was the 1920s before manufacturers switched to using it as the standard.[7] Canadian cookbooks, women's magazines, and recipe columnists long ago stopped using the terms "pint" and "quart" in favour of "cups" to avoid confusion.

For centuries, on either side of the Atlantic, households could purchase sets of tin or copper jugs with sizes ranging from a half gill, gill, two gills, pint, quart, and/ or gallon, even two gallons, for measuring liquids in kitchens, still rooms, home breweries, sculleries, and so on. Although stamped with the specific capacity, they were not further subdivided by horizontal markings. A cup size was never included in these sets, although one might find two gills, its equivalent. Cups were not unknown as a measuring device for dry ingredients, but gills, pints, and quarts were the norm. However, sometime in the early nineteenth century, American cooks started to dispense with jugs or a weigh scale and began using cups for both liquid and dry ingredients. Canadians who used recipes from American cookbooks, magazines, newspapers, and almanacs learned to follow suit when necessary. Today, while the rest of the world distinguishes between filling and weighing methods for fluid and dry ingredients, North Americans use volumes for all culinary measurements. Why this practice became standard is unclear, although several theories have been suggested.[8] Traill used both methods comfortably, sometimes even in the same recipe, depending on whether it was of British or American origin. Since the *Guide* gathers together recipes from Traill's circle of friends and family, it is likely that she retained the original recipe's measurement system. The classic mid-nineteenth-century American cake was the "cup cake," so-called because its elements were "one cup of butter, 2 cups of sugar, 3 cups of flour, and 4 eggs, well beat together, and baked in pans or

---

7 Strauss, *The Sizesaurus*, 68, 232n17; Driver, *Culinary Landmarks*, 188.
8 Sokolov, "Measure for Measure," 80–3; Schmidt, "Cakes," 159–60; Ross, "Measurement," 69–70.

cups,"[9] which contrasted with the old British pound cake and its one pound each of butter, flour, and sugar.

Living in the backwoods with American neighbours and having access to American cookbooks and magazines, Traill grew accustomed to using a cup, especially a teacup, as a measuring tool. Countless kitchens at historic sites still use teacups that have lost their handles and are therefore no longer useful at the dining table. Teacups vary in size, of course. The most experienced home baker, as well as the minimally equipped housewife in the colonial backwoods, had at least a favourite teacup and teaspoon for measuring, as well as a battered tin pint jug. Using the same teacup for years meant that proportions in that kitchen were the same, regardless of the actual capacity of the cup intended by the original cookbook author. Teacups as a measuring tool, although much less common in English cookbooks, are suggested by cookbook authors such as Eliza Acton, Maria Eliza Rundell, and Isabella Beeton.

Manufacturers saw an opportunity to sell a new product when domestic scientists began to extol exact measurements for "scientific" cooking and baking. Sets of nested measuring spoons and cups came on the market in the 1880s, designed to hold the exact amount of an ingredient when the "dip and sweep" technique was used with a palette knife. A little later, the need for cups of different styles to measure volumes of liquid and dry ingredients was recognized. Jugs of a larger capacity than required by the exact measurement were better for liquids as it prevented them from slopping over the top. Pyrex cups, which feature markings for fractions of cups and/or ounces on one side and, in Canada, millilitres on the other side, were introduced into the market in 1915, in sizes that range from one to eight cups (250 mL to 2L). To use the word "cup" is awkward when referring to the metric measure since it is also an actual measurement in the Imperial system; nevertheless, that is what we say in common parlance. Both are calibrated and we purchase them in the hopeful belief that they are scientifically accurate.

Historically, if a recipe specified quantity beyond "some" or "a little" or another inexact amount for small amounts of spices, the quantity was just as likely to be expressed as either ounces (weight) or spoonfuls (volume), according to the writer's personal preference. Weigh scales often included drachm or ounce pieces, while spoons came in an assortment of sizes that originally varied between manufacturers –

---

9 Child, *The American Frugal Housewife*. Copied by Traill into her *Guide*, although she (or whoever gave her the recipe) transposed the order of ingredients.

saltspoon, teaspoon, dessertspoon, tablespoon, or serving spoon. Frequently, a recipe just said "a spoon," leaving the final quantity up to the cook's discretion. The very first spoon sets for kitchen measurements, which ranged from an eighth of a teaspoon to a tablespoon, came on the market in the 1890s, and in Canada the metric sets of five mL to 25 mL arrived in the 1970s.

Some kitchens had a druggist's glass, which was a narrow upright container with horizontal lines indicating small volumes. If a recipe called for four drachms of diluted sulphuric acid, like Traill's remedy for Ague [210], she could have relied on her memory to judge the amount or used a druggist's glass.

TEMPERATURE AND TIME

Before 1900 recipe authors seldom bothered with any reference to the heat or time involved in cooking because numerical precision was problematical when the heat source was fire. Hardwoods, softwoods, and coal burn at different temperatures and speeds, and fires obviously varied in size and strength. Temperature fluctuates as wood or coal is added or flames die down, thereby altering the baking or roasting time. The best that could be suggested were helpful adjectives, such as a "quick" or "slack" oven or a "moderate" or "quite hot" fire.

Time-keeping in kitchens was first made possible by the hourglass, created in the Middle Ages, and eventually by clocks and watches. Traill's Canadian Croquets [109] were cooked for two minutes in boiling lard and the hops for Treacle Beer [144] had to be boiled in water for an hour before the treacle was added. Presumably Traill had an hourglass and/or a clock since a few recipes – although not many – stipulate time. She does recommend that settlers have one [30]. Perhaps she had brought one with her or Thomas Traill may have loaned his watch? Or was there a mantelpiece clock in the parlour? Mary Armstrong, who lived on a farm at Yonge and St Clair Streets, wrote in 1859: "[T]he house is very quiet now, I hear nothing but the ticking of the two clocks, one upstairs and one in the kitchen."[10]

It is safe to say, however, that even if the Traills' kitchen did have a way to keep time, it did not have a kitchen thermometer. Colonists were familiar with judging temperatures because they wrote constantly about the extreme cold and heat, but judging oven temperature was a special skill. As with their contemporaries, Traill and her daughters relied on experience developed by years of observation and empirical

10 Armstrong, *Seven Eggs Today*, 24 May 1859, 133.

competence to know when their breads were baked and cakes nicely risen. Long before thermometers became standard in kitchens in the twentieth century, cooks observed the changing colours, textures, sizes, viscosities, smells, and bubbling actions of, for example, fats for frying, sugars for candying, and meats roasting, to know the advancing stages of being done. Visual aids are still essential nowadays, even if we rely on a thermometer and timer: in addition to stating a length of time at a specific temperature, a modern cake recipe is expected to suggest a colour – "golden brown." You may not be able to describe it exactly, but you recognize it when you see it.

Thermometers took a long time making their way into home kitchens. Gabriel Daniel Fahrenheit had invented his temperature gauge in 1714 and Anders Celsius his in 1742, but not until the very early twentieth century did these instruments start to be used with any regularity in home kitchens. Until long after the simultaneous inventions of the scientific concept of temperature and an instrument to measure it, cooks and bakers judged the readiness of a brick oven or hearth fire by testing the heat with their hand or arm – the sooner they had to yank their arm out, the hotter it was. Sometimes the speed with which a small handful of white flour or a piece of white paper placed in the oven turned brown was used to indicate the heat level. They learned to develop a personal sensitivity to, even a rapport with, their own brick oven and, later, their iron cookstove. By Traill's time, thermometers were available but not yet much used in culinary activities. Plenty of families had thermometers to keep track of outdoor temperature, as we know from countless newspapers, settlers' letters, and journal entries commenting on Canadian sub-freezing cold and soaring heat. Some top-market iron cookstoves had thermometers, but this was several decades after Traill wrote the *Guide* and it was not until the 1920s that some gas and electric stoves had integrated thermostats. Only once there was the technological guarantee of a steady temperature could a thermometer be effectively used, and only then did recommended temperatures start to appear in recipes.

MEASUREMENT TERMS

Barrel Barrels were once essential containers for commodities conveyed from and to farmers, manufacturers, shops, businesses, and households. Made of waterproofed wood held together by iron rings and produced by highly skilled artisans, their size varied between thirty and forty gallons according to whether the article of trade they contained was dry (cornmeal, wheat flour, etc.), lump (apples, haddock, etc.), or liquid (wine, oil, etc.). They could be reused and, as Traill suggested, could be converted into cushioned armchairs for impoverished backwoods homes [31]. The word "cask" is sometimes used as a synonym.

Bushel   As with barrels, bushels were wooden containers for transporting agricultural products. A standard Winchester and then Imperial bushel contained eight gallons by volume, which varied by weight, according to the commodity. "The size of a Winchester bushel measure is a circular ring with straight sides 8 inches high and 18⅓ in diameter."[11]

Cup (c)   Chances are, if ingredients are measured in cups instead of pints or pounds, it is a North American recipe. By the mid-nineteenth century in North America, the cup – whether tin or china and of varying sizes – was the primary item used to measure everything, so much so that manufacturers starting making standardized cups and partial cups based on the two-cup pint. The British don't particularly use the cup measure, even today.

Cwt, *see* Hundredweight

Drachm or **Dram**   An obsolete term for a minute amount of a dry or fluid commodity, drachm is pronounced "dram"; the *ch* is silent. It comes from the Greek *drachma*, meaning weight. For apothecaries and doctors, it was one eighth of a fluid ounce and eight drachms were one fluid ounce in the Apothecary and the Winchester Systems. But in the Avoirdupois System, 16 drams made an ounce. An Imperial fluid dram is a teaspoon (3.55 mL). In the *Guide*, Traill uses the word drachm only once, in an ague remedy, but it was a very familiar measurement to any housekeeper or cook, or a mother following a doctor's orders in assembling remedies.

    Dram is also used for alcoholic drink, as in cider or whisky. To "down a dram" means whatever can be swallowed in a single swig.

Gallon   The American gallon never changed from the old Queen Anne Winchester Wine gallon of 64 fluid ounces. For Traill, a gallon was a common amount for her domestic duties: she made gallons of maple syrup, vinegar, and soft soap at any one time, enough to last her family for long periods. We cannot be sure whether Traill

---

11 *The Canadian Agriculturist*, 302.

used the old Winchester gallon of her English youth, now the American standard (most likely), or the newer 1826 Imperial gallon of 80 fluid ounces.

Gill   Pronounced "jill," it was equal to a quarter pint and therefore to four liquid ounces (Winchester Wine gallon), five liquid ounces (Imperial), and, after the introduction of the standardized eight-ounce cup, an American half cup. Traill only uses the term a few times.

Grain   Although mostly forgotten today, the grain was originally the smallest and most basic element in the Ancient Egyptian, Sumerian, Greek, and Roman measurement systems, and their European successors, the Troy, Apothecary, Avoirdupois, Winchester, and Imperial systems. Literally, it was a single grain of wheat in size and weight. Until the end of the nineteenth century it was used by doctors in their medical receipts. Traill used it only in the Ague remedy [210].

Hundredweight (cwt)   An Avoirdupois hundredweight is 100 pounds; this is called a short hundredweight. A long (Imperial) hundredweight is 112 pounds. Its short-form is *cwt*, the *c* representing the Roman numeral for one hundred, C, and *wt* for weight.

Ounce (oz)   Sixteen ounces in weight constitute an Avoirdupois pound. In cooking, an ounce or its parts or multiples were used for small amounts of powders, as in spices and leavening agents, but as the century wore on ounces were often converted to teaspoons or tablespoons. For example, one ounce of powdered cinnamon is four tablespoons (60 mL) and a scraped nutmeg is three and a half tablespoons. The "oz" abbreviation derives from *uncial*, Latin for one-twelfth.

Pint (pt)   A pint is one of the volumes that differentiates the Avoirdupois/Winchester/Wine (American) and Imperial Systems. In the former it is equivalent to sixteen fluid ounces (two cups), but in the latter to twenty fluid ounces (two and a half cups). Traill often suggested a pint basin (bowl) as a flour measurement; it was not necessarily an exact pint, but a generic reference to a medium-sized bowl.

Pound (lb)   An Avoirdupois and Imperial pound each weigh sixteen ounces. However, the volume of that pound can vary: since sugar is heavier than flour, the same weight fills a smaller container. The abbreviation "lb" stands for *libra*, Latin for pound.

Quart (qt) The old Avoirdupois and Winchester quarts were two sixteen-ounce pints and remain so in America today, but the Imperial quart was, and is, two twenty-ounce pints. This has long been a source of confusion for Canadian cooks.

Tablespoon (tbsp, T) The amounts that tablespoons contain vary. Before the standardized tablespoon measurements used in contemporary cookbooks, home cooks used household silver or tin spoons, which varied in size, for measuring small amounts. The most familiar amount is three teaspoons to a tablespoon, but internal evidence in some historic cookbooks indicates that a tablespoon sometimes refers to a serving spoon (about four teaspoons) or sometimes to a dessertspoon (about two teaspoons). Occasionally it may even indicate five teaspoons.

Teacup Cookbooks from the eighteenth and nineteenth centuries, and some in the early twentieth century too, suggest a teacup as a volume measurement. Teacup sizes varied from set to set, depending on the manufacturer, but charts included in cookbooks suggest that once a standard eight-ounce cup was generally recognized a teacup was usually – but not consistently – three quarters of a cup, so somewhat smaller than the new standard. However, sometimes it was equivalent to a cup. Since we don't know which set(s) of china the Traills owned, we cannot know what size her teacups were.

Teaspoon (tsp, t) Smaller than a tablespoon. Originally the small spoon for stirring tea leaves and/or sugar in a cup of tea, it moved into the kitchen as a measure for small amounts.

Wineglass Although stipulated by Traill only twice, a wineglassful was a common culinary measurement referring to a small amount. Just as with teacups, wineglass sizes varied, but charts usually stated it as equal to four tablespoons (American) or five tablespoons (Imperial). Two wineglasses made a teacup.

Measurement Chart

As the nineteenth century wore on, Canadian and American cookbooks began to include charts of comparisons to help cooks interpret weights as volumes. These frequently showed equivalencies for one pound, such as two cups of butter and four cups of flour. These charts didn't always correspond between cookbooks; for instance one pound of butter was sometimes two cups and sometimes two cups plus two tablespoons, and one pound of flour ranged from three and a half cups to four and a half cups, depending on locality, the wheat's type and refinement, and the author's individual cup. A tablespoon contained anywhere from two to five teaspoons.

Abbreviations in this chart:

c	cup	mL	millilitre
dr	drachm	oz	ounce
dsp	dessertspoon	pt	pint
fl	fluid	qt	quart
g	gram	tbsp	tablespoon
gal	gallon	tsp	teaspoon
L	litre	wg	wineglass

Word Used in Female Emigrants Guide	Avoirdupois		American Customary		Imperial		Canadian Culinary Metric	
	Fluid volume	Dry weight	Fluid volume	Dry weight	Fluid volume	Dry weight	Fluid volume	Dry weight
1 drachm / dram	1/16 fl oz	1/16 oz			1 tsp	1 tsp		
1 teaspoon					⅛ fl oz, ½ dsp	⅛ oz, ½ dsp	5 mL	5 mL/5 g
1 dessertspoon	2 tsp, ¼ fl oz, ½ tbsp	2 tsp, ¼ oz, ½ tbsp			2 tsp, ¼ fl oz, ½ tbsp	2 tsp, ¼ oz, ½ tbsp		
1 tablespoon			3 tsp	3 tsp	2 dsp, 4 tsp, ½ fl oz	2 dsp, 4 tsp, ½ oz	15 mL	15 g
1 ounce	1/16 cup	1/32 lb	2 tbsp	2 tbsp	2 tbsp, ½ wg, 437.5 mL	½ wg, 437.5 g	25 mL	25mL/25g
1 wineglass			2 fl oz, 4 tbsp, ¼ c, ½ gill	2 oz, 4 tbsp, ¼ c, ½ gill	2.5 fl oz, 4 tbsp, ¼ c, ½ gill, ½ teacup	2.5 oz, 5 tbsp, ½ gill, ½ teacup		
1 gill	5 fl oz		8 tbsp, 4 fl oz, 2 wg, ½ c	8 tbsp, 4 oz, 2 wg, ½ c	5 fl oz, ⅝ c, ¼ pt	¼ pt		

1 teacup	¾ c	¾ c	5 fl oz / 1 gill / 2 wg / ¼ fl pt / ¾ c	5 oz / 1 gill / 2 wg / ¼ pt / ¾ c		250 mL
1 cup	8 fl oz / 2 gill / 16 tbsp / ½ fl pt	8 oz / 2 gill / 16 tbsp / ½ pt	8 fl oz / 16 tbsp	8 oz / 16 tbsp	250 mL	500 g
1 pound	16 oz	16 oz	16 oz	16 oz		
1 pint	16 fl oz / 4 gill / 2 c / 0.47 L	16 oz / 4 gill / 2 c / 0.55 L	20 fl oz / 4 gill / 2½ c / 0.55 L	20 oz / 4 gill / 2½ c	500 mL	
1 quart	32 fl oz / 4 c / 2 fl pt / 0.94 L	32 oz / 4 c / 2 pt / 1.1 L	40 fl oz / 5 c / 2 fl pt / ⅛ fl gal / .95 L	5c / 2 pt	950 mL	1 L
1 gallon	16 c / 4 fl qt / 3.78 L	16 c / 4 qt	20 c / 10 lb / 4 fl qt / 4.54 L	20 c / 10 lb / 4 qt	4.55 L	

Interpreting Nineteenth-Century Recipes

Understanding a period recipe, or "receipt" as it was then spelled, can present a challenge to cooks accustomed to modern recipes that list ingredients followed by a step-by-step procedure that indicates temperatures and times. Sometimes a recipe is perfectly legible as is; sometimes it needs interpretation. Often a historical recipe is a mere aide-memoire for an experienced cook. In this section, we try to give contemporary cooks help in interpreting historical recipes. We want to show you how to produce these recipes with early twenty-first-century equipment and ingredients, although replicating them exactly is not possible with today's flours and dairy products. The following recipes are modern realizations of historical texts – equivalents in a new context. Any alterations we have made are explained. We suggest you read the original recipe before trying ours so that you see how we have modernized terminology and/or amounts, while maintaining each recipe's integrity to the best of our ability.

Original authors – in this case Traill and the friends from whom she acquired some of these recipes – naturally made assumptions about what their contemporaries knew. Certain familiar actions required no explanation, such as managing a cooking fire, or cracking, pulverizing, and sifting a hard white sugar loaf. Certain conventions were understood, such as letting cucumbers grow big and yellowish for stewing (instead of our own assumption that cucumbers should be young and green for salads). The final appearance and presentation of a dish was too familiar to explicate. For instance, flour was sprinkled over roasting beef to create a crisp golden surface, a practice obsolete now that roast beef is oven-baked by electricity or gas. However, since Traill was addressing an audience new to Canada, she does include many things that immigrant housewives could not know – how to employ hops in making a starter for bread and how to boil green corn, dry apples, or convert the dregs of maple sap into a viable vinegar.

Using Traill's advice and the comments in our modernized instructions, we invite you to go adventuring in your kitchen!

READING RECIPES

Preparing a recipe involves a few natural steps: reading it, assembling ingredients and equipment, making it according to the instructions, maybe enhancing it with some personal flourishes, then serving and eating. We can all do that. But an old paragraph-style recipe that reads as incomplete according to current standards does benefit from a few intervening steps.

Read it carefully. The first step is to write it out by hand in the modern format of three columns and numbered instructions – make a list of ingredients in the order they are to be used, along with the original measurements and the equivalent metric, then break the directions into a numbered sequence. This will help you understand what needs to be done.

The second step is to assess what is missing or unclear. Fill in what you can from your personal experience. Then look at similar recipes in your personal cookbook collection. Do a bit of research at the local library or online with cookbooks published in the decades surrounding that of your book. Much information can be gleaned through these comparisons because another author's quantities or directions may answer your questions. Adjust your interpretation to accommodate these new details.

The third step is to give it a try. As Traill said, "Try it!" [89]. Write notes during your first experiment. Perhaps you come to understand an unclear task, realize a quantity needs to be adjusted, or recognize that you misjudged the baking time. Taste it! Is it fine? Or do you want to give it a second try?

The fourth step is to try it again. And perhaps again. And again. Each occasion, change only one thing (an amount, an action, an ingredient, a time) to see what happens. Keep a log. The experimentation process fascinates some of us as we seek to understand historic recipes in today's kitchens.

MEASURING INGREDIENTS

Our instructions include both Metric and Canadian Imperial measurements, following common convention in Canadian magazines and cookbooks and as promoted by the various home economics associations within Canada. See pages 306 through 307 to learn more about how Canadians came to adopt the metric system of measurement.

Since the chemistry of baked goods succeeds best with exact measurements, we recommend that you measure your liquid ingredients into glass fluid cups at eye level and your dry ingredients by the dip and sweep method using dry cups and spoons (invented in the latter part of the nineteenth century, so Traill and her friends would not have done this). However, even baked goods benefit from the baker's personal touch – so if you prefer more or fewer sweet spices, then make that decision yourself, and if you decide that something is too dry, then go ahead and add a little more liquid, or vice versa.

BUYING INGREDIENTS

Almonds   Use whole skin-on ones that you blanche, de-skin, and pulverize yourself in a mortar or food processor to retain the oil. Packets of skinned almond pieces and pre-ground almonds are much too dry to replicate historic recipes effectively.

Baking soda   Use this as a substitute for saleratus and pearlash.

Butter   Use sweet (unsalted) at room temperature. Butter was once thoroughly salted for winter preservation but for baked goods, many nineteenth-century cooks took the time to wash their butter to remove the salt flavour. Summer butter was usually unsalted. For frying, clarified butter is a good idea, although Traill does not mention it: "Fresh butter, clarified from all foreign substances, pure 'British oil', is the most delicate substance in which meat [and fish] can be fried, as it communicates no predominating taste."[1]

Cornmeal   Use a fine yellow or white flint variety. Stoneground is even better because it contains the whole starch and oil. Modern sweet corns are not the same as hard flint corns. Prior to the 1860s, naturally dried stoneground cornmeal was moister than today's kiln-dried cut cornmeal. "If in using old [i.e. before the mid-1860s] receipts for corn-bread, one-eighth of the quantity of meal called for be omitted, the bread will be nearer what should be than it will if all the meal is used," wrote Maria Parloa in her *Kitchen Companion* of 1887.

Currants and Raisins   Use freshly packaged ones, but if shrivelled they can be re-plumped by being soaked in water, juice, or even rum or brandy. Until recently,

---

1 Dods, *The Cook and Housewife's Manual*, 124.

currants and raisins always required inspecting and cleaning to remove dirt and in-sects. "After currants are nicely washed, they should be dried in a cloth, and set before the fire. If damp, they will make cakes or puddings heavy. Before they are added, a dust of dry flour should be thrown among them, and shaken."[2]

Eggs   Use medium-size if you can get them since they are the best equivalent to an average of the varying sizes of eggs on early Ontario farms, but large-size are okay too. We do not recommend extra-large, since that can change the ratio of liquid to dry, resulting in a different outcome. Ten modern medium eggs equal a pound, which is the measurement often found in old pound cake recipes and measurement charts.[3] If the recipe calls for separating them, they "should be long beaten, whites and yolks apart, and always strained."[4] In Traill's time eggs were not kept in a cold room but simply stored at room temperature.

Flour   Use ordinary all-purpose white or whole-wheat flour since they are the most common in today's kitchens. Wheats, and therefore flours, are very different nowa-days, having gone through generations of genetic breeding and industrial process-ing. Neither drying nor sifting is necessary anymore. It is even better if you have access to unbleached stoneground white flour. It is fun to use stoneground red fife wheat if you can find it, since it is a genuine Canadian heritage variety. See page 485 for more on red fife.

Maple Syrup   Use a mid-brown (Number 2) syrup instead of a light (Number 1) since it is more like what used to be called maple molasses. Canadian maple syrup is classified by numbers, ranging from Number 1 (extra light, light, medium) through Number 2 (amber), to Number 3 (dark). The American equivalents are Grades A, B, and C.

Milk   Use 2% or 3% (whole) cow's milk. Sheep and goat's milk are fine too, although historically they were not much used in baking in Upper Canada.

---

2 *The Canadian Housewife's Manual of Cookery*, 253.
3 Lee, *The Cook's Own Book*, 10; Leslie, *Miss Leslie's New Cookery Book*, 25; Simmons, *The First Amer-ican Cookbook*, 37, and many others.
4 *The Canadian Housewife's Manual of Cookery*, 253.

Molasses   Use either maple syrup if Traill specifies it or an unsulphured (unbleached) light brown or dark brown sugar molasses. Don't use black-strap molasses, which is very dark, bitter, and actually lacks any sweetness. See also Treacle.

Oats   Use fine Scots or Irish *ground* (not rolled) oatmeal, preferably stoneground, instead of rolled oats, which are a milling innovation of the late nineteenth century. Rollers flatten the oats into what we call rolled oats (*flocons* in French) for breakfast.

Pease   Use dried green or yellow peas for pease pudding, either whole or split. Fresh green garden peas are not the same.

Raisins, *see* Currants and Raisins

Rice   Use a long-grain white variety, not a brown. Arborio is too starchy; Basmati too aromatic to simulate historic recipes, particularly rice pudding.

Spices   Use whole cinnamon bark, nutmegs, allspice berries, and so on. Pound with a mortar and pestle or grate as needed.

Sugar   Use ordinary white granulated sugar since that is the most common in today's kitchens. White sugar was certainly available to bush settlers who could get some groceries from town. However, using brown sugar of whatever grade or maple sugar (expensive though it is), would be equally appropriate, although each of them changes the flavour of baked goods. If you want to approximate the fine powder that resulted from pounding and sifting the hard pieces from a white sugar cone (*see* Loaf Sugar, 428), then either do that with a mortar and pestle or briefly whiz in a food processor. We do not recommend fruit or icing sugar because they are industrially pulverized.

Treacle   Use an unsulphured dark molasses (but not black-strap). Don't use golden syrup, which is called light treacle in some parts of England and Wales; although a product of that name was made by the Montreal company Redpath Sugars in the 1860s, it was not widely available until the 1880s.

Vinegar   Use apple cider, red wine, maple, or any herb vinegar instead of plain white vinegar.

Water Use tap water, though distilled water is better since it does not have the chemical additions that are present in municipal tap water. Traill and her backwoods neighbours used spring water or water from a well. The exception to tap water is if you want to make Salt-Rising Bread (345–7). Then use distilled or spring water to prevent chlorine and fluoride from interfering with the action of natural yeast.

Yeast Use modern granular or fresh compressed yeast dissolved in warm water or make your own starter. See pages 91 to 97 for directions on making starters with hops and yeasts.

PRESERVING FOODS SAFELY

Reading the *Guide* and other cookbooks available at the time, you realize how important preservation of the summer bounty was to individual farm and bush families who couldn't easily get to town, especially before canning industries succeeded in the late nineteenth century. With a family of seven children and an inadequate income, Traill became expert at preserving fruits with sugar, vegetables with salt, and hams in a dry cure or with a liquid brine. She was quite limited in her techniques, unlike other food writers, but she seems to have provided her readership with what worked for her.

Nowadays, awareness of food safety during the preservation process for jams, jellies, marmalades, and pickles is well understood. Covering the surfaces of preserves with egg-dipped paper or beeswax circles is insufficient to eliminate moulds and prevent spoilage, although these practices were once ubiquitous. And finding a room cold enough to keep the jars in is rare today, so we default to storing everything in the refrigerator, thus doubly ensuring its preservation. To ensure the safety and longevity of jams and pickles, we recommend that you follow the guidelines stipulated by government ministries of agriculture and such well-known companies as Bernardin, which specializes in preservation. Sterilize all equipment and jars before use, and submerge the filled jars in a boiling water bath to destroy unwanted organisms.

Instead of hanging hams and beef haunches in cloth bags from pantry beams or putting a bowl of leftover stew into a cupboard, as families once did, all meat products should be stored in the fridge at a minimum of 4°C (40°F) or the freezer at a minimum of -18°C (0°F).

Employ safety and caution at all times when storing perishable foodstuffs.

Recipes
in the
Guide

APPLE RICE [75]

We enjoy this very simple pudding, especially if lots of lemon peel is used to flavour it. No sugar is stipulated because the fruit adds natural sweetness, but a sweet sauce accompanies it well. Salt is not mentioned, but you could add 1 mL (¼ tsp) if you want. As Eliza Action explains, "A very *little* salt improves all sweet puddings, by taking off the insipidity, and bringing out the full flavour of the other ingredients, but its presence should not be in the slightest degree *perceptible*."[1]

For this typical nineteenth-century boiled pudding you will need a 47-cm (18") square muslin pudding cloth or at least ten layers of modern cheesecloth. Or you could use a pudding bowl. Before immersing the pudding, ensure that the water is boiling briskly. Submerge the pudding and then bring the water back to the boil. Turn the heat down to medium-low so that the water continues to simmer. This was so well understood by cooks that it was seldom mentioned, but Maria Eliza Rundell includes this useful explanation: the pudding cloth "should be dipped in boiling water, squeezed dry, and floured, when to be used ... The water should boil quick when the pudding is put in; and it should be moved about for a minute ... A pan of cold water should be ready, and the pudding dipt [*sic*] in as soon as it comes out of the pot, and then it will not adhere to the cloth."[2]

Yield: Serves six generously

2 c	500 mL	long-grain white rice
1 c	250 mL	unpeeled apple cubes (about 1½ apples; modern Granny Smiths are good)
2 tsps	10 mL	finely grated lemon peel (more if desired)

1 Put a stockpot three-quarters full of water on to boil. The pot has to be large enough that the pudding will be mostly submerged.

---

1 Acton, *Modern Cookery for Private Families*, 334.
2 Rundell, *A New System of Domestic Cookery*, 182.

2 Using tongs, dip the pudding cloth or cheesecloth in boiling water, let it drip into the sink for a few seconds to lessen the heat, then wring it out well. Place it flat on the counter, sprinkle lots of flour into the centre, where the cloth will come into contact with the batter, not on the edges, then shake the excess flour into the sink. Use the floured cloth to line a small mixing bowl, ensuring there are as few wrinkles as possible and letting the corners drape over the sides.

3 Place the raw rice in a sieve and dampen with enough water that the rice sticks together but does not lose its surface starch (which will allow the rice to bind as it cooks). Shake any excess water off, then pour two-thirds of the rice into the lined bowl. Use a spoon to gently smooth the rice up the bowl's sides to the top edges, creating a hollow. The rice should stick together nicely.

4 Quarter and core the unpeeled apples. Cut them into large cubes and place them in the hollow in the rice, tamping them down a bit to eliminate as many spaces as you can. Strew the lemon peel over the apples. Spoon the remaining rice on top of the apples and smooth it down.

5 Cut a piece of string about 30 cm (12") long. Gather up two opposite corners of the pudding cloth or cheesecloth and tie them, then repeat the procedure with the other two corners, leaving the cloth a bit loose so the rice can swell as it cooks. Wrap the two gathered corners several times with the string and make a firm knot. Trim the string ends.

6 Lower the ball of rice into the boiling water and cover the pan. Return to the boil, then reduce the heat to low to maintain a constant simmer. "Boil a full hour" [75].

7 Remove the pudding from the boiling water, using a pair of tongs to grip the tied corners. Dip the pudding into a bowl of cold water for a few seconds, then transfer it to a plate and let rest for about three minutes or until you can touch the string and cloth without hurting yourself. Snip the string and gently pull it away. Carefully peel the cloth down. Place another plate on top of the rice ball, and quickly turn the ball right side up, leaving the cloth behind.

8 Serve warm with a sprinkle of maple sugar or brown sugar, or a pudding sauce [31].

CURRANTS AND RICE [90–1]

Instead of apples, use ripe red or black currants. In fact, any fruit is suitable, including blueberries and raspberries. Traill says "serve with sugar and butter" [90].

COMMON BUSH TEA CAKES [109]

These are maple-flavoured shortbreads. For us, this is a true Canadian cake, one that was "common," or ordinary, in the backwoods. The maple sugar adds an unusual taste that is at first indefinable, especially when combined with caraway. Some people don't like the taste of caraways, so you can omit them, perhaps substituting "any spice you may have"; nutmeg and maple make a nice combination. The cakes are good as an accompaniment to hot milky tea.

Yield: about 48 cakes of 5 cm (2") diameter.
When saleratus was used, it was dissolved in a tiny amount of water, but that's not necessary with modern baking soda. If you use salted butter, don't add the teaspoon of salt.

1¼ c	315 mL	maple sugar
¼ c	65 mL	warm water
4 c	1 L	flour – whole wheat, white, or a mix
1 tsp	5 mL	baking soda
1 tsp	5 mL	salt
1 tbsp	15 mL	caraway seeds (or freshly powdered caraway)
1½ c	375 mL	soft unsalted butter

1 In a small bowl, dissolve the maple sugar in the warm water.
2 Measure the flour, baking soda, salt, and spice into a large bowl. Blend together. Using your fingertips, lightly rub the butter into the flour mixture. Make a well in the centre.
3 Pour the maple sugar and water mixture into the buttery flour mixture. Blend well and knead lightly until the dough forms a nice ball. Divide into three smaller sections. You can refrigerate two as you work with the third, which Traill, of course, would not have done.
4 Roll out on a lightly floured surface until about 5 mm (¼") thin. "Cut out with a tumbler [drinking glass]" or cookie cutter of 5 cm (2") diameter. Repeat with the remaining dough.
5 Either bake at medium heat in an ungreased iron frying pan on the stovetop until lightly browned, then flip and bake on the other side, from 10 to 12 minutes

altogether, OR, bake on a cookie sheet lined with parchment paper in a pre-heated oven of 180°C (350°F) for 18 to 20 minutes or until nicely golden. You can flip them halfway through if you like, but it is not necessary.

FERMENTATIONS AND BREADS

The Female Emigrant's Guide provides a great deal of information about the kinds of breads that were being made and eaten at home in mid-nineteenth-century Canada. For most rural families, and many urban families too, bread-making was a regular and necessary task, done every few days or once a week. But before the bread could be made came the time-consuming and sometimes tricky chore of preparing the yeast, "fermentation," "rising," or "barm." (The four words were used interchangeably.) A housewife might be able to obtain a cupful of hop-rising from a neighbour or buy an initial supply of thick frothy liquid beer yeast, also called barm, from the local brewer. If she was a brewer herself (uncommon in the backwoods, although British women had brewed beer at home for centuries), she had her own perpetual supply, as baking and brewing yeasts were usually seen as much the same. (See pages 378, 387, and 408 in the glossary.) By carefully feeding her yeast with a sugar, she could maintain an ongoing source in "a cool dairy or cellar" in summer "and in winter [in] some warm closet or cellar, which is too close to admit of frost" [94]. Families in the backwoods had a third option: they could capture wild airborne yeast spores and use them to ferment a flour gruel. Traill spent a lot of time explaining these options to immigrants.

People accustomed to hop-risen breads or breads activated by wild yeast, both of which take a long time to rise, allowing time for their textures and flavours to develop, often think them more interesting, similar to the sourdough breads some people prefer. Breads fermented this way are now a mostly forgotten taste and technique.

Starter Yeast

You can't make a risen bread without some sort of yeast, a "rising." If you are starting to explore this process, there is no escaping this fundamental fact. You can visit a brew-your-own shop to buy a brewer's yeast suitable for baking (keeping in mind that many strains have been developed since the mid-nineteenth century). You can use an airborne yeast, although its flavour and strength will be uncertain. Or you can use one of the risings whose care and use is described here, following the more detailed preparation instructions provided on pages 335–8.

1 Hop-rising (Barm #1)
Keep this in the fridge in a closely covered jug or glass bottle. Remove the quantity required for the recipe and bring it to room temperature. To test its viability if you are unsure after not having used it for a few weeks, feed it half a teaspoon of sugar. It's ready if you can see bubbles within a couple of hours.

2 Another American Yeast (Barm #2)
Same instructions as #1.

3 Leaven Cakes (Barm #3)
Once thoroughly dried, store the cakes in a cloth bag, wooden box, or cookie tin. Any moisture makes them damp, thereby ruining their effectiveness. "If rightly prepared these cakes will keep a year."[3] Two cakes dissolved in 125 mL (½ cup) of warm water works well for every half cup called for in an old recipe.

4 Granulated yeast
Soften 2 tsp/10 mL conventional granulated yeast in half a cup of warm water for five minutes, then stir to mix. As a general rule, this mixture should be substituted for every half cup of yeast called for in an old recipe for a baked product or barm. This can be the basis of an ongoing supply or be used for a single batch of bread.

   Important point: Do not use modern fast-acting granular yeast. It is engineered to be mixed directly into the flour without proofing, that is, without moistening the granules to begin the action.

5 Compressed cake yeast
Crumble 1 oz of compressed cake yeast in half a cup of water, leave for two minutes, then stir into a cream. Cakes of fresh compressed yeast wrapped in tinfoil are now hard to find, unfortunately, but some delicatessens and health food stores do carry them. They are also known as wet, fresh or

3 Hale, *Early American Cookery*, 30.

compressed yeast. Fresh compressed yeast is perishable and should be stored in the refrigerator.

Once you have a starter available, you can use some to activate the next batch. "Always take four [table]spoonfuls of the old to ferment the next quantity, keeping it always in succession."[4] Sourdough breads work on the same principle: a handful of dough is retained to activate the next batch of dough. Traill, however, does not use this term or the technique, even though it was well understood.

Our Tips about Hop-Risings

- Fresh or frozen hop flowers are available from the refrigerator of brew supply stores. If fresh ones are not used quickly, they should be put in the freezer until wanted. Buy hops, such as Willamette, which are used for English-style ales. Hops add flavour to the yeast, and therefore the bread. They also have an anti-bacterial function.
- One ounce of fresh hop flowers equals about three cups lightly packed.
- Don't be overly concerned with proportions of wet to dry ingredients. You can always adjust later when adding the flour.
- Barms are all slow-acting, so you must cultivate patience to allow fermentation; overnight is usually best.
- Make sure the hop batter is as lump-free as possible, otherwise the lumps will appear in your baked bread.
- Although the historic instructions say to pour the hop water into the flour, we find it easier to incorporate the flour into the hop water; as well, the resulting batter is smoother.
- If you are unsure of a barm's viability after a few weeks of life in the fridge, feed it with a generous tablespoon of maple sugar, honey, or brown sugar. It is good to use if it shows some bubbles the next day, although the dough may take longer to rise before baking. Even carefully nurtured hop barms eventually become too weak and sour to use, but we have kept barms going for several months.
- As an experiment, we left some hop barm (see recipe for Barm #1 below) out of the refrigerator for two weeks to track its viability. It remained bubbly, but when

4 Rundell, *A New System of Domestic Cookery*, 176.

combined with flour overnight for a bread next morning it developed a suspicious sour odour and grey streaks. So keep it refrigerated!

Advice from Historical Sources about Hop Yeasts

"Next in importance to the quality of the flour is that of the yeast. This should be light in colour and lively, effervescing easily when shaken, and emitting an odor like weak ammonia."[5]

"Tie the hops in a coarse muslin bag."[6]

"Never keep yeast in a tin vessel. If you find the old yeast *sour*, and have not time to prepare new, put in salaeratus, a tea-spoonful to a pint of yeast, when ready to use it. If it foams up lively, it will raise the bread; if it does not, never use it."[7]

THE FERMENTATION RECIPES

Don't be intimidated! These recipes really do work. After all, countless housewives used them successfully to make the family bread.

[COMMON] HOP-RISING (BARM #1) [92–4]

Five of Traill's fermentation recipes require hops. This flour-based one is the first and simplest one. With it as your guide, try your hand at the others!

Yield: about one quart (one litre). The recipe here is half the original.

1½ c	325 mL	hops, lightly packed (approximately ¼ oz/7 g)
6 c	1.5 L	water
2 c	500 mL	flour (whole wheat, white, or a mix)
½ c	125 mL	your choice of one of the five starter yeasts

5 Harland, *Common Sense in the Household*, 259.
6 Ibid., 262.
7 Hale, *Early American Cookery*, 29.

1 Using a stockpot, stir the hops into the water and turn on the heat. Once the water reaches a rolling boil, reduce heat to maintain a brisk simmer. The hops will rise to the surface, but within "an hour's fast boiling" they will sink and about half the water will evaporate. Aim for about 3 cups/750 mL. If the water evaporates too quickly, reduce the heat.

2 Strain the hops into a muslin- or cheesecloth-lined sieve resting over a large bowl. Gently press the hops with the back of a spoon to remove more water, then compost them. Rinse the stockpot. Return the hop water to the stockpot, bring to a boil again and remove from the heat.

3 A few spoonfuls at a time, whisk the flour into the boiling hop water, "stirring the batter quickly ... The flour will thicken up like paste. Stir it as smoothly as you can, then let it stand till blood warm," that is, lukewarm: about 38–45°C (110–120°F). It takes about an hour, sometimes less, to reach this temperature.

4 Mix in your choice of yeast. Cover the bowl and put it in a warm place to rise, about 10 hours or overnight. Once lots of bubbles are visible on the surface, use the quantity required for a recipe and transfer the rest to a large sterilized glass jar and store in the refrigerator.

ANOTHER AMERICAN YEAST (BARM #2) [95]

A potato-based yeast. Traill's recipe calls for two large spoonfuls of flour, which we interpreted as heaping tablespoons; halved, that's one heaping tablespoonful, or about five teaspoons. She said "it must be used fresh" but we found it can be kept in the refrigerator for a few days and still raise another batch of bread.

Yield: about 750 mL (3 cups). The recipe given here is half the original.

¾ lb	300 g	white potatoes (2 to 3 potatoes), peeled and cut into large chunks
1 c	250 mL	boiling water
½ c	125 mL	warm potato water
5 tsp	25 mL	whole wheat flour
1 tbsp	15 mL	maple molasses, maple syrup, or other molasses
½ tsp	2 mL	sea salt
1 c	250 mL	your choice of the five starter yeasts

TO BEGIN PREPARATION: AFTERNOON

1 Boil the potatoes until very soft, 20 to 25 minutes. Using a slotted spoon, put the potatoes in a bowl and mash them until "very fine." (Otherwise the potato lumps rise annoyingly to the surface during kneading and you have to stop and remove them. Other recipes advise rubbing the potatoes through a sieve.)

2 Pour 250 mL (1 cup) of boiling water over the potatoes, stir, and let the mixture sit until "only warm," 38–40°C (110–120°F), about 35 minutes. Measure out ½ cup of the potato water and either discard the rest or use it for another purpose.

3 Blend in the flour, molasses, and salt.

4 Mix in your choice of yeast.

5 Cover with a cloth and "leave it in a warm place all night," such as a gas oven with a pilot light or on top of a towel-covered radiator (in winter) or on the kitchen counter out of drafts in summer.

NEXT MORNING

6 When you remove the cloth you will see a thick potatoey crust over a thickish potatoey liquid that measures about 3 cups. Stir them together. The barm is now ready to use. Keep any that is not used in the refrigerator in a covered sterilized container, such as a mason jar. The crust will redevelop, so stir it in before using.

LEAVEN CAKES (BARM #3) [95]

This recipe is a more detailed copy of one in *The American Frugal Housewife*. It reads very much as if whoever shared it with Traill owned that book but paraphrased the recipe based on experience. Even more details appear in Sarah Hale's *The Good Housekeeper*, some of which are incorporated into our directions.[8]

Yield: about three dozen cakes (one-third of the original recipe).

3 c	750 mL	hops (lightly packed, about 1 oz/28g)
4 qt	4 L	water
1½ c	375 mL	rye flour

8 Child, *The American Frugal Housewife*, 80; Hale, *Early American Cookery*, 30.

½ c	125 mL	your choice of the five starter yeasts
3½ c	875 mL	cornmeal
½–¾ c	125–175 mL	white flour, if necessary

1 Using a stockpot, stir the hops into the water and turn on the heat. Once the water reaches a rolling boil, turn the heat down to maintain a brisk simmer. Boil the hops in the water "till reduced to a [third of a] quart," about three hours. Aim for about 1½ cups/375 mL. If it is evaporating too slowly, increase the heat. Pour the hops into a muslin- or cheesecloth-lined sieve resting over a large bowl. Gently press the hops with the back of a spoon to remove more water, then compost them. Return the hop water to the stockpot, bring to a boil again, and, if necessary, reduce it further. Strain again if necessary.

2 Remove from the heat. A few spoonfuls at a time, whisk the rye flour into the hop water. Let the mixture cool to lukewarm, about 38–45°C (110–120°F), about 30 minutes.

3 Mix in your choice of yeast. Let it rest until "it has begun to work well," which you can tell because the surface becomes puffy, usually about six hours or more. Stir occasionally to prevent formation of a skin.

4 Blend in the cornmeal half a cup at a time. Tip the rough ball of dough out onto a lightly floured counter. Knead, adding extra white flour until the dough it is very stiff, about 10 minutes. At first it will be difficult to handle, but it eventually turns into a nice ball. When almost ready, roll the ball in a bit of flour to dry its surface. If it feels too large, cut it into two.

5 "Roll it into cakes about an inch in thickness," and cut them into "two-inch squares" (approximately 10 cm × 10 cm). Reroll the scraps. "Prick them with a fork," said Mrs Hale, the only one who provides this practical suggestion to help improve the drying process.[9] Multiple fork holes allow each cake to dry more quickly and thoroughly.

6 "Let them dry on a clean board in the sun, for two or three days" [95] or "in a clean, dry chamber or storeroom where the sun and air may be freely admitted" up to "a fortnight."[10] Or, easier yet, place on a baking sheet in a gas oven with a pilot light or an electric oven with the light switched on for at least 72 hours.

9 Hale, *Early American Cookery*, 30.
10 Ibid.

Turn them over occasionally. They should become hard; in fact, other cookbooks call them hard yeast cakes.[11]

BREADS WITH HOP BARM RECIPES

You need patience to allow the slow-acting barms to raise the dough, hence the instruction to start the day before and leave overnight. As Lydia Maria Child observed in *The American Frugal Housewife*: "It is more difficult to give rules for making bread than anything else; it depends so much on judgement and experience."[12]

Our Tips about Bread Made with Hop Barms

- Barm-leavened breads rise slowly. The longer the rise, the better the texture and flavour. But they never double in bulk as so many modern bread recipes advise.
- Absorbability of flours varies, so adjust the quantities of flour and hop water as necessary.
- Before using the barm, pour off any liquid that has risen to the surface because it decreases the fermentation.
- If using leaven cakes, for every half cup of yeast required in an historic recipe, dissolve two yeast-cakes in 125 mL (½ cup) of warm water and stir in 15 mL (1 tbsp) of any flour to make a paste. Leave to activate overnight.

MRS. TRAILL'S BREAD [98]

Since by the early 1850s the Traills were a family of seven living children, Catharine and her eldest daughters, Katherine and Anne, were used to making large quantities of bread. We expect the Traill boys devoured lots of bread after their days working the farm. This recipe is typically large and was best made in a dough box, a common piece of furniture in a pioneer farmhouse. We have quartered the original quantities because you are unlikely to want eight loaves.

"Wash and pare half a pail of potatoes" – it is hard to know what size pail Traill intended. In her handwritten notes for the unpublished revision sometime in the

---

11 *The American Home Cook Book*, 111; Beecher, *Miss Beecher's Domestic Receipt Book*, 86.
12 Child, *The American Frugal Housewife*, 76.

early 1880s she crossed this out in favour of "a doz^n large potatoes."[13] Her instructions differ from those of several of her contemporaries, who said, in Eliza Acton's words: "the potatoes ... should be ... thoroughly boiled, thoroughly dried afterwards by having the water poured from them, and then standing by the side of the fire to steam ... They should be perfectly mixed with the flour while they are still warm."[14] Dry and warm mashed potatoes do make a very light loaf, but we follow Traill's method of mashing the cooked potatoes directly in their water. We have reduced the amount of salt she suggested from "a handful" to one tablespoon.

Yield: 3 loaves of about 450 kg (1 lb) each. The recipe given here is one quarter of the original recipe.

Either

4 c	1 L	white potatoes (3 to 4 large), washed, peeled, and cut into chunks and added to
4 c	1 L	cold water

or

3½ c	875 mL	leftover potatoes, moistened with ½ c hot water and mashed very smooth

1½ c	375 mL	whole wheat flour
2 tsp	10 mL	sea salt (more if you like salty bread)
½ c	125 mL	your choice of the five starter yeasts
7–8 c	1750 mL–2 L	flour – white, whole wheat, or a mix

AFTERNOON OF DAY ONE

1 If using raw potatoes, bring them to a boil. Reduce the heat to a simmer and cook "till reduced to a pulp," about 45 minutes. Mash the potatoes in the hot water to get a mixture that has "the consistency of a thick gruel." Or, if using mashed potatoes, blend the hot water in until they resemble gruel.

13 Traill Family Collection, 5883.
14 Acton, *The English Bread Book*, 157.

2 Let the potatoes sit for about half an hour until "cool enough to bear your hand in it": 38–45°C or 110–120°F.

3 Stir in the 1½ cups of whole wheat flour and salt. Stir in your choice of yeast. Transfer to a very large greased bowl, cover with a heavy cloth, and "set to rise in a warm place overnight." Rolling the dough in a lightly greased bowl helps retain the dough's moisture, since it helps prevent a non-pliable skin from forming on the fermenting dough. You can also ensure that the dough does not develop a skin by stretching plastic wrap over the bowl under the heavy cloth.

EARLY ON THE MORNING OF DAY TWO

4 Blend in the flour in three or four batches. We like to move the bowl to a low surface rather than using the kitchen counter, because it is easier to get your hands into the bowl and apply the necessary pressure to blend in all the flour. Once the flour is more or less blended, tip the mixture out onto a generously floured counter. Knead in the traditional manner, using the heel of your hand for about 15 minutes, sprinkling more flour on the counter if necessary, until the ball of dough is smooth and springy.

5 Transfer the dough to a lightly greased large bowl. Cover with plastic wrap and/or a damp cloth and return it to the warm place to let rise for at least three hours. An extra hour or two won't hurt it and will in fact help to develop its flavour.

LATE MORNING OR EARLY AFTERNOON

6 Deflate the dough by punching it several times.

7 Divide the dough into three equal balls. Knead each one for a few moments and shape into balls or lengths. Put into greased bread tins or onto a greased baking tray. Cover again and let rise for a further one or even two hours.

8 Pre-heat the oven to 230°C (450°F). Just before the loaves go into the oven, slash the tops in an ✕ pattern.

9 Bake for 15 minutes, then reduce the temperature to 200°C (400°F) to mimic a brick oven in which the heat gradually diminishes, and bake for a further 15 minutes. Reduce again to 180°C (350°F) for another 15 minutes. Check to see if the loaves are fully baked at the end of 45 minutes by tapping one sharply on its bottom. If it rings hollow, remove the loaves onto a rack to cool. If it sounds dull, return it to the oven and try again in 10-minute increments.

10 Tip the hot loaves out onto a rack. Brush the tops with a pastry brush dipped in milk, wrap them in a teacloth, "setting them up on one side against a shelf until cold" [98]. This softens the hard crust, so if you prefer a hard crust, it is best not to wrap them warm.

INDIAN-MEAL BREAD [98]

Yield: Two loaves of about 1 to 1.25 kg (2 to 2½ lb) each. The recipe given here is one quarter of the original.

We found that more starter than originally given is better, so we suggest 125 mL (½ cup) instead of 60 mL (¼ cup). We usually blend some whole wheat flour into the white flour for a better flavour and texture, about 250 mL (1 cup) of the total. This loaf keeps moist for several days, but be warned that it is heavy and dense. Delicious, though!

4½ c	1.125 L	yellow cornmeal
1½ tsp	7 mL	sea salt
4 c	1 L	boiling water
½ c	125 mL	your choice of the five starter yeasts
4–6 c	1–1.5 L	flour – whole wheat, white, rye, or a mix (we find the amount varies each time depending on the yeast, whether the flour is all-purpose or stoneground, and the exact mix of flours)

1 Measure the cornmeal and salt into a large mixing bowl. Stir in the boiling water with a wooden spoon until all of it is dampened. Leave it until it is "cool enough to work with the hand," about 38–45°C (110–120°F) or 18 to 20 minutes, stirring occasionally to bring the interior hot cornmeal into the air.
2 Mix in your choice of yeast. Add the flour a cup at a time, using one hand to mix the dough and the other on the bowl rim to hold it still, changing to both hands when the dough becomes too stiff to mix with just one. Blend thoroughly each time.
3 Tip the coarse dough onto a lightly floured surface. Knead in some of the remaining flour. Divide into two, and knead again, adding some flour if necessary. Shape into smooth balls. Flatten the balls and put them onto greased pans.

4 Cover with wax paper and a heavy cloth, and let rise in a warm place for at least two hours.

5 Bake at 230°C (450°F) for half an hour. Reduce the temperature to 200°C (400°F) and bake for a further half hour. If still not baked, reduce the temperature to 180°C (350°F) for 15 minutes or more, or until the surface is cracked and golden. Let cool on racks.

BUCKWHEAT PANCAKES [114]

Served with butter and maple molasses or treacle, buckwheat pancakes were "a favourite breakfast dish of the old Canadian settlers," including those in the early Atlantic provinces.

Yield: about 24 pancakes, 9 cm (3½") in diameter.

If you want fewer than 24, you can halve the ingredients or freeze the cooked pancakes for future breakfasts. The batter also freezes well too. When ready to use, leave it out overnight to reactivate the fermentation process and in the morning add ½ tsp/2 mL of baking soda.

Yeast Pancakes

These pancakes can be a bit heavy, more like crumpets in texture. Substituting white flour for half the buckwheat will lighten them, depending on your preferences. Use very little butter or lard, enough to prevent sticking but not so much that the cakes become greasy.

½ c	125 mL	your choice of the five yeasts
3 c	750 mL	warm milk or water (slightly more than lukewarm but not hot)
3 c	750 mL	buckwheat flour (or half buckwheat and half white)
½ tsp	2 mL	salt
		butter or lard for cooking the pancakes

EVENING

1 Blend the yeast into the warm water.

2 Measure the buckwheat and salt into a large mixing bowl. Stir and then make a well in the centre. Blend in the yeasty liquid. "[B]eat it well for a few minutes, till it is smooth." Cover with a cloth and "leave it in a warm place all night," especially in the winter. By the next morning it should have risen into a bubbly batter.

NEXT MORNING

3 Preheat the oven to about 80°C (170°F) and put in a heat-proof plate.
4 Heat the frying pan until "quite hot" and melt a teaspoon of butter or lard. "Into this drop a large spoonful or small teacupful" of the batter, 3 or 4 pancakes at a time, depending on the size of the frying pan, "but do not let them touch." "Fry of a light brown" until bubbles dot the surface as it dries out. Flip each pancake and cook the other side. Transfer to the plate in the oven. Melt more butter or lard in the frying pan and continue until the batter is finished.
5 "Serve quite hot, with maple molasses, treacle or butter."

Baking Powder Pancakes

Traill's last line says that baking powder can be used instead of yeast.

3 c	750 mL	buckwheat flour (or half buckwheat and half white)
½ tsp	2 mL	salt
4 tsp	20 mL	baking powder
3½ c	875 mL	warm milk or water

1 Measure the buckwheat, salt, and baking powder into a large mixing bowl. Stir and then make a large well in the centre. Blend in the milk or water. "Beat it well for a few minutes, till it is smooth." Let batter stand for five minutes.
2 Follow instructions for the yeast pancakes.

SALT-RISING BREAD [96–7]

Traill's directions for salt-risen bread read quite straightforwardly but the reality is a bit more complicated. Her facts were all correct but some subtleties were missing. She may have written the instructions down as she received them since she herself did not make this bread, as she "dislike[d] the peculiar flavour" [96]. Salt-risen bread does have a reputation for a bad smell while it is working and it can have a distinct flavour, but in our experience these are exaggerated. We have found the final loaf to be dense and moist – and delicious!

Recipes for salt-risen breads are often quite involved, but this simple wheat bread is quite possible without complications. See page 462 for its history.

Advice from Historical Sources about Salt-Rising Bread

"The usual plan in this country is to mix flour with warm salt and water, and set it by the fire to rise. But it must be carefully watched, the temperature must be kept even, no easy matter in cold weather. They usually put their vessel within another closed vessel of warm water, but even then it requires great attention, for if the fermentation is too long delayed it becomes sour. More-over, whenever the right degree of fermentation is attained, then and there you must mix your loaf at whatever inconvenient season it may happen to occur. If the operation is successful, you have very good bread, but there is great uncer-tainty in it."[15]

"[A]fter the barm has once reached its height, unless immediately made use of, it sinks, and rises again no more ... The water that surrounds the pot in which your rising is, must never be allowed to cool much below the original heat, more warm water being added (in the pan, not to the barm)."[16]

"[M]ake up your [salt-risen] bread into rather a soft dough ... [T]he softer is the dough, the more light and spongy will the bread be."[17]

Salt-Rising Bread

Yield: One loaf of about 1.125 kg (2½ lb).

Start this loaf by setting the bowl of ingredients into a warm water bath in the after-noon if you want to have bread for dinner the following day. Traill and other sources

---

15 Anne Langton, *A Gentlewoman in Upper Canada*, 11 December 1837, 163.
16 Traill, *Backwoods of Canada*, 138.
17 Bryan, *The Kentucky Housewife*, 320.

suggested it takes about six hours to raise the necessary creamy head of froth, but in our experience it can take as much as fifteen to eighteen hours (probably because our kitchens nowadays have far fewer ambient yeasts), so leaving it to rise overnight is a practical idea. As the dormant wild yeast spores awaken and the wet flour decomposes, they release bubbles of carbon dioxide, lactic acid, and beneficial bacteria. The key to this process is keeping the water warm so the gases can continue to develop and mingle with the natural airborne yeasts and those in the flour.[18]

After a lot of experimentation, we have found that distilled water and whole wheat flour make the best base, while finishing with white flour leads to the best texture and flavour. Municipal water has often been chlorinated or fluoridated, so using distilled water is important.

1 tsp	5 mL	sea salt
2 c	500 mL	warm distilled or spring (not tap) water or milk
2 c	500 mL	flour – whole wheat, white, or a mix (whole wheat ferments best)
3½–4 c	875 mL–1 L	flour – white, whole wheat, or a mix

LATE AFTERNOON OR EARLY EVENING OF DAY ONE

1 Dissolve the salt in the water or milk in a quart or litre jug. Whisk in the flour.
2 "Set the jug in a pan or pot half filled with water, warm but not too hot," between 38 and 45°C (110–120°F). "Set it in a warm place," such as in an oven with a light or on a towel-covered radiator, which maintains the water's gentle heat. Even in the summer the key is to keep the damp flour warm and to do this you have to keep the water bath warm. Nothing will happen for hours. Don't despair! Surface bubbles will slowly emerge and "the yeast will begin to rise in a fine soft creamy head." A faint odour may be detectable.

NEXT MORNING

3 Once the rising has developed, stir it and then pour it into a large mixing bowl. Blend in the flour, half a cup at a time, beating the batter until it is as

18 David, *English Bread and Yeast Cookery*, 299–301; Gill, *The Complete Bread, Cake and Cracker Baker*, 28–30; Oliver, "Salt Rising Bread."

smooth as possible. When it becomes difficult to beat, switch to blending with your hand.

4 When you have a rough ball, tip it onto a counter generously sprinkled with white flour.

5 Knead the dough well for about 15 minutes, until you have a smooth, compact ball. Sprinkle more flour onto the counter as the ball becomes sticky while kneading. Shape the dough into a nice dome and transfer to a greased and floured baking sheet or shape it into a rectangle and transfer it to a greased and floured bread tin. Cover with a damp cloth.

6 Set it to rise in a warm place for at least two hours, but probably more like three, until is nicely risen. It won't double in bulk as other breads do.

7 Pre-heat the oven to 230°C (450°F). Just before the loaf goes into the oven, slash the top in an ✕.

8 Bake for 15 minutes, then reduce the temperature to 200°C (400°F) to mimic a brick oven and bake for a further 15 minutes. Reduce again to 180°C (350°F) for another 15 minutes. Check if the loaf is fully baked at the end of 45 minutes by tapping it sharply on the bottom. If it rings hollow, remove it to a rack to cool. If the sound is dull, return the loaf to the oven and check it again in 10-minute increments.

GOOSEBERRY JAM [84–5]

Recipes for preserves in the old cookbooks usually call for large quantities of fruit and sugar since the goal was to fill the larder with supplies for winter. Nowadays, recipes tend to call for much smaller quantities, both because we don't need to store provisions in the same way, but also because food safety analysis has shown that preserving lesser amounts at one time is safer. Equal weights of sugar to fruit were stipulated most often, but sometimes recipes indicated a ratio of three to four.

On first reading even a straightforward, simple recipe such as this one raises many questions for contemporary preserve enthusiasts. We recommend finishing with a sterilization bath in accordance with the Ontario Ministry of Agriculture's guidelines for safety.

Yield: 4 half pints (four jars of 250 mL).

Only two ingredients go into this jam – gooseberries and sugar. Using maple sugar, although expensive, adds a subtle underlying flavour. The water bath is an old technique for reducing soft fruits to a pulp and avoids the risk that they will scorch if the pan is placed directly over the fire. It takes more time but not much effort because you can set the timer and do other tasks rather than watching the fruit closely to prevent burning. The result is somewhat runnier than a modern jam.

4 c	1 L	ripe and/or almost ripe gooseberries
2 c	500 mL	sugar, either white, brown, or maple

1 Bring a large pot half-filled with water to a simmer. Lay a flat tin plate on the bottom so the jar won't rattle. Wash a one-quart/one-litre preserving jar in hot soapy water, then carefully fill it right to the top with boiling water while you prepare the berries. Sterilize four half-pint preserving jars as well and keep warm until needed.

2 Fill the sink halfway with cold water; dump in the gooseberries. Top and tail them with your thumbnail and drop into a waiting colander.

3 Pour the hot water out of the preserving jar and immediately fill with the gooseberries; screw on the lid.

4 Lower the fruit-filled jar into the pan of simmering water and let cook gently for about two hours, until the fruit is very soft and juicy. If necessary, add some boiling water to top up the water level in the pan.

5 Remove the jar from the water, uncover, and gently stir in the sugar. Cover again and return to the water bath. Simmer for about an hour to give the gooseberries and sugar plenty of opportunity to blend. The water level should remain above the top of the gooseberries.

6 Remove the jar from the hot water and allow it to cool until touchable, about ten minutes. While the large jar is cooling, refill the pot with hot water and bring to a boil.

7 Using a sterilized spoon, transfer the fruit pulp to the four small sterilized jars. With a clean damp cloth gently wipe any stickiness off each lip, apply the jar lid, and lightly screw on the band.

8 Carefully submerge the filled jars in the hot water, cover the pan, bring to a boil, and boil for a full ten minutes. Remove the jars from the pan and set aside to cool completely. Listen for the pop as each lid seals itself. Once cool, wipe the jars to remove any remaining stickiness. Label them.

MAPLE SUGAR SWEETIES [152]

These are lovely little almost-hard candies, one of the few opportunities in the back-woods to have a sweet treat on which to suck. Traill, in her proposed revision, wrote that "They are nice and wholesome."[19] She assumed that the cook understood the basic steps of boiling sugar through the various stages. In modern terms, the maple syrup needs to reach the soft ball stage.

Candies were seldom mentioned in colonial domestic writings. Susanna Moodie commented on the flirtatious antics of a purveyor of bull's-eyes (striped candies) and lemonade while with her youngest son at the circus, and Anna Jameson commented on "lollypops from the village store" in Michilimackinac.[20] Undoubtedly, however, town confectionaries carried a wide variety of candies.

A word of advice if you have not boiled sugar syrup before. Beware of the hot syrup, which can burn you!

Yield: about 4 dozen sweeties.

Although Traill said to pour the syrup into a saucer, we suggest a tin pie plate or tray, or even candy moulds, just in case the hot sugar syrup causes a glass or ceramic saucer to crack from the sudden heat. The syrup needs to be hot, just as it would have been during the sugaring process.

2 c	500 mL	maple syrup
2 tbsp	30 mL	white flour
4 tbsp	60 mL	butter
¼ tsp	1 mL	essence of lemon, peppermint, or ginger (optional)

1 Pour the maple syrup into a heavy-bottomed saucepan. Stir in the flour. Add the butter and let it melt. Quickly stir to blend.
2 Bring to a boil on medium heat. Boil steadily for about ten minutes, until the temperature reaches the soft ball stage, 115°C (240°F). Do not stir while boiling!
3 Pour into a buttered tin pie plate. Let cool for a couple of hours. Turn out onto a wooden surface. Cut into squares with a sturdy knife.

19 Traill Family Collection, 6153.
20 Moodie, *Life in the Clearings*, 96; Jameson, *Winter Studies and Summer Rambles*, 430.

You can also turn this into toffee if you let the syrup cool to 80°C (170°F), turn it into a buttered tin plate, beat for a moment, and then work back and forth in your hands until pale and pliable.

RASPBERRY VINEGAR [85]

Except for lemonade, raspberry vinegar was the most popular and cooling of the non-alcoholic summer drinks in Upper Canada. Cold water was often considered unhealthy. Recipes varied with regard to the length of time the raspberries (or strawberries or cherries) should be soaked in the vinegar – anywhere from a few minutes to several days. Some recipes suggest replenishing the fruit a second time, or even a third, as Traill did, since the fruits grew abundantly in the backwoods. Although the drink is vastly improved in flavour intensity if the fruit is replenished, hand-picked summer raspberries are not inexpensive today.

Lydia Maria Child provided some additional detail about the advantages of this drink: "Raspberry shrub mixed with water is a pure, delicious drink for summer; and in a country where raspberries are abundant, it is good economy to make it answer instead of Port and Catalonia wine. Put raspberries in a pan, and scarcely cover them with strong vinegar. Add a pint of sugar to a pint of juice; (of this you can judge by first trying your pan to see how much it holds;) scald it, skim it, and bottle it when cold."[21]

Yield: approximately 500 mL (2 cups) of fruit syrup concentrate.

Our recipe is based on Child's, but with Traill's additions.

2 c	500 mL	vinegar (cider, red wine, even maple)
2 c	500 mL	raspberries (fresh or frozen)*
1 c	250 mL	sugar (white, brown, maple) – approximately

* 500 mL/2 cups or 1 L/4 cups more are needed if the fruit is doubled or tripled in the following days.

---

21 Child, *The American Frugal Housewife*, 82.

1   In a covered bowl or jug, soak raspberries for about 24 hours in the vinegar. Additional time is fine.

2   Strain the vinegar through a muslin- or cheesecloth-lined sieve. Press very gently with the back of a spoon to extract some of the juice, although Traill says "do not squeeze them," but avoid clouding the liquid. Discard the raspberries; they can be consumed, but we find them too vinegary.

3   Soak more raspberries once or twice if you want your syrup to have a really intense flavour and colour. Strain again.

4   Measure your liquid; you should have approximately 500 mL (2 cups). Stir in an equal quantity of sugar. Transfer the sugary vinegar to a large saucepan and slowly bring it to boil. Boil for ten minutes to concentrate the syrup. Skim off any scum that rises to the surface.

5   Pour the hot raspberry concentrate into two half-pint (250 mL) sterilized bottles.

To serve, we recommend a ratio of one part raspberry syrup to three parts water, but you may want to adjust that depending on your tolerance for the sharpness of the vinegar and the sweetness of the sugar.

SWEET INDIAN PUDDINGS

Cornmeal is a rare ingredient in puddings nowadays; in fact, puddings are rare nowadays. In the category of Indian puddings, there was a tremendous variety of ratios of milk to cornmeal, and sugar and/or molasses, and whether the pudding should be plain or have ginger (or nutmeg or cinnamon) added. Or whether eggs should be added and, if so, how many. These two cornmeal puddings demonstrate two styles: a firm boiled pudding with berries and a delicate baked pudding with chopped apples flavoured with traditional molasses.

INDIAN FRUIT PUDDING [126]

"An Indian-meal pudding, with ripe [red] currants, either baked or boiled, is very nice" said Traill in an earlier recipe for red currant puddings [90]. This is one of those recipes that challenges cooks today because the quantities of most ingredients are unstated. The main ingredient – cornmeal – isn't even specified in the instructions. The key is to compare this short-hand recipe with many of its more-or-less contemporaries, starting with the clue of six eggs. No one recipe we found matched this one completely, but several that call for six eggs suggest one quart of cornmeal, so that is the combination we went with. But we offer you the halved version.

Yield: serves 8 generously (half the original recipe).

You will need a pudding bowl, either the traditional ceramic kind or a glass Pyrex one, 2 L (2 qts) in volume.

1 c	250 mL	berries – red currants, gooseberries, cherries, or cranberries
½ c	125 mL	butter or finely chopped suet
2 c	500 mL	cornmeal (preferably stoneground)
2 c	500 mL	whole milk
2 tbsp	25 mL	maple sugar
½ tsp	2 mL	(sea) salt
3	3	eggs

1 Prepare whichever fruit you have chosen. Remove the currants and cherries from their stems, top and tail the gooseberries, check the cranberries. Wash and dry.
2 Fill a wide pot halfway with water. Put in the empty pudding bowl to see how far up the water level goes on the side of the bowl. Add or subtract water until the level is about three-quarters up the bowl. Remove the bowl, butter it well, and set aside. Heat the water to simmering.
3 Scald the milk in a large saucepan or double-boiler. Meanwhile, in a large bowl, blend the suet or butter and cornmeal with a fork. Pour the scalded milk slowly onto the cornmeal, stirring constantly. Pour the milky cornmeal back into the saucepan or double-boiler. Bring to a simmer, and cook gently for about ten minutes, stirring often to prevent lumps forming. It will thicken quite a bit.
4 Remove from the heat. Stir in the maple sugar and salt.
5 In a separate bowl, whisk the eggs well. Give the warm cornmeal a last stir, then gently and slowly blend in the eggs, stirring constantly. Stir in the prepared fruit.
6 Pour the batter into the buttered pudding bowl. Cover with tinfoil or a cloth and tie firmly with string.
7 Lower the bowl into the simmering water and cover the pan. The water must be boiling, or the pudding will be heavy. "Boil for two hours." If the water level drops too much, pour in more boiling water.

8 Carefully remove the hot bowl from the boiling water and set onto a counter for about ten minutes. Cut the string and lift off the tinfoil or cloth.

9 Serve warm with a pudding sauce [359].

BAKED INDIAN-MEAL PUDDING [125]

Yield: serves 4 (half the original recipe).

2 c	500 mL	whole milk
½ c	125 mL	soft butter or finely chopped suet
4 tbsp	60 mL	cornmeal (preferably stoneground)
½ tsp	2 mL	(sea) salt
1 tsp	5 mL	ginger or other spice, such as nutmeg
3	3	eggs
½ c	125 mL	dried currants or fresh apples, washed, cored, and roughly chopped
2 tbsp	30 mL	maple molasses or light molasses

1 Turn the oven to 150°C (300°F). Butter a 22 cm (9") pie dish ("pudding dish") and set aside.

2 Scald the milk in a large saucepan or a large double-boiler. Meanwhile, blend the suet or butter and the cornmeal together with a fork, and stir in the salt and spice. Stir the cornmeal into the hot milk and simmer on medium heat for about ten minutes, stirring often to prevent sticking and swelling. It will thicken somewhat.

3 While the milky cornmeal is simmering, beat the eggs well in a separate bowl and blend in the molasses.

4 Remove the milky cornmeal from the heat. Pour in the eggs in a thin stream, whisking quickly so the eggs don't coagulate. When well blended, stir in the fruit.

5 Pour the batter into the buttered dish. "Sprinkle a little suet over the top and grate a little nutmeg."

6 Bake for 1½ hours or until nicely puffed and a golden halo appears around the edge. Set on a rack for ten minutes.

7 Serve warm with a pudding sauce [359].

Additional Recipes

Traill referred to a number of dishes and beverages but did not supply recipes for them since they were commonly found in other cookbooks of the period. By way of inviting you to explore historical recipes of the period, we include some instructions for how to prepare these common dishes in a modern kitchen.

APPLE BEVERAGES

In directions for what to do with dried apples Traill said: "[A] delicious fever drink is made by pouring off the liquor after the apples have boiled a few minutes" [72–3]. Quite a few nineteenth- and early twentieth-century recipe books supply other instructions for such a drink. In a June 1854 letter, Traill says she gave her daughter Kate acid drinks and strawberries to cool her throat during an attack of fever.[1] Perhaps apple water was one of those drinks. This is a simple and delicious drink worth reviving, and not just when you are ill.

Apple Water for Sickness

The Cook Not Mad or Rational Cookery, 297.
"Cut two large apples in slices, and pour a quart of boiling water on them; or on roasted apples; strain in two or three hours, and sweeten lightly."

Apple Water

Child, *The American Frugal Housewife*, 32.
"This is given as sustenance when the stomach is too weak to bear broth, &c. It may be made thus, – Pour boiling water on roasted apples; let them stand three hours,

---

1 Traill to Ellen Dunlop, *I Bless You in My Heart*, 20 June 1854, 91.

then strain and sweeten lightly: – Or it may be made thus, – Peel and slice tart apples, add some sugar and lemon-peel; then pour some boiling water over the whole, and let it stand covered by the fire, more than an hour."

Apple Water

Leslie, *Miss Leslie's New Cookery Book*, 417.
"Pare and slice a fine juicy apple; pour boiling water over it, cover it, and let it stand till cold."

Apple Tea

Beecher, *Miss Beecher's Domestic Receipt Book*, 199.
"Take good pippins [apples], slice them thin, pour on boiling water, and let it stand some time. Pour off the water, and sweeten and flavour it."

BOILED PUDDINGS

Boiled puddings are not known to many people today, but in Traill's era people in all social strata and geographies were familiar with them. Variations were often chosen based on the family's ability to buy imported ingredients, since all kinds of dried fruits, spices, wines, and perfumed waters could be added to the basic duo of flour and suet. In North America, cornmeal was a substitute for wheat flour. (See Sweet Indian Puddings on pages 351 to 353.) Cooks are frequently cautioned to be careful when preparing boiled puddings as they can be easily spoiled by carelessness.

Eve's Pudding

The Cook Not Mad or Rational Cookery, 35.
Recipes for Eve's Pudding appear in many nineteenth-century cookbooks. "Eve," of course, because of the apple, Traill's favourite fruit.
   "Grate twelve ounces of bread, mix with it the same quantity of suet, the same of apples made fine, the same of currants, mix with these four eggs, a little nutmeg and lemon, boil three hours; serve with pudding sauce."

A Plum Pudding Boiled

The Cook Not Mad or Rational Cookery, 35.
"Three pints flour, a little salt, six eggs, one pound plums, half pound beef suet, half pound sugar, one pint milk; mix the whole together; put it into a strong cloth floured, boil three hours, serve with sweet sauce."

CURRY RECIPES

Anne Langton observed that her family made a lot of meat curries, especially in wintertime.[2] Indian curries entered the British culinary repertoire in the eighteenth century and pre-blended curry mixtures were available for sale or individual whole spices could be purchased and mixed at home.

The following three recipes would have been easy to prepare, even with limited resources in the backwoods, all of them from very well-known cookbooks of the early nineteenth century. In fact, in an amusing anecdote in *The Backwoods of Canada*, Traill refers to two of these authors in such a way that we realize she believed her readers would recognize them: "You may send down a list of groceries to be forwarded when the team [of horses] comes up, and when we examine our stores [i.e. purchases], behold rice, sugar, currants, pepper, and mustard all jumbled into one mess. What think you of a rice pudding seasoned plentifully with pepper, mustard, and may be a little rappee or princes' mixture added by way of sauce.[3] I think the recipe would cut quite a figure in the Cook's Oracle or Mrs. Dalgairn's Practice of Cookery, under the original title of a 'bush' pudding."[4]

Mulaga-Tawny Soup

Kitchiner, *The Cook's Oracle*, 222–3.
"Cut four pounds of a breast of veal into pieces, about two inches by one; put the trimmings into a stew-pan with two quarts of water, with twelve corns of black pepper,

---

2 Anne Langton, *A Gentlewoman in Upper Canada*, 3 August 1839, 252.
3 Rappee was a dark-brown snuff and Princes' Mixture a brand name of snuff.
4 Traill, *Backwoods of Canada*, 91.

and the same of allspice; when it boils, skim it clean, and let it boil an hour and a half, then strain it off; while it is boiling, fry of a nice brown in butter the bits of veal and four onions; when they are done, put the broth to them; put it on the fire; when it boils, skim it clean; let it simmer half an hour; then ... mix two spoonfuls of curry, and the same of flour, with a little cold water and a tea-spoonful of salt; add these to the soup, and simmer it gently till the veal is quite tender, and it is ready; or bone a couple of fowls or rabbits, and stew them in the manner directed above for the veal, and you may put in a bruised eschalot, and some mace and ginger, instead of black pepper and allspice."

Currie of Veal

Dalgairns, *The Practice of Cookery*, 148.
"Cut part of a neck of veal into cutlets, and make a gravy of the trimmings; season it with pepper, salt, and an onion; strain and thicken it with flour and butter, and add two spoonfuls of curry powder. Fry the cutlets with an onion minced very small, in butter, of a light brown colour, and then stew them in the prepared gravy till they become quite tender. Before serving, add the juice of half a lemon, and a little Chili pepper."

Chicken, Rabbit, and Veal &c. as Curry

Dods, *The Cook and Housewife's Manual*, 314–15.
"This common and favourite dish is at once economical, convenient at table, and of easy preparation. All kinds of viands, dressed or raw, may be dressed as curry. The only important rule is, to have good stock; and the sole art consists in hitting the medium in seasoning, or suiting the tastes of the individuals for whom the curry is prepared.[5] Cut up the chickens, fowl, rabbits, veal, lamb, &c. &c. into pieces proper to be helped at table, and rather small than clumsily large. Fry this cut meat in butter,

---

5 On page 190, Meg Dods instructed the reader: "Instead, however, of using curry-powder as obtained in shops, we would advise every cook to keep the several ingredients, each good of its kind, in well-stopped vials and to mix them when they are wanted, suiting the quantities of the various ingredients to the nature of the dish."

with sliced Spanish or whole button-onions, over a quick fire, till of a fine amber colour. When the meat is thus browned, add nearly a pint of good mutton or veal stock unseasoned; and when this has simmered slowly for a quarter of an hour, or more if the fowls are old, add from two to three dessert-spoonfuls of curry-powder and a spoonful of flour, both rubbed very smooth, and carefully stirred into the sauce. When the curry is just ready, add also a glass of good thick cream, and either the juice of a lemon or a proportionate quantity of citric acid. Skim off all fat, and if the sauce is not rich enough, stir in, before dishing, a small quantity of melted butter. If the sauce be too thick, add a little broth to thin it. Some cooks pound part of the meat and all the scraps to thicken the curry, and also the boiled livers, &c. Others marinade, in lemon-juice and sliced onion, the meat they curry. – Obs. Curry may be made of cold chicken, slices of veal, lamb, &c. and is a very acceptable variety at table, in place of *toujours* hash, though very inferior to curry of undressed meat. Some cooks add a few small onions that have been cooked in broth; other a few capsicums or fresh chili, which is peculiarly acceptable to those who like hot-spiced dishes."

SALADS AND SALAD SAUCES

We may not think that diners in centuries past ate much in the way of salads, although some people seem to have enjoyed them very much.

An English Salad and Salad-Sauce

Dods, *The Cook and Housewife's Manual*, 191–2.
"Let the salad herbs be fresh gathered, nicely trimmed and picked, and repeatedly washed in salt and water. Drain and cut them. Just before dinner is served, rub the yolks of two hard-boiled eggs very smooth on a soup-plate, with a little very rich cream. When well mixed, add a teaspoonful of made mustard, and a little salt, a spoonful of olive oil, one of oiled butter, or two of sour cream may be substituted, and when this is mixed smooth, put in as much vinegar as will give the proper degree of acidity to the sauce – about two large spoonfuls; add a little pounded lump-sugar, if the flavour is liked. Put this sauce in the dish, and lay the cut herbs lightly over it; or mix them well with it, and garnish with beet-root sliced and marked, rings of the white of the eggs, young radishes, &c. Onions may be served separately on a small dish. Some knowing persons like grated Parmesan put to their salad and sauce."

Salad Sauce

The Canadian Housewife's Manual of Cookery, 298–9.
"Boil one egg hard, when cold remove the yolk, put it into a basin, bruise it to a pulp with a wooden spoon, do not use iron, then add a raw yolk and a tea-spoonful of flour, a small teaspoonful of salt, and a quarter of pepper, then add half a spoonful of vinegar; stir it round, pour over a table-spoonful of oil by degrees, keep stirring, then a little more vinegar, two more of oil, until eight tea-spoonfuls of oil and three of vinegar are used; season with half a tea-spoonful of chopped onions, two of parsley, half of tarragon and chervil, a pinch of cayenne and six tea-spoonfuls of melted butter cold. The white of the egg may be chopped up and added. It will keep for some time if properly corked, and may be used in proportion with any of the following salads: a gill of whipped cream is good in it."

SAUCES

Sweet

Traill does not say much about sweet sauces, let alone provide any specific recipes. She does mention that pouring maple molasses over puddings or sprinkling them with sugar or blending sugar and butter were nice, but that is about it. Other cookbooks provide recipes, of which we give four, that would have been common even in the backwoods. For example, cream sweetened with maple syrup or sugar is delicious.

The Family Hand-Book, 240.
"Pudding sauce consists of melted butter, sweetened, and flavoured with good raisin wine, sherry or brandy."

A.B. of Grimsby, *The Frugal Housewife's Manual*, 8.
"One sauce answers for all kinds of puddings that require sauce. If you choose the old fashioned sauce, viz., sweetened cream, you will find a little nutmeg or cinnamon is an improvement."

Nourse, *Modern Practical Cookery*, 186.
"Make some thin melted butter; add some sugar, a glass of white wine, and a squeeze of lemon."

Leslie, *Miss Leslie's Directions for Cookery*, 297.
"Eat it with sweetened cream flavoured with wine and nutmeg."

Savoury

The basic English sauce for vegetables, fish, or boiled meat was butter thickened with flour, then flavoured with any number of savoury ingredients – mushroom ketchup, anchovy, lemon juice, mustard, walnut catsup, and more – to the cook's taste.

EXCELLENT SHORT CRUST

Traill assumed her readers already had a grasp of basic baking. Since she supplied only recipes for foods that would be largely unfamiliar to British immigrants, a basic pie pastry recipe was not included. The simple and effective recipe below is from a cookbook she undoubtedly knew of, given its popularity, although we do not know if she ever saw or owned a copy. Mrs Rundell's cookbook was first published in London in 1806 and went through multiple printings in Great Britain and the United States until 1880.

Rundell, *A New System of Domestic Cookery*, 164.
"Take two ounces of fine white sugar, pounded and sifted,[6] then mix it with a pound of flour well dried; rub it into three ounces of butter so fine as not to be seen – into some cream put the yolks of two eggs beaten, and mix the above into a smooth paste; roll it thin, and bake it in a moderate oven."

Our Modern Instructions

Yield: enough for a double-crust pie, two single crust pies, or twenty-four tarts.

Modern flours are thoroughly dried during processing, so the reminder that the flour be "well dried" no longer applies.

| ¼ c | 60 mL | white sugar |
| 3½ c | 875 mL | white flour |

6 See page 324 for information about pounding sugar.

¼ c	60 mL	salted or unsalted butter, cold but not hard
2	2	egg yolks, preferably medium
1½ c	375 mL	10% cream

1 Stir the flour and sugar together in a large mixing bowl. Rub the butter in with fingertips until it is "so fine as not to be seen," as Mrs Rundell instructed. Make a well in the centre.
2 Whisk the egg yolks in a medium bowl until they are pale yellow, four to five minutes. Pour the cream in slowly, whisking until smooth.
3 Using a fork, gently stir the eggy cream into the sugary flour. Carefully pull into a ball, divide into two sections, and refrigerate for about fifteen minutes.
4 Roll the first section to about 2 mm (⅛") thin on a lightly floured surface. Run a flat spatula or line under the pastry to separate it from the table. Carefully roll the pastry around the rolling pin, transfer over to the pie plate, and unwind it to line the plate.
5 Repeat with the other section.

Simple Fireplace Cooking at Home

Fig. 22 · Sketch of the "old fireplace" at the Canadian Historical Exhibition, 1899, showing a range of hearth equipment. Although a re-creation, it conveys the sense of busy activity that would have been typical around a real kitchen fireplace.

Simple cooking in your fireplace is quite doable at home. Next time the electricity fails, you can still prepare a hot meal for the family. Experience is the best teacher for hearth cooking. To paraphrase many cookbook authors, it is impossible to provide infallible rules for fireplace cooking. Too many variables exist: temperature fluctuations due to the fire's strength, the thickness of your pots, the height of your gridiron over the flames, the cake batter's density, and so on. Start by trying one recipe and cooking method, and then expand your repertoire to include others. If you doubt that you'll succeed, remember that for centuries whole meals, including state banquets, were cooked over fires.

One action that surprises new hearth cooks is how often the hearth (also called the apron or firestone) is used for the actual cooking. Three- or four-legged gridirons, skillets, or kettles can be positioned over small piles of coals on the flat hearth and controlled for small batch broiling, frying, and baking. Hot embers combined with flames are best for the high heat required for roasting and boiling. Grilling is the least intimidating because many cooks already know how to barbecue. Baking pancakes is easiest – in fact we bet many of you have cooked pancake breakfasts over a campfire. Try this first, then progress to the other techniques. If you have a wood fireplace and an iron bake pan with a well-fitted lid, you can bake a wide range of cakes, cookies, pastries, pies, biscuits, and breads.

BASIC EQUIPMENT

- A set of long-handled fireplace equipment including ash shovel, log tongs, fire poker, and ash brush.
- A set of long-handled barbecue equipment including tongs, spoon, and basting brush.

GENERAL ADVICE

1 Start by establishing a small but lively fire. Let it burn for at least half an hour to build some heat and develop a bed of glowing orangey-red coals. A longer burn time is better.
2 Smokiness indicates that the wood is new or damp or that the heat is not high enough to burn the wood cleanly.
3 Do not get too hung up on the cooking times given in recipes; some recipes did not even suggest a time. Use your judgement and all five senses.

GENERAL SAFETY NOTES

- Use caution at all times – watch for sparks, use oven mitts and/or pads, tie back long hair, avoid dangling aprons or shirtsleeves, use a thermometer (at least until you gain some confidence).

- Use dry hardwoods since they burn best – maple, oak, beech, ash, cherry.
- Have your chimney professionally cleaned annually.
- Have a bucket of water and a fire extinguisher nearby.
- Sweep the spent coals and ashes off the fireplace hearth and back into the fireplace as soon as you finish cooking.

GRILLING STEAKS OR CHOPS ON A GRIDIRON

SPECIFIC EQUIPMENT
- A low iron gridiron

1 Move two shovelfuls of coals onto your hearth. Insulate them with a layer of hot ashes. Replenish the coals as needed to maintain the temperature.
2 Position the gridiron. Let the coals warm it. Rub grease on the bars.
3 Grill your steak or chop as you would on a barbecue, three to seven minutes per side depending on the thickness of the meat.

Advice about Grilling from Historic Sources

"The gridiron should ... be placed at a distance of three, four, five or six inches above the fire ... The gridiron must be hot through (which will take about five minutes), before anything is put on it. It must be then rubbed with a piece of fresh suet, to prevent the meat from being *branded*, or sticking to the hot bars."[1]

"This culinary art is very confined, but excellent as it respects steaks. I will give you my practical rule: The fire should be clear, that the fumes from the drippings may draw up or from the meat; cut your steak crosswise of the grain, about three quarters of an inch thick. If it be beef, pound it the same as you would for frying; grease the gridiron that the steak may not stick when turning; salt it only on the upper side when you first put it down, for the salt will draw the juice out, and make it dry. When you turn it, first take a knife and fork, and lay one piece above the other that it may absorb the gravy one from the other, then turn and salt and pepper it. Cook it until it is done, (but not till it is dry) then take it up and put thin slices of butter between the pieces; lay them quite

---

1 Dods, *The Cook and Housewife's Manual*, 117–18.

compact, and turn a tin dish over them a few minutes, and they will be moist and good."[2]

BAKING PANCAKES ON A GRIDDLE

"[Pancakes] were ... baked on a large griddle ...; in a large family an expert hand was required to keep up the demand."[3]

See pages 114, 115, and 123 for Traill's pancake recipes and page 383 for our modern recipe for her buckwheat pancakes.

SPECIFIC EQUIPMENT
- A low iron trivet or gridiron
- A long-handled frypan
- Tinfoil
- Plate

1 Move two shovelfuls of coals onto your hearth. Insulate them with a layer of hot ashes. Replenish the coals as needed to maintain the temperature.
2 Position the trivet or gridiron and place the frypan on top. Heat the pan thoroughly to melt your cooking fat. Cook according to the recipe's instructions.
3 Keep pancakes warm on a plate loosely covered with tinfoil.
4 Warm the maple syrup in a ceramic jug placed near the embers. Turn the jug periodically.

BAKING BREAD IN A BAKE-KETTLE

"Many a beautiful loaf I have eaten, baked before a wood fire in a bake-kettle" [97].

See pages 97 to 100 for Traill's bread recipes and pages 332 through 347 for our modern equivalents.

SPECIFIC EQUIPMENT
- A cast iron bake-kettle or Dutch oven
- A rack that fits flat inside it

---

2 A. B. of Grimsby, *Frugal Housewife's Manual*, 67.
3 Haight, *Country Life in Canada*, 11.

- A tin loaf pan or flat plate that fits easily inside it on the rack with room to spare
- A low iron trivet or gridiron

1 Move two shovelfuls of coals onto your hearth. Insulate them with a layer of hot ashes. Replenish the coals as needed to maintain the temperature.
2 Position your trivet or gridiron over the coals and place the lidded bake-kettle on top, with the rack inside it. Shovel some coals onto the lid. Let it preheat for fifteen to thirty minutes. Once your oven is warmed, it is ready to warm the dough too.
3 Have the dough ready in its pan. Carefully lift the lid off the bake-kettle with the fire tongs, trying to avoid letting any coals fall into the pot. Tip the coals back into the fireplace. Quickly lower the bread dough into the pan and reposition the lid. Move the bake-kettle away from the coals on the firestone and shovel the coals back into the fireplace. Let the dough rise for about half an hour, turning the kettle occasionally to maintain the warmth evenly.
4 Shovel fresh hot coals onto the hearth, cover with a layer of insulating ashes, and again place the trivet and kettle on it. Shovel more coals onto the lid. Again, cover with a layer of ashes. Rotate several times so all the bread is evenly heated by the fire too. Bake for about half an hour before cautiously checking its progress.
5 Follow the recipe's instructions on doneness.

Advice about Baking Bread from Historic Sources

Don't repeat Susanna Moodie's first experience at baking bread! "It was my first Canadian loaf. I felt quite proud of it, and I placed it in the odd machine [bake-kettle] in which it was to be baked. I did not understand the method of baking in these ovens; or that my bread should have remained in the kettle for half an hour, until it had risen the second time, before I applied the fire to it, in order that the bread should be light. It not only required experience to know when it was in a fit state for baking, but the oven should have been brought to the proper temperature to receive the bread. Ignorant of all this, I put my unrisen loaf into a cold kettle, and heaped a large quantity of hot ashes above and below. The first intimation I had of the results of my experiment was the disagreeable odour of burning bread filling the house."[4]

4 Moodie, *Roughing It in the Bush*, 121–2.

"Those that bake what I term a *shanty loaf*, in an iron bake-pot, or kettle, placed on the hot embers, set the dough to rise over a few very embers, or near the hot hearth, keeping the pot or pan turned as the loaf rises; when equally risen all over they put hot ashes beneath and upon the lid, taking care to not to let the heat be too fierce at first."[5]

ROASTING MEAT ON A DANGLE STRING

The simplest method of roasting meat at a fireplace is a dangle string hung from a nail or hook imbedded in the mantle, which should be twisted regularly so that the meat turns in front of the fire. Mary O'Brien, for example, wrote that her "little quarter of pork was dangling before the fire at the end of a skein of worsted."[6] Metalsmiths did make several pieces of roasting equipment for those who could afford them, but they were not often found in the poor backwoods farms of old Ontario. Tin reflector ovens (also called tin kitchens), brass clock jacks that rotated the meat for the cook, and iron baskets that held birds and fish propped up on stands directly facing the fire are three examples. A tin kitchen, which is "a small tin oven with a slanting top, open at one side, and when required for use was set before the fire on the hearth"[7] are still available from tinsmiths who manufacture reproductions; antique stores sometimes have restorable clock jacks. But a dangle string is available to all cooks.

No matter the equipment, to effectively roast meat you need a good bed of radiant coals and a few energetic flames, but not a roaring fire. Feed the fire as needed. Keep the meat a couple of feet away at the beginning but towards the end move it closer to the heat and flames to increase the browning and crisping.

Roasting with fire often takes longer than in an oven, but of course you still want to reach the advised internal temperature. Check the recommended length of time for your meat or fowl in your favourite cookbook and use a probe thermometer to double-check the meat's internal temperature.

See page 158 for Traill's recipe for roast venison and 161 for roast pigeon.

5   Traill, *Backwoods of Canada*, 138.
6   O'Brien, *Journals of Mary O'Brien*, 6 November 1830, 141.
7   Haight, *Country Life in Canada*, 12.

SPECIFIC EQUIPMENT

- A dangle or drop string of sturdy cotton such as butcher's twine (measure to ensure that the meat will dangle at the correct height)
- A hook or nail under the mantel from which to dangle the meat
- A dripping pan
- A probe thermometer – not historical but useful and definitely safer

1 Encourage your fire so that you gain some good coals. Replenish the coals as needed to maintain the temperature.

2 Truss your meat or fowl firmly. Tie the drop string to the prepared meat. Place the dripping pan on the hearth with a bit of water in it so the first drippings do not burn. Hang the meat directly over it.

3 Twist the string and let it unwind. Its unwinding action provides the natural momentum to rewind, but gradually the momentum slows until it stops. Retwist the string as many times as required. You can also shift the meat back to front a few times. Baste regularly with melted butter and/or drippings.

4 Place a plate near the fire to warm up. Check the meat's internal temperature with the probe thermometer. When ready, lift the meat off the hook onto the warmed plate. Cut off the dangle string. Let the meat rest under a loose cover of parchment paper or tinfoil while you make a gravy of the drippings.

5 Snip off the truss strings. Transfer the meat to the serving plate.

Advice about Roasting from Historic Sources

"In roasting, the management of the fire is half the battle ... An hour before the roast is put down, make up a fire suited to the size of the joint; let it be clear and glowing, and free of ashes and smoke in front ... Place the meat at a due distance, that it may heat through without the outside becoming shriveled and scorched. To prevent this, baste diligently for the first half hour ... A radiant fire, due distance, and frequent basting, can alone ensure a well-roasted joint."[8]

"Cover the meat [beef, pork, lamb, mutton] for the first hour with kitchen paper [parchment paper], fastened on with twine."[9]

8 Dods, *The Cook and Housewife's Manual*, 93.
9 Ibid., 92.

BOILING PUDDINGS IN A LARGE POT

Puddings need a fairly high fire to maintain a brisk boil. Historically, this was best achieved by moving a crane that held the water-filled cauldron directly over the fire. Since your fireplace is unlikely to have a crane from which to hang a cauldron, you can manage with a large pot placed inside the fireplace on a tall trivet right over the fire.

Boiling a pudding on your stove is accomplished following the same method. See [90] and [113] for Traill's recipes and 355 for others from contemporary cookbooks.

SPECIFIC EQUIPMENT
- A cauldron or a very large pot
- A small rack inside the cauldron or pot (optional)
- A tall iron trivet
- A pudding cloth of linen or thick muslin, about 60 cm × 60 cm (24" × 24")
- A length of string 15 to 20 cm (6" to 8")

1 Encourage your fire so that you get some good coals. Replenish your coals as needed to maintain the temperature.
2 Place your trivet right over the coals, put the pot on it, and fill it three-quarters full with water. Let the water come to a rolling boil. Add wood to the fire as needed.
3 Meanwhile, mix your pudding batter according to the recipe instructions.
4 Dip your cloth into some boiling water, either with tongs or using two strategically placed fingers. Pull it out and let it drip briefly until you can squeeze out all the excess water without hurting your hands.
5 Lay it on a flat surface, generously sprinkle flour over it, and shake off the excess flour. Drape it inside a bowl, smoothing out the creases.
6 Fill the cloth with the pudding batter. Pull the edges of the cloth up into a tail and tie firmly into a ball with the string. Do not allow any edges to escape or water will leak in. Carefully lower the wrapped pudding into the boiling water. It should be submerged. Boil it gently while you do other tasks. Feed the fire as necessary to maintain a brisk simmer and if the water level drops, add some boiling water to keep the pudding submerged. Also, if you do not have a rack inside the pan, move the pudding ball occasionally so it does not stick to the bottom.
7 When done according to the recipe's instructions, use the tongs to pull the pudding out and transfer it to a plate. Dip it quickly in a bowl of cold water and then place it back on the plate. Clip the string and gently peel the cloth away. Place a

dry plate on top and carefully tip everything over so the hot pudding is sitting on the new plate.

8 Serve hot with a pudding sauce [359–60].

Advice about Boiling Puddings from Historic Sources

"If a Bread-Pudding, tie it loose; if a Batter-Pudding, tie it close."[10]

"Puddings ought to be boiled in an open pot, in plenty of water, which must be kept at a quick boil ... The common fault of boiled puddings, which are often solid bodies, is being underdone."[11]

"Be sure that the water boils before you put in the pudding, and keep it steadily boiling all the time ... Be scrupulously careful that your pudding cloth is perfectly sweet and clean ... Immediately before you use it, dip it in boiling water; squeeze it dry, and dredge it with flour ... When puddings are boiled in a cloth, it should be just dipped in a basin of cold water before you untie the pudding cloth, as that will prevent it from sticking."[12]

"The cloths in which puddings are boiled should be scrupulously clean, and kept in a dry place, as neglect in this particular will be sure to impart an unpleasant flavour to the pudding. They should always be dipped into boiling water, squeezed dry, and floured before using ... The water should boil quick when the pudding is put in; and it should be moved about for a minute ... A pan of cold water should be ready, and the pudding dipped in as soon as it comes out of the pot, and then it will not adhere to the cloth."[13]

10 Glasse, *The Art of Cookery*, 188.
11 Dods, *The Cook and Housewife's Manual*, 398.
12 *The Cook Not Mad*, number 273, 91–2.
13 *The Canadian Housewife's Manual of Cookery*, 210.

Glossary of Food and Cooking Terms

This glossary provides insight into the mid-nineteenth-century Canadian context by examining the many culinary words and phrases found in Traill's original edition of *The Female Emigrant's Guide*. The entries concentrate on the wide range of food-stuffs, kitchen equipment, and cooking terms Traill and her contemporaries used in the backwoods. We define only words that appear in the *Guide* and therefore include no explanations for such well-known foods as blueberry or trout, both of which were familiar and available to Traill, because she never mentions these foods in the *Guide*.

Abernethy Biscuit, *see also* Biscuits and Crackers   Abernethy, situated in central Scotland, is only indirectly the source of the name of these caraway-flavoured biscuits. They were apparently invented in London by Dr John Abernethy (1764–1831), whose family hailed from Abernethy originally. The doctor regularly ate Captain's Biscuits (probably the same as hardtack) at a baker's shop, but realized that adding caraway seeds improved their digestibility. Commercial companies still make them, often with a network of docked holes, which seems to suggest their naval origins.[1]

Acorn   Acorns are the fruit of oak trees (*Quercus*) and could be roasted as a coffee substitute, those from white and burr oaks in particular. They are "sweet and edible raw," although those of the red and black oaks are bitter. The Haudenosaunee employed them extensively as food and medicine.[2]

Allspice   Also called pimento and Jamaica pepper, *Pimenta dioica* was a popular dried berry from the West Indies and South America, used as an inexpensive multi-purpose spice by Traill and by today's cooks in a wide variety of sweet and savoury ways: ground to a powder for cakes, fruit, and meat pies, or kept whole in

1 McNeill, *The Scots Kitchen*, 250; Webster and Parkes, *Encyclopedia of Domestic Economy*, 749.
2 Erichsen-Brown, *Use of Plants*, 63–6.

tomato sauces, meat brines, and fish preservation. "[It] is called Allspice from a supposed resemblance in flavor to a mixture of cinnamon, nutmeg and cloves." It was considered to be the mildest and most benign of the common sweet spices, according to the *Encyclopedia of Domestic Economy* (1855).[3]

Almond, Bitter   Smaller than sweet almonds, bitter almonds (*Prunus dulcis* var. *amara*) contain a trace of bitter prussic acid. Although too strong to eat on their own, three or four were often pulverized with a handful of sweet almonds to intensify the distinctive almond flavour for cakes and confectionery. Traill's sole mention of them is in Lady Cake [108], but it is unlikely she could have afforded them, even if they had been available in the backwoods shops.

Almond, Sweet   Although imported, almonds (*Prunus dulcis* var. *dulcis*) were by far the most common nut used in nineteenth-century Canadian baking and confectionery. Many cookbooks specify the large sweet Spanish Jordan and Valencia varieties, the former the most esteemed. Today, California produces the largest almond crop in the world. Almonds have a long history in Mediterranean and Biblical cuisines, and were indispensable to upper-class medieval European cooking, including in the British Isles, because almond milk replaced cow milk as an essential ingredient in recipes acceptable on the Christian calendar of fasting days. By the end of the 1700s, almonds were pretty well restricted to use in sweet baking in Anglo-American cooking.

Today, almonds can be purchased whole with or without their skins, slivered, sliced, ground, or as a ready-made paste, but in Traill's era, bakers still had to prepare them themselves, one of the time-consuming tasks inherent in what we nowadays call scratch baking.

Almond Essence   Almond essence is oil of bitter almonds squeezed from the residue paste after the first extraction of the finest oil. Traill apparently had almond essence in her pantry at least occasionally because her Canadian Croquets recipe, an apparent favourite of hers, called for "three or four drops" [109] of lemon or almond essence.

Alum   A common chemical (a double-sulphate of aluminium and potassium), alum was used for many household tasks, such as whitening flour, keeping the colour in

3 Ward, *Grocers' Hand-Book and Directory*, 12; Webster and Parkes, *Encyclopedia of Domestic Economy*, 523.

green beans during cooking, and setting dyes for cloth; all these functions were familiar to Traill. It is one of the substances in some proprietary baking powders.

Apple Apples (*Malus sylvestris* var. *domestica*) were the most important and versatile fruit found in the backcountry. Dozens of varieties were obtainable but the McIntosh – once the quintessential Ontario apple – does not appear in her comprehensive list of apples for each season, even though it had come to market in 1835 from a Peterborough area farm. It took several decades to become prominent. The Traills planted their first orchard from "a little nursery of seedling apples of my own planting in a very thriving condition beside two ungrafted apple trees that were given me by a young settler last Spring and which my brother has promised to graft for me. I find by my own experience that it is better to grow the apple pips in the Fall than in the Spring."[4] Planting apple orchards in the new clearings was an indispensable settlement strategy because apples were a major source of sustenance due to their hardiness, keeping abilities, and culinary adaptability, particularly for the all-important cider. Sam Strickland recommended that the settler "devote a portion of his first cleared fallow for [this] purpose," advice echoed by his sister and many others.[5] Apples were preserved in several ways, most famously by drying them in slices, a technique learned from the German settlers of Pennsylvania. "Strings of apples were hanging from the ceiling to dry for the purpose of making applesauce in the winter," said Mary O'Brien. Such apple sauce "found its way to the table thrice a day … When they are wanted for pies, puddings and tarts, they are boiled with sugar, and prove very good for such purposes."[6] Traill's "Preserved Apples" recipe [73] is adapted from the October 1852 *Maple Leaf* (see 509).

By far the most common fruit sauce was made of apples; it appeared with great regularity as an element in all meals, not just as an accompaniment to meats. "They have a nice and cheap way of making Apple sauce by only paring them & cutting them in quarter's [*sic*] and boiling them in Cider – The longer they are boiled the longer they will keep."[7]

---

4 Traill to her sister Sarah, [April?] 1836, Traill Family Collection, 3461. See Custead, *Catalogue of Fruit & Ornamental Trees*, 8–9, and Woodhead, *Early Canadian Gardening*, 26–7, 57–61.
5 Samuel Strickland, *Twenty-Seven Years in Canada West*, 2:203.
6 O'Brien, *Journals of Mary O'Brien*, 20 October 1828, 19; Haight, *Country Life in Canada*, 26; Samuel Strickland, *Twenty-Seven Years in Canada West*, 2:296.
7 Deborah Mullet, 21 April 1825, quoted in Hoffman and Taylor, *Much to Be Done*, 301.

Apple Water Apple water (or Appleade as it was sometimes called) seems to have started as a Temperance drink in the 1830s, along with such other fruit syrups as Raspberry Vinegar. Similar recipes appeared in sections on sickroom cookery. See pages 354–5 for recipes.

Arrowroot, also Arrow-root The edible white starch of the rhizome *Maranta arundinacea*, from the West Indies. Since it was easily digested and nutritious, by mid-century it had become an ingredient for thickening milk puddings for invalids and weaned babies. In the backwoods, arrowroot was available, although expensive. A substitute was homemade potato starch. Frances Stewart received arrowroot in at least one annual box from home.

   Arrowroot was also used for starching linen. Explained Anne Langton, "We ladies have been exceedingly busy getting up our muslins, a very difficult operation with arrowroot as our starch."[8] In the backwoods, the roots of a native plant, Indian turnip (*Arum maculatum*), were pulped, pounded, and dried into an edible starch called Portland Arrowroot after a similar substance from the Isle of Portland in the English Channel.[9]

Asparagus Many people look forward to local *Asparagus officinalis* as one of the heralds of spring. Once fairly well-known, even in the kitchen gardens of backwoods farms, asparagus fell out of favour except with the wealthy until market farmers revived it in the mid-1980s in Canada, so successfully that imported asparagus is now available year-round in supermarkets. In May 1829, Mary O'Brien noted with anticipation: "asparagus in perfection."[10] Its nickname "sparrow grass" was considered vulgar.

Bachelor's Oven, also Roaster, Reflector Oven, Tin Kitchen, Tin Oven This was a small open-sided cylindrical or three-sided triangular oven that sat on short legs on the hearthstone facing the fire. Because it was made of tin, the fire's heat reflected off its back and sides onto the food, thus cooking or roasting from all sides, hence its other name, reflector oven. Sometimes it had shelves inside to accommodate pies and small trays of cookies, as well as a back door that could be opened to check the

8 Anne Langton, *A Gentlewoman in Upper Canada*, 2 April 1839, 220.
9 Traill, *Canadian Wild Flowers*, 10–11; Webster and Parkes, *Encyclopedia of Domestic Economy*, 765.
10 O'Brien, *Journals of Mary O'Brien*, 26 May 1829, 29.

baking or roasting process. Many were also designed to roast meat on a horizontal spit that was rotated by moving the spit's two ends around circles made of little holes on the two sides. The hot fatty drippings collected on the bottom. It was a handily portable piece of equipment in various sizes that could be shifted around the hearth as needed to adapt to the fluctuating heat levels generated by the fire and to make space for other equipment. These ovens arrived in North America from England sometime in the late 1700s and were in general use by the 1830s, although they were a bit expensive for poorer homes.[11] Bachelors may have liked them, but so did busy housewives – "This simple contrivance was a great convenience, and came into general use."[12] (See also the similar but much larger "tin hastener" standing to the right on the hearth in figure 22.)

Fig. 23a (*left*) · American oven; Fig. 23b (*right*) · Tin baker or reflector. Two versions of a tin oven, also called a "bachelor oven," "reflector oven," "tin kitchen," or "tin baker." The open side faces the fire and the back side absorbs and reflects the heat.

Bacon A true staple food, bacon is the salted (dry-cured) pork from the belly or sides of a pig. After curing, it was often smoked. Once an essential meat for Upper Canadians, it was to some extent associated with poverty, since it was so readily available and was less expensive than beef or lamb. Bacon could be cured at home, which many families, both farm- and town-based did, but pork butchery was one of the earliest food production businesses begun in colonial Canada.

11 Oliver, *Saltwater Foodways*, 10–13; Minhinnick, *At Home in Upper Canada*, 57–8.
12 Haight, *Country Life in Canada*, 12.

***Bake-Kettle**, also* Bake-Can, Dutch Oven   The bake-kettle was the most ubiquitous and essential iron pot for cooking over the fire and baking on the hearth. (See an example, centre, on the hearth in figure 19.) It served as stew pan, soup pot, sauce pan, bake oven, and water kettle, and could substitute for a mixing bowl or dish sink. Pans of cake batter, plates of tarts, or tins of bread dough could be carefully baked inside, usually on a trivet to buffer their bottoms from direct heat. For households without an indoor or outdoor oven, it was essential for baking "shanty bread" or "shanty loaf." In *The Backwoods of Canada*, Traill says: "I have eaten boiled potatoes, baked meats, excellent stews, and good soups, all cooked at different times in this universally useful utensil: so let it not be despised. It is one of those things peculiarly adapted to the circumstances of settlers in the bush before they have collected those comforts about their homesteads, within and without, that are the reward and the slow gleaning-up of many years of toil."[13] Descriptions of its utility appear frequently in immigrant writings, by both men and women. It was even used for baking wedding cakes laden with dried fruits.[14]

Bake-kettles always had a handle so that they could be hung from the crane over the fire; however, some also had three or four short legs and could sit directly on the embers, more of which were also piled on top of the kettle's lipped lid. Bake-kettles with flat bottoms were generally placed on trivets to raise them off direct heat, but were sometimes nestled directly into the embers.

Americans more commonly used the term Dutch oven instead of bake-kettle.

***Baking Powders**, also* Sodiac Powders; *see also* Cream of Tartar, Pearlash, Saleratus, Sal Volatile, Soda   Before the gradual adoption of chemical raising agents in the latter decades of the eighteenth century, both professional and home bakers relied on liquid yeasts, sourdough leavens, or beaten eggs to raise their baked goods. Nineteenth-century North American cooks came to employ a variety of chemicals as quick raising agents. The quality of these varied greatly, as domestic educator Catharine Beecher stressed: "In using alkalies with acids to raise mixtures, the poorest is pearlash, the next best is saleratus; ... and sal volatile is best of all."[15] All three were unfamiliar to British housewives, but as early as the first quarter of the eighteenth century were familiar to professional European bakers, particularly Dutch and

---

13 Traill, *Backwoods of Canada*, 138.
14 Traill, "The Interrupted Bridal," in *Forest and Other Gleanings*, 132.
15 Beecher, *Miss Beecher's Domestic Receipt Book*, 58.

German, as well as English gingerbread bakers. In America, German-speaking settlers introduced quick-acting pearlash to their receptive British neighbours.

In 1845, Eliza Acton noted in *Modern Cookery for Private Families* that "excellent dairy bread made without yeast" and quick breads "in which carbonate of soda and muriatic acid are substituted for yeast or other leaven, [have] within these few years been highly recommended" in the repertoire of cooks' ingredients.[16] Traill commented that "the use of acid and alkaline salts in fermenting flour food, has become very general of late years" due to their convenience and wholesomeness [96]. All of these were carbonates that released carbon dioxide bubbles when combined with an acidic activator. Purchased in crystalline lumps, they had to be rolled into a powder, sifted, and then kept in corked bottles to avoid exposure to air and moisture. When used, they had to be dissolved in a liquid to ensure that they were evenly distributed through the batter or dough to avoid little dark spots forming in the final baked product.

Chemical raising agents contributed to a major shift in baking styles and techniques by guaranteeing lift, simplifying mixing, and diminishing preparation time by eliminating the necessity to knead or wait until the mixture had risen: in fact, cake or biscuits had to be put into the oven immediately to capture the leavening strength of these agents. Quick breads became a North American staple. Of Traill's nineteen cakes, six call for beaten eggs alone and only two, both eggless, call for chemical agents alone; the others rely on a combination of beaten eggs and pearlash, saleratus, sal volatile, soda, or cream of tartar. Her biscuits and crackers are either unleavened or use saleratus or soda.

At first, the term "baking powder" was used to describe a wide variety of proprietary combinations of acid and alkali mixed by druggists and involving varying proportions of soda, alum, cream of tartar, ammonia, phosphates, and other chemicals. Traill recommends Durkee's Baking Powder [96], although in her unpublished early 1880s revision she expands this specific reference to say instead: "There are many kinds now in use, Cooks Friend, Snow Flake, Dunn's Best." Further on, she suggests that baking powder is best used for raising dough for small breads and buns.[17]

Balm Since Traill recommends bringing the seeds from England, she is not referring to the bee balm, also called oswego tea, that is native to North America and

---

16 Acton, *Modern Cookery for Private Families*, 495, 497.
17 Traill Family Collection, circa 1880?, 5881, 6104.

used to make a popular Amerindian hot drink. For her, balm might have been lemon balm (*Melissa officinalis*), which has a lovely lemony fragance and is suitable for a hot herbal tisane.[18]

Barley   Traill mentions barley as the base for beer – its main purpose – but it was also grown in Canada as cattle fodder, chicken feed, and a bread grain in hard times. Barley was also an occasional soup ingredient. Many farmers grew it; the Moodies certainly did. "Pot" barley has only its outer husk removed by milling. "Pearl" barley is milled further.

Fig. 24 · Barley

Barm, *also known as* Ale Yeast, Baker's Yeast, Beer Yeast, Brewer's Yeast; *see also* Brewer's Yeast   Barm had both specific and generic meanings, which can cause confusion in reading old culinary texts. Strictly speaking, barm is the wort or fermenting liquid in which yeast develops. By the sixteenth century it began to be the specific word for the thick creamy froth found on top of fermenting beers and ales that was skimmed off, rather like cream is skimmed off fresh milk, but it morphed into an ordinary synonym for any baker's or brewer's yeast and fermentation source. Certainly Traill considered barm and yeast to be synonymous; she and her contemporaries also used the terms "rising" and "fermentations."

Basil, Sweet   *Ocimum basilicum* is rare in Canadian kitchen gardens, says Traill [58]. It was also rare in English cooking of her era.[19] Today, it is a very popular herb for pairing with tomatoes and use in such dishes as pesto.

Bass   Several types of bass – members of the sunfish family – live in the waters of Rice Lake – largemouth, smallmouth, black. Susanna Moodie, and others, said that "black bass [is] a fish of excellent flavour that abounds in this place [Lake Katchewanook]."[20]

---

18 Woodhead, *Early Canadian Gardening*, 223–5.
19 Webster and Parkes, *Encyclopedia of Domestic Economy*, 491.
20 Moodie, *Roughing It in the Bush*, 328.

Beans, *see also* Broad, Bush, Green, Haricot, Kidney, Lima, Scarlet Runner, Speckled Red Bean   Beans were seldom mentioned in menus, notes about meals, grocery lists, and so on, and surprisingly few are included in recipes in Canadian cookbooks, yet they were clearly widely grown. Seed catalogues include many varieties,[21] and gardeners mention them frequently: for example, Sandford Fleming notes that he planted white beans.[22] In *The Backwoods of Canada*, in a letter dated 28 November 1834, Traill writes, "We have a great variety of beans, all of the French or kidney kind." In the *Guide* Traill cites several types without indicating how they were used, with the exception of stewed lima beans [139].[23] But Traill does not indicate that she is aware of the Haudenosaunee's proven agriculture technique of planting beans as companions to pumpkins and corn.

Worldwide, there are thousands of kinds of edible beans, which are divided into several genera, two of them central to Western foodways: the European *Vicia faba* (fava, broad) and the South and Central American *Phaseolus* (scarlet runner, kidney, lima, green, haricot, and many others). Their adoption in the eighteenth century transformed European agriculture and peasant cookery. Roasted beans were used as a coffee substitute.

Bear   To her surprise, Susanna Moodie agreed with her brother Sam that "Bruin makes very good eating": "The rest of the evening was spent in skinning, and cutting up, and salting the ugly creature, whose flesh filled a barrel with excellent meat, in flavour resembling beef, while the short grain and juicy nature of the flesh gave to it the tenderness of mutton. This was quite a Godsend, and lasted us until we were able to kill two large fat hogs, in the fall."[24] Boiled bear "tasted like tender boiled pork to" Anna Leveridge.[25] However, George Head decided it was "very disagreeable ... and extremely fusty," although his dog Rover "had no scruples" about eating it. Bear hams were among the winter stores of the productive Young family, whom Traill so admired. Many a bear also yielded its fur pelt to be a rug beside a bed, in front of a hearth, or as a covering in a winter sleigh.[26]

21 James Fleming, *Catalogue of Garden, Agricultural and Flower Seeds*.
22 Sandford Fleming, *Sir Sandford Fleming*, 12 June 1848, 124.
23 Traill, *Backwoods of Canada*, 219.
24 Samuel Strickland, *Twenty-Seven Years in Canada West*, 1:129; Moodie, *Roughing It in the Bush*, 402.
25 Tivy, *Your Loving Anna*, 77.
26 George Head, quoted in Hoffman and Taylor, *Across the Waters*, 318; Traill, "The Mill of the Rapids," in *Forest and Other Gleanings*, 63.

Beaver   Beaver tail was "a rare delicacy." The Young family considered beaver tail to be one of their "dainty meats."[27]

Beef   Beef, particularly grass-fed, was the most desirable of the meats, although pork was more prevalent. Boiled beef was mentioned more often in the colonists' personal accounts than roast beef, which had a better reputation due to its superior taste and higher status. Baby beef (veal) was less common: the Langtons once received an "opportune" present of veal from a friend, a "rarity, unseen here for two years" although readily available in town markets, says Moodie. She also says, "beef [here] is very inferior to the British, but ... there is a decided improvement in this respect." Most farms had one or two cows for milk and a pair of yoked oxen for use in the fields, but because they were usually killed only at the end of their lives, their meat tended to be lean and tough, necessitating long cooking. "Many people lost almost all their stock in winter from different causes such as starvation when fodder is not plenty, or perishing from cold or being lost in the woods when they cannot find any food," comments Stewart.[28]

Beer   So essential was beer to the daily diet of the British, the military, and the public that brewing businesses were established very early in the English-Canadian colonies. Brewing beers had been part of women's seasonal work in Europe and Britain, but from the beginning of settlement in Canada became largely men's work, although not exclusively. Mary O'Brien included this anecdote in the journal she maintained for her English family: "I have been gardening and learning to brew. The apparatus was arranged by the side of the stream and went on very prosperously. I had been watching the amber globules as they danced along the surface of the wort, exulting in the strength which bye and bye [sic] I was to imbibe from it, when lo! the temporary stage on which the mashing tub stood gave way. Down it fell and in falling upset the tub of wort and the precious beverage, together with the grain which was to have produced a second run. They all ran into the stream."[29]

---

27 Need, *Six Years in the Bush*, 16 July 1834, 99; Traill, "The Mill of the Rapids," in *Forest and Other Gleanings*, 63.
28 Anne Langton, *A Gentlewoman in Upper Canada*, 2 June 1840, 283; Moodie, *Roughing It in the Bush*, 52; Moodie, *Life in the Clearings*, 284; Stewart, *Revisiting "Our Forest Home,"* 10 December 1826, 121.
29 O'Brien, *Journals of Mary O'Brien*, 6 May 1831, 159.

Beef.

HIND-QUARTER.	FORE-QUARTER.
1. Sirloin.	11. Middle Rib; 4 Ribs.
2. Rump.	12. Chuck; 3 Ribs.
3. Edge-Bone.	13. Shoulder, or Leg of
4. Buttock.	Mutton Piece.
5. Mouse-Buttock.	14. Brisket.
6. Veiny Piece.	15. Clod.
7. Thick Flank.	16. Neck or Sticking-
8. Thin Flank	Piece.
9. Leg.	17. Shin.
10. Fore Rib; 5 Ribs.	18. Cheek.

Fig. 25 · Diagram of beef cuts

The number of breweries grew throughout the century as beer continued to be the main beverage, especially in English Canada.[30] Barley, as the main ingredient in beer, ale, and lager, was an essential agricultural product. In preparation for brewing, sprouted (malted) barley is mashed to create a dark liquid called beer-wort. Hops and eventually yeast are added to the beer-wort to cause fermentation. Weak, small, or table beer is produced from the second mashing of the malt. Flavourings include ginger, sugar molasses, spruce, and maple. Traill first mentions making a palatable maple beer with added ginger in a journal entry dated 22 January 1838. She also promises herself to try spruce beer since she has received a good recipe.[31]

Beet, *see also* Sugar Beet, Molasses   Common garden beets (*Beta vulgaris* var. *esculentat*) are a deep purple-red, while sugar beets (*Beta vulgaris*) are white. Mangel, or mangel-wurtzel (*Beta vulgaris* var. *rapa*), are fodder beets, also called turnip beets. Settlers planted all of these varieties in Canada. Beets overwintered well in sand pits in root houses, as long as the tops were kept above soil level. The blood beet referred to in the *Guide* [145] is an old variety often grown in early America and mentioned in early garden literature. It was known for its rich red juice.[32] Its leaves were boiled as a vegetable and served with butter, which is still done today, and its juice was used as a pink colourant in confectionery and fermented into vinegar and beer. In recent years, beet vinegar has begun to be used again.

Beetle   A wooden pounder of various sizes and uses in the kitchen that resembled the pestle for a mortar. Its name comes from the Scottish word "bittle," meaning to crush, flatten, or thresh.

Berries, Wild, *see also* Fruit, Bilberry, Blackberry, Chokecherry, Cranberry, Currant, Gooseberry, Huckleberry, Juneberry, Raspberry, Strawberry   Members of the First Nations in the area had long used wild fruit in remedies, eaten it fresh and dried, and incorporated it into pemmican, a mix of dried meat, dried berries, and fat shaped into small balls for winter food. Traill, an observant amateur botanist of her backwoods environment, was happy to pick wild fruits for eating, baking, and medications.

---

30 Heron, *Booze*, 81.
31 Traill, Traill Family Collection, 22 January 1838, 3430.
32 Weaver, *Heirloom Vegetable Gardening*, 82–4, 87; Woodhead, *Early Canadian Gardening*, 207.

However, despite her botanical knowledge, in the *Guide* she sometimes makes mistakes about identification, such as calling the tall juneberry a bilberry [82]. (The mistake was not repeated in *Studies of Plant Life* three decades later, although perhaps this is because local word use had been superseded by scientific nomenclature.) She owned and borrowed several plant identification books, such as Frederick Pursh's two-volume *Flora Americae Septentrionalis; Or, A Systematic Arrangement and Description of the Plants of North America*. Despite the abundance of available wild fruits, Traill and many other immigrants asked that seeds be sent from home and recommended that those following them bring fruit seeds of all kinds. One of the distinctions of *The Female Emigrant's Guide* is Traill's commentary on wild fruits, unusual in cookbooks of the nineteenth century.

Beverages, *see also* Apple Water, Beer, Brandy, Cider, Cocoa, Coffee, Dandelion Coffee, Diet Drink, Green and Black Tea, Hemlock Tea, Labrador Tea, New Jersey Tea, Raspberry Vinegar, Sassafras Tea, Sweet-Gale Tea, Water, Whisky, Wine   As hubs within small communities, wayside inns and taverns were the main sites of public drinking. This is where law courts first met, town meetings were held, early tradesmen started their shops, and many family events, such as weddings, took place. Drinking spirits together was how men of all classes confirmed and solidified their business, social, and fraternal relationships. Prior to the 1840s, public drunkenness was tolerated to a degree we find astonishing today. The temperance movement began in the United States about 1808 and began to have a social effect within a couple of decades: the national American Temperance Society was created in 1826, quickly followed by many grassroots societies in each of the Canadian colonies. Other community centres, such as theatres, billiard parlours, and hotel ballrooms, where alcohol was either prohibited or less available, began to take on some of the functions previously filled by inns and taverns. However, drinking continued to cause problems. Susanna Moodie exclaimed, "Alas! this frightful vice of drinking prevails throughout the colony to an alarming extent." Neither gin nor rum are mentioned by Traill in the *Guide*, but both were imported in large quantities.[33]

Tea and coffee were essential beverages for those who could afford them, but wild substitutes were also available, often based on knowledge learned from the local First Peoples. The leaves of several wild plants were infused as herbal teas, including

---

33 Heron, *Booze*, 278, 30–5, 45–9, 51–6; Moodie, *Life in the Clearings*, 68.

sweet gale, peppermint, and sage.³⁴ Cookbooks had recipes for other beverage options, such as apple water [72–3, 354], cinnamon water, ginger beer, lemonade (see lemon), raspberry vinegar [85, 350], and spruce beer.

Bilberry Black, blue-black, or red-black berries from North American shrubs in the *Vaccinium* family, which includes blueberries. Although not commercially cultivated, they were harvested by the settlers and added to pies and jams, giving a delicate almond flavour.

Biscuits and Crackers, see also Abernethy Biscuit, Breads, Damper, Fudge, Navy Bread, Rusk, Sippet Thin hard breads suitable for traveling, military and naval rations, and long-term storage in barrels have an ancient and world-wide history. Deriving from *panis biscoctus* (bread [panis] twice [bis] cooked [coquere]) in Latin, biscuit means "twice baked"³⁵ – first baked in an oven, then dried out in an oven. Mass production of very hard and dry ship's biscuit (navy bread) made of just flour and water began with the British Navy at their victualling yards, but their first commercial exploitation began with an American military baker, Josiah Bent, in Massachusetts, who picked up the new technology and in 1801 started manufacturing Bent's Biscuits, which quickly came to be colloquially called "crackers" in North America because the thin flour and water breads – thinner than ships' biscuit – cracked in the mouth. Bent's Biscuits became an extremely early brand name; the G.H. Bent Company still operates and is on the American National Register of Historic Places. Biscuits were usually purchased by the handful out of a cracker barrel, but in the backwoods and in times of poverty it was useful to have a recipe, so instructions for simple biscuits and crackers were included in early American cookbooks. Varying types of plain, savoury, and sweet biscuits, crackers, and cookies have proliferated ever since.³⁶

Soda biscuits/soda crackers were a mid-nineteenth-century evolution of water biscuits, with leavening soda and fat (butter or lard) added. Traill's recipe for Soda Biscuit [104] was taken from the September 1852 edition of *The Maple Leaf* (see pages 509–10 in the "Glossary of Sources and Influences").³⁷ The *Guide's* version adds the

---

34 Traill, "Rice Lake Plains," in *Forest and Other Gleanings*, 210; also Moodie, *Roughing It in the Bush*, 353.
35 Davidson, *Oxford Companion to Food*, 75; *Oxford English Dictionary*, 3:430.
36 Smith, "Crackers," 1:353.
37 *The Maple Leaf*, September 1852, 119.

adjectives "white" for the sugar and "square" for the shape. Today's mass-produced soda biscuits are familiar to soup lovers as they are a very common accompaniment.

Blackberry and Thimbleberry   An extensive group of wild brambles in the *Rubus* genus that grow throughout North America; several varieties are found in the eastern part of southern Ontario. The fruits are somewhat thimble-shaped when pulled off the vine, hence Traill's use of "thimble-berry" [82] as a nickname for the common conical blackberries (R. *villosus*) that grew in her Peterborough region, although only one of the *Rubus* genus (R. *parviflorous*) is officially called thimbleberry and it grows primarily in more northerly regions than the Rice Lake plain where the Traills lived. But she seems to have preferred the nickname. As Traill noted, blackberries make excellent pie fillings, jam, and jellies. Although blackberries were commonly a dark purply-black and thimbleberries an orangey-red, Traill gives a list of small fruit [82] that suggests she was familiar with a white thimble-berry, but what fruit she meant is unclear in her botanical writing.[38]

Blackbird   Traill does not specify which blackbirds should be used to make good pies [163], although several are native to Ontario. Sam Strickland wrote about three kinds, noting that those with the orange bars on the wings were more destructive than pigeons to the grain fields. We call these abundant migrant birds "red-winged blackbirds" (*Agelaius phoeniceus*) because of the males' bright red shoulders; they congregate particularly in cornfields during harvest-time.[39]

Black Pepper   Frequently used as a seasoning and often paired with salt just as today, black peppercorns (*Piper nigrum*) were expensive but popular and pervasive. Black pepper has been an essential trade commodity for millennia, one of the goods carried on the ancient spice trade routes from India into Arabia and Rome. Pepper has been a hugely important spice in European cooking and preserving since medieval times and was one of the earliest spices brought to North America.

---

38 Soper, Heimburger, and Garay, *Shrubs of Ontario*, 227, 247; Traill, *Studies of Plant Life in Canada*, 133.

39 Samuel Strickland, *Twenty-Seven Years in Canada West*, 1:299–300. See also Goodwin, *A Bird-Finding Guide to Ontario*, 441–3.

Bladder   The receptacle for urine within an animal body. Once emptied and thoroughly scraped and scrubbed, ox, veal, or sheep bladders in particular made excellent covers for kitchen containers, either put whole over a large container (a crock) or cut up into smaller pieces for smaller containers, such as pint preserving jars. Dampened and draped over the container or cork plug, they shrank rock-hard, forming a seal, although they could be softened around the edges sufficiently to allow them to be removed in one piece. They could be washed and reused several times; with care they could last a few years.[40] When used to protect fruit preserves, a disk of brandy-soaked paper was often laid over the fruit first, followed by the cork and/ or bladder. A piece of thin leather was often used as the final layer. Until the mid-nineteenth century, they were common in well-equipped kitchens, but were gradually replaced by mason jars with their own lids (1860s), waxed paper (1880s), tinfoil (1890s), and plastic wrap (1950s).[41]

Bran, see Shorts, Stone Wheaten Flour, Wheat

Brandy   Traill mentions brandy not as a drink but as a cake flavouring and a rubbed-on remedy for frost-bite. However, similar to spirits such as gin and whisky, brandy was imported and consumed in large quantities.

Breads, see also Biscuits and Crackers   Bread, potatoes, and salt pork were essential foodstuffs for less well-to-do immigrants. Backwoods breads were usually hearty, crusty loaves of wheat, bran, or cornmeal, although Anna Leveridge claimed "Heavy bread is unknown."[42] Rye and cornmeal were often combined in bread, and equal proportions of rye, wheat, and cornmeal were used to make "thirded" bread [99], which was leavened with one of the "risings." Traill's preferred bread was wheat and potato [98]. She considered the ability to make "REALLY GOOD HOUSEHOLD BREAD" an essential skill – as she made clear with her emphasis [16].

Frances Stewart, having just received a bread knife in a box of gifts from back home in Ireland, informed her family that, "Our home made loaves are a different shape from what you have I dare say seen at home, for we bake in what is here called

---

40 Dillon, "Bladders," 36–50.
41 Smith, *Oxford Encyclopedia of Food and Drink in America*, 2:289–90; Ward, *Grocer's Hand-Book and Directory*, 276.
42 Tivy, *Your Loving Anna*, 54.

a Bake kettle or Dutch oven & our loaves are like great huge cakes, more than loaves, so that a strong broad knife for cutting them adds considerably to the ease & expedition with which I may perform that operation, so necessary every morn & evening for a panel of impatient little animals called children."[43] Stewart and so many women baked bread at least weekly; it was one of their most insistent tasks.

Brewer's Yeast, *also known as* Ale Yeast, Baker's Yeast, Barm, Beer Yeast; *see also* Barm, Distiller's Yeast, Yeast   Until the early nineteenth century, a large proportion of British rural and farm households did their own brewing and baking. For millennia, brewer's yeast and baker's yeast (*Saccharomyces cerevisiae*) were the same thick creamy liquids and were used interchangeably, in contrast to today's strains of brewer's yeast, available in both liquid and dried forms from micro-breweries. Different regions had different properties in their *S. cerevisiae*, resulting in different flavours. When brewing beer and ale, the thick frothy topping was skimmed off and carefully stored in a jug as a source of ready yeast at home. In town, brewer's wives sold yeast, also termed barm, at the market. Eliza Leslie explained: "Those who live in towns where there are brewers have no occasion to make their own yeast during the brewing season, and in summer they can every day supply themselves with fresh yeast from the baker's. It is only in country places where there are neither brewers nor bakers that it is expedient to make it at home."[44]

Brewers regularly advertised their barm for sale. Often it was so bitter that it had to be washed, sometimes several times, by diluting it in cold water, allowing it to subside as a sediment, and carefully pouring off the bitter water. The froth's intense natural yeast was sufficiently active to raise bread, although it needed to be left to rise overnight.

In the backwoods, brewer's yeast was sometimes added to maple syrup to encourage it to sour into a type of vinegar.

Broad Bean   Also known as common garden beans and fava beans (*Vicia faba*), broad beans have been cultivated for thousands of years in cool damp climates, but did not do well in southern Ontario's hot and often dry summers. Before the many bean species from the Americas were introduced, broad beans were the sole kind used in Europe and were important foodstuffs when dried, broken into grits, or

---

43 Stewart to Honora Edgeworth, *Revisiting "Our Forest Home,"* 19 August 1827, 124.
44 Leslie, *Miss Leslie's New Cookery Book*, 406–7.

pulverized for flour.[45] Broad beans such as the Windsor Broad Bean (*Vicia faba* var. *maior*) eaten by the gentry and the English or horse bean more commonly eaten by the working-class were brought to North America by settlers and were once ubiquitous in kitchen gardens, as long as they could be harvested before it became too hot. Their popularity had declined by mid-century and lima beans assumed their place. In a set of instructions on how to cook vegetables properly found in the Traill papers, it was explained: "Green Windsors are beautifully green if the rule of '*put in boiling, keep boiling, take out boiling*' is duly observed.[46] Windsors are still available as heirlooms seeds.

Broccoli   Traill only mentions broccoli (*Brassica oleracea*), although she seems to have grown it; others certainly did. Early broccoli was not like the dark green, tree-like Calabrese variety most familiar to Canadians now but was thinner, leafier, and much less compact. Walcheren, the variety Traill mentions, takes its name from a coastal area of the Netherlands.[47]

Brown Sugar   Coloured from dark to light, the darker it was, the more molasses it held. The darkest and coarsest was muscovado. "Common" brown, that is, a dark yellowish colour, was for everyday use, such as sweetening coffee.

Brown and White Cane Sugars   "Cane sugar is the crystallized portion of the juice expressed from the sugar cane, and forms the main article of a grocer's stock."[48] Derived from the tropical grass *Saccharum officinarium*, sugar – sucrose – was the first mass-produced luxury to become available to the ordinary classes, although it was not often the best quality. By the mid-nineteenth century, when Traill was writing her *Guide*, it was readily available even in the colonial backwoods, although the best refined white sugar remained expensive and lesser grades sometimes required clarification by dissolving, draining, drying, and/or sifting at home. Refined sugars were imported from refineries in England, France, or New England, while muscovado and other unrefined sugars came via the West Indies. Canadian-manufactured sugar became available in early 1855 when John Redpath, a Scotsman, built the first refinery

45 Weaver, *Heirloom Vegetable Gardening*, 65, 97–8.
46 Traill Family Collection, vol. 4, file 22, folder 5, undated, unpaginated.
47 James Fleming, *Catalogue of Garden, Agricultural and Flower Seeds*, 2.
48 Ward, *Grocer's Hand-Book and Directory*, 220.

for imported raw sugar, in Montreal. The company's initial products included top level double-refined sugar, yellow refined sugar, crushed and ground sugar, golden syrup, and more.[49]

To simplify what is a complicated multi-step process: sugar cane was crushed to a black juicy pulp that was continuously skimmed while being boiled, filtered, re-boiled, evaporated, and then poured into conical moulds. The moulds were inverted, with their plugged tip facing downwards. When unplugged, the remaining molasses slowly dripped out, leaving behind a hard cone of compacted sugar crystals. Purer sugar was produced by pouring a thin sugar syrup through the cones, which drew out any remaining molasses, resulting in double-refined white loaves of the finest quality. Each level of production reduced the amount of molasses, thereby lightening the colour and reducing the caramel flavour. Today's manufacturing process is quite different: raw sugar is spun in a centrifugal machine that forces out the molasses, rather like a clothes dryer spins out water.

Described variously as "pounded," "sifted," "ground," "rolled," "scraped," or "powdered," hard sugar had to be prepared (see Loaf Sugar), not just scooped out of a bag in ready-to-use granular form. In the 1870s, advances in sugar industrialization increased output and dropped prices, and by the 1890s, ready-to-use granulated sugar had displaced the laborious preparation of loaf sugar at home.[50]

Buckwheat   *Fagopyrum esculentum*, buckwheat, the seeds of which are botanically fruit, not grain, is treated as a grain in cooking and baking. Originally from Asia, it entered Europe in the 1500s, and came to North America with the Dutch, who used it mainly for pancakes, breads, and filler in sausages. Buckwheat may have been "used for bread on the Continent [of Europe]; but ... is not considered of value for that purpose here [England]," said recipe authority Eliza Acton,[51] although buckwheat must have been grown occasionally in the English Midlands since "bockings" (yeast-risen buckwheat griddle cakes) appear in several nineteenth-century English cookbooks. Traill was not familiar with buckwheat before she emigrated, but it was easily cultivated in the northeastern states and Canada, making it a popular staple in the settler pantry. Traill approved highly of buckwheat pancakes, which suggests she must have fed them to her family, and they appear frequently in settlers' and visitors' accounts.

49 Ibid.; Feltoe, *Redpath*, 18–19, 48.
50 Feltoe, *Redpath*, 81.
51 Acton, *The English Bread Book*, 75.

The Christian Guardian of Toronto extolled their virtues: "the buckwheat cake is now firmly enthroned as the staple farinaceous food of all Northern and Western breakfasts," noting that buckwheat was also fed to horses.[52]

Bullace Plum   This old yellow or blue-black variety (*Prunus insititia*) is better for cooking than eating out of hand. Traill requested that their stones be included in the first box of supplies sent from her family in England.[53] They are now rare in Ontario.

Bush beans   Not a specific bean variety, but a generic adjective for any beans that grow on small bushy plants low to the ground. In 1834, Traill mentioned that they had planted a dwarf variety with a bright yellow seed.[54]

Butter   Many a colonial housewife, in both rural and urban households, churned cream into butter regularly, even daily. For many it was too dear to buy often, although its sale to local stores for families (and bachelors) who did not make their own was frequently an important source of income for colonial families. When Traill's *Guide* was written, farmwomen still undertook a lot of butter-making at home, some for their family's use but some for sale to provide part of the family income. By the 1880s in Ontario and elsewhere this skill was beginning to be commercialized through factories run by farmer-businessmen, elbowing out the product produced by skilled women.[55]

It was a source of puzzlement and vexation when churning was unsuccessful: "[T]he churning has bothered her wonderfully. She can't get the butter to come at all," exclaimed Frances Stewart.[56] Similar frustration was expressed by many dairywomen. Anne Langton wrote: "She [Mrs Hoare] makes her butter in the Devonshire fashion, and in winter I think it may be an improvement upon our own way, for we are sadly plagued with the cream getting a bitter taste, which many consider is in consequence of the cold."[57] In summer, housewives did their best to serve butter iced at the table. Many cautioned that salt was best washed out of the butter before

52 *The Christian Guardian*, 15 February 1855, 76.
53 Traill, *Backwoods of Canada*, 107.
54 Ibid., 219.
55 Beavan, *Sketches and Tales*, 79; Derry, "Gender Conflicts in Dairying," 31–47.
56 Stewart to Louisa Stewart, *Revisiting "Our Forest Home,"* 22 November 1866, 218.
57 Anne Langton, *A Gentlewoman in Upper Canada*, 10 June 1840, 286–7.

baking with it, although "Salt butter, if very good, and well washed, makes a fine flaky crust."[58] The "Epping" butter Traill comments on was a particularly famous for its yellow richness [194].

Traill recycled her 1853 "Prize Essay on Butter Making" after winning a prize for it at the annual fair sponsored by the Hamilton Township Agricultural Society, sending it for publication to the *Genesee Farmer*, where it appeared in January 1854, and to the *Canadian Agriculturalist*, which reprinted it in May of the same year.[59]

Buttermilk   Traditionally, this was a thin acidic liquid – rather like skimmed milk – left behind after cream was churned into butter. It is not to be confused with the thick commercial buttermilk available today, which has been treated with bacterial culture to thicken and sour it. In baking, both the old and modern kinds add an attractive light sour taste, suitable for breads or scones. It was also a refreshing drink when served cold.

Traill describes one possible way of draining buttermilk from churned butter [192–3]. As she had said earlier in *The Backwoods of Canada*, buttermilk was not something she had been familiar with before moving to Canada: "in this country most persons adopt the Irish and Scotch method, that of churning the milk, a practice that in our part of England [Suffolk] was not known. For my own part I am inclined to prefer the butter churned from cream, as being most economical, unless you chance to have Irish or Scotch servants who prefer buttermilk to new or sweet skimmed milk."[60] The Irish and Scottish often drank the thin buttermilk, often in the harvest fields, and sometimes thickened it by letting the whey drip out, leaving behind a thicker liquid eaten with sugar.

Butternut, see also Nuts   The nut of the butternut tree (*Juglans cinerea*), native to southern Ontario, is "sweet and pleasant, approximating a walnut." Nonetheless, Traill makes no reference to consuming them. They were used, however, to dye skeins of wool and cloth into a dark brown. And as "a hard fine wood of excellent grain ...

---

58 Abell, *The Skilful Housewife's Guide*, 65; *The Canadian Housewife's Manual of Cookery*, 231.

59 For another good explanation of historical butter-making, see Webster and Parkes, *Encyclopedia of Domestic Economy*, book 7, "Milk, Butter and Cheese," 408–10.

60 Traill, *Backwoods of Canada*, 132.

less liable to crack or warp than many others," butternut was used to line the walls of houses and carved into household objects, such as trenchers.[61]

Cabbage No less than eight varieties of cabbages are mentioned in Traill's *Guide*, indicating its overall importance [58–9]. Early York, a very old standby, and Vanoc (spelled Vannack), an old kind from Sussex and Hampshire, as well as Large Bergen and Portugal are all still available as heirloom seeds. Early York is in Custead's 1827 list and Fleming's 1855 list.[62] In *The Backwoods of Canada,* Traill says savoy cabbages keep well in cellars or root-houses all winter long.[63] Cabbage was fried up in drippings, pickled, and served in salads. The German and Dutch settlers in Waterloo district referred to pickled cabbage as sauerkraut, but the British colonists did not use this term.

Cake, *see also* Cookie, Cup Cake, Gold Cake and Silver Cake, Gingerbread, Johnny Cake, Lady Cake, Plum Cake, Pound Cake, Sponge Cake "Canada is the land of cakes" [110] is an oft-quoted Traill comment. Scottish poets Robert Fergusson and Robbie Burns had declared Scotland to be the Land o' Cakes in 1773 and 1789, something the well-read Traill surely knew. They, however, meant oatcakes, one of Scotland's national dishes, whereas Traill was referring to the many sweet varieties featured on the colonial tea-table, even in the backwoods. Many others commented on "sweet cakes in endless variety." English emigrant John Howison observed that Canadian "buck-wheat, rye, and Indian corn make excellent cakes," but he meant pancakes or griddle cakes.[64]

At the beginning of the nineteenth century, the term "cake" encompassed three basic categories: plum cake (large yeasted or egg-raised fruit breads; also called "great cake"), pound cake (plain butter cakes), and sponge cake (plain cakes made very light by the addition of eggs, yolks and whites beaten separately until very airy; also called biscuit cake and savoy cake). It was also a generic word that covered any sweet, flour-based baked item such as small currant queen cakes, small dropped cakes,

61 Anne Langton, *A Gentlewoman in Upper Canada,* Ellen Langton to William Langton, 28 October 1837, 155; Stewart, *Revisiting "Our Forest Home,"* 15 July 1822, 70.

62 Custead, *Catalogue of Fruit & Ornamental Trees,* 14; Woodhead, *Early Canadian Gardening,* 32; James Fleming, *Catalogue of Garden, Agricultural and Flower Seeds,* 2.

63 Weaver, *Heirloom Vegetable Gardening,* 99, 101, 107; Custead, *Catalogue of Fruit & Ornamental Trees,* 14; Woodhead, *Early Canadian Gardening,* 32; Traill, *Backwoods of Canada,* 219.

64 Haight, *Country Life in Canada,* 14; Howison, *Sketches of Upper Canada,* 256.

shortbreads, and many more. The three Strickland siblings would have grown up understanding this tradition. The colonists had to adjust to the differences in Yankee cakes – the grains, the leavening agents, the textures, and the nomenclature. During the nineteenth century American women developed many other types of cakes that are now familiar to us but were only starting to become known in Traill's time; examples are black cake (fruit cakes with molasses), golden cake (pound cake with extra egg yolks), angel cake (sponge cake with egg whites only), and numerous others.[65]

All the cakes Traill chose for her *Guide* were essentially plain cakes made tastier by a range of accessible flavourings: ginger predominated due to the gingerbreads, but of the twenty-two flavourings she used, singly or combined, caraway seeds, cinnamon, lemon, and nutmeg were used three times or more. None of the cake recipes contain her wording, with the likely exceptions of Bush Cakes and Canadian Croquets. Her selections are all distinctly American and provided for British immigrant women unfamiliar with them. They were measured mostly by volume (cups) rather than weight (pounds), were raised with pearlash, saleratus, or soda rather than yeast or multiple eggs, and moistened with molasses, milk, or sour cream instead of softened butter. They were inexpensive, quick, small, and simple, with few eggs to whisk, and very unlike the fruit-laden, yeasted great cakes of her Suffolk childhood. They were exactly what was needed by busy mothers in the bush who had no domestic staff.

Belying the notion that white sugar was costly and unavailable, her choices are amply sweetened with it, brown sugars being substituted only if necessary, although sometimes molasses was texturally preferable, as in gingerbreads and cornmeal cakes. Her last two cake recipes also reveal an elegant adaptation to scarcity: Canadian Croquets [109] were inexpensive, thinly rolled, egg-rich pastry, cut into shapes and deep-fried, then sprinkled with sugar and Sweet Fruit Cake [109–10] was apple marmalade between two layers of easy-to-make shortcrust.

Canaille Although *canaille* is the French word for rabble or coarse and vulgar people, in the backwoods, it was a corruption of the term canel/cannel and referred to a coarse grade of wheat.

Caraway Seed, *also* Carraway Seed   Originally from the Mediterranean, and naturalized in the British Isles, the umbelliferous caraway plant (*Carum carvi*) grew readily

65 Schmidt, "Cakes," 159–61.

in Canada. In the eighteenth and nineteenth centuries the seeds and tiny dried fruits were so popular in cakes that "seed cake" became a category of its own in Anglo-European baking. They were often used in sweet biscuits, such as Shrewsbury cakes, a type of butter shortbread that appeared in many cookbooks. Traill even suggests that settlers plant caraway so they can sell the seeds [58]. Caraways were not used to flavour bread or cheese in Anglo-Canada, as they were in German and Mennonite communities. Candied caraway seeds, called comfits, were used for sweetening the breath and decorating cakes.

Carrot Traill, via Fleming, names some carrot varieties (*Daucus carota*) that are still grown in the twenty-first century. The Common Early Horn was a Dutch cultivar common in England, Canada, and the northeastern United States, while the Long Orange was developed as a fodder carrot. Custead's 1827 *Catalogue* lists Early Horn and Long Orange, noting that the former has a chunky cylindrical root and the latter a thin taper.[66] Carrots were eaten raw when very young, boiled as a vegetable, or added to soups and stews. Carrot juice was also used as a food colourant.

Catsup Today, we think of catsup or ketchup (also catchup) almost exclusively as a thick tomato condiment for fries, hot dogs, and hamburgers, although its flavour bases and applications were once more varied. Traill's savoury fish and meat recipes call for spoonfuls of flavourful salty and vinegary catsup, either mushroom, walnut, or tomato, once the three most prevalent kinds. Anchovies, oysters, mussels, and fish were also familiar catsup flavours. They were not thick sauces, but thin, usually extracted juices. The English words are derived from *kē-tsiap*, Mandarin for a sauce of fermented soy-beans. Dutch traders brought *kē-tsiap* to Europe, where highly flavoured vinegar and verjuice sauces, pickles, and brines were already common.[67]

Cauliflower The Purple Cape variety (*Brassica oleracea* var. *botrytis*) included in Traill's *Guide* [59] originally came from the South African Cape and was brought first to England from Cyprus in the seventeenth century, and then on to North America

---

66 Weaver, *Heirloom Vegetable Gardening*, 123–4; Woodhead, *Early Canadian Gardening*, 207; James Fleming, *Catalogue of Garden, Agricultural and Flower Seeds*, 2.
67 Smith, "Ketchup," 2:5; Davidson, *Oxford Companion to Food*, 430–1.

as a new introduction in the 1840s. In colour it is "a greenish bronze-purple, shifting to rose."[68]

Cayenne, *also* Red Pepper   Although originally a tropical plant, cayenne was in-cluded in nursery seed lists as suitable for planting in Ontario. It is not actually a pepper but a member of the *Capsicum* family (which includes chilies and bell pep-pers). It was employed both fresh and ground (after being dried and pulverized to a powder), and Traill's recipes do not always make it clear which is intended. Cayenne is particularly suited for use with cooked tomatoes, which is how she uses it most [137, 138]. "This powerful spice has become a necessary article at table," said Webster and Parkes.[69] Cayenne lozenges were thought to be good for sore throats.[70]

Celery   Traill quotes a Fleming passage about celery, but eliminates this sentence: "It requires considerable attention to grow it to perfection."[71] Since successful celery plants require considerable care and water, eliminating the sentence was a curious decision. Celery was generally used to flavour soups and stew dishes and only oc-casionally eaten raw; after Traill's time a solid-stalked variety suitable for eating raw and in salads was propagated. By the end of the century, this variety was being served at the dinner tables of the well-to-do in cut-glass vases. Today, heritage varieties of celery, more flavourful than mass-produced varieties, continue to make excellent additions to soups and stews.[72]

Cheeses, *see also* Cheshire Cheese, Cream Cheese, Gloucester Cheese, Rennet, Wiltshire Cheese   In nineteenth-century Canada, cheese was made largely of cow's milk, rather than sheep's or goat's. Sheep were kept primarily for their wool and to provide some meat. A single cow or two produced enough milk for a small family, but once farm families started to expand and become prosperous, they could main-tain a herd of cows that produced enough milk to make butter and cheese, both for

68 Weaver, *Heirloom Vegetable Gardening*, 114–16.
69 Webster and Parkes, *Encyclopedia of Domestic Economy*, 521. See also Custead, *Catalogue of Fruit & Ornamental Trees*, 15; Woodhead, *Early Canadian Gardening*, 33.
70 Moodie, *Flora Lyndsay*, 101.
71 James Fleming, *Catalogue of Garden, Agricultural and Flower Seeds*, 2, 63; Weaver, *Heirloom Vege-table Gardening*, 127–30; Woodhead, *Early Canadian Gardening*, 203.
72 Webster and Parkes, *Encyclopedia of Domestic Economy*, 487.

their own needs and to sell at market. Keep in mind that Traill's simple farm cheeses were all made from raw, unpasteurized milk. Traill was proud of her cheese-making and butter-making skills, which she probably learned as a youth in Suffolk. Cheese-making was an ancient female skill that was eventually taken over by men working in factories, starting in the 1860s and accelerating in the 1880s, after the *Guide* was published. Interestingly, for her proposed republication she intended to write "Something about the Cheese Factories," according to a handwritten note.[73]

By the end of the eighteenth century, cheeses identified by their geographical name were being transported around Great Britain rather than remaining local and some of them gained excellent reputations.[74] We can conjecture that the Strickland siblings had tasted a number of these before leaving England. English cheddar and French gruyere, popular then as now, were also imported into Canada.

Cheese was consumed in sandwiches, as an accompaniment to puddings and pies, as a custardy cheesecake, and on its own with pickles, much as we still consume it today. One diarist said that, after a meal of fried pork with onions and mashed potatoes, "a nice cup of tea and a nice apple pudding with some good cheese concluded our meal," although unfortunately she does not specify which kind of cheese.[75]

Cherry, *see also* Chokecherry   Orchards of cherry and peach were first planted in the Niagara region in the mid-1790s and soon flourished. They were planted in the eastern parts of Upper Canada as well, but Traill herself seems to have had minimal experience with cherry cultivation. Besides being a dessert as fresh fruit for a brief season, cherries were put into whisky and brandy and were the basis of cordials.

Cheshire Cheese   Cheshire cheese is thought to be Britain's oldest surviving named cheese. It is made from whole milk, including all the cream. Shaped into a drum typically weighing 30 kg (70 lb), it has a crumbly texture, mild flavour, and a rich orange colour from annatto or marigolds.[76] Its well-known size was used as a visual reference in *The Backwoods of Canada* when Traill relates the story of building her house with the help of sixteen neighbours: "Some huge joints of salt pork, a peck of potatoes,

---

73 Traill Family Collection, circa 1880?, 6218.
74 Dalby, *Cheese*, 76, 95; Paston-Williams, *The Art of Dining*, 217.
75 Armstrong, *Seven Eggs Today*, 9 March 1859, 112.
76 Dalby, *Cheese*, 35; Davidson, *Oxford Companion to Food*, 164; Webster and Parkes, *Encyclopedia of Domestic Economy*, 411.

with rice-pudding, and a loaf as big as an enormous Cheshire cheese, formed the feast that was to regale them during the raising."[77] It was already arriving in Halifax by the 1750s.[78] Cheshire is a county in North West England.

Chicken Traill lists seven breeds of chicken living on early Canadian farms [201]. They all laid different size and colours of eggs, and had very different feathers. Although the word "chicken" was and still is used loosely and collectively, it actually refers to male birds up to three months old, after which they are called roosters, and females up to four months old, when they start laying eggs and are called hens. By far the most common breed was the Cochin-China, which Moodie describes as "stately" when she saw them as part of a display of "improved and foreign breeds of poultry" at the Provincial Agricultural Show in Toronto circa 1850.[79]

Chive These appear only once in the *Guide*, in fish soup [167], but were very useful as pot-herbs. *Allium schoenoprasum* is a widespread native of the northern hemisphere.

Chokecherry These are late summer berries, which turn from scarlet to black when ripe, from a shrub (*Prunus virginiana*) that is widespread in North America. Seldom eaten raw because the berry is so "astringent that it causes a painful contraction of the throat if many berries are eaten at the same time," as Traill said in her *Studies of Plant Life in Canada*, chokecherries can be successfully combined with sweeter berries and/or sugar to make nice jellies. Traill did not include all her culinary knowledge in her *Guide*; in *Studies of Plant Life in Canada* she continues: "The leaves also have a pleasant aromatic, bitter flavor like those of the peach and almond, and form a good flavoring, resembling ratafia; when boiled in milk for puddings and custards one or two are sufficient, and may be removed when the milk has boiled. This flavoring is harmless and pleasant and easily obtained."[80]

Wild cherries of all kinds, and their barks and roots, had multiple medical applications, both for the First Peoples and the settlers, and were used particularly for ague, fever, cough, and diarrhea.[81]

---

77 Traill, *Backwoods of Canada*, 114.
78 *Halifax Gazette*, 1752.
79 Moodie, *Life in the Clearings*, 287; Webster and Parkes, *Encyclopedia of Domestic Economy*, 416.
80 Traill, *Studies of Plant Life in Canada*, 119.
81 Erichsen-Brown, *Use of Plants*, 159–62.

Chowder   Usually "a dish composed of fish, pork, onions, biscuit, etc. stewed together."[82] Traill misunderstood this, describing it as a dish of potatoes and fish mashed together, then browned [131]. She probably got this idea from one of the many magazines circulating at the time. In 1793, Lady Simcoe had twice happily eaten a "chouder" of salt pork, fish, potatoes, onions, and pulverized crackers at a picnic with visitors.[83] The word chowder is thought to be derived from *chaudière*, meaning pot in Breton, spread by sailors from Brittany to the Newfoundland Banks and New England coast.

Churn   Butter makers need to agitate the cream to extract its butterfat content and that was the purpose of a household churn. By the early twentieth century, commercial butter operations were taking over this female domestic task. Most churns were small barrels with a dasher inside (a rod with an X-shaped wood attachment at the bottom end), although inventive farmers designed others.

Cider   All apples can be juiced for cider, but the old English Pearmain, which Traill lists as both a summer and winter type, were considered best.[84] Fermented apple juice, called hard cider, contained alcohol and could be further soured into vinegar. Casks of cider were stored in the cold cellar. A small cider mill was a common piece of agricultural equipment for farms.

Cinnamon   The most popular spice in nineteenth-century Anglo-American foods was the fragrant cinnamon bark (*Cinnamomum verum*), imported from Ceylon (now Sri Lanka). It had to be pounded in a mortar and pestle and then finely sifted. Cassia is inferior cinnamon.

Citron   In old colonial recipes that called for citron or candied citron, it was frequently unclear whether the reference was to the citrus fruit (*Citrus medica*) or to one of the many common red-, yellow-, or white-fleshed watermelons (*Citrullus lanatus*) from Africa, whose smooth thick rinds candied very well. There is also a green citron muskmelon (*Cucumis melo* var. *reticulatus*; also confusingly sometimes called citron melon), but its rough rind is not suitable for candying.

---

82 Ward, *Grocer's Hand-Book and Directory*, 39.
83 Simcoe, *The Diary of Mrs. John Graves Simcoe*, 26 June 1793, 172, and 29 September 1793, 203.
84 Woodhead, *Early Canadian Gardening*, 59.

One of the earliest Asian *citrus* introduced to Europe, citrons have sweet greenish-yellow flesh but were primarily grown for their thick peels, which were candied for cake decoration and confectionary. The African *melon* flourished in American gardens and as early as the late eighteenth century its candied rind was being substituted for the expensive imported citrus citron. A recipe for "The American Citron" appeared in *American Cookery* (1796), the first published North American cookbook to use indigenous fruits and vegetables.

Citron melons/citron watermelons (*C. lanatus* var. *citroides*) grow well in southern Ontario and, because they keep very well in dry-cold cellars late into the winter, were often eaten after a little cooking to soften their flesh. Although the flesh was firm enough for pies, similar to firm cooking apples, citron melons do not appear to have been much used for this purpose in Ontario, even in the winter, despite being called pie melon in the southern US. They were, however, made into marmalade and various sweet condiments.[85]

Clove *Syzygium aromaticum*, the unopened flower buds of an evergreen tree indigenous to the Molucca (Spice) Islands, have been imported into Europe since the Middle Ages. They are dried and smoked to a dark brown colour.[86] Cloves were recognized early as a versatile spice for broths, gravies, meat and fish soups, fruit preserves, and cakes. Traill's recipes for pickled ham and beef [155, 157], venison fricassee and pie [158–9], potted fish [168], tomato catsup [138], and preserved melons [136] demonstrated this versatility.

Cocoa Traill does not refer to cocoa or chocolate, but Vere Foster included it in the list of rations that could be supplied to emigrants on board ship. In the early 1850s, when Traill was compiling her *Guide*, cocoa preparation was time-consuming and consisted of scraping

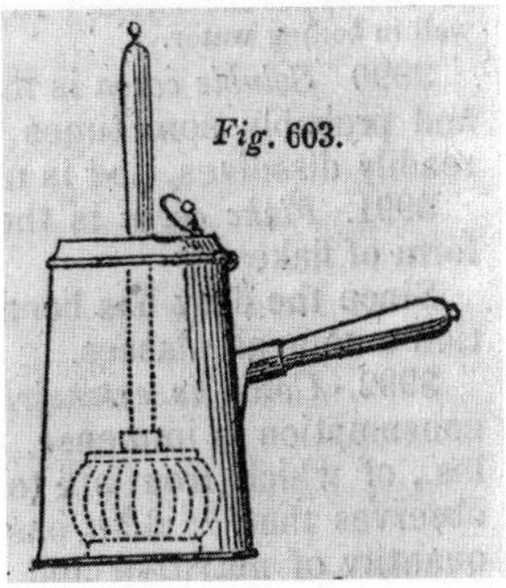

Fig. 603.

Fig. 26 · Chocolate (cocoa) pot. This cross-section shows the mouliquet that was used to blend the chocolate so the cocoa butter wouldn't separate.

---

85 Weaver, *Heirloom Vegetable Gardening*, 379–81; James Fleming, *Catalogue of Garden, Agricultural and Flower Seeds*, 2. Also an email from Bob Wildfong, executive director, Seeds of Diversity, 30 June 2016, who notes that citron melons seem poorly documented in Ontario.

86 Webster and Parkes, *Encyclopedia of Domestic Economy*, 522.

the cake of hard chocolate, gently melting the gritty powder, boiling it, and then milling it, that is, twirling it with a special stick called a mouliquet to make it smooth and ensure that the cocoa butter didn't separate into a greasy layer on top. Historical cocoa is not to be confused with modern fatless cocoa powder which, when combined with hot milk or water, becomes our familiar hot beverage or when blended into a batter renders it brown and chocolatey.[87]

Cod   Ocean cod, particularly as salt cod, was a major foodstuff and economic driver in Europe, North America, and the Caribbean for centuries, even before Europeans settled the Americas. Fresh cod was available in the towns of Canada East and West for those who could afford it, which probably did not include the Traills.

Coffee, *see also* Dandelion Coffee   Green coffee beans could be roasted in a small roaster over an open fire. Roasted coffee beans could be purchased whole, so coffee grinders were screwed to the wall or sat on many a kitchen sideboard and tavern table in Canada. The Stewarts brought a coffee mill in their luggage when they arrived in 1823 but found themselves using it to grind wheat into flour each evening for the next day. Some people pronounced coffee prepared in Upper Canada "vile," but others, like Susanna Moodie, loved coffee with "plenty of trimmings ... good sugar and sweet cream."[88]

Cookie, *see also* Biscuit, Cake   Although only one recipe is identified as a cookie in the *Guide*, Traill includes three others that were already being classed as cookies in other cookbooks – Excellent Gingerbread [106], Drop Sweet-cakes [107], and Common Bush Tea-cakes [109]. Sweet cake, small cake, sweet biscuit, and tea cake were all terms used interchangeably for what colonial New Yorkers in their vernacular culinary speech had begun to identify as cookies in the mid-seventeenth century, an anglicization of their Dutch neighbours' word "koekje." According to the Scottish culinary authority, F. Marian McNeill, this use was not related to the Scottish word "cookie" derived from "cukie," which was a traditional yeast-risen bun served with jam and cream like a scone. North American cookies didn't have yeast, although they might have a chemical leavener, as two of Traill's recipes do. "Cookie," now a quintessential American word, would have been new to a lot of Traill's original readers.

87   Ibid., 717; Grivetti and Shapiro, *Chocolate*, 129–31; Lane, *Jane Austen and Food*, 30.
88   Lewis, *From Dublin to Douro*, 9; Moodie, *Roughing It in the Bush*, 264.

It first appeared in print in 1786, and the first recipe for a cookie was in *American Cookery* of 1796.[89]

Oatmeal cookies are often erroneously associated with pioneer Canada. Although earlier recipes in periodicals may await discovery, the first known recipe for oatmeal cookies appeared in the 1892 Canadian *Galt Cook Book,* compiled by the Ladies Aid Society of the Central Presbyterian Church, whose congregation had a strong Scottish element. The result appears to bridge the transition from the sugarless oatcakes of Scotland to oatmeal cookies.[90] The first American recipe came four years later in Fannie Farmer's *Boston Cooking-School Cook-Book.*[91]

Cooking Equipment, *see also* Bachelor's Oven, Bake-kettle, Beetle, Bladder, Churn, Fish Kettle, Kneading Trough, Milk Dish, Oven, Pudding Cloth, Stove, Sugar-kettle, Tundish   Traill was writing for women who had a range of culinary skills and kitchen equipment, domestic abilities, and household supplies. When it comes to cooking technology, the *Guide* dealt with both the old hearth fireplace and the new iron cookstove. Traill herself had experience with both in her various homes so the recipes often refer to both fire and stove. The other cooks who provided recipes were also dealing with this change – some recipes assume the cook has a hearth and bake-kettle only, while others assume a stove. Another important point, although she did not address it, was how cooking fuels differed in Canada and Great Britain: in the old country, fuel was coal, peat, gorse or furze, or bundles of twigs and sticks called faggots which were put into small closed iron grates or hobs, whereas the great forests of the Americas supplied endless stacks of wood logs for open fireplaces and, eventually, cookstoves.

We in the early twenty-first century are so accustomed to stainless steel and plastics of all sorts in the kitchen, along with some wood, that we forget that tin, iron, brass, bronze, copper, pewter, and silver, as well as the all-important woods and ceramics, were once common materials for kitchenware. Settlers brought little equipment with them, so had to buy it at great cost or make it themselves. A lot of young housewives started out with minimal equipment. In a detailed inventory of the contents of her bridal home, Sarah Hallen Drinkwater reports that her kitchen held: "rough shelves, a

89 McNeill, *The Scots Kitchen,* 231; Davidson, *Oxford Companion to Food,* 212, 214; Smith, *Oxford Encyclopedia of Food and Drink in America,* 1:317–18; Simmons, *The First American Cookbook,* xvi–xvii.

90 Driver, *Culinary Landmarks,* 376–80; Driver, personal communication, April 2016.

91 Farmer, *Boston Cooking-School Cook Book,* 406.

carpenter's bench for a table and five spare barrels, a clock (a treasure), two iron pots, one kettle, a saucepan to hold about a pint, a large iron spoon, one dozen knives and forks, four German silver teaspoons, six teaspoons, two German silver candlesticks, snuffers and a tray [for the candles], a black tin teapot, one dozen teacups and saucers, seaweed pattern blue and white, half dozen small plates, four dishes, two pie dishes, soup tureen, two vegetable dishes, half dozen tumblers [water glasses], two salt sellers [*sic*], two water jugs, cream jug."[92]

Sarah was lucky to have so much in the beginning. But she does not include a gridiron for the iron pots, an iron ash rake, a butter churn, crocks to store her vinegar, a bowl to mix her batters, and so on. Either her inventory was incomplete or she acquired such necessities in later weeks. After she acquired a cookstove, she would have required flat-bottomed iron pots and pans to sit on its flat cooking surface; the price of many cookstoves included such basic equipment.

Cooking Fats, *see also* Drippings, Lard, Shortening, Suet   Today we tend to choose cooking oils (safflower, sunflower, corn, and canola) instead of fats for frying, with the ongoing exception of butter. Italian and Spanish olive oil was imported and used in small quantities, but is not cited by Traill in any of her writings, nor is clarified butter, once commonly used in high-quality cookery in the eighteenth- and nineteenth-centuries.

We tend to forget that our predecessors found uses for all sorts of items we routinely discard. Leftover fats, drippings, and grease were kept in refuse containers, ready to be combined with ash lye and converted to soap. Even the fat that rises to the surface when meat boils in water could be strained and thrown into the grease storage. Some fats were rendered into tallow. Melted, carefully strained of impurities (blood vessels, connective tissues), and cooled, tallow developed a soft buttery texture that never resolidifies and was thus ready to be combined with scents to make into face creams, shaving creams, and lip balms, or remelted and poured into candle moulds [178]. A well-fed pig could yield a lot of fat for such household and culinary uses: "Father killed ten fat hogs ... [s]ome of them were four inches thick in fat."[93] Anna Leveridge received a much welcomed thank you gift of forty pounds of dripping early in 1885.[94]

92 Sarah Hallen Drinkwater, October 1840, quoted in Hoffman and Taylor, *Across the Waters*, 218.
93 Deborah Mullett, 21 January 1825, quoted in Hoffman and Taylor, *Across the Waters*, 307.
94 Tivy, *Your Loving Anna*, 68.

Corn, see Indian Corn

Cornstarch   The first Canadian cornstarch production facility opened in 1858 in Edwardsburg, Canada West (now Cardinal, Ontario).[95] Traill twice says that American-made cornstarch was best used for starching (stiffening) cotton and linen [132, 126], but she also approved of it as a basis of delicate puddings, much liked by people who were accustomed to heavy suet and flour puddings. Today, cornstarch is notorious for over-stiffening moulded puddings and over-thickening sauces and gravies, but if not too generously used and not overcooked, the results are delicate, as Traill notes.

Cracker, see Biscuits and Crackers

Cranberry   The crimson acidic berries of two types of unrelated evergreen shrubs, both common in southern Ontario: the low-bush, small or marsh cranberry (*Vaccinium oycoccus*) and the high-bush cranberry (*Viburnum opulus*). Botanically, the brightly translucent fruit of the latter is not a true cranberry, despite its visual similarity. As Traill herself writes later, "The name Cranberry has been improperly applied to Viburnum Opulus, as it has no affinity with the low creeping Marsh Cranberry."[96] It was, however, delicious: "my husband soon stripped the boughs of their tempting treasure, and I, delighted with my prize, hastened home, and boiled the fruit with some [maple] sugar, to eat at tea with our cakes. I never ate anything more delicious."[97] High-bush cranberry, a European guelder rose, was introduced as an ornamental bush and eventually naturalized, becoming known as the American guelder rose. Traill suggests that the First Peoples used them medicinally and gives one recipe each for a sauce and a jelly [87, 88].[98] "The low-bush cranberries are brought in great quantities by the Indians to the towns and villages. They form a standing preserve on the tea-tables in most of the settlers' houses," she noted.[99] They were also known for their medicinal properties, especially as a tea for easing stomach and leg cramps. Preserved cranberries, of both types, were once a popular topping for hot cakes and an accompaniment to bread and butter, and form "an excellent sauce for

95   Driver, *Culinary Landmarks*, 114.
96   Traill, *Studies of Plant Life in Canada*, 140.
97   Traill, *Backwoods of Canada*, 105.
98   Soper, Heimburger, and Garay, *Shrubs of Ontario*, 471.
99   Traill, *Backwoods of Canada*, 106.

roasted venison or mutton," although Traill does not make the connection between turkey and cranberry sauce, already familiar to many eastern North Americans.[100]

In *Canadian Wild Flowers* she adds, "So much in request as Cranberries are for household use, it seems strange that no enterprising person has yet undertaken to supply the markets of Canada" even though "this fruit is successfully cultivated for market in many parts of the Northern States of America,"[101] an observation she repeated almost twenty years later in *Studies of Plant Life in Canada*.[102] Since then, cranberry marshes have been successfully cultivated in Ontario.

Cream Cheese   Traill's cream cheese was made of cream, but other cream cheeses were made of rich milk. All of them, however, were intended for quick consumption without maturation. They were generally made in August and September, when the cream or milk was at its richest. Some commentators pointed out that they were not, therefore, true cheeses, but "nothing more than cream dried sufficiently to be cut with a knife."[103]

Cream of Tartar, see also Leavening Agents   Refined potassium tartrate or bitartrate (the principal acid in grape juice) is the substance that remains at the bottom of the barrel after fermented wine is siphoned off. It was purified into a white crystalline powder that was used for a number of household tasks, such as cleaning leather, and when combined with various acidic carbonates became an element in commercial baking powders.

Croquets, see also Fritters   In French cuisine, croquettes are mixtures of finely minced and highly flavoured meat, fish, vegetable, or potato that are shaped into small balls (or cylinders, triangles, squares), often coated in breadcrumbs, and deep-fried until crisp. "*Croquer*" means to crunch. Very occasionally there were sweet versions. Croquets became fashionable in English cooking in the mid-eighteenth century. Traill's "Canadian Croquets" had no filling and no breadcrumbs, but were deep-fried pieces of thin dough on which sugar was sprinkled – more like wafers actually.

100 Traill, *Studies of Plant Life in Canada*, 140.
101 Traill, *Canadian Wild Flowers*, 51.
102 Traill, *Studies of Plant Life in Canada*, 129–30.
103 Webster and Parkes, *Encyclopedia of Domestic Economy*, 413.

It is fun to make these in all sorts of shapes with children, and also fun to think about Traill providing these simple sweet treats for her youngsters.

Crushed Sugar   This "inferior sort of loaf sugar" [73] could be used as is or clarified by boiling with egg whites to attract the impurities, which became scum and sediment and were discarded. Cookbooks often gave instructions on how to accomplish this successfully. It was also called granulated sugar or powdered sugar.

Cucumber   We think of cucumbers as the long thin-skinned English or short tender field varieties for eating raw and in salads, but if certain cucumbers (*Cucumis sativus*) are allowed to grow large, until they begin to turn yellow, they can be cooked like squash, a familiar way to serve them until the mid-nineteenth century. Traill writes about cultivating them but not about actually consuming them.

Cup Cake, *see also* Pound Cake   Of plain Cup Cake, Traill states: "This is a regular American cake" [108]. Said the influential Mrs Child: "Cup cake is about as good as pound cake, and cheaper."[104] These were plain cakes made in little cups (sometimes literally teacups), which were sometimes lined with paper – the predecessor to the decorative icing-laden treats that became all the rage in the early twenty-first century. Traill's recipe is taken without attribution from Mrs Child's in *The American Frugal Housewife*.

Currant, Black and Red, *see also* Currant, Zante   Berries within the large Ribes family, which includes gooseberries. Wild black currants (*Ribes nigrum*, although Traill identifies them as *Ribes floridum*) and red currants (*R. rubrum*) grew abundantly in the Ontario wilderness, but once cultivated they lost some of their sourness. Though considering the plant "more ornamental than useful," Traill liked black currants for jams, jellies, and adding to puddings. The black "is used extensively as a preserve." She was less approving of the red: "In its wild state the fruit is small, very acid, and not unpalatable or unwholesome, but has a flavor of the astringent bark."[105] Thomas Macgrath bluntly said they were sour.[106] Traill makes no comment on white

104   Child, *The American Frugal Housewife*, 71.
105   Traill, *Studies of Plant Life in Canada*, 117.
106   Magrath and Radcliff, *Authentic Letters from Upper Canada*, 27 July 1832, 58.

currants. European currants were brought to North America in the seventeenth century, and Traill recommends that their seeds be brought by emigrants [81].

Currants were also the basis of wines and cordials. "In all the farmhouses here they still follow the old custom of making wine, mostly from Currants and Raspberry."[107] Indeed, there was a Currant Cordial in the Traill papers.[108]

Currant, Zante, *see also* Currant, Black and Red   Also called black Corinths, the Zante currant was a small, black, seedless type of raisin originating in Greece and grown throughout the eastern Mediterranean. Used similarly to raisins, they were immensely popular in cakes and suet puddings before seedless raisins were cultivated and were therefore imported into Canada in vast quantities. The distinction between the wild black currant berries of Europe and Canada (*Ribes nigrum*) and the dried grape also called a currant (*Vitis vinifera*) is made clear in Traill's statement: "Many people use the dried fruit of currants or huckleberries as a substitute, in cakes and puddings, for the Zante currants" [84]. They were tightly packed in casks for transport, so had to be dug out with a strong instrument when purchased.[109]

Dairy Foods, *see also* Butter, Buttermilk, Cheeses, Iced Creams, Milk   Traill's section on the dairy suggests that even ill-equipped farms could manage to produce basic cheeses with a few loose-weave baskets, some cloths, and a press. She warns about allowing cows to roam freely in the forests – not an English practice – which often led to lost cows or cows who ate greens that tainted the milk with unpleasant flavours. Traill and frugal housewives like her were not lavish in their use of milk and butter, but they did take pride in the quality available. "Women's duties in this country include the management of the dairy, etc." said Anne Langton in the journal she wrote for her family.[110] Quite a few established farms had an outbuilding specifically for dairying – "a little bark-lined recess adjoining the house" was one description.[111] Traill's simple description of a good dairy room [191–2] recalls the cool and commodious ones of her childhood.[112]

---

107 Erichsen-Brown, *Use of Plants*, 131.
108 Traill Family Collection, 4(22): unpaginated (#41).
109 Webster and Parkes, *Encyclopedia of Domestic Economy*, 507.
110 Anne Langton, *A Gentlewoman in Upper Canada*, 10 June, 1840, 286.
111 Beavan, *Sketches and Tales*, 30.
112 Anne Langton, *A Gentlewoman in Upper Canada*, 10 June, 1840, 286.

Damper   An Australian term for unleavened white bread baked directly in the ashes, similar to the ashcakes of North America. One of the three items in the most primitive colonial cooking in the outback – damper, salt meat, and hot tea – it eventually became part of the Australian culinary identity.[113] This reference to an Australian foodstuff shows that Traill was continuing her education through newspapers.

Damson Plum   This small, dark purple plum (*Prunus damascena*) was native to Syria, but transplanted easily to Europe and then to Canada. In England it grew wild in the hedgerows.[114] Traill first requested the stones be sent to her in 1833 and then in 1854 recommends it as one of the English stone fruits that emigrants should carry in their baggage [80]. The damson is best suited for jam. Today, farmers' markets often have baskets of them in early autumn.

Dandelion   *Taraxacum officinale* came as seeds from Europe and naturalized rapidly in North America. The leaves were eaten as salad and the roots roasted as a coffee substitute [142]. Susanna Moodie writes that the boiled green tops were fermented with hops into beer.[115]

Dandelion Coffee   Roasted dandelion and chicory roots used as successful coffee substitutes figure in many colonial accounts. Traill borrowed Moodie's directions for dandelion coffee, which Moodie had discovered in an article by a Dr Harrison of Edinburgh in the New York *Albion* in 1832. Moodie, who loved coffee, published her recipe and a short commentary in *The Victoria Magazine* in September 1847 and later in *Roughing It in the Bush* with the ringing endorsement that it was "equal in substance and flavour to the best Mocha coffee."[116] Although Traill includes a fairly lengthy paraphrase of her sister's instructions, she avoids making the same claims about the excellence of the result and suggests that her own attempts were not as successful as her sister's [142]. However even Harriet King, ever the complainer, conceded that "chicory or dandelion ...with a little sugar and milk, is tolerably nice."[117]

---

113 Symons, *One Continous Picnic*, 30, 44, 159.
114 Davidson, *Oxford Companion to Food*, 242.
115 Moodie, *Roughing It in the Bush*, 355.
116 *The Victoria Magazine*, September 1847, 1:22; Moodie, *Roughing It in the Bush*, 353–5; Hutchens, *Indian Herbology of North America*, 110.
117 King, *Letters from Muskoka*, 40.

Today, packages of roasted dandelion roots are available as a caffeine-free coffee substitute in some health food shops.

Diet Drink   An old term for any medicinal beverage, such as "medicated wines, ales, meads, and wheys," often prescribed by doctors.[118] Recipes abounded in published and manuscript cookbooks.

Distiller's Yeast   Just as beer and wine need yeast to ferment, so too does hard liquor such as whisky. At the time Traill was writing, most distilleries in Canada were small operations run by flour millers,[119] and they sometime sold their yeast, which had a reputation for being weak, as Traill also implies [92]. "Many people are not aware of the difference between brewer's and other yests [*sic*], such as distiller's. A wedding day was set; to make a wedding cake the recipe book said, 'take one pint of yest,' when unluckily brewer's was used; the cake was spoiled and the wedding postponed."[120] Either this distiller's yeast was considerably weaker than a brewer's yeast or the brewer's yeast was so lively, it caused this wedding cake to rise too much! The next paragraph confirms this: "Half a teacupful of brewer's yeast is as much in effect as a pint or even a quart of distiller's."[121]

Dripping(s)   Flavourful leftover bits of fat and oil from frying salt pork, bacon, and ham were still useable as fat in pastry dough or cake batter if pure butter or lard were unavailable. Despite an unfair reputation for being used only by lazy and poor housewives, and certainly more homely than butter or lard, drippings were much used in cooking by all classes. Unlike today's kitchens, a pot of drippings stood by the hearth or cookstove, ready to be spooned into a frying pan; the dregs were often returned to the pot.

Drippings were also essential in soap making and leftover fats were thrown into crocks or barrels for eventual conversion into soaps or candles.

Duck, *see also* Wild Duck   "Ducks require great care in this country, the winter does not suit them, but we intend to make the experiment" with a newly purchased flock

---

118 Quincy, *Pharmacopoeia Officinalis & Extemporanea*, 534.
119 Heron, *Booze*, 20–2; Gruber, "Whiskey," 2:608.
120 *The Cook Not Mad*, number 265.
121 Ibid.

of ducklings,[122] wrote Anne Langton. The Traills seem to have raised duck flocks on several occasions.

Dutch Oven, *see* Bake-kettle

Eel   Although a mostly unfamiliar fish today, eel was once common and popular in daily family meals. The Moodies ate eel pies on several occasions. While on a camping trip north of Peterborough, Sandford Fleming and his companions ate "stewed duck & eels & fresh bread for breakfast."[123] Eel was also caught in winter through a hole in the ice.

Eggs   Traill is not overly generous in the quantities of eggs in her recipes, but since she raised chickens, ducks, and geese, she must have had plenty. A prime concern was preservation. Advice about preserving eggs in all manner of ways for when the chickens were not laying was a common entry in recipe books. The key was to prevent oxygen passing through the shell, which dries out the egg inside. "To preserve eggs, take butter without salt [some said to use suet instead of butter], and rub the shell with it to prevent the salt soaking through; then lay them down in layers of salt. Or make a solution of gum-arabic and immerse the eggs in it; lay them separately on basket-lids to dry. Set them on the shelf overhead in the cellar," instructed the anonymous author of *The Frugal Housewife's Manual*. Or they could be kept in salted unslaked lime water,[124] or just salt, small end pointing down. There were any number of ingenious ways to lengthen the shelf life of eggs before refrigeration made it easy.

Candling was a technique to determine freshness – "To ascertain if they are good and fresh, 'candle them;' hold them upright between the thumb and fore-finger before a candle by which means you will be enabled to detect any spots that may be in them; if a few white spots only, they will do for puddings, &c,; if a black one, it is bad. If light and transparent, they are fresh."[125]

Endive   Today, we think of endive (*Cichorium endiva*) not as a vegetable but as a salad leaf.

122   Anne Langton, *A Gentlewoman in Upper Canada,* 9 June 1840, 286.
123   Sandford Fleming, *Sir Sandford Fleming,* 25 September 1851, 201.
124   A.B. of Grimsby, *The Frugal Housewife's Manual,* 20; Abell, *The Skilful Housewife's Guide,* 11; Child, *The American Frugal Housewife,* 11. For lime water, see Lime.
125   *The Canadian Housewife's Manual of Cookery,* 158.

Eschalot   A mild-tasting member of the *Allium* genus, "Eschalotts are now [1707] from France [and have] become an English plant."[126] By the 1820s, perhaps earlier, they had become a Canadian plant too. Shallot (*A. cepa* var. *aggregatum*) is now the current term; they are related to leeks and chives. Both of Traill's tomato sauce recipes include some eschalot [138].

Fine Sugar, *see* Loaf Sugar

Fish, *see also* Bass, Cod, Eel, Herring, Masquinonge, Perch, Salmon, Whitefish   In Traill's part of Canada West, fish of the "finest quality" [165] were abundant in the waters of Rice Lake, Sturgeon Lake, Stoney Lake, Lake Katchewanook, and the Otonobee River. On one camping trip on Stoney Lake in October 1849, the Strickland men caught thirty-four salmon trout, eight masquinonge, and several large lake bass, which together weighed 437 pounds. Presumably they preserved them; vast quantities of fish were dried, pickled, or smoked, as well as eaten fresh. The Young family "was never without the finest fish, which they all knew how to spear in the lakes – white fish, salmon, trouts, and bass, which were either dried after the Indian fashion, and exposed to a few hour's smoke in the chimney, or pickled if they could not dispose of them fresh."[127] Fish was one of the wild commodities most bartered by the First Peoples in exchange for such products as white flour and salt pork. The colonists were fascinated by the First Peoples' methods of winter ice-fishing and summer spear-fishing and described them many times.

Fishing from shore or a rowboat was socially acceptable for women: "The great charm of a new settlement to young men is the abundance of hunting, shooting and fishing; the latter alone of which women can enjoy."[128] Susanna Moodie and Catharine Parr Traill enjoyed fishing. Catharine's favourite book was Izaak Walton's *The Compleat Angler* (1653) because she had learned to fish and prepare tackle as a child with her father, who introduced the book to her.[129]

Barrels (called hogsheads) of fresh, salted, and pickled oysters and lobsters were shipped from the Atlantic coast to the dinner plates of affluent customers in towns.

126 *Oxford English Dictionary*, 5:387, quote from a 1707 husbandry book.
127 Traill, "The Mill of the Rapids," in *Forest and Other Gleanings*, 62–3.
128 Samuel Strickland, *Twenty-Seven Years in Canada West*, 2:198.
129 Traill, *Pearls and Pebbles*, 156.

They certainly did not appear in the backwoods, so there is no reference to them in the *Guide*.

Fish Kettle Although likely familiar with this sophisticated piece of kitchen equipment, Traill is unlikely to have had one in Canada. It was an oblong copper pan with an interior perforated tray fitted with handles on which the fish would be laid to poach before being pulled up to allow the excess poaching liquid to drip off.

Fricassees and Hashes, see also Soups and Stews Although fricassees and hashes have largely disappeared from home cooking in Ontario, they were once regular dishes on the farm because they were quickly prepared and hard to spoil, allowing the farm wife to take on other tasks while they cooked. A fricassee contains small pieces of fried meat – venison, rabbit, or black squirrel are Traill's suggestions [158, 162] – that are then gently simmered in a flavourful gravy. A hash is minced meat simmered in the same way.

Fritter, see also Croquet These are small balls or patties of battered fruits or vegetables, sometimes seafood, which are deep-fried. The ingredients can be chopped (as in Traill's Green Corn Fritters [122]) or whole, as in apple slices or clams. Fritters made of all sorts of ingredients appear in a multitude of cuisines.

Fruits, see also Apple; Berries, Wild; Currant, Black and Red; Currant, Zante; Grape, Cultivated; Grape, Wild; Hawthorn; Lemon; May-apple; Medlar; Melons; Peach; Pear; Plum; Quince; Raisin; Rhubarb It was recognized early that stone-fruit trees (apricot, cherry, nectarine, peach, plum) thrived in the Niagara area of Ontario (as well as in the Detroit, Michigan, area) and could be transported to other parts of the colony and also to Quebec. The Peterborough area also had wonderful orchards, despite a lack of peaches. Based on his own success, Sam Strickland advised "the emigrant, who becomes an agriculturalist, to pay great attention to orchard planting, and indeed, to devote a portion of his first-cleared fallow for that purpose ... I do not know any thing that gives a greater air of comfort to a farm, than a well-loaded orchard."[130] Nurserymen made a point of providing a remarkably extensive range of fruit trees for these orchards.

---

130 Samuel Strickland, *Twenty-Seven Years in Canada West*, 1:205.

Kitchen gardens were so critical to the family endeavor that all members of the family participated in their maintenance, from seed to harvest. Wild berries were transferred to such gardens for cultivation. Many fruits were preserved in maple molasses and sugar molasses. Some people loved this, while others thought they "shall get used [to the flavour] in time."[131]

While lemons were mentioned frequently, oranges were not, nor were two other tropical imports, pineapples and coconuts, even though they were available in town shops. The West Indian shaddock, predecessor to the modern grapefruit, "an excellent fruit," was already available in August 1792, according to Elizabeth Simcoe.[132]

Frypan   A frypan (frying pan) was as essential as a bake-kettle. "[A] frying pan, that desideratum in a bush settler's house [was] the only cooking utensil, saving the aforesaid tin tea-pot, that Tom's kitchen boasted of – in this he cooked his meat and baked his bread, varying his modes of dressing his meat by either making it a frying or stewing-pan, adding a plate turned over the top to keep in the steam." But, adds Traill, "Do not spoil good food by frying, or stewing in a frying-pan."[133]

Fudge, Fadge   Not to be confused with the sweet creamy treat known as fudge today, fadge was a flat, plate-sized unleavened bread made of inferior flour (and sometimes potato) moistened with buttermilk, baked on the griddle, and served at breakfast. Although Traill wrote that the Irish in her environs "call these coarse cakes by the odd name of 'fudge'" [101], the Scots spelled and pronounced it "fadge," a derivative of *fouace*, a French flat cake or bannock that had enjoyed a long usage in Scotland and Ireland.[134] Eliza Acton's recipe: "Break up very small an ounce and a half of butter into a pound of meal just as it comes from the mill (wholemeal is meant by this), and make it into a paste with about half a pint of milk. Roll it out to the size of a plate, and to the third of an inch thick, and bake it on a griddle or in an oven ... about 20 minutes."[135] As the simplest of breads it was associated with poverty, although Fannie Farmer included a recipe for whole wheat fadges in *The Boston Cooking-School Cook Book* of 1896, which was not a book for poor families.[136]

131 Jameson, *Winter Studies and Summer Rambles*, 23 January 1836, 54.
132 Simcoe, *The Diary of Mrs. John Graves Simcoe*, 6 August 1792, 132.
133 Traill, "The Settlers Settled," 110.
134 Connery, *In an Irish Country Kitchen*, 128; McNeill, *The Scots Kitchen*, 213, 318.
135 Acton, *The English Bread Book*, 154–5.
136 Farmer, *The Boston Cooking-School Cook Book*, 77.

Gage Plum   Gages are green, yellow, or purple and can be enjoyed raw, cooked, or stewed. However, green gages (*Prunus italica*) are prized for their flavour and were the first to be planted in North America.[137] Whether Traill planted any is uncertain.

Garlic, *see* Wild Garlic

Ginger, *see also* Gingerbread   Ginger (*Zingiber officinale*) was absorbed into European cookery after arriving from Asia. An underground rhizome, it can be used young and fresh or mature and dried, but by the time it reached the kitchens of early Canada it was thoroughly dry. In Traill's time, most came whole from the West Indies.

Gingerbread   Traill's gingerbread recipes include one European hard cookie dough and three American soft batters, including a cupcake raised with one of the new chemical leaveners. Gingerbreads were prominent in nineteenth-century Anglo-Canadian recipe books, as they were in European and American cookbooks. Medieval gingerbreads were unleavened and often uncooked mixtures of breadcrumbs, honey, pulverized ginger, and sometimes ground almonds. Flour and sugar or treacle gradually replaced the breadcrumbs and honey, and leavenings of yeast and/or eggs were added. Gingerbread was traditionally rolled out thin and either stamped into fanciful shapes or imprinted with a mould. It was long associated with fairs and festivals, and was considered to be good for travelling and troops' rations. By the end of the eighteenth century, a new cakey version had been developed in the northeastern United States and appeared in Simmons' *American Cookery*.[138]

Traill's Ginger Cup-Cake [106] was a very close copy of the recipe in Eliza Leslie's 1840 version of *Seventy-Five Receipts*. The original specified "rich" milk as well as a few other minor alterations and called for half a cup of allspice and cloves in addition to half a cup of ginger. Traill's recipe indicated "add the ginger and other spices," as did Leslie's, but either the printer forgot to typeset "allspice and cloves" or whoever gave the recipe to Traill assumed whatever spices the cook wanted would be acceptable. We think it was more likely a typesetting error.[139]

Gizzard   The second part of a bird's stomach, which it uses for grinding its food. Although edible and delicious if cooked, recipes using it seldom appeared in cookbooks.

---

137 Woodhead, *Early Canadian Gardening*, 64.
138 Simmons, *The First American Cookbook*, xv–xvi, 36; Davidson, *Oxford Companion to Food*, 338–9.
139 Leslie, *Seventy-Five Receipts*, 22.

Gloucester Cheese   Mild-tasting Gloucester cheeses were (and are) produced as Single and Double (which is often larger). As Traill says, Single starts with the skimmed evening milk, to which is added the full morning milk. Double has whole milk and more cream blended in. They cut well with a knife due to their smooth, waxy texture. Gloucester is the main town of the southwest English county of Gloucestershire.[140]

Gold Cake and Silver Cake   A pair of decoratively iced gold and silver cakes were featured on many a tea-table through the mid-nineteenth to early twentieth centuries. An American development within the English tradition of egg-rich pound cakes, making them involved separating numerous eggs so that the yolks could be used to make half the batter "gold" while the whites made the other half "silver."[141] In the old country such cakes were baked in decorative moulds and served in wedges, but in North America they were baked in "square, flat pans ... and cut in square, thick pieces" [107]. Traill's recipes for gold and silver cakes are taken, with minor alterations, from the August 1852 edition of *The Maple Leaf*, a magazine for juveniles that circulated in the backwoods. (See page 509.)

Goose, *see also* Wild Goose   Traill maintained flocks of domestic geese in some years. Besides being consumed for dinner, geese provided feather quills for writing and soft feather down for stuffing pillows.

Gooseberry   Another member of the *Ribes* family of berries, which ripens later than currants. Traill collected wild gooseberry plants for transplantation into her kitchen garden [66] and also recommended that emigrants bring gooseberry seeds from home [81]. She was familiar with three wild varieties: the inedible Swamp Gooseberry (*R. lacustre*), the "most palatable," dark purple Smooth Gooseberry (*R. oxyacanthoides*), and the edible Prickly Gooseberry (*R. cynosbati*). The last was "rough and spiny and is troublesome to gather, but in old times it was sought for by the settlers in the backwoods as a welcome addition to their scanty fare." It was sometimes called "thornberry" due to its thorns. In a letter to her English sister, Sarah, Traill explained that "some varieties are smooth and as large as our common sized garden gooseberries[;] others [are] armed with sharp thorns – these latter with propriety might be termed thornberries – they can be used by scalding and rubbing the fruits in a coarse

140 Webster and Parkes, *Encyclopedia of Domestic Economy*, 412.
141 Schmidt, "Cakes," 158–9, 161.

cloth which takes off the thorns[.] [T]hus prepared they are equally good for pies &c as the smooth sort."[142]

Grains and Flours, *see also* Barley, Buckwheat, Indian Corn, Oats, Rice, Rye, Wheat "In August the wheat fields were ready for the reapers. This was the great crop of the year. Other grains were grown, such as rye, oats, peas, barley and corn, but principally for feeding [animals]."[143] Wheat was the preferred grain in Eastern Canada, although good breads of many forms could also be made from buckwheat, rye, and oats – all ancient European staples – and corn, the grain of the Americas. Distinct differences defined the evolving culinary culture of the new country of the United States of America, a major one being the emphasis on Indian corn. Yankees moving to the Canadas brought their corn-based recipes with them.

Traill chose to write little about planting imported grains because that was men's work, instead explaining the culture of Indian corn [117–21] and Indian rice [111–13]. Her letters and journals, however, often refer to the important wheat harvest: "I strolled up the road by the side of the wheatfield today to look at the state of the grain and consult with JL about getting a few sheaves threshed to send to mill as we are reduced like all our neighbours to our last handful of flour. What a season this has been[,] so cold, so wet, and the harvest so. late."[144] Fortunate farmers could realize a good income from wheat, "the pride of the province."[145]

The "inferior grains" used in times of "scarcity in wheaten flour" [115] could be lightened with wheat to make a variety of breads. Once the West had been opened up by settlers from the Eastern Provinces, it became "universally acknowledged that the soil of the plains produces the finest quality of wheat and wheat stands so high in the estimation of the flour merchant that it is eagerly bespoken from the grower before it is thrashed – the flour is finer and whiter and sweeter than elsewhere," writes Traill in her journal, probably around 1851.[146]

Grapes, Cultivated, *see also* Wild Grapes   Some native wild grapes were successfully cultivated in gardens, as Traill managed to do, but other varieties (*Vitis vinifera*) came from Europe. In a letter from Toronto, Moodie told her sister Traill that

142   Traill, *Studies of Plant Life in Canada*, 116; Traill to Childe, (1836?), Traill Family Collection, 3461.
143   Haight, *Country Life in Canada*, 55.
144   Traill, Journal, 4 September 1836, Traill Family Collection, 3404.
145   *Unterricht Für Einwanderer in Ober Canada*, quoted in Hoffman and Taylor, *Across the Waters*, 359.
146   Traill Family Collection, 3513.

"A near neighbour sent us about a bushell of grapes which grew on the roof of their house and shed. They were excellent. Most of the folks train them over the roofs of outhouses and they bear abundantly, and are very ornamental and make nice pies and preserves."[147] The variety could have been a cultivated wild grape or one of the dessert grapes offered in Custead's catalogue of 1827, carefully nurtured to survive the winter.[148]

Gravy, *see* Sauces

Green "Green" meant (1) fresh, when applied to fruits and vegetables, as in "green corn" which referred to fresh corn, not unripe corn, and (2) young, as in green goose. Some very fresh cream cheese was also called green cheese.

Green Bean The tender beans of early and mid-summer, best eaten fresh, pod and all, rather than dried for winter consumption.

Green Corn, *see* Indian Corn

Green Peas The English had learned to cultivate many sub-varieties of peas (garden, marrowfat, and sugar, all *Pisum sativum*) expertly, but the summers of the northeastern states and southeastern Canada were generally too hot for traditional varieties, so other suitable varieties had to be developed as well.[149] The Traills first planted garden peas in 1834. Not to be confused with field peas for drying, sugar peas were eaten fresh. Advice that appeared in several publications said green peas could be kept until Christmas if shelled, dried well, bottled, and covered with a layer of mutton suet and then a bladder and piece of leather. Resuscitation was possible with a bit of water, sugar, butter, and mint.[150]

Ham Ham (the salted and/or smoked back leg of a pig or any large animal, such as deer and mutton) was a commonplace food. Since it kept well for months and travelled well, cold ham was frequently taken to picnics, as recorded by numerous

---

147 Moodie to Traill, *Letters of a Lifetime* [fall 1881], 348

148 Custead, *Catalogue of Fruit & Ornamental Trees*, 10; Woodhead, *Early Canadian Gardening*, 28.

149 Weaver, *Heirloom Vegetable Gardening*, 237.

150 Simmons, *The First American Cookbook*, 46; *The Cook Not Mad*, number 44; *The Canadian Housewife's Manual of Cookery*, 178.

settlers, but was equally valued at fancy ball suppers. "A few small hams" were among the meagre stock that the Traills had in April 1846, so they may have been prepared as potato hash, slices fried with gravy, baked with mustard sauce, in a pie, with eggs, or any number of simple ways. Hams were hung in the smoke-house or chimney as a way to preserve them through smoking, although there was the risk of seeing one crash into the fire, as happened once to the Langtons – since meat was scarce, they simply dusted it off and ate it anyway. Let's hope it was not "leathery," as one person derided the ham served to him.[151]

Traill suggests that ham be boiled with hay, an old method of reducing its saltiness and adding some sweetness.[152]

Hare   Most historical comments about Canadian hare as a food, like Traill's, were unenthusiastic [162]. They were considered best in summer for soup.

Haricot Bean   Haricot is the English word for a wide number of cultivars in the genus *Phaseolus vulgaris*, such as the species of kidney, navy, pinto, black, flageolet, snap, and string beans, and is also the generic French word for bean.

Hasty Pudding   Between Traill's Breads and Biscuits sections are three recipes for thick hasty puddings that she calls "homely dishes ... intended for homely people" [103]. Such simple preparations seldom appeared in printed sources, so they were true vernacular dishes. She likely served these and similar but thinner gruel recipes to her children.

Hawthorn   "It had fruit as large as cherries, pulpy and of a pleasant flavour, not unlike a tamarind."[153] Hawthorns (*Crateagus pruinosa*) were wild, not cultivated, although Traill did try to plant them in her gardens.

Hedge-Bullace   This was Traill's term for the bullace plums that grew in hedges around her Suffolk home. She felt they would grow well if their stones were brought to Canada West.

---

151 Traill to Susanna Moodie, *I Bless You in My Heart*, 16 April 1846, 57; J.J. Bigsby, quoted in Guillet, *Early Life in Upper Canada*, 189.

152 Davidson, *Oxford Companion to Food*, 369.

153 Traill, *Pearls and Pebbles*, 170.

Hemlock Tea   Caught out in the bush on several occasions without adequate provisions, Sam Strickland drank a hot tea made from hemlock without sugar but "with a dash of whiskey in it, merely to assist the flavour, as the best preventative" from damp. He dismayed his sister by drinking a lot of it enthusiastically because she felt "this proved to my taste, a vile decoction."[154] The Eastern Hemlock tree (*Tsuga canadensis*) is part of the pine forests of Canada and the northern states and featured in the Amerindian pharmacopeia.[155]

Herbs, see also Balm; Basil, Sweet; Endive; Lettuce; Marjoram, Sweet; Mint; Parsley; Peppermint; Sage; Savoury; Thyme; Wild Greens   The term "herb" encompassed more then than it does now, including salad greens, edible flowers, pot herbs, and garden herbs. Some were culinary, some strictly medicinal, some served both purposes. Some could be overwintered in pots on warm sunny windowsills, hence "pot herbs" or "seasoning herbs."[156] Dried at home in a bake-kettle or bake oven, they were tied into paper bags or placed in little bottles (perhaps left over from other purchases) that could be tightly closed, similar to the supermarket commodities of today. Traill mentions nine herbs and salad leaves, although some she does not mention (chicory, rocket, burnet, tarragon, rosemary, horehound, comfrey, and oregano, for instance) were used in Anglo-Canadian cooking.

It is a mistake to think that Canadian Victorians did not eat salads. They were much esteemed by many, including Traill, even though some medical authorities thought the raw vegetables fermented in the stomach. On salads, *The Canadian Housewife's Manual of Cookery* (1861) quoted Alexis Soyer, the celebrated mid-nineteenth-century French cook: "'What is more refreshing than salads when your appetite seems to have deserted you, or even after a capacious dinner – the nice, fresh, green, and crisp salad, full of life and health, which seems to invigorate the palate and dispose the masticating powers to a much longer duration.' Experience has taught us to say that Soyer is right, and salads should be brought into more general use, viewing them at once as food and a purifier of the blood; to that end we here insert some of the numerous herbaceous plants, which, with a few 'fixins,' nicely finishes up a dinner at small cost. Use a wooden spoon and fork."[157]

---

154 Samuel Strickland, *Twenty-Seven Years in Canada West*, 1:279; Traill, *Backwoods of Canada*, 54.
155 Erichsen-Brown, *Use of Plants*, 15–18.
156 Webster and Parkes, *Encyclopedia of Domestic Economy*, 489.
157 *The Canadian Housewife's Manual of Cookery*, 298.

Herring   "Lake Ontario abounds with herring, of much the same flavour as the sea species, but not so strong and oily, nor so large."[158] Traill suggests preserving them [168]. Pickled herring had an honourable history in Scotland, off whose shores considerable ocean herring were caught. The herring listed in Foster's extract (mentioned on page 43) was pickled herring, intended to last for the sea trip to Canada.

Hominy, see also Supporne   Hominy is a vegetable porridge made from the dried kernels of flint-variety maize that have been scalded in lye water (made of ashes) to soften and remove the unwanted outer hard skins [121].[159]

Honey   Throughout the nineteenth century, honey was seldom available except in Lower Canada, which was developing a small industry in it. Establishing and maintaining hives was not a colonial priority for a long time, although we found one rare mention of its occasional availability: "Rode after dinner to see our washer woman who has the ague ... sent her some honey & etc. were so very thankful."[160] Perhaps this was wild honey. Young Louis Perron in *Canadian Crusoes* looked forward to when he could collect wild honey in the autumn to add it to their limited edibles; when he returned in November, he filled a pail with rich honey-comb. Haight remembered eating so much as a child he made himself sick.[161]

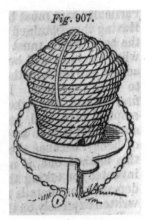

Fig. 27 · Beehive

Hop-Rising, see also Hops   Hops played an important role in Canadian backwoods bread fermentations, not for aerating the dough but for improving its longevity (shelf-life) and flavour by reducing the sourness inherent in naturally fermented dough. Hop-rising was also called "American yeast." The process was simple: an infusion was made by boiling the small yellow hop flowers when fresh, straining it, then stirring in flour to make a batter, which was left to either ripen on its own by attracting wild

158 Samuel Strickland, *Twenty-Seven Years in Canada West*, 2:77.
159 Davidson, *Oxford Companion to Food*, 470–1; Smith, *Oxford Encyclopedia of Food and Drink in America*, 1:615.
160 Pengelley, The Diaries of Harriet Pengelley, 5 October 1835.
161 Traill, *Canadian Crusoes*, 70; Haight, *Country Life in Canada*, 275.

airborne yeast spores or was assisted by a few spoonfuls of a previous batch. Countless loaves of hop-risen bread were made by settlers in Ontario.

Hops, *see also* Breads, Hop-Rising   Although many hop varieties grow around the world, only *Humulus lupulu* is native to North America. Starting in the seventeenth century, Europeans brought others, which escaped into the wild and naturalized. Many a stoup or verandah of a Canadian farmstead was wreathed with luxuriant, fast-growing hop vines. The female flowers (the "hops") produce a bitter yellow powder that brewers used for its flavour and antiseptic qualities. Sometime in the eighteenth century, American housewives began including hops in their yeast mixtures as a preservative agent and for flavour. See pages 92–5 for more on hops in yeast.

Huckleberry   The soft black fruit of the low-growing North American shrub *Gaylussacia*, of which only *G. baccata* is found in Ontario. Huckleberries are frequently mistaken for blueberries (the related *Vaccinium*) because their reddish purple to blackish berries are similar and they also ripen in July and August. Huckleberries, however, are full of tiny seeds. Since Traill refers to them as "sweet" [79] and suggests using them dried or fresh for puddings, cakes, pie filling, and jams without ever mentioning removing seeds, she was probably referring to wild high-bush blueberries (*Vaccinimum corymbosum*) rather than true huckleberries. She treated them, both in the *Guide* and in *Studies of Plant Life*, as synonymous and says that they "abound[ed] ... in our back lakes."[162] Huckleberry seems to have been the more common local word but they were also called whortleberries.[163]

Iced Cream   One of the luxuries that came with an ice-house was the possibility of keeping ice to make iced cream when cream was available. Confectioners sometimes made it, such as an Italian immigrant in York in the early 1830s.[164] Ice cream without the "d" in iced had become the more usual term by the early twentieth century.

---

162 Traill, *Studies of Plant Life in Canada*, 121.
163 Soper, Heimburger, and Garay, *Shrubs of Ontario*, 379; Erichsen-Brown, *Use of Plants*, 184–7; Traill, *Canadian Crusoes*, 62.
164 Guillet, *Early Life in Upper Canada*, 204.

Ice-House "Building for the storage of ice collected during the winter for use in summer, usually wholly or partly underground, often of two walls insulated with sawdust or other material, fitted with a drain at the base, and frequently of circular vaulted form."[165] The hole in the ground was an inverted cone, so that the melting ice water closest to the top flowed easily downward to the distant drain. A thick door minimized the possibility of cold air escaping and allowing warm air to take its place.[166]

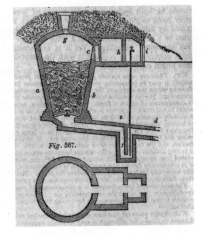

Fig. 567.

Fig. 28 · The ice-house, built deep in a hillside, kept ice cold for year-round use in storing food. A door in the hill allowed ice to be put in.

Indian Corn, *see also* Cornmeal, Maize

"Indian corn" was the colonial term for maize, *Zea mays*, the American grain, used to distinguish it from "corn," the old English term for wheat. Indian corn quickly lost its native connection, despite its name. Before the introduction of sweet corn in 1828, there were only flint and dent corns, which are ground to make cornmeal.[167] Green corn is immature (unripe) field corn. "[W]ith the exception of wheat, there is not a more valuable grain, or one more various and valuable in its uses to man" [116]. Traill spends considerable time explaining how to use this valuable but unfamiliar, versatile, and ubiquitous grain in its edible form of Indian meal (today's cornmeal). It could be prepared and served as vegetable, bread, gruel, sweet or savoury pudding, sweet or plain cake, muffins, biscuits, stuffing, coating for fried fish, and many kinds of griddle cakes, as well as animal fodder. Corn husks and cobs had other practical uses, which she enumerates, some similar to practices in the British Isles (using husks for mattress stuffing instead of straw) and some not (burning the cobs to make fine white ashes that could be used as an alkali for raising cakes). Like their Amerindian counterparts, housewives had to be ingenious in employing

165 Curl, *Oxford Dictionary for Architecture and Landscape Architecture*, 381.
166 Webster and Parkes, *Encyclopedia of Domestic Economy*, 677–8.
167 Woodhead, *Early Canadian Gardening*, 217; Plaisted, "Corn," 1:343.

materials at hand: shredded corn husks were woven into mats, corn silks were used before toilet paper was invented, corn ashes leavened cakes, dried corn cobs corked European glass bottles, and the stalks made effective floor brooms. Corn was also converted into whisky. At harvest time, "Husking Bees" were often called, which were community gatherings to husk the corn, followed by "an evening frolic" [119].

Her twenty-five recipes for corn and their internal variants are the most provided for one food article. Loosely speaking, they can be categorized into First Nation–style dishes and Europeanized dishes: the former include hominy, supporne, and corn on the cob; the latter substitute cornmeal for wheat flour in the gamut of puddings, breads, and cakes basic to northeastern North American foodways and therefore essential in a settler's guide. Traill's Green Corn and Green Corn Patties recipes [122] originally came from *The Maple Leaf*.

Indian Meal, *see* Indian Corn

Indian Pudding   Recipes for sweet and plain cornmeal puddings are ubiquitous in old American and Canadian recipe books and follow the age-old Anglo tradition of boiling a flour batter that contains spices and dried fruits. The first printed recipes for boiled and baked Indian puddings appear in Amelia Simmons's *American Cookery* (1796). Typical accompanying sauces were plain molasses, a sugar and wine combination, or a meat gravy.

Indian Rice, *also* Wild Rice   Wild rice (*Zizania aquatic*) – actually a grass, not a grain – was an important exchange product between the indigenous peoples and the settlers. First Nations women harvested it and taught settler women how to parch, wash, and parboil it, but settlers then combined it with milk and eggs to make puddings.

As an enthusiastic botanist, Traill cannot resist informing her readers about indigenous methods of growing and harvesting wild rice, though they were "rarely practised by the settlers" [112], who purchased it from their First Nations neighbours instead. Living near Rice Lake, Traill was intrigued by its grassy leaves and the First Nations women's harvesting and parching methods [111–13], which she also outlines in detail in *Canadian Crusoes*; clearly she liked its flavour and that it could be the basis of either sweet (sugar, spices) or savoury (salt, butter) dishes. Her recipes are "the most approved" Wild Rice Pudding, Stewed Rice, and Indian Rice in Soup [113]. She cautions that wild rice must be well soaked and drained to avoid a fishy smell

[113], unlike the bright white rice from Carolina.[168] In *Studies of Plant Life*, she repeats this advice, adding: "It used to be a favourite dish at many tables, but it is more difficult to obtain now."[169] For her, wild rice "if properly cooked is very delicious."[170]

Jerk   Jerking is an ancient method of preserving meat. The meat was cut into thin strips and hung up in a drafty and/or smoky location to dehydrate.

Johnny Cake, *also* Johnnie Cake, Jonny Cake, Jonnycake   In northeastern American and eastern Canadian baking, the many varieties of hearth breads – johnny cakes, hoe cakes, ash cakes, pones, bannocks – were similar quick breads based on cornmeal. "We are going to have a good supper tonight. We are going to have a johnny cake which Margaret is making. It is very healthy."[171]

At their simplest, American johnny cakes were unleavened flatbreads of cornmeal and water baked on a board (plank), stone, hoe, or griddle angled towards the fire or, if wrapped in leaves, in the fire itself (and thus called ash cakes) and were similar to countless ancient flatbreads of other grains prepared around the world. Its first evolution was as a thicker batter enriched with such things as molasses, scalded milk, and shortening, as in the first recipe published in New England in Simmons's *American Cookery* (1796), but it was still baked in front of the fire. Later a looser batter was poured into a greased frypan or skillet that was baked near the fire. Traill's two typical recipes [125] are cake-like batters enhanced with the fat inherent in milk, butter, buttermilk, or eggs and were poured into square pans inserted into a bake kettle or oven. Pouring maple syrup or molasses over johnny cake was a deliciously typical way of serving it.

Johnny cake's origin, etymology, and development are much disputed among culinary historians, but there is no doubt about its ongoing popularity in the eighteenth and nineteenth centuries, and its association with journeying. The word may derive from journey, Shawnee, jonniken, or jannock, which is related to bannock, the Scottish oatcake baked on an iron griddle (see figure 22 for a flat griddle). It may or may not have antecedents in American First Nations breads of ground cornmeal

---

168   Traill, *Canadian Crusoes*, 125–9.
169   Traill, *Studies of Plant Life in Canada*, 104.
170   Traill, *Pearls and Pebbles*, 128.
171   Catherine Bell Van Norman, 25 January 1850, in Hoffman and Taylor, *Much to Be Done*, 102.

baked in hot ashes or Scottish oatcake. Perhaps cornmeal was an easy substitution for oats.[172]

Juneberry   Several types of purply-black or purply-red juneberry, both dwarf (*Amelachier spicata*) and what she called tall (unidentified) were familiar to Traill. She describes their almond-like flavour as "luscious" [129]. In some Canadian provinces this fruit is called "saskatoon" (*A. alnifolia*) or "serviceberry" (*A. canadensis*). Similar-looking juneberries, blueberries, and huckleberries grow close to the ground in some Canadian Shield districts and ripen at the same time in July and August but are distinguished by the bloom on blueberries and the shiny surface of juneberries.

Kidney Bean, *see also* Scarlet Runner Bean   A haricot variety. Traill uses "the size of kidney beans" [142] as an indication of how small dandelion roots should be cut for roasting, so clearly she expected her readers to know their size. She grew kidney beans at least in her first years in Upper Canada.[173]

Kneading Trough, *also* Bread Trough, Bread Box, Dough Box   A large rectangular wooden box with sloping sides that often stood securely on four legs. The opening was larger than the base and was fitted with a protective lid that doubled as a hard work surface. Since bread was often made in large quantities at home, the trough served as an enormous mixing, proofing, and kneading bowl. Not every household that made its own bread had one, but they were fairly common.

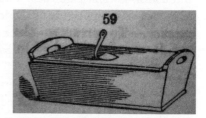

Fig. 29 · Trough for kneading bread. On the kneading trough's lid is a scraper, used to remove the dried bits of dough.

Labrador Tea   A shrub (*Ledum greenlandim*) found across much of Canada and the northern United States. It grows in acid bogs and blooms in June and July, when the

172 For discussions of this fascinatingly complex subject, see Simmons, *The First American Cookbook*, xiii; Randolph, *The Virginia Housewife*, 277–9; Stavely and Fitzgerald, *America's Founding Food*, 29–39; Oliver, "Bannock," 3–6; Smith, "Bread," 1:120; *Dictionary of Canadianisms on Historical Principles*, 394, 396.

173 Traill, *Backwoods of Canada*, 219.

pretty white flowers were collected for a wholesome anti-scorbutic tea very popular with the colonists. "Canadians and Yankies [*sic*] use an infusion of the leaves as tea," approving of its "resinous aromatic flavor," a flavour Traill did not particularly like although she preferred it over hemlock tea. Its fresh leaves can be applied to wounds.[174]

Lady Cake   A simpler variant of Silver cake, usually flavoured with bitter almonds or almond essence and/or rosewater. Recipes for such white-coloured cakes started appearing in American cookbooks in the 1830s.

Fig. 30 · Cake mould

Lamb, *see also* Mutton   Sheep are not native to the Americas but were among the livestock brought by European settlers. It took considerable time to clear the land and erect the fencing and housing necessary to keep them safe from the winter cold and predators such as wolves and wolverines, so the meat and wool from sheep were only available after earlier priorities of housing, wheat fields, orchards, and cattle herds had been accomplished. "Sheep are the greatest source of comfort the settler can possess. Let him get to the length of keeping a small flock, and he will never need to go to the store for comfortable and decent clothing for his family. Besides the wool, he can have fresh meat and plenty of candles."[175] Since fresh lamb was not as common as pork or beef it was often considered a treat. "House-lamb is in season in March; grass-lamb comes in the end of May. Although preference is generally given to the former, both, nevertheless, are favourite dishes."[176]

Lamb's Quarters, *also* Wild Spinach   An invasive species (*Chenopodium album*) from Europe, popularly served as a cooked side vegetable similar to spinach.

Lard   Lard is the abdominal fat of pork meat after it has been melted, strained, and resolidified, a process called rendering. It was an abundant source of fat for cooking and soap-making throughout the nineteenth century. Lard consumption dropped as the number of milch cows increased and butter became more common, but it

---

174   Traill, "Rice Lake Plains," *Forest and Other Gleanings*, 210; Traill, *Studies of Plant Life in Canada*, 136; Erichsen-Brown, *Use of Plants*, 195.
175   Traill, "Bush Wedding and Wooing," *Forest and Other Gleanings*, 92.
176   *The Canadian Housewife's Manual of Cooking*, 144.

remained an essential ingredient for the never-ending frying and for baking, especially for pie pastry.

Traill provides only cursory instructions for rendering raw lard because the process was so straightforward that details were not necessary. Mary Armstrong, living on a busy farm at Yonge and St Clair Streets in Toronto, noted that she was "well satisfied and [thought] it a good day's work" in February 1854 when she and her "girl" melted sixty-five pounds of raw lard down into forty-seven "good" and six "inferior" pounds, leaving the remainder for scraps "which we did not value."[177] "Sweet lard" was nice lard that had not turned rancid.

Lard was an important ingredient in homemade soaps when combined with lye.

Leavening Agents, *see also* Baking Powders, Yeasts   Before the easy availability of packets of reliable granulated yeast and tins of infallible baking powder, both familiar to housewives by the late nineteenth century, home and professional bakers raised their breads and cakes with leaven, beaten eggs, and yeasts. Leaven (a lump of risen dough) was retained for raising a subsequent batch, a principle well understood for centuries but not a technique included in the *Guide*. Besides enriching cake batters and bread dough, eggs separated into yolks and whites were beaten vigorously to incorporate air; when heated, the trapped air caused the batter to rise. Traill's recipes do not include many that use this time-honoured technique, and those that do are fancy cakes. By the last quarter of the eighteenth century, chemical pearlash had begun to be familiar to household bakers in eastern North America, a forerunner to a new category of reliable leavening agents, "baking powders."

Lemon   "This fruit is not an article of mere luxury, but is almost an essential for culinary and many other purposes," stated Webster and Parkes.[178] Lemon (*Citrus limon*) was the most commonly suggested flavouring in the *Guide* but was always subtle since the suggested amount is so often "a little bit." Lemons came to early Canada from Italy, Sicily, and Spain. Lemons from California and Florida did not start to displace this trade until the end of the nineteenth century. Simmons's *American Cookery* (1796) called for lemon and all the nineteenth-century cookbooks published in the United States and Canada, including the *Guide,* contain recipes that called for fresh lemons. But when did fresh lemons actually first arrive in English Canada? They were

177 Armstrong, *Seven Eggs Today*, 4 February 1859, 96.
178 Webster and Parkes, *Encyclopedia of Domestic Economy*, 504.

in French Canada by the late 1600s[179] so; wrapped individually in paper and packed in barrels of sand, they likely came to York (now Toronto) before the War of 1812. After a sea voyage of several weeks, they may not have been quite as pretty as they were when picked. Bottled lemon and lime juice were advertised by shopkeeper J. Cawthra in *The Upper Canada Gazette* in 1806 and Mrs Simcoe mentions (bottled) lemon juice at least twice.[180] Hannah Jarvis's manuscript household book of 1792 to 1815 had multiple recipes requiring fresh lemons.[181]

Candied lemon peel was homemade throughout the eighteenth and nineteenth centuries, as was candied orange peel, and was considered essential not only for fruit cakes and mincemeat, but also for the occasional gingerbread, cheesecake, and ice cream.

Homemade lemonade is not cited in the *Guide*, but it was certainly familiar and popular at all sorts of family gatherings and public events. Susanna Moodie and her son once drank lemonade while attending a circus.[182] Lemonade had been popular for centuries, but for the temperance movement it, along with such beverages as raspberry vinegar, apple water, and plain water, had the extra benefit of being non-alcoholic.

Lemon Essence Lemon essence, the light, colourless, and odiferous essential oil extracted from the rind, was a common flavouring agent. It was a frequent commodity in grocers' advertisements, starting with one in the 19 May 1804 edition of *The Upper Canada Gazette*.

Lettuce Nowadays, lettuce (*Lactuca sativa*) is primarily served raw in salad, but earlier varieties were also blanched as a full head and served hot with a piquant sauce or added to soups, especially a "spring soup." Many kinds were available but Traill does not list any. "Solid headed lettuce did not seem to be grown then [1853] as the curly variety had the run at the time," said Charlie Peterkin, reminiscing. Traill does say in 1834, however, that "lettuces are very fine, and may be cultivated easily, and very early."[183]

179 LaFrance and Desloges, *The Taste History*, 9.
180 Simcoe, *The Diary of Mrs. John Graves Simcoe*, 8 September 1795, 290, and 8 June 1796, 315.
181 Jarvis, *Every Comfort in the Wilderness*.
182 Moodie, *Life in the Clearings*, 96.
183 Peterkin, *A Boyhood Journey*, 41; Traill, *Backwoods of Canada*, 219.

Lima Beans Originally from Peru, *Phaseolus lunatus* was brought back to Europe by the invading Spanish and Portuguese. Although Traill said white lima beans were a good soup ingredient [139], she did not follow with any soup recipes. They grow well in hot southern Ontario summers.

Lime, *also* Burnt Lime, Quick Lime, Quicklime Lime starts out as calcium carbonate ($CaCO_3$) derived primarily from limestone but also from chalk, bone, or such sea creatures as oyster shells and coral. When limestone is roasted in a kiln, its inherent carbon dioxide evaporates, leaving greyish lumps of calcium oxide (CaO), also known as quicklime, but frequently shortened to lime. "Quick" is an old synonym for lively and when pulverized or powdered calcium oxide melts in water it bubbles quickly. At this point it becomes calcium hydroxide ($Ca(OH_2)$), but is also called quicklime or lime. The action of mixing the powder with water is called slaking (as in "slaking your thirst"), hence the common term slaked lime.

Lime was an ingredient in an astounding number of household, agricultural, and garden applications on the pioneer homestead, such as making soap [55, 171–5], whitewash, glue, and house cement, and sprinkling around as an insecticide or fertilizer [70, 76], as well as many other possibilities [50, 148, 201]. Crystalline lime powder could be purchased or made by the settlers themselves. Although Traill does not mention this, it was also used medicinally, as a liniment and antacid among other things. Traill quotes from her brother's section "Description of a New Settlement" [48–51] on the making of lime and there are many other settler accounts of excavating limestone for the fiery task of manufacturing domestic lime.

Liquor A generic word for liquid used in cooking and baking.

Loaf Sugar, *see also* Brown and White Cane Sugar, Lump Sugar This was the best quality white sugar, the kind that went on the table for tea or sprinkling over fruit, or was used in concocting the best sweetmeats and finest preserves. Until the late nineteenth century, cones – called loaves – of compacted sugar crystals that varied from eight to fourteen pounds were the main form in which white sugar was sold. They were usually wrapped in white and then purplish-blue paper. Before use, the rock-hard loaf had to be smashed with a hammer and then broken into lumps with special scissor-like nippers; if wanted for baking, the lumps were further pulverized in a mortar with a pestle and sifted. It was a tedious process, but necessary, and in colonial Canada was a job sometimes given to children.

Lump Sugar, *see also* Loaf Sugar   A general name for white sugar of better or best quality that was sold in lumps off the loaf. It was often found on the tea table in pretty sugar bowls.

Mace, *see* Nutmeg

Maize, *see also* Indian Corn   The grain on which the North and South American nations built their cuisines. The immigrant English Americans called it Indian corn, as opposed to European corn, which was what we now know as wheat. The English word derives from French *maïs* or Spanish *maiz*, originally from the now-extinct Carib language Arawakan.

Mangel-wurtzel, *see* Sugar Beets

Maple Molasses   Thicker and stronger tasting than maple syrup, a pot of maple molasses – the residue that drained from "solid cakes" of cooling maple sugar [149] – would be found on rural kitchen tables at all meals throughout much of the nineteenth century in Ontario. As Traill explained to her mother in 1833, "The molasses boiled from maple-sap is very different from the molasses of the West Indies, both in flavour, colour, and consistency. Besides the [maple] sugar, I made about three gallons of molasses, which proved a great comfort to us, forming a nice ingredient in cakes and an excellent sauce for puddings."[184] However, in January 1860, the Traills were reduced to "dry bread and tea without milk or sugar" and just "molasses and butter" for dinner, which in their poverty they "greatly relished."[185]

Maple Sugar   Maple sugar was a major agricultural product manufactured largely by farmwomen and their children for their own family meals, as a cash crop for barter, or to take to market rather than for foreign export. Due to the unusual production techniques required to get maple sugar and its identification with successful settlement, instructions for edible maple products appear in many emigration manuals, settler's accounts, and periodicals. Traill's notes on how to achieve "sparkling" and "good grained" [149] maple sugar of appropriate quality for a "cakes, puddings, tea, or coffee" [149] sweetener are extensive (and mostly taken from the book by her brother,

184 Traill, *Backwoods of Canada*, 114.
185 Traill, Journal, 31 January 1860, Traill Family Collection, 2965.

Sam Strickland, *Twenty-Seven Years in Canada West*). Sap was boiled for several hours until its water evaporated and it formed a condensed syrup, which could be further evaporated and stirred until it crystallized into sugar. This was then tipped into tin or wood moulds to harden into "cakes." If the cakes were carefully drained of any remaining syrup, they could become pale yellow, or even a white equal to the best English loaf sugar. A maple cake could be scraped or pounded into a fine granular powder for baking and baked goods and confectionery requiring white sugar at home in Britain could be replaced by maple sugar, a distinctive flavour of the colonies. Susanna Moodie once took a cake of maple sugar and "drained [it] in a wet flannel bag until it was almost as white as loaf sugar."[186]

Fig. 31 · A couple work together to produce a year's supply of maple sugar.

With time Traill became an expert sugarer. The Traills' first maple season was in 1833, and though their only help was an Irish lad, Traill was proud of the result: "Considering it was a first attempt, and without any experienced person to direct me,

186 Moodie, *Roughing It in the Bush*, 420.

otherwise than the information I obtained from S—— [Sam] [,] I succeeded tolerably well, and produced some sugar of a fine sparkling grain and good colour."[187] It is delightful to imagine Sam and his sister consulting each other during sugar-making in the bush. The First Peoples usually made maple sugar, since syrup was liable to spoil due to its natural fermentability; European technology had improved their ancient methodology by allowing them to replace wood equipment with iron. Maple sugar was stored in a well-covered barrel or ceramic crock in a cool place to help inhibit spoilage.

Traill's delicious Common Bush Tea-Cakes [109] specify maple sugar, but on several occasions she wrote that it suited all sorts of purposes, for instance, "Raspberry vinegar is a cheap luxury to those who have home-made vinegar and home-made sugar" [85]. One spring, Traill wrote to Frances Stewart that she was "sorry to say our sugar-making was on so small a scale that it will not enable us to be as liberal in the way of preserves as I had hoped to be."[188] Did her British readers pick up on her unstated distinction between using maple sugar with native fruits, but white sugar with orchard fruits to make preserves?

In the 1850s, maple sugar, "this Canadian luxury" so critical to backwoods survival, though "not as it used formerly to be" [146] was beginning to be less essential to most settlers than it had been in previous decades, as either a flavour or commodity, because inexpensive West Indian cane sugars were increasingly available. Also, the forests were disappearing and with them a good portion of the maple groves. By 1864, the handwritten additions for Traill's proposed new edition of the *Backwoods of Canada* included this note: "Maple sugar broken into small pieces is sold in all the confectioners' stores as a sweetmeat … [and] is sold as a sweetie as easily as sugar candy."[189]

Maple Syrup   A distinction was made between what we think of now as maple syrup (a term seldom used in the colonial literature, unlike today) which resembled "virgin honey" [152], and the thicker, darker syrup, which was known as maple molasses. Forty litres of fresh sap were required to make one litre of syrup. Carefully boiled for several hours, sometimes even overnight, sap was evaporated into concentrated

187   Traill, *Backwoods of Canada*, 113.
188   Traill, letter to Frances Stewart, undated (c. 1844–1869), Frances Stewart Papers, S215. Toronto Public Library.
189   Traill Family Collection, 6153.

syrup. If boiled further and stirred it crystallized into sugar. The later it is collected in the season, the darker the sap; nowadays the resulting syrups are graded according to colour. The last lingering and weak sap that still flows at season's end was sometimes fermented into vinegar.

Marjoram, Sweet   Mrs Simcoe drank a tea of sweet marjoram (*Origanum marjorana*) for a headache. Other marjorams were grown for cooking and medicines, but the sweet was the preferred one, hence its common name.[190]

Masquinonge   A large North American pike. Spelling the Algonquian word flummoxed lots of writers – maskalongy (Need), masquinonjé (Traill), maskilonge (Strickland), mascquinonge (Captain Basil Hall), and others.[191] Today, we write it as muskellunge; muskie is the short form. Adjectives such as "noble" and "mighty" often described this large fish, which could weigh up to fifteen kilograms (about thirty-five pounds). Thomas Need said its best flavour was in winter, before the river ice melted in April. John Langton salted some in a barrel of mashed potatoes, which he froze, then "when any is wanted for use take out a sufficient quantity and fry it in little round cakes."[192]

May-Apple   May-apple, American mandrake, or wild jalap (*Podophyllum peltatum*) is a perennial of Ontario, Quebec, and the northeastern United States. Although its young seeds, rind, and roots are poisonous, its ripe fruit and roots have medicinal properties recognized by North America's First Nations communities.[193] Anna Jameson said that may-apples made "an excellent preserve."[194] For Traill, the fruit was a favourite, and the first native fruit she tasted after her arrival in Canada. She describes it in her *Studies of Plant Life in Canada*:

190 Simcoe, *The Diary of Mrs. John Graves Simcoe*, 7 September 1795, 290; Webster and Parkes, *Encyclopedia of Domestic Economy*, 491.
191 Need, *Six Years in the Bush*, 25 February 1833, 43; Traill, *Canadian Crusoes*, 126; Samuel Strickland, *Twenty-Seven Years in Canada West*, 1:270; Basil Hall, quoted in Williamson, *"To Fare Sumptuously Every Day*,*"* 14.
192 Need, *Six Years in the Bush*, 4 April 1835, 104; John Langton, quoted in Guillet, *Early Life in Upper Canada*, 200.
193 Hutchens, *Indian Herbology of North America*, 19; Erichsen-Brown, *Use of Plants*, 324–8.
194 Jameson, *Winter Studies and Summer Rambles*, 30 May 1837, 174.

The fruit of the May-apple is a large fleshy berry; the outer rind when ripe is yellow, otherwise darkish-green and of a rank, unpleasant flavor; the inner or pulpy part is white, soft, and filled with somewhat bony light-brown seeds. When not over-ripe this pulpy part may be eaten; it is sub-acid and pleasant. The fruit makes a fine preserve with white sugar and when flavored with lemon-peel and ginger, but the outer coat I would not make use of. The fruit is ripe in August, and should be gathered when the first yellow spots on the outer coat indicate ripeness, and laid in a sunny window for a few days. The medicinal value of the root of this remarkable plant is now so well established that it has superseded the use of calomel in complaints of the liver with most medical practitioners in this country, but so powerful are its properties that it should never be used by unskilful persons. Ignorant persons have been poisoned by mistaking the leaves for those of the Marsh Marigold (*Caltha palustris*) and using them as a pot herb. A case of this kind occurred some years ago whereby several persons were poisoned. At that time there was no attempt made by the backwoods settlers to cultivate vegetables, and they made use of many of the wild herbs with very little knowledge of their sanative or injurious qualities.[195]

Meats, *see also* Beef, Fish, Lamb, Mutton, Pork, Poultry, Veal   Killing animals for food was familiar to all farm families, and this home-based butchery was not necessarily a man's job. In autumn 1828, Mary O'Brien commented that "Mama has bought a dead pig and she is cutting and carving and very happy" and "Richard has bought a pig to begin his winter stock of provisions. He is cutting it up under Mama's directions whilst Fanny is looking on." She then made a third comment: "A day of slaughter – three pigs must bleed today for part of the winter's store and the summer supply of bacon. Southby has his pigs shot, which saves them from suffering and us much annoyance from their dying groans."[196] But Traill has no reference to eating any of the organs at butchering time – kidneys, livers, lungs (lights), sweetbreads (thymus) – or the heads and feet, which undoubtedly her family consumed. While most meat was preserved, some fortunate families with ice-houses had fresh meat all year long. "We are still eating fresh beef from the ox which was killed at Christmas and we shall probably have it for a month or two longer. It is kept in the ice house and brought

195 Traill, *Studies of Plant Life in Canada*, 40–1. See also Traill, *Backwoods of Canada*, 179.
196 O'Brien, *Journals of Mary O'Brien*, 2, 18, and 24 November 1828, 23, 25, 26.

indoors in time to be thawed before we want it."[197] In general, though, fresh meat was "a luxury which we can seldom obtain in the summer."[198]

Meat was preserved by two major methods: wet cure or dry cure. Wet cure involved packing the meat into a barrel between thick layers of salt and then pouring in a cold brine of salt, saltpetre, molasses or sugar, and/or vinegar, and often herbs or spices, which penetrated the meat fibres. The presence of saltpetre in this boiled and cooled brine, called "the pickle," inhibited destructive bacteria and added an attractive pinkish colour. The meat stayed completely submerged in the barrel until wanted, which could be several months, and then was rinsed and cooked by boiling. If scum rose to the barrel's surface, it was skimmed off and the brine reboiled. Dry cure meant rubbing salt thoroughly onto the surface and into all the crevices of the meat pieces to draw off the interior moisture, which combined with the salt to create its own pickle. Although this curing environment was wet, it was still called dry because brine was not involved. The length of time the meat stayed in its own salty pickle depended on the type, size, and degree of saltiness wanted. The second step in a dry cure was smoking; in fact "to cure" usually meant to dry cure and smoke.[199]

The quality of meat improved as the farms improved. "The condition of all the meat sent to market now-a-days [early 1850s] is ten per cent better than the lean, hard animals, we used to purchase for winter provisions, when we first came to the province."[200] Cookbooks that appeared prior to the Second World War regularly contained detailed advice on how to recognize and purchase good-quality fresh meats.

Medlar A small brown apple-like fruit (*Mespilus germanica*). Traill recommends that settlers bring its seeds [80], but it never became a familiar fruit in Ontario. It was boiled down into jam, although it became edible as a fruit after almost becoming rotten.

Melons, see also Citron Melon, Nutmeg Melon, Watermelon "My garden supplied the dessert, which consisted of melons, raised from English seed, but far exceeding their parent stock in size and flavour."[201] The Traills' first melon patch was planted in

---

197 Ibid., 11 Febuary 1829, 37.
198 Jameson, *Winter Studies and Summer Rambles*, 14 January 1837, 25.
199 Davidson, *Oxford Companion to Food*, 689; Sheppard, *Pickled, Potted and Canned*, 54–5.
200 Moodie, *Life in the Clearings*, 284.
201 Need, *Six Years in the Bush*, 16 July 1834, 99.

1834, only two years after their arrival, thus showing their significance as food. Musk melon, cantaloupe, nutmeg melon, and watermelon all thrive in Ontario soil. Traill also lists rock melon [136], which seems to have been a cantaloupe variety, but that term, unlike the others, does not appear in the nursery catalogues of Custead (1827) or Fleming (1855).[202] Autumn frost can damage these plants, so almost-ripe melons were good candidates for pickling and pickled melons were often among the many condiments at a winter meal.

Milk   Most farms had at least one or two milch cows to provide milk, although newcomers often had to wait to get their first one, which left them without milk for the first months, particularly in winter – "We can get no milk for love or money."[203] Dairy-women worried about cows getting loose in the woods because they ate the wild leek that grew abundantly there and tainted the milk's flavour, rendering it unfit for butter and cheese.[204] By 1885, Traill confidently wrote that there were "no more complaints of leeky milk and butter."[205] Goats were rare in Ontario, but not unheard of: John Langton had a pair of goats in the early 1830s that provided him with milk.

Milk Pan, *also* Milk Dish   The fresh warm milk was poured into these wide shallow bowls with flaring sides to let the cream rise to the top for skimming. Earthenware was considered best for this because, unlike tin, it had no crevices that could harbor old milk to spoil the new; whichever was used, it had to be thoroughly scalded between milkings.

Mince Pie   Traill's statement that an apple-marmalade pastry "sold in the confectioners under the name of mince-pie, and pie-cake" [110] is puzzling. Perhaps it was a long-vanished localism. Mince pie had two meanings, neither of them an apple-marmalade pastry. One was a mixture of minced meat (usually beef) and suet, dried fruits, and/or chopped apples, along with sweet spices; the other was the same mixture without the meat but still called mincemeat or minced meat. Particularly rich

---

202 Custead, *Catalogue of Fruit & Ornamental Trees*; James Fleming, *Catalogue of Garden, Agricultural and Flower Seeds.*

203 Pengelley, The Diaries of Harriet Pengelley, 1835–36.

204 Anne Langton, *A Gentlewoman in Upper Canada*, 21 April 1839, 231.

205 Traill, *Studies of Plant Life in Canada*, 37.

versions also had nuts, candied citrus and citron peels and juices, and brandy. By the end of the nineteenth century, the actual meat had disappeared from recipes on both sides of the Atlantic and it had evolved into a sticky, spicy, dark brown, raisiny mass.

Such pies had long been most often associated with Christmas. "This morning I made a lot of mince pies to last over the holidays"[206] and "We had roast beef and mince py for dinner."[207] At the end of January 1869, Mary Armstrong wrote: "Came home to dinner at twelve and had the last roast of our Christmas Beef and tonight a good mince pie, but we are not nearly at the end of our mince meat."[208] Although ambiguous, Mary seems to have been saying that her mince pie did not include beef. Traill and her newly widowed sister-in-law shared a piece of mince pie in February 1867.[209]

Mint, *see also* Peppermint   Various *Mentha*, classified as sweet herbs, that includes peppermint, spearmint ("common"), and pennyroyal; Traill mentions only peppermint.

Moist Sugar   A brown muscovado sugar with a fair amount of molasses retained in it, but cleaner, a bit brighter and dryer, sold in the shops as somewhat better.[210]

Molasses, *see also* Treacle, Pumpkin   Sugar cane molasses was a derivative of processing raw sugar cane into granulated white sugar. It was the thick brown liquid drained from raw sugar crystals: "When the sugar is becoming dry or crystallized the syrup drops from the grains as honey does from the comb."[211] However, its quality depended on the sugar's quality, so molasses also varied from coarse to fine table quality. Mrs Child even said, "it is a prodigious improvement to boil and skim it before you use it" – as if the housewife and mother didn't have enough tasks already! Frances Beaven, a resident of the New Brunswick backwoods, called it "the staple commodity in transatlantic housekeeping."[212]

206 Mathilda Bowers Eby, 23 December 1868, quoted in Hoffman and Taylor, *Much to Be Done*, 243.
207 Hallen, *Eleanora's Diary*, 25 December 1835, 124.
208 Armstrong, *Seven Eggs Today*, 29 January 1869, 138.
209 Traill to Kate Traill, *I Bless You in My Heart*, 2 February 1867, 166.
210 Webster and Parkes, *Encyclopedia of Domestic Economy*, 721.
211 Ward, *Grocer's Hand-Book and Directory*, 134.
212 Child, *The American Frugal Housewife*, 16; Beaven, *Sketches and Tales*, 28.

Beets and pumpkins could also be crushed, simmered for a long time in water, and the resulting juices strained and further boiled down into a concentrated syrup. It sounds like a tedious homemade procedure that Traill's two recipes do not really explain sufficiently.

Muscovado Sugar, *also* Muscavado Sugar, Barbados Sugar   A low-quality, unrefined sugar of dark brownish colour and oily texture, it was full of impurities since it had not been strained. The word derives from *más acabado,* Spanish for "more finished," since it was a level up from raw sugar. Imported West Indian muscovado is "quite as cheap" [146] as local maple sugar, says Traill, although Anne Langton states that "maple sugar, if made by hired labour, comes as dear as good Muscovado."[213] These sugars could be used interchangeably in recipes. White loaf and crushed sugars were manufactured from raw muscovado, which was transported to refineries, including those in Britain, but also, after the late 1850s, to Redpath's refinery in Montreal.

Mustard   A standard hot-tasting condiment and ingredient in English kitchens from at least the early Middle Ages. It's hard to imagine English foodways without mustard. Archaeological digs, merchants' advertisements, and estate inventories all reveal that commercial mustard powder, or flour as it was called, was available in small glass bottles or ceramic pots from at least the 1750s in Canada. Mrs Simcoe had it in her food supplies.[214] Brands were seldom identified, but two familiar English brands, Keen's and Colman, began to be manufactured in 1742 and 1814, respectively. However, the first (and continuing) Canadian mustard mill was Hamilton's G.S. Dunn Dry Mustard, established in 1867.

Mustard is part of the *Brassica* family; black (*B. nigra*) and yellowish-red white (*B. alba* or *hirta*) are native to Europe. Both were planted in early Ontario. Today, huge quantities are grown in the Prairies. Before the 1950s, English paste mustards were judicious blends of black and white with additions such as turmeric and rice flour for colour and body, but nowadays often include brown (*B. juncea*).[215]

213 Anne Langton to Thomas Langton, *A Gentlewoman in Upper Canada,* 29 November 1837, 162.

214 Olive Jones, *Glass of the British Military,* 60; Simcoe, *The Diary of Mrs. John Graves Simcoe,* 4 October 1791, 44.

215 Vaughn and Geissler, *New Oxford Book of Food Plants,* 142; Woodhead, *Early Canadian Gardening,* 33, 213; James Fleming, *Catalogue of Garden, Agricultural and Flower Seeds,* 2.

Despite being unmentioned in the *Guide*, mustard poultices, emetics, diuretics, and snuffs were widely employed in the sickroom. Steamed mustard greens were also very occasionally described in cookbooks, as were baby mustard leaves for salads.

Mutton "The Canadian grass-fed mutton is not so large as it is in England, and in flavour and texture more nearly resembles the Scotch," says Susanna Moodie. (Since it had been many years since she was in Scotland, how did she remember that?) She continues, "It has more of a young flavour, and, to my thinking, affords a more wholesome, profitable article of consumption."[216] Anna Jameson considered the local mutton "bad" but Mrs William Radcliff "heard about its excellence."[217] "Sheep between four and five years old produce the finest quality of mutton, but it is seldom got above three, and often under two years. The flesh should be a darkish, clear, red colour; the fat white."[218]

Stronger tasting mutton is making a comeback in Canada, due to influences such as the Slow Food movement and increasing numbers of Muslim shoppers. Butchered sheep sold as lamb is allowed to be up to twelve months old, while mutton must be more, preferably between two and four years.[219]

Navy Bread, also Hard Tack, Ship's Biscuit; *see also* Biscuits and Crackers A cheap, hard, and thick unleavened cracker fed to sailors – and often soldiers too – as part of their rations from the mid-seventeenth century onward. Its extreme dryness due to its being saltless and twice baked (baked and dried) rendered it more advantageous than yeast-risen bread on board ship: its portability and resistance to humidity meant that it could be stored in barrels much longer, both as rations during voyages and as foodstuffs destined for the colonies. After decades of hand production, in the late 1700s the British Navy invented machines for kneading and cutting the dough.

New Jersey Tea Traill claimed: "There is an historical interest attached to the name of this very attractive shrub which lingers still in the memories of the descendants of

216 Moodie, *Life in the Clearings*, 283.
217 Jameson, *Winter Studies and Summer Rambles*, 1 April 1837, 151; Magrath and Radcliff, *Authentic Letters from Upper Canada*, Mrs Radcliff, 14 June 1832, 43.
218 *The Canadian Housewife's Manual of Cookery*, 135.
219 Farm Products Grades and Sales Act, R.R.O. 1990 [Ontario], https://www.ontario.ca/laws/regulation/900380 (accessed 20 July 2016).

the U.E. Loyalists in Canada and in the State of New Jersey, where the leaves of the *Ceanothus* were first adopted as a substitute for the Chinese Tea-plant. Even to this day Americans will cross to Ontario in summer to gather quantities of the leaves to carry back from our plains, where it is found in great abundance. And while they commend the virtues of the plant, they, no doubt, recount the tales of war, trouble and privation endured in the old struggle waged by their grandfathers and great-grandfathers for independence, when, casting away the more costly tea, they had recourse to a humble native shrub to supply a luxury that was even then felt as a want and a necessity in their homes." She added, "The flavour of the leaves is slightly bitter and aromatic."[220] The scent was "delicate."[221]

Nutmeg and Mace   Mace is the lacy outer covering of the nutmeg (*Myristica fragans*). Both were popular spices, although mace's fragility meant transportation was difficult. Nutmeg graters were common little kitchen items, although some recipes suggested slicing and pounding nutmeg to a useful powder instead of grating. Mace was also pounded in a mortar, although pre-ground bottles were available. A whole nutmeg was sometimes "concealed in a [bride]cake and the happy person who cut the piece containing it was the next to be married."[222]

Nutmeg Melon   Nutmeg melon is a musk variety, with a sweet green flesh. It is listed in Custead's 1827 nursery catalogue.[223]

Nuts, see also Almond, Butternut, Walnut   It is curious that Traill is not more expansive in her treatment of the edible nuts of her region – acorn, beech-nut, black walnut, butternut, chestnut, hazelnut, hickory. It's true that the Peterborough area was on the outer geographical range of black walnut and American chestnut, but the others were not. She wrote often of the beech tree and oak trees in the forests and informed readers in her *Studies of Plant Life in Canada* that hazelnuts were "sweet and well-flavoured," so why didn't she discuss their fruits, the nuts, as food? The children in *Canadian Crusoes* are well aware of their efficacy and realize at the start of

220 Traill, *Studies of Plant Life in Canada*, 152, 160.
221 Traill, *Canadian Crusoes*, 8.
222 O'Brien, *Journals of Mary O'Brien*, 28 October 1829, 77.
223 Custead, *Catalogue of Fruit & Ornamental Trees*, 15; Woodhead, *Early Canadian Gardening*, 33, 212.

their ordeal they have plenty of nuts of different kinds such as "bushels and bushels of [sweet acorns] for the roasting," plus "sweet and pleasant" butternuts and hickory nuts among their "catalogue of forest dainties." Later they pick dwarf filberts (hazelnuts).[224]

Many First Nations relied on nuts transformed into oils, flours, and butters or various pottages, as well as a dye, but these uses do not appear to have been passed along to these particular colonists. An exceptions was the settlers' use of butternuts for a rich brown dye [182].[225]

Oats, see also Cookie   Some held that the oats grown in Upper Canada (*Avena sativa*) were "very indifferent, and much inferior to those raised in Europe, being small and light in the grain, and comparatively not nutritious."[226] Traill begged to differ: since oats helped the Scottish and Irish communities grow "strong in muscle" they made "good food" in Canada [115]. Oats were brought by the Scots, for whom it was the staple grain, and had the advantage that they flourished in cold climates where wheat and barley did not. Frances Stewart said in 1847 that "it was always very difficult to procure."[227] Traill supplies recipes for pancakes and two porridges, plus instructions for the use of oats in a fever drink and a stomachic, but she deems it "presumptuous in an Englishwoman to give a recipe for Oat-cakes" to women of northern England, Scotland, and Ireland [116]. She lacked a corresponding aversion to giving American recipes to Englishwomen because she was a North American resident now.

Oatmeal is not to be confused with rolled oats, which appeared after the development of rollers for milling grains in North America and were first introduced in Canada in 1882.[228]

Onion   A member of the wide genus *Allium*, which also includes eschalot, garlic, and chives, each mentioned in the *Guide*, as well as shallots and leek, which were not. Many types were grown in early Canada. The most widely cultivated was the yellow

224 Traill, *Studies of Plant Life in Canada*, 109; Traill, *Canadian Crusoes*, 62, 147.
225 Traill, *Studies of Plant Life in Canada*, 151; Erichsen-Brown, *Use of Plants*, 58–62, 70, 74.
226 Howison, *Sketches of Upper Canada*, 233.
227 Stewart, *Our Forest Home*, 5 May 1847, 212.
228 Thornton, *The History of the Quaker Oats Company*, 37.

Spanish onion, still familiar now.[229] In the earliest years and in places like lumber camps which did not have a kitchen garden, onions were considered to be a luxury on a par with tea and sugar. Onions fried up with beefsteak or ham slices were a common dish.

Oven: Brick, Stone, or Clay   Which oven Traill is referring to requires looking at her sentences in full context. Sometimes it was a bake-kettle acting as an oven, sometimes the oven within an iron cookstove, and sometimes a constructed bake oven made from brick, stone, or clay.

Building an effective bake oven that did not leak hot air required a skill that not many settlers had when they arrived, so for the first decades of colonial life ovens of brick, stone, or clay were rare, either inside or outside log cabins. Once the family built its second and bigger house, an oven was more likely to be included, either incorporated into or beside the fireplace or placed outside, away from the cabin. They took skill to manage since the firewood had to be laid in appropriately, the fire left to burn for long enough to heat the brick, clay, or stones, the coals quickly scraped out and the food put in at the right temperature. Lacking thermometers, several ways were used to judge the oven's readiness: throwing in a handful of flour or a piece of paper to see how quickly it browned, or thrusting in one's arm to see how long it took to become too painful to leave in. Each cook became familiar with how many seconds her method took in her oven. Removing the door during baking to check was not a good idea because too much heat could be lost, possibly damaging the food. And once the heat started to fade it could not be restored.

Bread was usually put in first, as it required the most intense heat. Pies and cakes went in after some heat had faded, followed by custards and small cupcakes and biscuits. Leftover heat was suitable for such tasks as drying pigeon feathers for pillows or tomatoes for winter storage. Traill says to bake many things in the oven, but did not assume readers would have one.

Panada, Pap   Both of these easily eaten and digested compounds were similar to a very soft bread pudding, and thus designated as invalid and baby foods. Pap was milk thickened with arrowroot or sago powder, or pieces of white bread moistened by water or milk, while panada was crustless soft white bread stirred into a pulp with

---

229 Woodhead, *Early Canadian Gardening*, 210; James Fleming, *Catalogue of Garden, Agricultural and Flower Seeds*, 2.

very hot water or milk. Sometimes they were flavoured with personal choices such as rosewater, nutmeg, and/or sugar, and occasionally a few raisins or currants were blended in. They were easily spooned into a waiting mouth.

Parsley   As in our time, the two types of parsley (*Petroselinum crispum*), flat-leaved and curly-leaved, were the most popular daily herb, both chopped as an ingredient for countless dishes and used in sprigs as a garnish.

Parsnip   (*Pastinaca sativa*). One of parsnip's characteristics is to improve in flavour and sweetness if left to overwinter in the ground instead of being moved to a root cellar. They were roasted or boiled and mashed with potatoes and butter.[230]

Partridge   In Traill's children's novel, *Canadian Crusoes*, the three lost children gather "a dozen fresh partridge eggs from the inner shade of a thick tuft of grass and herbs that grew beside a fallen tree ... [W]hile a stone flung by the steady hand of Hector stunned the parent bird, ... not the first partridge [he had] killed that way."[231] The boiled partridge eggs, wild strawberries, and cold spring water were the first meal the forlorn children shared. The roasted partridge was their second. Many colonists referred to cooking a brace of partridges in autumn, the season when they were best. Neither the wood partridge nor the spruce partridge migrate. Through the winter, they eat wintergreen berries, spruce buds, and the red bark of the wild raspberry, "which imparts a red tinge and much bitterness to the flesh, and by the month of February renders it unfit for food."[232]

Peach   Nine varieties (and two nectarines) (all *Amygdalus Persica*) were offered in the 1827 Toronto Nursery catalogue.[233] Niagara was early recognized as having the necessary warm climate to grow peach trees. So plentiful were peaches in Niagara, "that bushels may be seen lying rotting under the trees, their only consumers apparently being the pigs."[234] They did not thrive in the Peterborough region.

230 James Fleming, *Catalogue of Garden, Agricultural and Flower Seeds*, 3.
231 Traill, *Canadian Crusoes*, 24–5.
232 Traill, *Pearls and Pebbles*, 78–9.
233 Custead, *Catalogue of Fruit & Ornamental Trees*, 10–11; Woodhead, *Early Canadian Gardening*, 28–9.
234 Samuel Strickland, *Twenty-Seven Years in Canada West*, 1:152.

While the *Guide* was being typeset and bound, the section on peaches was put in the wrong place: it was placed following the section on wild fruits instead of being grouped with the stone fruits.

Pear   As with apples, Traill's list [77] only hints at the varieties of common or European (*Pyrus Communis*) pears available; about 150, suggested the *Encyclopedia of Domestic Economy*.[235] None of those in *the Encyclopedia* matched hers nor did those in Custead's 1827 list. No pear was native to North America. Some varieties were eaten as dessert, while others were best for stewing or poaching. Yet others were turned into alcoholic perry. Of those on Traill's summer list, Bartlett, named after the man who brought the trees to the United States, remains well known.[236]

Pearlash, *also* Pearl Ash, Pearl-ash, Pearlashes   Potassium carbonate, a partially refined version of potash. Vegetable potash is the white ashy by-product of thoroughly burned green hardwood, particularly oak, beech, and elm and some ferns. Pine has too much resin to make good potash. Barrels with perforated bottoms had a layer of straw and lime powder (see entry for lime, above) put in the bottom and were then filled with the ashes and rinsed with water. The damp ashes were burned again and dried into hard glassy lumps of pearly white potassium carbonate. The water that was rinsed out became lye and was used in laundering as a bleach. Rural housewives carefully stored cold ashes from the fireplace and cookstove to make lye to use in their homemade soap.

As vast acres of ancient forest were razed by European colonists, a huge potash industry developed in early Ontario to supply the European market. In the early years, ashes were often the main, even sole, source of cash for the bush farmers and ashery kilns sprang up in numerous small towns and villages. Pearl and pot ashes were so important to the economy that smugglers cultivated an illicit trade across the Canada–United States border. Potash appeared on countless export lists through the 1860s, then gradually disappeared as the hardwood forests vanished and deposits of mineral potash were found in Germany. By the 1880s, the agricultural industry had vanished, but mineral potash is mined today in Saskatchewan and serves as an essential ingredient in such products as agricultural fertilizer. Both potash and pearlash were already important ingredients in many household and industrial products, such

235 Webster and Parkes, *Encyclopedia of Domestic Economy*, 498–9.
236 Custead, *Catalogue of Fruit & Ornamental Trees*, 9; Woodhead, *Early Canadian Gardening*, 27.

as bleach, soap, furniture polish, varnish, matches, and dye mordant. Pearlash was also used to soften hard water, to give white paint a pearly grey tint, and in manufacturing explosives and imitation jewels.

Pearlash is an alkali and when combined with an acid (buttermilk, sour milk, molasses, lemon juice, wine) and then moistened releases bubbles of carbon dioxide into a cake batter or bread dough, causing it to rise. It was also used to aerate beverages. As a baking ingredient in a household cookbook, pearlash first appeared in *American Cookery* (1796), although its use by professional bakers preceded this date by several decades. Dutch settlers in the United States are credited with being the first to use pearlash in baking.

Peas, Green, *see* Green Peas

Pease Pudding   Peas were important provisions for soup and pudding. The white, yellow, or green peas in "pease" pudding or "pease" soup (the "e" was often retained in these two dishes) were ripened, dried, and then often split naturally into two pieces, hence the phrase "split peas." After soaking overnight, they cooked quickly and conveniently. Pea soup was mentioned by settlers as easy to prepare.

The British Army stationed in the Canadas was constantly looking for supplies of dried peas for rations, as numerous ads inserted in the early years of the *Upper Canada Gazette* attest.

Pepper-Grass   Pepper-grass or pepperwort (*Lepidium sativum* or *campestre*), common garden cress, is part of the mustard family. A peppery-tasting herb, it is a pleasant salad green. Although it is included in a list of vegetables Traill quotes [61] she indicates no specific knowledge of it in her botanical writings. It was a European introduction, now considered a nuisance weed.

Peppermint, *see also* Mints   Cultivated mostly for its cooling oil, which was sold as peppermint essence. *Mentha piperita* was known for its "highly odiferous and pungent essential oil."[237]

Pickles and Preserves   It is hard to overestimate the importance of pickles and preserves year-round on the Canadian table. In *The Backwoods of Canada,* Traill sum-

237 Webster and Parkes, *Encyclopedia of Domestic Economy*, 490.

marizes the importance of pickles to everyday meals: "The great want of spring vegetables renders pickles a valuable addition to the table at the season when potatoes have become unfit and distasteful."[238] Vast quantities of home-made pickles, jams, jellies, chutneys, sugared fruits, marmalades ("that pet sweet of the Scotch"[239]), and catsups filled pantry shelves, but imported and locally produced varieties were also available in the shops. In Canadian

Fig. 32 · Preserving pan.

cookbooks of the nineteenth century, the four most included pickles were made from beets, cucumbers, cabbage, and onions. Pickled green beans were also common, as was horseradish [164]. By the latter part of the century, mixed pickles like chow chow were regularly appearing in cookbooks.

As for sweet preserves, strawberry and raspberry were most favoured, as they are today. "The ladies make jams and jellies after the orthodox European fashion," noted Sam Strickland, but he also remarked that plum, raspberry, and strawberry jam were used to make something resembling what we today call fruit leathers by being "spread, about half an inch thick, on sheets of paper, to dry in the sun. This will be accomplished in a few days; after which the papers are rolled up, tied, and hung up in a dry place for use."[240]

Although the underlying scientific causes of spoilage were just starting to be understood, the need to take measures to conserve foodstuffs safely was definitely understood, especially the need to exclude air. Some pickle jars were covered with stretched bladders, which dried tight as a drum. Fruit preserves often had rounds of white paper dipped in brandy placed directly on the fruit, with more paper tied over the top and glued with egg white. All too often, however, "at sundry times afterward, unless the luck is unusual, the preserves continued 'working,' [moulding] and the boiling and skimming has to be done again,"[241] as many a recipe laments. The possibility of poisoning from eating food that had been improperly cooked and stored was partially understood. Tin pots, for example, were safer than those made of brass

238 Traill, *Backwoods of Canada*, 147.
239 Moodie, *Flora Lyndsay*, 125.
240 Samuel Strickland, *Twenty-Seven Years in Canada West*, 2:296.
241 "Preservation of Fruit," *The Canadian Agriculturalist*, August 1855, 8: 244.

when cooking with vinegar for pickles because the green that arises when vinegar interacts with brass is verdigris, which is poisonous. "Stone [i.e. stoneware] and wood are the only suitable materials in which to keep pickles."[242] "Pickles should be kept closely covered; always use a wooden spoon, all mettle [sic] being improper. The large jars should be seldom opened; and small ones, for the different pickles in use, for common supply. Acids dissolve the lead that is in the tinning of saucepans. When necessary to boil vinegar, do it in a stone[ware] jar on the hot hearth, or in an enamelled saucepan. Pickles should never be put into glazed jars, as salt and vinegar penetrate the glaze, which is poisonous."[243]

In *The Backwoods of Canada*, Traill remarked that, lacking a good vinegar, "I have heard [cucumber pickle] much commended, [that] putting the cucumbers in whisky and water, which in time turns to a fine vinegar, and preserves the colour and crispness of the vegetable; while the vinegar is apt to make them soft, especially if poured on boiling hot, as is the usual practice."[244] Amusingly, Dr Tiger Dunlop, a Scot known in Upper Canada as the Backwoodsman, cited bad cucumber pickle as an example of bad Canadian cooking.[245]

Pies, *see also* Cooking Fats, Mince Pie   Then, as now, "If properly made, few articles of cookery are more generally liked than relishing pies; they may be made of a great variety of things," stated *The Canadian Housewife's Manual of Cookery*. One Moodie meal included pumpkin, raspberry, cherry, and currant pies. A skilled pastry maker was much admired: "The girls, in those days, ... could handle a rolling pin with more satisfaction than a sketch book," reminisced Caniff Haight about his 1830s boyhood. All fruits, vegetable, meats, poultry, fish, and wild game could be encased in pastry and could appear at all three daily meals.[246]

Nowadays we usually think of commercial shortening, particularly the Crisco brand, available in Canada from the mid-1910s onwards, as pastry fat, but cooks used to employ a wider variety: suet (beef, mutton, veal), lard, drippings, beef marrow,

242 Abell, *The Skilful Housewife's Guide*, 63. Also *The Frugal Housewife's Manual*, 20. Many cookbooks remarked on these matters.
243 *The Canadian Housewife's Manual of Cookery*, 310; Webster and Parkes, *Encyclopedia of Domestic Economy*, 795.
244 Traill, *Backwoods of Canada*, 148.
245 Ibid., 73–4; Dunlop, *Statistical Sketches of Upper Canada*, 57.
246 *The Canadian Housewife's Manual of Cookery*, 195; Moodie, *Roughing It in the Bush*, 333; Haight, *Country Life in Canada*, 47.

or butter. "Drippings, especially from beef, when very clean and nice, are frequently used for every-day crusts and pies, and for such purposes are a satisfactory substitute for butter [and] lard."[247] (Interestingly, butter and lard are returning to favour in early twenty-first-century pies.) Traill provides no recipe for puff pastry, the most time-consuming of all pastry, although it was a standard recipe in most other cookbooks, including Canadian ones.

Her savoury pie flavourings are homemade vinegar and cheap mustard, with a few herbs, in contrast to the sophisticated range of flavours in recipe books such as Dods's *The Cook and Housewife's Manual* (1826) and *The Canadian Housewife's Manual of Cookery* (1861), which suggested white wine and oyster liquor for fish pies, and anchovy and veal gravy for meat pies. Winter fruit pies could be made of summer preserves, but summer fruit pies followed the succession of harvest, from rhubarb (the first) through strawberry, red and black raspberry, black currant and gooseberry, to cherry, then to huckleberry, blackberry, and blueberry, followed by apricot, peach, and plum, and (the last) apple and pumpkin. Apple pies were by far the most common and popular in nineteenth-century Canada. Apples could also be combined with other fruits. Other sweet pie fillings could be raisin, lemon, lemon custard, mincemeat, tomato, or sweet potato. A lemon pie recipe extant in the Traill Family Papers was actually an apple pie flavoured with lemon.[248]

Pigeon   The pigeon in Traill's *Guide* is the now-extinct passenger pigeon (*Ectopistes migratorius*), also called the wild pigeon, once so numerous that the immense migrating flocks struck witnesses with awe. Their annual arrival in Ontario in mid-March was a harbinger of spring. They were sometimes destructive to field crops such as wheat, buckwheat, and peas, but they were delicious eating and were consumed in the millions in pot pies [161], stews, and soups, and preserved with either salt or smoke. The squabs were extra fat and delicate. So approving was Traill that she provides six recipes. By the very early 1880s they had disappeared from Traill's Peterborough area, although a few were sighted in Toronto until circa 1900; the last known passenger pigeon in Ontario was seen in 1902, in Penetanguishene.[249] Pigeon feathers were used as stuffing in pillows.

---

247 *The Cook Not Mad*, number 273.
248 Traill Family Collection, 4(22): unpaginated.
249 Mitchell, *The Passenger Pigeon in Ontario*, 21, 106–9, 133; Samuel Strickland, *Twenty-Seven Years in Canada West*, 2:297–302.

Plum, *see also* Bullace Plum, Damson Plum, Gage Plum, Hedge-Bullace, Wild Red Plum The fourth most important fruit tree crop cultivated in nineteenth-century Ontario was plums (*Prunus domestica*), following apples, peaches, and pears. Although a native red plum was well liked by the European colonists, they planted a wide variety of imports. Seventeen varieties were already available in York (Toronto) in 1827, according to *The Catalogue of Fruit & Ornamental Trees*, put out by the Toronto Nursery.[250]

Plum Cake, *see also* Cake, Pound Cake, Sponge Cake "Plum" in this context – and plum pudding – was an old word for dried fruits, particularly currants and raisins, and sometimes dates and apricots. Traill's Plain Plum Cake [106], with its limited currants or raisins and bit of carbonate of soda, is descended from the long British tradition of great yeast-risen fruit cakes. In the eighteenth century, the air incorporated into the batter from beating eggs intensely became the leavener instead. Distinctions between "better" or "good" versus "plain" or "common" plum cakes (less fruit, spice, egg) originally arose out of the limited household baking facilities of families in industrialized cities, then were translated to backwoods conditions. Plum cakes had gone out of fashion by the end of the Victorian era but survive as Christmas cakes.

Plum Pudding Plum pudding has a long history in Anglo-American cooking and cookbooks. In this context, plum means dried fruit, particularly currants and raisins but also dates, figs, and apricots. With roasted beef, it was part of many a meal. "[He] drove to [the] Gosses with a piece of beef and a plum pudding for them as we thought it would be a treat for them as they were not well off but very respectable people," said Eleanora Hallen.[251] It was perhaps a bit old-fashioned by mid-century, as implied in these remarks by Armstrong: "I am cooking roast Beef & plum pudding for the sake of old times." Then, on 1 July, "Papa & I took our lamb & green pease with a plum pudding quietly alone."[252]

Plum pudding also has a long association with Christmas: "We got up by candlelight [and] we made a large plum pudding before breakfast as the pensioners['] children are coming to dinner" wrote Elizabeth Hallen. Almost two decades earlier, John Langton wanted to make a plum pudding for his lumbermen at Christmas, but

250 Woodhead, *Early Canadian Gardening*, 28.
251 Eleanora Hallen, 25 December 1845, quoted in Hoffman and Taylor, *Across the Waters*, 131.
252 Armstrong, *Seven Eggs Today*, 26 March 1869 (Good Friday), 144, and 1 July 1869, 148.

"currants and suet were scarce, the eggs entirely wanting, and flour by much the preponderating ingredient."[253]

Porcupine   Traill says in passing that lumbermen sometimes ate porcupine. Others at least tried it: "We killed a porcupine here the other day, and ate it. It is said to resemble sucking-pig, but I thought it more like lamb," wrote John Langton. Alexander Ferrier thought it "very like rabbit." For Indiana in *Canadian Crusoes*, it was "white and good to eat."[254]

Pork, *see also* Bacon, Ham, Lard, Meats, Salt Pork   Pigs were the most significant source of meat in early Canada. Their only functions were to provide meat for sustenance and skin for leather (unlike cows, which could also provide milk, and sheep, milk and fleece) but pork was still so essential to the provincial economy that it was often used as payment in lieu of cash and early settlers' accounts tell us how much they relied on salt pork and bacon for their daily fare. Recognizing its supremacy, Patrick Shirreff called fried pork "the standard dish of the country" and Anne Langton called boiled pork "the national dish." She reported on 1 January 1841, that "Besides pork barrels we have now six sides of bacon and thirteen hams decorating our ceiling."[255] At butchering time, some meat was used fresh, while the rest was preserved for later consumption.

"We had some meat [pork] hanging in a bag on the side of the house, which your brother tied up tightly to prevent depredation" from the animals, said Mrs King.[256] Vast quantities were prepared for family consumption: "Mary is having a hundredweight of sausages made to furnish our winter breakfast table, and Bill and Anthony are building a smoke house for drying the bacon and hams on three pigs for the coming year" and "[g]reat cooking of pigs still going on. The smoke house is now full of hams and bacon, and will continue to be so for a month or weeks to come."[257] Some families took their hams out of the brine in spring and only then smoked them.

253 Mary Hallen, 29 December 1851, quoted in Hoffman and Taylor, *Across the Waters*, 244; John Langton, quoted in Guillet, *Early Life in Upper Canada*, 200.

254 Anne Langton, *A Gentlewoman in Upper Canada*, 16 September 1842, 351; Alexander Ferrier, quoted in Hoffman and Taylor, *Across the Waters*, 317; Traill, *Canadian Crusoes*, 147.

255 Patrick Shirreff, quoted in Guillet, *Early Life in Upper Canada*, 199; Anne Langton, *A Gentlewoman in Upper Canada*, 21 October 1838, 189, and 1 January 1841, 310.

256 King, *Letters from Muskoka*, 113.

257 O'Brien, *Journals of Mary O'Brien*, 27 November 1828, 26.

Fig. 33 · Diagram of pork cuts

Interestingly, Traill did not refer to pork sausages, once an utterly common way of preparing pork.

There were varying opinions on the quality of pork. Anna Jameson considered it "excellent and delicate, being fattened principally on Indian corn," while the Tom Wilson character in *Life in the Clearings* complained of "fat pork ... morning, noon and night, swimming in its own grease" and "the horrid sight of swine's flesh for ever spread before him."[258] One reason pork was so flavourful was the farmers' habit of allowing their pigs to range freely through the forests, particularly their autumn diet of hickory nuts and corn. Only by mid-century, when farms included much greater acreage, were pigs less likely to be allowed to roam freely. Once penned, they were fed a diet of table scraps, food waste, and weeds pulled from the garden.

258 Jameson, *Winter Studies and Summer Rambles*, 1 April 1837, 151; Moodie, *Life in the Clearings*, 80.

Traill's allusion to "chine fashion" [154] relates pork ribs to the image of barrel ribs projecting above the top lip before they are sawed off.[259]

Potash, *see* Pearlash

Potato   By far the most planted and most consumed vegetable in Upper Canada in Traill's era were common white potatoes (*Solanum tuberosum*), called English White in Custead's catalogue of 1827[260] but also widely known as Irish potatoes (as differentiated from yellow and orange sweet potatoes, *Ipomoea batatas*). Their original habitat was South America; they were taken from there to Europe, and then to North America. A few potato varieties from before the Irish Famine of the 1840s survive as heirlooms.

Pork and potatoes were repeatedly referred to as the settlers' main food, especially in the early years. Even if no other vegetables were planted, potatoes were. Sam Strickland suggested that a family needed to overwinter twenty or thirty bushels of them, but other accounts suggest many more – that's a lot of potatoes![261] The need for potatoes is summarized in this 1852 comment: "Large farmers in the old cleared country live remarkably well, and enjoy within themselves all the substantial comforts of life. Many of them keep carriages, and drive splendid horses. The contrast between the pork and potato diet, (and sometimes of potatoes alone without the pork), in the backwoods, is really striking."[262] Potatoes were occasionally eaten with buttermilk.

Some farmers and housewives had difficulty growing them. Frances Stewart said of the 1851 harvest: "all crops are excellent except potatoes which in most places about here seem bad. The leaves are all black & shriveled & no roots ... [T]he potatoes are all wet & small & scanty."[263] Indeed, the same blight that decimated the potato harvest in Ireland in the 1840s affected some Canadian harvests too.

Traill names several common varieties of potatoes, some early season, some mid-season and some late, so that they were constantly available for harvesting. Storing them properly was a major concern because they could turn mushy and smelly if there was insufficient air circulation. No one liked the task of sorting out rotted potatoes.

259   *Oxford English Dictionary*, 127.
260   Custead, *Catalogue of Fruit & Ornamental Trees*, 15; Woodhead, *Early Canadian Gardening*, 211.
261   Samuel Strickland, *Twenty-Seven Years in Canada West*, 1:65.
262   Moodie, *Life in the Clearings*, 94.
263   Stewart, *Our Forest Home*, 25 August 1851, 185–6.

Potato Yeast Potato mash was a popular medium for growing yeast. Potatoes were cooked, mashed, and left out to attract wild yeasts. The yeasty potatoes were then blended with flour to make loaves.

Poultry, *see also* Chicken, Duck, Gizzard, Goose, Turkey Hens were the most common farmyard poultry, but some farmwomen kept ducks, geese, and turkeys too, although they were harder to maintain. Mary Armstrong commented that the "market was well supplied with all kinds of provisions[,] ... such an abundance of poultry both alive and dead, such a crackling of fowls[,] quacking of chicks as well as geese and turkey was never surpassed in the genial days of spring." Sometimes the settlers complained that their poultry were subject to the predations of wolves, foxes, eagles, and wolverines, and even of the free-range pigs. Frances Stewart lamented the loss of "a dear little black hen with a large *topping* of black and white feathers" who was "so tame she came to me whenever she saw me and [would] eat bread out of my hand. I was very sorry. The Wolverines cry at night like some person screaming. They are like a very large cat." Traill mentioned once that "a horrid beast ... called here a scunck" got several of her "best fowls." She started her Canadian farm life with "a fine brood of fowls, ... some ducks, and I am to have turkeys and geese this summer [1835]."[264]

Pound Cake, *see also* Cake, Cup Cake, Plum Cake, Sponge Cake Pound cake recipes, so-called because the flour, butter, and sugar each weighed a pound, appeared in the early eighteenth century. The best ones were a lot of work because the butter had to be laboriously creamed by hand until very light, then the sugar worked in, then the stabilizing flour added. This buttery batter was lightened by many yolks and whites that had been whisked for a long time to achieve the light custardy texture and airy peaks that trapped enough air to elevate the batter while baking in the hot oven. A century later in America, the same ingredients were converted to one cup of butter, two of sugar, three of flour, and four eggs, enhanced with a baking powder, then quickly baked in individual cups – cup cake.

Early cookbooks often had two pound cake recipes, one plain and one fine or rich. The latter had additions such as caraway seeds, rosewater or brandy, or "candied

264 Armstrong, *Seven Eggs Today*, [20] February 1859, 106; Stewart, *Revisiting "Our Forest Home,"* 25 March 1868, 230; Traill, *Backwoods of Canada*, 224.

lemon peel cut thin, and blanched and chopped sweet almonds" and "half a pound of currants."[265] Other recipes called for spices and candied seeds.

Pudding Cloth   A pudding cloth enclosed pudding batter so that it could be cooked by boiling in a liquid, usually water. Kitchens had at least one drawerful of closely woven cloths of plain cotton or muslin for this use. A common size was 24 × 24 inches (61 cm × 61 cm) or bigger; a square was essential to ensure an even ball-shape when the four corners of the cloth were pulled up and tied above the lump of pudding batter. Greasing and/or flouring the inside of the cloth created a barrier between the boiling water and the pudding and helped to preventing a waterlogged mess. These cloths had to be scrupulously cleaned before reuse, otherwise the next pudding might taste of soapy water or dirty dishcloth. Just when they began to be used as containers for boiling food is unclear, but they are found in English recipes starting in the very early seventeenth century. Until then, the cylindrical membranes of beef, pork, and lamb intestines had been used for savoury (not sweet) puddings, as in sausages, but these casings could only be used once, were laborious to clean after butchering, and often broke. The pudding cloth revolutionized pudding-making because it was much easier to use than intestines and was re-usable.

A pudding bag was a rectangular pudding cloth folded in half and seamed on the two edges. A drawstring pulled the top closed. Pudding cloths and bags had been almost replaced by ceramic bowls and metal shapes by the mid-nineteenth century.

Puddings, *see also* Hominy, Indian Pudding, Panada and Pap, Pease Pudding, Plum Pudding, Rice Pudding, Sauces, Supporne; *also* Pudding Sauces [359]   Traill's choice of pudding recipes for her *Guide* was limited to those that needed explaining to her immigrant audience. These came from the Anglo pudding tradition via New England. The term "pudding" has a more circumscribed meaning in Canada today and is often associated with packages of instant milk-based puddings stirred on top of the stove (as in chocolate or butterscotch pudding), although sometimes also with homemade versions of these packages as well as baked rice pudding or baked lemon pudding. In Traill's time, however, "pudding" had a range of meanings and the results were a mainstay of all sorts of meals, from those of the very poor to the elite. The one constant at a meal was the presence of a sweet and/or savoury pudding – or two or

265 Hale, *Early American Cookery*, 405.

three. They could be based on wheat, corn, sago, tapioca, rice, arrowroot, or some other grain or starch and were baked, boiled, steamed, or boiled and then baked; thick, runny, soft, hard, delicate; spicy, salty, sweet, plain; floury, eggy, fruity, fatty; sauced, sprinkled with sugar; round like a ball, long like a sausage, moulded in a castle or turban shape, baked in a pie-dish, baked in a patty-pan; hasty, slow – the variations were endless. By the mid-nineteenth century the prevalence of pudding started to wane, but its dominance in Canadian household menus took a long time to disappear.

Pumpkin Botanically, pumpkins belong to the genus *Cucurbita* and are actually squash. Larger varieties were grown in fields as important crops for cattle feed, with small sweet ones grown in the garden for household meals. Pumpkin flesh could be converted to many dishes: it could be stewed like a vegetable, baked in a pie, reduced to a mash and turned into soup, or filtered into a syrup or a molasses called sass (although Traill does not use this American term; see her recipe for pumpkin molasses [135]). Sliced pumpkin dried well for reconstitution in winter. "How delicious the large piece of pumpkin pie tasted," sighed Canniff Haight.[266] Pumpkin pies have been associated with Thanksgiving since the late eighteenth century, but Traill does not acknowledge this in any of her writings, though many of her neighbours were Yankees. Pumpkins were also carved for lanterns for Hallowe'en.

Quail Quails (*Colinus virginianus*) "are the most delicate eating," said Anna Jameson, and "I lived on them when I could eat nothing else." They were once bountiful, but are nowadays found mostly in southwestern Ontario and are better known as Northern Bobwhites.[267]

Quince Although the hard, raw, yellow quince (*Cydonia oblonga*) is unpalatable ("austere"),[268] it cooks down into a fragrant pink jam, jelly, or paste. Traill does not provide any recipes, but mentions it as a fruit seed to bring during emigration [80]. She would have been familiar with it at home in Suffolk, where it grew well. Quince

266 Haight, *Country Life in Canada*, 9.
267 Jameson, *Winter Studies and Summer Rambles*, 1 April 1837, 151; Goodwin, *A Bird-Finding Guide to Ontario*, 384.
268 Webster and Parkes, *Encyclopedia of Domestic Economy*, 499.

recipes regularly appeared in British recipe books of the sixteenth through eighteenth centuries but seldom in any Canadian or American cookbooks.

Radish   Dishes of sliced carrot-shaped red or yellow raw radishes (*Raphanus sativus*) were a common feature on Canadian breakfast and dinner tables from mid-spring to early frost, whereas today we think of the little ball type and associate them with salads and garnishes. Young seedlings were sometimes included in salads. Occasionally the old varieties are found at farmers' markets.[269]

Raisin   Raisins are dried grapes; those dried in the sun were called sun raisins and sometimes jar raisins since they were packed for export in jars. The large Muscatel or Malaga raisins were an element in elegant desserts. While travelling by coach down the St Lawrence River shore from Montreal to York (Toronto) Rebecca Radcliff was "uniformly" served "a dessert of raisins, almonds, biscuits and wild fruits," even "at all the poorest taverns." Common raisins were lesser quality grapes. Until the latter part of the nineteenth century, raisins were less widespread than currants (see Currant, Zante) because they required seeding before use, a tedious task before raisin seeders were invented in the 1890s, one of the many clever Victorian inventions that eased kitchen work. For cakes on special occasions – weddings, Christmas – such extra work was worth it, but not ordinarily to busy housewife-cooks. Our modern-day seedless Thompson raisins started reaching the Canadian market late in the 1800s.[270]

Raspberry, Wild Red and Black   Wild red (*Rubus idaeus*) and black (*R. occidentalis*) raspberries grew prolifically in the backwoods in clearings, along creek banks, on upturned tree roots, and in "every waste and neglected spot," as many settlers, Traill included, noted with awe. One family made "more than a bushel of" dried raspberries.[271] They were important sources of fresh fruit for jam, jelly, and beverages (wine, tea, and juice), as well as of twigs, bark, and roots for poultices and decoctions. Sam Strickland described wild raspberries, both red and black, as "a delicious fruit, and particularly grateful on a hot day to a weary traveler."[272]

269 Weaver, *Heirloom Vegetable Gardening*, 207.
270 Magrath and Radcliff, *Authentic Letters from Upper Canada*, Mrs Radcliff, 27 June 1832, 58; Webster and Parkes, *Encyclopedia of Domestic Economy*, 507.
271 Tivy, *Your Loving Anna*, 80.
272 Traill, *Studies of Plant Life in Canada*, 132; Samuel Strickland, *Twenty-Seven Years in Canada West*, 2:310.

Raspberry Vinegar   A refreshing drink of raspberry syrup made with vinegar instead of water was one of several non-alcoholic drinks created in the mid-nineteenth century by the temperance movement in an attempt to combat daily consumption of beer, gin, whisky, and cider. See page 85 for a delicious version to make at home.

Receipt   The old word for recipe, both for cooking and medications.

Rennet   A digestive enzyme found in the stomach lining of unweaned calves and a very few plants, rennet is used for coagulating milk and/or cream into curds and whey (junket) and in most cheeses. During butchery time the stomach lining was a highly prized product but was not useable until it had been cleaned and then either thoroughly dried or soaked in a brine for several months. In Traill's time a dry piece was steeped in milk as an early step in cheese-making, but two decades later it was more conveniently available as a liquid extract.[273] One dried stomach could be cut into enough coin-sized pieces to last for a season of making cheese at home.

Rhubarb   Other than recommending it be planted, it is surprising that Traill says nothing more about cooking this much-loved early spring fruit (*Rheum*), also called "pie plant" because it is the first fresh ingredient to appear in spring for pies and was so often used as a pie filling. However, perhaps she did not grow up with it, since Webster and Parkes say in their *Encyclopedia of Domestic Economy* (1855) that it was comparatively little known in British kitchen gardens until about 1825.[274]

Rice, see Indian Rice, White Rice

Rice Pudding   Fruited rice puddings were popular in rural Canada and appeared regularly on breakfast, midday, and supper tables, and also at gatherings such as housing or quilting bees since they were easy to make and kept well. Anne Langton once saw "twelve very large" ones at a breakfast accompanied by cranberry jelly. Sandford Fleming's teas on 12 and 29 June 1853 consisted of rice pudding.[275]

273 Ward, *Grocer's Hand-Book and Directory*, 176.
274 Webster and Parkes, *Encyclopedia of Domestic Economy*, 492.
275 Anne Langton, *A Gentlewoman in Upper Canada*, 29 June 1842, 345; Sandford Fleming, *Sir Sandford Fleming*, 12 and 29 June 1853, 275, 277.

As with so many culinary practices in the backwoods, rice pudding has a long history. Recipes for baked rice puddings began appearing in English cookbooks in the early 1600s, although rice was recorded as having arrived in the British Isles in the mid-1200s.[276] Nutmeg and raisins were common additions. Over a century later, *The Art of Cookery Made Plain and Simple* (1747) has twenty-two recipes featuring rice, including nine puddings (five baked, four boiled). *American Cookery* (1796) has six, all baked. Traill's boiled Apple-Rice is untraditional; no eggs to bind, no sugar to sweeten, no butter to enrich, just plain rice and acidic apples, and a little flavour from lemon and/or cloves if available, plus a sprinkling of sugar as sauce. A true poverty dish.

Robin   Traill's sentence about Canadian robins being edible was crossed out in the version being prepared for possible republication in the early 1880s.[277] Presumably the effort required to capture and prepare such a small bird for cooking was no longer necessary in the now well-settled Ontario farmlands.

Root-House   The root-house was a food storage cellar effective in the harsh climate of North America that settlers borrowed from the First Peoples: "a house to preserve roots [vegetables] from the frost. This is a pit of six or eight feet deep and roofed with logs which are again covered with earth," says O'Brien. In *Canadian Crusoes*, Traill explains that they were "built over deep excavations below the reach of the frost, or the roots [that is, root vegetables such as potatoes and carrots] stored would be spoiled." Traill has a further explanation of its utility: "[W]ith the addition possibly of barrels of pork and beef, or a firkin of salted butter; sometimes, if floored with boards, or paved, they are made to answer the purpose of a winter dairy; as it must be frost-proof, or the vegetables would be spoiled, it answers the purpose of keeping the milk well." If the cellar got too warm during the winter thaw, the vegetables sometimes inconveniently started to sprout.[278]

Rosewater   Before vanilla became the preferred flavouring for baking in the Western world, rosewater and orange-flower water were the two most prominent non-spice

---

276 Davidson, *Oxford Companion to Food*, 663, 665.

277 Traill Family Collection, 5811.

278 O'Brien, *Journals of Mary O'Brien*, [?] October 1828, 71; Traill, *Canadian Crusoes*, 168; Traill, "Canadian Lumberers," *Forest and Other Gleanings*, 146.

flavours. This had been true since medieval times, when these waters began to be imported at great expense from the Arabian Peninsula. By the 1600s, they had become important substances that were distilled by skilled housewives in their still-rooms, not just for baking but for cosmetics and medicines too. Only one Traill recipe – doughnuts [108] – specifies rosewater, although undoubtedly Traill grew up with it.

Rusk   As Traill says, rusks were twice-baked slices of bread, like thick crackers. Mary O'Brien once turned bread dough that had risen too high into rusks: "I cut from the top of the loaf the exceeding portion and placed it, much to my satisfaction, before the fire on a plate. There I hoped it would soon be converted to capital rusks."[279]

Rye   In Upper Canada, rye (*Secale cereale*) was grown in considerable quantities to be used in some breadstuffs, animal feed, and for distillation into whisky. In the *Guide* it is used once, in the American-style recipe for leaven cakes but is mentioned twice as a bread flour in times of scarcity. As a woman from southeast England, Traill had no personal cultural affinity for rye bread but, although she does not mention it in her book, the Traills planted a field of rye in 1836.[280] The Yankees often blended rye with corn and/or wheat for their daily bread.

Saffron   When Traill suggests colouring apple jelly and cheese with saffron [73], she likely meant the florets of the safflower (*Carthamus tinctorius*), known as bastard saffron and American saffron. These seeds were sold by some Canadian nurserymen; it was included in the medicinal herb seeds available in the 1827 *Catalogue of Fruit & Ornamental Trees*.[281] Some housewives used it to dye cloth.[282] True saffron is the dried stigma of *Crocus sativus* and expensive due to its rarity; it was once much cultivated (and coveted) in England at Saffron Walden, Essex, but now comes primarily from Spain, France, Italy, and Iran.[283]

Sage   An ancient plant, sage (*Salvia officinalis*) is a perennial in the mint family used in poultry cooking, as a medicine, and as a tea. Sage was also used to flavour some cream cheeses. Sage was traditionally combined with onion and breadcrumbs

279 O'Brien, *Journals of Mary O'Brien*, 7 November 1830, 141.
280 Traill Family Collection, 3461.
281 Custead, *Catalogue of Fruit & Ornamental Trees*, 33, 233–4.
282 Woodhead, *Early Canadian Gardening*, 233–4.
283 Davidson, *Oxford Companion to Food*, 680.

to stuff geese for roasting in British cuisine, as Traill suggests in the lone recipe that calls for it, even though she considers it an essential potherb [58, 163]. Some stuffing recipes for poultry still call for sage and onion, but many have substituted chopped parsley. Sage "correct[s] the too great lusciousness of strong meats, as in goose, duck or pork."[284] One 1960s Canadian cookbook, *Chatelaine's Adventure in Cooking,* provides a basic stuffing recipe with parsley and also an "old-fashioned" one with sage. Madame Benoit's authoritative *New and Complete Encyclopedia of Cooking* (1975) also has no sage in her recipes for stuffing.[285]

Saleratus, *also* Salaratus, Salaeratus   Potassium bicarbonate – the "bi" meaning twice refined – or, later, sodium bicarbonate (common baking soda); literally, aerating salt. Saleratus is an American term used from the 1820s to 1910s to designate an advanced form of pearlash that had greater leavening power and a less acrid taste. It was later applied to baking soda. Like pearlash, saleratus only provides the alkali and requires an acid to become active. It was used alone as a leavener or as the main component in proprietary baking powders. Although Traill always distinguishes between saleratus and pearlash, the term "saleratus" could be confusing as it was used indiscriminately to describe all alkali carbonates.

Salmon and Salmon Trout   Atlantic salmon used to come up the St Lawrence River into Lake Ontario for their annual spawn; construction of the early sawmills made this difficult and construction of the dams, locks, and canal system known as the St Lawrence Seaway in the 1950s blocked all access. They were once so prolific that Anna Jameson noted her host "family had speared two hundred salmon in a single night," a number Sam Strickland repeated: "I have known two fishermen in this manner kill upwards of two hundred salmon in one night." Sometimes, the salmon were actually salmon trout, and it is not always clear from the context which was intended to be understood. Salmon trout were also "taken in vast quantities," said Sam.[286] Considerable salmon and salmon trout were salted for winter eating. Atlantic salmon are being restored to Lake Ontario and its tributaries through the auspices of the Ministry of Natural Resources.

284 Webster and Parkes, *Encyclopedia of Domestic Economy,* 490.
285 *Chatelaine's Adventure in Cooking,* 95–6; Benoit, *New and Complete Encyclopedia of Cooking,* 217.
286 Jameson, *Winter Studies and Summer Rambles,* 30 May 1837, 169; Samuel Strickland, *Twenty-Seven Years in Canada West,* 1:76.

Salsify, *also* Oyster Plant, Vegetable Oyster   Although salsify (*Tragopogon porri-folius*) is seldom grown in Canadian home gardens nowadays, it was very popular for a time in the nineteenth century. Its flavour resembles mild oysters, hence its other name. Traill provided a recipe in her May 1855 column for *Canadian Farmer*; the grated salsify was simmered in milk, thickened with flour and eggs, and fried in little patties so "the resemblance to oysters is complete."[287]

Salt   Salt (*sodium chloride*) is a major international commodity and has been for mil-lennia, of course, but in home kitchens of the early twenty-first century, we mostly buy it in small amounts since its main purpose is to enhance a dish's flavour during cooking, baking, and at the table, although home cooks who like to make their own breads and pickles need larger amounts. Not many people need or want to regularly or seasonally preserve their own meats or make their own butter, unlike home cooks of Traill's era or any time before the widespread adoption of household refrigerators and freezers after the Second World War. Kitchens in Traill's rural world, and count-less others, needed sacks or barrels of salt that could be used to dry, cure, ferment, pickle, and smoke the quantities of meats, fishes, vegetables, butters, and cheeses required for the coming cold months. Of course, any number of butchers, fishers, farm women, bakers, bread-makers, and other small processors of foods sold their products to housewives, but the fact remains that large quantities of household food production continued until well into the twentieth century. And salt was needed in all of them.

Industrially, salt has been an essential commodity too. Manufacture of ceramics, leathers, fertilizers, chemicals, baked goods, pickles, de-icers, soaps, and the ubiqui-tous salt cod, salt pork, salt beef, and so on, all required vast quantities. Many places in the world developed salt works eons ago. Prior to the discovery of the vast rock salt formations that lie under much of southwestern Ontario and the Great Lakes region, salt was imported into British North America from England, the Turks and Caicos Islands, and Onondaga, New York. The familiar Canadian brands of Sifto (1866) and Windsor (1893) post-date the *Guide*, so Traill likely bought either Onondaga salt or

---

287 Traill, "Ladies' Department," *Canadian Farmer*, May 1855, 158. This was one of several vegetable recipes copied from *Soil of the South*, which was both a book from 1850 and a periodical in the early 1850s but we don't know which one was the source of these recipes. Did Traill identify these as recipes she wanted to see reprinted as they would be useful for her Canadian readers?

"Liverpool salt," the generic name for the trusted salts produced in Cheshire but exported through Liverpool. It is also possible that she bought Ontario salt since the Niagara area salt springs had been producing since the earliest days of settlement.[288]

Sea salt is derived from sea water, which is methodically evaporated in very large and shallow flat pans until only the coarse flaky crystals remain. Rock salt is the salt minerals from prehistoric seawater that has been compressed with sand into rock; it is not food grade but is suitable for freezing ice cream in churns. Salt can also be derived from evaporation of the salty rainwater pumped up from salt or brine springs or streams imbedded in rock salt. Salt varies in quality based on origin and the shapes and sizes of its crystals. Traill is careful to specify "clean," "good," or "fine" salt [154, 155] for pickling since some impure sea salts retained magnesium, which limits sodium's ability to inhibit the growth of harmful bacteria, hence its critical importance in preserving meats. Not having access to enough salt created real hardship.[289]

Historically, salt has been paired with black pepper as the most favoured seasoning duo. "A little salt" appears on numerous occasions in Traill's recipes. But that "little salt" was a bit more work for her than just shaking the salt bottle or dipping a spoon into the salt cellar: salt crystals often hardened or clumped in damp weather, requiring pulverization in a mortar. The boon of free-running salt was invented by the American company, Morton, in 1911 when they added the anti-caking agent magnesium carbonate.[290]

Saltpetre, also Saltpeter   Saltpetre is *potassium nitrate*, a white crystalline chemical with many purposes in pioneer homes, chief among them as an ingredient in brines for preserving meat and butter. Its "considerable antiseptic power"[291] improved the colour of pickled meat, the flavour of tainted milk, the keepability of butter, and also the flammability of candle wick. Using it in brines for preserving meats was a well-established technique, although too much could cause the meat to turn green and hard. Today it is used sparingly. It was also part of gunpowder.[292]

288 Kurlansky, *Salt*, 240, 241, 246, 315; Fielding, *The Salt Industry*, 6–7, 47; Russell, *The Edward Ross Store*, 34, 66.
289 Fielding, *The Salt Industry*, 6–7; Hyun Jung Lee, "Salt," 2:390–6.
290 Mescher, "Salt of the Earth," 7.
291 Ward, *Grocer's Hand-Book and Directory*, 189.
292 McCalla, *Consumers in the Bush*, 108–11, 208; Hartley, *Food in England*, 326; Smith, *Oxford Encyclopedia of Food and Drink in America*, 2:71; Sheppard, *Pickled, Potted and Canned*, 55–6.

Salt Pork, *see also* Pork   Pork absorbs salt so well that salting it became an import-ant preservation technique, either in dry salt or wet salt (brine). Ham and bacon are specific forms of salt pork.[293] Although it was a staple meat, especially in winter and spring, not everyone liked it. Children, in particular, found it hard to tolerate, wrote Harriet King about her grandchildren. So much was consumed in Upper Canada that Ohio had to provide some too, said John Langton. He described salt pork as "the standing dish for breakfast, dinner and tea" from November through April.[294]

Salt-Rising, *also* Salt-Barm, Salt Yeast   Traill's instructions on salt-rising bread in *The Backwoods of Canada* were the first published in North America,[295] even though this bread had obviously been long familiar to Yankee housewives in both the north-ern States and Canada. Despite being notoriously temperamental, especially in win-ter, salt-rising was "much used among the old Canadian and Yankee settlers" although "the peculiar flavour it imparts to the bread renders it highly disagreeable to some persons," Traill included [96].[296] Anne Langton's family, however, said "the votes were in favour of it."[297] After the 1836 publication of Traill's information about salt-rising, recipes appear in many nineteenth-century cookbooks, manuscript collections, news-papers, and almanacs, but by the early twentieth century had largely disappeared because packaged yeast had become readily available in the shops.

As with hop-rising, milk-rising, bran-rising, and others, the salt-risen dough relied on natural fermentation due to the presence of wild yeasts in the air and the flour, although its chemistry was not understood until the early twentieth century when the bacterium *lactobacillus* was recognized as an additional active agent. The base for salt-risen dough was cornmeal, wheat flour, or potato mash, and to ensure a light bread the sponge was mixed the night before. Writers often comment on the distinct odour and whiteness of salt-risen bread. Its texture is dense and moist, and it is an excellent vehicle for fresh butter.

Sal Volatile, *also* Baker's Ammonia, Hartshorn   Now the chemical compound am-monium carbonate, once a distillation made from the shaved horn of a hart (male

293   Davidson, *Oxford Companion to Food*, 689.
294   King, *Letters from Muskoka*, 69; John Langton, quoted in Hoffman and Taylor, *Across the Waters*, 307.
295   Craigie, *Dictionary of American English*, 3:1450.
296   Traill, *Backwoods of Canada*, 137.
297   Anne Langton, *A Gentlewoman in Upper Canada*, 10 October 1838, 180.

deer), which led to its being called hartshorn. Unlike pearlash and saleratus, sal volatile contains both alkali and acid and hence has greater leavening power: "Sal volatile must be kept powdered, and closely confined in glass bottles with ground glass
stoppers. It is certain to make any mixture light that can be raised by anything."[298]
When dissolved in alcohol, sal volatile was the acrid agent in smelling salts, which
were used to revive people (especially women) who had fainted. It was also used to
remove stains in fabrics.

Sassafras Tea   Traill refers to the evergreen sassafras tree (*Sassafras officinalis*) and
its many medicinal applications [140], although it was not native to the Peterborough
area, but to southwestern Ontario and throughout the United States. In *Canadian
Crusoes*, the Ojibwa people who captured young Catharine Maxwell considered sassafras tea to be special because their Credit River Chippewa guests had brought it as
a gift.[299]

Sauces, see also Catsup; and Pudding Sauces   The British were teased for having
one sauce – melted butter – into which they put a vast array of ingredients to create
the sweet and savoury British repertoire: anchovy, apple, celery, chopped egg, mushrooms, mustard, oysters, parsley, shallots, sugar, walnut catsup were among the various additions. A sauce of "proper" gravy consisted of elaborately browning bones
with vegetables, then gradually adding meat juices and/or water, whereas plain gravy
was just meat juices thickened with flour. The truth was more complicated, although
Traill's backwoods sauces are of the easy butter or gravy varieties. No nurturing of a
stock pot for soups and fine gravies was involved. Ready-to-use maple syrup accompanied many a quick pudding. Tart cranberry sauce to accompany turkey was already
well-established in American cooking by the 1850s, but Traill does not refer to this
link in her recipe for it [87].

The word *sauce* (pronounced sass, sarce, or sace) had a variant meaning in New
England and could also refer to cooked vegetables accompanying the main meat;
English people found the word as used by New Englanders in Upper Canada to be
amusing and vaguely vulgar.[300] As Bridget Lacy described it to her friend in Ireland:

298 Beecher, *Miss Beecher's Domestic Receipt Book*, 202.
299 Traill, *Canadian Crusoes*, 211–12, 249.
300 Moodie, *Roughing It in the Bush*, 94–5; Samuel Strickland, *Twenty-Seven Years in Canada West*,
     2:205; Webster, "Sauce," *A Dictionary of the English Language*; *Dictionary of Canadianisms on Histor-
     ical Principles*, 659.

"*Sace* is anything you could name – potatoes, vegables [*sic*], butter, pickles and sweet-meats – they're all called *sace* – only mustard, pepper and vinegar are not. And Mary my jewell, the people here must have *sace* at all their meals."[301]

But the best sauce, as Traill quips, was an appetite! [166]

Scarlet Runner Bean   In the *Guide,* Traill recognized only the aesthetic beauty of the scarlet runner's flower, not the edibility of the bean (*Phaseolus coccinea*), a type of kidney bean. But earlier, in 1834, she wrote: "There is a very prolific white runner ... bearing a profusion of pods, which are cut and boiled as scarlet-runners, or else, in their dry or ripe state, stewed and eaten with salt meat."[302]

Sharps, *see* Shorts

Shortening   Originally a generic Yankee term for cooking fat, whatever the cook had on hand. "Short" means brittle, exactly what a cook aims for when she wants to achieve a reputation for flaky pastry or light quick breads. Today, shortening refers to the industrially produced white vegetable fat that was first manufactured in Canada by Crisco in 1915 in Hamilton, Ontario (1911 in Cincinnati, Ohio).[303] The first printed use of the word is in Simmons's *American Cookery* (1796).

Shorts   The distinction between "shorts" and "sharps" is now hard to pinpoint. Both were part of the cannel or canaille (see entry above), the coarse elements of bran, germ, and husk that were sifted out of the desirable white interior starch, that is, the flour. Both were synonyms for "middlings," meaning middle quality flour (neither fully refined nor too rough). But middlings seem to have had grades too; in the better grades the shorts were smaller, somewhat more finely ground and sifted than "sharps." The coarse sharps helped keep the tiny mesh holes of bolting (sifting) cloths open on humid days, otherwise the tiny holes gummed up with moisture. A farmer who took his grain to be milled received back whole wheat flour, meal, bran, and

---

301 Magrath and Radcliff, *Authentic Letters from Upper Canada*, December 1832, 136. Despite the title of the book, Bridget Lacy is a fiction, created by one of the letter writers to express "far better than her master or mistress the ideas of the majority of settlers," in contrast to "the percentage of families with resources like theirs," according to Talman in his introduction (xi).

302 Traill, *Backwoods of Canada*, 219.

303 Driver, *Culinary Landmarks*, 528–9.

shorts. At home, the meal could be further sifted to separate the flour from the other elements and the leftover shorts could become animal food. Alternatively, the shorts could be mixed back into the flour to extend it.[304]

In *The English Bread Book* (1857), after explaining the finer wheats, Eliza Acton states: Sharps or middlings "come next to that inner portion of the grain which contains the flour, and is good, *cheap*, nourishing, and excellently adapted to making bread, if mixed with [white] flour for the purpose." Acton said it required a bit more yeast to raise it into light loaves.[305] Shorts were "seldom used as a mixture in bread" [100], but instead were eaten as a porridge [101]. But Traill seems to like brown breads, recognizing their nutritive quality. Shorts were also used as chicken and animal feed, unless poverty forced human consumption. Ironically, because shorts and sharps retained a considerable portion of bran specks and wheat germ, they were healthier than the white flour many people preferred.

Silver Cake, *see* Gold and Silver Cakes

Sippet   These were triangles of buttered toasted bread decoratively arranged around a platter of meat or served with soup.

Smoke-House   Smoke-houses were small wooden structures for drying and/or smoking meat, turning pork shoulders and haunches, for instance, into bacon and ham. Pieces of meat were hung above a continuously smouldering fire and the door was kept tightly closed to hold the smoke in. Meat was also smoked by hanging it inside the kitchen chimney. Hickory wood was considered to deliver the best flavour, but most hardwoods and fruitwoods were suitable. Using green wood or resinous pine led to unpleasant flavours.

Soda, *see also* Baking Powders, Saleratus   "Baking soda" is the more common term nowadays for carbonate of soda, and the more refined bicarbonate of soda or sodium bicarbonate. It was one of the new chemical agents that were mixed with a little liquid such as milk and used to introduce fast carbonation into a cake, cookie, bread, or biscuit dough to cause it to rise in the oven. Soda is an alkali that needs to be combined with an acid to be an effective leavener, hence recipes using it also call for

304 Leung, *Grist and Flour Mills*, 109, 110, 154, 234, 239, 241; McCalla, *Consumers in the Bush*, 123–4.
305 Acton, *The English Bread Book*, 83, 132–133; Leung, *Grist and Flour Mills*, 241.

acidic sour milk, buttermilk, molasses, or cream of tartar. Foods such as flat pancake batters and sluggish yeasts could be rescued if soda was added to encourage more carbon dioxide bubbles. Until the late nineteenth century, the single word "soda" was often synonymous with baking powder, as Traill showed when she used it as a substitute [94], but soda was, and is, actually only one element in baking powders. The term "bread soda" was used by Vere Foster [43].

Sal-soda was sodium carbonate, washing soda. It was used to soften water for laundry, thereby improving the sudsing action of soap.

Soda Biscuit, *see* Biscuit

Soups and Stews, *see also* Chowder, Fricassees and Hashes   Soups and stews were simple preparations of infinite variety that were easily made in the backwoods using only a cauldron or large stew-pot over the fire (see figure 22), so it is surprising that Traill does not include many actual recipes. Instead, she makes suggestions within a limited listing of "dishes that are more peculiar to the cookery of Canada" [131]. No time-consuming consommé or complicated mock turtle soup, nor, interestingly, any Scottish national soups such as cock-a-leekie or barley broth that her husband may have grown up with. Traill's three soup recipes were of fish, venison, and potato, all easily procurable on bush farms, but she says wild rice and beans were good too. Her preferred seasonings were tomato catsup, onions, herbs, and the inevitable salt and pepper.

As for partridge and squirrel stew, Traill offers no direct opinion but says they were frequent ingredients. Irish Stew, to which Traill compares her ultra-simple Irish Mash [131], was layers of mutton chops, sliced potatoes, and sliced onions cooked slowly together over low heat for several hours until they blended.[306] "Stewed" was also a common adjective for gently simmered foods, such as corn or berries. Parboiled porcupine made an excellent stew, notes John Langton, who was also partial to potato soup.[307]

Speckled Red Bean   Likely one of the *Phaseolus vulgaris* beans; several had the word speckled or mottled in their local names, referring to their appearance.

---

306 Dods, *The Cook and Housewife's Manual*, 377–8; Mrs N.K.M. Lee, *The Cook's Own Book*, 99; Connery, *In an Irish Country Kitchen*, 70, 72; Smith, "Soups and Stews," 2:467.
307 John Langton, quoted in Hoffman and Taylor, *Across the Waters*, 317.

Spices, *see also* Allspice, Black Pepper, Caraway Seeds, Cayenne, Cinnamon, Cloves, Ginger, Nutmeg and Mace, Mustard, Saffron   When Traill wrote her *Guide* in the 1850s, vanilla bean – so ubiquitous and recognizable to us today – was exotic and unusual. She must have eventually become familiar with it, because four decades later the fragrance of the Indian grass (sweetgrass or *Hierochloe odorata*), which was woven into household items such as table mats, reminded her of vanilla.[308]

Fig. 34 · Mortar and pestle

Traill's readers would have been accustomed to cloves and the cinnamon-nutmeg-allspice trio for baking. Mustard was essential for making pickles and sauces, and as accompaniment to meats. The seeds of anise, coriander, dill, fennel, and lovage were all featured in Anglo-American cooking, and could be successfully grown in Canada; Traill does not mention planting them, although she did grow caraway. Other spices not mentioned by Traill were cardamom and turmeric, although grocers did import them. In fact, from the earliest years of settlement grocers imported many whole spices, such as cinnamon, cloves, mace, nutmeg, and cayenne, and advertised them.[309]

Curried dishes had become fashionable by the time the Traills left the British Isles. Recipes for homemade mixtures of curry spice appear in many cookbooks of Traill's era and before, but in the backwoods many settlers may have been too poor to purchase the individual ingredients, such as cumin, fenugreek, coriander seed, and turmeric. Alternatively, shopkeepers in the villages near Traill may not have had them on their shelves; they were not included in the shop inventories catalogued in *Consumers in the Bush*.[310]

Spikenard   *Aralia racemosa*. The First Peoples from Quebec to Manitoba, down to Kansas, used it widely as a food and an ingredient in many medicines. Whole purple-black berries were infused in spirits for cordials, and their juice blended into

---

308 Traill, *Pearls and Pebbles*, 132.
309 Custead, *Catalogue of Fruit & Ornamental Trees*, 13; Woodhead, *Early Canadian Gardening*, 33; *Upper Canada Gazette*, passim, from 11 December 1802, onward; McCalla, *Consumers in the Bush*, 205; Williamson, "Seasonings and Flavourings in Canada before 1840," 16–26.
310 McCalla, *Consumers in the Bush*, 205. McCalla's research includes a shop in Lakefield, Ontario, Sherin's, which listed Traill in its customer accounts as of 1861.

a syrup for coughs, chest complaints, and stomach ailments. It is in the same family as ginseng and sarsaparilla.[311]

Spinach *Spinachia oleracea* has a long history in upper-class European and British cuisines, particularly in egg dishes, such as egg and spinach pies, which often had intricate pastry decorations on the upper surface. Spinach was invariably served cooked, whereas nowadays we have tender varieties bred to be eaten raw in salads. Spinach juice, expressed from either raw or cooked spinach, was a major colourant in confectionery, both professional and homemade. Traill planted it in her garden but specifies no uses.

Sponge Cake, *see also* Cakes, Cup Cake, Plum Cake, Pound Cake   Light sponge cakes, in which separated egg whites and yolks, well-whisked, cause the batter to swell during baking, were invented later than plum or pound cakes, which date back to the seventeenth and eighteenth centuries respectively. British sponge cake evolved from the small Italian and French bisket or biscuit cake that consisted of only three ingredients (white flour, white sugar, and eggs – and flavourings); alternate names were Savoy cake, diet-bread, and spunge cake. Jane Austen is credited with a very early use of the name "sponge cake," but clearly such cakes were already familiar to her readers since she did not need to describe them.[312] By the 1830s, American cookbooks had reduced the number of eggs and supplemented their lift capacity by adding a baking powder, exactly as demonstrated in Traill's Farmer's Sponge Cake [108]. Sponge cake and jelly, that is, circles of sponge cake with jelly or jam between them, was becoming popular, and in fact Traill received one in 1867 as a friendly gift.[313]

Squash   Eaten raw when new and cooked when older. Like dark green marrows and orange pumpkins, they are members of the *Cucurbita* genus. Specific native types still available that could have been familiar to Traill and her Peterborough neighbours are crookneck, hubbard, and pattypan (cymlin) (*Cucurbita pepo*).[314]

311 Hutchens, *Indian Herbalogy of North America*, 256–7; Erichsen-Brown, *Use of Plants*, 353–4.
312 *Oxford English Dictionary*, 16:303; Lane, *Jane Austen and Food*, 68.
313 Traill Family Collection, 3705. See also Schmidt, "Cakes," 160.
314 Custead, *Catalogue of Fruit & Ornamental Trees*, 15; Woodhead, *Early Canadian Gardening*, 33, 215; Weaver, *Heirloom Vegetable Gardening*, 282, 285.

Squirrel   Black, grey, and occasionally red squirrels were eaten in large numbers in fricassee, soup, pie, roast, and stew – far more often than the occasional mentions in emigrant papers would suggest. John Herbert, a young bachelor immigrant, made squirrel soup and Mary Frances Cleveland stated in her diary that she "ate a whole black squirrel along with about three slices of bread."[315] Sam Strickland thought "the flesh is excellent eating, far superior to that of the rabbit."[316] Thomas Need explained one way to catch them: "Accompanied an Indian to the forest, to learn the art of barking squirrels: this is performed by striking the bark of the tree with a rifle ball, just under the animal, which is thus killed by the splintered bark, without injury to the fur or flesh."[317] Snaring them was easier.

Starches, see also Cornstarch   Some household products were by-products of food. Starch is a good example. Traill gives clear directions for manufacturing homemade potato and bran starches [131–2, 132–3] but by mid-century commercial cornstarch had become a boon for busy housewives and laundresses. Other starches were manufactured from rice, wheat, sago, and farina. They were put to a variety of household uses, such as stiffening fabric in aprons, bonnets, lace trimming, and men's dress shirts. Fabrics permeated with starch were stouter and could repel dirt for a longer time, thus reducing the need for laundering, which in the centuries before automatic clothes washing machines was understandably desirable.

In Traill's time the word starch was not used to denote an element in a meal, in the way potato, rice, or pasta are considered starches in today's meals.

Stone Wheaten Flour, see also Shorts   This "is the wheat ground into a proper state for bread-making without *any part* of it being taken away. Neither the bran nor any other portion of it is withdrawn."[318] "Stone" refers to the stone grinding wheel that turns the wheat into flour. Our modern term in North America is whole wheat flour. Another historic term not much used anymore was "meal," as in wholemeal flour. "The substance of edible grain [wheat, corn, oat, rye, etc.] ground to fine particles,

---

315   Herbert in King, *Letters from Muskoka*, 211; Cleveland, quoted in Hoffman and Taylor, *Across the Waters*, 173.

316   Samuel Strickland, *Twenty-Seven Years in Canada West*, 1:302.

317   Need, *Six Years in the Bush*, 31 October 1833, 77.

318   Acton, *The English Bread Book*, 82.

and not bolted or sifted ... The word meal is not generally applied to the finer part, or flour, at least in the United States."[319]

Stove   Heating stoves were manufactured before cooking stoves. In 1829 merchants in Brockville, Upper Canada, were advertising the arrival of new-fangled iron cook-stoves from the United States, complete with pots and utensils. The Traill's first house had one; on 9 May 1833, she writes: "The weather is now very warm – oppressively so. We can scarcely endure the heat of the cooking stove in the kitchen."[320] This heat often caused families to move the stove to a temporary outdoor location, an open but roofed outdoor summer kitchen, or an extension at the back of the house, away from the living area. The Langtons had one in their backwoods house, which Anne described in detail for her English family: "This stove stands about ten yards from the back door, under a little shed. It measures 2 feet by 7 inches each way. The chimney pipe rises at the top, an oval kettle fits into one side, a deep pan with a steamer above it into the other side, and a large boiler on a bake-pan at the bottom, each hole having an iron lid, when the vessels are not in, on which you may then place smaller sauce-pans, or heat irons, &c. The front of the stove has an upper and lower door and a little hearth – formerly there was something of an oven within, but it was out of repair before I was acquainted with it."[321]

The first Canadian-made stoves arrived in the late 1830s, first from the Van Norman works in Long Point, Ontario, on Lake Erie, then from their new location in Marmora, Ontario. Other manufacturers began making them soon thereafter.[322] Culturally, the cookstove coincided with the introduction of a new repertoire of quick breads and cakes raised by the new chemical leaveners. Physically, it transformed how women cooked their family's meals. Instead of needing to bend over to hearth level, the cook-top was now at table level; rather than having to be wary of sparks while moving around the fire, the fire was contained; and instead of moving the crane in and out of the fire as a way to control heat under the cauldron or griddle (see figure 22 for a cauldron and griddle), the pots remained stationary on the stovetop; and instead of having to estimate and deal with the ebbing heat of a bake oven, oven heat could be maintained by simply adding another log to the cookstove's fire box. Cookstoves also

319   Webster, "Meal," *A Dictionary of the English Language*, unpaginated.
320   Traill, *Backwoods of Canada*, 114.
321   Anne Langton, *A Gentlewoman in Upper Canada*, 10 October 1838, 179.
322   MacDonald, "How the Cooking Stove Transformed the Kitchen," 3–11.

Fig. 35 · Canadian kitchen, 1862. The iron stove has a prominent place in the cabin's main room.

meant that less wood had to be chopped and hauled in to fill the perpetually empty-ing woodbox. The portable (although very heavy) cookstove also brought about a change in kitchen layouts and eventually in the kitchen's location within the home because placement of the kitchen was no longer restricted by the fixed position of the solid masonry hearth. However, the cook no longer had the benefit of the hearth's firelight, which led to larger kitchen windows.[323]

Strawberry   Tiny wild strawberries (*Fragaria virginiana*) were abundant in natural and recently burned clearings both for eating fresh and preserving as jam. Many au-thors wrote of their delight in these delicious strawberries, despite their smallness. Traill decided early that she would cultivate beds of the wild ones in her kitchen garden. Cultivated strawberries were also planted. One party table at the Armstrong household starred "red ripe straw berries" that "contrasted beautifully with the snowey blancmanges [*sic*]."[324]

---

323 Lucas, *Hearth and Home*, 8–11; MacDonald, "How the Cooking Stove Transformed the Kitchen," 8–9.

324 Traill, *Canadian Crusoes*, 106; Armstrong, *Seven Eggs Today*, 7 July 1869, 149.

Suet   Suet is the hard white fat surrounding the kidneys and loins of cattle and sheep. Due to its high melting point, it is ideal for making stiff hot water paste, frying chops, and combining with fruit and flour in plum and sponge puddings and dumplings. A batter for Yorkshire pudding crisps up very well in melted hot suet under a cut of beef roasting in front of the fire. At butchering time raw suet was peeled off the kidneys and kept as cold as possible in its original shape. The required amount was later grated or finely chopped and sometimes coated with some flour. Surprisingly, considering that it was such a common English ingredient, suet is seldom specified in the *Guide*, probably because lard was so readily obtainable in the backwoods, in contrast to beef. *The Canadian Housewife's Manual of Cookery* (1861), on the other hand, uses considerable amounts of suet.

Sugar Beets, *also* White Beets   *Beta vulgaris,* an inedible root vegetable known as mangel-wurtzel. Now more or less a forgotten crop except as animal food and agricultural fertilizer, in nineteenth-century Ontario it was grown in farm fields and kitchen gardens for transformation into beer, vinegar, and molasses. Its intrinsic sucrose was extracted by boiling crushed slices in successive waters, then straining. Although its sucrose is chemically identical to cane sugar, it did not catch on for baking, let alone confectionary. Traill made "a trial of boiling mangel-wurtzel into molasses. The produce was not so pure nor so agreeable as that from the maple." Adding a red beet – "blood beet" – turned the molasses pinkish, she said. She also converted its syrup into an acceptable beer.[325] A Canadian sugar beet industry flourished briefly in the decades before the First World War, but nowadays is found only in Alberta.

Sugar-Kettle   A sugar-kettle was an enormous iron boiler used for boiling maple sap into syrup and then further reducing it to sugar. People in the backwoods often shared their large equipment. In summer 1837, Traill loaned "my big kettle and two small boilers" in exchange for payment of "three gallons of fine molasses and five gallons of vinegar. This paid me well for the use of the utensils for three weeks." Susanna Moodie reports having had the misfortune of breaking a borrowed sugar-kettle.[326] (See figures 13 and 31.)

---

325   Traill Family Collection, 3334, 3442.
326   Traill Family Collection, 3403; Moodie, *Roughing It in the Bush*, 418–20.

Sugars, *see also* Brown and White Cane Sugars, Brown Sugar, Crushed Sugar, Loaf Sugar, Lump Sugar, Maple Sugar, Moist Sugar, Muscovado Sugar, Sugar Beets, Syrups Sugar and molasses were common ingredients in Traill's recipes, but the modern reader cannot always tell whether she meant maple sugar, a white or brown sugar, or maple or sugar cane molasses, all of which were produced in an array of qualities and prices. Since terminology for grades of sugar was not fixed until the late 1800s, her meaning sometimes has to be surmised from the context and/or her adjectives.

Cane sugars and molasses were imported commodities, but maple sugar and molasses are indigenous to northeastern North America and were much used by the First Nations. At first produced for family consumption by the colonists, in the 1880s maple production began to be commercialized, following the development of new techniques, such as the covered evaporating pan. Maple sap could be converted into vinegar, wine, ink, beer, and also "sweeties" as an "indulgence" for the children [152].

Sugar had a long association with the slave trade, a fact that Traill does not acknowledge in her writings, although she was undoubtedly aware of it through reading the circulating newspapers.

Sugar Yeast   Traill admits to not having tested "Sugar-Yeast" and Leaven Cakes but included them on the authority of their commonness. Interestingly, she must later have tried Sugar Yeast, because her early 1880s revision reduced the original amount of "two pounds of sugar" to half a pound.[327]

Summer Savoury   *Satureja hortensis* was considered good as a seasoning for fish and known for preventing flatulence. Other types included winter savoury, its name referring to its harvest time in its native Italy.[328]

Supporne, *also* Supawn *or* Suppawn; *see also* Hominy   A dish of corn or cornmeal served as porridge, but not just at breakfast. Frances Stewart, not recognizing the word, called it "seppane,"[329] and "sessane."[330] Other people called it mush or mush-

---

327 Traill Family Collection, 5880.

328 Woodhead, *Early Canadian Gardening*, 222; Webster and Parkes, *Encyclopedia of Domestic Economy*, 494.

329 Stewart's original phrase was "smoking Seppane" but her daughter Ellen altered it to "'suppone,' or Indian cornmeal stirabout" for her 1902 publication (Stewart, *Revisiting "Our Forest Home*," 144; Stewart, *Our Forest Home*, 13, 212).

330 Aoki, "Culinary Themes in the Writings of Frances Stewart," 3.

and-milk. Traill describes it to her family in *The Backwoods of Canada*: "The [corn] flour makes a substantial sort of porridge, called by the Americans "Supporne;" this is made with water, and eaten with milk, or else mixed with milk; it requires long boiling." She adds that it could be "fried in slices, and eaten with maple syrup." In *Canadian Crusoes*, it was "a common dish in every Canadian or Yankee farmer's house" and for Joseph Pickering "a favourite dish [which] most people are fond of from its wholesomeness and lightness for a supper meal."[331] Italian polenta is an adapted version, with barley replaced with maize, which arrived in Italy in the seventeenth century. Traill even has a character in a short story make that connection: "Mrs. Gibbons ... was a famous compounder of 'supporne' (a sort of porridge made from Indian meal, somewhat resembling the Italian polenta)."[332]

Sweet-Gale Tea, *also* Sweet-Fern   Another wild plant (*Comptonia asplenifolia*) that made a reputable hot tea. The *Guide* repeats information provided in *Canadian Crusoes* – that it smelled like nutmeg and "was highly esteemed among the Canadians as a beverage, and also as a remedy against the ague"; it grew "in great abundance on dry sandy sands."[333] It is still made into tea by knowledgeable foragers.

Syrups, *see also* Cane or Beet Sugars, Maple Molasses, Maple Syrup, Molasses, Treacle
Liquid sugar has been used in confectionery and baking for centuries. Sugar crystals can be carefully melted into syrup for conversion into a wide variety of candies, but this was seldom done in rural homes. However, liquid sugar in the form of molasses was indispensable. Depending on the context in old Canadian sources, molasses was either maple molasses or sugar cane molasses, very occasionally sugar beet molasses. Treacle was the English word for molasses. Being dark brown and viscous, molasses was preferable for gingerbreads and cornbreads (Indian cakes) because of its texture, and was also used in pickling hams, making beer, and moistening pork and beans.

Tea, Green and Black . The tea available in Canada until the early 1840s was mostly green China tea, not black India tea. "An old friend, one of the sons of a U.E. Loyalist, told me that for some years after leaving the United States (this family was from

331 Traill, *Backwoods of Canada*, 135, 197; Traill, *Canadian Crusoes*, 115; Joseph Pickering, 1826, quoted in Guillet, *Early Life in Upper Canada*, 199.
332 Traill, "The Settlers Settled," 110, 137.
333 Traill, *Canadian Crusoes*, 93.

Vermont), the genuine Chinese Tea was rarely to be met with in the houses of the settlers, especially with such as lived in lonely backwoods settlements, that for the most part they made use of infusions of the leaves of" wild plants.[334] Soon though, tea was "the inseparable beverage of every meal in New Brunswick"[335] and in Upper Canada/Canada West too. It was offered to visitors, drunk at meals, shared at social events, and featured at temperance meetings. Drinking it from china cups recalled the gentility of the remembered English homes of numerous backwoods settlers. Many colonial women noted that they shared tea together during their social visits (starting with Mrs Simcoe, whose 1790s journal has constant remarks about taking tea with others), although the light meal called afternoon tea did not become popular until the 1870s in Canada, and then particularly in towns. In 1866, Susanna Moodie emphatically stated, "Tea is an article we cannot do without."[336]

Tea's cost dropped as the nineteenth century progressed because its cultivation expanded from China, becoming a large agricultural industry in India, Sri Lanka (Ceylon), and Japan. Inexpensive black Bohea, Pekoe and the costlier green Hyson, smoky Lapsang Souchong, and Gunpowder from China appear commonly in purveyors' advertisements; Twankey and Imperial came later but were available by the 1800s. Strong Darjeeling and Assam black teas from India were introduced later in the century. (These were loose leaf, not bagged, as bags were an American invention in the pre-First World War decade.) Complaints about quality and adulteration were rife. Served tea at a tavern during her travels, Anna Jameson pronounced it "for all the world like musty hay." Harriet King colourfully agreed; she deemed that tea available in the Muskoka stores was "using up the refuse of all the slops in Toronto ... full of sloe-leaves, wild raspberry leaves, and other natural productions that never grew in China; and it was so full of bits of *stick* that my son informed the people at the store that we had collected a nice little stock for winter fuel."[337]

Loose tea leaves were measured out at the store, tied up with string in packets of blue, brown, or grey tea paper[338] and taken home where they were stored in special wooden boxes called caddies that were designed to keep the leaves dry and fresh and could be locked to stop pilfering. They usually had three compartments, one for green

334 Traill, *Studies of Plant Life in Canada*, 115.
335 Beavan, *Sketches and Tales*, 34.
336 Moodie to Traill, *Letters of a Lifetime*, 18 November 1866, 235.
337 Jameson, *Winter Studies and Summer Rambles*, 23 January 1837, 54; King, *Letters from Muskoka*, 39.
338 Russell, *The Edward Ross Store*, 37.

leaves, one for black leaves, and a middle one for blending. A fourth compartment might be for sugar lumps. Ceramic tea sets were valued household items as many settlers had only metal sets. A large copper tea kettle sits on the hearth and a smaller one on the mantel in figure 22.

Tea and coffee were sometimes considered to have no nutritional value, except when milk or sugar were added. Certainly being served "tea without the agreeable accompaniment of cream or even milk" was a source of vexation, opined Thomas Magrath. Children were cautioned not to drink tea (or coffee). Black teas eventually superseded green teas in popularity, so much so that *The Galt Cook Book* (1898) stated "Beware of green tea, it is the unripe leaf and bears the same relation to the real article that the green does to the ripe peach," a feeling echoed by others.[339] Now we understand that green tea has great health benefits.

Thimbleberry, *see* Blackberry

Thornberry, *see* Gooseberry

Thyme   *Thymus vulgaris* was often used interchangeably with summer savoury. It is rare, says Traill, although it was a standard sweet herb in English cooking.

Tomato, *see also* Catsup   Traill clearly liked tomatoes – at least when they were cooked. She devotes more pages to their cultivation and use than to any other vegetable. Many kinds were planted in the southern parts of Upper Canada, but she does not specify which she used. Interestingly, in contrast to the many varieties of other vegetables listed in the 1827 *Catalogue of Fruit & Ornamental Trees*, the tomato is given only as "Tomato or Love Apple."[340] A tremendous amount of hybridization has been done with the common garden tomato (*Lycopersicon lycopersicon*) since the mid-nineteenth century, so most of the kinds Traill grew would be unrecognizable today, despite the popularity of heirloom kinds, most of which date to after 1850. One of the best known in Traill's time was the Early Large Red Tomato, which was

---

339 Magrath and Radcliff, *Authentic Letters from Upper Canada*, December 1831, 14; Taylor and McNaught, *Galt Cook Book*, 375.
340 Custead, *Catalogue of Fruit & Ornamental Trees*, 15; Woodhead, *Early Canadian Gardening*, 33, 218.

considered to be best for cooking and drying due to its redness and pasty quality, exactly as Traill suggests.[341] *The Canadian Housewife's Manual of Cookery* states:

> Tomatoes deservingly class among the most wholesome of vegetables, but are frequently spoiled by the manner in which they are prepared for table; it is very seldom they are sufficiently cooked, and they are more often served as a sour porridge than otherwise. They should always be well cooked, from one to three hours, according to the nature of the cooking, which, when thoroughly done, may be closely sealed in cans or bottles, and kept for years; or the pulp may be spread upon plates and dried in the sun or in a slow oven, it will keep as well as dried pumpkin, apples, peaches, &c., and will be equally acceptable in the winter time. For every-day use, as much as the family will consume in a week may be cooked at once, which can be eaten cold or warmed up.[342]

By the late 1860s, the tomato was being "grown by every one who makes any pretensions to keeping a garden," an attitude still common among home vegetable gardeners.[343] The Leveridges came to grow lots of them annually for both cooking and eating raw: "We had a quantity of tomatoes. I gave away several pecks, and made sweet pickles and ketchup, and the children eat them raw. We did not care about them at first, [but] we all like them now. They are nice sliced up and just sprinkled with sugar. They are reckoned very wholesome things."[344]

Treacle   While today treacle is a cane syrup that can range from black to golden in colour, depending on the country of origin and brand name, in Traill's day it was the light molasses that drained out of muscovado sugar.[345] It was poured over buckwheat pancakes and spread on bread. Quality treacle imported from England was sometimes associated with Christmas: the *Globe* newspaper had small advertisements for English treacle inserted by Fulton, Michie & Co., 6 King Street West, in November

341 Weaver, *Heirloom Vegetable Gardening*, 338, 344.
342 *The Canadian Housewife's Manual of Cookery*, 304.
343 D.W. Beadle, 1872, quoted in Von Baeyer and Crawford, *Garden Voices*, 229.
344 Tivy, *Your Loving Anna*, 15 October mid-1880s, 83.
345 Webster and Parkes, *Encyclopedia of Domestic Economy*, 722.

and December of 1851 and 1852. Clearly it was a treat then, even if we don't think so anymore.[346]

Tundish, *also* Tun Dish A vat or cask for fermenting beer, used by Traill as a generic term for a container to hold maple sap.

Turkey, *see also* Wild Turkey Some farmwomen kept flocks of turkeys, which by the 1850s were associated with both Thanksgiving and Christmas dinners. "For [Christmas] dinner we had an immense turkey."[347]

Turnip White turnip (*Brassica napa*) was not only human food, but excellent feed for cattle and poultry. They were grown in England, but were particularly widespread in Canada. Rutabaga (swede turnip; *Brassica napus*) was introduced to England from Sweden in the late eighteenth century, and to North America soon after. Readers cannot always tell which one Traill means in her text.[348] Edward O'Brien's Swedish turnips stayed successfully frozen in the field all winter, but Asa Burham's "fine crop" rotted because he "covered them up too warmly."[349] Since they were a new vegetable, the colonists had to learn "by experience how they should be treated."[350] They were eaten alone, mashed or cooked in soups and stews, and the tender young leaves put in salads.

Vandyke-shaped Pieces Diamond shapes. Sir Anthony Van Dyck (1599–1641) was a famous and influential Flemish portrait painter at the court of the English King Charles II. Fashionable men and women in his paintings wore elaborate lace collars with a series of points along their edges.

Veal Veal is baby cow. Some thought that Canadian meat was "not of the best quality ... excepting veal, which is very good."[351]

346 *Globe*, 24 and 25 November and 1 December 1851, page 3, identical advertisement repeated three times in 1852.
347 Sarah Hallen Drinkwater, 25 December 1846, quoted in Hoffman and Taylor, *Across the Waters*, 242.
348 Weaver, *Heirloom Vegetable Gardening*, 356–7; Woodhead, *Early Canadian Gardening*, 208–9.
349 O'Brien, *Journals of Mary O'Brien*, 19 November 1829, 79; Asa Burnham, speech at a 30 November 1864 dinner, quoted in Guillet, *Early Life in Upper Canada*, 196.
350 Webster and Parkes, *Encyclopedia of Domestic Economy*, 481.
351 Magrath and Radcliff, *Authentic Letters from Upper Canada*, Mrs Radcliff, 27 July 1832, 56.

Vegetables, *see also* Asparagus, Beans, Beets, Broccoli, Cabbage, Carrot, Cauliflower, Celery, Cucumber, Green Peas, Herbs and Wild Greens, Onion, Parsnip, Potato, Pumpkin, Radish, Salsify, Squash, Spinach, Tomatoes, Turnip; *see also* Root-House   Although not always mentioned in the extant colonial literature, a wide variety of vegetables were planted and consumed, as can be seen in the seed lists of contemporary nurseries.[352] Besides the seeds brought with the immigrants and those saved by the farmers and gardeners, several British and American seed growers had agents in Upper Canada. The American Shakers were famous for inventing the logical idea of counting good quality seeds into tidy paper packets; prior to this innovation, seeds were scooped out of bulk containers and weighed at time of purchase at the nursery or village store. Overall, farmers and gardeners had access to a very extensive range of vegetable seeds and cultivars for their crop fields and kitchen gardens.[353]

Further information about which vegetables were grown are found in casual remarks such as, "Cucumbers and onions are coming up in the open ground; asparagus in perfection, early potatoes just sprouting."[354] On 10 June 1833, Thomas Need, who lived on a Peterborough bush farm, noted that he had "sowed the seeds of cucumber, melon, lettuce, parsley, endive, mustard and turnip. I also planted some potatoes for seed next year, and picked out cabbages and brocoli [sic]." He harvested some tender salad greens for dinner for a few weeks, until in late July a pair of oxen trampled most of his young plants. To his satisfaction, two weeks later they were "recovering [from] the rude treatment of the oxen."[355] In the early decades of settlement, most settlers did not have as much choice, since vegetable plots were not a priority, as many writers note. Potatoes, Indian corn, pumpkins, cabbage, and perhaps turnips were the most likely to be part of early plantings. By the time the Stewarts, Langtons, Traills, and Moodies arrived in the 1820s and 1830s, vegetable plots were considered essential, but substantial time and human effort was required to fell the trees and prepare the ground, so for their first year the Traills planted only small fields of oats, corn, pumpkins, turnips, and potatoes. In their third year, they started a small garden for

352 Such as James Fleming's *Catalogue of Garden, Agricultural and Flower Seeds*, 1855, which Traill consulted and copied from, and William Custead's *Catalogue of Fruit & Ornamental Trees*, 1827, which is the subject of Eileen Woodhead's *Early Canadian Gardening*. Other catalogues are referenced in her book, starting with that of merchant Quetton St. John in 1808.

353 Woodhead, *Early Canadian Gardening*, 13–14, 179, 198.

354 O'Brien, *Journals of Mary O'Brien*, 26 May 1829, 52.

355 Need, *Six Years in the Bush*, July 1833, 66–70.

other vegetables (marrowfat peas, carrots, spinach, celery, beans, onions[356]) as well as herbs and fruits. Once their homes were established, skilled gardeners such as the Langtons built hotbeds for delicate seedlings in their kitchen gardens.[357] Cultivating these gardens was an important contribution children made to the household economy [63]. In Traill's opinion, "vegetables are in general fine."[358]

Traill reprints advice about growing particular vegetables from James Fleming's *Catalogue of Garden, Agricultural and Flower Seeds* and the *New England Farmer* (1855) [58–60], from which we can infer that these are the ones she grew and fed to her family. However she reprinted only the entries for beans, beets, broccoli, cauliflower, cabbage, cucumber, carrot, celery, and melons, not the remainder of the alphabetically organized list of lettuce, onion, parsnip, radish, rhubarb, salsify, spinach and turnip that had appeared in the original publications. Perhaps this was a printing error? Traill does not mention giant vegetable-marrow, which the Kings and Langtons grew.[359] Other common vegetables not mentioned in the *Guide* are leeks, brussel sprouts, and jerusalem artichokes. The latter were important to the original people of North America, and are undergoing a revival in interest from gardeners, cooks, and chefs. Still to be developed were bell peppers, so familiar in our salads these days, although hot peppers were well known, particularly cayenne.

One of the challenges was winter storage. Traill does not provide much information on this topic, but many clever techniques were utilized, such as overwintering parsnips in the garden, hanging cauliflowers upside-down from the ceiling, burying green beans in salt, and converting mushrooms into pickle.[360]

It was recognized that eating vegetables made an important contribution to good health, even though the medical and scientific reasons for this were not yet understood. Cooks once had a reputation for over-boiling vegetables. "Every sort of vegetable should be cooked until tender, as if the least hard or under-done they are unpalatable and unwholesome," said Eliza Leslie in *Miss Leslie's Directions for Cookery*.[361] Other authors cautioned against overcooking: "Most people spoil garden things by over-boiling them. All things that are green should have a little crispness,

---

356 Traill Family Collection, 26 April and 4 May 1837, 3389.
357 Anne Langton, *A Gentlewoman in Upper Canada*, 17 April 1839, 229.
358 Traill, *Backwoods of Canada*, 219.
359 King, *Letters from Muskoka*, 87.
360 Lucas, "Every Woman Prided Herself," 13–17.
361 Leslie, *Miss Leslie's Directions for Cookery*, 183.

for if they are over-boiled, they have neither any sweetness or beauty."[362] *The Canadian Housewife's Manual of Cookery* concurred: "if overboiled, they may lose their beauty and crispness."[363] Miss Leslie suggested carrots and cabbage be boiled for two hours and cauliflower for one,[364] but many other writers considered this was too long. (Keep in mind that modern varieties are often smaller and have usually been bred to be sweeter and tenderer than earlier ones.) We think that Traill was fairly moderate in her approach to cooking vegetables: in her papers there is a handwritten four-page note about how to successfully cook green vegetables which suggests, "to secure a beautiful colour and fine flavour, put in boiling water, keep up boiling water[,] take out [of] boiling water ... When boiled tender take them at once off the fire and pour them through a cullender or strainer[,] do not let them touch the water[.] Then they are safe. But if boiled ever so green and permitted to stand by in cooking water the colour becomes a dirty yellow and the flavour and smell are alike abominable."[365]

Venison The most socially approved wild meat was deer – venison. For centuries venison had been reserved for European royalty and the aristocracy, who had the sole right to hunt deer in their estate parks. In Canada, it did not have this reputation or restriction and emigrant manuals include access to venison as an encouraging factor. Quite a few colonial writers, men and women, include accounts of exhilarating hunting expeditions, both successful and not, that pay tribute to their quarry's swiftness and spiritedness. In the first decades deer were plentiful, but by the 1870s they were being pushed out of their former territories by farms and growing townships. Anna Jameson pronounced venison (in the 1830s) "good and abundant, but very lean, unlike English venison."[366]

Canadian game laws were different from British ones. Thomas Need commented: "According to the Provincial Game Laws, deer hunting begins in July and ends in February, but this law, like many others in a growing colony is only in use inasmuch as it serves as a moral restraint upon the gentlemen: the mere backwoodsman regards it lightly enough, and the Indian not at all. Of all the natives of the forest, the poor deer

362 Glasse, *The Art of Cookery*, 29.
363 *The Canadian Housewife's Manual of Cookery*, 177.
364 Leslie, *Miss Leslie's New Cookery Book*, 183.
365 Traill Family Collection, 4(22); no date, unpaginated pages labelled "Settler's Guide: misc ms recipes [undated]."
366 Jameson, *Winter Studies and Summer Rambles*, 23 January 1837, 52.

are most persecuted and least protected." In 1853, Sam Strickland added, in recalling the 1830s: "This is one of the great charms of a Canadian life, particularly to young sportsmen from the mother-country, who require here neither license nor qualification to enable them to follow their game; but may rove about in chase of deer, or other game, at will."[367]

Vinegar   In 1837, Traill received five gallons of maple vinegar in exchange for the loan of her big kettle and two small boiling pans.[368] She later learned to make it herself.

Vinegar is probably as old as wine, since wine vinegars are wines that have become overly fermented; the English word vinegar derives from *vin aigre*, French for "sour wine," which is caused by aerobic (air-breathing) bacteria combining with oxygen to create acetic acid, which produces the characteristic acidic quality of vinegar. But in a pioneer household all red and white wines, ciders, fruit juices, very soft fruits, malted liquors, tree saps, honey, and wood waters could become vinegar. (Wood water vinegar is pyroligneous acid, mentioned by Traill as useful for artificially flavouring meat with "smoke" [155], what we call "liquid smoke."[369])

Vinegar was achieved after a process of fermentation, either spontaneously, as in wine gone sour and in Traill's directions for Currant Vinegar [89], or deliberately. One deliberate method involved using a cask that had recently contained vinegar to promote development of the next batch, similar to the way lingering micro-organisms in a dough or hop-rising stimulated the growth of more such organisms. Another method was adding yeast, as described by Traill in her maple vinegar and beet vinegar recipes [152, 145]. These mixtures were allowed to ferment peacefully in gentle warmth, such as beside a kitchen chimney corner or behind a cookstove [153], until a "mother of vinegar" formed on the surface. A third method was inculcating a liquid base with the necessary bacterial culture by adding the mother. Whichever method was used, keeping the developing vinegar carefully bunged in its cask or corked in its bottle minimized air absorption and helped prevent the formation of excess bubbles of carbon dioxide. Some vinegars were made quickly, others allowed to develop and mature slowly, as is the case today.[370]

367 Need, *Six Years in the Bush*, [?] July 1838, 109–10; Samuel Strickland, *Twenty-Seven Years in Canada West*, 2:179.
368 Traill Family Collection, 6 August 1837, 3403.
369 "Pyroligneous acid," Wikipedia, accessed 1 August 2016.
370 Webster and Parkes, *Encyclopedia of Domestic Economy*, 655–61; Davidson, *Oxford Companion to Food*, 827–8; Dillon, *Various Vinegars for Assorted 17th- and 18th-Century Uses*; Hillman, *Kitchen Science*, 183–4.

As a final step, commercial vinegars were distilled, that is, vaporized, chilled, and clarified for the most effective long-term keeping. Historically, pure distilled vinegar was recommended for the most successful pickling since it had no colour and flavour to interfere with either the pickled vegetables or meat.[371] But distillation required special equipment that the average overworked colonial housewife did not have, so she made do without. Today's supermarket distilled vinegar is a corn-based product.

Walnut, *see also* Nuts   The walnuts mentioned by Traill [66] were English trees (*Juglans regia*), not the Ontario black walnut (*Juglans nigra*), whose growing range was outside her geographical area of southern Ontario. Black walnuts are edible, although hard to extract from their casing. They easily stain whatever they touch, so were used as a cloth dye and as writing ink. They were also one of the bases of early catsups. The wood also made fine furniture.

Water   We take the ease of obtaining water from a tap or bottle for granted today, but before the development of municipally treated piped water, it was often medically suspect. Urban water could be tainted by sewage, and farm water by manure. Often, water had to be boiled to make it palatable. While in general water was approved as the "best and most wholesome beverage,"[372] some were adamantly opposed to it: Dr Tiger Dunlop had an "almost rabid antipathy to water," according to Susanna Moodie, although she herself greatly enjoyed a glass of cold water and often referred to its refreshing quality throughout her writings. She purchased a glass of water and peaches while on a visit to Niagara Falls, "which proved a delicious refreshment" because she was "parched with thirst." Newcomer Harriet King welcomed "iced water to drink" as a "great alleviation to the fatigue of travelling."[373]

Watermelon, *see also* Citron, Melon   Originally from Africa, watermelons (*Citrullus lanatus*) reached the Americas as early as the 1630s via African slaves and the Portuguese and Spanish settlers. There are many varieties.[374]

Wheat, *see also* Shorts, Stone Wheaten Flour   Wheat flour was preferred for most baking in Anglo-American foodways, as it still is, because the resulting baked goods

---

371 Webster and Parkes, *Encyclopedia of Domestic Economy*, 665–72.
372 Ibid., 692.
373 Moodie, *Life in the Clearings*, 29; King, *Letters from Muskoka*, 15.
374 Weaver, *Heirloom Vegetable Gardening*, 375–84.

are lighter in texture and weight. The finer and whiter the
flour, the better. Until the late eighteenth century, white
wheat flour was generally a prerogative of the affluent
and the aspiring middle-classes, but by Traill's youth this
was becoming less so. In the Canadian colonies, wheat
grew well as a staple grain. "Spring" or "summer" wheat
was planted in those seasons, but harvested in autumn;
the grains were harder, brittle, and contained the gluten
that makes for good quality bread flour. "Fall" or "winter"
wheat was sown in the autumn and overwintered for
early summer harvesting. It had less gluten so was more
suitable for cakes and pastries.[375]

Fig. 36 · Winter wheat

Grist mills once ground and sifted wheat into several
grades of flour, from a fine white called superfine down
through a series of ever-coarser inferior grades that are
no longer commercially marketed; Traill specifies sharps
and shorts, but there were other grades as well. Each wheat berry has three parts:
the outer shell (bran), inner starch and gluten protein (endosperm), and seed (wheat
germ). For centuries, wheat berries were milled between two round burr stones (hence
the term "stoneground") into a flour that consisted of all three elements, which was
then sifted to remove the bran and wheat germ. Some took their flour home from the
grist mill and spent time sifting it further to avoid the miller's extra fee. The elements
removed by sifting, called shorts or sharps, were used for a rough bread or added to
the hog meals. Removing as much bran as possible led to finer flour and removing as
much wheat germ as possible removed most of the natural oils that can make whole
flour go rancid. Many old recipes reminded bakers to dry the flour first by warming
it by the fire. Wheat flour was a creamy buff colour due to the wheat's natural colour
and because it retained some specks of bran, no matter how finely sifted it was at the
mill or at home.

Through the nineteenth century an ongoing theme was the confrontation between
advocates of whole grain flours and breadstuffs versus those who preferred white
flours and breadstuffs. Two well-known campaigners for unadulterated, unprocessed
whole foods were Doctor Sylvester Graham (1794–1851) and William Cobbett (1763–

375 Leung, *Grist and Flour Mills*, 34, 103.

1835) (see page 506).[376] Traill herself seems to have preferred homemade brown breads that incorporated some bran, echoing Cobbett [99]. Several culinary authors also espoused similar regimens of healthy eating, particularly Sarah Hale and Catharine Beecher, and suggested avoiding pies with heavy white pastry.

In the 1880s roller-milling started to supersede ancient stone grinding. Instead of tearing the wheat berries, the rollers crushed them with precision, separating the bran, starch, and wheat germ, resulting in a finer powder from which it was easier to sift out the bran and wheat germ. Additional improvements in sifting techniques eventually removed the germ altogether. By the late 1800s, almost half a century after publication of the *Guide*, flour could be consistently white and better keeping. The next century saw the introduction of bleach, sterilization, and fortification with vitamins, and further development of the harder wheats, that is, those with more protein gluten for breads.[377]

Wheat grown in Canada West eventually became an essential export commodity. Approximately six bushels of wheat resulted in one barrel of superfine flour when ground on the old burr stones.[378] The most famous wheat produced in nineteenth-century Canada was red fife, first grown in the 1840s on the Peterborough farm of David Fife, although it was the 1860s before its commercialization really took off. It is fun to consider that Traill may have been among the first Canadians to use local red fife wheat, although her family probably did not actually grow that variety. Often destitute, Traill was habitually in need of flour and accepted the gift of a barrel of flour from her brother Sam in November 1863.

Whisky Breweries for beer were founded early in Canada's settlement, and so were distilleries for spirits. At first they were small operations associated with grist mills, but by the 1840s were beginning to be larger enterprises. One of the first, which eventually became internationally known and one of the most important in the nineteenth century, was Gooderham and Worts in Toronto, founded in 1832. Distillation of rye and corn into alcoholic beverages was linked to the whole economy because excessive grains found a market, grist mills had a second product, and one of its

---

376 Smith, *Oxford Encyclopedia of Food and Drink in America*, 2:573–4.
377 Kelleher, "Flour from Mill to Market," 1–2.
378 Mika, Mika, and Turner, *Historic Mills of Ontario*, 11–13; Leung, *Grist and Flour Mills*, 250–67.

by-products, swill, was an important source of food for hogs and milch cows. Scottish and Irish whiskys were also imported in ever-increasing quantities.[379]

Whisky was often served diluted with water or as whisky-punch, not necessarily neat. To the regret of many colonial commentators, it was popular at all levels of Canadian society. "Drinking is the curse of Canada, and the very low price of whisky places the temptation constantly in everyone's reach," writes Susanna Moodie, suggesting that Canadian whisky was "that invidious enemy of souls."[380] It was an essential element at barn-raisings, ploughing matches, housing bees, weddings, and all sorts of social gatherings. Farmers made their own whisky to share with their workers.[381] Casual labourers were sometimes even paid in whisky. Several times Traill comments on her fear when in the presence of men under the influence of whisky, and many colonists commented on the prevalence of drunkenness, such as this pointed comment by Traill's brother-in-law John Moodie: "The fact is, that in no country I have ever seen does *drunkenness* prevail to such a degree as here. Temperance Societies may, *for a time* do some good; – but in general the remedy is about as effectual as amputation of the leg would be for a sore foot. This vice prevails most in *new settlements*. As the country becomes improved, and the inhabitants of all classes become less intermixed the people settle down into more regular habits."[382]

Whitefish   Of the whitefish in the waters off Michilimackinac, Anna Jameson wrote: "I have never tasted anything like it, either for delicacy or flavour." Traill, and many others, concurred on the excellence of the celebrated Canadian whitefish. Great quantities were salted, barrelled, and shipped to other colonies and the eastern United States. The most extensive fisheries were on Manitoulin Island, in Lake Huron, and the eastern section of Lake Ontario.[383]

White Rice, *also* Carolina Rice; *see also* Rice Pudding   This long-grain type of rice was imported in large amounts to Canada from South Carolina, even if backwoods people, Traill says, prefer wild rice [113]. Eliza Acton comments that, "the highest in

---

379 Heron, *Booze*, 20–1.
380 Moodie, *Life in the Clearings*, 70, 66.
381 Anne Langton, *A Gentlewoman in Upper Canada*, 2 January 1839, 201.
382 John Dunbar Moodie to James Traill, 8 March 1836.
383 Jameson, *Winter Studies and Summer Rambles*, 394; Samuel Strickland, *Twenty-Seven Years in Canada West*, 1:76–7.

price, and the best for general purposes, is that which we derive from America, – the Carolina – which is large-grained and very white."[384] Carolina rice (*Oriza sativa*) was famous for its brilliant whiteness. Although white rice stored well and was not expensive, Traill provides only two recipes, both simple fruit puddings, one with apples [75] and one with ripe currants [90]. Her "Farmer's Rice," made from moistened flour rolled between the fingers, then cooked in milk, was easily made by and for children in families who could not afford real rice.

Wild Duck, *see also* Wild Game   Migrating wild duck were a prime catch in spring and fall. Immense and noisy flocks filled the skies and marshes. Sam Strickland said, "Wood-duck is a delicious bird" and "I am particularly fond of" it. The finely plumaged wood duck (*Aix sponsa*) is fairly common in Ontario's wooded wetlands.[385]

Wild Game   The Traill family probably ate much more wild game than is apparent from Traill's writings. Certainly the Langtons ate a lot of it: "[T]he larder presents a very different spectacle to what it did last year. There is neither beef nor mutton, the remains only of one solitary haunch of venison; nor have the woods furnished us with either pigeons or partridges this year, but there is plenty of pork!"[386] Faunal remains from archaeological investigations of the Stewart homestead, Auburn, show a lot of wildlife consumption.[387] Migratory wildfowl provided quick fresh meat. Raccoons were mentioned by others, but not Traill.

As settlement overtook the forests, wild game became scarce, a devastating problem for the Native Peoples who had been displaced from their hunting grounds and one that came as an unpleasant shock to newcomers expecting to use the forest as a larder: "I certainly arrived with the vague notion that passing deer might be shot from one's own door, that partridge and wild-duck were as plentiful as sparrows in England, and that hares and rabbits might almost be caught by hand. These romantic ideas were truly dispelled! There is little game of any kind left, and to get that good dogs are wanted, which are very expensive to keep."[388]

384 Acton, *Modern Cookery for Private Families*, 74; Ward, *Grocer's Hand-Book and Directory*, 177.
385 Samuel Strickland, *Twenty-Seven Years in Canada West*, 1:66; Goodwin, *A Bird-Finding Guide to Ontario*, 368.
386 Anne Langton, *A Gentlewoman in Upper Canada*, 30 November 1842, 364.
387 Aoki, "Culinary Themes in the Writings of Frances Stewart," 3.
388 King, *Letters from Muskoka*, 42.

"Many young men are attracted to the Backwoods by the facilities they present for hunting and fishing. The wild, free life of the hunter has for an ardent and romantic temperament an inexpressible charm. But hunting and fishing, however fascinating as a wholesome relaxation from labour, will not win bread, or clothe a wife or shivering little ones."[389]

Wild Garlic   In spring "the hungry cattle hasten to browze on the tender shoots and swelling buds of the sugar maple and the basswood, or search out the oily succulent blades of the wild garlic" (*Allium canadense*).[390] Dislike of wild garlic was predicated on the cultural dislike of garlic held by most of the British. With a few exceptions, such as in a piquant sauce, Canadian cooks had little use for garden garlic (*Allium sativum*). It was similarly dismissed by early American cooks: "Garlicks, tho' used by the French, are better adapted to the uses of medicine than cookery."[391] But *The Canadian Housewife's Manual of Cookery* of 1860 cites it as an ingredient in over three dozen sauces, gravies, and sausage mixes.

Wild Goose, *see also* Wild Game   "The wild goose is excellent eating when well cooked," reported Anna Jameson. The Canada Goose (*Anser canadensis*) was readily domesticated. They were notorious for raiding the grain fields, grumbled Frances Stewart, among others.[392]

Wild Grapes, *see also* Grapes, Cultivated   The woods were often described as abundantly "festooned with the wild grape" by newcomers, in this case Anna Jameson, but while they "were rich in hue and beautiful in appearance," they were deemed "small and crude" (Sam Strickland), and "unhappily, tasteless to the palate" (Thomas Need).[393] These native climbing grapes (*Vitis raparia*) were an important foodstuff for the indigenous peoples and the settlers, and in time were carefully cultivated. "I have got two bearing shoots of a purple wild grape from the island near us, which

389 Moodie, *Life in the Clearings*, 11.
390 Traill, "A Glance Within the Forest," *Forest and Other Gleanings*, 249; Erichsen-Brown, *Use of Plants*, 454–5.
391 Simmons, *The First American Cookbook*, 12.
392 Jameson, *Winter Studies and Summer Rambles*, 1 April 1836, 151; Stewart, *Revisiting "Our Forest Home,"* 18 March 1869, 234.
393 Samuel Strickland, *Twenty-Seven Years in Canada West*, 2:29; Need, *Six Years in the Bush*, 16 July 1834, 99.

I long to see in fruit," says Traill in 1834, because, she told her sister, "they are very good for preserving as a jelly."[394]

Traill has a fascinating throw-away line about how wild grapes softened by early frost are suitable for wine [26], repeated in her *Studies of Plant Life in Canada*, which seems to be an early reference to what has become known as ice wine, although the grape varieties are different today.[395]

Wild Greens, *see also* Dandelion, Herbs, Lamb's Quarters, Pepper Grass, Wild Garlic, Wild Leek   Of the many available wild greens, Traill mentions dandelion, lamb's quarter, pepper grass, wild garlic, and wild leek in her *Guide*, but many appear in her other writings, such as nettles, watercress, American cress ("mild and tender and fit for the table"), and wintergreen. "An aromatic essence obtained from the leaves of this plant, known as 'Spice Wintergreen,' enter largely into the sugar confections sold in the stores."[396] In the present book she does not mention spring fiddleheads, the edible young sprouts of ostrich fern (*Matteuccia struthiopteris*), but she does mention other edible ferns in *Studies of Plant Life in Canada*.[397]

Wild Leek, *also* Ramps   Similar to wild garlic, wild leek (*Allium tricoccum*) notoriously tainted the flavour of milk, making it undrinkable and unsuitable for making butter or cheese for a few days. Therefore, it was seldom consumed by the colonists, but certainly was by the First Peoples.

Wild Red Plum   Wild red plum (Wild Canada Plum, *Prunus nigra*) trees once grew abundantly along river edges, and once fences started appearing in Upper Canada, they grew well along them as well. Traill liked them boiled down with maple molasses into a "capital preserve" [80]. "These make admirable preserves, especially when boiled in maple molasses, as is done by the American [that is, Canadian, as in non-British] housewives," and had also been similarly prepared by early French nuns. Wild red plums were popularly consumed for centuries before the Europeans, according to plentiful archaeological evidence.[398]

394 Jameson, *Winter Studies and Summer Rambles*, mid-July 1837, 267; Traill, *Backwoods of Canada*, 225; Traill Family Collection, letter to Sarah Strickland, undated, c. 1836, 3461.
395 Traill, *Studies of Plant Life in Canada*, 124–7.
396 Traill, Journal, Traill Family Collection, 3390; Traill, *Backwoods of Canada*, 236.
397 Traill, *Studies of Plant Life in Canada*, 256.
398 Traill, *Backwoods of Canada*, 104; Erichsen-Brown, *Use of Plants*, 163–5.

Wild Rice, *see* Indian Rice

Wild Turkey   Wild turkeys were prolific in Upper Canada and are making a come-back in parts of Ontario, such as Prince Edward County. Sometimes they were very common on the table, although others commented that "occasionally we had a wild turkey for a treat." They were not easy to catch, complained one colonist, Thomas Need, although others said their reputation for stupidity made them easy to catch.[399]

Wiltshire Cheese   Wiltshire cheese is a cylindrical semi-hard fresh cheese, moister and flakier than cheddar. Occasionally it is mentioned by name in Canada, for instance in banquet menus. Such cheeses were sometimes flavoured and coloured by green sage leaves. Wiltshire is a county located in southwest England.[400]

Windsor Bean, *see* Broad Bean

Wine   Shopkeepers imported wine "of the best and costliest kind" for gentlemen and caterers.[401] Claret, port, sherry, madeira (all reds) and champagne, moselle, and hock (whites) all appear on the grand menus, personal inventories, and importation lists of the earliest French and English Canadians, such as those in the *The Upper Canada Gazette*.

The grapes of North America did not lend themselves to good wine in the Mediterranean style, although many attempts were made. Traill says of wine made by the Reverend George Wilson Bridges, "I have tasted excellent grape-wine, made ... from the fruit gathered on Grape Island."[402] Some housewives made fruit wines (cordials) of raspberry, currant, elderberry, blackberry, mulberry, and raisins. Frances Stewart said a "currant cordial (home-made)" was part of a late-night supper she served in July 1841 to people who attended the raising of their second house.[403]

"In this highly-favoured Canada, this adopted country of ours, where all kinds of food are abundant and cheap, but wines comparatively scarce and high-priced, from

---

399 Mallory and Gordan, "Recollections of Early Days in Guilds, Kent Co.," 346; Need, *Six Years in the Bush*, 3 August 1831, 31–3.
400 Webster and Parkes, *Encyclopedia of Domestic Economy*, 412.
401 *Cobourg Star*, 10 January 1855, quoted in Guillet, *Early Life in Upper Canada*, 191.
402 Traill, "Rice Lake Plains," *Forest and Other Gleanings*, 208.
403 Stewart, *Our Forest Home*, 15 July 1841, 176.

the following carefully selected receipts the want may be supplied at a trifling expense. If carefully made and kept, say three or four years, a proportional strength being given, they would answer every purpose of foreign wines for health, culinary, or other domestic purposes."[404]

Woodchuck   "The woodchuck climbs like the raccoon and burrows like the rabbit ... The flesh is white, oily, and in the summer, rank, but is eaten in the fall by the Indian and the woodsmen ... [A] stone or stick well-aimed soon kills them."[405]

Yeasts, *also* Fermentations; *see also* Barm, Brewer's Yeast, Distiller's Yeast, Hop-Rising, Potato Yeast, Salt-Rising, Sugar Yeast   Until the mid-nineteenth century, yeast was yeast. Nothing was understood of the biology or chemistry of yeast fermentation, although centuries of observation meant that in practice yeasts could be controlled for certain qualities when they were intended for use in making breads, beers, ales, lagers, wines, and spirits. The primary yeast genus is *Saccharomyces* and the primary strain is *cerevisiae*, but the various properties of numerous *S. cerevisiae*, identified and classified through scientific experiments, are exploited for different purposes by industrial brewers, bakers, wine makers, and distillers. Today, yeast is no longer just yeast.

In addition to comments on the recent arrival of chemical leaveners, Traill includes no fewer than eight recipes for Canadian-style bread yeasts [91–7] all of which rely on wild airborne yeast spores, which once filled the atmosphere when bread was baked at home regularly. Anne Langton writes: "The usual plan in this country is to mix flour with warm salt and water, and set it by the fire to rise,"[406] so as to capture the wild yeasts, but that simple method was often augmented by other leavenings. Sharing and lending yeast starters was also a neighbourly action in the backwoods. Traill's instructions for colonial yeasts, or "fermentations" as she called them, are more thorough than those in *The American Frugal Housewife* (1832), *The Frugal Housewife's Manual* (1840), and *The Canadian Housewife's Manual of Cookery* (1861), because she considered it particularly important that British newcomers learn to make hop-risen and salt-risen breads . She makes a point of saying that "there is a

---

404   *The Canadian Housewife's Manual of Cookery*, 319.
405   Traill, *Canadian Crusoes*, 42.
406   Anne Langton, *A Gentlewoman in Upper Canada*, 11 December 1837, 163.

great difference in the materials she [i.e. the female emigrant] will have to make use of, and in the managing of them" [91].

Yeast was notoriously temperamental: "My last loaf is bad owing to the cold weather [-30°F]."[407] Many a bread-maker had similar laments. Yeast was never kept in tin cans, because tin "destroys its life."[408] Instead, yeasts were kept in tightly covered ceramic jars or crocks in a semi-warm place, often on the kitchen fireplace mantel, and occasionally fed a little sugar – in Canada, maple sugar or maple molasses – to keep them lively. The jar sometimes burst, if its bubbly contents were exceptionally spirited. When used, a few spoonfuls were retained to "ferment the next quantity, keeping it always in succession."[409] Many a recipe simply said "take a cup of yeast," but the cook had to understand the temperament and activity of her particular yeast. Recipes sometimes called for differing quantities, knowing that some were naturally less active than others. For example, a choice of "1 T. brewer's yeast or 2 T. hop yeast" is given in one recipe for buckwheat pancakes.[410] When translating an historic recipe for today's use, one must take into account that extra liquid is needed to substitute for the cup or other volume of yeast used in the original.

Commercial compressed yeast (*Saccharomyces cerevisiae*) was first marketed in Germany and the United States in the 1860s and reached Canada soon after. In 1871, Harriet King was grateful for "Twin Brother's Yeast" because she found her own rising made her bread "either bitter, sour, or salt."[411]

407 Pengelley, The Diaries of Harriet Pengelley, 15 December 1835.
408 Child, *The American Frugal Housewife*, 79.
409 Rundell, *A New System of Domestic Cookery*, 219.
410 Haskell, *The Housekeeper's Encyclopedia*, 189.
411 King, *Letters from Muskoka*, 39.

Glossary of Traill's Sources and Influences

By examining a cookbook's direct and indirect influences, published and unpublished sources, and identifying derivative material, one can trace how culinary knowledge was disseminated and modified between families, regions, eras, and cultures.

Traill had dealt both clearly and obliquely with household management topics in her writing for many years. However, early in the 1850s, several factors and influences, including family dynamics and her ongoing financial privation, coalesced to prompt Traill to produce her *Guide*. Having decided on this new project, she reached out to many people and publications for applicable recipes, quotations, excerpts, and advice to supplement her own hard-won knowledge. *The Female Emigrant's Guide* incorporated a considerable amount of previously published material, some without explicit acknowledgment (which was not unusual practice at the time).

Throughout her life Traill read widely in poetry, emigration literature, literary and agricultural journals, botanical and horticultural books, the Bible, and local and imported newspapers; she also corresponded prolifically with dozens of people. Evidence of this wide knowledge was readily apparent in her writings. Biblical quotes, both accurate and misremembered, and lines and phrases from the poems and Shakespeare plays she knew by heart are scattered throughout the *Guide*. This new edition does not identify these numerous quotations and paraphrases taken from non-culinary sources, although the glossary below provides a brief biography of the two poets Traill mentions by name, Mrs Southey and Robert Southwell.

FAMILY

Traill's survival novel, *Canadian Crusoes,* about three lost but resourceful adolescents who forage, fish, and hunt in the bountiful wilderness in and around Rice Lake, was published in 1852, a testimony to Traill's intimate knowledge of the local habitat as well as her own survival skills. In the same year, her sister Susanna Moodie's autobiographical book, *Roughing It in the Bush*, a mordant account of adjustment to backwoods housewifery in the 1830s and a not-so-veiled commentary on the cheerful optimism of Traill's 1830s *Backwoods of Canada,* was published. The next year their brother Sam added to the expanding library of emigration literature by publishing the enormous and well-received *Twenty-Seven Years in Canada West* (see pages 515–16), relating yet more stories of male-centred settlement. Catharine was exasperated by its price ("beyond the reach of a large proportion of the emigrants and poorer settlers" [47, 152]) and his lack of explanatory instructions for women, even as she was proud of his accomplishments. He wrote the book while vacationing in England following the death of his wife, Mary; while there he proposed to an old friend, Katherine Rackham. Katherine wrote to Catharine for Canadian housekeeping advice,[1] which must have made her realize how ill-prepared her new sister-in-law was, even though she would have help at Sam's substantial Lakefield household from his daughters, raised by Canadian-born Mary.

These family dynamics refocused Traill's attention on the possibilities of a new book project, one aimed at emigrant women. Since she had been a neophyte immigrant before becoming a seasoned bushwife, had already published on the topics of female emigration and frontier housewifery, and continued to meet immigrant women who needed assistance, she must have felt uniquely qualified to write a practical handbook for her unprepared compatriots. Her voice was that of a kindly moralizing teacher, a wise and practical old-timer, who speaks in a didactic but cheerful, cautionary but still encouraging, tone. Her new book would both replace traditional grandmother to mother to daughter instruction and mediate between educated gentlewomen and women of varied backgrounds who were entering a new geographical, psychological, and social environment.

Susanna Moodie had also become one of those experienced settlers, although in *Roughing It in the Bush* she rather overstates her initial incompetence for narrative effect. Since the sisters depended on each other throughout their lives and lived as neighbours for their first several years in Upper Canada, it would have been natural to discuss their housekeeping chores regularly, and furthermore, to talk with their nearby sister-in-law, Mary Strickland, who apparently said repeatedly, "Wait till you have been in Canada a few years, and then you will better understand the difficulties of a bush settler's wife."[2] Their brother was enormously helpful and informative to his sisters in their early years in the bush. An agreeable image involves siblings Sam and Catharine in their orchards consulting each other about grafting and soaping fruit trees, and in their maple groves with Susanna discussing sugar making, which

1 Katherine Rackham to Traill, dated early 1854, Traill Family Collection, 5–12.
2 Traill, "Ramblings by the River" in *Forest and Other Gleanings*, 162.

they undertook together (along with Jenny, Susanna's faithful servant) in the winters of 1835 through 1838.[3] Traill spends considerable time explaining maple sugaring [146–52], including a long extract from Sam's *Twenty-Seven Years in Canada West*.[4] She also uses her sister's previously published directions for a dandelion coffee [142–3] (also see page 407).

Susanna probably helped Catharine in other ways too, such as identifying possible recipes, as requested. Catharine also asked for help from their sisters Elizabeth and Agnes, who remained in England, not just for content but for publication assistance, which they had helped with for previous endeavours. Early in 1854, she sent out a second call to friends and family in England, to which several responded with enthusiasm, if not utility. "Eliza ... highly approves of [the *Guide*]," Catharine informed Susanna,[5] and apparently one of Eliza's recipes appears in it,[6] although which one is not obvious. Agnes, however, never understood the reality of her younger sisters' frontier lives for she condescendingly advised them to "be sure to warn ladies not to make the worst of everything for no one can avoid trials even in the most luxurious homes."[7] Sarah, the third sister, known as "the baker" in the family circle because of her light breads,[8] sent "a large stock of standard recipes almost big enough for a whole book" via Jane, the fourth sister.[9] None of them were deemed suitable for the *Guide*, but some may be still be among the stash of mostly uncredited recipes in the Traill papers.

FRIENDS AND NEIGHBOURS

The most effective expertise had been gained in the crucible of personal pioneer experience and generously shared through conversations and letters. In her "adopted

3 Traill Family Collection, 22 January 1838, 3430; 17 March 1838, 3432; 5 April 1838, 3435.
4 Samuel Strickland, *Twenty-Seven Years in Canada West*, 2:298–311.
5 Traill to Susanna Moodie, 6 January 1854, *I Bless You in My Heart*, 88–90.
6 Traill to Ellen Dunlop, 1 September [1855], Traill Family Collection, 1953.
7 Agnes Strickland to Traill, 3 April [1854], Traill Family Collection, 550.
8 Peterman, *Sisters in Two Worlds*, 12; Gray, *Sisters in the Wilderness*, 21.
9 Jane Strickland to Traill, 4 April [1854], Traill Family Collection, 56. Sarah had apparently published recipes in the first and second volume of *The Home Circle* (7 July 1849 to mid-1851) for which Agnes and Catharine both wrote stories and poems. Sarah's authorship of any of the recipes in volumes 1 and 2 is not obvious, but two of her sisters had stories with their bylines (Traill, *I Bless You in My Heart*, 22).

country," Traill wrote, her best teachers were "old settlers' wives, and choppers and Indians," plus her "own powers of observation."[10] In addition to her own twenty-two-year repertoire of bush farm experience, Traill's text and private letters reveal that she sought help from established and resourceful neighbours, friends, and acquaintances who lived in the backwoods and nearby towns, as well as from her family, both nearby and far away. Scattered throughout Traill's surviving records are cooking, medical, and housekeeping recipes in both her and others' scribbles. Such informal borrowing and loaning was as much a part of backwoods culture as the constant verbal sharing of gained experience. The extent of friendly exchanges of advice on all manner of settlement skills, as well as actual provisions, has surely been underestimated; women in particular relied on verbal communication, due to their higher level of illiteracy and the scarcity of relevant printed material.[11] We can easily imagine conversations between settlers starting with "How do you do this?"

Catharine credited Frances Stewart, who had already been resident on a rough Otonobee River farm for a decade by 1832, with being her first colonial teacher.[12] "By the bright blazing fire in the parlour of Auburn, enlivened by the conversation of its genial, intellectual host and hostess, I learned more practical lessons for my guidance in the new life of a settler's wife in the backwoods than any book could have given me, had any book then been written on the subject. I learned ... how much could be done by practical usefulness to make a home in the lonely woods the abode of peace and comfort."[13]

Leaving the hospitable Stewarts, the Traills moved ten miles north to live with Sam and Mary Strickland in their comfortable lakeside log house for the autumn months, while building their own cabin in a small clearing. Frances and Mary helped Catharine, the ever-curious botanist, in her initial identifications of the edible local berries, herbs, and mushrooms, as well as by demonstrating the manufacture of bush yeasts,

10 Traill, *Studies of Plant Life in Canada*, 3.
11 *History of the Book in Canada*, 1:170. Similarly, garden historian Eileen Woodhead says, "The contributions made by conscientious gardeners – their exchange of information as well as actual seeds and plants – has played an almost unrecognized role in our past" (Woodhead, *Early Canadian Gardening*, 28).
12 Traill, *Studies of Plant Life in Canada*, 3.
13 Traill, from the obituary letter for the Peterborough *Review*, later printed in the second edition of Stewart, *Our Forest Home*, 143–6; a short extract is quoted in Traill, *I Bless You in My Heart*, 13. See the Stewart entry below for further details.

breads, soap, and cooking with the indigenous cornmeal and wild rice. They also had learned from the very few settlers who had preceded them; in Frances' case she identified them as British women who had been neighbourly in the short months she had spent in Cobourg village before moving to their farmland.[14]

In her preface Traill notes "her obligations" to Mrs Stewart and her family, but also to the McKyes family and the Misses A. and M. Ferguson [13], who are all described in separate entries below. Letters and autobiographical stories reveal the identities of other "ladies of my acquaintance who kindly supplied me with hints from their own experience on various matters" [13]. The sisters Betty and Nora Young, featured in an 1838 story, inspired rapturous praise for their backwoods industry and talents. Susanna Moodie knew them too, calling them "excellent housekeepers."[15] Clearly, such women were inspirations. Maria Wright and Eliza Brown were "nice" Yankee women; Eliza provided one recipe, although Traill does not specify which one.[16] Mostly, these women remain tantalizingly unidentified. The art of grafting, for example, she "learned … from a Canadian lady in her own parlour" [69]. The Pumpkin-Pie recipe came from "a Canadian lady who is celebrated for the excellence of her pumpkin-pies" [133] and "A Rich Cheese" was made from "a secret told me by a dairy-woman, famous for the manufacture of the blue cheese" [198]. Her dairy section gives a good idea of how much she communicated with the local expert butter and cheese makers who were "old country farmer's" wives [194] from the English shires.

At least one recipe, "Pickle for Beef or Pork," was "furnished by a gentleman" at whose table Catharine had "eaten excellent meat" [154].

Of her medical knowledge, Catharine told Ellen Dunlop: "You know darling I am a regular old quack but I learned some of my wisdom from respectable sources. I was always a pet of the doctors, and they used to tell me many things good for myself and others – and praise my nursing of their patients."[17] Traill knew several physicians. "Canada too has her simplers and herbalists among the old settlers – especially among the old UELoyalists and their children – [who] extract virtues from the wild plants of the forests and swamps and though they have few written recipes they have

---

14 Stewart, *Our Forest Home*, 19, 23, 25, 38, 39.

15 Traill, "The Mill of the Rapids" in *Forest and Other Gleanings*, 59–71; Moodie, *Roughing It in the Bush*, 352.

16 Traill to Ellen Dunlop, 17 September [1854, incorrectly dated 1855 in finding aid of Traill Family Collection], 1953; Driver, *Culinary Landmarks*, 292, 293.

17 Traill to Ellen Dunlop, *I Bless You in My Heart*, 22 June 1856, 102.

much valuable knowledge which they practice among themselves remedies which they have gleaned from the Indians and can give names for every weed or herb of the field – It was from such sources that I myself learned the common names of most of our native plants and some of their sanitary virtues."[18]

She also seems to have learned some of this information directly from the local Mississauga Anishinaabe women, especially around Rice Lake.[19] That Traill was interested in the First Nations peoples of Canada was apparent even in her *Young Emigrants* (1826). With first-hand knowledge, she developed this theme in her *Backwoods* letters and again in *Canadian Crusoes*, whose Mohawk heroine, Indiana, taught the Canadian-born heroine, Catharine Maxwell, basic survival skills that came in handy when she was later captured by the Ojibwa (which Traill spelled Ojebwa). In *The Female Emigrant's Guide*, this theme was muted. The most widespread influence of the First Nations found there is in the cultivation of corn, pumpkin, squash, sweet potato, cranberry, and other wild fruits, and harvesting maple sap, although by the 1850s this indigenous produce had been so thoroughly absorbed into the North American culinary mainstream that its original source had disappeared from immediate memory. Traill sometimes wrote about her trade relationships with the nearby First Nations people, as discussed in our Introduction [xiv–xvii].[20]

NEWSPAPERS, JOURNALS, AND BOOKS

In addition to extensive conversational and hands-on practical guidance, some of Traill's influences and sources can be traced to publications circulating in the bush that discussed relevant aspects of emigration, agriculture, horticulture, botany, housewifery, and cooking. As educated people, the Traills continued to read a great deal after they left England; some of that content reappeared in the *Guide*, adjusted and transformed.

The *Guide* includes numerous quotes from authoritative male authors. Traill wanted to reach a large audience and, with the exception of her own *The Backwoods of Canada* and Susanna Moodie's *Roughing It in the Bush,* no woman had published

---

18 Traill, Journal, note in Traill's handwriting added to November 1865 entry, transcript by Sara Eaton, Traill Family Collection, 2989.

19 Martin, McGillis, and Milne, *Gore's Landing*, 15.

20 Traill, *Backwoods of Canada*, 117.

advice on agriculture, horticulture, or emigration.[21] Advice from male writers became springboards for some of her own recommendations on successful emigration and she expanded on it to include advice about family concerns and creating a comfortable homestead. From the eighteenth century on, a considerable amount of emigrant advice literature had been available for British men coming to North America, such as Howison's *Sketches of Upper Canada*, Dunlop's *Statistical Sketches of Upper Canada*, and Brown's *Views of Canada and the Colonists* [506] and her brother's *Twenty-Seven Years in Canada West* [47–51, 150–2] and Catharine had read a great of it once her brother left for Canada, not realizing she would follow him seven years later. In all of these works women as emigrants and active settlers in their own right were all but ignored. If they and their gendered tasks were mentioned, it was typically in a dismissively summary way, often in tandem with the children: "Married persons are always more comfortable, and succeed sooner, in Canada, than single men; for a wife and family, so far from being a burden here, always prove sources of wealth. The wife of a new settler has many domestic duties to perform; and children, if at all grown up, are useful in various ways."[22] "The family, when industrious, find their time fully employed in spinning and other female occupations; and, when it is considered that almost every article of convenience or luxury must be made at home or dispensed with, it may easily be imagined that the duties of a Farmer's Wife and grown up Daughters are numerous and unceasing, – for in proportion with their industry and abilities will be their domestic comfort and happiness."[23] While granting that the male writers may have felt ill-qualified to comment extensively, such statements nonetheless revealed a stunning and systemic disregard for the importance of women's industry in successful settlement.

Catharine Parr Traill, of course, critiqued the fundamental inadequacy of previous guides by aiming *The Backwoods of Canada* and the *Guide* at the other half of the immigrant population, the females "on whose responsibility the whole comfort of a family depends."[24] Others had observed that there was an abundance of wild fruits, for instance, but Traill, freshly arrived in Upper Canada, was already taking that ob-

---

21 A. B. of Grimsby is something of an exception because the second half of her *Frugal Housewife's Manual* of 1840 duplicates much of Charles F. Crosman's *The Gardener's Manual*. See Lucas and Williamson, "Frolics with Food."

22 Howison, *Sketches of Upper Canada*, 239.

23 Widder, *Information for Intending Emigrants*, 5. Widder was company commissioner for The Canada Company in Guelph, Canada West, from 1839 to 1864.

24 Traill, *Backwoods of Canada*, 1.

servation a step further by noting how they could be cooked and cultivated, work that could be expected to fall to women.

Printed advice on using wild forest berries and herbs for food and medicine was scarce, because botanies of North America were few; the most prominent was Frederick Pursh's two-volume work, published in 1814 and 1816,[25] which included occasional notes on culinary and medical uses and was prized by literate women. Frances Stewart owned a copy of Pursh, which Traill was able to borrow. Books and periodicals relevant to Canada were becoming increasingly available, even if most were written by Americans.

Catharine enjoyed reading literary periodicals as well as farming and agricultural magazines, and had access to several. In April 1853, for instance, she was receiving four: "*The Anglo*," "*The Horticulturalist*," the "*Snowdrop* from Montreal," and "the *M Leaf*."[26] The "Rochester Horticulturalist" [137] refers to the *Horticulturalist* from Rochester, New York. She acknowledges *The Genesee Farmer* from Genesee, New York [87]. She also copied from the *Old Countryman,* a Toronto newspaper she considered "popular and useful" [61],[27] as well as the *American Fruit Book* (1849). The *Guide's* "A Few Hints on Gardening" and the following pages on horticulture, orchards, and foraging have a slapped-together quality that nevertheless exudes confidence, as it was based on Catharine's own experience and advice, and extracts from published sources that she considered provided information suitable to the Peterborough region.

She also recycles her own material that had appeared in periodicals, most obviously her "Prize Essay on Butter Making," originally published in *The Canadian Agriculturalist* of May 1854 after winning a prize at the annual fair sponsored by the Hamilton Township Agricultural Society.[28] It was shortened for the *Guide.* She took particular pride in her skill as a dairywoman, but liked learning new hints, such as pre-warming milk pans to better raise the cream, which came from a "North-Lancashire paper [193]."

25 Pursh, *Flora Americae Septentrionalis.*
26 Traill to Frances Stewart, *I Bless You in My Heart*, 28 April [1853], 78–9.
27 According to Stuntz, *List of the Agricultural Periodicals of the United States and Canada*, 113, there were six periodicals titled *New England Farmer*. The one Traill would have seen, which circulated in Canada West and is the one extracted in *The Old Countryman*, was a weekly from Boston, 9 December 1848 to 25 August 1864.
28 Traill, "Prize Essay on Butter Making." It was written in 1853.

Traill's section on fashioning a comfortable home out of a log cabin is full of practical and inexpensive ideas. For her original readers, one idea must have stood out as strange, that of converting barrels into furniture, such as chairs. She provides simple but adequate directions. Interestingly, such barrel chairs had been described and illustrated in an influential 1850 book called *The Architecture of Country Houses*.[29] There is no way to know whether she had seen the book or whether barrel chairs were already being used in the Canadian bush.

COOKBOOKS AND RECIPES

The more one reads old cookbooks, handwritten recipe manuscripts, and recipe columns in women's magazines, the more one recognizes identical and paraphrased recipes that appear in multiple places. All culinary authors borrowed from each other, despite claims otherwise: borrowing previously published recipes without attribution has a long history, starting with the earliest published cookery books. Recipe collections were often built on goodwill exchanges, with friends being honoured by having their names written beside their recipe(s), an identification technique that continued in most community cookbooks once they became a publishing phenomenon in the last third of the nineteenth century.[30] Another widespread custom was taking recipes from cookbooks for inclusion in magazines, newspapers, and almanacs, both as filler and as a nod to female readers. However, in mid-century, once a few enterprising women began to build careers around housewifery advice (Americans Eliza Leslie, Sarah Josepha Hale, and Catharine Beecher especially), recipe copying began to pose a serious drawback to their credibility as professional writers. For her *Guide* Traill borrowed recipes freely, with and without accreditation, and without necessarily testing the recipe herself, which she does not mind admitting. A friend's recommendation was sufficient. The fancifully named California Cake [107] was certainly not a title Traill herself would have used for an utterly ordinary butter cake that clearly came from somewhere other than a backwoods neighbour.

Investigating the cookbooks she could have had access to, the periodicals with recipes to which we know she subscribed, and other common publications with

---

29 Downing, *The Architecture of Country Houses*, 414.
30 On community cookbooks, see Driver, *Culinary Landmarks*, xxii–xxv, and Driver's introduction to *The Home Cook Book*.

domestic columns that circulated in Canada West, it is possible to compile a short but inevitably incomplete list of the sources in which her recipes were originally printed.

According to bookseller lists and shop advertisements placed in the local newspapers,[31] many English, Scottish, and American cookbooks were sold in pre-Confederation Canada, such as Amelia Simmons's *American Cookery* (1796), Eliza Maria Rundell's *A New System of Domestic Cookery* (1806), Dr Kitchiner's *Cook's Oracle* (1817), Mary Randolph's *The Virginia Housewife* (1824), Meg Dods' *Cook and Housewife's Manual* (1826), as well as the many recipe books by Americans Eliza Leslie, Sarah Hale, and Catharine Beecher, all familiar names to North American homemakers for much of the nineteenth century. Some immigrant women carried their trusted cookbooks with them across the ocean and Traill points out that "it was quite amusing for a looker-on to watch the curious anxious faces peering over one another's shoulders onto the various cookery-books, English and American, that had been privily borrowed from the most accomplished housewives in the neighbourhood."[32] However such cookbooks, written for a middle-class urban audience, had limited application to modest Canadian households in the bush, as Catharine indicates when she says her *Guide* was not "a regular cookery book" [110, 160].

No correlation exists between the *Guide* and the two well-known cookbooks aimed at a middle-class audience that she references in *The Backwoods of Canada*: Dr Kitchiner's *Cook's Oracle* (1817) or *The Practice of Cookery* (1829) by Catherine Dalgairns.[33] Although detailed handbooks written specifically for rural English homemakers had been published up until the end of the eighteenth century, the very few in the early part of the new century were nostalgic polemics against encroaching industrialism and were quite short on practical details.[34]

Judging by the number of reissues and the frequency with which newspapers, magazines, almanacs, handwritten recipe collections, and other cookbooks, the *Guide* included, copied recipes from it, with and without accreditation, the book that appears to have been most familiar to Canadians was Lydia Maria Child's *American Frugal Housewife, Dedicated to Those Who Are Not Ashamed of Economy* (1829; 1832).

---

31 Williamson, "Recipe and Household Literature," in *The Book in Canada*, 1:275, and Peterman, "Literary Cultures and Popular Reading in Upper Canada," in ibid., 1:403.
32 Traill, "The Interrupted Bridal," 132.
33 Traill, *Backwoods of Canada*, 91.
34 Attar, *A Bibliography of Household Books Published in Britain, 1800–1914*, 27–8.

The cake section in the *Guide* seems to contain the most recipes taken from other sources, particularly two published cookbooks: Leslie's *Seventy-Five Receipts* and Child's *American Frugal Housewife*. Traill used four of Child's recipes: Cup Cake [108], Doughnuts [108], Leaven Cakes [95], and Excellent Bread without Yeast [100]. Only the latter was attributed.

Three cake recipes closely resemble those found in Eliza Leslie's *Seventy-Five Receipts*, although not the original 1828 edition. The book was republished many times, and the 1840 version, which was sold packaged with Mrs Lee's *Cook's Own Book*, includes Ginger Cup Cake [106], Doughnuts [108], and Indian Pound Cake [124], obvious precedents to the recipes in the *Guide*.[35] Traill's versions probably came through an intermediary, because they have been slightly changed. Also, these three recipes, as well as Common Gingerbread [106], Plain Plum Cake [106], Cookies [107], and Drop Sweet Cakes [107], use a colon between ingredients, rather than the semi-colons, commas, or periods found in other recipes, which suggests that one person supplied them, even though they are not grouped together in the *Guide*.

The only other semi-culinary author Traill references by name is William Cobbett, whose *Cottage Economy* (1822) extols the virtues of homemade bread. Catharine paraphrased his recipe for bran bread [99].

None of the recipes in the *Guide* seem to have come from the *Canada Farmer* (in which she published a domestic column), the *Horticulturalist* [86], or the *Canadian Horticulturalist*, despite the wide variety of recipes they published that presumably were suitable for the farm families who constituted their readership. For instance, the latter periodical cherry-picked some recipes from Alexis Soyer's *Modern Housewife* and *Miss Beecher's Domestic Receipt Book*, among others. The *Old Countryman* ([39, 61, 225]; also see below) may also have had a recipe column and, if so, perhaps some of the *Guide's* recipes come from it, as the gardening advice does, but since only two issues survive we cannot know.

Some recipes were taken from *The Snow Drop* and *The Maple Leaf*, short-lived publications aimed at Canadian juveniles to which Catharine regularly contributed sketches, discussed below.

Catharine borrowed Susanna's twice-published directions for Dandelion Coffee, an idea Susanna had first read about in an article by a Dr Harrison of Edinburgh published in the New York *Albion* in 1832. The recipe and a small commentary appeared

---

35 Leslie, *Seventy-Five Receipts*, 22, 23, 25. Miss Leslie added and deleted recipes in her various editions so each collection of recipes differs somewhat from the one that precedes it.

in the first issue of the Moodies' literary venture, *The Victoria Magazine*, in September 1847, and were reprinted in an alternate order in *Roughing It in the Bush*. Using quotation marks to acknowledge its origin, Catharine paraphrased her sister's words but scoffed at Harrison's claim that roasted dandelion roots were "equal in substance and flavour to the best Mocha coffee" [142] and carefully avoided including Susanna's similar opinion that "the coffee proved ... far superior to the common coffee we procured at the stores."[36] In her autobiographical novel *Flora Lyndsay*, which recounts the months prior to arrival in Canada, Moodie makes it clear she likes "fragrant and exhilarating" coffee, and states she possesses "quite an Asiatic taste in that respect."[37]

The origins of some recipes remain mysterious, but they could have come from friends and family.

A last note: several recipes are indisputably Traill's own. Besides her self-identified "Mrs Traill's Bread [98], others had a similar expansiveness and chattiness that seem very much like her – certainly Canadian Croquets [109], Bush Tea-Cakes [109], and Buckwheat Pancakes [114].

PEOPLE AND PUBLICATIONS THAT TRAILL IDENTIFIED

A note on punctuation and font: The titles of books, newspapers, and journals that Traill drew upon for inspiration are presented here within quotation marks because she often identified them incorrectly. Accurate titles are italicized.

"Advice to Emigrants" and "Emigration to America"

Traill copied a page of advice from an unidentified issue of one of the missing *Old Countryman* newspapers about the routine treatment afforded each emigrant ship when it docked [39–40], to which she added a long "Extract from Mr. Vere Foster's Advice to Emigrants" about ship stores and other voyage essentials, calling it "Emigration to America." Both are incorrect titles. Foster's booklet is actually *Work and Wages*, published in 1851, and reprinted at least five times with updates. Its thorough subheading gives a clear indication of its content: *The penny emigrant's guide to the United States and Canada: for female servants, laborers, mechanics, farmers, &c.:*

36 Reprinted in the Editor's Table column of the Moodies' *The Victoria Magazine* 1 (1) (September 1847): 22; Moodie, *Roughing It in the Bush*, 353–6.
37 Moodie, *Flora Lyndsay*, 47, 77.

containing a short description of those countries, and most suitable places for settlement, rates of wages, board and lodging, house rent, price of land, money matters, &c., together with full information about the preparations necessary for the voyage, instructions on landing, and expenses of travelling in America: with an appendix.[38]

Traill begins, "I have been allowed by the author" [40], suggesting that Foster had given her permission to reproduce the text; if so, the correspondence is now lost. Vere Foster (1819–1900), a well-known Irish philanthropist and benefactor, was known to have provided information about and funding for immigration to thousands of nine-teenth-century Irish (mostly female) who were immigrating to North America. Traill obviously had access to a copy and makes it seem as if only "a few words [were] added or omitted as the case may be" [44], although in fact she extensively paraphrased and abridged Foster's words. The least altered quotations were those that concerned the British and American laws on sea stores and extra provisions, although she inexplic-ably changed his "baking powder," a term she uses elsewhere, to "bread soda for rais-ing cakes" [43]. She inserted a line about eating fruits and vegetables sparingly to avoid upset stomachs [44], perhaps based on her own memories and also following the medical wisdom of her day.

American Fruit Book

In planting her own orchards, a task generally considered men's work in Britain, Traill relied on "an old-fashioned book on orchard-planting" [70] called *The American Fruit Book; Containing Directions for Raising, Propagating, and Managing Fruit Trees, Shrubs, and Plants; With a Description of the Best Varieties of Fruit, Including New and Valuable Kinds* (1849) by William Cole. Although she does not name the author, she quotes and paraphrases the book extensively, perhaps from a personal copy or one of the copies "found in most of the district libraries" [75]. She notes that it was "to be regretted that so few plain practical gardening-books have as yet been published in Canada, devoted to vegetable and fruit culture, suited expressly for the climate and soil of Canada" [86]. Her text was an early attempt to capture this information.

Although enthusiasm for growing fruit trees in Britain and the long-settled parts of North America was the impetus behind many books, the first original book on horticulture for English Canada, *The Canadian Fruit-culturalist*, was not published until 1867, many years after Traill's *Guide*.

38 Foster, *Work and Wages*, Canadian Institute for Historical Microreproductions 35643.

"Brown's View's [*sic*] of Canada" [47]

The full title was *Views of Canada and the Colonists, Embracing the Experience of an Eight Years' Residence; Views of the Present State, Progress, and Prospects of the Colony and Practical Information for Intending Emigrants* by James Bryce Brown. First published in 1844, it was apparently the second edition of 1851, "corrected throughout and greatly enlarged," according to the title page, with which Traill was familiar.

Cobbett, William (1763–1835)

Englishman William Cobbett was a well-known radical newspaperman, reform politician, farmer, and soldier who championed the age-old skills of rural self-sufficiency in an era when industrialism and capitalism were leading to a loss of homemade foodstuffs and agricultural knowledge. Traill was familiar with his writings. Among his many books are *Cottage Economy* (1822) and *Rural Rides* (1830), which promoted and explained techniques for brewing beer, baking bread, keeping livestock, selecting grasses to make hats, and constructing ice-houses in the American style, among many other topics in agriculture and handcrafts.[39] He advocates a return to such tasks as regular bread baking by housewives and the destruction of farm machinery that had replaced farm labourers, among other idealistic and impractical ideas for England; in Canada, regular bread baking and machineless farm labour was the reality for most colonists starting out on bush farms. Cobbett lived in New Brunswick, Virginia, New York State, France, and the countryside of England, always advocating for farm families who were being subjected to the political and cultural forces undermining the rural countryside. Traill mentions him in *Backwoods of Canada*, disagreeing with him about the possibility that English farmers could effectively grow American corn, as it requires a longer and hotter growing season than that in the British Isles.[40]

Ferguson, Misses A and M

A and M Ferguson were the daughters of Frederick Ferguson (1802–1867), an Irishman who had arrived in Upper Canada in 1834 and settled as a merchant in the village of Ashburnham, now part of east Peterborough, where he later served "with

---

39 Cobbett, *Cottage Economy*; originally printed as several pamphlets in 1820 and 1821. The book was sold by the Lesslie Brothers in Toronto in 1837. Also Cobbett, *Rural Rides*, serialized in his *Cobbett's Weekly Political Register* from 1822–26, and repackaged as a book in 1830. Well-known at the time was Copley's *Cottage Comforts*.

40 Traill, *Backwoods of Canada*, 135.

integrity and ability" as county treasurer and twice stood unsuccessfully for election to Parliament.[41] According to the 1851 census, which was actually conducted in 1852, he and his West Indian–born wife, Mary Elizabeth, had four children: Alithea M., (also born in the West Indies), age nineteen "at next birthday," that is, in 1853, Mary I., age seventeen, Elizabeth, age twelve, and William, age eleven. According to the birth records of Dr Hutchison of Peterborough (who also delivered several Traill, Moodie, Stewart, and Strickland children; see also page [35]), Mary's birthday was 1 June 1836 and Elizabeth's was 4 May 1841.[42] In 1854, therefore, in the months leading up to the publication of *The Female Emigrant's Guide*, Alithea would presumably have been twenty-one and Mary nineteen. How did they help Traill sufficiently to warrant mention in the preface? They do not appear in the Traill papers, as far as we can see. As young women, did they help in the Traill household, even though there were several Traill daughters? They lived in Ashburnham, where the Traills lived in the 1840s.

"Fleming's Printed Catalogue"

Traill drew upon an early 1850s pamphlet she misnamed "Fleming's Printed Catalogue," actually the annual *Catalogue of Garden, Agricultural and Flower Seeds* by James Fleming (1812–1888), a Scotsman who arrived in Toronto in 1836. Fleming was a market gardener with a seed store and greenhouse on three acres west of Yonge and Elm Streets in Toronto.[43] Ontario seedsmen's catalogues provided valuable information about local conditions for planting and those of Torontonians William Custead and James Fleming were particularly well known in their day. Of Fleming's annual catalogues, the *Canadian Agriculturalist* says: "They are adapted to the soil and climate of this part of Canada, and as Mr. Fleming ranks as A No. 1, as a gardener and as a seedsman, we publish his directions with much confidence."[44] From Fleming's "Brief Hints on Sowing and Raising Culinary Vegetables," a section of three and a half pages, Traill reprinted slightly altered versions of the first half of his entries, those for kidney beans through celery [58–60], but oddly not the second half, which dealt with lettuce, onions, parsnips, radishes, rhubarb, salsify, spinach, tomatoes, and

41 Poole, *A Sketch of the Early Settlement*, 54, 59, 61, 121; Traill, *I Bless You in My Heart*, 88n4.

42 1851 Census, Canada West, Peterboro County, Town of Peterboro. The handwitten name "Alithea" is hard to read; it could also be Alitten or Alithen. See also Jean Cole, *Peterborough in the Hutchison-Fleming Era*, 17.

43 "James Fleming" in *The History of Toronto and County of York*, 2:50.

44 *The Canadian Agriculturist*, 1855, 150–2.

more turnips, all of which were equally important and familiar. Perhaps her copy was missing the pamphlet's last two pages and she could not get a full copy in time for publication. She does not provide a similar level of instruction for the missing list of vegetables elsewhere in her vegetable section, except for tomatoes, to which she devotes two pages. Her notes for rhubarb are quite different from Fleming's, so she appears to have disagreed with his methods in that case.

Foster, Vere, Esq., *see* "Advice to Emigrants"

Genesee Farmer, The
Subtitled "A Monthly Journal Devoted to Agriculture, Horticulture, and Domestic Rural Economy," this was an agricultural newspaper published in Rochester, New York, from 1840 to 1865, when it merged with *American Agriculturalist*. It circulated widely in Upper Canada. To its editor, in a letter offering some of her short writings on Canadian wildflowers, Traill said, "The ladies I assure you sometimes read the Genesee Farmer, as well as their husbands and brothers."[45]

Harrison, Dr, of Edinburgh, *see* Dandelion Coffee [407]

Horticulturalist
When Traill wrote of the "Horticulturalist" [86] and "Rochester Horticulturist" [137], she was referring to the *Horticulturist and Journal of Rural Art and Rural Taste*, first published in Albany and Boston between 1846 and 1852, then in Rochester from 1853 to 1855, and in Philadelphia and New York from July 1855 to December 1875.[46] The publisher was James Vick. Traill had a subscription to the *Horticulturist*, which she described as a "very beautiful got up work," elegant enough for "a drawing room table."[47] The editor sent her the numbers with coloured illustrations. Four of her literary sketches on flowers appeared in it in 1853. Instructions on training tomatoes over a trellis, a practice that she appears not to have followed but perhaps was familiar with from neighbours' gardens, also came from the *Horticulturalist* [137].

---

45 Traill, to editor of *The Genesee Farmer, I Bless You in My Heart*, [September 1852], 76.
46 Stuntz, *List of the Agricultural Periodicals*, 80.
47 Traill, *I Bless You in My Heart*, 28 April [1853], 78.

"Letters from the Backwoods of Canada"

In the preface to her *Guide,* Traill misidentifies her own book from 1836, *The Backwoods of Canada: Being Letters from the Wife of an Emigrant Officer, Illustrative of the Domestic Economy of British America.* See page xxxv for more on this groundbreaking publication. Traill often got her own titles wrong in her letters and journal entries. Although she did not quote directly from the *Backwoods* for the *Guide,* she did rely on its subject matter.

Maple Leaf, The

Among the periodicals Traill saw regularly was "the *M Leaf,*"[48] which in full was *The Maple Leaf, A Juvenile Monthly Magazine,* published in Montreal and edited by Robert Lay and then by his widow, Eleanor Lay, between June 1852 and July 1854. (Not to be confused with Henry Rowsell's *The Maple Leaf, or Canadian Annual, A Literary Souvenir,* from Toronto, 1847, 1848, and 1849). It was a short-lived publication for Canadian juveniles to which Traill regularly contributed literary sketches. Her novel, *Lady Mary and Her Nurse; or, A Peep into the Canadian Forest* was originally serialized as a twelve-part story, "The Governor's Daughter," in the *Maple Leaf* in 1853.

The other magazine produced by Montrealers Robert and Eleanor Lay from 1847 to 1853 was *The Snow Drop, or Juvenile Magazine.* As well as plentiful and original Canadian material, the Lays reprinted – with credit – items "of a refined and improving character ... adapted to the young ... [and] edifying to older, and more cultivated minds" from other periodicals.[49]

The first several issues of the *Maple Leaf* had an anonymous column called "Domestic Recipes" that covered items ranging from Windsor Soap to Mock Preserved Ginger to Indelible Ink, but later issues replaced this column with occasional articles on food, such as English strawberries and Arabian coffee. In accordance with her aim of including only recipes appropriate to Canadian farm houses, Traill selected seven recipes from four 1852 issues: from August, Cheap Family Cake [107]; from September, Green Corn [122], Green Corn Patties [122], and Soda Biscuits [104]; from October, Preserved Apples [73]; and from November, Golden Cake and Silver Cake [107]. Most were taken verbatim except for tiny grammatical alterations. Only Silver Cake has the identifier "from the Maple Leaf" appended to its title. The Soda Biscuits show

---

48 Ibid., 78–9.
49 Publisher's introductory letter to readers, *The Maple Leaf,* 30 June 1852, 1:30.

her personal adjustments in the method. Perhaps she chose these seven because they were Traill family favourites. Why not Preserved Pumpkin from the September 1852 issue? (Perhaps its influence can be detected in Melons Preserved [136].) Eleanor Lay had probably also purloined these seven recipes from elsewhere. From the *Snow Drop* came Farmer's Sponge Cake [108] and Johnny Cake [125].

McKyes, Mr, Mrs, and Miss

Willis and Clarissa (or Clarisa) McKyes were Americans who lived with their daughter Anne in Hamilton Township in Amherst village, now inside Cobourg. Clarisa McKyes was still there in 1871, according to the census, which also indicates she was age seventy-one and had been born in Vermont, although of English origin.[50] McKyes was an eminent name in the area, but Willis's relationship to the other McKyes is not clear.[51] The McKyes and Traill families were good friends and Thomas Traill mentions the McKyes several times in his extant journals. For instance, while his wife was away, he dined with them on 21 July 1856; later that summer, the day after the Traills' house, Oaklands, was largely destroyed by fire, the McKyes provided them with "a small quantity of flour and some necessary articles of crockery."[52] Since Willis was a farmer and miller, providing flour seems to have been the logical way he could help. Was Willis McKyes the "highly intelligent Scotchman" on page 129?

How did the three of them contribute to *The Female Emigrant's Guide*? There is no mention of Miss Anne McKyes, but Catharine related a story about her parents to Frances Stewart. In September 1853, on their way home from a quick trip into Cobourg, Thomas and Catharine Traill's horse was severely lamed when another cart crashed into theirs. Badly shaken and almost fainting without a parasol in the hot sunshine, Catharine made her way to the nearby McKyes home for help. She called them good Samaritans for unexpectedly hosting them overnight and pasturing the horse for quite a while.[53] Could it be that she was acknowledging this recent munificent assistance instead of something else toward production of the *Guide* specifically?

50 1851 Census, Canada West, Peterboro County, Town of Peterboro, accessed on 11 August 2016, http://data2.collectionscanada.gc.ca/1851_pdf/e095/e002361025.pdf; 1871 Census, microfilm reel C-9983, accessed 7 August 2004, via http:/data4.collectionscanada.ca.

51 Poole, *A Sketch of the Early Settlement*, 60.

52 Thomas Traill, Journal, 21 July and 26 August 1857, Traill Family Collection, 2804 and 2805.

53 Traill to Frances Stewart, *I Bless You in My Heart*, 4 September 1853, 85–7.

"Mrs Child's Frugal Housewife"

In her day, Lydia Maria Child (1802–1880) was a very well-known activist, abolitionist, feminist, domestic educator, novelist, and journalist. Her *Frugal Housewife, Dedicated to Those Who Are Not Ashamed of Economy* (1829) was and is best known as *The American Frugal Housewife*. The eighth edition of 1832 included the adjective "American" to distinguish the book from the familiar *Frugal Housewife* by Sarah Carter, published in London (1765), and then in New York and Boston (1772) and Albany (1796). It was a small packed book that declared itself "adapted to the wants of this country,"[54] that is, the United States, but it was equally relevant in Canada. It was reprinted at least thirty-five times before 1860.

Mrs Child's was undoubtedly the best known American recipe and household advice book among poor Canadian country housewives from its publication until the early 1850s. Her recipes were republished in many other places, for example, nineteen in the *Canadian Farmer's Almanac* (1837) and five in A. B. of Grimsby's *The Frugal Housewife's Manual* (1840). Most of Child's material and advice was suitable for backwoods households, but Traill picked only four. Traill did not necessarily own a copy, but a neighbour or two probably did because she notes that "I have been told it is a good receipt" [95]. Similarly, the Sugar-Yeast Cakes "I have not myself tested" [95], although the original has altered to clarify it, so, someone probably gave her the altered version to use.

Mrs Child lived with the frugality she championed because she and her lawyer husband spent their money on social causes; like Catharine Parr Traill, Lydia Maria Child was the main breadwinner.[55] There are strong similarities between the points of view and content in *The American Frugal Housewife* and *The Female Emigrant's Guide*: both blended cooking and non-culinary advice for "persons of moderate fortune," although Child's tone was much more dictatorial. The book is full of advice, such as "make your own bread and cake" rather than purchase it from a convenient but costly baker or confectioner.[56] Traill echoes this sentiment: "My female friends must bear in mind that it is one of the settler's great objects to make as little outlay of money as possible" [15].

54 See Longone introduction to the Dover edition of the 1844 *The American Frugal Housewife*, iii.
55 Longone, Introduction, Child, *The American Frugal Housewife*, iv.
56 Child, *The American Frugal Housewife*, 9.

New-England Farmer

Six periodicals entitled *New England Farmer* circulated in Upper Canada/Canada West. The *Old Countryman* in Toronto extracted material from the *Boston Weekly* published from December 1848 to August 1864.[57] Traill in turn copied the cultivation of asparagus, small fruits, and ornamental flowers [61–2].

"North-Lancashire newspaper"

Such specificity about its geographical location seems to ensure accuracy, but the newspaper's title remains unidentified, despite searches. (Perhaps it has not yet been digitized for the online British Newspaper Archive, or was short-lived.) Our guess is that it was most likely an item sent in a package from England, but who first received it in the Rice Lake farming community and then shared it? Lancashire is located on the coast of northwest England.

Old Countryman

Old Countryman was a Toronto weekly newspaper published by Reverend Henry Payne Hope from September 1853 until sometime in 1861. Traill considered it "popular and useful" for both established immigrants and newcomers [61]. Only two partial issues survive: Wednesday, 19 October 1853, and Saturday, 15 April 1856. It carried popular and political news from Britain, agricultural articles reprinted from newspapers in the northern United States, and many advertisements. In 1857 its name was changed to the *Toronto Times*.[58] Traill published articles in and copied material from *Old Countryman*. Since it carried recipes, some of them may have been reprinted in the *Guide*, although we think not because the recipes in the extant copies are for the usual middle-class fare (Prince Albert's Pudding, Orange Pudding, Imperial Drink, Lemon Brandy, and more). The *Guide* was advertised for sale in its pages. One lost *Old Countryman* issue included an extract [61] from the *New England Farmer* concerning the cultivation of asparagus, small fruits, and ornamental flowers.

Henry Hope was Traill's agent for *The Female Emigrant's Guide*. He had a close working relationship with its first publisher Thomas Maclear, and under the auspices of his *Old Countryman*, issued the fifth edition – renamed *The Canadian Settler's Guide* – as well as the seventh edition, brought out by the *Toronto Times*.

---

57 Stuntz, *List of the Agricultural Periodicals*, 113.
58 Firth, *Early Toronto Newspapers, 1793–1867*, 52.

"Old-fashioned book on orchard planting," see *American Fruit Book*

"Rochester Horticulturist," see *The Horticulturist*

Southey, Mrs

Caroline Anne Bowles Southey (1787–1854), the second wife of Robert Southey, the poet-laureate, was a well-respected English poetess herself. Her major works included *Ellen Fitzarthur* (1818), a metrical tale that she sent to her future husband and which led to their friendship.[59]

Southwell, Robert (1561?–1595)

Father Robert Southwell was an English Jesuit who was executed as a traitor for being an activist Catholic priest in Elizabeth I's Protestant kingdom. Three volumes of his religious verses were published after his death.[60]

"Mrs. Stewart of Douro" (1794–1872)

Frances Stewart (née Browne) was Traill's dearest and lifelong friend. Older by eight years and experienced in bush housekeeping for a decade by the time they met in August 1832, Frances Stewart was described by Traill as her first colonial teacher.[61] Sam Strickland introduced the Traills to the Stewarts very soon after they arrived in Upper Canada, and they lived for a few months with the Stewarts at "Auburn" on the Otonobee River. As the wife of Thomas A. Stewart, whom she married in 1816, Dublin-born Frances was a member of the Anglo-Irish group of gentry who settled the forest wilderness of Douro Township in the early 1820s, preceding Peter Robinson, founder of the Irish settlement of Peterborough in Douro in 1826.[62] The Stewarts were kin to the Reids, the family with whom they immigrated. Maria Reid was Thomas Stewart's sister, hence Frances's sister-in-law. Their daughter, Mary Reid, married Samuel Strickland. Stewart's story was posthumously told in *Our Forest Home, The Letters of Frances Stewart,* edited by her daughter Eleanor ("Ellen") Dunlop in 1889, a book suggested to her by Traill.[63]

59 Gibbon, *The Casquet of Literature,* 289.
60 *Dictionary of National Biography,* 53:294–9.
61 Traill, *Studies of Plant Life in Canada,* 3.
62 Edmison, *Through the Years in Douro,* 11, 15–16; Needler, *Otonabee Pioneers,* 11, 15, 19.
63 Traill, *I Bless You in My Heart,* 271. First edition was 1889, second was 1902. See also Stewart, *Revisiting "Our Forest Home,"* edited by Jodi Aoki.

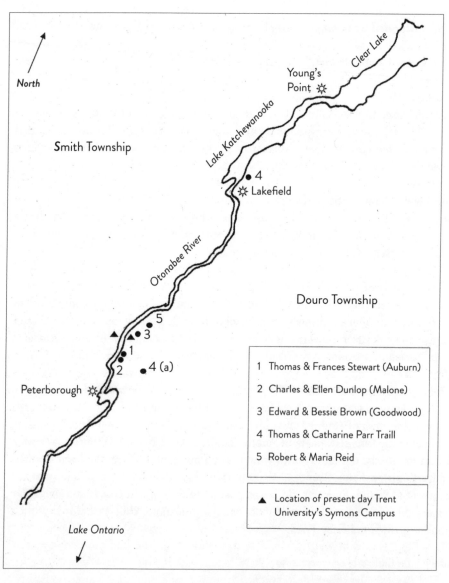

North

Clear Lake

Young's
Point ☼

Lake Katchewanooka

Smith Township

● 4
☼ Lakefield

Otonabee River

Douro Township

● 5
▲ ●● 3
● 1
● 2 ● 4 (a)

Peterborough ☼

1	Thomas & Frances Stewart (Auburn)
2	Charles & Ellen Dunlop (Malone)
3	Edward & Bessie Brown (Goodwood)
4	Thomas & Catharine Parr Traill
5	Robert & Maria Reid

▲ Location of present day Trent
University's Symons Campus

Lake Ontario

Fig. 37 · From December 1832 to February 1839 the Traills lived on Lake Katchewanooka as neighbours to the Moodies and Stricklands in what is now Lakefield. Then they moved into the Ashburnham area, near the Stewarts, now part of Peterborough. In 1846 they moved to Rice Lake, south of Peterborough. This map also shows the homes of the two Stewart daughters, Ellen Dunlop and Bessie Brown, as well as that of the Reids.

The lives of the Stewart and Traill families were intertwined for decades. Catharine Parr Traill and Frances Stewart shared books, homes, child-rearing, a lifetime of writing letters to each other, their religious faith, and interest in literature and botany. They did not often see each other but kept in close contact with regular letters. Their daughters were also good friends. When the Traills' farmhouse, "Oaklands," burned to the ground in August 1857, the widowed Frances offered a temporary cottage to them. When Frances died, Catharine wrote a heartfelt obituary.

Cultured and musical, Frances Stewart disembarked in Cobourg, Upper Canada, in the summer of 1822 utterly unprepared to be a farmer's wife on a raw bush farm. Ten years later, when she met Traill, she was an experienced housewife who had much to teach her new friend. Stewart's first teachers were English women, mostly wives of naval or military officers. Said Frances's daughter, Ellen, "Mrs Henry and several other ladies very kindly came to her assistance and taught her how to make yeast, bread and soap, etc." Leaving Cobourg for Douro in snowy February the next year, she was met by her husband at their unfinished log cabin with its doors not yet hung and the chimney not yet complete. "Pease-soup and boiled pork make our dinner each day." By the end of July she lamented to her journal, "This place is so lonely that in spite of all my efforts to keep them off, clouds of dismal thoughts fly and lower over me. I have not seen a woman except those in our party for over five months."[64] Loneliness and depression would dog her the rest of her long stressful life.

Strickland, Major Samuel (1805–1867)

In 1825, when he was twenty, Samuel Strickland, the adventurous younger brother of Catharine Parr Traill and Susanna Moodie, immigrated to a farm in Upper Canada. He married a young settler named Emma Black, daughter of the family he had come to join, who died in the summer of 1826 soon after the birth of their son; he died at age three. Sam was employed by John Galt's Canada Company to help open the towns of Goderich and Guelph. By 1832, however, when his sisters and their husbands arrived – to Samuel Strickland's utter surprise – he was farming and lumbering on the shore of Lake Katchewanooka in Douro Township with his second wife, Mary Reid, whom he married in 1828 and with whom he had fourteen children. Mary Reid had arrived with her family in 1822 together with the Stewarts, three years before Sam. She was the eldest daughter of Robert and Maria Reid and was Frances Stewart's niece by marriage. During the Rebellion of 1837, Strickland supported the

---

64 Stewart, *Our Forest Home*, 28 August 1822; 25 April 1823; July 1823: 19, 25, 32, 39.

government, became a major in the Northumberland militia unit, and was later a justice of the peace. His farm acted as an agricultural school for newly arrived Englishmen. The three Strickland siblings in Upper Canada maintained close contact all their lives, with Sam providing early settlement support to the Traills and Moodies, and important financial assistance during later crises. He is often incorrectly credited with being a founder of Lakefield, just north of Peterborough, where he died a much respected elder.

Sam's account of being an early settler, *Twenty-Seven Years in Canada West or the Experience of an Early Settler*, published in two volumes in 1853, was written at the behest of his sisters Agnes and Jane while he was vacationing in England following Mary's death. They were appalled at what they considered to be Susanna's indiscreet negativity and indecorous literary style in *Roughing It in the Bush*. His third wife was Katherine Rackham, a cultured Englishwoman who became a good friend to Catharine.

As she often did, Traill again misquoted a title, in this case three times, inserting "Residence" between "Twenty-seven Years" and "Canada West" [47, 48, 51]. Under her subtitle "Description of a New Settlement," she quoted more or less correctly from chapters 7, 8, and 13 in Sam's first volume on basic cooking utensils and how to chop wood, burn weedy fields, and build a log cabin, with her editorial comments added in square brackets, along with a few transcription alterations and a few clarifications, mostly minor.[65] Her considerable explanations for maple sugaring [146–52], include a long extract from Sam's directions in book two. He was describing the 1830s, but Traill must have thought the information still relevant for newcomers in the early 1850s.

Most emigrant guidebooks were written from the perspective of managing agricultural resources and investments, however minimal these were upon arrival, while immigrant memoirs were exciting narratives by educated gentleman farmers or townsmen about their transformation into knowledgeable settlers, as exemplified by Tiger Dunlop's *Statistical Sketches of Upper Canada* and Sam Strickland's *Twenty-Seven Years in Canada West*.

"27 Years Residence in Canada West," *see* Strickland, Major Samuel

---

65 Samuel Strickland, *Twenty-Seven Years in Canada West*, 1:91–5, 96–9, 165–71; 2:298–311.

Bibliography

A. B. of Grimsby. (1840) *The Frugal Housewife's Manual*. Toronto: J.H. Lawrence.

Abell, L.G. (1848) *The Skilful Housewife's Guide; A Book of Domestic Cookery, Compiled from the Best Authors*. Montreal: Armour & Ramsay.

Abella, Irving. (1990) *A Coat of Many Colours: Two Centuries of Jewish Life in Canada*. Toronto: Lester & Orpen Dennys.

Abusch-Magder, Ruth. (1997) "Cookbooks." In Paula Hyman and Deborah Dash Moore, eds, *Jewish Women in America: An Historical Encyclopedia*, 281–7. New York: Routledge.

Acton, Eliza. (1990 [1857]) *The English Bread Book*. Introduction by Elizabeth Ray. Lewes, UK: Southover Press.

– (1993 [1845]) *Modern Cookery for Private Families Reduced to a System of Easy Practice, in a Series of Carefully Tested Receipts, in which the Principles of Baron Liebig and Other Eminent Writers Have Been as Much as Possible Applied and Explained*. Introduction by Elizabeth Ray. Lewes, UK: Southover Press.

An American Lady. (1999 [1854]) *The American Home Cook Book: With Several Hundred Excellent Recipes, Selected and Tried with Great Care, and with a View to Be Used by Those who Regard Economy, and Containing Important Information on the Arrangement and Well Ordering of the Kitchen*. Facsimile. Whitstable, UK: Pryor Publications.

Aoki, Jody. (2005) "Culinary Themes in the Writings of Frances Stewart, Genteel Pioneer of Douro Township." *Culinary Chronicles: The Newsletter of the Culinary Historians of Ontario* 46 (Autumn 2005): 3–7.

Armstrong, Mary. (2004) *Seven Eggs Today: The Diaries of Mary Armstrong, 1859 and 1869*. Edited by Jackson Webster Armstrong. Waterloo, ON: Wilfrid Laurier University Press.

Attar, Dena. (1987) A *Bibliography of Household Books Published in Britain, 1800–1914*, London: Prospect Books.

Atwood, Florence. (1936) Atwood, Florence – Transcript: Memoirs of Annie Atwood. Traill Family Collection, MG29, D81, 7(16): 10887–10914. Library and Archives Canada, Ottawa.

– (n.d.) Atwood, Florence – C.P.T. Transcripts. Traill Family Collection, MG29, D81, 7(15): 10841–10886. Library and Archives Canada, Ottawa.

Baird, Elizabeth, and Bridget Wranich. (2013) *Setting a Fine Table: Historic Desserts and Drinks from the Officers' Kitchen at Fort York*. Vancouver: Whitecap Books.

Ballstadt, Carl. (1984) *Catharine Parr Traill and Her Works*. Downsview, ON: ECW Press.

Beavan, Frances. (1845) *Sketches and Tales Illustrative of Life in the Backwoods of New Brunswick, North America, Gleaned from Actual Observation and Experience during a Residence of Seven Years in that Interesting Colony*. London: George Routledge.

Beecher, Catharine Esther. (2001 [1858, 3rd ed.]) *Miss Beecher's Domestic Receipt Book: Designed as a Supplement to Her Treatise on Domestic

Economy. Introduction by Janice Bluestein Longone. Mineola, NY: Dover Publications.

– (1842) *A Treatise on Domestic Economy, for the Use of Young Ladies at Home, and at School*. Boston: T.H. Webb.

Beeton, Isabella. (1968 [1861]) *The Book of Household Management*. London: Jonathan Cape, Ltd. (Republished in facsimile by several companies; entries in the text refer to this edition.)

Benoit, Jehane. (1975) *New and Complete Encyclopedia of Cooking*. Ottawa and Montreal: Les Messageries du Saint Laurent Ltée.

Black, Maggie. (1985) *Food and Cooking in 19th Century Britain: History and Recipes*. London: English Heritage.

Brown, James Bryce. (1851) *Views of Canada and the Colonists Embracing the Experience of an Eight Years' Residence Views of the Present State, Progress, and Prospects of the Colony: With Detailed and Practical Information for Intending Emigrants*. 2nd ed. Edinburgh: A. and C. Black; London: Longman & Co.

Bryan, Lettice. (n.d. [1839]) *The Kentucky Housewife*. Bedford, MA: Applewood Books.

Burnham, Harold B., and Dorothy Burnham. (1972) *"Keep Me Warm One Night": Early Handweaving in Eastern Canada*. Toronto: Royal Ontario Museum and University of Toronto Press.

Canadian Housewife's Manual of Cookery, The. (1861) Hamilton, ON: William Gillespy, "Spectator" Office.

Canadian Oxford Dictionary, The. (1998) Toronto: Oxford University Press.

Canadian Receipt Book, The. (1867) Ottawa: Ottawa Citizen.

Chatelaine's Adventures in Cooking. (1969) Toronto: Maclean-Hunter.

Child, Lydia Maria. (n.d. [1833]) *The American Frugal Housewife, Dedicated to Those Who Are Not Ashamed of Economy*. 12th ed. Bedford, MA: Applewood Books. (Applewood Books

reproduced the 1833 printing, but in 1832 Child added "American" to her title and this is the date frequently cited in bibliographies.)

– (1999 [1844]). *The American Frugal Housewife*. 29th ed. Introduction by Janice Bluestein Longone. Mineola, NY: Dover Books.

Cobbett, William. (1822) *Cottage Economy, containing information relative to the brewing of beer, making bread, keeping of cows, pigs, bees, goats, poultry and rabbits and relative to other matters deemed useful in the conducting of the affairs of a labourer's family*. London: C. Clement.

– (1830) *Rural rides in the Counties of Surrey, Kent, Sussex…: with economical and political observations relative to matters applicable to, and illustrated by, the state of those counties respectively*. London: W. Cobbett. http://galenet.galegroup.com/servlet/ MOME?af=RN&ae=U106508549&srchtp= a&ste=14&locID=mlin_m_tufts.

Cole, Jean Murray. (1993) *Peterborough in the Hutchison-Fleming Era, 1845–1846*. Occasional Paper 5. Peterborough, ON: Peterborough Historical Society.

Cole, Samuel W. (1849) *The American Fruit Book Containing Directions for Raising, Propagating, and Managing Fruit Trees, Shrubs, and Plants: With a Description of the Best Varieties of Fruit, Including New and Valuable Kinds*. Boston: J.P. Jewett.

Connery, Clare. (1992) *In an Irish Country Kitchen: A Cook's Celebration of Ireland*. New York: Simon & Schuster.

Cook Not Mad or Rational Cookery, The. (1972 [1831]) Introduction by Roy Abrahamson. Toronto: Cherry Tree Press.

Copley, Esther. (1825) *Cottage Comforts, with Hints for Promoting Them, Gleaned from Experience*. London: Simpkin and Marshall.

Copway, George. (1847) *The Life, History, and Travels of Kah-ge-ga-gah-bowh (George Copway), a young Indian chief of the Ojebwa *nation, a convert to the Christian faith, and a missionary to his people for twelve years; with a sketch of the present state of the Ojebwa nation, in regard to Christianity and their future prospects.* Albany, NY: Weed and Parsons.

Craigie, William A. (1940) *Dictionary of American English.* Chicago: University of Chicago Press.

Crosman, Charles F. (1835) *The Gardener's Manual: Containing Plain and Practical Directions for the Calculation and Management of Some of the Most Useful Culinary Vegetables.* Albany, NY: Hoffman and White.

Crowen, Mrs T[homas J.] [A Lady]. (1846) *Every Lady's Book: An instructor in the Art of Making Every Variety of Plain and Fancy Cakes, Pastry, Confectionery, Blanc Mange, Jellies, Ice Creams, and Other Useful Information for Ordinary and Holiday Occasions.* Niagara: A. Davidson.

Curl, James Stevens. (2006) *A Dictionary of Architecture and Landscape Architecture.* 2nd ed. Oxford: Oxford University Press.

Custead, William W. (1827) *Catalogue of Fruit & Ornamental Trees, Flowering Shrubs, Garden Seeds and Green-House Plants, Bulbous Roots & Flower Seeds, Cultivated and for Sale at the Toronto Nursery, Dundas Street, near York.* York [Toronto]: W.L. Mackenzie.

Dalby, Andrew. (2009) *Cheese: A Global History.* London: Reaktion Books.

Dalgairns, Catherine. (1829) *The Practice of Cookery Applied to the Business of Every-Day Life.* London and Glasgow: Richard Griffin and Company.

Dana, Richard Henry Jr. (1968) *The Journals of Richard Henry Jr.* Vol. 1. Cambridge, MA: Harvard University Press.

David, Elizabeth. (1977) *English Bread and Yeast Cookery.* London: Allen Lane.

Davidson, Alan. (1999) *The Oxford Companion to Food.* Oxford: Oxford University Press.

DeLisle, Susan B. "Coming out of the Shadows: Asserting Identity and Authority in a Layered Homeland: The 1979–82 Mud Lake Wild Rice Confrontation." PhD dissertation, Queen's University, 2001.

Derry, Margaret. (1998) "Gender Conflicts in Dairying: Ontario's Butter Industry, 1880–1920." *Ontario History* 90 (Spring): 931–47.

Dictionary of Canadianisms on Historical Principles. (1967) Lexicographical Centre for Canadian English, University of Victoria, BC; Toronto: W.J. Gage.

Dillon, Clarissa F. (2004) "Bladders." *Petits Propos Culinaires* 75 (March): 36–50.

– (2012) *Various Vinegars for Assorted 17th- and 18th-Century Uses.* Self-published: Hayesville, PA.

Dods, Margaret. (1833 [1826]) *The Cook and Housewife's Manual: A Practical System of Modern Domestic Cookery and Family Management.* Edinburgh: Oliver & Boyd.

Downing, Andrew Jackson. (1859) *The Architecture of Country Houses.* New York: D. Appleton.

Driver, Elizabeth. (2008) *Culinary Landmarks, A Bibliography of Canadian Cookbooks, 1825–1949.* Toronto: University of Toronto Press.

Dunlop, William "Tiger." (1833) *Statistical Sketches of Upper Canada, for the Use of Emigrants.* 3rd ed. London: John Murray.

Edmison, John Alexander. (1967) *Through the Years in Douro: Peterborough County, 1822–1967.* Peterborough, ON: A.D. Newson Co.

Emery, Sarah Anna. (1879) *Reminiscences of a Nonagenarian.* Newburyport, MA: W.H. Huse & Company.

Encyclopædia Britannica, The: A Dictionary of Arts, Sciences, Literature and General Information. (1911) 11th ed. New York: Benton Foundation.

Erichsen-Brown, Charlotte. (1979) *Use of Plants for the Past 500 Years.* Aurora, ON: Breezy Creeks Press.

The Family Hand-Book; or Practical Information in Domestic Economy; Including Cookery,

Household Management, And All other Subjects Connected with the Health, Comfort, and Expenditure of a Family: With a Collection of Choice Receipts and Valuable Hints. (1840) London: Parker.

Farmer, Fannie Merritt. (1896) *The Boston Cooking-School Cook Book.* Boston: Little Brown.

Fee, Margery. (2009) "Stories of Traditional Aboriginal Food, Territory, and Health." In Nathalie Cooke, ed., *What's to Eat? Entrées into Food History*, 55–78. Montreal: McGill-Queen's University Press.

Feltoe, Richard. (1991) *Redpath: The History of a Sugar House.* Toronto: Dundurn Press.

Fielding, Andrew and Annelise. (2006) *The Salt Industry.* Buckinghamshire: Shire Publications.

Firth, Edith. (1961) *Early Toronto Newspapers, 1793–1867.* Toronto: Baxter Publishing Company in cooperation with the Toronto Public Library.

FitzGibbon, Theodora. (1970) *A Taste of Scotland in Food and Pictures.* London: J.M. and Sons.

Fleming, James. (1855) *Catalogue of Garden, Agricultural and Flower Seeds.* Toronto: W.R. Robertson. Also available as Canadian Institute for Historical Microreproductions 68163.

Fleming, Sir Sandford. (2009) *Sir Sandford Fleming: His Early Diaries, 1845–1853.* Edited by Jean Murray Cole. Toronto: Natural Heritage Books.

Foster, Vere. (1852) *Work and Wages, or, The Penny Emigrant's Guide to the United States and Canada: for Female Servants, Laborers, Mechanics, Farmers, &c.: Containing a Short Description of Those Countries, and Most Suitable Places for Settlement, Rates of Wages, Board and Lodging, House Rent, Price of Land, Money Matters, &c., Together with Full Information About the Preparations Necessary for the Voyage, Instructions on Landing, and Expenses of Travelling in America: With an Appendix.* London: W. & F.G. Cash. (5th edition is available as Canadian Institute for Historical Microreproductions 35643)

Frandsen, Julius Herman. (1958) *Dairy Handbook and Dictionary.* Amherst, MA: J.H. Frandsen.

Gibbon, Charles. (1873) *The Casquet of Literature: Being a Selection in Poetry and Prose.* London: Blackie & Son.

Gill, J. Thompson. (1881) *The Complete Bread, Cake and Cracker Baker.* 5th ed. Chicago: J. Thompson Gill.

Glasse, Hannah. (1995 [1747]) *The Art of Cookery Made Plain and Easy By a Lady.* Devon, UK: Prospect Books.

Goodwin, Clive E. (1995) *A Bird-Finding Guide to Ontario.* Revised ed. Toronto: University of Toronto Press.

Gray, Charlotte. (1999) *Sisters in the Wilderness: The Lives of Susanna Moodie and Catharine Parr Traill.* Toronto: Penguin.

Grivetti, Louis Evan, and Howard-Yana Shapiro, eds. (2009) *Chocolate: History, Culture and Heritage.* Hoboken, NJ: John Wiley and Sons.

Gruber, Mark C. (2004) "Whiskey." In Smith, *The Oxford Encyclopedia of Food and Drink in America*, 2:607–10.

Guillet, Edwin. (1933) *Early Life in Upper Canada.* Toronto: The Ontario Publishing Company.

Haight, Canniff. (1986 [1885]) *Country Life in Canada – Personal Recollections and Reminiscences of a Sexagenarian.* Introduction by Arthur R.M. Lower. 3rd facsim. ed. Belleville, ON: Mika Publishing.

Hale, Sarah Josepha Buell. (1996 [1841]) *Early American Cookery: "The Good Housekeeper," 1841.* Mineola, NY: Dover Publications.

Hallen, Eleanora. (1994) *Eleanora's Diary: The Journals of a Pioneer Girl, 1833–1838.* Edited by Caroline Parry. Richmond Hill, ON: Scholastic Canada.

Harland, Marion. (1878) *Common Sense in the Household: A Manual of Practical Housewifery.* New York: Scribner, Armstrong & Company.

Hartley, Dorothy. (1963 [1954]) *Food in England.* London: Readers Union MacDonald.

Haskell, E.F. (1872) *The Housekeeper's Encyclopedia.* New York: D. Appleton & Co.

Hawker, Peter. (1816) *Instructions to Young Sportsmen, on the Choice, Care, and Management of Guns… Second Edition, with Explanatory Plates, Considerably Enlarged and Improved.* London: R. Hunter; J. Ridgway & Sons.

Heron, Craig. (2003) *Booze: A Distilled History.* Toronto: Between The Lines.

Hillman, Howard. (1989 [1981]) *Kitchen Science, A Guide to Knowing the Hows and Whys for Fun and Success in the Kitchen.* Rev. ed. Boston: Houghton Mifflin Company.

History of Toronto and the County of York, Ontario containing an outline of the history of the Dominion of Canada, a history of the city of Toronto and the county of York, with the townships, towns, villages, churches, schools, general and local statistics, biographical sketches, etc. (1885) Vol. 2. Toronto: C. Blackett Robinson.

Hoffman, Francis, and Ryan Taylor. (1999) *Across the Waters: Ontario Immigrants' Experiences, 1820–1850.* Milton, ON: Global Heritage Press.

– (1996) *Much to Be Done: Private Life in Ontario from Victorian Diaries.* Winnipeg: Hignell Printing.

Home Cook Book, The. (2002 [1877]) Introduction by Liz Driver. Vancouver: Whitecap Books.

Howison, John. (1970 [1821]) *Domestic, Local, and Characteristic: to Which are Added, Practical Details for the Information of Emigrants of Every Class; and Some Recollections of the United States of America.* Facsimile. Toronto: Coles Publishing.

Hughes, Kathryn. (2005) *The Short Life & Long Times of Mrs. Beeton.* London: Fourth Estate.

Hutchens, Alma R. (1983 [1969]) *Indian Herbalogy of North America.* Windsor, ON: Merco.

Jaine, Tom, ed. (1989). *The Cooking Pot: Proceedings, Oxford Symposium on Food & Cookery, 1988.* Papers presented at the Oxford Symposium on Food and Cookery, London.

Jameson, Anna Brownell. (1990 [1838]) *Winter Studies and Summer Rambles in Canada.* Afterword by Clara Thomas. Toronto: McClelland and Stewart.

Jarvis, Hannah. (1994) *Every Comfort in the Wilderness: A Personal Journal, with excerpts from the housewifery book, diaries and letters of Hannah Jarvis, Upper Canada, 1792–1845.* Edited by Gloria Troyer. Toronto: Green Dragon Press.

Jones, Olive. (1985) *Glass of the British Military, 1755–1820.* Studies in Archaeology, Architecture, and History. Ottawa: National Historic Parks and Sites Branch, Parks Canada, Environment Canada.

Jones, Peter. (1860) *History of the Ojebway Indians with Especial Reference to Their Conversion to Christianity.* London: A.W. Bennet.

Kander, Lizzie. (1901) *The Settlement Cook Book: Containing Many Recipes Used In Settlement Cooking Classes, The Milwaukee Public School Cooking Centers and Gathered From Various Other Reliable Sources.* Milwaukee, WI: S.N.

Kelleher, Tom. (1994) "Flour from Mill to Market." *Food History News* 6 (2): 1–2.

King, Harriet Barbara. (1878) *Letters from Muskoka.* London: Richard Bentley and Son. This work was originally published anonymously, under the pen name "An Emigrant Lady."

King James Bible. (1996) Project Gutenberg.

Kitchiner, William. (1818) *The Cook's Oracle; And Housekeeper's Manual.* 2nd ed. New York: J. & J. Harper.

Knowles, Valerie. (1997) *Strangers at Our Gates: Canadian Immigration and Immigration Policy, 1504–1990.* Toronto: Dundurn.

Kurlansky, Mark. (2002) *Salt, A World History*. New York: Walker and Company.

LaFrance, Marc, and Yvon Desloges. (1989) *The Taste of History: The Origins of Québec's Gastronomy*. Ottawa: Canadian Park Service.

Lane, Maggie. (1995) *Jane Austen and Food*. London: Hambledon Press.

Langton, Anne. (2008) *A Gentlewoman in Upper Canada: The Journals, Letters, and Art of Anne Langton*. Edited by Barbara Williams. Toronto: University of Toronto Press.

– (1881) *The Story of Our Family*. Manchester: Thos Sowler & Co.

Langton, John. (1926) *Early Days in Upper Canada. Letters of John Langton from the Backwoods of Upper Canada and the Audit Office of the Province of Canada*. Toronto: The MacMillan Company.

Laviolette, Gontran. (1957) "Notes on the Aborigines of the Province of Ontario." *Anthropologica* 4: 79–106.

Lawrence, Bonita. (2012) *Fractured Homeland: Federal Recognition and Algonquin Identity in Ontario*. Vancouver: UBC Press.

Lee, Hyun Jung. "Salt and Salting." In Smith, *The Oxford Encyclopedia of Food and Drink in America*, 2:390–6.

Lee, Mrs N.K.M. [A Boston Housekeeper]. (1997 [1832]) *The Cook's Own Book: Being a Complete Culinary Encyclopedia: Comprehending All Valuable Receipts for Cooking Meat, Fish, and Fowl and Composing Every Kind of Soup, Gravy, Pastry, Preserves, Essences, &c. that Have Been Published or Invented During the Last Twenty Years. Particularly the Very Best of Those in the Cook's Oracle, Cook's Dictionary, and Other Systems of Domestic Economy. With Numerous Original Receipts, and a Complete System of Confectionery*. Merrifield, VA: Rare Book Republishers.

Leslie, Eliza. (1999 [1851 ed.]) *Miss Leslie's Directions for Cookery*. Introduction by Jan Longone. Mineola, NY: Dover Publications.

– (1857) *Miss Leslie's New Cookery Book*. Philadelphia, PA: TB Peterson.

– (1988 [1828]) *Seventy-Five Receipts for Pastry, Cakes and Sweetmeats*. Cambridge, MA: Applewood Books. Traill (or the person who gave her some Leslie recipes) used the 1840 edition (Cambridge, MA: Munro and Francis), which differs from other editions.

Leung, Felicity. (1981) *Grist and Flour Mills in Ontario from Millstones to Rollers, 1780s–1880s*. Ottawa: Parks Canada, National Historic Parks and Sites Branch.

Lewis, Joyce C. (1994) *From Douro to Dublin: The Letters of Frances Stewart*. Peterborough, ON: Peterborough Historical Society, Publications Committee.

Lincoln, Mrs. D.A. (Mary). (1996 [1884]) *Mrs. Lincoln's Boston Cooking School Cook Book: What to Do and What Not to Do in Cooking*. Introduction by Janice Bluestein Longone. New York: Dover Publications.

Lucas, Fiona. (2006) "'The Condition of Turkey Will Be Seriously Considered Today': Thanksgiving in Ontario." *Food History News* 18 (2): 1, 6–8.

– (1997) "'Every Matron Prided Herself'": Preserving Nature's Bounty Before the Mason Jar." *Seeds of Diversity* 10 (1): 13–17.

– (2006) *Hearth and Home: Women and the Art of Open-Hearth Cooking*, Toronto: James Lorimer.

Lucas, Fiona, and Mary F. Williamson. (2010) "Frolics with Food: The Frugal Housewife's Manual by 'A.B. of Grimsby.'" In B.K. Grant and J. Nicks, eds, *Covering Niagara: Studies in Local Popular Culture*, 147–68. Waterloo, ON: Wilfrid Laurier University Press.

MacDonald, Eva M. (2005) "How the Cooking Stove Transformed the Kitchen in Pre-Confederation Ontario." *Culinary Chronicles, The Newsletter of the Culinary Historians of Ontario*, 43 (Winter): 3–11.

MacKenzie, Colin. (1854) *Five Thousand Receipts in All the Useful and Domestic Arts, Constituting* a Complete and Universal Practical Library, and Operative Cyclopedia. Philadelphia, PA: Hayes and Zell.

Magrath, Thomas William, and Thomas Radcliff. (1953 [1833]) Authentic Letters from Upper Canada: With an Account of Canadian Field Sports. Introduction by James John Talman. Toronto: The MacMillan Company of Canada.

Mallory, Mary C., and Lucy Grant Gordan. (1982) "Recollections of Early Days in Guilds, Kent Co." Families 21 (4): 344–7.

Martin, Norma, Donna S. McGillis, and Catherine Milne. (1995) Gore's Landing and the Rice Lake Plains. 2nd ed. Bewdley, ON: Clay Publishing Co.

McCalla, Douglas. (2015) Consumers in the Bush: Shopping in Rural Upper Canada. Montreal: McGill-Queen's University Press.

McNeill, F. Marian. (1929) The Scots Kitchen: Its Traditions and Lore, with Old-Time Recipes. London: Blackie & Son.

Mescher, Virginia. (2005) "Salt of the Earth." Food History News 17 (3): 7.

Mika, Nick, Helma Mika, and Larry Turner. (1987) Historic Mills of Ontario. Belleville, ON: Mika Publishing Company.

Minhinnick, Jeanne. (1994 [1970]) At Home in Upper Canada. Toronto: Stoddart Publishing and Boston Mills Press.

Mitchell, Margaret Howell. (1935) The Passenger Pigeon in Ontario. Toronto: University of Toronto Press.

Mongrain-Dontigny, Micheline. (2003) L'Érable: son histoire, sa cuisine / A Taste of Maple: History and Recipes. Saint-Irénée, QC: Les Éditions La Bonne Recette.

Moodie, John Webberburn Dunbar, to James Traill. (8 March 1836). The Patrick Hamilton Ewing Collection of Moodie-Strickland-Vickers-Ewing Family Papers (51). Library and Archives Canada, Ottawa, accessed via https://www.collectionscanada.gc.ca/

moodie-.traill/027013-119.01-e.php?rec_id_nbr=51&anchor=027013-4998-e.html.

Moodie, Susanna. (1847) "The Captive." The Victoria Magazine 1 (1): 36.

– (2014 [1854]). Flora Lyndsay; or, Passages in an Eventful Life. Edited by Michael Peterman. Ottawa: University of Ottawa Press.

– (1985) Letters of a Lifetime. Edited by Carl Ballstadt, Elizabeth Hopkins, and Michael Peterman. Toronto: University of Toronto Press.

– (1993) Letters of Love and Duty: The Correspondence of Susanna and John Moodie. Edited by John Ballstadt and Michael Peterman. Toronto: University of Toronto Press.

– (1989 [1853]) Life in the Clearings Versus the Bush. Afterword by Carol Shields. Toronto: McClelland and Stewart.

– (1989 [1852]) Roughing It in the Bush, or, Life in Canada. Toronto, ON: McClelland and Stewart. (Page numbers in the text refer to this edition.) Reprint. (1990). Edited with an introduction by Carl Ballstadt. Centre for Editing Early Canadian Texts, Ottawa: Carleton University Press.

Moxon, Elizabeth. (1758) English Housewifery Exemplified in above Four Hundred and Fifty Receipts, Giving Directions in Most Parts of Cookery. Leeds, UK: T. Wilson, and C. Etherington, in York: Printed for George Copperthwaite.

Murray, Rose. (2008) A Taste of Canada: A Culinary Journey. Vancouver: Whitecap Books.

Need, Thomas. (1838) Six Years in the Bush: or, Extracts from the Journal of a Settler in Upper Canada, 1832–1838. London: Simpkin, Marshall.

Needler, G.H. (1953) Otonabee Pioneers, the Story of the Stewarts, the Stricklands, the Traills and the Moodies. Toronto: Burns and MacEachern.

Norman, Alison. (2012) "'Fit for the Table of the Most Fastidious Epicure': Culinary Colonialism in the Upper Canadian Contact Zone." In Franca Iacovetta, Valerie Korinek, and Marlene

Epp, eds, *Edible Histories, Cultural Politics: Towards a Canadian Food History*, 38–69. Toronto: University of Toronto Press.

Nourse, Mrs. (1845) *Modern Practical Cookery, Pastry, Confectionery, Pickling and Preserving with a Great Variety of Useful and Economical Receipts*. Montreal, QC: Kingston; Hamilton, ON: Armour & Ramsay.

O'Brien, Mary Sophia Gapper. (1968) *The Journals of Mary O'Brien, 1828–1838*. Edited by Audrey Saunders Miller. Toronto: Macmillan.

Oliver, Sandra L. (1989) "Bannock: Jonnycake, Dodgers, Ashcake, and Hoecake." *Food History News* 1 (3): 3–6.

– (1989) "Sauce, Garden Sauce, Sass." *Food History News* 1 (1): 5.

– (2001) "Salt Rising Bread." *Food History News* 13 (4): 3–5.

– (1995) *Saltwater Foodways: New Englanders and their Food, at Sea and Ashore, in the Nineteenth Century*. Mystic, CN: Mystic Seaport Museum.

Oxford English Dictionary, The. (1989) 20 vols. Oxford: Oxford University Press.

Parloa, Maria. (1887) *Miss Parloa's Kitchen Companion: A Guide for All Who Would be Good Housekeepers*. Boston: Estes and Lauriat.

Paston-Williams, Sara. (1993) *The Art of Dining: A History of Cooking & Eating*. London: National Trust.

Pengelley, Harriet. (1835–36) The Diaries of Harriet Pengelley. Folder 4, Box 1. Trent University Archives, Peterborough, ON.

Perkins, John T. (1934) *John T. Perkins' Journal at Sea, 1845: From the Original Copy Owned by Mrs. Grosvenor Ely*. Mystic, CN: Marine Historical Association.

Peterkin, Charles R. (2015 [1925]) *A Boyhood Journey, Scotland to Canada in 1853*. Edited by Mary F. Williamson. Toronto: self-published.

Peterman, Michael. (2004) "Literary Cultures and Popular Reading in Upper Canada." In Patricia Lockhart Fleming, Gilles Gallichan, and Yvan Lamonde, eds, *The History of the Book in Canada,* 1:395–408. Toronto: University of Toronto Press.

– (2007) *Sisters in Two Worlds: A Visual Biography of Susanna Moodie and Catharine Parr Traill*. Toronto: Doubleday Canada.

– (1990) "'Splendid Anachronism': The Record of Catharine Parr Traill's Struggles as an Amateur Botanist in the Nineteenth Century." In Lorraine McMullen, ed., *Re(dis)covering Our Foremothers: Nineteenth-Century Canadian Women Writers*, 173–85. Ottawa: University of Ottawa Press.

– (1996) "Strickland, Catharine Parr (Traill)." *Dictionary of Canadian Biography,* vol. 12. Toronto: University of Toronto Press.

Plaisted, Susan McLennan. (2004) "Corn." In Smith, *The Oxford Encyclopedia of Food and Drink in America*, 2:341–4.

Poole, Thomas W. (1867) *A Sketch of the Early Settlement and Subsequent Progress of the Town of Peterborough: and of Each Township in the County of Peterborough*. Peterborough, Canada West: Office of the Peterborough Review.

Prince, William. (1827) *1827 Wholesale Catalogue of American Trees, Shrubs, Plants, and Seeds, Cultivated and for Sale at the Linnaean Botanic Garden and Nurseries, near New-York*. 24th ed. New York: T. and J. Swords.

Pursh, Frederick. (1814–16) *Flora Americae Septentrionalis; Or, A Systematic Arrangement and Description of the Plants of North America*. 2 vols. Volume 1, London: Printed for White, Cochrane and Co., 1814; volume 2, London: Printed for James Black and Son, Covent Garden, 1816. Canadian Institute for Historical Microreproductions 47846.

"Pyroligneous acid." Wikipedia, accessed 1 August 2016.

Quincy, John. (1724) *Pharmacopoeia Officinalis & Extemporanea. Or a Complete English*

Dispensatory in Four Parts. 5th ed. London: J. Obsorn and T. Longman.

Randolph, Mary. (1984 [1824]) *The Virginia Housewife, with Historical Notes and Commentaries*. Edited by Karen Hess. Columbia: University of South Carolina Press.

Rogers, Edward S. (1978) "Southeastern Ojibwa." In Bruce G. Trigger, *Northeast*, vol. 15, *Handbook of North American Indians*, 15760–71. Washington, DC: Smithsonian Institution.

Ross, Alice. (2004) "Measurement." In Smith, *The Oxford Encyclopedia of Food and Drink in America*, 2:68–70.

Rundell, Maria Eliza. (1998 [1806]) *A New System of Domestic Cookery: Formed Upon Principles of Economy; and Adapted to the Use of Private Families*. Introduction by R. Arthur Bowler. Youngstown, NY: Old Fort Niagara Association.

Russell, Miles. (1992) *The Edward Ross Store in New Ross, Nova Scotia, c. 1835 to 1845*. Halifax: Nova Scotia Museums.

Schmidt, Stephen. (2004) "Cakes." In Smith, *The Oxford Encyclopedia of Food and Drink in America*, 1:157–65.

Secombe, Thomas. (1898) "Robert Southwell." *Dictionary of National Biography*, 53:294–9. London: Smith Elder.

Shephard, Sue. (2000) *Pickled, Potted and Canned: The Story of Food Preserving*. London: Headline Book Publishing.

Shorter, Edward. (2013) *Partnership of Excellence: Medicine at the University of Toronto, and Academic Hospitals*. Toronto: University of Toronto Press.

Simcoe, Elizabeth. (1911) *The Diary of Mrs. John Graves Simcoe, Wife of the First Lieutenant-Governor of the Province of Upper Canada, 1792–6*. Edited by John Ross Robertson. Toronto: W. Briggs.

Simmons, Amelia. (1984 [1796]). *The First American Cookbook, A Facsimile of "American Cookery."* Introduction by Mary Tolford Wilson. New York: Dover Publications.

Simpson, Leanne. (2011) *Dancing on Our Turtle's Back, Stories of Nishnaabeg Re-creation, Resurgence and a New Emergence*. Winnipeg, MB: Arbiter Ring.

Simpson, Leanne Betasamosake. (2016) "Land & Reconciliation." *Electric City Magazine* 7 (January). http://www.electriccitymagazine.ca/2016/01/land-reconciliation/.

Smith, Andrew F., ed. (2004). *The Oxford Encyclopedia of Food and Drink in America*. Oxford: Oxford University Press.

– (2004) "Bread." In Smith, *The Oxford Encyclopedia of Food and Drink in America*, 1:116–24.

– (2004) "Crackers." In Smith, *The Oxford Encyclopedia of Food and Drink in America*, 1:353–4.

– (2004) "Ketchup." In Smith, *The Oxford Encyclopedia of Food and Drink in America*, 2:5–7.

– (2004) "Soups and Stews." In Smith, *The Oxford Encyclopedia of Food and Drink in America*, 2:461–7.

Smith, Andrew, and Shelley Boyd. (2009) "Talking Turkey: Thanksgiving in Canada and the United States." In Nathalie Cooke, ed., *What's to Eat? Entrées in Canadian Food History*, 116–44. Montreal: McGill-Queen's University Press.

Sokolov, Raymond. (1988) "Measure for Measure – Only in America Do We Measure with a Cup." *Natural History* (July): 80–3.

Soper, James, Margaret Heimburger, and Leslie Garay. (1957) *Shrubs of Ontario*. Toronto: The Royal Ontario Museum.

Soyer, Alexis. (1849) *The Modern Housewife or Ménagère: comprising nearly one thousand receipts for the economic and judicious preparation of every meal of the day, and those for the nursery and sick room; with minute directions for family management in all its branches*. London: Simpkin, Marshall, & Co.

Spicer, Kay. (n.d.) *The Metric Kitchen*. Toronto: Premium Readers Club/Trans Canada Readers Services.

Stavely, Keith, and Kathleen Fitzgerald. (2004) *America's Founding Food: The Story of New England Cooking*. Chapel Hill, NC: The University of North Carolina Press.

Stead, Jennifer. (1985) *Food and Cooking in 18th Century Britain: History and Recipes*. London: English Heritage.

Stevens, Daniel. (2010) *The River Cottage Bread Handbook*. Berkeley, CA: Ten Speed Press.

Stewart, Frances. (1902) *Our Forest Home: Being Extracts from the Correspondence of the Late Frances Stewart*. Edited by E[leanor]. S. Dunlop. Montreal: Gazette Printing and Publishing Company.

– (2011) *Revisiting "Our Forest Home": The Immigrant Letters of Frances Stewart*. Edited by Jodi Aoki. Toronto: Dundurn and Natural Heritage Press. This edition includes materials not in the origial 1902 compilation, as well as Stewart's original wording for letters that her daughter Ellen Dunlop modified for publication.

– (1833) To Maria Nagle, 18 September 1833. Frances Stewart Fonds (1757–1890), 02-011. Trent University Archives, Peterborough, ON.

Strauss, Stephen. (1995) *The Sizesauras: Making Measures Fit for Human Consumption*. Toronto: Key Porter Books.

Strickland, Catharine. (1826) *The Young Emigrants; or, Pictures of Canada, Calculated to Amuse and Instruct the Minds of Youth*. London: printed for Harvey and Darton, Gracechurch-street. Canadian Institute for Historical Microreproductions 21199.

Strickland, Samuel. (1970 [1853]) *Twenty-Seven Years in Canada West, or, The Experience of an Early Settler*. Two volumes. Edmonton, AB: Mel Hurtig.

Stuntz, Stephen Conrad. (1941) *List of the Agricultural Periodicals of the United States and Canada Published During the Century July 1810 to July 1910*. Miscellaneous Publication No. 398. Washington, DC: US Government Print Office, United States Department of Agriculture.

Symons, Michael. (2007) *One Continuous Picnic: A Gastronomic History of Australia*. Melbourne: Melbourne University Publishing.

Taylor, Margaret, and Frances McNaught. (1898) *The New Galt Cook Book*. Toronto: McLeod and Allen.

Thomas, Clara. (1967) "Happily Ever After: Canadian Women in Fiction and Fact." *Canadian Literature* 34: 43–53.

Thornton, Harrison John. (1933) *The History of the Quaker Oats Company*. Chicago: University of Illinois.

Tivy, Louis. (1972) *Your Loving Anna, Letters from the Ontario Frontier*. Toronto: University of Toronto Press.

Traill, Catharine Parr. (1997 [1836]). *The Backwoods of Canada: Being Letters from the Wife of an Emigrant Officer, Illustrative of the Domestic Economy of British America*. Edited by Michael Peterman. Centre for Editing Early Canadian Texts. Ottawa: Carleton University Press.

– (1994 [1851]) "Bush Wedding and Wooing." *Sharp's London Journal* 13: 90–3. In Traill, *Forest and Other Gleanings*, 180–6.

– (1852) *Canadian Crusoes, A Tale of the Rice Lake Plains*. Preface by Agnes Strickland. London: Arthur Hall, Virtue & Co. Reprint. (1986) Edited by Rupert Schieder. Centre for Editing Early Canadian Texts. Ottawa: Carleton University Press. Page numbers in text are to this edition.

– (1868) *Canadian Wild Flowers*. Montreal: John Lovell.

– (1854) *The Female Emigrant's Guide, and Hints on Canadian Housekeeping*. Toronto: Maclear and Company. (Retitled as *The Canadian Settler's Guide* in reprints after 1855.) For further information on reprints see xlii.

– (1994) *Forest and Other Gleanings: The Fugitive Writings of Catharine Parr Traill*. Edited by

Michael Peterman and Carl Ballstadt. Ottawa: University of Ottawa Press.

– (1996) *I Bless You in My Heart: Selected Correspondence of Catharine Parr Traill*. Edited by Carl Ballstadt, Elizabeth Hopkins, and Michael Peterman. Toronto: University of Toronto Press.

– (1994 [1849]) "The Interrupted Bridal. A True Story of the First Rebellion in the Colony." *The Home Circle* 1 (1): 6–7 and 1 (2): 19–21. In Traill, *Forest and Other Gleanings,* 129–40.

– (1822–75) Journal (with Thomas Traill). Traill Family Collection, MG29, D81, 2(34): 2794–2991. Library and Archives Canada, Ottawa.

– (1831–1895). Journal. Traill Family Collection, MG29, D81, 2(37): 2992–3385; 3(1): 3386–556; 3(3): 3617–3811. Library and Archives Canada, Ottawa.

– (1856) *Lady Mary and Her Nurse, or a Peep into the Canadian Forest*. London: Arthur Hall, Virtue & Co.

– (1994 [1838]) "The Mill of the Rapids, A Canadian Sketch." *Chambers Edinburgh Journal* 7 (November 1838): 322–3. In Traill, *Forest and Other Gleanings,* 59–71.

– (1999 [1894]). *Pearls and Pebbles*. Edited by Elizabeth Thompson. Toronto: Natural Heritage/Natural History.

– (1854) "Prize Essay on Butter Making." *The Canadian Agriculturist* 6 (5): 140–2.

– (1853) "Ramblings by the River." *Anglo-American Magazine* 2 (May): 181–4. In Traill, *Forest and Other Gleanings,* 160–7.

– (1852) "Rice Lake Plains – The Wolf Tower." *Anglo-American Magazine* 1 (4): 417–20. In Traill, *Forest and Other Gleanings,* 202–13.

– (1880) Settler's Guide. Traill Family Collection, MG29, D81, 4(18–22): 5782–6252, 19. Library and Archives Canada, Ottawa.

– (1849) "The Settlers Settled; or, Pat Connor and His Two Masters," Part One. *Sharp's London Journal* 10: 110, 139–40.

– (n.d.) A Slight Sketch of the Early Life of Mrs. Moodie. Traill Family Collection, MG29, D81, 7(13): 10789–10809. Library and Archives Canada, Ottawa.

– (1885) *Studies of Plant Life in Canada: or, Gleanings from Forest, Lake and Plain*. Ottawa: J.S. Woodburn.

– (1861) To Agnes FitzGibbon, 29 October 1861. Thomas Fisher Rare Book Library, University of Toronto.

– (c. 1870?) "Tom Nixon's Forest Home." Ms. Fragments. Traill Family Collection, MG29, D81, 3(31): 4906–4938. Library and Archives Canada, Ottawa.

– [1880s] Memoirs. "Under the Pines." MG29, D81, 6(3): 8638–8773. Library and Archives Canada, Ottawa.

Vaughn, J.G., and C.A. Geissler. (1997) *The New Oxford Book of Food Plants*. Oxford: Oxford University Press.

Von Baeyer, Edwinna, and Pleasance Crawford. (1995) *Garden Voices: Two Centuries of Canadian Garden Writing*. Toronto: Random House of Canada.

Wallace, William Stewart. (1927) *A History of the University of Toronto*. Toronto: University of Toronto Press.

Walton, Izaak. (1992 [1653]) *The Compleat Angler; Or, the Contemplative Man's Recreation*. Waltham Abbey, UK; Toronto: Coles.

Ward, Artemas. (1886) *The Grocer's Hand-Book and Directory for 1886*. Philadelphia, PA: The Philadelphia Grocer Publishing Co.

Weaver, William Woys. (1997) *Heirloom Vegetable Gardening: A Master Gardener's Guide to Planting, Seed Saving, and Cultural History*. New York: Henry Holt and Company.

Webster, Noah. (1832) *A Dictionary of the English Language*. London: Black, Young and Young.

Webster, Thomas, and Mrs Parkes. (1855) *Encyclopedia of Domestic Economy*. New York: Harper and Brothers, Publishers.

Widder, Frederick. (1850) *Information for Intending Emigrants*. Toronto: Scobie & Balfour. Canadian Institute for Historic Microreproductions 22194.

Williamson, Mary F. (2004) *"To Fare Sumptuously Every Day": Rambles Among Upper Canadian Dishes and Repasts Together with Authentic Menus and Culinary Receipts*. Occasional Paper 25. Peterborough, ON: Peterborough Historical Society.

– (2004) "Seasonings and Flavourings in Canada before 1840." *Petits Propos Culinaires 75* (March 2004): 16–26.

– (2004) "Recipe and Household Literature." In Patricia Lockhart Fleming, Gilles Gallichan, and Yvan Lamonde, eds, *The History of the Book in Canada*, vol. 1: 275–7. Toronto: University of Toronto Press.

Wilson, Carol. (Spring 2005). "Wedding Cake: A Slice of History." *Gastronomica* 5 (2): 69–72, also at http://www.gastronomica.org/spring-2005/. Accessed 19 November 2016.

Woodhead, Eileen. (1998) *Early Canadian Gardening: An 1827 Nursery Catalogue*. Montreal: McGill-Queen's University Press.

Wright, Richard. (1934) *The Story of Gardening, from the Hanging Gardens of Babylon to the Hanging Gardens of New York*. New York: Dodd, Mead and Co.

Zupko, Ronald Edward. (1985) *A Dictionary of Weights and Measures for the British Isles: The Middle Ages to the Twentieth Century*. Philadelphia, PA: American Philosophical Society.

ARCHIVES

Letters and memoranda concerning the publication and distribution of *The Female Emigrant's Guide* by Bureau of Agriculture and Statistics, and the Government Emigration Department. Library and Archives Canada. (1855) RG1, E7: Submissions to the Executive Council Office of the Province of Canada Fonds, vol. 43.

United Church of Canada and University of Victoria Archives, University of Toronto, ACC.83.06C, UCC Publications, Series III, Box 50, oversize ledger, Wesleyan Methodist Book and Publishing House, 1854–1859, 155.

JOURNALS

Canada Farmer. Toronto. 1864–68.

Canadian Agriculturist, The. Toronto. August 1855. Vol. 8, 1855.

Christian Guardian, The. Toronto. 1829, 1840, 1855.

Genesee Farmer, The: A Monthly Journal Devoted to Agriculture & Horticulture, Domestic and Rural Economy. Genessee, New York. 1840–65.

Globe. Toronto. 1851 and 1852.

Halifax Gazette. 1752.

Home Circle, The, A Magazine of Literature, Science, Domestic Economy, Arts, Practical Information, General Knowledge, and Entertainment, London. 1849–54.

Horticulturist and Journal of Rural Art and Rural Taste, The [Rochester, NY]. 1853–55.

Maple Leaf, The, a Juvenile Monthly Magazine. Edited by Robert Lay and Eleanor Lay. 1852–54. Published in Montreal by E.H. Lay.

New England Farmer. Boston. 1848–64.

Old Countryman. (1853–1861) Toronto. Archives of Ontario, L23 container 17-1. Only two issues survive: 19 October 1853 and 15 April 1856. Mary F. Williamson has scoured North American archives for other issues, to no avail.

Upper Canada Gazette, The. York, Upper Canada. 1793–1810.

WEBSITES

Farm Products Grades and Sales Act, R.R.O. 1990 [Ontario], accessed 20 July 2016,

https://www.ontario.ca/laws/regulation/
900380.

Hiawatha First Nation, accessed 20 November
2016, http://www.hiawathafirstnation.com/
about-us/history/.

1851 Census, Canada West, Peterboro County,
Town of Peterboro, accessed 11 August 2016,
http://data2.collectionscanada.gc.ca/1851_pdf/
e095/e002361025.pdf.

1871 Census, microfilm reel C-9983,
accessed 7 August 2004, via
http:/data4.collectionscanada.ca.

Index

doughnuts, *108*; hop-rising, 419–20; from hops, 26, *92–4*; liquid, 376; to make vinegar, 482; to make wine, 153; making, xxvi, 16, 332–9; in modernized bread recipe, *344–7*; modernized recipes for, *339–43*; in pancake recipes, *114, 125, 343–4*; potato-based, 95, 452; rescuing sluggish, 466; sharing knowledge about, 496, 515; sugar-yeast, *95*, 473

– substitutes for, 393; buttermilk, 95–6; salt-rising, *96–7*, 462
– *See also* barm, brewer's yeast, distiller's yeast, hops, leavening agents

Zante currant. *See* currant, Zante